THE
NAUGHTY NINETIES

Also by David Friend

The Meaning of Life

More Reflections on the Meaning of Life

Watching the World Change: The Stories Behind the Images of 9/11

THE
NAUGHTY NINETIES

THE TRIUMPH OF THE AMERICAN LIBIDO

DAVID FRIEND

TWELVE

NEW YORK BOSTON

Twelve
Hachette Book Group
1290 Avenue of the Americas, New York, NY 10104
twelvebooks.com
twitter.com/twelvebooks

First Edition: September 2017

Twelve is an imprint of Grand Central Publishing. The Twelve name and logo are trademarks of Hachette Book Group, Inc.

The publisher is not responsible for websites (or their content) that are not owned by the publisher.

The Hachette Speakers Bureau provides a wide range of authors for speaking events. To find out more, go to www.hachettespeakersbureau.com or call (866) 376-6591.

Library of Congress Cataloging-in-Publication Data

Names: Friend, David, 1955- author.
Title: The naughty nineties : the triumph of the American libido / David Friend
Description: First edition. | New York : Twelve, [2017] | Includes bibliographical references and index.
Identifiers: LCCN 2016040005| ISBN 9780446556293 (hardcover) | ISBN 9781478940128 (audio download) | ISBN 9781455567553 (ebook)
Subjects: LCSH: Sex—United States—History—20th century. | Sex in popular culture—United States—History—20th century. | Sexual ethics—United States—History—20th century. | Sex scandals—United States—History—20th century. | United States—Moral conditions—20th century.
Classification: LCC HQ18.U5 F745 2017 | DDC 306.70973/0904—dc23 LC record available at https://lccn.loc.gov/2016040005

ISBNs: 978-0-446-55629-3 (hardcover), 978-1-4555-6755-3 (ebook)

Printed in the United States of America

LSC-C

10 9 8 7 6 5 4 3 2 1

Contents

1. A Wednesday in November 1

2. Down the Rabbit Hole.. 12

3. The Night We Met the Clintons 20

4. The Bubba Boomer 40

5. On the Third Wave.. 59

6. Empowerment Icons 74

7. The Crying Game 99

8. A Vagina Travelogue 116

9. The Glory of O 134

10. Culture Warriors, Man Your Battle Stations.................... 152

11. Wanderlust 168

12. The Wild Blue Web 182

13. Don't Ask, Don't Tell 197

14. The Age of the Long Lie...211

15. The Oversexed, Underexamined, Media-Soaked
    Yadda Yadda of Everyday Life..219

16. Botox, Booties, and Bods 244

17. The Bust Boom 261

18. Celebrity Sin 274

19. Four Moments That Changed the Narrative 292

20. The Boomsie Twins 322

21. Objects in Mirror Are Tinier Than They Appear............339

22. Shadows on the Wall of the Man Cave 360

23. Dudes and Subdudes... 382

24. Porn Goes Pop 405

25. Chez Fleiss 420

26. Hard Currency.. 428

27. The Lowest-Hanging Fruit 445

28. Culture Wars, Part II 457

29. The Hardener's Tale 472

30. Homo Erectus..493

31. The Internet and the Intern...518

Afterword: *The Trumpen Show*.. 543

Acknowledgments 557

Sources... 563

Index..611

For Nancy

[Independent counsel Kenneth Starr was] not just prosecuting Bill Clinton; he was prosecuting the entire culture that gave birth to what Bill Clinton represents.

—*Wall Street Journal*, editorial
(September 11, 1998)

There is a cultural war at the heart of this political war. Since Watergate, there has been a pendulum of partisan revenge. And right now Republicans want their payback for Watergate, for [Robert] Bork, for Iran-contra, even for Woodstock. Like Kenneth Starr, the Republicans are attempting to repeal the 1960s.

—Maureen Dowd, *New York Times*
(December 13, 1998)

I believe that we probably have lost the culture war.

—Paul Weyrich, open letter to fellow conservatives
(February 16, 1999)

Marx has been turned on his head. Class struggle, of course, continues. But the boil and froth of primary elemental history is now the account of the struggle between sexuality and public life—the struggle of sexual classes.

—Lionel Tiger, *The Decline of Males*
(1999)

CHAPTER 1

A Wednesday in November

November 15, 1995, at first glance, was a rather eroticized day in Washington, D.C.

At 10 a.m., the Justice Department announced that fashion designer Calvin Klein and his company's ad agency had not violated U.S. law, even though they had hired inordinately youthful-looking models for a suggestive new jeans campaign.

Later that morning, supporters of Hooters—the restaurant chain known for its bosomy, T-shirt-clad waitstaff—staged a rally in D.C.'s Freedom Plaza. They had come to protest a federal sex-discrimination ruling that called for male employees to be phased into the ranks of its women-only service crew. In response, dozens of "Hooters Girls" assembled, citing political correctness run amok. Some lofted signs with such messages as "Men as Hooters Guys— What a Drag."

Outside the capital, too, there seemed to be Eros in the air. Throughout the day, newscasts ran accounts of Britain's Princess Diana's adulterous relationship with James Hewitt, an officer in the Household Cavalry Regiment. Theaters showed trailers for the new James Bond film, *GoldenEye*, in which a sultry assassin named Xenia Onatopp crushes men to death with her thighs (and reaches orgasm as they expire). On the R&B charts, R. Kelly was rolling out "You Remind Me of Something," with lyrics comparing his "babe" to a Jeep, which he said he wanted to "wax," "ride," and "get inside." ABC-TV aired *The Naked Truth*, featuring Téa Leoni as an accomplished photojournalist who works at a tabloid where she's asked to do things like pilfer a sample of Anna Nicole Smith's urine to determine if the model is pregnant. And atop the *New York Times* Best Seller List, General Colin Powell's autobiography, *My*

American Journey, was supplanted by *Miss America*, a provocative memoir by radio renegade Howard Stern, who appeared in drag on the book's front cover.

Back in Washington, a government shutdown was in effect, a tactical ploy by Speaker of the House Newt Gingrich, who had sought to force the president's hand in a nasty budget battle. As a result, most federal employees had not reported for work—and at the White House a scaled-down staff was on duty. Shortly after 10 p.m.—as outlined in the official report of the independent prosecutor—President William Jefferson Clinton and a White House intern named Monica Lewinsky, then twenty-two, repaired to a "windowless hallway adjacent to the study...off the Oval Office" and shared the first of what would be many intimate encounters over the course of the next two years. Their ensuing relationship would ultimately contribute, by the end of the decade, to the president's impeachment.

But was that particular Wednesday, in hindsight, really out of the ordinary? One could make a persuasive case that it was a fairly *representative* twenty-four hours in the nation's erotic life—a day in a decade that followed thirty years of evolving exploration, from the sexual revolution of the '60s through the women's and gay rights movements of the '70s and '80s. The 1990s, as it turns out, were marked by several milestones that would force Americans across all sectors of society to reexamine their views on sexual politics, on physical attraction, on their tolerance for others' sexual orientation, and on innumerable other subjects related to human intimacy.

Sex had gone mainstream in, of all places, the historically puritanical United States. Long discussed sotto voce, individuals' sexual desires and hang-ups and biases were now an integral part of a larger social conversation. Indeed, the fractious debate about private sexuality and public life would begin to color many facets of the national psyche well into the twenty-first century.

————

Call it the Naughty Nineties.

The decade began with blaring tabloid headlines about real estate mogul Donald Trump and his inamorata Marla Maples, a young model and actress. (Over the winter holiday break, 1989, the pair had been confronted by Trump's wife Ivana on the slopes at Aspen. The Trumps would soon divorce.) The decade ended on the eve of the 2000 election with an America in suspended agitation, doubtful that presidential hopeful Al Gore could emerge from the shadow of his predecessor's sex scandal and impeachment (he couldn't) and uncertain that computer programs could evade a global "Y2K" meltdown (they did, even though tech fortunes would evaporate a few months later when the dot-com bubble burst).

The decade began, in strictly economic terms, with day one of the bull market, on October 11, 1990. It ended with the inauguration of George W. Bush on January 20, 2001, after a contentious, disputed election that signaled the collapse of the high-living, free-spending, balls-out era from Reagan-Bush up through Clinton-Gore. The pivotal midpoint of the decade, one could argue, was that Wednesday in November 1995 when a president and an intern began their relationship, a week coincident with a Wall Street watershed, when the Dow Jones Industrial Average, according to the *New York Times,* "tied the 20th century record of 59 new highs in one year, previously achieved only in 1925 and 1964." (The financial newswires that day were reporting that Netscape, the company behind Mosaic, the first major Web browser, was about to reward its shareholders with a two-for-one stock split.)

Though we hardly realized it at the time, the 1990s turned out to be a period in which significant issues related to sexual conduct and mores—and an inundation of erotically explicit stimuli—saturated the culture and stoked the Internet, reaching across age groups and demographic frontiers. This book will explore these implications through interviews, reporting, and cultural analysis. Its chapters will alternate between discussions of female and male sexuality; social change and popular culture; the ongoing culture war; and, as a sort of through line, the presidency of Bill Clinton. *The Naughty Nineties,* by focusing on the stories of well-known personalities—and accidental players caught up in decisive events—will show how our paradoxical value system helped shape the decade in ways that still resonate and confound us.

First off, the lay of the land, if you'll excuse the expression.[1]

In the 1990s, Baby Boomers had finally come of age and settled into the executive suites of Hollywood, Madison Avenue, and, for the first time, 1600 Pennsylvania Avenue. The counterculture, around which so many Boomers had

---

1. In these pages, I will avoid making excuses for double entendres. As novelist David Foster Wallace wrote in his memorable 1998 essay for *Premiere* magazine about visiting a Las Vegas porn-industry awards ceremony, "It's going to be a constant temptation to keep winking and nudging and saying 'no pun intended' or 'as it were' after every possible off-color entendre . . . [so] yr. corresps. have decided to try to leave most of them to reader's discretion." Policy so adopted, under the Wallace Rule. (David Foster Wallace, "Big Red Son" [1998], in *Consider the Lobster and Other Essays* [Boston: Back Bay/Little, Brown, 2005], 10.)

rallied in their youth, had now *become* the culture. And the "culture wars" of the 1980s and early '90s, under Republican presidents Ronald Reagan and George H. W. Bush, had pitted the advocates of so-called family values (on the right) against those espousing what many would refer to as "moral relativism" (on the left). That skirmish would turn into all-out combat once a young Democrat—socially liberal and politically centrist—commandeered the Oval Office.

With Boomers now calling the cultural shots from the left and center, sexually suggestive fare became not an anomaly but a staple of music and film, the advertising and fashion industries, the tabloids and the mainstream press, as well as network and cable television, where the early-evening entertainment-news shows (chockablock with titillating gossip) segued into a nightly smorgasbord of cheesecake and innuendo. A Kaiser Family Foundation study would determine that by the 1999–2000 TV season, 68 percent of a given evening's lineup contained programming with "sexual content"—a 12 percent increase over the year before.

And yet popular culture was merely the outward mantle. There were seismic shifts occurring at society's core.

On the medical front, Viagra would bestow consistent and credible tumescence on an entire generation of older men. With much fanfare and little stigma, many elderly individuals were sexually awakened over the course of less than seven months (from the FDA's approval of the drug, in March 1998, to the announcement, the following October, that the Nobel Prize had been awarded to the scientists who'd discovered the biochemical signaling mechanism that made the medicine work). At the same time, estrogen replacement therapy was back in vogue, altering the experience of menopause for hundreds of thousands of women. Even more dramatically, fertility treatments were now allowing women to conceive well into their forties and beyond. Such methods helped recast society's traditional definition of childbearing years and forever altered mating behavior, parenting decisions, childcare habits, and women's workplace opportunities. (There was also a steep increase in multiple births due to assisted reproductive technology and the fact that many women were choosing to have children later in life. Some studies would suggest that the rising percentage of children born with autism may have been partly a function of the rising percentage of older men becoming fathers.)

On the other end of the age scale, many preadolescent girls were suddenly confronting their sexuality at an earlier stage than ever before. In 1997, the journal *Pediatrics* appeared to confirm a trend that had been troubling endocrinologists. According to a hotly debated study, the onset of puberty's "secondary signs" (such as the growth of pubic hair and breast buds) had dropped to age seven or eight for as much as 15 percent of the female population. In a relatively narrow window of time, then, genuine sexual self-awareness had become a crucial part of life for a much older and, quite often, much younger set.

Meanwhile, many men were existentially adrift. Caught in the tidal currents of second- and third-wave feminism, males of every stripe were struggling to get their bearings. They began to segregate and gather in sweat lodges, en masse (crammed into sports stadiums for Promise Keepers conclaves), and on the National Mall in Washington (for the Million Man March).

At the same time, many women felt themselves empowered, united not by a single cause but by their personal drive and a social conscience. Many began to identify with a new breed of empowerment icon: the self-assured sisters who placed their sexuality front and center. There was Madonna, the pop provocateur who scuttled sexual boundaries and gender stereotypes. And Ellen DeGeneres, who came out twice: first in real life ("Yep, I'm Gay" was *Time* magazine's cover line), and then as Ellen Morgan (in the ABC sitcom *Ellen*). And Terry McMillan, whose novel *Waiting to Exhale* became a field guide to female bonding. And Eve Ensler, whose play *The Vagina Monologues*—an "oral history" of modern female sexuality—became a '90s touchstone.

There were also figures who defied category and convention. There was Anita Hill, whose allegations about Supreme Court nominee Clarence Thomas would make her the face of sexual harassment. (Thomas would deny her charges.) There was Lorena Bobbitt, who after a moment of madness and rage in which she cut off her husband's penis, would become an unwitting symbol of domestic sexual assault. There was Paula Jones, who sued a sitting president, claiming he had made crude sexual overtures to her while she was an Arkansas state employee. (Clinton would deny her charges.) And hovering above them all were two women central to the president's life in the 1990s: Hillary Rodham Clinton, possibly the most powerful, most polarizing, and (according to polls) most respected American woman for much of the decade; and Monica Lewinsky, who would emerge a generation later to tell a tale of how partisan politics, tabloid journalism, and the Internet had combined to create a national contagion of society-sanctioned voyeurism that compromised civility, invaded privacy, and dashed reputations on gossip's altar.

As the 1990s progressed, new technologies would heat up the sexual climate. The World Wide Web, whatever else it did, helped usher in a digital age of erotic communication and exhibitionism, sexual inquisitiveness and role-playing, online anonymity—and predatory activity. Platforms for personal expression and interaction (chat rooms, blogs, AOL Instant Messenger, and nascent social networking services) would permit people to connect both online and off. What's more, the Internet's ability to efficiently and cheaply deliver all manner of intellectual property—including porn—would bring an abundance of unadulterated "adult content" into the hands of the newly tech-savvy, whether young or old, urban or rural, rich or poor.

Biotechnology also reshaped our understanding of humankind's genetic and sexual building blocks. The decade brought about early experiments with human embryonic stem cells to treat illness and birth defects; the first cloned animal (a sheep, named Dolly, "created" in Scotland); and the near completion of a rough draft of the human genome, which would begin to probe the mysteries of the aging process, identify genetic markers for potential disease and disability, and begin to break the code of what fundamentally makes us men and women.[2]

Fiscal forces entered the picture as well. The American economic boom of the 1980s and '90s—echoing the Gilded Age of the previous century, the Roaring Twenties, and the Swinging Sixties—helped spur the shift toward increased sexual exploration, allowing more and wealthier Americans to engage in leisure pursuits and in unbridled personal gain and self-expression, often to excess and with little regard for the consequences.

Global geopolitics were at a hinge moment too: the Soviet bloc was dissolving; China was suppressing dissent with an iron fist; Islamist extremism was advancing (Al-Qaeda first attacked the World Trade Center in 1993). On the home front, however, Americans were in a giddy interregnum of narcissism, solipsism, and skyrocketing mutual funds. Of that span from 1989 to 2001, historian and biographer Walter Isaacson has noted, "We had coasted

---

2. A series of '90s films—including *Jurassic Park, Judge Dredd, Multiplicity, Gattaca, The Fifth Element,* and *Alien: Resurrection*—fired the public imagination, warning of the potential dangers of cloning and similar advances. "These movies, some of them sci-fi horror films," science writer David Ewing Duncan reflects, "struck a similar chord to Mary Shelley's *Frankenstein* in its day, which was then a reaction to the new science around electricity and electromagnetism." (Interview with Duncan.)

through the '90s with irrational exuberance.[3] Between the fall of the Berlin Wall until the fall of the twin towers, there was nothing unnerving us."

And then there was the pitched political battle on the home front, which helped transform society's attitudes toward sexuality, marriage, diversity, and inclusion. At the 1992 Republican National Convention, conservatives called for a "cultural war" against the left, charging liberals with contributing to the erosion of "traditional values." And President Bill Clinton, upon taking office six months later, would begin to introduce a slate of progressive initiatives focused on reproductive rights, women's rights, domestic violence, and the family. (In an early misstep he championed the Pentagon's policy called "Don't Ask, Don't Tell," which would prove to be a myopic and much-derided attempt to allow gays and lesbians to continue to serve in the armed forces.) Meanwhile, three same-sex couples sued the state of Vermont for denying them marriage licenses, and by decade's end the state supreme court would rule that Vermont was legally obligated to accommodate lesbian and gay partners seeking civil unions. Politicians, with unprecedented frequency and candor, were beginning to speak openly of their support for the rights of what would become known as the LGBT community.

———

New social customs emerged, altering Americans' rites of passage. On campuses, "hooking up" took hold. Twenty-somethings were assembling in chum scrums: groups of postadolescent, irony-clad friends who hung out after work and sometimes moved in together as roomies (keenly rendered in Douglas Coupland's 1991 novel *Generation X* and a rash of films and TV shows).

New trends came with new names: the booty call, the belly ring, the tramp stamp, the Brazilian bikini wax, the V-chip, the sex tape, the sex tourist, the Rabbit, the little blue pill. There was the Peter Pan complex and the man cave, the bromance and the metrosexual, the MILF and the cougar. Increasingly, media outlets turned tabloid, providing 24/7 scandal coverage that would spool out episodically for months at a clip. Greater swatches of everyday life became erotically inflamed. Sexual addiction counseling emerged from therapy's shadows. Pornography

———

3. "Irrational exuberance" is the term that Federal Reserve chairman Alan Greenspan famously used in a 1996 speech to question whether investors' unrealistic estimates of the market had "unduly escalated asset values, which [might] then become subject to unexpected and prolonged contractions [i.e., market corrections]." (Alan Greenspan, "The Challenge of Central Banking in a Democratic Society," federalreserve.gov, Francis Boyer Lecture, American Enterprise Institute for Public Policy Research, December 5, 1996, http://www.federalreserve.gov/boarddocs/speeches/1996/19961205.htm.)

became, if not yet respectable, then at least consumer-friendly, slinking out of the bottom dresser drawer and into ever more visible corners of the culture.

During the 1990s, there appeared to be an increase in sexual experimentation and, among Gen-Xers, diminished levels of guilt and dread surrounding sexual activity. This change in behavior was partly a result of a heightened awareness of safe-sex practices and the more open, sophisticated, and graphic conversations—in households, schools, doctors' offices, and even houses of worship—that had come about in the '80s in the wake of the AIDS pandemic. Also playing a significant role was a shifting attitude toward reproductive rights. In the mid-'90s, for the first time, a majority of Americans, 56 percent according to one key study, supported a woman's right to choose. This pivot in opinion—along with the widespread use (and ever more aggressive marketing) of contraceptives—would alter the whole pro-life/pro-choice dynamic, further empowering *and dividing* radical activists on either side.

The changing state of matrimony was a driver as well. Although it sounds self-contradictory, couples in the '90s were increasingly cohabiting before marriage and/or delaying marriage, if they were marrying at all. Those who did marry would frequently end up separated or divorced.[4] And the divorced, in a curiously American phenomenon, often remarried serially, as Johns Hopkins sociologist Andrew J. Cherlin would later outline in his book *The Marriage-Go-Round*.

Then, of course, there was Bill Clinton himself. The '90s were, after all, the kickoff of the Clinton years. And the public had come to regard the president, not inconsequentially, as a man of deep-seated passions—social, political, personal, and sexual. A purported extramarital affair had first threatened to shatter his candidacy, in 1992. An ongoing court case, mentioned earlier, would dog his presidency. And midway through his second term, a sex scandal almost forced him from office. Indeed, the details of Clinton's private behavior became so prevalent in the day's headlines that the news cycle began to acquire a perplexing sexual overlay.

In effect, the sex acts of the president of the United States had helped recalibrate the public's perception of what in fact constituted "sex." Many Americans began to consider oral sex as being outside the bounds of *actual* sex, claiming to have taken their lead from the leader of the free world, who

---

4. Though divorce rates rose to a bracing 50 percent during the 1970s and '80s, they actually settled down in the '90s. (Claire Cain Miller, "The Divorce Surge Is Over, but the Myth Lives On," *New York Times*, December 2, 2014.)

had sworn he "did not have sex" during the above-mentioned West Wing encounters—presumably because those liaisons were nonpenetrative. In a reliable yardstick of the changed tenor of the conversation, the *New York Times*, for the first time in its 147-year history, published the word "fuck" (while quoting a secretly recorded audiotape related to discussions about the president).

Nonetheless, America's tolerance only went so far. The Republican base became incensed by the off-hours dalliances of a sitting president, the social policies championed by Bill and Hillary Clinton, and the laxity of popular culture in general. Such animus culminated in the mobilization of the conservative faithful and the eventual eight-year reign of President George W. Bush, elected in 2000 with the promise of "bringing dignity" back to a defiled White House. Neither the passage of time nor the presidencies of Bush or Barack Obama could resolve the "dignity" matter.

Presently there has been a veritable '90s revival. (Witness reboots of everything from *Baywatch* to *Twin Peaks* to *Beauty and the Beast*.) And many of the decade's sex-charged narratives, scandal-scarred personalities, and polarized culture clashes remain with us. Recent docudramas have revisited the sagas of Anita Hill (facing a Senate panel) and O. J. Simpson (facing an L.A. jury), reengaging audiences with the lessons of dueling agendas, values, and codes of justice. Some view this revival as harmless nostalgia: millennials attending '90s-themed parties and following '90s-inspired fashion and design trends. But the blood, red and blue, runs deep. Most telling of all, of course, has been the defeat of a '90s liberal icon (Hillary Clinton) by an '80s iconoclast-cum-reality-TV-star (Donald Trump). Indeed, Trump's hard-right recycling of Reagan-Bush social policies and his codependence on Fox News—not to mention the resurrection of characters like Roger Stone, Newt Gingrich, and Rudy Giuliani on a sort of Golden Oldies tour—have made it plain that too many Boomers are still settling the same culture-war scores.

The Naughty Nineties, in many ways, laid the groundwork for our current age. It is evident in the voyeurism and virulence aroused by social media; in the thirst for scandal incited by tabloid news and the 24/7 news cycle; in the false narratives concocted by reality TV; in the breakdown of private barriers in the Internet age. It is evident in the social sanction to lie about personal and political conduct, and in the partisan rancor perpetuated by the culture war. This book, in this regard, can be seen as a codex for understanding how America arrived here—how, a generation after Clinton was sworn in as president, promising

"American renewal," we have ended up in the Trump-tinged Teens, with a president promising that "this American carnage stops here."

Yes, in 1999, Paul Weyrich, an eminence of the New Right, had decreed in a letter to the conservative faithful: "I believe we probably have lost the culture war." The left had won—or so it seemed. But the right, as it turned out, continued to play the long game. This strategy and its ramifications were not lost on Hillary Clinton. In fact, she had offered a prescient observation a year and a half before she would lose the 2016 election (which was partly a referendum on the social values championed and institutionalized when her husband took office). "Winning the culture wars is not enough," she had warned in a conversation with the *New York Times Magazine*'s chief national correspondent, Mark Leibovich. "It's never final. There's always the rearguard actions." The war, both sides knew, would wage on, and on.[5]

———

In the 1990s, Americans, as never before, confronted an expanding public encroachment on their private lives. They were entertained, and alarmed, by tales of public figures ensnared in scandal. They grappled with matters surrounding sexuality, sexual identity and expression, reproductive choice, LGBT rights, domestic violence, sexual abuse and harassment, and the cultural ramifications of porn, the Web, and social media. Sex, in ways large and small, moved to the forefront of individuals' civic and personal lives: from the legal validity of marriage equality to new laws that criminalized anti-LGBT violence, from Riot Grrrls to the Spice Girls, from *American Pie* to *American Beauty*.

The Naughty Nineties were a fin de siècle inflection point when an array of forces aligned—cultural, social, political, legal, economic, medical, and technological—and prompted a customarily prudish nation to face its deep fascination with, and trepidations toward, human sexuality in all of its complexity and ubiquity. The decade, in sum, reconditioned Americans to accept themselves as profoundly sexual creatures.

Sigmund Freud, some say, had set the stage decades before. He argued that civilization persisted, indeed it flowered, when members of the body politic sublimated many of their primal instincts. Freud believed, as the radical

———

5. War terminology will be used in these pages to refer to American culture clashes at the turn of the century. Such phrases—battle, skirmish, front lines—can come off as histrionic. But given the lives and livelihoods destroyed by these clashes, they seem, for the most part, to be fitting and justified.

social theorist and leftist icon Herbert Marcuse would later put it, that "the full force of civilized morality was mobilized against the use of the body as [a] mere object, means, instrument of pleasure.... Precisely in his gratification, and especially in his sexual gratification, man was to be a higher being, committed to higher values; sexuality was to be dignified by love." Imagine it. Romantic passion, followed by commitment and fidelity, devotion and shared contentment. The stuff of storybooks, perhaps.

What, then, of a "liberated" society, one that preferred a looser definition of love? Such a society, Marcuse argued, would have great potential upside: a social contract in which work would become play, oppressive toil would be abolished, and amity and love would be ascendant. This society might in time become the foundation of a utopian world. Marcuse, one of the great sages of the '60s counterculture, understood this to the very marrow. And yet he cautioned that there was a dark dimension to this idealized vision. Once the age of technology arose in the 1950s (and with it more free time)—followed by the coming Age of Aquarius in the '60s (and with it more variations on the theme of "free love")—there arose a distinct possibility that traditional monogamous love, in Marcuse's pessimistic assessment, would beat a fast retreat.

In his 1961 preface to *Eros and Civilization*, his mid-'50s treatise on Freud, sex, capitalism, and modern culture, Marcuse had forecast a "transition to a new stage of civilization." He foresaw sexual emancipation and accelerated automation. But for all the benefits of these breakthroughs, he saw that they also augured great risk. These advances, he wrote, might subvert traditional culture by "the liberation of instinctual needs and satisfactions which have hitherto remained tabooed or repressed." He anticipated that society might experience "the methodical introduction of sexiness into business, politics, propaganda, etc., [whereby] sexuality obtains a definite sales value"; he anticipated that the culture might fall prey to "the destruction of privacy, the contempt of form, the inability to tolerate silence, the proud exhibition of crudeness and brutality." Marcuse even warned of the possibility "that instinctual liberation [could] lead . . . to a society of sex maniacs."

It would take a generation before such seeds, planted in the '60s, would sprout. And it has taken another generation to gain a bit of perspective on that crucial decade.

To the Naughty Nineties, then.

CHAPTER 2

Down the Rabbit Hole

The story of '90s sexuality really starts more than four million years ago, beginning with the earliest bipeds, up through the Bushmen, and on through the Boomers. Indeed, the sexual codes of our species did not begin with Madonna, or the Virgin Mary, or even with Eve. Nor did America's ingrained debates about sex begin in Puritan times, let alone the free love '60s.

The tale goes back epochs. "Our earliest ancestors copulated with just about everybody," writes anthropologist Helen Fisher in her book *Anatomy of Love.* "And yet gradually serial monogamy emerged [and, over time] we evolved three basic drives: the sex drive, romantic love, and attachment to a long-term partner. These circuits are deeply embedded in the human brain. They're going to survive as long as our species survives."

This is not to say, as Fisher tells me today, that monogamy, anthropologically speaking, means sexual fidelity. "In all hunting/gathering societies, men and women form pair-bonds, but they are also adulterous. We are sexual animals. And we often have many sexual partners....Hunter-gatherers practice sexual social monogamy *and* clandestine adultery."

If what Fisher and her colleagues say is true, then how does the species balance this dialectic? And how is it possible to get an anthropological fix, in the here and now, on a tribe *from the 1990s* that is pursuing both its own sex drive *and* its hardwired instinct for romance?

I ask Dr. Helen Fisher to join me on a field study. I ask her to travel back with me to the land of Manolos, Cosmo's, and Rabbits.

———

We embark with the intention of observing a small band of women suspended in a sort of '90s time warp. Fisher has agreed to interpret the clan's behavior in the context of four to five million years of intimate interaction. We settle on our target: a group of passengers riding around on a Manhattan tour bus and visiting sites featured in HBO's '90s megahit *Sex and the City*. Our study sample consists of fifty-three women in a tint-windowed coach, a contemporary tribe exploring the mysteries of urban romance while taking their cues, quite literally, from four characters on cable television: Carrie, Samantha, Charlotte, and Miranda.

The passengers on our bus are a mixed bag: tourists in their twenties and thirties from Ireland, New Zealand, Miami; three retirees from Australia; giggly knots of gal pals in flats, designer sunglasses, and smart scarves from New Jersey and the outer boroughs. They're here because each of them has paid $49 for a three-and-a-half-hour tour of locations from *Sex and the City*. First stop: the Pleasure Chest, a popular West Village sex-toy emporium. And yours truly, as one of only six males in their midst (the other men have come with "dates"), is grateful to have the good doctor in attendance.

Fisher is a vivacious sixty-something Rutgers anthropologist. Trim, attractive, and full of zest, she is wearing a black turtleneck and carrying a chic knapsack. Her specialty is the neurochemical basis of interpersonal attraction. But she has also studied the prehistoric roots of human sexuality and love. She has pondered the torrid dusks before the last Ice Age and the frigid midnights of Victorian England. It is my hope that Fisher, playing a latter-day Margaret Mead, might shed some light on this phenomenon: an effulgence of women, by the dozen, pouring out of tour buses twice a day, six days a week, as they visit destinations (Bergdorf Goodman, Magnolia Bakery, the stoop outside Carrie's brownstone) that were once prominently featured on a cable TV series—one that has not aired an original episode since 2004. Fisher is more than game.

We follow the women into the Pleasure Chest, where they wander among tubes and jars of lubes and jellies. They eye rhinestone-studded handcuffs and a wall of dildos. One friend asks another to photograph her mock-gagging on a pink plastic thermos-y thing—a large, penis-shaped "Dicky Chug Sports Bottle."

They pass a display case of cutting-edge vibrators, each with external clitoral stimulators, each a different shade and shape, some bearing distinctive names: Little Dolly, Big Boss, Meany. One by one, as the tour bus waits outside, the women file by to gawk. Hand after outstretched hand swoops down to finger the shafts, stroking neon purple or midnight blue. The women laugh in sly cahoots and then move on, some toward the cash register.

In season 1, episode 9, from August 1998, *Sex and the City*'s Miranda (played by Cynthia Nixon) visits the Pleasure Chest and introduces the Rabbit vibrator to the initially reluctant Charlotte (played by Kristin Davis). "I have no intention of using that," Charlotte says, balking. "I'm saving sex for someone I love." She is persuaded, however, to bring one home for a trial run. And she ends up hooked. ("Oh, it's so cute," she squeals. "It's pink, for girls! And, look, the little bunny has a little face, like Peter Rabbit.") Peter, indeed. She becomes a hermit, so enraptured with her cunny bunny that her *City* sisters have to barge into her apartment and perform a "Rabbit intervention." Soon the sex toy, thanks to Charlotte's segment, would hit the big time. Because of a TV program, a long-vaunted masturbatory accoutrement— a "marital aid," as it was referred to in polite company—would become a down-the-middle diddler for the open-minded woman.

The women in the tour group are hardly here incognito. It is a bright Indian summer Saturday, at high noon. And many seem to be pregaming, kicking off a girls' weekend. In groups of three and four, oblivious to passersby, they enter or exit the store and gather outside for snapshots next to the window display. In the glass case behind them sits a black-and-silver LELO Smart Wand body massager (a sleek and gleaming twelve inches) that doubles, says a shop attendant, "as a clit vibe." One young British woman shouts to her friends, "Orgasm poses!" and her companions oblige.

———

If the Sex Decade had a pop-culture apotheosis, it was surely *Sex and the City*. Premiering in the summer of '98, the series aired for six seasons (and two follow-up films) to help educate, thrill, and, some say, corrupt a generation of young women. Here was a program that was more like a movie: steamy subject matter, zero laugh track, scenes often filmed with a single camera, characters obsessed with wardrobe. Here were four brainy, attractive strivers all hyperconscious of their career paths, their social status, and their Manolos. Here were BFFs who believed that there was nothing more natural or rewarding in life than convening over a liquid brunch or an after-work round of Cosmo's (or two or three) and openly talking about their sexual tastes; bemoaning their romantic fiascos; and, once they'd dashed off into the night, openly having sex—on screen—with a motley string of lover-boys. (Samantha: "Ladies, can we cut the cake and get out of here?—I have a three-way to go to.")

In its Sunday night perch on HBO, *Sex and the City*—based on Candace Bushnell's sex-and-lifestyle column in the *New York Observer*—first attracted a more urban, upscale, "bobo"[1] viewership. But it soon caught on with a broad audience, at first jarred by—and then enamored of—its barrage of adult situations.

Sex and the City clicked on many levels. With its quartet of intertwined story lines. With its zippy writing, snappy dialogue, and social insights. With its confessional voice. (In every episode, Carrie, as narrator—played by Sarah Jessica Parker—offered pearls of wisdom: "Twenty-something girls are just fabulous, until you see one with the man who broke your heart.") In all, the series had precisely the right recipe for the times: sex, sisterly candor and cattiness, savage sarcasm, *more* sex—and binge shopping. The show was groundbreaking in placing its characters in a succession of overtly sexual circumstances; in its ability to derive humor, however dark, from the moral quandaries of social rituals; in its consistent ability to look at the world from a female perspective (often at the collateral man's expense); and in its focus on single women preoccupied with their romantic lives. It was what many considered to be television's first uncensored feminist comedy.[2] It made the case that the women's movement had not only delivered gender and sexual equity but had liberated women to pursue their sex lives on their own terms.[3]

---

1. "Bobo" is short for "bourgeois bohemian," a phrase coined by David Brooks and developed in his '90s primer *Bobos in Paradise* (2000) as a shorthand for describing the nouveau global-citizen-minded, latte-loving American meritocracy.

2. Dr. Jamieson Webster, a Freudian psychoanalyst, holds a contrarian view. She insists that *Sex and the City* rarely depicts genuine, healthy sex. Of the four main characters, she tells me, "One is single, hung up on unavailable men, and has more libido in her closet. Ironically she writes a quasi–advice column on love. The other is a careerist lawyer who dates passive men. The other is [virtually] a man and fucks like a man and is terrified of commitment. And the last one is a prude obsessed with having a baby. Who is really enjoying themselves? No one is having a full, loving sex life." (Interview with Webster.)

3. Come the 2010s, HBO's millennial-era successor to *Sex and the City*—Lena Dunham's *Girls*—would go one step beyond (by way of Brooklyn, not Gotham). "Over all, it's a show that reminds you that the sexual revolution is a done deal," Margaret Talbot would profess in the *New Yorker*, "that few women today see sex as a bargaining chip in a bid for commitment, and that gender parity tends to go along with more sex.... Studies have shown it to be true: societies in which the sexes are more equal are societies in which people have more sex." (Margaret Talbot, "Girls Will Be Girls," *New Yorker*, April 16, 2012, 39.)

In its first season *Sex and the City* tackled the ménage à trois and adultery; spanking and anal. (Miranda: "If he goes up your butt, will he respect you more or respect you less? That's the issue." Samantha: "You could *use* a little backdoor.") Also on the tote board: the high anxiety of the late period, and how to handle a male underwear model—or a dude with a "gherkin" dick.

Here, then, some fifteen years later, Fisher and I witness the all-American spin-off of the show: the glib, postmodern guided tour. From the comfort of an air-conditioned coach, the passengers listen to a woman standing at a microphone. On today's trip, she's a young, perky part-time singer-actress who goes by the name of Lou. In sync with her shpiel, four overhead monitors run clips from episodes that correspond to the sites outside. Pass the Madison Square Park dog run and Lou recalls the scene where a half dozen pooches, freed from their leashes, start humping one another. ("Remember the doggy gang bang?" she asks.) Pass the Plaza Hotel and Lou mentions the Oak Room, "where Samantha met the senior-citizen millionaire." It is time for the ride's first test. "And what distinctive trait," she asks, "did *he* have? Did I hear you say, 'Saggy ass'? Repeat after me"—and the riders, in a dulcet chorus, chime in, "*Sag-gy . . . ass.*"

As we crawl south through traffic, Lou speaks in code, yet the passengers nod at the references and shout out rejoinders. "How about Friar Fuck? Mr. Too Big? The no-happy-ending massage guy? The hot priest guy?" (She's referring, I find out later, to the nicknames of men with whom Samantha— played by Kim Cattrall—did *not* consummate.) "How about Sarah Jessica Parker's EPT test, when she'd just found out she was pregnant?" The bus pack sighs, in unison, "*Awwww.*" (Lou, of course, means the actress's *character* Carrie, but the distinction seems immaterial since Lou also refers to a few recent on-the-street Sarah Jessica sightings.)

The event operators, On Location Tours, have been hosting these junkets since 1999, capitalizing on sexually charged entertainment *as nostalgia.* Historian Daniel Boorstin, back in the '60s, had described the mind-set of the modern tourist as being magnetically drawn to "pseudo-events." But today we have turned this anomaly into an industry. In trying to intuit vanished civilization, many of us have dispensed with walking the cold stones of the Appian Way and prefer instead to meander through invented ruins—in this case the remnants of a televised fable.

While I express an unguarded cynicism, Dr. Helen Fisher views the bus ride experience as healthy and hopeful. Fisher is pleasantly surprised by the unfettered vibe. The bus riders seem largely uninhibited—and happy. Their mothers and grandmothers, she notes, came from uptight generations. "We're still a sex-negative society in America," she says. But watching this group smiling together among the vibrators, or pointing out oddities from the windows of their coach, Fisher sees only the slightest hint of inhibition. "In the past, they would have had no outlet for such expression," she says. "Now they *dare* do it. In public. They're back to doing it like they did fifteen thousand years ago. *Avidly.* I think they're almost *feigning* embarrassment."

What Fisher observes, she posits, is women returning to their natural habits, courtesy of this Potemkin habitat. "In ancient hunting-and-gathering societies," Fisher explains, "women would go off and do their gathering together every day. I traveled very briefly with a hunting-and-gathering society in Tanzania, called the Hadza. The women go together to do their gathering, and the men often go individually to do their hunting. The day I was there, [the women] were gathering berries out of a tree, and some tubers that tasted like potatoes. They would all go together—fifteen women, with older children. (Very small children stayed in camp, as they're too heavy to carry.) Their interaction consisted of giggling, chatting. They were talking in a click language. They were very relaxed with each other, talking constantly. In many respects, it had a sense of community that is missing, really, in much of America, because these people live with each other day and night—there's no privacy—and know everything about each other."

She continues, "When you read some of the famous ethnographies of the !Kung Bushmen from tribes from Botswana and Namibia, who share the same basic heritage as the Hadza, the women get up in the morning, and they go out gathering, and they start saying, 'Oh, my back hurts,' and 'Boy, he took forever—I don't want to do *that* again' kind of thing. They're making all kinds of comments about the men and the other women.

"Gossip was the first form of social control. It was the first form of spreading the news in very basic forms of language, most likely as early as a million years ago. They were probably gossiping by then: 'Johnny's a pretty bad lover, and Jim has three wives and can't seem to manage. Jody is sleeping with—' I mean, come on. The oldest human conversation was probably about the weather. The *second* oldest was probably about who's sleeping with whom. Because, from a Darwinian perspective, *love matters.* I mean, who you have sex with is going to lead to who you have babies with, and who you have babies with is going to make an enormous difference in the future of your DNA."

Fisher moves on to discuss the role of the menstrual hut in certain cultures. "Men perceived that women were consigned to being 'cast out' to the menstrual hut," she says, "but women *like* it there. In traditional societies, menstrual blood was regarded as very powerful. So a woman who was menstruating couldn't touch a man's hunting gear, for instance. Blood was a polluting substance. I talked to an anthropologist some time ago who lived in an Amazonian community for a long time, and he discovered that these women loved going to the menstrual hut because it was five days off from work. It's some distance away from the village, somewhere they can talk about life and sex with their best friends." In short, *Sex Before the City*. The long brunch. The gals' getaway. No men allowed.

Fisher, with a knowing grin, stands outside the Pleasure Chest, her arms folded. "They appear to be doing it for female bonding," she says. But there is much more going on. "By watching videos and discussing these old sex stories from the program—stories they're already familiar with—they're empathizing and identifying with the characters. They're sharing in other people's joys and sorrows. You see love, sex, heartbreak. You can jack up your whole limbic system, but you don't have to go through it yourself. Plus, they're picking up sex tips and the mores of fashion so they can discuss it among themselves. It's the whole package."

The women—each with a souvenir Pleasure Chest spanking wand—reboard the bus, which starts purring again. "The bus is a wonderful image of a world that is entirely changed. What's *in* the bus—the women—hasn't changed for two hundred thousand years. It's the bus—the culture—that's changed. The bus itself is the expression of a dominant culture in which women are now free to express their sexuality. Marriage was the only women's 'career choice' for ten thousand years. In agrarian societies around the world, until the beginning of the Industrial Revolution, pairs were stuck together, economically, until 'death do us part.' Along with that, we [adopted] a whole lot of ideas about what a man is and what a woman is, and among those ideas was that women were less sexually interested, that their place was in the home, that they were less intellectual . . . that they were less economically competent. They were second-class citizens.

"A hundred years ago, on a Saturday like this one, an upper-class woman would be getting the children ready for the park, perhaps taking a ride on her horse, sidesaddle so that nothing would be damaged—because she was a vessel in which a man put his seed. Her point was to have babies and pass on the male line. And the male was *equally* stuck. The bottom line: there wasn't an opportunity for a woman to get on the bus.

"But at the beginning of the Industrial Revolution you see women beginning to move back into the job market. So, as women were reemerging to be financially liberated, they began to be emotionally and sexually liberated, and that's exactly what they're doing now. Can you imagine? A bus that takes women on a sex tour? In other cultures, they'd be in chadors, covered up, hidden, and out of touch with their own sexuality."

She makes a final observation. "For millions of years, we lived in these little hunting-and-gathering bands, and in those bands women were just as economically, socially, and sexually powerful as men. They commuted to work—to do their gathering every day. They came home with 60 to 80 percent of the evening meal. Women were no less adulterous than men.

"The hallmark of our modern world is that women are piling into the job market in cultures around the world, and with that, their natural sexuality is emerging. They can once again express it.

"Sexually speaking, we're closer now to how we were a million years ago than we have been in centuries."

––––––––

For a million years, give or take, nighttime had been a time of rest, a time for storytelling, a time to retreat from the daily threats to one's survival. Nighttime also became the time for romance. Fast-forward to the mid-1950s. As television became the national (and then the global) hearth, nighttime again emerged as the time for stories—especially Sunday night, when families gathered in the cathode gloaming. Indeed, each one of the ninety-odd episodes of *Sex and the City* first aired on a Sunday night. And groups of women, sometimes mothers and daughters together, would sit down to watch Carrie and friends talk about love, pine about wayward partners, and screw their brains out. (Meanwhile, the menfolk, to be completely sexist about it, would sit down in another room, glued to sports.)

And sports it is. It is time to click the remote and travel back to one such enchanted evening: Super Bowl Sunday 1992.

CHAPTER 3

The Night We Met the Clintons

Until a few weeks before the New Hampshire presidential primary in 1992, we had never really met them—met the Clintons, that is.

We were unfamiliar with Hillary Clinton's unwavering resolve. We'd never seen her up close, this proud feminist, litigator, and children's rights advocate. We didn't know that she'd helped plot her husband's campaigns, held her own as a political infighter, and joined the fray when Team Clinton went after his detractors.

Nor had we really met her husband, Bill. We didn't yet understand how a hard-charging bear of a man could be the same sort of guy who'd bite his lip and turn all misty-eyed when his emotions welled up. We'd never seen the way he'd lean in with that raspy whisper, his face a few shades shy of a garden beet's, and place his hands on listeners, male or female, making them feel he was theirs alone.

At the time—January 1992—Hillary and Bill Clinton, the first couple of Arkansas, were little more than a blip on the electorate's radar. And then, in an instant, they were Breaking News.

On the most media-hyped night of the year—Super Bowl Sunday—they were on network television. There was the forty-five-year-old governor with the salt-and-pepper mop offering a confession that would make the public jaw drop.

A no-name candidate. Dropping the A-bomb. With his wife perched right beside him. Then pushing ahead full throttle with his campaign. This was an all-in gamble to get out in front of a sex scandal, to deflate it and to *own* it by owning up to it.

I have acknowledged causing pain in my marriage, he allowed, with the cameras rolling. *I have said things to you tonight—and to the American people from the beginning—that no American politician ever has.*

And his wife had nodded in support, adding that she empathized with the other party in the equation, a private individual who'd been besieged by the media and the circumstances (not by her spouse, necessarily)—as if, in Hillary's words, the poor woman *"got hit by a meteor and it's no fault of [her] own."*

It had all begun to snowball two weeks earlier. Bill Clinton had appeared in his first high-profile cover story, for *New York* magazine. The headline got right to the point: "Who Is This Guy?" The article inside, by journalist Joe Klein, quoted an influential fund-raiser who branded Clinton "the very heavy favorite" to win the Democratic presidential nomination. The next week, there he was again, beaming from the cover of *Time*. The cover line: "Is Bill Clinton for Real?" The magazine described how this untested politician, just a month before the breakout New Hampshire primary, had been "anointed—prematurely—as the front runner" against the Republican incumbent, George H. W. Bush.

Dee Dee Myers, Clinton's first press secretary, vouches for his relative obscurity. Those were drowsier days, she points out, when daily papers controlled the narrative flow of the race; when just one cable news network, CNN, was on the air; when the terms "weblog" and "blog" wouldn't be coined for another five years. "It wasn't like it is now," she recalls over lunch at an outdoor restaurant in Washington, D.C., "where [candidates] are out there for two years and actually get covered [by the press]. They weren't on TV. People didn't know who Bill Clinton *was.* His name-ID, I'm sure, was under 20 percent." Indeed, at an event in South Carolina at the time, a local newspaper editor had confronted the candidate, point-blank, "Aren't you the guy who gave that awful speech for [Governor Mike] Dukakis at the 1988 Democratic Convention?"

That guy, exactly. If Clinton had made any national impression whatsoever, it was thanks to his interminable nominating speech, a numbing thirty-three minutes in all, delivered four years earlier in Atlanta. Its crescendo had come as he announced, "In *closing*…"—the very phrase inciting the delegates to bellow their approval.

If *he* was ill-defined, then so too was his wife. Hillary Rodham Clinton had gained early fame as Wellesley's first-ever student commencement speaker. She had a raft of accomplishments in the civil justice and legal

arenas. But she was a newly minted public figure outside her home terrain (Illinois, Yale Law, Arkansas power circles, and the corporate board
of Walmart). "This was the first time that anybody had ever seen Hillary,"
recalls CBS News correspondent Steve Kroft. "She had never really been on
[national] television before."

All that changed on January 26, 1992.

If ever there was a time to introduce a presidential aspirant, it was the
night when some eighty million viewers would tune in for the nation's most
hallowed secular fiesta. During the game, CBS had aired a ten-second teaser.
To the sound of a ticking stopwatch, a video clip showed flash bulbs popping.
A telegenic candidate and his wife waved at a crowd from a podium. The
voice-over promised, *After the game, a* 60 Minutes *exclusive interview with
Governor and Mrs. Bill Clinton.*

Super Bowl XXVI turned out to be a rout. The Washington Redskins
pummeled the Buffalo Bills, 37–24. And for other such blowouts, most fans
would have bolted midway through the third quarter. But on this night,
thirty-four million stayed glued to their Barcos and their Naugahyde. They
stayed through the postgame interviews and the locker-room champagne.
They stayed for what was, back in the day, an unprecedented televised morality play.

In the months and years that followed, that particular Super Bowl Sunday would come to be remembered as the evening when much of America
would first lay eyes on a married pair who, respectively, would become the
forty-second and *not-quite*-forty-fifth presidents of the United States. And
due to the topic that night—a politician's implied admission of adultery—
the nation was getting a nasty foretaste. They were meeting a man who,
before the decade was out, would become the second American president
ever to be impeached, a man undone by the most politically divisive and personally destructive sex scandal in Washington history.

————

It had come together in a blur.

Bill Clinton was under siege. Though he'd gained traction among Democratic mandarins, not a single primary voter had yet gone to the polls. On
top of it, he was suddenly getting a punishing share of unsolicited publicity.
His face was gracing not just *Time* but also the front page of the *Star*, a supermarket tabloid.

Eura Gean Flowers went by the name of Gennifer. As a reporter for the NBC affiliate in Little Rock, Arkansas, Ms. Flowers in 1977 had met and become familiar with the state's attorney general, Bill Clinton. By 1992 she was working as a local nightclub singer and by day as an employee of the Arkansas Appeal Tribunal—a $17,500-a-year position she had recently managed to land through then-governor Clinton's good graces. Gennifer Flowers—yes, *Flowers*; yes, Gennifer *with a G*—was a thistle-teased ersatz blonde with a fetching swagger. She seemed to have a soft spot for shoulder pads. She possessed, as Norman Mailer once described a bottle blonde in his novel *Tough Guys Don't Dance*, "a full pout on the mouth, [that made her appear] as spoiled and imperious as the breath of sex." She was self-assured, articulate, and, incredibly enough, quite credible.

In the *Star*'s exclusive—for which Flowers was paid $150,000—she went into salacious detail about what she claimed was a twelve-year romance with the guv, a liaison that both she and Clinton had previously, and vehemently, denied.

The *Star* was on a tear. The week before, the tabloid had printed a story saying that Clinton had had relations outside his marriage with at least five women, including Flowers—a conjecture that Clinton's rapid-response troops had successfully downplayed, if not discredited. But now the *Star* was publishing a three-part bombshell ("Mistress Tells All—The Secret Love Tapes That Prove It"... "They Made Love All Over Her Apartment"). The first installment's most salient revelation was that Flowers had squirreled away an hour's worth of cassette recordings, which captured recent personal phone conversations she had had with her nominal boss. Flowers praised her lover's stamina in the sack. And, as if to pride herself on a discerning palate, she divulged that theirs was "the best sex I ever had." This was steamy stuff for reporters who, in those weeks before the primaries, tended to get their jollies from sitting in coffee shops with farmers, talking Medicare and crop rotation.

To be sure, the press corps was in a bind. For the last half of the twentieth century, legitimate news organizations had resisted using unsubstantiated reports about officials' personal slipups. Journalists were also loath to recycle the morsels dished out by the tabs, which occupied the lowliest strata on the editorial food chain. White House correspondents, for example, had been aware of both JFK's and LBJ's extracurriculars, and yet they'd remained mum to maintain the dignity of the office *and* their own privileged niche on the West Wing's perimeter.

But now that technology could provide proof—in the form of clandestinely recorded conversations—such civility was in eclipse. Here was corroboration. Here were the delicious echoes of Watergate. And despite the assertion that Flowers, in the words of Clinton's spokesmen, appeared to be peddling "trash for cash," the presence of the tapes suggested that her revelations were hardly garbage.[1] Flowers's threat of releasing the evidence was a major buzz kill for the high-flying campaign.

As Clinton continued with his public appearances, the media felt newly emboldened. It wasn't so much that reporters resented being misled by a politician (though they certainly did). Or that they would somehow seem complicit in an act of press-pack self-censorship (which they certainly would have been). But the idea of being upstaged by a tabloid skeeve-sheet like the *Star*? Not a chance.

Journalists began hounding Clinton, who held his ground, or, more accurately, his quicksand. "The allegations in the *Star* are not true," he said at one campaign stopover. "She's obviously taken money to change her story." But the denials—including a refutation by Hillary Clinton—were falling on deaf ears. Besides, the governor's reputation was being cited by Republican operatives, who didn't disguise their glee. One GOP strategist remarked sniffishly to *New York* magazine, "We hear [Clinton has] a history with the ladies. Are we worried? *You* guess."

Clinton, truth be told, had sown his share of nummy oats. One of his closest aides, Betsey Wright, had actually come up with a phrase—"bimbo eruptions": a code blue that would go out when one of the governor's alleged lady friends came tumbling out of the bushes.

Many of the rumors, it turned out, proved bogus. But not infrequently

---

1. Shortly afterward, as outlined in a retrospective article in the *New York Times*, private investigator Jack Palladino was hired by the campaign, reportedly with Hillary Clinton's consent, to look into Flowers's past. As part of a concentrated plan, drafted in March 1992, Palladino supposedly urged that "every [Flowers] acquaintance, employer, and past lover should be located and interviewed." According to Megan Twohey in the *Times*, Flowers began to get feedback "from boyfriends and others who said they had been contacted by a private investigator. 'They would say that he would try to manipulate them,' Ms. Flowers recalled, 'or get them to say things like I was sexually active.'" (Megan Twohey, "Her Husband Accused of Affairs, a Defiant Clinton Fought Back," *New York Times*, October 3, 2016, A, 15; Dick Morris, *Behind the Oval Office: Getting Reelected Against All Odds* [New York: St. Martin's, 1999], xxi–xxii.)

they had legs. And curves. Five years before, when Clinton was pondering a presidential run, Wright reportedly presented him with a veritable scroll of rumored companions. According to David Maraniss in his Clinton biography, *First in His Class*, Wright sat down with the governor in the quiet of her own living room and went over the names of some of his purported liaisons—not once but twice. "Okay," she said, according to Maraniss's account. "Now, I want you to tell me the truth about every one." (Clinton decided to sit out the 1988 race—for other reasons. As he persuasively claimed at the time, he was only forty, and both he and Hillary worried about "the impact of prolonged absences" on their daughter, Chelsea, then seven years old.)

But with this new election cycle, new squalls of warrantless rumor began to lash the campaign. In *Vanity Fair*, Sidney Blumenthal—who would become a close adviser to (and sometime apologist for) both Bill and Hillary Clinton—provided a laundry list of slurs. The governor did coke in his office. The governor had romped with the 1982 Miss America, Arkansas's Elizabeth Ward, who quickly batted down the story. According to Blumenthal, such scabrous fictions were partly the invention of campaign reporters who, hoping to impress their peers with "inside dopesterism," sometimes floated stories to sound as if they were on the cusp of the gossip curve. "In recent months," wrote Blumenthal, "a partial list of unsupported rumors [had depicted supposed incidents in which] Bill Clinton propositioned the young daughter of Ron Brown, the chairman of the Democratic National Committee.... Hillary Clinton has had a number of affairs. Hillary is gay. And so on."

If such innuendos weren't enough, the Clinton camp had to squelch one persistent and plainly libelous allegation. As shown in the campaign documentary *The War Room*, George Stephanopoulos, Clinton's deputy campaign manager for communications, would bark during a phone call, "If you went on the radio and said that Bill Clinton is the father of an illegitimate black child, you would be laughed at." On the other end of the line, according to the movie, was an ally of the formidable independent candidate for president, Ross Perot. "Believe me," Stephanopoulos continued, "it's been looked at by every major national news organization. Everything. And it is completely bullshit.... People would think you're crazy.... People will think you're scummy."

As time went on, this drip-drip-drip of dubious tips, according to historian and legal scholar Ken Gormley, among others, would have Clinton propositioning "the lead baton twirler for the University of Arkansas football squad"; Clinton fathering more than a dozen out-of-wedlock children; Clinton appearing in photos (as stated in a memo by a lawyer for a plaintiff in one anti-Clinton lawsuit) with his former Whitewater land-deal partner "[Susan] McDougal on the hood of [a] car having sex.... (Them, not the car.)" All, in the end, pure hooey.

But back in 1992, it mattered little if a thousand Flowers bloomed. That January, there was but one thorn that mattered.

———

A press release about the *Star* story was faxed to ABC News, as described in Hedrick Smith's PBS documentary *The People and the Power Game*. ABC's field reporter Jim Wooten read the release and, with a video cameraman in tow, broached the subject with the candidate. "Well, first of all, I read the story," Clinton insisted. "It isn't true." Wooten, who felt he needed other sources to support or counter the *Star*'s say-so, telephoned New York and gave the segment a thumbs-down. "There isn't enough substantiation," Wooten said, "so it's unfair." Peter Jennings, the anchor of ABC's *World News Tonight*, agreed. "There was a great battle royal here about whether you put it on the air," Jennings would later tell PBS. The ABC team decided to sit on the footage.

Stations subscribing to ABC's news feed, however, had no such compunctions. Local news shows had hours to fill, stiff competition, and generally less-accountable news executives calling the shots. News staffs in ABC's supply chain received an uplink of the actual snippet of Wooten and Clinton, and several channels simply ran the clip, unexpurgated. Their justification: a candidate actively *denying* an unsubstantiated tabloid report was, in its way, *news*.

Some news outlets naturally followed suit. Soon, others used the occasion as an excuse to "cover the media covering the story," as Clinton campaign mastermind James Carville would note, allowing the media "to cover its favorite subject, which is, of course, the media." Still others would come at it sideways, as "a tortured colloquium on whether or not infidelity was a legitimate issue," in the words of David Brock (at the time a right-wing muckraker, who would dissect the scandal in the *American Spectator*).

One night that week, the phone rang as Clinton's campaign manager, David Wilhelm, was sound asleep. A threatening voice, as Sidney Blumenthal would report a few months later in *Vanity Fair*, began to tick off a roster of supposed Clinton mistresses. "You're through, Wilhelm," the stranger said, before hanging up. Another Clinton aide fielded an even more foreboding call after he'd turned in for the night: "Your heart is going to be torn out. You're going to be dead."

Daylight hours brought little relief. Traveling reporters whispered quiet zingers. Fund-raisers grew uneasy with Clinton's viability, insisting that peter problems, once made public, invariably incinerated a candidate's chances. Chief campaign strategist Paul Begala saw the handwriting on the parapet wall. "If we don't turn this into a positive," he remarked, "we're going down."

Hillary Clinton herself—initially resistant to having her husband engage in a full-dress discussion of their marriage (believing it would rob them of their privacy, to say nothing of the effect it might have on their daughter, Chelsea, by then age eleven)—eventually bought into the plan for a counterattack. "I was persuaded that if we didn't deal with the situation publicly," she would explain in her memoir *Living History*, "Bill's campaign would be over before a single vote was cast."

The Clinton camp began to scramble. George Stephanopoulos was the campaign's floppy-banged pivot man for communications. Two weeks shy of his thirty-first birthday, he had not yet evolved, as he would by year's end, into politico-dreamboat status. At the Holiday Inn in Manchester, New Hampshire, Stephanopoulos hunkered down with James Carville, the campaign's top strategist. Carville was a roguish, shoot-from-the-lip veteran of numerous election bouts.

The pair were the governor's most invaluable aides: Stephanopoulos, the former altar boy, a Greek American with an Ivy League degree and a jones for a tussle (he'd been conditioned from his stint on the well-pummeled Dukakis campaign); Carville, the wily, wiry consultant with his chaw-jawed speaking manner, whose competitive juices and heavy Louisiana accent had first bubbled up from the stewpot of the bayou. (Some of the GOP's most outspoken seers respected Carville's hot-under-the-collar TV persona. He had an admirable ferocity, and screen presence, that opponents sometimes spoke of in zoological terms: he could look, in the words of Fox News founder Roger Ailes, "like a fish who's swum too close to a nuclear reactor.")

James and George had their work cut out for them. On Thursday, the campaign had discussions with ABC's *Nightline* to have the governor appear that night. But late in the day, as Carville would recall, the notion was nixed; Bill and Hillary Clinton insisted that they face the cameras together. And since Mrs. Clinton was traveling in Georgia, she couldn't connect with her husband in time. So the telecast was scrubbed.[2]

The next morning Stephanopoulos got on the phone with *60 Minutes'* Steve Kroft. They had to move fast, and both of them knew it.

Kroft was a forty-six-year-old correspondent who had joined the *60 Minutes* stable three years before. Among his more famous elders at TV's preeminent weekly newsmagazine, he was beginning to throw his weight around. The night before, Kroft recalls, he happened to be having drinks with Anne Reingold, an ex-CBS colleague then working for the Democratic National Committee. They'd both wondered: if the rumored *Nightline* broadcast didn't materialize, might Clinton consider a *60 Minutes* interview? Reingold was eager to help and, according to Kroft, put him in touch with Stephanopoulos.

"Our situation was so serious," Stephanopoulos would observe in his memoir, *All Too Human*, "that the only hope was the media equivalent of experimental chemotherapy. *60 Minutes* was strong enough to cure us—if it didn't kill us first." (Stephanopoulos declined to be interviewed for this book.) For Kroft, any further delay could be disastrous; he couldn't risk losing the story to, say, a local reporter, should Clinton decide to issue a mea culpa on some windswept tarmac. And so: the Hail Mary pass on Super Bowl night.

"Do you want to do this?" Stephanopoulos pressed him.

"Yeah, but you've got to understand something," Kroft said, explaining that his boss was traveling in San Francisco. "We don't have a show. I have to go to Don Hewitt. I have to ask him about this to see if we can get some time back from the network to do it."

According to Kroft, Stephanopoulos—possibly preoccupied by the primary maelstrom—asked, "What do you mean you don't have a show?"

"Well, we've got the game."

"What game?" Stephanopoulos supposedly inquired.

"The Super Bowl?" said Kroft.

Stephanopoulos, recalls Kroft, paused a moment. "You mean this would be on after the Super Bowl?"

---

2. Others say the *Nightline* appearance never had a prayer. An Arkansas death row inmate was set to be executed the next night and the governor didn't want to be seen on TV yapping about the state of his marriage while his state was dispensing with a prisoner.

Today Kroft sits in his *60 Minutes* office overlooking the Hudson River, two decades after that conversation. He contends that the lure of the big game helped close the deal. "The subtext was clear," says Kroft, who recalls that he also conferred with Clinton campaign chairman Harold Ickes. "There was a mutual need that [Bill Clinton] wanted to address this *once*. And we said, 'Look, if you come on *60 Minutes* you can say, "I talked about this on *60 Minutes*, and I'm not going to talk about it again." ' "

The legendarily aggressive *60 Minutes* interview had acquired a dedicated following as a Sunday night blood sport. But it had always afforded the producers an unfair advantage. As the Mother of All Public Grillings, the show's segments had elements of a show trial. The victim, many times at the darkest hour of his or her public life, was paraded before a stern inquisitor. He sat in surreal light and shadow in a sterile setting: a hotel room, a book-lined office, a nondescript conference room. He faced a series of queries, each more pointed. Even his appearance had a funereal aspect: he had likely chosen somber attire and had been ceremonially daubed in makeup. The encounter, despite its theatricality, had the high seriousness of an inquest.

For the Clintons, however, the format had distinct advantages. If they could paint Prosecutor Kroft as a stand-in for the rest of the press, they might win sympathy as yet another political couple being placed under the media microscope. If they could bristle indignantly about the adultery question, they might get the audience wondering: why should *anyone's* extramarital matters have any bearing on his fitness for public service? And the governor, on top of it all, might get points just for *showing up*. Viewers, in the era before reality TV, sometimes believed that one's willingness to occupy the hot seat implied he might have less to hide than met the eye.

At this stage, though, Kroft held most of the cards as he and Stephanopoulos set some ground rules. First, the interview would have to be done on Sunday morning, at the Ritz-Carlton in Boston, to give CBS time to edit the show and ready the tape for broadcast. Second, the program would run as a short "special edition" (ten to fifteen minutes, tops), which was all the time the network could spare on such a crowded, coveted night. What's more, the thrust of the segment would have to focus on the *Star* controversy. "We want to talk about Gennifer Flowers," Kroft recalls saying to both Stephanopoulos and Ickes. " 'That's the only thing *we* want to talk about, and that's the only thing *you* want to talk about.' We [didn't] want to get into a situation where we're going to put him on after the Super Bowl and talk about health care." (Some Clinton insiders would later contend they'd settled on a more wide-ranging interview and that CBS had agreed to air the tape largely unedited—claims that, to this day, the *60 Minutes* camp refutes.)

Finally, as Kroft recollects, CBS would have to agree to a key campaign demand. "How would you feel," Stephanopoulos asked, "about Mrs. Clinton appearing with him?"

"Great," Kroft replied. "*Better.*"

———

To prepare for the interview, Clinton's team arrived in Boston late Saturday. They were met by Kroft and his boss Don Hewitt, the producer who'd created *60 Minutes*—TV's first newsmagazine—in 1968.[3] The producers walked the Clintons through the hotel suite where the interview would be taped the next day. It had a fireplace, two lapis vases, some potted plants, assorted porcelain. The couple would be seated on an eggshell-white couch; Kroft would sit across from them in an upholstered armchair. A water pitcher would be kept full and at the ready. Hillary discussed camera placement, the positioning of the chairs. "She was in control," Kroft would later tell *Vanity Fair*'s Gail Sheehy. "[If] you didn't know she was his wife, you'd have thought she was a media consultant. She didn't do it in a dictatorial sort of way.... She was very delightful and charming. When they left the room, everybody pretty much said, 'Boy, she's terrific.'"

Outside, however, bedlam reigned. "Governor Clinton!"..."Did you have *an affair*?!"..."*Governor!* What about *Gennifer Flowers*?!" James Carville was struck not just by the number of reporters who had come to town on the eve of the broadcast but also by their level of frenzy. "We were in Boston [surrounded by] the hordes of the media," Carville recalls, speaking from his home in New Orleans. "For, like, five seconds I thought I was going to die. It musta been kinda like being at a Brazilian soccer match and trying to get out of the stadium, and you have *no* control. You're pinned. You're just at the mercy of this throng. And they were, like, throwing microphones at him and everything." Carville remembers literally being lifted off his feet at one point, swept along on a tide of journalists' torsos and elbows. Cameras were

———

3. Considered one of the forefathers of modern network news, Hewitt had been the pioneer behind the storied Kennedy-Nixon face-off of 1960, the first presidential debate to be telecast.

hefted up and pointed down, shooting the mayhem. Grown men snarled. Flash bulbs and tempers flared. "I think this, of its time, was the worst," he concedes, never having experienced a press scrum more intimidating. "That's the most [ravenous] I remember."

Clinton's top aides took refuge in a hotel room and strategized their battle plan. Each was acutely aware that their jobs were riding on the way that a few hot minutes of television would play out twenty-four hours hence. "We discussed whether he should make a general admission of adultery—explicitly, unequivocally, using that word instead of a euphemism," Stephanopoulos would recall in *All Too Human*. But no dice. "Both Clinton and Hillary were adamant about not using the A word, arguing that it was too grating, too harsh, too in-your-face to the viewers at home."

Carville and Mandy Grunwald, the canny media adviser, stuck to the essentials. It was important that they admit to previous marital strain. But they had to underscore a larger issue: what had this nation come to when it paid more attention to a potential nominee's private life than to how he might address the nation's economic, political, and international challenges?

The session broke well after midnight. "No one could sleep," Stephanopoulos recounted in his autobiography. So the team repaired to pollster Stan Greenberg's room to unwind. "We talked about the day ahead and whether we'd even be together a week from now. For us, no matter how tomorrow turned out, it would be a war story, the day we bet a whole campaign on a single interview.... Tomorrow the whole country would be discussing [the Clintons'] marriage."

Jotting down notes, Clinton's young communications chief drafted what turned out to be a game-day memo. It urged Clinton, in straightforward terms, *Use your family as a metaphor for character. You've had problems in your marriage, you've faced them, you've worked through them, and you're coming out stronger than ever.*

James Carville had barely slept. Due to nervous exhaustion and the anxious anticipation, he spent much of the night crying in his room. ("I don't mean tearing up," he would write in his campaign memoir, *All's Fair*.[4] "I mean sobbing for hours, drained, weeping piteously.") Nonetheless, he had

---

4. Carville cowrote the book with his wife, Mary Matalin, who in 1992 was helping to run the campaign of Clinton's eventual opponent George H. W. Bush.

found time to draft a parallel set of bite-the-bullet bullet points with Paul Begala. Among their pearls, according to Carville's book:

> * [Remain] calm.... Reporters and voters are like horses and dogs—they can sense when someone is fearful.
> * [Hillary] is our ace in the hole.... When y'all feel like Steve is going too far... Hillary needs to interrupt and say: "Look, Steve... it's our relationship; our marriage; our family—and at some point we have to draw a line."

Begala and Carville advised the governor to don a sweater: "We can't think of anyone who wears a suit on Super Bowl Sunday." (Clinton ignored them and wore a dark suit.) They quoted Confucius, referenced Elvis, and cited Hemingway's *A Farewell to Arms*: "The world breaks everyone and afterward many are strong at the broken places."

Clinton had also fielded advice from Dick Morris, the battle-hardened operative who would later become ensnared in his own sex scandal. Morris, according to his memoir *Behind the Oval Office*, counseled Clinton to be contrite, apologize to his wife in front of the nation, and tick off a list of past presidential infidelity—possibly citing Eisenhower, Kennedy, and Johnson by name. As a kicker, Morris said, Clinton should ask voters—at the risk of sounding presumptuous—that they believe "his past sins would no more interfere with his ability to serve the nation than it had interfered with these other great presidents." The governor took a pass, not wanting to offend Hillary. "That's a good line," Clinton supposedly told Morris, "but if I said it I'd have to find a new place to live."

Steve Kroft, meanwhile, was getting his own ducks in a row. This was an act that had elements of the high wire and the tripwire. How, then, to delicately ask a candidate about alleged infidelity without appearing sleazy oneself? To prepare, Kroft sought counsel from his producer L. Franklin Devine, and the program's most confrontational interviewer, Mike Wallace.

Wallace, according to Kroft, "told me, 'Don't be mean to him; don't push him too hard; don't be too aggressive with the questions.' Why Mike told me that I have no idea, because I don't believe that Mike would have handled the interview that way....I felt like I had to protect the record. [Since this would be the only such interview,] I had to ask him every question that everybody else wanted to ask, and I had to ask him it two or three different ways." Later, Kroft says, he discovered "from a number of CBS executives [that] Mike Wallace spent a couple of days trying to get it away from me, behind the scenes," lobbying to be allowed to conduct the interview himself. Hewitt, however, stuck with Kroft, who had brought in the scoop.

Clinton's widely dispersed team tuned in from Arkansas, Iowa, New Hampshire, and across the country. Gary Ginsberg had left his job as a young corporate lawyer in Manhattan—on the very day the Flowers story had broken—to begin work as Clinton's new advance-operations director. A Buffalo Bills fan, Ginsberg (now an executive at Time Warner) was sitting with his father in a bar in Minneapolis, the site of that year's Super Bowl. He was convinced, he now puts it, that "this was going to be the shortest leave of absence anyone has ever enjoyed from a Wall Street law firm. I thought I was going to be back in New York by the end of that week."

What they witnessed, along with the rest of the nation, was a condensed version of an interview that had gone on for a relentless hour or so, a session with so much offstage intrigue it could have sustained an operetta.

––––––

The Clintons sat beside each other on the couch. Two cameras stayed focused on the couple: Bill, with his hands held as if in prayer, positioned between his knees; Hillary, with her arm cozily draped behind his back or straying occasionally to settle on his arm. She wore a thin black headband and a turquoise suit with matching turtleneck. From time to time she examined her husband lovingly, yet she maintained a commanding air, nodding approvingly as he spoke, then jumping in as necessary.

Her husband's responses were measured, firm, and softly delivered. His tone was emphatic and empathetic. Often, the impression he conveyed was that of an earnest choirboy with all the naughty scolded out of him. At some points, a viewer couldn't help thinking that he was a nimble actor as well, patting his heart and leaning forward thoughtfully—the Clinton whom columnist Maureen Dowd would come to call the "maestro of faux sincerity." Now and again he appeared hurt, even vaguely aghast, his bottom lip resolutely chewed or his eyebrows gone all circumflex. At other times he shook his head or narrowed his eyes to express exasperation with his interrogator, who got right to the point.

Kroft: [Gennifer Flowers] is alleging and has described in some detail in the supermarket tabloid what she calls a twelve-year affair with you.

Clinton: That allegation is false.

Hillary Clinton: When this woman first got caught up in these charges, I felt as I've felt about all these women—that, you know, they've just been minding their own business....

Clinton: It was only when money came out, when the tabloid went down there offering people money to say that they had been involved with me, that she changed her story. There's a recession on. Times are tough. And I think you can expect more and more of these stories as long as they're down there handing out money.

Kroft: I'm assuming from your answer that you're categorically denying that you ever had an affair with Gennifer Flowers.

Clinton: I said that before. And so has she.

Kroft pressed on, posing The Question from every conceivable angle. Clinton's responses were even-tempered, but his answers always fell short of the drum-tight categorical.

Kroft: You've said that your marriage has had problems.... What do you mean by that?... Help us break the code. I mean, does that mean that you were separated?... Had communication problems?... Contemplated divorce? Does it mean adultery?

Clinton: I think the American people, at least people that have been married for a long time, know what it means and know the whole range of things it can mean.

Kroft: ... Are you prepared tonight to say that you've never had an extra-marital affair?

Clinton: I'm not prepared tonight to say that any married couple should ever discuss that with anyone but themselves.... I think most Americans who are watching this tonight, they'll know what we're saying; they'll get it, and they'll feel that we have been more candid. And I think what the press has to decide is: Are we going to engage in a game of 'gotcha'? . . .

Kroft: I don't like some of these questions any better than you do. . . .

But that didn't stop him from pressing on.

Clinton, while he appeared calm and even chastened on camera, would later admit that he was fuming. After denying a romance with Flowers, he would later recall in his autobiography that Kroft "asked if I had had any affairs." Then, after stating that he'd "caus[ed] pain" in his marriage, Clinton was gobsmacked. "Kroft, unbelievably, asked me again. His only goal in the interview was to get a specific admission."

The exchange, which came off as civil, was actually getting progressively testier. To make matters worse, the mood in the room was already at full boil. Off-camera, Stephanopoulos stood to the side, offering the Clintons moral support. Hewitt was ensconced in the adjacent "control room," with producers and several Clinton aides, including a tightly wound Carville.

Twice there was a break in the taping. And twice, Carville now says, he would shout out encouragement, like an exuberant coach on the sidelines. "When they'd reload the camera and put another magazine in, I said, 'That's great, man! You're doing great!'" Hewitt, in parallel, would swoop in and get on his haunches right next to the couch, making a direct appeal to the governor. "It was kind of crazy," says Kroft. "Don would come out, in between takes, and knelt down next to Clinton . . . and said, 'Look, you've got to come clean. You've got to tell us.' Because Don, I think, wanted some resolution. He thought the headlines would be bigger or the story would be bigger if Clinton were more direct and honest about it.

"Nobody knew who James Carville *was*," Kroft recalls. "I knew his name, but he was certainly known only to political people at that point. Don threw him out of the screening room because he was saying how good [Clinton was doing]." (Hewitt, in his memoir, *Tell Me a Story*, recounted saying, "Will someone please shut this guy the fuck up or get him the hell out of here!")

"Hewitt was pissed at me," Carville insists, "because he didn't want Clinton to think he was doing well. He wanted Clinton to think he was doing shitty. [Hewitt] kept telling him, 'You got to come clean with the whole thing.' Clinton just looked at him like he was crazy." (Hewitt, says Carville, later wrote him "a taut letter, kind of a shitty letter, you know: 'I've been in this business for all these years, I've never seen [behavior like that]!' ")

Finally, Kroft tripped the switch. He tried to articulate what many viewers were thinking. But he made an observation that might as well have been supercharged in a cyclotron: "I think most Americans would agree that it's very admirable that you've stayed together—that you've worked your problems out, that you've seemed to have reached some sort of understanding and an arrangement."

"I wanted to slug him," Clinton would concede. Here he was—alongside the woman he'd admittedly aggrieved, her hand on his forearm—hearing their sixteen-year marriage characterized as *an arrangement*. "Instead, I said, 'Wait a minute. You're looking at two people who love each other. This is not an arrangement or an understanding. This is a marriage.' "

Instinctively, Hillary pounced. Her candid, coolheaded response was the sound bite heard round the world—the one that would turn Bill and Hillary into household names: "You know, I'm not sitting here, some little woman standing by my man, like Tammy Wynette. I'm sitting here because I *love* him, and I *respect* him, and I honor what he's been through and what we've been through *together*. And, you know, if that's not enough for people—then, heck, don't vote for him."

Heck yeah. The wallflower political wife? The pitiable victim of her husband's philandering? That caricature of a candidate's spouse had been suddenly, irrevocably sent packing. In a single stroke, Hillary Rodham Clinton had broken it all down to what mattered to viewers—and voters:

- The way that a couple behaves, and forgives, is ruled by its own dynamics.
- Love shouldn't be judged by fixed moral codes. (When it comes to long-term romantic relationships: *It's complicated.*)
- The press (and the political opposition research squads), damn it, should just steer clear of people's private affairs.
- And, take that, Gennifer-with-a-G.

Hillary Clinton's broadside was a bracing rejoinder to Kroft's statement, which had come off to many as patronizing. She had projected righteous indignation and political backbone. (Indeed, as journalist Gail Sheehy would point out, the governor had long recognized his wife's political appeal: "Some say the wrong Clinton is in the statehouse.... It doesn't bother me for people to see her and get excited and say she could be president. I always say she could be president, too.") She had also displayed her steadfast commitment to this newest curiosity on the national stage—this likable, complex, beguiling man.[5]

Dee Dee Myers was watching the broadcast with other staffers in the open bullpen of the Little Rock campaign headquarters. "People were kind of hanging on every word," she reflects. "It was pretty quiet; there was no applause moment. And afterward they didn't have this instantaneous talking-head thing that you would have now, where you go right to a panel of pundits to talk about, 'How'd he do?,' where you've got MSNBC and Fox and CNN. We thought it went pretty well. We didn't *know*."

Mark McKinnon, who would become media adviser to George W. Bush, as governor and then as president, had also tuned in that night. "I remember thinking two things watching the broadcast," says McKinnon, who had recently been working in Texas on Ann Richards's campaign for governor. "It was going to be impossible for Clinton to recover because the charges were so humiliating. *And* that Clinton *was* going to recover because the confession was just so candid and audacious. Never before had the American public seen a candidate for president air his dirty laundry so publicly—with his spouse by his side."

Perhaps the best measure of the segment's impact was how the opposition viewed it. Carville's partner at the time (later his wife) was Mary Matalin, the political director of President George H. W. Bush's reelection campaign. Today she calls the Clintons' appearance "masterful."

"All campaigns," Matalin says from her New Orleans home, come down to "looking at somebody else's playbook. But they had no playbook to look at. They had to make a brand-new event. And they had to get the wife on board. And they had to get everyone to execute perfectly. And the timing of

---

5. Hillary Clinton's defense of her husband's behavior (and her slam of Gennifer Flowers later that week as a "failed cabaret singer" possibly seeking a payday and "fifteen minutes of fame") would sow the seeds for the electorate's long-term wariness of HRC's candor and motives. In 2016, Politico's Michael Kruse would quote one of Hillary Clinton's Wellesley friends, Nancy Wanderer, about that post–Super Bowl appearance: "I just said the other day, 'When did this business start, when people began to not like her, not trust her?' And I think it's the *60 Minutes* interview." (Michael Kruse, "The TV Interview That Haunts Hillary," Politico.com, September 23, 2016; Sam Donaldson, "The Other Woman," *Primetime Live* interview, January 30, 1992, https://www.youtube.com/watch?v=jUOhUei6aTM.)

it. There are very few things in politics that are *purposefully* make-or-break; there are very few things that are make-or-break, period. But that you *on purpose* set up a make-or-break moment? That never happens. *Nobody* does that. That took so much courage.

"Politically, [the Clinton campaign] had to lance the boil," she reflects. "That has never been done as well before or since. That Super Bowl moment was so brilliant—because it paid forward. [It] was like shooting the elephant in the room, with not a drop of blood on the floor."

———

And then the sky fell in—almost literally.

The overhead lights for the shoot, which had been rigged up by a Boston freelance crew, somehow became unmoored, along with their wood-beam mount. The rigging toppled over, barely missing Hillary. "They just kind of popped off," Kroft remembers, "and came crashing down on the back of the sofa behind the Clintons, and it knocked over a pitcher of water, and they lurched forward [to avoid the] burning filaments and flying glass.

"And she said, 'Jesus, Mary, and Joseph!'—I'll never forget that. Which wouldn't have been the first words out of *my* mouth. That's one thing I've learned about Hillary, starting then: she has a tremendous amount of self-control."

Bill Clinton, a tragedy averted, took his wife in his arms, clutched her close, and kept telling her softly that he loved her and that everything would be okay.

Taping was halted. The mood was broken. The TV lights might as well have been the Clintons' wider world, which all week had seemed to be collapsing around them. But in that instant there was security and love and a ray of hope.

Jim Kennedy, who would later become a Clinton "crisis manager" during his second term as president, recently reviewed the unedited tape. "That scary moment," he says, "when Bill Clinton grabs hold of Hillary Clinton in a very immediate and protective way and they keep holding on to each other, reveals a deeper truth at the heart of the entire one-hour interview. It was touching because it said something about their relationship that I think is important: that they were together, they were a team, they cared about each other, they were *in love*. There's a real bond there despite whoever or whatever tries to come between them." Kroft, in fact, says that friends of his who knew the Clintons would later tell him, "Bill said that that moment won him six months of good favor with Hillary. He had come to her rescue. He was there to console her"—admittedly after she, on national television, had come to rescue *him*.

Just as the session ended, Carville was next. He rushed over to Clinton's side and began weeping. The governor, as he had with Hillary, held Carville and comforted him, saying, as Carville remembers it, "Yeah, we got through this, buddy."

Carville now insists he was experiencing a mess of emotions: "I probably felt exhaustion, relief, and just the utter sadness of watching these people have to sit there for an hour or however long it was, and to answer these questions. It was just like a fucking—just painful, you know? We'd been four or five days of dealing with this. I probably hadn't slept.... [But despite] the exhaustion, [it] was, like, 'It was over.' And I'd pushed for the *60 Minutes* alternative.

"It was just a relief that, you know, my whole standing in the campaign, if that thing would have gone poorly, [might have been at risk]. But it was fine"—even though, he adds, "like everybody else on *60 Minutes*, I thought we got kinda like a shitty edit."

Clinton—and his reputation—seemed to have tolerated the antidote. Yet his aides weren't quite sure. "The takeaway from the night was, 'Okay, we put our case out there,'" says Dee Dee Myers, "'but we have no frickin' idea how it's going to play.' None. Because we were in unchartered territory.... That moment was not something we'd seen a lot of: a politician acknowledging infidelity."

"In all my years in politics, in running statewide races, I had never—*nobody*—had [ever] seen this," Carville says, adding, with a laugh, "I think everybody was a virgin on this kind of thing."

And with that, as Carville remembers it, the whole group went upstairs to a feast of cold cuts and an ice chest crammed with longneck beers. "I just never tasted a beer that tasted so good in my life."

Matalin is careful to point out that her husband doesn't easily tear up. "Campaigns are emotional," she says. "James has never run to me and sobbed, even at the birth of our kids. That's just not how he is. But when you're doing something for someone that's never been done before, [it] evoke[s] emotion. Maybe James was crying. But that's not evidence of James being an emotional person. That's evidence of, 'Wow, did we just not only dodge a bullet? We just landed on the beach.'"

CHAPTER 4

The Bubba Boomer

Bill Clinton represented a new masculine archetype.

Not that American males ever emulated him, not consciously. But many men across the land already shared some of his propensities. Clinton was that rare public figure who encapsulated the whole brash package: the perpetually horny, ever-prevaricating, irrepressibly optimistic, in-touch-with-his-inner-Hillary, emotionally expressive (if artificially sweetened) Bubba Boomer.

As the dominant figure of '90s America, he had a persona, a worldview—and a rash of peccadilloes—that helped shape and scar the national psyche. As such, any psychosocial assessment of the national manhood in that decade requires a deep dive into Clinton the man.

———

Bill Clinton, alone among American presidents, is the leader we associate, in a single breath, with sex.[1] And Clinton's studly reputation—as archaic as that sounds today—may have worked in his *favor* in the '92 election, especially in light of his opponent: incumbent president George H. W. Bush.

During the previous election cycle, Vice President Bush had been por-

———

1. In all, one out of every three presidents has been a straying spouse, according to the conservative commentator and political theorist William Bennett, citing Brown University professor James Morone, who has calculated that fourteen U.S. presidents have exhibited extramarital behavior that "set off whispers." The dean of campaign reporters, Teddy White, felt confident in his belief that of the presidential candidates he'd covered, all but three—Harry Truman, Michigan governor George Romney, and Jimmy Carter—had entertained "casual partners." (William J. Bennett, *The Death of Outrage: Bill Clinton and the Assault on American Ideals* [New York: Simon & Schuster, 1998], 24; Matt Bai, "How Gary Hart's Downfall Forever Changed American Politics," *New York Times Magazine*, September 18, 2014; Theodore H. White, *In Search of History: A Personal Adventure* [New York: HarperCollins, 1978], 529.)

trayed by the media and his Democratic foes as lacking a requisite manliness. *Newsweek* put it plainly in a low-blow cover story: "George Bush: Fighting the 'Wimp Factor.'" Writer Margaret Garrard Warner asserted that "Bush suffers from a potentially crippling handicap—a perception that he isn't strong enough or tough enough for the challenges of the Oval Office. That he is, in a single mean word, a wimp."

Going after this particular candidate's machismo was a cheap shot, and unjustifiable. Bush had been a Navy aviator, a war hero, the chief of the CIA, the head of the Republican National Committee, and an envoy to both China and the U.N. His single-term foreign policy record was sterling: removing strongman Manuel Noriega from power in Panama; coordinating the West's measured response as the Berlin Wall fell and the Soviet Union collapsed; and rebuffing Iraq's invasion of Kuwait. All in four years.

Even so, the slur stuck. The same month as *Newsweek*'s takedown, a *Doonesbury* cartoon strip also used the wimprimatur. (*Doonesbury*'s creator, Garry Trudeau, had previously accused Mr. Bush of being so deferential to Ronald Reagan that he'd agreed to place his "manhood in a blind trust.") Half of the nation's voters, in fact, told pollsters that Bush had an image problem. On TV, his voice came across as reedy. And as he hit the stump and the airwaves, the man who seemed to be forever shrouded in the shadow of the Great Communicator appeared "stiff or silly," by *Newsweek*'s gauge, and unable to "project self-confidence, wit or warmth to television viewers."

It was partly a function of manner. Bush was levelheaded, a centrist, an experienced diplomat. He was a politician who'd gotten into the game not for the power jag but *to serve*. In an age when voters were eager for ego, Bush quashed his own for the sake of the common good—or, in one infamous instance, a bipartisan tax deal.

But H.W. couldn't shake the W. tag. Yes, he'd managed to defeat an even wimpier adversary in 1988: the diminutive Mike Dukakis, who in one campaign photo op had posed punily in the commander's hatch of a tank. And yet the president was still perceived as that privileged son of a senator, Connecticut's honorable Prescott Bush. As a boy, he'd been "chauffeured to the Greenwich Country Day School," according to *Time*, and was occasionally "spanked by his father with a squash racquet." He was an Episcopalian swell, as Texas governor Ann Richards once quipped, "born with a silver foot in his mouth." He had a wife (Babs!) with such a snow-white coif that people sometimes mistook her for his mum. He had nicknames (Poppy! Gampy!) that made it sound as if he was already bound for assisted living.

And his biggest campaign gaffe of all against Bill Clinton? Bush was accused of being utterly flummoxed one day on the campaign trail when he came across a grocery barcode scanner. The implication? This pampered preppie had rarely set foot in a supermarket and therefore couldn't grasp the everyday financial strains of the common voter.

The incident became Bush's albatross. It wasn't just a matter of the old boy being out of the loop. It was a reflection of the anemic economy he was overseeing. For that rough patch in the late '80s (when Wall Street took a nosedive), to the oil-price spike-and-plummet after Iraq's 1990 invasion of Kuwait, to the 1992 election, Bush had been the helmsman of a listing ship. The captain—who had vowed never to raise taxes and then had done exactly that—would have to be relieved of his duties and replaced by a more strapping and daring sort of sailor.

———

From the 1890s to the 1990s, the presidential role model had gone from the backwoodsy, gun-toting Rough Rider (TR) to the prepster from Phillips Academy and Yale (GHWB). And in the second half of the century, four mucho macho men stood out.

There was John Kennedy, who today might arguably be categorized as a sexual predator. Though JFK was praised as a family man—married to the most glamorous first lady of the twentieth century—the press corps and the public wink-winked throughout his presidency.[2] (Kennedy would privately insist that he needed to have sex daily—to avoid headaches, as he put it. And in a story that might have even been true, he supposedly bragged that he wasn't satisfied with a lover unless he'd "had her three ways.")[3] The Camelot myth, however, painted JFK as a picture of potency. He possessed the Kennedy pedigree, a combat veteran's bravura, and the vigor of youth (age forty-three when he took office). He also projected an athleticism that masked his physical ailments (Addison's disease, chronic back pain).

———

2. Never more so, perhaps, than the night Marilyn Monroe serenaded him with a breathy rendition of "Happy Birthday, Mr. President."

3. JFK's sexual rapacity was reckless and, by several inside accounts, abusive. Journalist Timothy Noah, in a review of Mimi Alford's memoir *Once Upon a Secret*, called Kennedy nothing less than "a compulsive, even pathological adulterer [who] treated women like whores…[and] had an appetite for subjecting those close to him to extreme humiliation." (Timothy Noah, "JFK, Monster," *New Republic*, February 8, 2012.)

Lyndon Johnson, following suit, was a legendary philanderer in chief. Rabelaisian, proud, and occasionally vulgar, he was known to flabbergast acquaintances by whipping out his Texas longhorn of a pecker. Historian Robert Dallek has attested that on one occasion the president got so angry with newsmen who were pressing him to justify America's role in the Vietnam War that he went full johnson. "According to [U.N. ambassador] Arthur Goldberg," Dallek writes, "L.B.J. unzipped his fly, drew out his substantial organ and declared, 'This is why!' "[4]

In 1981 came Ronald Reagan, the first *divorced* president—a daring social precedent. Not only did the conservative ex-governor exude Hollywood allure, as did his movie-star wife, but he was actually a product of the entertainment trade, having started out as a radio sports announcer, then a player in the studio system, then the head of the powerful Screen Actors Guild. His was not sex appeal as much as it was celebrity glam.

Ron in black tie and Nancy in sequins, dancing across a 1985 cover of *Vanity Fair*, did the Kennedys one better. And when the photographer for that shoot, the legendary Harry Benson, persuaded them to pose for a close-up kiss—"like a big-screen, Technicolor fade-out, just before the credits roll," as Benson now puts it—the picture would run across two full pages in the magazine. In the accompanying text, none other than William F. Buckley Jr. would gush that "the Reagans think it altogether splendid to dance together in their own version of Camelot." And the lines began to blur irrevocably between Washington and Hollywood, politics and marketing, power and romance.

And then up jumped Bill.

---

4. Next came three shades of bland. Richard Nixon, by turns gawky and gruff, seemed practically asexual. (In an attempt to throw interviewer David Frost off guard—or to establish a kind of conspiratorial rapport—Nixon joshed with him before one of their postpresidential Q&As in 1977, "So, did you do any fornicating this weekend?" The agonized phrasing betrayed someone unaccustomed to making manly small talk—let alone fornicating.) Gerald Ford was a well-known straight arrow whom comedians would depict as a stumblebum. And the devout peanut farmer Jimmy Carter proved to be the National Prude. His Baptist beliefs—he would admit to none other than *Playboy*—helped him wrestle with his own private sex fantasies. "I try not to commit a deliberate sin," he confessed, but "I'm human and I'm tempted....I've looked on a lot of women with lust. I've committed adultery in my heart many times....And God forgives me for it." While the nation's youth were getting their groove on, the Oval Office had become, for a time, a hormonal no-fly zone. (David Greenberg, "The President Who Never Came in from the Cold," Slate.com, December 4, 2008; Robert Scheer, "Playboy Interview: Jimmy Carter," *Playboy*, November 1976.)

———

The tale of Clinton's roots is hardly that of Moses in the bulrushes. But it has the requisite predestination of the best presidential lore.

By now the story has become familiar. William Jefferson Blythe III came into this world in 1946 in a town called Hope (population 6,000), an Arkansas hollow of watermelon patches, buttermilk churns, and phones with party lines. He was conceived, almost to the very week, on the leading edge of the Baby Boom. And ever the true Boomer, he would adopt the pop-culture fascinations of his peers: *Flash Gordon* movie serials, *Baby Huey* cartoons, TV's *Howdy Doody*. He favored Hostess fried pies and Royal Crown Cola. He attended Saturday matinees for a dime, finding inspiration in *High Noon*'s Marshal Will Kane, played by Gary Cooper. He took up the tenor sax (attending band camp six summers running), formed a high school trio, and revered Ray Charles and Elvis Presley. (Elvis became the moniker bestowed upon the guv by his '92 staff. The name of his campaign plane? *Air Elvis.*)

As destined births go, Billy's was not without its auguries. Three months before, his father W. J. Blythe Jr., had been the victim of a freak car accident. Ejected from his vehicle during a crash, he'd crawled from the wreckage, only to drown in a waterlogged ditch. Blythe was twenty-eight years old.

When his widow, Virginia Dell Blythe, gave birth on August 19, 1946, "there had been record heat the day before," writes David Maraniss in the Clinton biography *First in His Class*, "exceeding a hundred degrees, followed by a ferocious thunderstorm that cracked and boomed all night, igniting three fires in town. The local moviehouse happened to be showing a film that captured [the] twenty-three-year-old mother's predicament: *The Young Widow*, starring Jane Russell."

Virginia was a let-loose, life-of-the-party gal. And it didn't take a slide rule for local folks to float the rumors. Nine months before his son was born, W.J. Jr., a salesman turned World War II mechanic, had *not* been in Hope, some said—or even in Arkansas. He'd reportedly been in war-torn Italy servicing the U.S. Army's tanks and transport vehicles. "There were whispers in Hope about who little Billy's father was," Maraniss contends, "[partly] spawned by Virginia's flirtatious nature." And yet Maraniss's research shows that Virginia Blythe gave birth a month ahead of schedule—by C-section—which would place the child's conception at a time when Blythe had already returned stateside. What's more, contemporaneous acquaintances of Bill's have said that he bore an uncanny resemblance to W. J. Blythe.

Blythe himself had hardly been a choirboy. Unbeknownst to Virginia, he had already fathered two children over the course of three broken marriages. Clinton, in his memoir *My Life*, would later describe his father in terms that would suit them both: "a handsome, hardworking, fun-loving man." Blythe's loss left the son "with the feeling that I had to live for two people.... The knowledge that I, too, could die young drove me...to try to drain the most out of every moment."

At age four, Billy would gain a stepdad, Roger Clinton, the owner of the local Buick dealership. The elder Clinton had been a runaround and a violent one at that, even while he was dating the boy's mom. In court papers, Clinton's ex-wife had claimed her husband was a batterer, and he would go on to repeat that pattern, abusing Virginia during drink-fueled outbursts.

Early on in their marriage, Roger Clinton pulled out a gun in the middle of one of his rages and fired a bullet into a nearby wall, just missing his wife and stepson; the cops were summoned. When Bill was fourteen, one altercation got so heated that when he rushed to his mother's aid and found Roger smacking Virginia, Bill took matters into his own hands. "I grabbed a golf club out of my bag," Clinton would recall. "I told him to stop and said that if he didn't I was going to beat the hell out of him.... We didn't have any more trouble for a good while."

In 1962, Virginia sought and received a divorce. But as sometimes happens with couples mired in codependency, they reconciled and remarried. And young Bill, of his own volition, decided to legally change his last name to Clinton.

Bill Clinton, like many presidents, may have had what men's movement activist Robert Bly has called "father hunger." The boy had never known the male parent listed on his birth certificate. He assumed the name of a struggling alcoholic whom he called Daddy. He was forever striving to prove himself worthy of his elders. He faced absence and anguish—his mother's, his younger brother Roger Cassidy Clinton's, and his own. "I came to accept the secrets of our house as a normal part of my life," Clinton would later concede, insisting that he suffered in silence, never daring to mention to a soul this cycle of addiction and abuse. "Secrets can be an awful burden to bear, especially if some sense of shame is attached to them.... I now know [my personal spiritual] struggle is at least partly the result of growing up in an alcoholic home and the mechanisms I developed to cope with it."

With his central father figures sometimes absent or aberrant,[5] Bill Clinton grew up devoted to his large-hearted, effervescent protector, a woman of Cherokee and Irish stock: Virginia Dell Cassidy Blythe Clinton Dwire Kelley. Mother, he called her—a nurse-anesthetist by trade. She had a hankering for the horses and was a regular at the Oaklawn Jockey Club. She was the daughter of an overbearing mother who had become addicted to morphine. Virginia also bore a second son, Roger Jr., who would battle his own substance issues. Over time, she would go on to compare her tumultuous life to "a country song."

Clinton's love for Mother was complete and altogether genuine. Transfixed by the woman's quotidian rituals, he would recall the care with which she'd comb out her wavy black hair. "I liked watching her brush it until it was just so," he would write dotingly in his autobiography. Then there was the "game face," as Clinton called it, that she applied to meet the day. "When I could get up early enough I loved sitting on the floor of the bathroom and watching her put makeup on that beautiful face. It took quite a while, partly because she had no eyebrows." She would draw them on instead, he remembers, "with a cosmetic pencil. Then she put on her makeup and her lipstick, usually a bright red shade." (Virginia became known for her spider-leg lashes and her "skunk stripe" coif.)

By the time Bill entered fourth grade, the Clintons had resettled in Hot Springs—Arkansas's "Sin City." Fifty miles from Little Rock, the raucous enclave was famous for its spas and sulfur springs.[6] The place liter-

---

5. Though the Clinton household lacked a trustworthy father figure, Bill would later recount that he had an extended family, with relatives "in fifteen of Arkansas' seventy-five counties." They were a colorful bunch. The first strong male presence in his childhood was his mother's father, James Eldridge Cassidy, a grocery store proprietor who taught him to treat all men and women, black or white, as equals. Buddy, his great-uncle, had conquered his own struggles with drink, swearing off alcohol one day and keeping that vow for half a century. The first time young Bill met his stepdad's father, a parole officer, the man was en route to the state pen, escorting an inmate. As Bill would recount that initial encounter with "Poppy Al": when his step-granddad first walked up to the family house in Hope, he was accompanied by a prisoner—*handcuffed to his wrist.* (Bill Clinton, *My Life* [New York: Random House/Vintage, 2004], 10–11, 15, 31).

6. The area's healing waters had persuaded sixteenth-century explorers like Hernando de Soto to believe they'd stumbled upon the proverbial "fountain of youth." As psychoanalytic pioneer Otto Rank pointed out, many heroes of history and the great myths had their origins in or around water, sometimes involving vessels that float along a river, echoing the birth trauma. Rank cites Babylonia's Sargon, the Israelites' Moses, the Hindus' Karna, as well as Oedipus and Romulus and Remus. (Clinton, *My Life*, 25; Otto Rank, *The Myth of the Birth of the Hero* [1914] *and Other Writings* [New York: Random House/Vintage, 1964], 14–44.)

ally bubbled with temptation. (For grins, a ten-year-old Bill Clinton and his pals would place prank calls to Maxine Harris's whorehouse to try and tie up the telephone lines.) Hot Springs, to put it bluntly, had vaporous moral guidelines—as Gail Sheehy once observed in *Vanity Fair* when discussing the effect of Clinton's upbringing on his marriage—and appealed to certain residents and visitors as "a warm bath of half-truths and hypocrisy where gamblers and bookies and fugitive mobsters from New York and Chicago found a resort just right for their tastes." It was a town, in Sheehy's view, "where a proliferation of Baptist churches attempted to put proper Sunday faces on the bathhouses, betting parlors, and brothels that were supported by the local government. 'In Hot Springs, growing up here, you were living a lie,' [said] a local prosecutor, Paul Bosson." Indeed, by the time Clinton rose through the Arkansas political ranks, several of his detractors would contend that the governor, having spent his formative years in that seatbed of vice, had been unavoidably schooled in the art of compromising one's conscience.

What, in fact, *were* Bill Clinton's ethical underpinnings? Faced with a home life marred by addiction and codependency, he improvised. And in time, he relied on several guideposts.

First came a commitment to Christ. Arkansas, in that curious American duality of the sacred and the profane, sat along the main artery of the Bible Belt. And even though Clinton's parents were not observant, their son made it his mission to attend Park Place Baptist Church almost every Sunday. By age nine or ten, Clinton's faith had become such an integral part of his life that he persuaded Mother to let him get baptized. "I had absorbed enough of my church's teachings," Clinton would recall, "to know that I was a sinner and to want Jesus to save me." At twelve, he sat in Little Rock's War Memorial Stadium and found inspiration in hearing Billy Graham, the prevailing moral authority of America's white Southern Baptists, preach to a biracial congregation. (Segregationists had urged Graham to ban African Americans from the assembly, an ultimatum he had refused.)

Next came Clinton's embrace of the life of the mind. He excelled at school, seeking refuge and edification in books and falling under the spell of a series of authors and educators. And then Clinton had a political awakening, partly shaped by the region's racial divide. In the summer of 1963, he was voted one of two student "senators" who would represent Arkansas at a conclave in Maryland for the Boys Nation public service program. And in his speech to the assemblage, Clinton spoke of the Little Rock Nine and the forced integration of schoolchildren that in 1957 had divided and riveted the nation. "We have grown up in a state," he announced, "ridden with the shame of a crisis it did not ask for." Most important and providential of all: that same week, the student delegation was invited to the White House, and Clinton positioned himself up close so he could shake hands with John Fitzgerald Kennedy—and have his picture snapped as he did.[7]

The Kennedy-Clinton Shake. Though the photograph would serendipitously show America's first "New Generation" presidents meeting face-to-face, nothing about Clinton's political trajectory had been foreordained. It would take a singularly driven individual to fulfill the promise presaged in that single frame. And William Jefferson Clinton was such a one. He'd been forced by circumstance to concoct his own survival skills. He'd stood up to the most threatening figure in his limited universe, taking the very name of that man. He'd embraced a new religion, of his own accord. His mental acuity and genuine grit would propel him to Georgetown and Oxford and Yale Law. He would fall in love with a woman of strength who was by every measure his intellectual equal. He would become one of the country's youngest governors. And those were just acts 1 and 2.

———

As a president, there was something entirely fresh about Bill Clinton. Unlike his generation's models, he was not the righteous, reliable fatherly type; not the tough-love coach; not the strong, silent war hero. Instead, he was a modern-age hybrid: the softie with a perpetual hard-on. He was a country lawyer with a wonkish precision, who telegraphed his every emotion in big, sloppy strokes. He was a cutthroat political infighter, who wore his heart on his sleeve and who desperately needed love—from both friend and foe. He was a dervish who would stop in his tracks to blabber a blue streak; a

———

7. Arnie Sachs, the local cameraman who chronicled the scene, would remember Clinton making a beeline for JFK: "This kid barrels through the line [of American Legion representatives] and grabs the president's hand, so I took the shot." Sachs, who ran a company in Washington, D.C., called Consolidated News Photos as well as a photo shop just steps from Capitol Hill, had been assigned by the American Legion that day to cover the students' visit and managed to catch the fateful shake on 2¼-inch film. (Clinton, *My Life*, 62; Adam Bernstein, "News Photographer Arnie Sachs; Took Pictures of 11 Presidents," *Washington Post*, November 7, 2006; interview with J. P. Pappis.)

free-spirited lefty who kept to the political center; a born-again Christian who entertained a catering hall of appetites. He was a man of faith who was, in his marriage, unfaithful.

How could Bill Clinton be so brainy and yet be ruled by his sensory organs? How could he be such a people person and yet so classically self-absorbed? So inexhaustibly hyperactive and yet convinced that the perfect getaway was the Renaissance Weekend, where he and Hillary, amid old friends and several hundred others, could chill out and spend a few days trading ideas, schmoozing about policy, and sharing stories of "personal growth"? He and his wife were forever being accused of "using" people for political gain, and yet he had a profoundly generous streak, always handing out well-considered gifts, some of which he would wrap himself. (In an Oval Office interview I conducted with him at the end of his presidency, Clinton told me, "When I got here, fortuitously, I found that in the President's Bathroom there is a closet with several shelves. It goes back kind of deep. It's narrow. And I just started, you know, acquiring things [as presents] and squirreling them away—a few books, a few CDs, few items of jewelry.")

Here was someone cut from distinctly different cloth than the American macho man. Bill Clinton was, in fact, an alpha male who understood his feminine facets. He could fly off the handle in private (some insiders referred to Clinton's passing storms as "purple fits"; adviser David Gergen would call them "morning vents"), but in public he had measured manners and a southern unction that cast a honeysuckle spell. In a period when men were torn and frayed and turning inward, his was the high-beam gleam of a more compassionate generation. He was a man whose first inclination was not to restrict or judge but to tolerate and include. He was a good boy *and* a good ol' boy *and* a naughty, naughty boy. He was, in his way, "the sensitive guy at the dogfight."[8]

Former Clinton strategist Dick Morris once identified this Sunday-morning/Saturday-night dichotomy—a sort of Bifurcated Bill. Sunday-morning Clinton "is the one we have all seen so often on television," Morris would write in his memoir *Behind the Oval Office*. "Brilliant, principled,

---

8. This phrase was originally meant to describe the contributors and readers drawn to the hipster magazine of the New South, the beloved *Oxford American*, launched in 1992. (Dwight Garner, "It Was the New Yorker with Hot Sauce," *New York Times*, December 3, 2012.)

sincere, good-willed, empathetic, intellectual, learning, and caring." Saturday-night Clinton, by comparison, "is pure id—willful, demanding, hedonistic, risk-taking, sybaritic, headstrong, unfeeling, callous, unprincipled, and undisciplined. The Sunday man adores his family. The Saturday-night counterpart risks its destruction." In Morris's view, "Each side of Clinton seems unaware of the other"—as if the two Bills were separated by a "wall of denial."

Clinton was complex, postmodern, and defined by his double personality—politically and socially, emotionally and psychologically. In a period when men were flailing at maintaining their traditional patriarchal dominance of the womenfolk, he was Robert Bly's so-called soft male, deferring to the one who wore the pants in the family, even if his were occasionally coming off.

———

In a time of cynicism, Clinton was the Boy from Hope. In a time of fad diets and white wine spritzers, he was snarfing down the Wendy's. (At a Camp David team-building retreat that Clinton convened for his top aides nine days after he took office, he reportedly admitted to being "a fat kid when he was five or six and [discussed] how the other kids taunted him.") As if defined by his childhood persona, he was, deep down, "just a guy in the [school] band," as Gennifer Flowers once described him. "He wasn't a big, muscular football hero who had girls falling all over him. Then all of a sudden, he became a politician and started getting the kind of attention he had only dreamed of."

He'd started out, as we've seen, as something of a mama's boy. And he went on throughout his career to surround himself with forceful women. "Clinton was just comfortable with women," says his first White House press secretary, Dee Dee Myers. "That should be followed by a punch line, right?...[But] he liked being in the company of women. And he liked all different kinds of women. He was very comfortable around women in a way [that stood out back then]. Some, [like] Susan Thomases, were Hillary's friends that she brought in, and a lot of them weren't. He was very comfortable with Mandy [Grunwald], with Betsey [Wright]. She was very strong, and women were allowed to be that around him. You know"—Myers stops to laugh—"he just liked women. That was great. Washington is very much a boys' club....If you look back, he had a lot of women in the cabinet. He promoted women."

The public perceived Clinton as a man who was concerned with others' needs and who strove to project that sensitivity. He was so sensitive, in fact, that comedian Dana Carvey once portrayed him in a TV skit as a man who could actually lactate. While impersonating Clinton in 1996, Carvey announced himself to be such "a caring, nurturing president" that he'd reached the stage where he could suckle a child. "I could be both father and mother to our nation," Carvey's Clinton declared. "I've taken this a step further. With the employment of estrogen hormonal therapy, I have developed the ability to breastfeed." And, bingo, Carvey took a doll to his chest and began nursing it. "I'd like to see Steve Forbes do this."

Clinton, of course, could lay it on thick. And his tendency to weave over the median from suave to slick had earned him no less a nickname than Slick Willie.[9] While Slick Willie's was also the name of a popular pool-hall chain in the South, the alias was first affixed to Bill Clinton by journalist Paul Greenberg (later the editorial page editor of the *Arkansas Democrat-Gazette*), who had charted the candidate's rise. In September 1980, Greenberg, then at a paper called the *Pine Bluff Commercial*, wrote an editorial that criticized Clinton, as Greenberg would later recall, for giving "a speech before the state Democratic convention in which he depicted himself as in the tradition of progressive governors in this state." In the view of Greenberg and his colleagues, Clinton, who would lose his gubernatorial reelection bid, was a zigzagger who tailored his views to suit voters. He was, said Greenberg, a "classic waffle[r]" who carefully worded many policy stances in a way "that would allow him later to take whatever side looked popular"; he was a budget-cutter "who had broken this succession of reform governors [who had preceded him]. And so we used the sobriquet Slick Willy on that occasion and it caught on."

Clinton was also the consummate charmer. My friend Jamieson Webster, a Freudian psychoanalyst, calls him the Last Charismatic. Indeed, Clinton's early appearances on the stump, like JFK's and RFK's before him, had a rock-star shimmer, drawing his share of comely swooners.[10] Young supporters

---

9. Often written as "Willy."

10. Leave it to Boomers to call a politician a rock star. *Rolling Stone*'s founder, Jann Wenner, had reportedly dubbed Clinton the "first rock and roll president." But before the phrase "he/she's a rock star" became devalued through overuse, its application in connoting an iconic personality

were attracted by his populism, his pop-culture references, his small-town earthiness. They took to his unabashed directness and at the same time his preacherlike expansiveness and reassurance.

There was an unspoken thrill that issued from those rope-line bear hugs, from his laying on of hands. Clinton was uncommonly physical: touching, feeling, connecting. He had, it bears repeating, sex appeal. He could set his lapis gaze on a voter in a public session in such a way as to make that voter feel courted, special, set apart. But it was more than that. "Bill Clinton is one of those very rare people who can walk in and change the chemistry of a room," James Carville has written. "The molecules in the room were one way and he would walk in and after he got there the molecules were arranged slightly differently." At six foot two, the president, mano a mano, had a way of sidling up, close and conspiratorially, as Lyndon Johnson liked to do. Clinton's voice was often hoarse and guttural, quasi-carnal, coming from somewhere deep inside. His ruddy complexion hinted of ardor—with a touch of the blush of a boy who'd just been punished. He was an adult and a man-child, presidential *and* intimate—a seductive combination.[11]

My wife, Nancy, and I were once invited to a White House dinner in

---

was evidence that the rock idol, above all else in the Boomersphere, was the epitome of rebellious individualism, a person in whom success, excess, popularity, and cool had found full flower. In the '80s you were "the King of Pop" or "the Pope of Print" or a "Master of the Universe." By the '90s, however, Top Dog had one designation: Rock Star. The jargonauts at Merriam-Webster trace the first use of the term to 1991, when novelist Stephen King was dubbed "a rock star of an author— his horror movies routinely go multiplatinum, and his byline operates like a brand name." In fact, the term—as applied to non–rock stars—was prefigured by the term "superstar," the most obvious example being the title character in the '70s rock opera *Jesus Christ Superstar*. (Joe Eszterhas, *American Rhapsody* [New York: Knopf, 2000], 3; William Safire, "A Star Is Born," *New York Times*, March 26, 2006; Sarah Crompton, "Andrew Lloyd Webber Interview: The Second Coming of *Jesus Christ Superstar*," *Telegraph* [U.K.], September 21, 2012.)

11. While Clinton had exuded heat, Barack Obama was a throwback, exuding cool. Author Ishmael Reed called him "the president of the Cool," comparing Obama's demeanor to the great jazz masters of bebop, who possessed "an intensity and focus that lurk[ed] underneath the detached exterior." Columnist David Brooks made a similar observation, noting, "Obama has displayed a kind of ESPN masculinity: post-feminist in his values, but also thoroughly traditional in style—hypercompetitive, restrained, not given to self doubt, rarely self-indulgent....He has defined a version of manliness that is postboomer in policy but preboomer in manners and reticence." Obama and fellow postboomers (from "the era of the workout gym," as Brooks puts it) had adopted a "low friction manner" to suit the prevailing tone of their generation, which "was cool, not hot." (Ishmael Reed, "The President of the Cool," *New York Times*, December 19, 2013, A39; David Brooks, "The ESPN Man," *New York Times*, May 15, 2012, A27; Brooks, "The Generation War," *New York Times*, October 12, 2012, A27.)

1997. Long after the meal and the speeches, Gladys Knight and the Pips were about to leave the bandstand after they'd played "Midnight Train to Georgia." But then Clinton, as I remember, called for an encore. And later, as we departed, we stood off to one side among the other attendees, and the president moved swiftly alongside the crowd, making his exit, shaking hands and trading shout-outs. When he got to Nancy, he dallied long enough for me to snap two photographs with the point-and-shoot camera I'd brought along.

Admittedly, my wife had been known to cause passersby to pivot. Her chic demeanor, prematurely silver tresses, and smooth, glowing complexion are often an irresistible combination to men of Clinton's age or older. But when I developed the roll of film, I was surprised to see that it was *Nancy* who had flushed hot pink. As the president took her hand, she had simply melted, offering an uncharacteristic attaboy wink. Even in a scrum of strangers, he'd managed to elicit a cozy little contact high. "I've never seen a man be so casually magnetic," she now recalls.

In a similar vein, an L.A.-based journalist I know, who has worked on stories with dozens of major studio stars, confides that she has rarely met anyone with more charisma in all her years covering Hollywood. (She requests anonymity, given her high profile in the business.) "He takes your hand and lasers you with those baby blues," she explains, her voice catching, "and you go so weak. In one second, [you project ahead and] you see yourself gathering up your clothes in the dark and fumbling for change in the back of the cab on the way home. I imagine Warren Beatty had it in his prime. For Clinton, it's only compounded by the fact that he's been the leader of the free world."

———

This new masculine archetype was, in fact, several men in one.

By one measure, Clinton was the First Bro. On the campaign trail, he hung out in jogging shorts, a baseball cap, and an Arkansas Razorbacks T. He played a lot of hearts and solitaire and, in off hours, habitually wedged an unlit cigar in his mouth. The candidate's team, meanwhile, seemed more like dorm rats than the eagle squadron. Stephanopoulos, for example, could sometimes be spotted blowing chewing-gum bubbles; Carville, munching popcorn. (Those in Clinton's cadre of intimates and supporters—in line with the vibe—were not called donors or supporters but "FOBs": Friends of Bill.)

Bro-ness had long been Bill Clinton's métier. While governor, he'd inaugurated Casual Fridays and, as he would later recall, "encouraged everyone to go for a long lunch at a nearby haunt that had first-rate hamburgers, pinball machines, and a shuffleboard game." Upon reaching Pennsylvania Avenue, he chaired meetings that had a stoner's rhythm, starting late and running long, with *every* staffer allowed to pipe in with opinions. (Carville would joke to *Vanity Fair*'s Marjorie Williams in 1994, "If God had wanted us to be on time, He wouldn't have made us Democrats.") In *The Agenda*, a book on Clinton's attempt to reboot the economy, journalist Bob Woodward characterizes the indiscipline of the first-term White House: "The staff was too often like a soccer league of 10-year-olds. No one stuck to his part of the field during a game. The ball—any ball—would come on the field, and everyone would go chasing it."

But what else were we to expect? This was a guy who played sax—*in shades*—on *The Arsenio Hall Show*. He sometimes drove a Mustang convertible. He had a rack of loud ties and a fondness for loud underwear. Clinton was so at ease with the kicked-back vibe that when MTV hosted a town hall session two years into his presidency and a teenage girl in the crowd asked him, "Boxers or briefs?," he was taken aback but fielded the question anyway. "Usually briefs," he said. "I can't believe she did that." (By answering, many railed, he was demeaning his high office.)

The First Bro, lest we forget, was also the First Bubba. Though the word "bubba" had entered the vernacular in the late '70s, Clinton would come to own it, whole hog.[12] During the 1992 campaign, the *Wall Street Journal* focused on the vital "Bubba vote," which stood for "conservative whites, many of them Democrats." A bubba, however, according to David G. Cannon's 1990 book *Hey, Bubba!: A Metaphysical Guide to the Good Ol' Boy*, connoted something more socially relevant. He was not a redneck, which implied "an ignorant, mean-spirited individual," but was instead a more temperate southern male. He was a Dixie-bred "mellow hedon[ist]" and "a plain-spoken, salt-of-the-earth sort," often sporting a baseball or John Deere

---

12. "Bub" was used in the late nineteenth century as a term of endearment when one male wanted to convey brotherly closeness to another. If we are to believe the *Dictionary of American Regional English*, "bubba" was used in similar fashion among black males in certain parts of the South. But by 1979 the word came to signify a southern white male who held more or less conservative values. Though generally acceptable among certain bubbas, according to linguistic watchdog William Safire it was a synonym for "redneck" when applied to poor rural whites. (William Safire, *Safire's Political Dictionary* [Oxford: Oxford University Press, 2008], based on Random House edition, 1993 [revised], 85.)

cap, wearing "Duck Head khakis [and a] possum-eating grin." On the sexual side, writes Cannon, bubbas were romantics who "genuinely like women, an appreciation uncluttered by sexual guilt"; they "tend to be gallant lads with a touch of old-school chivalry"; and they "exude a low-key masculinity for which they don't find it necessary to apologize, openly preferring that women not look and act like men."

At one point in the '92 race, in fact, Clinton defended the characterization, saying of his running mate, Al Gore, and himself, "There's a little bubba in both of us—in the sense that we both come from small towns, where people have old-fashioned values and want their country to be the best country in the world—and I don't think that's all bad." Clinton's upbringing was southern working class, and yet this good ol' boy was a crossover type. As Bob Woodward would later note, Clinton had kicked off his campaign in 1991 at the Old State House in Little Rock by stating that "his central goal was 'restoring the hopes of the forgotten middle class.' He made ten references to the middle class."

Clinton, without apology, was also the nation's First Boomer, quaffing generously from the trough of pop culture. One telling anecdote is worth repeating. At the end of my above-referenced Clinton interview, in 2000 (in which we talked about his personal memories of his eight years in Washington), I gave the president a copy of a new coffee-table book, *Vanity Fair's Hollywood*, that the magazine's editor, Graydon Carter, and I had just published. Though our Q&A session had ended, the president was still on a roll, and he flipped through the book, providing running commentary. "This is a famous picture," he said, lingering over the classic Slim Aarons portrait of four of cinema's most dashing leading men. "This is Gable, Cooper, Stewart...and Van Heflin, who was in *Shane* with Alan Ladd. I think this was, like, late '50s, in Hollywood.[13] I know because [Gary] Cooper didn't live many more years and [Clark] Gable only lived a [couple more]. But they were great-lookin' guys." For a wonkish politico, his knowledge of cinema icons was refreshingly fanboy.

---

13. The photo, in fact, was taken on New Year's Eve 1957 at Romanoff's in Beverly Hills. And Cooper, as it happens, was the star of Clinton's favorite film, *High Noon*, which the president reportedly screened seventeen times in the White House. (Graydon Carter and David Friend, eds., *Vanity Fair's Hollywood* [New York: Viking, 2000], 10–11; Glenn Frankel, *High Noon: The Hollywood Blacklist and the Making of an American Classic* [New York: Bloomsbury, 2017], 294–95.)

"I love this," he continued, stopping at a photo. "[Jack] Nicholson, my golf partner...Kim Basinger, one of the all-time gorgeous women. Nice person. Alec Baldwin [her husband at the time], he's a good friend of ours... I love this...Oh, look at this old picture of Sammy Davis...Is this [Julie Andrews in] *Victor/Victoria*?...Whoopi [Goldberg]...Great picture of young Harrison Ford. Look at this. This is unbelievable."[14]

As a Boomer, Clinton inevitably came with Boomer baggage. His contemporaries were arguably the country's most spoiled, self-willed, whiny, and (up until the millennials) voyeuristic generation. But hold it right there. The Boomers had been the ones who'd ushered in an era of inclusiveness, diversity, and Aquarian dreams for a more humane society. They'd exported constitutional democracy across the globe, along with mass culture, high technology, medical advances—and good vibes. The Greediest Generation they were not, or at least not completely. Clinton, to his credit, had taken JFK's torch and run with it.[15]

Columnist Michael Kinsley would try to set the record straight in the *Atlantic* in 2010, balancing the Boomer ledger (and by extension, the Clinton legacy) against that of the Greatest Generation (those who survived the Depression, defeated fascism during World War II, and forged a prosperous postwar America): "It was the Boomers, not the [Greats], who forced the nation to address civil rights. And it was the Greats, not the Boomers, who got us addicted to debt." By Kinsley's count, the Greats ushered us into Vietnam too, a war from which the Boomers extracted us. The Greats may have taught us the virtues of self-sacrifice, even as the hippie-cum-yuppie Boomers " 'sold out' and eased into middle-class life." But Clinton's generation— indeed, the generation of Bill *and* Hillary Clinton—had "changed it for the

---

14. Clinton's attraction to Hollywood was more than just the starstruck fascination of a film geek. Players in the entertainment world—most of them Boomers—had been among his most visible supporters and fund-raisers. According to *Time*, the president did not hide the fact. During his "first 125 days" in office he hosted "Billy Crystal, Barbra Streisand, Sharon Stone (twice), Richard Gere, Richard Dreyfuss, Paul Newman and Joanne Woodward, Quincy Jones, Sinbad, Christopher Reeve, John Ritter, Sam Waterston, Hammer, Lindsay Wagner and Judy Collins." One had to stifle the urge to call the Lincoln Bedroom the Boom Boom Room. (Kurt Andersen, "The Clinton-Hollywood Co-Dependency," *Time*, June 7, 1993.)

15. And all while making whoopee. Clinton, according to his sometime strategist Dick Morris, was asked a theoretical question on President's Day 1995: "If you could ask your idol, John Kennedy, one question and only one question, what would it be?" The president later joked to Morris that what he'd really wanted to say was, "How did you do it? How did you get away with it?" (Morris, *Behind the Oval Office*, xviii.)

better. They made environmentalism, feminism, gay rights so deeply a part of middle-class culture that the terms themselves seem antiquated."

————

There was one more aspect that made Bill Clinton a new breed of American male. He was, like many of his Boomer peers, more publicly emotive than men of previous eras. He fairly oozed empathy. He repeatedly said he could *feel* a voter's *pain*.[16]

Early on, Clinton had learned how to put on his game face by watching Mother in that mirror. By adulthood he'd become the national champ at playing the choked-up, chin-quivering card. For years, going moist had been verboten in presidential politics. In 1972, Senator Edmund Muskie, many believe, had lost the Democratic nomination for president to George McGovern because of a misty incident in New Hampshire. Muskie, at a press conference in a snowstorm, had appeared to shed tears. (He would later insist the water on his cheeks was merely melted snow.) The scene registered in reporters' and voters' minds as an indication that Muskie was the sort of man who might crack under the strain of the office.

But no longer. Thanks in large part to Clinton, dry eyes soon meant: heartless. The power male who could take a tear to the brim, and yet hold it back, was exhibiting compassion *and* reserve. There were no histrionics, no bawling. (That would come later, with men like the former House Speaker John Boehner, who became known as something of a human faucet.) Instead, the politician, male or female, became comfortable exhibiting a measured mistiness.[17] It allowed a public official to show a sentimental side, to show some *heart*, yet to safely fall just a drop shy of anything mawkish.

Being a Cry Guy,[18] however, was really less a calculated effort to snag votes than an outward expression of being a man in tune with a full range

————

16. None other than Kenneth Starr, Clinton's nemesis, would eventually deign to praise him on this score: "His genuine empathy for human beings is absolutely clear. It is powerful. It is palpable. And the folks of Arkansas really understood that about him, that he genuinely cared. The 'I feel your pain' is absolutely genuine." (Nick Gass, "Ken Starr Praises, Laments Bill Clinton's Legacy," Politico.com, May 25, 2016.)

17. Indeed, Hillary Clinton *won* the 2008 New Hampshire presidential primary after appearing to mist up at a much-photographed gathering with voters in a coffee shop. (Karen Breslau, "Hillary Clinton's Emotional Moment," *Newsweek*, January 6, 2008.)

18. The era even created a new movie genre: the "guy cry" picture, epitomized by *Field of Dreams* (the 1989 absent-father baseball classic that would cause legions of grown men to weep) and 1994's *The Shawshank Redemption*, which *Vanity Fair* would call "the ultimate in 'guy cry' cinema."

of emotions. This was Naughty Billy, Slick Willie, and the Boy from Hope. This was the First Bro, the First Bubba, and the First Boomer. This was, after JFK, the first president not to have emerged from the Greatest Generation, who would come to represent bold youth and unbounded prosperity. This was the first president to eventually support his life partner, Hillary Clinton, as a worthy successor.

This was a new sort of man in a grave new world.

And what, pray tell, of the new women in that world?

(Margaret Heidenry, "The Little-Known Story of How *The Shawshank Redemption* Became One of the Most Beloved Films of All Time," VanityFair.com, September 22, 2014.)

CHAPTER 5

On the Third Wave

From Washington State to Washington, D.C., women were inspired, involved, and, in many cases, enraged. Then, in a matter of months, there was a surge. And on April 5, 1992, between 500,000 and 750,000 pro-choice supporters attended the March for Women's Lives, one of the largest protests in the nation's capital in twenty years.

The previous fall, a young black law professor named Anita Hill had made headlines when she told a Senate committee—all white and all male—about a pattern of sexual harassment by her former superior, Clarence Thomas. The jurist, who was being vetted for a seat on the Supreme Court, would dismiss Hill's allegations, and would go on to narrowly win confirmation. Angry and driven and politicized, women would mobilize: running for public office in record numbers, joining the ranks of national and local women's organizations, and preparing for a showdown. Thomas and his fellow justices would soon meet and decide, in a key case, whether to uphold, modify, or strike down *Roe v. Wade*, the 1973 decision that guaranteed a woman's legal right to an abortion. It was time for feminists to reclaim the national stage.

Amid the sea of women on the Mall that day, every one of the Democrats running for president—including Bill Clinton—arrived to express his support. But as author Sara Marcus would recount in her book *Girls to the Front*, "None of the candidates was given a turn at the microphone during the rally. Patricia Ireland, the president of NOW [the National Organization for Women], addressed the crowd. 'We are tired of begging for our rights from men in power,' she intoned. 'We are going to take power.'"

And so they did.

The women's movement came in waves. There was the first wave, which started with the first formal women's rights gathering in the United States (in Seneca Falls, New York, in 1848) and culminated in the 1920s as women secured the right to vote. There was the second wave: the "women's liberation" movement of the late '60s and '70s that sought to educate and politically organize women to combat sex discrimination and social and cultural inequities. Then, in the early '90s, came third-wave feminism.

That wave directed a fresh focus on vital issues across classes, races, and backgrounds. It built on the advances achieved by the previous generation's feminists and yet it forged something indie and indigenous. It gained much of its momentum from the punk, grunge, and hip-hop scenes, and from the bottom-up, homegrown networks that were then animating the infant Web. It was more about individual self-discovery and less a unified crusade. "We have inherited strategies... from the Second Wave [to take on] modern problems of our own," Jennifer Baumgardner and Amy Richards would point out in 2000 in their influential book *Manifesta: Young Women, Feminism, and the Future.* "Prominent Third Wave issues include equal access to the Internet and technology, HIV/AIDS awareness, child sexual abuse, self-mutilation, globalization, eating disorders, and body image."

And yet the accomplishments attributed to third-wave activists were not solely the product of a coterie of twenty-somethings. Many of the changes, according to historian Kirsten Swinth, were driven by second-wave originators who by the 1990s were "maturing into positions of continued political and social influence" and had joined forces with their younger counterparts. Despite what sometimes appeared as a generational split, the women of this double wave would help spearhead new policies in the workplace regarding maternity and medical leave; recommendations for ways to promote corporate advancement; and a system of redress for incidents of sexual harassment and misconduct. While the movement continued to concentrate on reproductive choice, the struggle was also directed at proper access to health care, childcare, and education; the drive to register female voters; the rights of the LGBT community; a new surge in breast cancer awareness and research advocacy; and the achievement of full legal equality for women. It decried the objectification of women by the media, advertising, and popular culture, as well as the creation of an idealized body type, which had contributed to the prevalence of anorexia and bulimia.

But this was a movement that lacked a cohesive message, and many young women were questioning whether the very term "feminist" was even viable anymore. In 1998, *Newsweek* would cite a respected *New York Times* poll indicating that "the number of American women who think the word 'feminist' is a compliment has halved since 1992.... Current discussions of women's issues tend to emphasize individualism over collectivism, and personal success over political action."[1]

One of the most animating issues of the period involved attempts to clearly define sexual assault. In response to campus incidents of date rape, Antioch College, in a highly controversial decree, set up a binding sexual-offense code that governed students' after-hours behavior. Among the provisions: "Do not take silence as consent; it isn't" and "You must still ask each and every time." Critics reacted forcefully, with journalist and author Katie Roiphe declaring in a 1991 column entitled "Date Rape Hysteria," "This so-called feminist movement peddles an image of gender relations that denies female desire and infantilizes women."[2] *Newsweek*'s Sarah Crichton, in a cover story titled "Sexual Correctness: Have We Gone Too Far?," spoke for many in rejecting such stringent guidelines. "We are not creating a society of Angry Young Women [but] Scared Little Girls," she insisted. While acknowledging grievous incidents such as the Navy's Tailhook scandal,[3] Crichton found dangerous repercussions in rules that further victimized females and demonized males. "It is polarizing men and

---

1. Closer to our day, Andi Zeisler, the creative director of Bitch Media, has noted that there is also a palatable, roll-your-own, consumer feminism—"marketplace feminism"—that has largely decoupled feminism from politics, positioning the movement as "a cool, fun, accessible identity that anyone can adopt." This is, in its way, a kind of progress. But as Zeisler warns, the privatization of feminism is at a perilous remove from the feminist waves of the past, which were grounded in collective action intended to affect policy and bring down oppressive hierarchies. (Andi Zeisler, *We Were Feminists Once: From Riot Grrrl to CoverGirl, the Buying and Selling of a Political Movement* [New York: PublicAffairs, 2016].)

2. Themes set out in Roiphe's article were explored more deeply in her widely read book *The Morning After: Sex, Fear, and Feminism.*

3. In 1991, at the annual Tailhook gathering of Navy and Marine aviators, a gauntlet of intoxicated officers and others manhandled dozens of female military personnel, without their superiors objecting. A Pentagon report would later describe a variety of other sexually coercive or offensive acts at the convention. ("Excerpts from the Pentagon Report," *New York Times*, April 24, 1993, A1; Eloise Salholz and Douglas Waller, "Tailhook: Scandal Time," *Newsweek*, July 6, 1992; "One Lesson from a Messy Scandal," editorial, *New York Times*, November 14, 2012, A28.)

women...rather than encouraging them to work together, to trust one another."

Date rape, however, remained no minor matter, and the testimonies of young women across the country amounted to a national wake-up call. On college campuses, Take Back the Night marches served to underscore the gravity of the situation—and to galvanize a generation of undergraduates. The subject began to take center stage in courts of law and in counselors', deans', and therapists' offices, over the clamor of the popular press, which often sensationalized legitimate concerns or mischaracterized the matter. (Many believed that applying the phrase "hysteria" to date rape, for instance, was needlessly reviving a term that for four millennia had been ascribed to disorders of "the female temperament.") Americans young and old were recognizing that peer-to-peer sexual assault was an ingrained and grave problem to be minimized at one's peril.

Third-wave feminism had another unique and contentious aspect, which some referred to as sex-positive feminism.[4] Others called it pro-sex or sexual-empowerment feminism—in marked contrast to the antiporn activism that had been championed in the previous decade by Catharine MacKinnon, Andrea Dworkin, and others. Esquire ran a 1994 story with a button-pushing cover line: "The Rise of 'Do Me' Feminism." But in reality, the issue was more significant and nuanced than Esquire implied—and it hardly warranted a snide label from a magazine that, from its 1933 inception, had aimed to be "the common denominator of masculine interests."[5] Many feminists were boldly expressing their sex appeal; giving space to an active erotic life; and "thinking through the meaning of the sexualization of wom-

---

4. The term had been in use, according to writer Ariel Levy, since at least the mid-'70s, around the time Susan Brownmiller published her seminal *Against Our Will: Men, Women and Rape.* The phrase, insists Levy, "was employed by the members of the women's movement who wanted to distinguish themselves from the antiporn faction. But, of course, all of the feminists thought they were being sex-positive." (Ariel Levy, *Female Chauvinist Pigs: Women and the Rise of Raunch Culture* [New York: Free Press/Simon & Schuster, 2005], 63.)

5. *New York Times* columnist Anna Quindlen, among many others, would rail about the *Esquire* story, declaring that it reduced many activists in the contemporary women's movement to proponents of a kind of "babe feminism," espousing a handful of issues that would make the discerning male salivate: (a) "Good Feminism = Great Sex"; (b) women are "too busy eviscerating one another to take [men] on"; and (c) "anyone who has been suspicious of the movement heretofore can have his fears confirmed: we're angry because we're ugly." (Tad Friend, "Yes," *Esquire*, February 1994; Anna Quindlen, "Public & Private; And Now, Babe Feminism," *New York Times*, January 19, 1994.)

en's bodies," says Swinth, the social and cultural historian, "re-examin[ing] how to be physically sexy without being objectified." While the movement for decades had emphasized the importance and wonder of female desire, the '90s feminist was stating unequivocally that men—and the larger culture—did not define a woman's sexuality. Only *women* did.

Among the most provocative commentators on this score was the humanities professor Camille Paglia, who would cause fits in some circles when she declared that women and men needed to acknowledge and accept the darker, complex, and sometimes dangerous truths and consequences that had forever defined the erotic. Male lust, in her view, "was the animating factor in culture." At the same time, Paglia stated, it was women who held the upper hand, sexually speaking. They created life. They were mysterious. ("Woman," she wrote, "remains *the hidden*, a cave of archaic darkness.") And they were the ancient keepers of "the elemental power of sex." Paglia's was one of the rare voices to announce, "The problem with America is that there's too little sex, not too much."

Beyond all of these stateside concerns, the third wave also sought a reaffirmation of solidarity among women worldwide. The larger fight was not just economic or social or legal, but a fight for human rights. It addressed a woman's status in many countries as a second-class citizen; widespread malnourishment, illiteracy, and insufficient health care for girls and women; unhealthy environmental conditions where women labored and lived; sexual slavery and prostitution; community- and state-sanctioned maiming, stoning, or burning; genital mutilation; forced sterilization; and rape being used from the Balkans to Rwanda to Indonesia as a weapon of war. This was a struggle involving matters of life and death.

———

Glass ceilings were shattering. Women were becoming political heavyweights in Washington, serving in key posts as attorney general (Janet Reno), head of the EPA (Carol Browner), and press secretary (Dee Dee Myers), as well as secretaries of state (Madeleine Albright), energy (Hazel O'Leary), and health and human services (Donna Shalala). At various times in the 1990s, women served as the U.S. trade representative, director of the Office of Management and Budget, chairperson of the Council of Economic Advisers, and chief of the Small Business Administration.

In the armed forces, Defense Secretary Les Aspin opened up previously restricted positions to women. In the judiciary, the president named Ruth Bader Ginsburg to the Supreme Court and, as the *New York Times* would point out, appointed "a record proportion of women...to the Federal bench." In the legislature, the incoming congressional class, elected in 1992—in what would come to be called the Year of the Woman—doubled female representation in the Senate, while women in the House ranks swelled to forty-seven members. (After the GOP took over two years later, however, that progress would stall and then level out. "I really felt that we were paving the way for a huge number of women," said Iowa state senator Jean Lloyd-Jones, twenty years later, "but the promise of 1992 was never realized.")

While the feminist movement was sometimes downplayed by (and often at odds with) mass media, there was evidence nonetheless of a ripple effect throughout mainstream culture. So-called chick lit came on strong as a genre, thanks to titles such as *Bridget Jones's Diary* and *The Girls' Guide to Hunting and Fishing*. Terry McMillan's bestselling novel *Waiting to Exhale* (1992) presented female friendship as being as vital as oxygen. McMillan explored the lives of four Arizona friends—Savannah, Bernadine, Robin, and Gloria—chilling out in the steam room, smoking a cig outside the yogurt shop, or shuttling between board meetings for Black Women on the Move. "Let me ask you sistahs something," Savannah inquires. "What is it we all have in common?" Gloria responds, "We're black and female." What Savannah means, she continues, is that "none of us have a man." Bernadine chimes in, "I don't want one, either." This is precisely Savannah's point, she says: one's loyalty to one's sisters takes precedence. "Don't ever think a man would have that much power over me that I'd stop caring about my friends." Or, as the Spice Girls pop group would advise potential suitors, "If you wanna be my lover, you gotta get with my friends." Self-help fare, meanwhile, climbed the bestseller lists, addressing everything from the differences between women and men (*You Just Don't Understand*) to personal empowerment (*Yesterday, I Cried*) to menopause (*The Silent Passage*). *Women Who Run with the Wolves* offered ten General Wolf Rules for Life, the last five being "Cavil in the moonlight. Tune your ears. Attend to the bones. Make love. Howl often."

There was a femme fatale renaissance on TV and in cinema, epitomized by bad-girl characters played by Shannen Doherty and Jennifer Love Hewitt. The movie *Thelma & Louise*—in which the protagonists, after one of them is sexually assaulted, go on a road-warrior rampage—was the ultimate outlaw chick flick, and it floored moviegoers upon its 1991 release. The film, starring Susan Sarandon and Geena Davis, was praised for its pitch-perfect exploration of female rage. It also took serious heat. Some critics considered it emasculating, others an invitation to vigilantism. Richard Johnson, gossip columnist at the time for the New York *Daily News*, would allege, "It justifies armed robbery, manslaughter and chronic drunken driving as exercises in consciousness raising."

The chick flick, in fact, became a genuine '90s genre. For her book *Why Women Should Rule the World*, Bill Clinton's former press secretary Dee Dee Myers, now director of corporate communications at Warner Bros, interviewed Sherry Lansing, who was running Paramount Pictures and greenlighted the 1996 comedy *The First Wives Club*, about a trio of commiserating divorcées. Typically Lansing would finance films by partnering with other studios. But for this film she had no takers. "No one thought anyone would go see [it,]" she would recall. "That was the only movie I couldn't get a partner on....And it was a hit. People were shocked." In Myers's view, "the 'female empowerment' chick flick" was now on the map, thanks to the cult status of a succession of '90s films (as distinctive as *Go Fish* and *10 Things I Hate About You*) as well as the box-office success of many others (from *Clueless* to the screen version of *Waiting to Exhale*).

At the same time, formidable challenges remained, especially for girls,[6] even as American society began recognizing gender inequity and trying to reach girls in need. Educators, for example, were heralding the success of girls' schools,

---

6. Part of the issue was physiological. As mentioned elsewhere in these pages, many preteens were demonstrating an anatomical acceleration in their sexual maturity. In 1997, a study of thousands of girls in the United States and Canada was published to much fanfare—and controversy. New statistics suggested that the age of the onset of secondary signs of puberty (which for five decades had typically hovered around thirteen years of age) had recently dropped to age eight for as many as 15 percent of the children surveyed. The possible causes influencing such premature development: additives in milk and beef, an obesity epidemic, longer daily exposure to light in industrialized society, and the environmental disruptions to the food supply due to substances like DDF and PCBs. "It's as if an entire generation of girls has been put on hormonal fast-forward," *Time* declared in a cover story. "Childhood is short enough as it is, with kids bombarded from every direction by sexually explicit movies, rock lyrics, MTV videos and racy fashions." In a relatively narrow window of time, then, profound sexual self-awareness had become a crucial part of life among a much younger population. (Michael Lemonick, "Early Puberty: Why Girls are Growing Up Faster," *Time*, October 30, 2000; Gina Kolata, "Doubters Fault Theory Finding Earlier Puberty," *New York Times*, February 20, 2001, A1, 16.)

showing how all-female classes helped foster educational advancement, independence, and self-esteem. By the '90s, as the writer and culture-wars arbiter Kay S. Hymowitz points out in her book *Manning Up*, girls were participating in team sports roughly as often as boys were—a consequence of Congress's Title IX law that had demanded parity in how schools treated their athletic programs.[7] When experts began to identify an epidemic in diminished self-confidence among adolescent girls, Gloria Steinem and Marie Wilson, the president of the Ms. Foundation, set up what would become, in 1993, the first nationwide Take Our Daughters to Work Day. The program would educate girls about the professional world and encourage them not to let gender hamper them as they pursued their education and career. The next year, Hymowitz recalls, "saw the passage of the Gender Equity in Education Act, which provided extra funds for educators to help girls succeed." (Such initiatives, of course, often failed to address the persistent obstacles faced by a large percentage of girls, many of whom came from disadvantaged backgrounds and neglected communities.)

Popular culture offered new (or revised) models too. Young girls looked up to strong female protagonists in Disney films such as *Beauty and the Beast* and *Aladdin*, or superheroines such as Xena or Linda Hamilton (in *Terminator 2*), and the likes of the Powerpuff Girls, Sailor Moon, and Marvel's Spider-Girl. Sarah Michelle Gellar battled vampires on *Buffy the Vampire Slayer*. U.S. soccer star Brandi Chastain became a triumphant national icon in 1999 when, following her penalty kick that gave America the victory over China in the Women's World Cup final, she tugged off her jersey, sank her knees into the green carpet of the Rose Bowl, and clenched her fists, revealing her black bra and ripped abs.

But the wider culture offered its own impediments to progress. In her signal book *Reviving Ophelia: Saving the Selves of Adolescent Girls* (1994), clinical psychologist Mary Pipher would argue that even as the women's movement had improved the lot of girls and adolescents, opening access to areas of life inconceivable in earlier generations, many girls upon reaching puberty would "crash into junk culture...a girl-poisoning culture [that is] more dangerous, sexualized and media-saturated." In the 1980s, the record

---

7. "It was parents, particularly fathers, who translated Title IX into a middle-class lifestyle known as 'soccer parenting,'" writes Kay S. Hymowitz in *Manning Up*. "They loved having daughters who played sports....It sure beat jump rope and tea parties." (Kay S. Hymowitz, *Manning Up: How the Rise of Women Has Turned Men into Boys* [New York: Basic Books, 2011], 67.)

increase in preteen suicide rates as well as physical violence and sexual assault against girls had set the stage. By the '90s, as described in *Reviving Ophelia*, therapists, educators, and medical professionals were alarmed even further. There was a pattern of victimization by predatory boys, relatives, and stepparents; a steep rise in sexually transmitted diseases; a steep demand for counseling and intervention to address behaviors such as self-mutilation, anorexia, and bulimia; and a widespread contempt among many young girls toward their parents.

"Many of the pressures girls have always faced are intensified in the 1990s," Pipher would write, citing contributing factors such as "more divorced families, chemical addictions, casual sex and violence against women." But perhaps the most oppressive component of all, in her view, was the barrage of warped messages being projected on the ever-present scrim of pop culture. "Something new is happening," she declared. "The protected place in space and time that we once called childhood has grown shorter.... One way to think about all the pain and pathology is to say that the culture is just too hard for most girls to understand and master at this point in their development. They become overwhelmed and symptomatic."

For a time, a young, rebellious vanguard ruled. They were part of the Riot Grrrl wave, a '90s feminist movement-within-the-movement that sought to rejuvenate feminism—and recast society—partly by shocking the system with punk-band power chords.

If the Riot Grrrl movement had a catalytic moment—a couple of transformational months when its full force erupted, pure and undiluted—it might very well have been in Washington, D.C., in June and July of 1991. The writer and musician Sara Marcus lays out a convincing argument in her study of the Riot Grrrl scene, *Girls to the Front*. That spring and summer, the "three-fourths female" punk band Bikini Kill, as Marcus tells the tale, had left its home in Olympia, Washington, to go on tour. Back home, their young audiences had often been too disengaged to wholly connect with their message. ("I'm a revolutionary feminist," the band's drummer, Tobi Vail, would put it, "[and] I won't rest until sexism is obliterated.") Many fans in the heartland, in fact, had already come to know them through their cassette tapes. "For a while," writes Marcus, "no other music mattered [to me], just that breastbone-shaking bass line and Kathleen Hanna's voice singing with all the concentrated fury of a firehose, 'Dare you to do what you want! Dare you to be who you will!' "[8]

For the last concert of their tour, on June 27, Bikini Kill was pumped. Hanna, the lead singer, had been an abuse counselor, artist, spoken-word performer, creator of the zine *Fuck Me Blind*, and musician who'd fronted the bands Amy Carter and Viva Knievel. Tobi Vail was a fellow rocker and punk scholar of sorts, who'd started the zine *Jigsaw* and had dated Nirvana's Kurt Cobain.[9] And as Bikini Kill powered through its set, the bandmates were floored by the reaction, as Marcus reports, when the audience literally rushed the stage. "It was almost like an earthquake, the reverberations that went out through the scene," Mark Andersen of the activist punk collective Positive Force would tell Marcus some twenty years later.

The tremors foretold a groundswell. A week or two after that breakout show, Hanna joined a few compatriots (Molly Neuman, Jen Smith, and Allison Wolfe) and created the first issue of a weekly photocopied zine to distribute free at concerts. Its name: *Riot Grrrl*. Its first-edition cover grrrrl: Madonna, double fist-pumping. Then, by month's end, the first Riot Grrrl meeting convened, in D.C., kicking off what Hanna, according to Marcus, would call a movement created around the problems of sexual and emotional abuse—"an angry girl movement."

Thus began what amounted to a Riot Grrrl crusade. A committed corps of antiestablishment women—first in tight, separatist communities and then across the country—were forging a broad coalition, using what amounted to rudimentary social media: public protest, art projects, and zines. Riot Grrrl

---

8. The group, with albums and song titles like "Pussy Whipped," "I Like Fucking," and "Suck My Left One," says culture writer Julianne Pepitone, "became a seminal part of the Olympia, Washington, and Washington, D.C., punk-rock scenes, proving grunge and grit weren't just for the boys." (Charles R. Cross, *Heavier Than Heaven* [New York: Hyperion, 2001]; interview with Pepitone.)

9. Hanna, one bleary night in 1990, had spray-painted the bedroom wall of Vail's boyfriend Kurt Cobain, emblazoning the phrase KURT SMELLS LIKE TEEN SPIRIT. Hanna, according to Cobain biographer Charles R. Cross, "was referring to a deodorant for teenage girls, so her graffiti was not without implication: Tobi used Teen Spirit, and by writing this on the wall, Kathleen was taunting Kurt about sleeping with [Vail], implying that he was marked by her scent." After Vail and Cobain's subsequent breakup, he would write a cycle of songs that were ostensibly Vail-inspired, becoming the centerpiece of Nirvana's decade-shaking *Nevermind*. (Cobain would meet his future wife, Courtney Love, in 1990.) (Charles R. Cross, *Heavier Than Heaven*, 167–69; Sara Marcus, *Girls to the Front: The True Story of the Riot Grrrl Revolution* [New York: Harper Perennial, 2010], 49–50; David Fricke, "Life After Death," *Rolling Stone*, December 15, 1994.)

gatherings, teach-ins, and even national chapters became as central to the scene as chat rooms were to the growing online community. And the background soundtrack was not male-dominated grunge (Nirvana, Pearl Jam, Soundgarden) but feminist punk rock, emanating from bands like Bikini Kill, Bratmobile, L7, and (out of the U.K.) Huggy Bear.

Journalist Julianne Pepitone, who writes about the arts, business, and technology, summarizes the Riot Grrrl ethos. It embraced radical feminist values, pushed sexual boundaries, and never shied away from haranguing male-centric commercial culture. It delved into its participants' own histories, which sometimes involved sexual assault, domestic abuse, rape, or abortion. "It became an underground subculture of the feminist movement," she explains, "that embraced a DIY spirit of self-sufficiency, feminist theory, sexual power, art, and activism. Much like the gay population, which had reappropriated the term 'queer,' riot grrrl bands reclaimed words like 'bitch' and 'whore' and turned them into battle armor."

Rock, since its birth, had always been essentially sexual. (The phrase "rock and roll," like "jazz" before it, had been a euphemism for intercourse.) But in the '90s, rock clubs had ceased to be boys' clubs. "The corporate music industry," feminism scholar Rebecca Munford would observe, was no longer a "gendered relationship between (male) production and (female) consumption." Indeed, the very feminists[10] who were having their way on the stage and in the studio were just as hormonal as their male peers. Lisa Palac, the sex-positive feminist, editor, and writer, would observe in the 1990s, "In the world of rock, unprecedented numbers of female artists were going public with the power and pleasure of sexual desire. Wholesome-looking Liz Phair softly sang, 'I want to be your blowjob queen.' Courtney Love, in her baby-doll dress and crooked lipstick, screamed 'Suck my clit!' during Hole performances before stage-diving into a sea of fans.... Women's erotic awareness had reached critical mass."[11]

Much of the point was self-definition, according to Munford: "Riot Grrrl

---

10. Grrrls, womyn, and other terms were coined, often ironically.

11. There was a girl band surge, with groups such as TLC, Salt-N-Pepa, Indigo Girls, and Destiny's Child drawing a large fan base. A mania arose for the Spice Girls, the British pop group. "The Spice Girls were having fun," says the actor Alan Cumming, who would appear in the performers' 1997 film *Spice World.* "They were very sexy and confident but it wasn't all just for men's enjoyment. It was very pro-women, [projecting] really good sort of messages for young girls. They were sexy but not

provides a response to dominant representations of patriarchal girlhood by forging spaces in which girls and young women are empowered to resist and, moreover, to produce their own self-representations." Riot Grrrl, in a way, was about women finding their individual voices—and comprehending the economic and social forces behind their very personal struggles. It was also a movement that would make political and legal inroads while influencing everything from fashion to film to the Lilith Fair tour (the star-studded "Celebration of Women in Music" festival that would soon outshine Lollapalooza).

This new model of feminism would persist even as it has evolved to the present day. "Today feminism is more about personal identity," Ann Friedman would note in *New York* magazine's *The Cut* in 2016. "There are points of collective action, but mostly it's a belief system that we adhere to individually, and in highly individualized ways.... Most of us...consider problems like racism and transphobia to be just as pernicious as sexism." Friedman today recalls second-wave sessions at which the movement's leaders would "decide which issues to prioritize and which candidates to support. In the past, that perceived unanimity gave feminism more political clout, but made it less inclusive. We just don't work like that anymore."

Looking back twenty years later, Bikini Kill's Hanna would reveal to journalist Melena Ryzik the method to her (and her generation's) radness: "I didn't just hit the glass ceiling, I pressed my naked [breasts] up against it."

––––––––

Within the space of two years, February 1990 to October 1991, four new voices emerged in the women's movement, in the form of three new books—and an accidental pioneer. Together, they hit like a series of tropical storms, amplifying the early impact of the third wave.

First, Camille Paglia, the aforementioned art historian and humanities professor, published *Sexual Personae: Art and Decadence from Nefertiti to Emily Dickinson*. Paglia—a thorn in the side of many fellow feminists—was one of the greatest hype-meisters to have ever come out of academia. The professor would brag that *Sexual Personae*, at seven-hundred-plus pages, "may be the longest book yet written by a woman, exceeding in this respect even George Eliot's hefty *Middlemarch*." She was also a media darling, dubbed

––

inappropriate. They were very concerned about empowering women. That was their whole thing: Girl Power." (Interview with Cumming.)

"the intellectual pinup of the Nineties" by *Newsday*. She appeared, sword in hand, as a "Woman Warrior" for a *New York* magazine shoot, and was called out on the cover of the *Advocate*: "Attack of the 50-Foot Lesbian."

On its surface, *Sexual Personae* was a survey of erotic representation in art. Deeper inside, Paglia attacked PC academics who wanted to do away with the Western canon and PC feminists who wanted to do away with naughty sex. While she was at it, Paglia went after '60s liberals (who'd gone too far with their excesses) *and* conservative prudes everywhere. She urged readers to get in tune with their outer Apollo (the taming force that guaranteed social order and traditional measures of achievement) *and* their inner Dionysus ("The amorality, aggression, sadism, voyeurism, and pornography in great art have been ignored or glossed over").

Paglia saw in our obsession with pop culture—especially with rock music and Hollywood's "Imperial" star system—the signs of a healthy return to humanity's pagan roots. She lauded contemporary attachments to drag, to façades, to the "malleable but elastic" self, to personae, as she would write in her preface,[12] which she considered "the hidden masks of our ancestors and heirs." She deplored modern society's dismissal of the brutish Male, insisting that men were largely responsible for Western progress ("If civilization had been left in female hands, we would still be living in grass huts"). At the same time, Paglia would affirm the secret force of the Female, her life-giving power, her "intuition," her ability to collude with her sisters in "a secret conspiracy of hearts and pheromones." And in a rash of contrarian op-ed pieces, interviews, and talks, she trashed the notion that there was a date-rape epidemic; defended sex-trade workers as empowered beings; and pegged liberal feminism as having created a culture of victimization. A humanities scholar, of all people, was stirring up gale-force headwinds.

Into those winds swept another bright sail. In 1991, Susan Faludi published *Backlash: The Undeclared War Against American Women*. (That same year she would win the Pulitzer Prize for her reporting on labor issues.) The book argued that even though women had succeeded in making substantive, real-world gains, society had shifted in an attempt to undermine their advances and return to the male status quo. After the breakthroughs of the

---

12. The preface actually appeared separately, two years after *Sexual Personae* was published. (Camille Paglia, *Sex, Art, and American Culture: Essays* [New York: Random House/Vintage, 1992], xi, 101–24.)

second wave, Faludi stated, well-organized conservatives had been conveniently standing in the wings. Energized by their new status as a declining minority, leaders on the far right were soon buoyed by a backlash, reasserting their power in more exaggerated fashion and thriving by having been recast as the underdog.

Despite this pushback, the 1980s had ultimately *strengthened* women, according to Faludi: "The backlash decade produced one long, painful, and unremitting campaign to thwart women's progress. And yet, for all the... blistering denunciations from the New Right, the legal setbacks of the Reagan years, the powerful resistance of corporate America...women never really surrendered." Instead, she contended, "At the start of the '90s, some forecasters...began declaring that the next ten years was going to be 'the Decade of Women.'"[13]

Faludi's book became a feminist landmark. And it was often read alongside another title published that spring, Naomi Wolf's *The Beauty Myth: How Images of Beauty Are Used Against Women*. Wolf, who would go on to informally advise the Clinton reelection campaign and to serve as a Gore campaign consultant on women's issues and messaging, offered a powerful thesis. She argued that even as women were progressing on various fronts, their traditional roles—and the straitjackets applied by capitalism, marketing, pop culture, and male institutions—held them in perpetual check. American women, in a close reading of Wolf, were forever being treated as subordinates in a manner similar to the way the ruling class treated the underclass, immigrants, and minorities.

The Beauty Myth was a wholesale indictment. Wolf squared off against the economic system, the power elite, Hollywood, the advertising community, the porn business ("during the past five years...[it has become] the main media category"), and the cosmetics and fashion industries. Although the '60s' "sexual revolution [had] promoted the discovery of female sexuality," she claimed, "'beauty pornography'...invaded the mainstream to undermine women's new and vulnerable sense of sexual self-worth." Although feminism in the '70s and '80s "gave us laws against job discrimination based on gender," she wrote, "immediately case law evolved in Britain and the United

---

13. The political triumph of Donald Trump a generation after Faludi's book was published would exemplify, to many, a sort of Angry White Male whiplash that had finally resurfaced after the backlash to the backlash.

States that institutionalized job discrimination based on women's appearances." Despite the pervasive advances women had enjoyed in recent years, society was still rigged to screw them.

The beauty myth, as Wolf defined it, held that "strong men battle for beautiful women, and beautiful women are more reproductively successful. Women's beauty must correlate to their fertility, and since this system is based on sexual selection, it is inevitable and changeless. None of this is true." Instead, she argued, "there is no legitimate historical or biological justification for the beauty myth; what it is doing to women today is a result of nothing more exalted than the need of today's power structure, economy, and culture to mount a counteroffensive against women.... The beauty myth is not about women at all. It is about men's institutions and institutional power."[14] Gloria Steinem would insist that "every woman should read" Wolf's book. Fay Weldon called the author a '90s heroine, describing the volume as "essential reading for the New Woman." Germaine Greer endorsed it as "the most important feminist publication since *The Female Eunuch*"—her own 1970 classic.

The books of Paglia, Faludi, and Wolf would be taught for decades and their exploration of '90s feminist paradigms would echo long after. But right in their midst, in the autumn of 1991, another voice spoke to the nation with a force that was even more immediate. That voice was unwavering and indignant—and its message would touch every American worker. It was the voice of a stoic thirty-five-year-old law professor named Anita Hill.

---

14. Some argued that female beauty, in counterpoint to Wolf's proposition, was not a social construct manufactured to perpetuate male supremacy. It was instead an expression of aesthetics, taste, sex appeal, perceived fecundity (or virginity), animal magnetism, fear (or envy) of women's creative power, physical and indeed metaphysical attraction. Psychologist Nancy Etcoff, for one, in her 1999 book *Survival of the Prettiest*, would express the belief that "beauty is a universal part of human experience.... It provokes pleasure, rivets attention, and impels actions that help ensure the survival of our genes." The point: the female form, from epoch to epoch, has always been idealized and aggrandized, largely *because* of its sexual components. (Nancy Etcoff, *Survival of the Prettiest: The Science of Beauty* [New York: Doubleday, 1999].)

CHAPTER 6

Empowerment Icons

The women, though incomparable, invited comparisons. "Hillary Rodham Clinton," in the opinion of the *Washington Post*'s Martha Sherrill, was "replacing Madonna as our leading cult figure." "For years," author Lorrie Moore would assert, "we watched [Hillary Clinton] looking like a nerdier Tina Brown, who in turn looked like a nerdier Princess Di (the 1990s were confusing!)."

These writers, while spot-on, were nonetheless comparing mangoes to kiwis. In the '80s and '90s a new brand of feminist was emerging. And yet it wasn't a matter of Hillary versus Madonna versus anyone. In fact, a diverse *range* of empowerment icons was on the march, advancing in proud formation. And before we engage with one of them firsthand—Professor Anita Hill—there are a few other trailblazers who deserve special mention.

———

Later we would come to know **Hillary Rodham Clinton** as senator, foreign policy architect, humanitarian, and, yes, the first female nominee for president in the 240-year history of the republic. In incalculable ways, she had altered the very perception of what power looked like in this country. But in the '90s we watched her grow in another way: as a role model for contemporary American women.

Hillary Clinton had always been spiritual, but had resisted drawing undue attention to her Methodist roots. She had always been bent on social change, insisting in her 1969 college commencement address that despite that era's advances (such as the civil rights struggle and the Peace Corps), "we arrived at Wellesley and found . . . that there was a gap between expectation and realities." She had always been a principled, committed feminist.

She had advocated for family and children's rights, later writing a book on the subject, *It Takes a Village*. She had been a Walmart board member, an accomplished attorney, and a partner in a buttoned-down corporate law firm—at the time an almost exclusively male enclave. She had firmly held the reins—as a spouse, a strategist, and a political scrapper—when her life partner sought higher office.

Hillary Clinton was also a champion of women in the workforce. During her husband's 1992 presidential campaign, one of her most memorable declarations came as she spoke unapologetically about being a working mother: "I suppose I could have stayed home and baked cookies and had teas, but what I decided to do was to fulfill my profession which I entered before my husband was in public life." Contrary to the complaints of her detractors, however, she was *not* belittling American homemakers. She would go on to state, expansively, "Women can make choices…whether it's full-time career, full-time motherhood, or some combination."

A feminist. A lawyer. A political strategist. A working mom. A defender of children's and women's rights. These were the cornerstones for building a new type of First Lady (even the title today sounds anachronistic)—and a new type of American politician.

Inevitably, upon first occupying 1600 Pennsylvania Avenue, she *became* the public's. In her memoir *Living History*, Clinton professed to understand the bargain: "Over the years, the role of First Lady has been perceived as largely symbolic. She is expected to represent an ideal—and largely mythical—concept of American womanhood." Indeed, she assumed the mantle uncomfortably at first, in full public view.

It is instructive to hear law professor Joan Williams on the subject. Williams, who has written often on sex, gender, and power, tells me, in her office at UC Hastings College of the Law, in San Francisco, that when the Clintons came to power they were a turn-off to many Americans. "The fact that they were both so openly feminist is what made Hillary into [a martyr, a] Saint Stephen," Williams recalls. "She gradually began to understand it, through color-by-numbers. . . . Uppity women get sanctioned every day in workplaces throughout the United States. Hillary [was] the archetype of the Uppity Woman in the early ['90s]. She's gotten more savvy. She gradually understood that she had to go more 'femmy.' Remember the hairstyle change? The problem is, she was acting like a Yale Law graduate. How infuriating. It sets off even more class conflict, because if there's anything a blue-collar guy feels more affronted by is an upper-class woman who is lording it over him. These were gender rules. [In the 1990s] Hillary did not understand how deeply traditional society still was, and still is.[1]

"Do I admire Hillary for being Hillary?" Williams wonders aloud. "I admire her *so* much. But you know what began Hillary's rehabilitation? When she stood by her man. That's when Hillary began to get it. She didn't diss him. And she didn't leave him.... She lived with someone who humiliated her, and that's very femmy.... I think she, in her DNA, had begun to understand what you have to do to connect to a deeply sexist public."

From the early '90s onward, Hillary Clinton, even more than her husband, was reviled by the right. A solid wall of Lynch Hillary books would swell the shelves at Borders and Barnes & Noble. The sexist slurs were rampant: radio haters and conservative journals routinely called her a witch, the "Lady Macbeth of Arkansas," and much, much worse. Some, in time, would attack her feminist bona fides head-on, calling her pro-woman stance duplicitous because of her outsize role in the slut-shaming of women who had accused her husband of sexual advances.

Others saw in Clinton a handy caricature of the classic feminist emasculator. Essayist and poet Katha Pollitt would recount the time that conservative pundit Tucker Carlson went so far as to remark, " 'When she comes on television, I involuntarily cross my legs' ... in a jokey segment about the Hillary Nutcracker, which crushes walnuts between its steely thighs, yours for only $19.95. The ball-busting theme looms large in the male Hillary-hating imagination—that's why she can be both a lesbian and a siren who has Bill by the short hairs."

And while we're on the subject of hair? Culture critic Laura Kipnis would make the case that many of those who were most disparaging of Hillary Clinton—especially male commentators—would make much ado about her hairdo, possibly as a way of transferring their larger angst onto convenient symbols of female display. They zeroed in on her blondeness, her yokelly

---

1. Congresswoman Nancy Pelosi, in contrast—a political contemporary of Clinton's—innately understood that to succeed at the time, in the words of journalist Leslie Bennetts, she had to "cloak her authority in gender mufti." Pelosi, for example, would describe "her ability to order congressmen around [by] using her 'mother-of-five voice.' " (Leslie Bennetts, "Pinning Down Hillary," *Vanity Fair*, June 1994.)

big-hair-ness, her *lack* of a sense of style as well as her *preoccupation* with style. David Brock, according to Kipnis, would denigrate early Headband Hillary for coming from the "look-like-shit school of feminism." R. Emmett Tyrrell—"who sounds like an aspirant," writes Kipnis, "for the Vidal Sassoon endowed chair on the Clinton-hating Right"—would lambast her for having "run through scores of appalling coifs."[2] (Clinton, years later, would enter the same thicket, calling her presidential opponent Donald Trump "an id with hair.")

So much about her came down, dismissively, to appearance. Clinton, going from wispy bangs to bouffant, feathery to teased, was a perfect mother superior for the Makeover Decade. Her pantsuits alone could merit a grad-school dissertation. To supporter and foe alike, she possessed, by turns, the secret powers of *Bewitched*'s Samantha, the liberal conviction of Murphy Brown, *and* the utilitarian chilliness of Martha Stewart. But the barbs, taken one way, were enough to make any rebel proud. To earn this much wrath, Hillary Clinton had to be doing *something* right. She was, in fact, shaking up the perceived role of women in power in America. And in the process, she was shaking men, and many women, to the core.

How did she reshape what a First Lady was supposed to be? First, she raised the bar in terms of political engagement and policy, obtaining, as Virginia Woolf might have put it, a West Wing room of her own. She raised the bar for First Family power-sharing—taking on the ambitious (albeit ill-fated) health care initiative. She raised the bar for thoughtfulness and empathy in political life, calling for a "politics of meaning"—echoing activist rabbi Michael Lerner's notion that all people are in need of healing—and advocating for some semblance of a "zone of privacy" that would cocoon individuals' personal data but also the lives of public officials.[3]

---

2. Even Joe Klein, in his roman à clef about the Clintons, *Primary Colors*, would conjure a sex scene in which the Hillary character has an encounter with the protagonist, campaign strategist Henry Burton. Burton's reaction: "I'd never, I realized, made love before to a woman who used hair spray." (Anonymous [later revealed to be Klein], *Primary Colors: A Novel of Politics* [New York: Random House, 1996], 247.)

3. In 1998, Clinton foresaw a not insignificant downside of a no-holds-barred Internet, calling the new technology "exciting," but wondering how the medium, "without any kind of editing function or gatekeeping function...[would protect your] right to defend your reputation, or to respond to what someone says?" Then in Philadelphia, in 2016, upon accepting her party's nomination as its presidential candidate, she would allow, "The truth is, through all those years of public service, the 'service' part has always come easier to me than the 'public' part." (Rebecca Eisenberg, "First

She even raised the bar for Washington poise—in response to her husband's extramarital conduct. (Writer Ariel Levy would contend that Clinton became "a walking Rorschach test for our feelings about infidelity.")[4] She led through example, exhibiting survival skills, the value of an iron will, and, as novelist Robert Stone would say in another context, "the courage to go on, which may be the most admirable and irreplaceable of human virtues."

Through the roughest gales, it was steady Hillary Clinton who assumed the role of the stay-the-course captain. It was she, not Bill, who made the case, after his relationship with Monica Lewinsky came to light, that the Clintons were battling a "vast right-wing conspiracy." (Though it sounded truly paranoid, paranoia is often the midwife of Washington crisis management.) "Every time he goes down," Gail Sheehy would comment in *Vanity Fair*, "she rears up and turns into a lioness, tearing into the political veld to rip the flesh off their enemies." (Neither Bill nor his minions actually *needed* "enabler Hillary." They were in large measure rather expert at such dark arts.) But whatever the case, much of the country venerated her, learned from her, *felt* for her. Hillary Clinton, during six of her years as First Lady, would occupy the top slot in Gallup's annual ranking of the most admired women in America. (Starting in 2002, she would top the list fifteen years running.)

True, Hillary, like Bill, had a credibility gap. She was accused of massaging the truth as it suited her. She found herself at the center of political whodunits: the missing Travelgate documents; the missing Whitewater billing records—harbingers of the missing State Department emails that would dog her as she sought the presidency. (At one point during the 2016 campaign, a Quinnipiac poll found that 57 percent of voters did not consider Hillary Clinton to be "honest and trustworthy." And the most frequent "first word" that came to voters' minds when her name was mentioned? "Liar.")[5]

Lady Just Doesn't Get It," SFgate.com, January 22, 1998; "Hillary's DNC Speech, Annotated," *Los Angeles Times*, July 28, 2016.)

4. Columnist and critic Barbara Lippert would call her "a walking Rorschach test for our own ambivalences. In the stereotypical labeling of things male and female, it's easy to feminize him and masculinize her." (Barbara Lippert, "The Hillary Mystique," *New York*, February 9, 1998.)

5. *New York Times* media columnist Jim Rutenberg would observe, "There are more 'gates' affixed to her last name—Travelgate, Whitewatergate, now Emailgate—than there are gates in the Old City of Jerusalem." And the *Times*'s Frank Bruni would declare, the morning after Clinton lost the election to Donald Trump, "She was forever surrounded by messes...all of them exhausting to voters who had lived through a quarter century of political melodrama with her." (Jim Rutenberg,

Not unlike her husband, she possessed a sense of entitlement that is unseemly in a public servant. "Hillary has an 'I' message [on the campaign trail]: I have been abused and misunderstood and now it's my turn," the *New York Times*'s columnist Maureen Dowd would write during that race. "It's a victim mind-set that is exhausting, especially because the Clintons' messes are of their own making." While loyal and legendarily generous to staffers, she was regarded by various critics as a creature of political expediency, who sometimes used people and then cast them aside.

"She has flip-flopped on so many issues of image," wrote the playwright Wendy Wasserstein in 1998, "that her behavior can justifiably be called erratic. First she defiantly wasn't baking cookies, then suddenly we were barraged with her recipes for Christmas cookies. Initially, she sandwiched 'Rodham' within her name, and then it magically disappeared. When the coast was clear, it slinked back out again." During Clinton's 2008 presidential campaign, in fact, strategists working for her Democratic opponent, Barack Obama, drafted a memo that identified an Achilles' heel: "She's driven by political calculation, not conviction....She prides herself on working the system, not changing it." Eight years later, when she lost her second bid for the White House, it was said that voters had long ago tired of Madame HRC, ascribing to her personality traits that might have been readily levied against her opponent: greedy,[6] vengeful, suspicious, secretive, mercenary, entitled, infuriating, power-hungry, out-of-touch, cold-blooded, untrustworthy...Need I go on?

To others, of course, none of the above was a sign of outright deceit. "Sure, Clinton's calculating," columnist Nicholas Kristof would admit as Clinton made her 2016 bid. "She's not a saint but a politician, and to me this notion that she's fundamentally dishonest is a bogus narrative." Author Jonathan Rauch would echo Kristof, citing hacked emails in which Secretary Clinton, in almost Lincolnian fashion, made the case for occasional evasion, for establishing "both a public and a private position." In Rauch's view, "she understands that

---

New York Times, August 8, 2016, A1, 14; Frank Bruni, "Donald Trump's Shocking Success," *New York Times*, November 9, 2016.)

6. In their post–White House years, Clinton and her husband reportedly took in nearly a quarter of a billion dollars in pretax income, much of it in speaking fees. (Dan Alexander, "How the Clintons Have Made $230 Million Since Leaving the White House," *Forbes*, October 13, 2015.)

hypocrisy and two-facedness, when prudently harnessed to advance negotiations or avert conflicts, are a public good and a political necessity."

Hillary Clinton would win a seat in the U.S. Senate, twice. She would go on to run for the presidency, twice, serving in between as the nation's secretary of state. In that role, she would visit 112 countries, help make advances in women's rights a global priority, orchestrate the deal that pushed Iran into nuclear negotiations, and restore a level of respect and prestige in American diplomacy that had been squandered during the Bush years.[7] She was a feminist, a Democrat, a Boomer, a social activist, a political infighter, a diplomat, and a grandmother. And she was, above all, another inevitable, inescapable Clinton.

But in the 1990s, if there was a cause she championed, first and foremost, it was, in a word, the empowerment of women. And her shining hour of the decade came with her address in China. In 1995, before the U.N.'s Fourth World Conference on Women—an event that attracted fifty thousand attendees from across the globe—Clinton decreed from the podium:

> If there is one message that echoes forth from this conference, let it be that human rights are women's rights, and women's rights are human rights once and for all....As long as discrimination and inequities remain so commonplace everywhere in the world, as long as girls and women are valued less, fed less, fed last, overworked, underpaid, not schooled, subjected to violence in and outside their homes—the potential of the human family to create a peaceful, prosperous world will not be realized.

In the audience that day in Beijing, many of the listeners cried openly. Here was a woman of conscience, power, and valor who was giving voice to their deepest beliefs as women and as members of the human family. Indeed, to this day, the credo "Women's rights are human rights" remains a vital rallying cry.

---

7. When praising her at the 2016 Democratic National Convention, President Obama, her onetime opponent, would state unequivocally, "There has never been a man or a woman—not me, not Bill, nobody—more qualified than Hillary Clinton to serve as president of the United States of America." He then looked up at the ex-prez in the balcony seats, adding, "I hope you don't mind, Bill, but I'm just telling the truth, man." (Barack Obama, "Remarks by the President at the Democratic National Convention," Philadelphia, July 28, 2016, www.whitehouse.gov.)

Few contemporaries had more influence in busting gender norms. Or recalibrating women's personal style and comportment. Or navigating the dynamics of sex and social interaction. In all of the discussions and interviews I've conducted for this book, with dozens of women, Madonna's is the name that has emerged more frequently than any other as a personal inspiration or as a catalyst for changing the way American women in the '90s were perceived by society—and how they perceived themselves.

In a broader context, **Madonna Louise Ciccone** was a master of celebrity longevity through protean reinvention. She was the tastemaker who shape-shifted in response to (and in anticipation of) the ebbs and flows in the tastes of the times. Indulge me a bit of a recap.

Madonna was the one, in the 1980s, who'd helped popularize the crucifix and rosary beads as fashion accessories, undergarments as outerwear, and the navel and the shaggy pit as bad-girl monograms. She'd donned matrimonial white to open the virginity conversation[8] and vowed "I'm keeping my baby" to address teen pregnancy (in the song "Papa Don't Preach"). In concert she sported torpedo-shaped breastplates to assert her alpha femme. In one music video she wore a neck manacle; in another, she kissed a black Jesus figure as crosses flickered in flame.

At every turn, the ruling class shuddered, which only increased Madonna's hold on the hoi polloi. Her lyrics rankled parents and legislators. Catholic groups in Italy called for a boycott of her performances. Even MTV, which prided itself on '80s edge, banned her video for "Justify My Love," a peep-and-drag show of sado-teasing and bi-curious couplings. (Camille Paglia praised the clip as a "truly avant-garde [work that succeeded in] restoring lesbian eroticism to the continuum of heterosexual response.") In Alek Keshishian's 1991 warts-and-all documentary, *Truth or Dare*, Madonna gave head to a bottle of H_2O. And her then partner, Warren Beatty, would say of her as the tape rolled, "She doesn't want to live off camera, much less

8. "Virginity is mine to claim, is Madonna's message," columnist James Wolcott would write, duly impressed in the summer of 1985. "I'm pure as long as I belong to myself. This seems to me healthier than Brooke Shields's campaign to make a national shrine out of her hymen." (James Wolcott, "Let the Mascara Run," *Vanity Fair*, August 1985, 71.)

talk.... Why would you say something if it's off camera? What point is there of existing?"

She was also a force of nature—and stature—in the entertainment industry. In 1990, *Forbes* would name Madonna "America's smartest businesswoman," well before she started Maverick, her own boutique talent incubator under the Time Warner umbrella. She certainly acted the part. Taking to the stage on one tour in a pair of businessman's slacks—and a bustier—she "looks out at the crowd of 35,000 fans," as *Forbes* put it, "grabs her crotch, raises her fist, and yells, 'I'm the boss around here.'"

Her most risky venture of all came in 1992. That was the year Madonna published an opulent book of pornographic photos and erotic musings called *Sex*. Published in five languages, it would sell out every last copy—all five hundred thousand in the United States and more than a million more globally. Throughout the volume, Madonna portrays a character named Mistress Dita, who gamely play-acts (along with models, celebrity friends, and social swells) for fashion photographer Steven Meisel. In the pictures she is being eaten out by a succession of partners. She nibbles some man ass. She portrays lynxes and Lolitas as well as porn princesses straight out of stroke books and bondage films (replete with SS garb). *Sex* contains scenes of gang assault, mock bestiality, and domination. There is also a good deal of humor: Madonna in her birthday suit, hitchhiking; a live-action porn comic; liquid streams (fountains, sun-lotion eruptions) that appear as a running joke.

In the end, however, the joke was on her. Major critics blanched at the book's pretensions. The *New York Times'* Vicki Goldberg, for one, found the words wanting ("when it comes to writing, she makes a good plumber") and the pictures a corny sort of porn: "either too artificial or what would be too ordinary if...such extravagant effort had not been made to achieve high-class calendar art." Michiko Kakutani, also in the *Times*, called the book's imagery "secondhand, borrowed from the work of Robert Mapplethorpe...Calvin Klein's annoying Obsession ads and self-important S&M movies like *The Night Porter*." In fact, two of Mapplethorpe's friends—critic Ingrid Sischy and Howard Read, director of the photography department at Mapplethorpe's dealer, the Robert Miller Gallery—would tell me of their dismay for how the physical book, stamped with an "(X)" on the jacket and tucked away in a heat-sealed Mylar sack, seemed a commodified echo of Mapplethorpe's breakthrough portfolios from the '70s and '80s (labeled "X," "Y," and "Z," and shrouded in discreet cases).⁹

Even so, Madonna was venturing into new and crucial terrain. *Sex* was a mongrel mating of erotica and fame, and it amounted to a celebrity endorsement of the porn turn. Here was a star's inoculation against overexposure: *complete* exposure. The culture's Mistress of Persona, in effect, was breaking down the last barrier between one's public personality and one's private—if fantasized—sex life, and she was doing it with her own body as her canvas. (What's more, she was doing it under the imprint of Warner Books, a mainstream publisher that was part of Time Warner, a massive, publicly traded company.) Madonna was boldly updating Warhol: *In the future*, she was predicting, *everyone will open the kimono for fifteen minutes*.

Be that as it may, let's put aside the dancer-singer-actress-fashionista-entrepreneur-provocateur's transfigurations: punk to siren, material girl to spiritualist, hellion to mom, vamp to pornographer. Madonna's real-world impact had little to do with self-promotion or brand enhancement. More meaningful were the three principles of conduct that Madonna seemed to be espousing in the '80s and '90s, principles that, when articulated today, might seem tame.

First, she taught women, men, and those across the gender spectrum to disregard taboos and to explore and express their sexual selves. In songs like "Express Yourself," the singer was advocating a kind of polymorphous pride,

---

9. I discussed the book with Sischy, the respected critic of the visual arts and longtime editor of *Interview*, over lunch, and in a follow-up email exchange in 2015, two months before her death from breast cancer. Sischy's take: "[*Sex*] seemed to want to be a fetish object for the masses.... Madonna had such a strong track record of tapping into underground ideas and bringing them into the mainstream in a smart way. This time it didn't work. In contrast to what was going on in the art world, Madonna's *Sex* book felt like it was too manufactured and very commercial. The thing that's interesting about the subject of sex is that when it is commercialized it loses its zip. The audience can tell. This project failed because it had such an aura of commerce that took over. It had an advertising sensibility—models were cast in a big open call, as I remember—and the whole project was accomplished in a matter of days, as opposed to something that was actually *lived*. With *Sex* there was a feeling in the art community that the real battles of the day [over AIDS awareness and action, LGBT rights, sexual exploration, gender roles, and so on] had been exploited and that people who had no real investment in these struggles had come in and made a flashy and portentous product of it all. It was a shame because Madonna genuinely cared about these issues and she herself had been on the front line, and continued to be. But this was a misstep."

which espoused that only *you* should define your sexual self—your gender identity and expression, your relationship choices, your manner, your masks, your sex appeal—independent of the biases or mores of other individuals or society at large. The *Truth or Dare* documentary, for instance, was ahead of its time in showing out-and-proud dancers in her retinue being sexually expressive for the camera. In one particularly steamy scene, two men French kiss during a round of "Truth or Dare"; the exchange, according to journalist Jim Farber, reviewing a 2016 film (about the documentary and the 1990 Blond Ambition tour),[10] was "an extremely rare sight for a mainstream movie at the time. For a generation of gay people, it was a transformative moment.... In large part, [*Truth or Dare*] was about revealing truths to erase shame—specifically about being gay or H.I.V.-positive at a time when AIDS paranoia ran rampant."

Second, Madonna encouraged women to preempt their victimization by confiscating the language of oppression—along with words, behaviors, and outward displays—as their own. (One of her companies, for example, was named Slutco; another, Boy Toy Inc.) As Madonna would tell Norman Mailer in a 1994 interview for *Esquire*, "Feminists were beating the fuck out of me: 'What are you doing? You're sending out all the wrong messages to young girls. They should be using their heads, not their tits and their asses.' My whole thing is you use all you have, all you have, your sexuality, your femininity, your—any testosterone you have inside of you, your intellect—use whatever you have." She was, as essayist Emily Nussbaum put it, "our sacrificial anti-victim."

Third, Madonna reinforced the American virtues of self-reliance, of self-definition, and finally, of finding one's own path even as one strove to live in a culture promoting social equality. Hers was an ethos of restless independence. Her lyrics, videos, and actions were a club-kid-turned-pop-diva's version of sentiments expressed by Austen and Brontë and Woolf, of figures as disparate as Mae West and Angela Davis.[11]

And so it goes. Thirty years after the star's debut, the producer-musician

---

10. The 2016 documentary, *Strike a Pose*, was directed by Ester Gould and Reijer Zwaan.

11. No one said it better than Madonna's soul mate academician, Camille Paglia: "Madonna has a far profounder vision of sex than do the feminists. She sees both the animality and the artifice. Changing her costume style and hair color virtually every month, Madonna embodies the eternal values of beauty and pleasure. Feminism says, 'No more masks.' Madonna says we are nothing but masks. Through her enormous impact on young women around the world, Madonna is the future

Diplo would conclude, "No one stands this long. All the women start with Madonna. No matter where you come from, no matter what you're doing now—if you're a powerful woman, the genesis is Madonna."

———

All these years later, it's hard to imagine the tumult. But in 1997, America went a little bananas when **Ellen DeGeneres**, star of the sitcom *Ellen*, appeared on the cover of *Time* alongside the headline—stilted even back in the day—"Yep, I'm Gay."

For a while, the actress's sexual orientation had been something of an open secret. A few weeks before *Time's* issue hit newsstands, she'd appeared in press photos taken at the *Vanity Fair* Oscar Party, clearly bonding with actress Anne Heche, whom she'd met that night. And DeGeneres's real-life situation mirrored an on-air plot development on *Ellen*, the series: her TV alter ego, Ellen Morgan (as the magazine put it), was set to "discover that she—the character, that is—is a lesbian.[12] For DeGeneres, 39, the decision was the culmination of a long process of struggling with feelings about her own sexuality, her fears about being rejected for it, her wish to lead a more honest and open life in public, her weariness at the effort it took her not to [come out]."

Here was TV's first openly gay big-name star playing an openly gay lead character, and doing it on ABC, part of the family-friendly Disney company. As a consequence, her very personal disclosure was an inspiration to many of the forty-two million viewers who would watch the episode.

"There was some commercial calculation in it," says Bruce Handy, who wrote *Time's* cover story twenty years ago. "Coming out as gay in her real life/ professional life just as her character [did], brought her a lot of attention. . . . But what she did was brave. There were risks. There was no way of knowing in advance that it would turn out so well. True, the show got cancelled a year later, but she's since been one of the great hosts of the Oscars telecast, and she's an extremely successful talk-show host [which capitalizes] on her gift, which is in being herself. Coming out allowed her to do that."

———

of feminism." (Camille Paglia, "Madonna—Finally, a Real Feminist," *New York Times*, December 14, 1990.)

12. Among those to appear in cameos on the broadcast: Melissa Etheridge, k. d. lang, Demi Moore, and Oprah Winfrey—the latter portraying Ellen's therapist. (John J. O'Connor, "Coming Out Party: The Closet Opens, Finally," *New York Times*, April 30, 1997.)

DeGeneres was up against a still-resistant society. Many Americans had little experience in addressing sexual orientation in a substantive manner. Many inside and outside that conversation had trepidations about confronting their own biases or conflicts. Anti-LGBT discrimination and prejudice remained widespread; the Reverend Jerry Falwell would call her "Ellen DeGenerate." And as antibias gains were made, incidents of assault often rose.

For many viewers, the newly uncloseted *Ellen* (and the program's exploration of themes related to her character's sexual orientation) went a bit overboard. Yet DeGeneres herself would upbraid those who criticized the show as "too gay." "Everybody's saying, 'O.K., enough already,'" she remarked. "If it was enough already, we wouldn't have the crime that we have—the hate crimes. We wouldn't have the suicides. We wouldn't have...gay-bashing. It's not enough already. It's not nearly enough."

Ellen/*Ellen*'s magic moment was part of what some would downplay as the pinnacle of "lesbian chic," an attempt to glamorize women the culture had stereotyped.[13] Yet lesbian chic, to some, was just another male- or hetero-affixed baggage tag. Writer Kara Swisher would complain that "even with the welcome warmth of the spotlight, lesbians shouldn't allow anyone to exploit them for their trendiness." Even more cynically, another kind of trend had been set in motion. As Alyssa Rosenberg would later insist in the *Atlantic*, DeGeneres's orchestrated rollout became the template for how public figures proclaimed their orientation—in TV sitdowns, in the popular press, and on social media. It was yet another card to play in firmly establishing one's franchise. "Coming out remains a fraught process for many Americans," Rosenberg would write. "But for some famous, secure people, official confirmation of their sexual orientation isn't just a matter of honesty: It's a highly valuable commodity. The coming-out process has become yet another celebrity experience to be packaged up for consumption."

And yet in 1997, Ellen DeGeneres's reveal had broad impact. As more and more straight people accepted gay and lesbian friends, family members,

---

13. Glamorize, and how. Two weeks after the *Time* story, DeGeneres and Anne Heche would be invited to the annual White House Correspondents' Dinner. They would meet President Clinton—glam himself, in black tie—and laugh along with the audience when comedian Jon Stewart said from the dais that the actress's coming out had really been "an elaborate ruse to keep Larry King from hitting on her." (Patrick Rogers, "Girls' Night Out," *People*, May 12, 1997.)

and coworkers; as the marriage-equality movement made greater strides; as formerly hesitant or insular Americans made everyday acquaintance with what would come to be called the LGBT community, the wider culture was moving light-years beyond "Yep."

———

Demi Moore, the screen star with the ice-queen demeanor and a striking coltish quality, was the quintessential '90s movie star. And like her contemporary Michael Douglas, she excelled at portraying characters who forcefully challenged assumptions about society's codified sex roles.[14]

Her greatest role of all, however, would come in front of a still camera. In 1991, Moore was scheduled to be the subject of a *Vanity Fair* cover story. There was one problem, though. How would photographer **Annie Leibovitz** depict the actress—seven months pregnant at the time—in a way that made her *presentable* (the word sounds obsolete today) on the front of a commercial magazine?

The photographer and her subject were already comfortable with each other. When Moore married Bruce Willis, Leibovitz had shot their wedding photos. When Moore was carrying the couple's first child, Leibovitz had agreed to take some private nudes. For the *Vanity Fair* session, things started off slowly. Moore posed seminude, draped in a green silk robe. At another point, she put on a black lace bra. "Toward the end of the shoot," as Leibovitz would recall in her book *Annie Leibovitz at Work*, Moore dispensed with clothing altogether. "The fully nude picture...was intended just for Demi. I was taking some companion photographs to the ones I had made during Demi's first pregnancy. As I was shooting, I said, 'You know, this would be a great cover.'"

What Leibovitz saw through her lens was the most arresting film actress of the day wearing nothing but a pair of diamond earrings and a thirty-carat diamond ring. In the resulting photo, Moore discreetly shrouded her breasts and held her protruding belly. Her posture—upright, forthright, head tilted slightly upward—was statuesque, iconic. Her full figure, her openness, her

———

14. In eight films from 1990 to 1997, Moore plays a woman who communicates with a deceased lover (*Ghost*); who may have murdered an abusive husband (*Mortal Thoughts*); who serves as legal counsel in the staunchly male bastion of the Marine Corps (*A Few Good Men*); who considers a one-night stand in exchange for a million dollars (*Indecent Proposal*); who sexually harasses a male underling at work (*Disclosure*); who incurs her community's wrath after falling for the local pastor (*The Scarlet Letter*); who, as a single mom, works as an exotic dancer (*Striptease*); and who volunteers to go through grueling Navy SEAL training (*G.I. Jane*).

natural beauty referenced Rubens and Titian, Botticelli's *Birth of Venus* and sculptor Jacob Epstein's *Genesis*. And when it appeared on the August cover of *Vanity Fair* it set off cultural shock waves.

As I have recounted elsewhere, certain newsstands sold out the day it was published. Many convenience stores and grocery chains banned the issue from their shelves. In much of America, retail outlets and distributors would carry copies only if they were shrouded in a white paper wrapper. Conservative commentators railed about the fact that an expectant mother was expressing herself as an unapologetically sexual creature. *Interview* magazine, meanwhile, would compare the cover's "cross-cultural recognition and infamy" with the power of "a hit movie."

The cover's immediate impact, in the period before the prevalence of the World Wide Web, was measured in its echoes across the print press: fifteen hundred newspaper articles mentioned the photo; twelve major cartoonists lampooned it; the *Atlanta Journal-Constitution* conducted a poll gauging public reaction and noted that "5,000 responded, with opinion dividing right down the middle." *Vanity Fair* received a similar mix of mail, pro and con, the most thoughtful perhaps coming from Shannon Marmion of Plano, Texas, who commented, "Is America really this messed up? Have we actually come to a point where exploitative magazines full of naked women are displayed openly at newsstands while sensitive pictures of pregnant women are banned or covered up so as not to offend anyone?"

Leibovitz and Moore, in fact, had created something lasting. Their "Madonna with Child" reprised a theme that sculptures, paintings, and totemic figures had conveyed for millennia: the primal link between fertility and sensual power. "I thought about how people in this country don't want to embrace motherhood and sensuality," Demi Moore would later comment. "While you're pregnant you're made to feel not beautiful or sexually viable. You're either sexy or you're a mother. I didn't want to have to choose, so I challenged that."[15] Elsewhere she would remark that the photo was a "feminist statement.... People were moved by something I did that was very natural to me, and that in the process I could have done something to make women look at themselves differently."

---

15. Later in the decade the term "MILF" would enter general parlance, popularized by the 1999 film *American Pie*.

Fashion experts would credit the picture with having started the trend of snug-fitting maternity clothes that accentuate curves instead of hiding them. To many women, the cover helped destigmatize *appearing* pregnant. As odd as it sounds, what had sometimes amounted to a nine-month "predicament"— in the male-dominated workplace or in youth-oriented popular culture—was becoming, more to the point, a point of pride.

The framework, thanks to Moore and to Leibovitz, had expanded for depicting and understanding mothers-to-be. And millions of Americans would readily acknowledge that a childbearing woman inherently embodies the promise of new life, certainly, but also sensual allure and the irrefutable power of creation.

Anita Hill grew up on a working farm in Lone Tree, Oklahoma. The youngest of thirteen children, she was raised in the Baptist faith. "Every other week I attended our local Baptist church, and Sunday school every Sunday," says Hill, a professor of social policy, law, and women's studies at Brandeis (in one of our two long interviews in Newton, Massachusetts). "It was a rural church, exclusive to African Americans. Women sat on one side with the children; men on the other. Female deacons were not allowed and still aren't. My mother's father helped found the church." Her farming parents instilled in their children the virtues not only of a spiritual grounding but also of a good education. In high school, Anita—studious, popular, and active in Future Homemakers of America—would become her class valedictorian before going off to Oklahoma State University, then Yale Law.

Faith, like the law, would continue to be a strong component in her life. (She would join the Presbyterian Church in 1992.) But contrary to her public image as a prim, sober sort, she is in fact a shrewd woman of the world; active in the legal, academic, and women's rights communities; possessed of a sparkling and sometimes withering wit. She has maintained a longtime relationship with a male partner. She enjoys the occasional dry martini.

And yet never in her life, before or since, would she be compelled to take on as public a role as she did in October 1991.

It all began three months earlier. To fill the vacancy of the retiring Thurgood Marshall, President George H. W. Bush had designated Clarence Thomas as his new Supreme Court designee. The nomination, though sure to receive strong resistance from many Democrats because of Thomas's far-right views and rulings, nevertheless seemed a fairly safe bet. He was a conservative serving on the U.S. Court of Appeals for the D.C. Circuit and, like Marshall, a black jurist. He had served under Ronald Reagan and— en route to securing his federal judgeship on President Bush's watch—had developed relationships with powerful congressmen and prominent Washington conservatives.[16] Moreover, right-wing strategists had mobilized to avoid a repeat of the contentious 1987 hearings at which Democrats had scuttled the confirmation of Robert Bork, Reagan's archconservative pick for a Court vacancy. Justice Thomas, all in all, seemed to have the wind at his back, his bid championed by savvy negotiators on the Bush-Quayle team and by lobbyists who moved in to tamp down opposition. He even felt reassured by the Senate Judiciary chairman, Joe Biden, who'd reportedly told him, "I'm in your court."

But accusations soon surfaced. A decade before, so the rumors went, Thomas, while a government appointee, had made sexually charged statements to one or more people, including an employee who was reporting directly to him—charges he would categorically deny. That person turned out to be Anita Hill.

Hill had been Thomas's assistant when he was head of the Department of Education's Office for Civil Rights. She would continue working for him when he was asked to lead the Equal Employment Opportunity Commission (EEOC)—the federal agency tasked, among its other roles, with processing claims arising from accusations of workplace harassment. At the time, Hill chose not to air her grievances about Thomas's alleged behavior. While she

---

16. Among Thomas's supporters for the appeals court position was Patrick McGuigan, part of hard-liner Paul Weyrich's Free Congress Foundation, according to journalists Jane Mayer and Jill Abramson in their book *Strange Justice: The Selling of Clarence Thomas*. During Thomas's fight for the Supreme Court post, wrote Mayer and Abramson, far-right figures Gary Bauer and William Kristol played key roles, as did an important Thomas mentor, Senator John Danforth, the Missouri Republican, who during the hearings would pray with Thomas and his wife, Virginia, in the senator's office bathroom. As reported by Jeffrey Toobin in the *New Yorker*, Thomas would officiate the 1994 wedding of conservative radio personality Rush Limbaugh and currently counts among his friends Limbaugh's fellow talk-show eminence Mark Levin. Virginia Thomas would later become an important force in the Tea Party movement. (Jane Mayer and Jill Abramson, *Strange Justice: The Selling of Clarence Thomas* [New York: Houghton Mifflin, 1994], 152–55, 170–71, 192–94, 289; Virginia Lamp Thomas, "Breaking Silence," *People*, November 11, 1991; Jeffrey Toobin, "Partners," *New Yorker*, August 29, 2011, 46; Harrison Smith, "Supreme Court Justices Officiate Lots of Weddings," *Washingtonian*, May 18, 2015.)

could have done so, such complaints were not at all common—which was part of the problem. What's more, as a woman with a rising career, she had not wanted to alienate her politically connected boss.

Eventually, Hill switched jobs. She says she felt the need to escape what she would come to characterize as a hostile working environment. For all that, however, she stayed in touch with Thomas professionally over the years, once asking him to write her a letter of recommendation.

The incidents, she claims, had plagued and puzzled her. At the time of the encounters, she sought others' confidence and discussed the details— and her distress—with three of her colleagues. And while meeting with an American University faculty member, who was encouraging her to apply for a prospective position as a visiting professor, she was asked why she'd left the EEOC. She decided to confide in him as well. (That law professor, Joel Paul, happens to have been a friend and college classmate of mine.)

Hill, for the most part, had made a decision to remain silent; what was past was past. But then, in the late summer of 1991, a Senate aide looking into Thomas's history phoned Hill and asked about a purported pattern of behavior by the judge. She declined to answer, she now says, describing the initial inquiry as "very general—something like, 'Did I know anything about rumors that Thomas had harassed women who worked for him?'" Even so, she encouraged the caller to have the committee investigate further. By her way of thinking, according to Jane Mayer and Jill Abramson in their book *Strange Justice: The Selling of Clarence Thomas*, Hill "'feared' that unless other women came forward with similar accounts, her description of Thomas's outlandish behavior would be dismissed as 'an isolated incident by someone who had recently been divorced.'" (Thomas and his first wife divorced in 1984; Hill has never married.) Accusations of workplace sexual harassment at the time were relatively rare.

Her fears were justified. If she were to come out with her charges, she realized, she would have to dredge up long-ago incidents that were embarrassing, shameful, and personal. She would be navigating new legal and social terrain, without fixed guidelines. She would be putting Thomas's career on the line, as well as her own, risking her privacy and reputation.

For three weeks, Senate aides continued to probe into the matter, and, Hill says, their questions became more pointed—as did the pressure to go public. Finally, in late September she agreed to cooperate and describe her experiences to an FBI agent, she recalls, "but only if I could put in the record a statement in my own words about what happened with Thomas along with [the mandatory] FBI report." The next step was inevitable. The Senate committee announced that its hearings would be expanded to include testimony from both the nominee, Thomas, *and* his accusers: Hill, along with four "witnesses" (Joel Paul and the three others who were willing to discuss Hill's past disclosures to them about Thomas). Her appearance was scheduled for October 11, 1991.

It was hard to believe, as many would contend, that Anita Hill was politically motivated. She had told others, for instance, that she objected to the treatment of Robert Bork—one of her former teachers at Yale—who had been one of the most conservative modern-era judges proposed to serve on the Court. Indeed, as Paul would state under oath, "I know from numerous conversations with her that she served faithfully in the Reagan administration, that she was generally in sync with the goals of that administration."

Hill's rationale, instead, was straightforward, she now says: "What I thought I was doing was to give testimony that was relevant to the proceeding at hand that went to the behavior of a person who was going to be put on the Supreme Court for life. And it went specifically to how he had comported himself in the workplace with regard to rules that he was in charge of enforcing.

"At the time," Hill continues, "I might have been seen as embodying a liberal cause. Over time—even now—it came to be, to some, an embodiment of 'conservative values.' You become the embodiment of whatever people project onto you.... I was never there to embody a cause."

———

On the first day of her testimony, Anita Hill appeared in a conservative blue-green skirt suit, speaking courteously, softly, forcefully. She sat before an all-male, all-white panel of senators, before TV cameras, before a national audience estimated at thirty million. She was addressed throughout the proceedings as Professor Hill.

She would assert that while she worked for Thomas at the Department of Education, he had asked her out on dates and she had refused, believing, as she told the committee, "that having a social relationship with a person who was supervising my work would be ill-advised." After a time, she said, Thomas would call her into his office to discuss work matters, then speak graphically about sexual topics. "His conversations were very vivid," she stated. "He spoke about acts that he had seen in pornographic films involving such matters as women having sex with animals, and films showing group sex or rape scenes. He talked about pornographic materials depicting individuals with large penises or large breasts involved in various sex acts....Because I was extremely uncomfortable talking about sex with him at all, and particularly in such a graphic way, I told him that I did not want to talk about those subjects."

Once Thomas and Hill began working at the EEOC, she claimed, Thomas would comment about the outfits she wore. "One of the oddest episodes I remember," she added, "was an occasion in which Thomas was drinking a Coke in his office. He got up from the table at which we were working, went over to his desk to get the Coke, looked at the can, and asked, 'Who has put pubic hair on my Coke?' On other occasions he referred to the size of his own penis as being larger than normal."

She went on to allege that he once referred to the penis size of a particular porn-film actor. When committee chair Joe Biden pressed her on specifics— "Do you recall what it was?"—she responded, "The name that was referred to was Long Dong Silver." This methodical chronicle of adult movies, sex acts, and body parts in the halls of Congress seemed to many to have turned the hearings, in the words of Judge Thomas, into "a circus."[17] Indeed, he would bluntly tell the committee that the accusations played "to the worst stereotypes we have about black men in this country."

When Thomas, in turn, took his seat before the lawmakers, he dismissed Hill's charges in their entirety. He also questioned how the behavior and motives of the committee and the press could have allowed such an important process to devolve into farce and spectacle. "I have endured this ordeal for 103 days," he said. "Reporters sneaking into my garage to examine books I read. Reporters and interest groups swarming over divorce papers, looking for dirt.... This is not American. This is Kafkaesque. It has got to stop.... I

---

17. None other than Robert Bork would reflect, "During the worst of the Clarence Thomas hearings, [he] was subjected to scurrilous and vulgar sexual allegations that were telecast internationally. The shock of seeing how far our government processes had descended was so great that I went to a friend's office and said, 'Television is showing the end of Western civilization in living color.'" (Robert H. Bork, *Slouching Towards Gomorrah: Modern Liberalism and American Decline* [New York: HarperCollins, 1996], 335.)

am not here to be further humiliated by this committee, or anyone else, or to put my private life on display for a prurient interest or other reasons."

He would go on to say, "As far as I'm concerned, it is a high-tech lynching for uppity blacks who in any way deign to think for themselves.... I will not provide the rope for my own lynching or for further humiliation. I am not going to engage in discussions, nor will I submit to roving questions of what goes on in the most intimate parts of my private [life] or the sanctity of my bedroom."

Thomas also spoke of the psychic costs. "I have never, in all my life, felt such hurt, such pain, such agony. My family and I have been done a grave and irreparable injustice.... I have been racking my brains and eating my insides out trying to think of what I could have said or done to Anita Hill to lead her to allege [these charges].... This is a person I have helped at every turn in the road since we met. She seemed to appreciate the continued cordial relationship we had since day one. She sought my advice and counsel."

Several lawmakers could barely conceal their contempt for Hill's imputations. Senator Orrin Hatch, the Utah Republican, wondered aloud if Hill had purloined her charges from printed sources. He cited an Oklahoma lawsuit that mentioned Long Dong Silver, implying that Hill could have lifted the reference from an old legal case. He held up a copy of the horror novel *The Exorcist*, then read a passage that might have inspired Hill, in which a character reportedly spoke of "an alien pubic hair floating around in my gin." Senator Strom Thurmond of South Carolina would declare, "I do not believe Judge Thomas is capable of the kind of behavior Professor Hill described."[18]

Wyoming's Alan Simpson—who had put through his own legislation to combat sexual harassment—would say ominously, "I really am getting stuff over the transom about Professor Hill. I have got letters hanging out of my pockets. I have got faxes... statements from people that know her, statements from Tulsa, Oklahoma, saying, 'Watch out for this woman.' But nobody has the guts to say that because it gets all tangled up in this sexual harassment

---

18. In 2003, it would be revealed that unapologetic segregationist Thurmond—who spoke out often against the mixing of races—was in fact the father of a biracial daughter, Essie Mae Washington-Williams. Her true lineage had been kept a family secret for nearly seventy years. (Jelani Cobb, "The Segregationist's Daughter," *New Yorker*, February 7, 2013.)

crap.... Mr. Chairman, you know all of us have been through this stuff in life, but never to this degree.... This is all Shakespeare. This is about love and hate, and cheating and distrust.... What a tragedy. What a disgusting tragedy."

Hill still bristles about the outburst: "With Alan Simpson it was, 'People are saying, "Watch out for this woman."' [He was implying] that I was some kind of threat to all of them: You are a threat not only to Clarence Thomas—you are a threat to *America*. And [Senator Arlen] Specter accused me of flat-out perjury."

Meanwhile, some of those on the Judiciary Committee who might have been Hill's ardent supporters were themselves hamstrung. Senator Edward Kennedy, she recalls, "couldn't help. He was hardly a person in a position to shed light on what appropriate behavior was.... He had his own indiscretions and episodes of bad behavior. He was neutralized. Some of the other things that could have compromised the other senators were not as obvious. The behavior that was documented shortly thereafter [involving sexual misconduct accusations against Republican senator] Bob Packwood was well known to the other senators. The 'page scandals' were part of Senate history.

"Those things were in the air. [The committee members] either had to know or they chose not to. So at the time, I thought, 'How *dare* you say, "I must not be telling the truth—I had to be inventing it,"' if there was so much like this in their world. They could shield their eyes from it and pretend it didn't happen when it suited them politically."

To top it off, Chairman Biden, for reasons that remain unclear, decided not to call for the testimony of several additional people who might have backed up Hill's version of events (or might have called Thomas's into question). It was a decision that some considered a procedural blunder—one that could have very well swayed the outcome. As Hill would say on the twentieth anniversary of the hearings, "Everybody has to take responsibility for what he did during that time, including Joe Biden, who should have called the witnesses."

In the end, Thomas was confirmed by a narrow Senate vote: 52 to 48. And much of the country had found *Thomas* to be the more credible presence in the harsh glare of the TV lights. "After the hearings, when people were polled," Hill recalls, "six out of ten people did not believe me."

Hill, however, saw a silver lining. "The fact that I was able to get up there and say [what I said] was a triumph," she insists. "I was able to tell the truth of what happened in the face of all those people trying to completely silence me. I could not have done it without the four people on that panel—corroborating witnesses—people I'd told years before the nomination. But what people don't know is that they volunteered. They came on their own. They called the committees or called me after this whole thing erupted in the press."

And what of Hill's reputation? It continued to suffer blow after blow. Thomas's wife, Virginia, would put it this way, in *People* magazine that November: "What's scary about her allegations is that they remind me of the movie *Fatal Attraction* or, in her case, what I call the fatal assistant. In my heart, I always believed she was probably someone in love with my husband and never got what she wanted."[19] Soon thereafter, journalist David Brock would construct a damaging story in the *American Spectator* impugning Hill as "a little bit nutty and a little bit slutty." He would then expand it into a 438-page "character assassination"—his own characterization—in a 1993 book called *The Real Anita Hill: The Untold Story*, which sought to help exonerate Thomas by undermining Hill and her testimony. And yet a decade later, Brock would recant many of the facts, indeed the foundation of his case against Hill, in his 2002 memoir *Blinded by the Right*. "I was a liar and a fraud in a dubious cause," he wrote. "I had missed significant evidence that showed that Hill's testimony was more truthful than Thomas's flat denials." Even after admitting to himself the error of his ways ("my version of the Thomas-Hill controversy was wrong"), Brock would go on with his smear campaign—in his words, "continu[ing] to malign Anita Hill and her liberal supporters as liars."

Hill would gain a measure of rehabilitation with the publication of Mayer and Abramson's *Strange Justice*. In their book, the authors interviewed witnesses who were prepared to testify but had never been called to do so, along with other women who claimed to have been sexually harassed by Thomas. The authors also unearthed people who had known Thomas and could recall what they considered to be his porn habit. The authors tracked down the owner of a video rental parlor in Washington who disclosed that "Clarence Thomas was a regular customer of adult movies." There was no

---

19. In 2010, Virginia Thomas would leave a voicemail message on Anita Hill's telephone answering machine, actually requesting an *apology*. (Charlie Savage, "Clarence Thomas's Wife Asks Anita Hill for Apology," *New York Times*, October 19, 2010.)

crime in this, of course. But the recollections ran counter to the image of probity that Thomas conveyed at the hearings. And a report that Thomas had rented such materials as late as 1989, wrote Mayer and Abramson, made it "all the more difficult to dismiss tales of his earlier interest in pornography as a youthful indiscretion."

What of Hill's legacy over time? It was, inarguably, irreversible. By shining a light on the untenable work environments that many Americans found all too familiar—and by standing up as a woman, a person of color, and a legal scholar who dared to speak truth to power in the corridors of the white male establishment—she would help breathe a new kind of energy into the women's movement. In the year after her Senate testimony, the EEOC saw a twofold rise in the number of women filing on-the-job harassment grievances. Aided in part by Hill's public disclosures, the coffers began to swell at EMILY's List, a group that backed the candidacies of female pro-choice Democrats. And by the fall of 1992, in what many would call the "Anita Hill Class," twenty-eight new female members were voted into Congress, an unprecedented number.[20] Even committee member Arlen Specter, who came close to losing his seat in the 1992 election partly due to his tough grilling of Hill, would eventually reflect, "Professor Hill produced the year of women in the Senate. That proceeding was a real lesson to me. I heard from so many women who saw themselves in her place, who felt their veracity was being questioned along with hers."

What has come to matter most to Hill are the tales of strangers who approached her to explain how her courage had helped embolden them. "The best thing that happened," she says, were "the stories. Women sat down and talked for the first time with their mothers, their daughters about their own incidents of sexual harassment. They'd never filed a complaint. They had never discussed this with people they were closest to." It continues to this day. "A few months ago on the street here, in [nearby] Waltham," Hill attests, "a woman came up and told me she got involved in the priest sex abuse movement locally and she was employed by the diocese. She said the hearings had

---

20. In but one example, Carol Moseley Braun of Illinois, according to a *New York Times* story written during the 1992 campaign, "specifically ran for the Democratic Senate nomination out of anger that Professor Hill had been ignored and Justice Thomas confirmed." (Deborah Sontag, "Anita Hill and Revitalizing Feminism," *New York Times*, April 26, 1992.)

been one of the inspirations for her finally coming forward and divulging what she knew."

The ironies were rich. Clarence Thomas, the man in charge of the EEOC—the arm of government that oversaw compliance with laws protecting American workers' civil rights—had himself been accused of on-the-job sexual harassment. And six years later, the same man would join the unanimous Supreme Court ruling that would permit the Paula Jones case to move forward, a lawsuit that ostensibly hinged on the principle of workplace harassment.

Professor Hill addresses the power dynamic in another office relationship that became politically charged that decade: that of Bill Clinton and Monica Lewinsky. "She was an intern—there was a big age [and authority] difference," Hill concludes. "So the idea of 'consensual,' to me, is a misnomer here. The second problem I have is the whole affair does contribute to the devaluing of young women in the workplace, whether at the White House or anywhere else. What if your daughter *doesn't want* to engage in sexual relations with the president? What is the message to *that* young woman? The message coming out was: being intimately involved with *the president*? That's what she *should* want. There wasn't a counter[argument] to that."

Anita Hill's impact ultimately was profound. She would alter the way Americans interact at the office, the way bosses treat employees, the way workers file grievances, the way we *respect* coworkers, consciously and unconsciously. Sexual harassment, she tells me, "is partly about men and women, but it's also about the powerful over the less powerful." She shares a private letter she received from a Pasadena woman, one of many she has treasured for nearly three decades:

> That day you gave testimony, I was home waiting to go to work. As I watched, tears started rising behind my eyes.... I was remembering my own feelings at fourteen when the principal (in whose office I worked at school) kept asking me what I did with my boyfriends.... When I got to work there were four women talking at the sign-in sheet. They were exhilarated. "This'll change everything." "It's finally been said." I joined in, thrilled that I wasn't alone. Several of us hugged. There were no questions. We were just swimming in the same water.

CHAPTER 7

The Crying Game

When we last left Bill and Hillary Clinton, in New England, they were suspended in the eye of a media storm. Many pundits saw the governor's presidential hopes in tatters. Many voters, meanwhile, admired the couple's unflinching commitment to each other. But there was at least one TV viewer who was utterly aghast on Super Bowl night—and not about the Buffalo Bills' performance.

"I was seething with outrage," Gennifer Flowers would recount in her memoir *Passion and Betrayal*. "To watch the two of them sit there with innocent looks on their faces, lying to the entire county, was infuriating."

America might have thought that the postgame show had been the last word on the subject. But now came the ultimate Monday morning quarterbacking. Flowers the very next day showed up at a packed press conference at New York's Waldorf Astoria, accompanied by her Arkansas attorney, Blake Hendrix. And the media free-for-all—350 people by one Clinton campaign estimate, with CNN covering the proceedings live—represented a new nadir in real-time television news. If *60 Minutes*, as many believed, had sunk to the gutter by questioning a candidate about his love life, CNN was down in the cesspool.

To start things off, a huddle of photographers shoved their way onto the podium. As Flowers appeared, their flash heads blazed like squad-car beacons. The *Star*'s editor, Dick Kaplan, stood between two easels with blow-up covers of the tabloid (headline: MY 12-YEAR AFFAIR WITH BILL CLINTON). He kept raising his voice at the swarm—"That's it, fellas, please, that's it"—as if feigning displeasure. After remarks from Hendrix, Flowers appeared on the dais.

She wore a bright honeysuckle suit with black lapels and some majorly

'80s shoulder pads. Her lips were full and red and almost cartoonishly solemn. Her pyrotechnic blondeness, with its cascade of dark roots, wreathing her face like a spray of goldenrod. She stood tall at the Waldorf lectern, which oddly resembled a bedroom vanity, all pink Lucite with gold trim.

And yet she somehow managed to project a magisterial quality, offering the refreshing tang of truth. She had the *wiretaps* and they would speak volumes.

Gennifer Flowers opened the proceedings by reading prepared remarks, admitting to an affair with Clinton, expressing "disgust" for his appearance on *60 Minutes*, and telling the restive crowd, "The truth is I loved him. Now he tells me to deny it. Well, I'm sick of all the deceit and I'm sick of all the lies." She also disclosed, "There are one or two conversations in the tapes that embarrass me now"—though not enough to dissuade her from playing them on national television.

The recordings, with all of their echoes of Nixon at the Watergate battlements, were what prosecutors might call smoking guns. And smoking they were. Both voices on the tapes, clearly Clinton's and hers, disparaged New York governor Mario Cuomo for his "mafioso" ways. The Arkansas governor worried aloud about competition from fellow candidate Bob Kerrey: "Because he's single, looks like a movie star, and won the Medal of Honor . . . nobody cares who he's screwin'." They discussed an earlier conversation they had had—before he'd announced his candidacy—in which they talked about what she might say if reporters asked about the rumored affair. Her idea, she recalled with a naughty laugh, was that she would tell them, "You ate good pussy."

Most damning of all, though, was one Clinton clip in which he seemed to be urging Flowers to deny what sounded very much like an affair. "If they ever hit you with it, just say, 'No,' and go on. . . . If everybody sort of hangs tough, they're just not going to do anything. . . . They can't, on a story like this . . . if they don't have pictures."

The press conference soon devolved from farce to vaudeville. One female reporter asked if Flowers would "be so kind as to elaborate on the sex and the relationship you say you had with him over twelve years? We want you to talk about it. That's why the cameras are all here." (Flowers declined, telling her to read the *Star*.) As the crowd continued to fire off questions, one man distinguished himself from his peers—the comedian "Stuttering John"

Melendez, a fixture on the Howard Stern radio show, who'd made his name by finagling his way into the path of celebrities and ambushing them with comically confrontational queries. He'd then play the tapes of his escapades for Stern's audience.

Stuttering John asked, straight-faced, "Did Governor Clinton use a condom?"

It became clear at once that the retaining wall had fallen between news and entertainment. And why not? CNN, using the *60 Minutes* segment as journalistic camouflage, was now rerouting a tabloid story into the legitimate news cycle. So a certain poetic justice was served when a mock reporter appeared, using tabloid language to lampoon the press, politicians, and their pieties.

Stuttering John's follow-up question was even more outrageous—and funnier: "Will you be sleeping with any *other* presidential candidates?"[1]

His one-liners underscored why the pack was there in the first place. This was the dawn of the sex-scandal lynch mob. They had come to listen in on what they shouldn't hear. They had come to see for themselves what Clinton might have seen in Ms. Flowers. And they had come, cheeky devils, to be in the same room with a woman lusty enough to charm a governor—and crafty enough to switch on a tape player. The Waldorf, with its barkers and its jostling crowd, had a touch of the carnival midway: . . . *And over in the next tent!* One wondered: would there be *others* still to come?[2]

---

1. "You can YouTube it—it's hilarious," Carville says. "It's so funny you can't stop laughing. So then when Stuttering John said, 'Did [Governor Clinton] wear a condom?,' [the attorney says,] 'Well, that's enough, we're going to cut this off, it's getting out of hand now." (Flowers's lawyer actually says, "We're going to put this to a stop if there are any further questions that are degrading in my opinion.") (Interview with Carville.)

2. "It got to be quite a big circus," remembers Dan Payne. The Democratic consultant, along with a Republican counterpart, Todd Domke, had been asked to show up at Boston's local ABC studio to be ready to comment on air as soon as the Flowers press conference ended. Payne recalls watching the raw feed with Domke and a few Channel 5 staffers. "It's sort of looking like a press-chaos scene, with nobody knowing where this is going. . . . Everybody's yelling at the same time. Domke, at the very end, [turns to us and] says, 'Boy, I feel like I need a *cigarette* after that'—it was so raunchy." But Payne had to shift gears—and fast. When asked on camera for his assessment of the fallout, if any, from the press conference, he gave a withering comment that in context seemed sensible at the time, but would become the stuff of prognostication legend. Payne's sound bite would later be showcased in the Clinton campaign documentary *The War Room*: "The friction in this is going to be too much for Clinton to survive. I think it's really a matter of days before he'll have to get out [of the race]. If not hours." That pronouncement, now considered something of a classic misjudgment,

While the press conference was still going on, Dee Dee Myers was traveling with Clinton on a swing through southern capitals. She recalls, with a cringe, that at one campaign event in Louisiana, Governor Edwin Edwards tried to buck up Clinton's spirits. According to Myers, mimicking Edwards's strong southern drawl: "So Ed Edwards goes to Clinton, 'Aww, is that true they paid that girl $150,000 for huh story? Hay-yell. If they paid all my girls $150,000, they'd be *broke.*' And Clinton loved that. He laughed his ass off. It was just comic relief."

Gennifer Flowers's appearances in the *Star*, it turned out, wasn't the half of it. At the end of the year, she would appear unclad in a gauzy-lensed photo spread in *Penthouse*. More descriptions of supposed trysts would come out in a Flowers 1995 tell-all book. ("I met him at the door wearing my fur coat with nothing on underneath but a white bustier.... I called mine 'Precious,' and his penis was 'Willard...Willard for Willy.'") There were various stories involving spanking, mascara, dripping honey, silk scarves, and a blindfold. Clinton, for all his protestations, would later admit under oath that the two of them *had* in fact been sexually intimate. (He would, of course, leave out the colorful details.)

It appeared that New Hampshire couldn't get much grimmer for Governor Clinton. Until it did.

In a matter of days, both the *Wall Street Journal* and ABC's *Nightline* raised questions about whether Clinton, as a student (on a Rhodes Scholarship at Oxford), had used connections to avoid military service during the Vietnam War. *Nightline*, which had lost out to *60 Minutes* for that first big interview, unearthed a letter from December 1969 in which Clinton, then twenty-three, had thanked an Arkansas-based higher-up, Colonel Eugene Holmes, for intervening and, in Clinton's words, "saving me from the draft." The note went on to outline Clinton's active stance against U.S. involvement in Southeast Asia ("I have written and spoken and marched against the war") and his pride in being able to count himself among the "many fine people [who] have come to find themselves still loving this country but loathing the

would usher in twenty-five years' worth of dead-wrong political punditry. (Interview with Payne; *The War Room*, Chris Hegedus and D. A. Pennebaker, directors [Cyclone Films, McEttinger Films, Pennebaker Associates, 1993].)

military"—this from a man who would have intentions of becoming America's commander in chief.

Clinton even admitted that one of the reasons he'd initially signed up for the draft—before changing his mind—was "to maintain my political viability in the system." Here was a young man who seemed to be genuinely grappling with the war's rationale and with his own fate and fears, but who was making precocious noises about a future role at home after his postgraduate studies in England. In his early twenties, Bill Clinton was already tying himself up in ethical knots and, with semantic finesse, making a case for why he'd wanted it both ways.

Commentators howled. The GOP growled. And shortly thereafter, on one critical night at a Days Inn in Manchester, New Hampshire, Stephanopoulos "was curled up on the floor, practically in tears," Clinton would relate in his memoir. "He asked if it wasn't time to think about withdrawing." Carville instead advised the candidate to go on the offensive. In Carville's eyes, the long-forgotten letter showed the young Clinton to be articulate, reflective, and principled beyond his years. "Carville paced the floor," Clinton would note, "waving the letter around and shouting, 'Georgie! Georgie! That's crazy. This letter is our friend. Anyone who actually reads it will think he's got character!'" Clutching the viper to its breast, the campaign took out big ads in the state's papers and ran the letter *in full*.

The strategy was risky, especially coming a week before New Hampshire voters went to the polls. And as D-Day approached—so historian Michael Takiff would recount in his oral history of the Clinton years, *A Complicated Man*—there were ominous auguries. According to Takiff, when pollster Stan Greenberg phoned up the governor's mansion around this time, "My first word was *meltdown*. Then I gave them the numbers. A 15-point drop—from 45 to 30." Carville registered the jolt in the pit of his stomach: "I would describe the feeling as a gut-shot Confederate soldier leaning against a tree ready to die." Soon, many seasoned observers were in agreement: it was inevitable that the governor bow out. Mike McCurry, who would become the White House spokesman for Clinton, recounted a comment from Senator Bob Kerrey's campaign chief, Tad Devine: "I think Clinton's toast. We better get ready for the fact that he'll be out of this race within a matter of hours."

"We went into that final weekend [before the New Hampshire primary] in total meltdown," says Dee Dee Myers. "But somehow by sheer force of will, he just refused to go down. He was bleeding. He was, like, unconscious. But he just stayed on his feet. I've never seen anything like that. It was super-human. He dug so deep. And he's never more focused than when he's stand-ing on the edge of the cliff and he's about to go over it."[3] Carville felt the same way: "I have never seen a human being perform like he performed that week in New Hampshire. It was stunning. It was more like an athlete than it was a political candidate."

Clinton went on a last blast across the state, taking his case to as many potential voters as he could. What they saw, day after day, was scrappiness, indefatigable optimism, and what they believed to be a man candidly address-ing his own vices and appetites—and wearing them all on his sleeve. They also saw a man raised in faith and in small-town surroundings, who therefore *connected*; he cared about them because he'd lived through the same prob-lems they were experiencing. They could see it in those off-the-cuff moments. When Clinton seemed moved by a voter's story, he would not only gnaw at his bottom lip sympathetically, but sometimes go over and embrace the voter like a relative. ("The whole thing about biting his lip—that was coached," Paul Begala would later declare to Takiff. "Because he would answer so fast. We'd say, 'Take a beat. Pretend you're thinking about it. Pretend you haven't already got an answer.' It was a studied thing to give himself a second to force himself to slow down.") Through it all, political chronicler Joe Klein could sense a spark, an alternating current between Clinton and those New Hampshire crowds. "There was a physical, almost carnal, quality to his pub-lic appearances," Klein would observe in his Clinton biography *The Natural*. "He embraced audiences and was aroused by them in turn.... There was a needy, high-cholesterol quality to it all; the public seemed enthralled by his vast, messy humanity."

In addition to this powerful dynamic, what many witnessed, and wel-comed, was sexual brio. Media executive Patricia Steele, having watched the

---

3. In a recent oral history of the New Hampshire showdown, Myers would recount a single, shining eleventh-hour rally at an Elks Club in Dover, New Hampshire, at which an exhausted Bill Clinton took the podium. "The place was full of union guys who were skeptical," Myers told the *New York Times*. "Who is this guy? A draft dodger, a womanizer? But then Clinton talked about their lives and said, 'I'll be with you till the last dog dies.' ... As long as I live, there will never be a political event that could come anywhere near that one in Dover." (Patrick Healy, "Bill Clinton's 1992 Make-or-Break Stand in New Hampshire," *New York Times*, February 9, 2016, A14.)

Flowers press conference on television, recalls her thinking at the time: "Men were criticizing Clinton, but many women were talking about the power of his libido and how we viewed it as a common trait of someone capable of succeeding in a high-wire arena like D.C. We thought: that's the sort of guy who *should be* running the show. Because all extreme people seem to be built this way. They have outsize peccadilloes, which are often sexual in nature, [that] seem to channel some of their vociferous energy. It goes with the territory."[4]

The night before the primary, the polls were looking almost uniformly bleak. Clinton, true to form, put up a hopeful front. He told his staffers—many of whom feared that this was the campaign's twilight hour—that he was determined to stick with it, no matter the numerical outcome. Stephanopoulos, in an interview for a 2001 ABC-PBS documentary, would retain the distinct election-day vision of the Clinton contingent hunkered down in Carville's New Hampshire hotel room: "What I remember most vividly, waiting for the exit polls, was James walking around the suite in his undershirt, lashing himself on the back with a piece of rope, like a medieval penitent and—just lashing himself, lashing himself."

But no. Out of some polling-booth alchemy of tenacity (the candidate's), fascination (the voters'), and hype (by the Clinton spinmeisters), his fortunes rose out of the storm cellar. Votes at the eleventh hour were shifting to the governor's column. The first exit polls showed him running a brisk second. True, the former senator Paul Tsongas—who had the advantage of hailing from neighboring Massachusetts—would actually *win* that night, coming in with more than a third of the Democratic votes cast. But it was Clinton, defying virtually every expectation, who had second place all to himself, and by a large margin.

Having secured 26 percent of the ballots, Clinton had a healthy enough

---

4. On an entirely different level, Clinton was also capitalizing on the electorate's growing unease with the media. Many viewed a vote for the Arkansas governor to be a vote *against* what he'd identified on *60 Minutes* as the press's perpetual "game of 'gotcha.'" While many were put off by what they considered flimflam, others envied Clinton's ability to work the angles—to keep his wife *and* maintain an affair or two; to run as a fortysomething outsider *and* run an entire state government. You had to hand it to the guy. Bill Clinton might be precisely the kind of crafty character who could stand down the snakes and clowns in Washington. (That same resourceful penchant for working the angles—even a similarly checkered reputation as a "player"—were not insignificant in stoking voter fascination with Donald Trump, the man who in 2016 would defeat Clinton's wife for the presidency.)

showing to now declare himself "the comeback kid"—which he did at a memorable press conference. The Clinton script doctors had adroitly dictated the narrative. And by getting out in front of Tsongas and giving the press a handy headline, they helped their candidate come off as the big winner in the battle for New Hampshire.

History, contrary to Churchill's maxim, was no longer written by the victors. In the media age, history was spun by the slickest spinners.

———

Many New Hampshire citizens had endorsed Clinton enthusiastically that winter. But when it really came down to it, his reputation in the public mind amounted to a caricature. If voters in others states thought of Clinton at all, it was, as Dee Dee Myers puts it, "as a presidential candidate with acknowledged infidelity."

So the question arises: what *was* it in the culture at that juncture that had allowed primary voters to accept an admitted adulterer as a serious contender for high office?

A handful of forces, by rough count, came into play.

First and foremost were the nation's shifting demographics. In 1992, for the first time, Baby Boomers (postwar offspring born between 1946 and 1964) made up a large segment—41 percent—of eligible voters. And many of these seventy-five million people, some thirty years after John Kennedy's assassination, had come to realize that JFK, their standard-bearer, had his own checkered romantic history. In fact, many of these same Boomers had had no problem marking their ballots for Ronald Reagan, the first president to have been previously divorced. The Boomer voter, come 1992, was saying: *Cut the Clintons some slack.*

Second, society's mind-set was changing with regard to "the sinner." In religious and secular spheres alike, people were no longer judging the adulterer as having a profoundly flawed character. Mainstream America instead had become more willing to give individuals who acknowledged their weaknesses their fair shot at redemption. The era's most beloved advice columnist, Ann Landers,[5] would note, apropos of Clinton's extramarital admissions later in the decade, that voters in "Middle America...Des Moines; Muskegon; Tyler, Texas," instead of chastising his actions as ethically repugnant, were

———

5. Real name: Eppie Lederer.

showing him a new and admirable brand of dispensation. "We're getting to be more forgiving as a people," Landers told columnist Frank Rich in the *New York Times*. "[The public is] more permissive. They are more realistic. This is the way life is. Not all husbands are faithful.... I've been doing this 43 years. The country has been going in this direction for some time." Clinton seemed to be the beneficiary of a New American Mercy, one overlaid with a kind of real-world clarity. "The American people," Landers concluded, "are pretty solid, they're pretty savvy, and they know what's important. That's why they're not screaming and yelling about Bill Clinton and some of these females."[6]

Third, the country was becoming one grand *audience*. The Zeitgeisti-est Generation was spending a third of every day in front of a screen. And the Clintons of Arkansas were effectively the stars of a new style of episodic political reality series, broadcast live: *The Powerful Knocked from Pedestals*. Indeed, celebrity schadenfreude was becoming a national pastime; viewers could feel slightly better about themselves by watching the public indignity of the mighty suddenly brought low.

The fourth change agent was the badass political operative. A generation after Nixon's "dirty tricks" team had single-handedly unraveled his presidency, modern political consultants were using sabotage like a power tool. On the right was Lee Atwater, the GOP swami who emerged as the Darth Vader of political dark ops.[7] On the left was the Clinton hit squad, so loaded for bear that they'd set up what they called a war room[8] for rapid media response, day or night, so as to meet each slam with their own.

The fifth factor was the public's queasiness about the press's pivot. More and

---

6. To put the most cynical spin on it, as *Rolling Stone*'s Hunter S. Thompson observed, "The net result of the Gennifer Flowers flap was a nine-point gain for Clinton in the New Hampshire popularity polls. The pro-adultery vote had spoken." (Hunter S. Thompson, *Better Than Sex: Confessions of a Political Junkie* [New York: Ballantine/Random House, 1994], 50.)

7. A generation after Atwater, Donald Trump's chief strategist, Steve Bannon, would tell journalist Michael Wolff, "Darkness is good. Dick Cheney. Darth Vader. Satan. That's power. It only helps us when they"—which Wolff would translate as liberals and the media—"get it wrong. When they're blind to who we are and what we're doing." (Michael Wolff, "Ringside with Steve Bannon at Trump Tower as the President-Elect's Strategist Plots 'An Entirely New Political Movement,'" *Hollywood Reporter*, November 18, 2016.)

8. The campaign "war room" catchphrase has been variably attributed to Hillary Clinton and to James Carville.

more news outlets in the early '90s were tarting things up, tabloid-style. With CNN's need to feed its news maw (Fox News and MSNBC did not yet exist) and with a Boomer-fueled entertainment industry that was growing steroidally through merger madness, News Lite (gossip, trivia, soft features, infotainment) crept in on little tab feet. As the '80s had had their junk bonds, the '90s developed junk news.

In what surely seems archaic and circuitous in our day, stories that were too tawdry for the American press would often surface first in the tropics (the prime U.S. tabloids were based in Florida). Or in faraway Britain, where London's Fleet Street papers had long plied a trade in rumormongering. The scandals—sometimes with only a thin filament of sourcing—would germinate on foreign soil, acquire the piquant aroma of muck, then migrate back across the Atlantic to run as "news" in papers that were not infrequently under the control of the same owner, in some instances Mr. Rupert Murdoch, the Australian press baron long known to back causes and candidates on the right of the political spectrum. "It was more like a chain reaction, triggered under fixed laws of media thermodynamics," according to Howard Kurtz, a seasoned observer of the Washington press, "[in which] accusations were laundered through [the tabloids].... The phenomenon had begun back in 1992 with Gennifer Flowers."[9] Indeed, CBS and Steve Kroft of *60 Minutes*, as soon as the Clintons' segment aired, were raked over the briquettes, and not only by

---

9. Over the previous decades, the Washington and campaign press corps had been a relatively genteel bunch; only the most persistent rumors seemed to withstand transcontinental vetting. But then came an avalanche. Legions of young journalists, post-Watergate, began striking out in search of bombshells. Talk radio metastasized. The '80s debate programs (such as CNN's *Crossfire* and *Capital Gang*, along with the PBS program *The McLaughlin Group*) got ever more heated. On top of that, certain reporters, as Joe Klein would describe in his book *The Natural: The Misunderstood Presidency of Bill Clinton*, were acting like gumshoes at publications that were late-'80s outliers (the alternative newspapers, the tabloids, and opinion journals with a political bent). Borrowing the sleuthing tactics of their British and Aussie cousins (some of whom had migrated to stateside newsrooms), they obtained video store rental records in 1987 and found out which movies the Supreme Court nominee Robert Bork had rented. Two years later they examined the horndog rumors that were dogging defense secretary nominee John Tower. Routinely, many of these journalists had been given their tips by sources with political axes to grind. And once the embarrassing stories emerged—and one party received a brushback pitch—the other party would demand an equalizer. Reporters in the press box followed the bloodsport. "There was a gleeful, voyeuristic quality to much of the reporting," Klein would write about the 1992 race. "Politicians were now, routinely, presumed guilty—especially on the new, witlessly contentious television sound-bite shows: 'Groups' and 'Gangs' of journalists screaming at each other and making facile judgments about complicated issues." (Joe Klein, *The Natural: The Misunderstood Presidency of Bill Clinton* [New York: Doubleday, 2002], 99.)

the public but by members of the Fourth Estate. Kroft remembers colleagues asking him incredulously, "How can you stoop so low as to report this stuff from *Star* magazine?"[10]

A sixth (and final!) factor: while each constituency had shifted—the voter, the culture at large, the home audience, the political operative, and the press—so had America's methodology for public reckoning. Society, in the media age, was starting to develop a new set of norms for the ritual of public shaming and public contrition. High-profile figures, when tarnished by scandal, were beginning to realize that in certain circumstances a high-profile, unqualified apology might give them a shot at resurrection.

And in this regard, Bill Clinton proved to be the culture's dean of reputational redemption. He had understood—indeed, he had begun to perfect—what historian Susan Wise Bauer has ingeniously termed "The Art of the Public Grovel" (in her book so named; subtitle: *Sexual Sin and Public Confession in America*).

To succeed convincingly, a big-ticket mea culpa had to appear to be self-initiated. It had to be leavened with credible expressions of remorse. It had to contain a clear admission of transgression, preferably addressed directly to the victimized party. Furthermore, it had to be delivered before a large audience (for maximum impact and to assure that the person enscandaled was thoroughly braised in shame). The ultimate goal, of course, was that the penitent, once liberated from his burden of sin, was now in a position to control and tame his impulses.

---

10. In Kroft's judgment, once Flowers's claims had pulsed up on a competing network, it was not unreasonable to cover them, even if only as a news item. "It was the policy of the mainstream media to ignore anything that was in the tabloid press because they considered it to be rumor, gossip—unreliable," he says. "We didn't really pursue [the story at first] because it was unseemly and, aside from this woman's word, there was no corroboration.... [But] once somebody breaks the wall of silence, then everybody does it. So it began building. I believe it was NBC that broke through, and for the first time actually reported something that had been in the supermarket tabloids.

"There were a lot of people who said afterwards, 'This is a low point for *60 Minutes* to go and have this conversation about that.' I never felt that way because the glass had been broken the week before [and it was] hard to ignore. Particularly if you're talking about a presidential candidate and if it's the only thing that people on the street and on the campaign trail are talking about, and that it may end the presidential aspirations of the front-runner. I think that it demanded coverage.

"If *60 Minutes* had been the first, would we have gone on that night and done a story about Bill Clinton based on a report in the *Star* or based on Gennifer Flowers's allegations? No. I'm sure we wouldn't have." (Interview with Kroft.)

Bill Clinton, of all people—first on *60 Minutes* and then in a sequence of scandals later in the decade—was applying some of the lessons he'd learned from his spiritual upbringing. "As a Southern Baptist," contends Susan Wise Bauer, Clinton "had watched rituals of public repentance and confession all his life.... Clinton was imbued with the ideal of Protestant confession as both public and well-informed, involving full consent of both the will and the mind, and performed before a witnessing community that could testify to that full consent." Moreover, she writes, the payoff for the apologist was immeasurable: "public admission of moral failing, along with public repentance, led inevitably to forgiveness."

————

Clinton's ordeal had come on the heels of four other scandals—prominent test cases that had helped define the dos and don'ts of the Ethical Spectacle.

In 1987, it was revealed that televangelist Jim Bakker had had impious relations with a young church employee named Jessica Hahn. But Bakker, instead of issuing a grand apology to members of his ministries and to his wife (the monstrously eyelashed and perennially weepy Tammy Faye), chose to chastise "treacherous former friends and then colleagues, who victimized [and] betray[ed] me... at a time of great stress in my marital life." The graceless Bakker was disgraced, his goose irrevocably microwaved.

A year later, televangelist Jimmy Swaggart was photographed at a Travel Inn motel with a lady of the night. But unlike Bakker, he decided to give a textbook confession. Standing before his Family Worship Center congregation, he atoned at Old Testament length to everyone he'd wronged by his behavior. And as a result, he would be forgiven, and would go on to preach another day. (That is until 1991, when Swaggart was caught yet again with a woman in the flesh trade.)

Dovetailed between the Bakker and Swaggart scandals was the conflagration of Democratic presidential aspirant Gary Hart. Though a married man, the Colorado senator was discovered to have spent quality time with A-Woman-Not-His-Wife. Her name was Donna Rice, at the time a brainy model, occasional actress, and drug-firm sales rep. And once the revelations came to light, Hart, instead of standing his ground or offering a public explanation, withdrew from the race, holding a press conference at which, like Bakker, he lambasted his antagonists—in Hart's case, the heedless media. (Many members of the press actually *agreed* with Hart's critique of a process that, as he had articulated that day, seemed to condone "reporters in bushes; false and inaccurate stories printed; photographers peeking in our windows; swarms of helicopters hovering over our house... [and] ponderous pundits wondering in mock seriousness why some of the best people in this country choose not to run for high office." As E. J. Dionne would write in the *New York Times* on the morning of Hart's withdrawal, "The process that Gary Hart underwent was in many ways a cruel one, unprecedented in American political history.... No candidate has ever had his home watched for the purposes of finding out about his romantic life." Dionne concluded that the media pile-on would "certainly provoke a needed debate on his contention that the system has gone out of control.")[11]

If Bill Clinton had gone to school on any late-'80s scandal, however, it had been the humiliation of Barney Frank, the popular Massachusetts congressman. Frank in 1987 had come out as homosexual. Two years later, he

---

11. Hart had adamantly refused the Public Grovel. And from a purely cosmetic perspective, his wife, Lee, in making only brief appearances on the stump that week, did the same. "One of the things that killed Gary Hart," posits Steve Kroft of CBS News, "was the fact that his wife stood in the background [as Hart dropped out of the race]. There was kind of this sense that she was really upset with him and didn't believe him. So I think the Clintons were very smart, [realizing] they would be much better having [Hillary] there and know[ing] that she was a very strong character. And they carried the day. So I think they learned a little bit from the Hart scandal."

The press's decision, in the TV era, to probe a presidential candidate's extramarital relationships "went back to Gary Hart," Lanny Davis says today. Davis, who had attended Yale Law with the Clintons and would serve as a White House crisis adviser in the late '90s, recalls the transition. "[Prior to the Hart scandal] the argument had always been: If it affects public policy or abuse of power and it involves sex—then it's okay to write about it. But if it's just about a personal peccadillo or weakness, or you can't resist touching a nice tush with a thong over it, it has nothing to do with anything [and] we're *not* going to write about that.... Something changed, and it started with Gary Hart."

Journalist Matt Bai, who would write the definitive study of the Hart scandal, agrees. "What you can see now, some 25 years on," Bai would state in his 2014 book *All the Truth Is Out,* "is that a series of powerful, external forces in the society were colliding by the late 1980s, and this was creating a dangerous vortex on the edge of our politics. Hart didn't create that vortex. He was, rather, the first to wander into its path." Bai would add a coda, both cynical and insightful: "If post-Hart political journalism had a motto, it would be: 'We know you're a fraud somehow. Our job is to prove it.'" Bai rightly points out that part of the impetus for such reporting was that many bright, hungry journalists, after Watergate, had gone into the business to become another Bob Woodward or Carl Bernstein—"which is to say, there was no greater calling than to expose the lies of a politician, no matter how inconsequential those lies might turn out to be or in how dark a place they might be lurking." (Matt Bai, *All the Truth Is Out: The Week Politics Went Tabloid* [New York: Alfred A. Knopf, 2014], 32; interviews with Kroft and Davis; Bai, "Legend of the Fall," *New York Times Magazine,* September 21, 2014, 39, 60.)

admitted to having sex for money with a male escort named Steven Gobie, whom he later took on as a personal assistant. But instead of covering up that relationship, Frank agreed to cooperate with a House ethics panel looking into the charges.

The signature moment of the whole imbroglio came when Frank called a one-of-a-kind press conference, having forewarned reporters, as his media consultant Dan Payne now remembers it, "I will stay here and answer every question, no matter how ridiculous, so pack a lunch." Frank's passive-aggressive posture, remarkably, did the trick. "The only way to end this story," Payne says, "was if he stood up there and took *everything*...demonstrat[ing] that this was not necessarily a fatal event." Though Frank would eventually be reprimanded by Congress for his dealings with Gobie, he would beat the ethics rap and breeze to reelection. "I don't know that the Clintons studied [it,]" Payne insists, but "now it has become the model: the only way you can survive is if you stand there and take the heat. You can't say, 'This is private or this is personal or this is irrelevant to my stewardship as a public official.'"

For all of the precedent provided by these '80s dustups, there was a single factor that determined the success of that *60 Minutes* appearance: the presence, and persuasiveness, of Hillary Clinton. Had she refused to participate, her husband's candidacy in all likelihood would have sunk right into the cushions of that hotel-room couch in Boston. The thinking of the time was, and remains, that if she and her husband had chosen to stay in their marriage and go forward, who were we to judge? "Hillary was the key," concedes Mark McKinnon, the political consultant and George W. Bush adviser. "The public knew she was tough enough to probably have taken an inch of Bill's hide in private, but brave and loyal enough to stand by her man when the klieg lights went on. If his wife could forgive him, then surely we could.

"The larger truth we learned that night about the Clintons, and about the larger electorate, was that American voters were willing to accept fallibility as long as it is mixed with authenticity. And [we learned] that the Clintons had political survival skills that would have impressed Darwin—survival capabilities the likes of which we may never see again in American politics."

Steve Kroft goes so far as to say that "the interview went a long way towards winning him the presidency. I think it showed that he was able to perform in a very difficult situation—and you don't always get a presidential candidate in the middle of a campaign where they're forced to confront a serious personal crisis. And he and his political team and his wife dealt with it—artfully."

———————

Bill Clinton became the exemplar of political resuscitation through open confession. The Clintons' joint appearance became the gold standard for closing ranks in a crisis; for how to use the media to one's advantage when faced with revelations of indiscretion; for what an elected official and his partner need or needn't talk about when they talk about love. Together, they lit the torturous path that would await every public personality ensnared in scandal in the years to follow.

By playing the A-card, Bill Clinton decoupled it from its political context. And thereinafter, an elected official's romantic choices were mainly portrayed—and accepted by many observers—as a predominantly private matter. While the perceived fraying of one's moral fiber was still open for public discussion (and tabloid consumption), a politician's longings or lapses tended to be perceived as holding little bearing on his or her corresponding ethical choices in the government realm—a guideline that Clinton would try to reestablish once and for all, and not altogether successfully, during the impeachment crisis seven years later.

Such acceptance didn't come overnight. Commentators on the left and especially the right made a convincing case that a public official's marital vows *were* germane. The argument was a clear one. As part of an implicit social contract, an elected representative needed to be held—as Gary Hart himself had said in 1987—to "the very highest standards of integrity and ethics, and soundness of judgment." But with the passage of time, voters dispensed with the canard. Unfaithfulness, or even unlawfulness, did not automatically imply unfitness for public service. In 1994, for instance, Marion Barry—after serving jail time for smoking crack (caught on a hidden video by the FBI)—was reelected as the mayor of Washington, D.C. Later in the '90s, New York mayor Rudy Giuliani would weather accusations of maintaining a more-than-friendly involvement with his communications director—a charge both parties denied. (Then, after beginning an affair in 1999 with the woman who would become his third wife, Giuliani would famously convene a 2000 press conference announcing his separation from his second.)

Bill Clinton's political revival after admitting infidelity, according to Raymond Strother (who had served as an adviser to both Senator Hart and

Governor Clinton), "was like Roger Bannister breaking the four-minute mile.... Prudishness has never been the same." And more than two decades later, a string of politicians caught in extraconjugal quandaries would be forgiven by voters,[12] among them Louisiana's David Vitter and South Carolina's Mark Sanford. Their rebounds would not have been conceivable had Clinton not blazed the trail.

In truth, Clinton had been winging it. But it worked like a charm because he was in tune with his audience and the confessional culture, speaking the language of the clergyman and the psychotherapist, twelve-step programs and New Age gurus, self-help bestsellers and empowerment retreats. He understood the power of Oprah Winfrey, the national shrink, and when he related his own personal trials, he was also referring to his listeners', who were reminded of those nights when they themselves had had to fight the quickened pulse or the ache of the heart.[13]

---

12. For scandals PBC (post–Bill Clinton), a Doppler-like shift affected the dynamic. Due in part to the sheer abundance of celebrities caught in compromising positions, memories began to foreshorten in the ADD era. And today the more distant the scandal, the more indistinct the initial transgression appears in the public's rearview mirror, almost regardless of its original scuzz quotient.

13. Oprah Winfrey's TV talk show, which had begun modestly in 1984 as *AM Chicago*, had zigged while its competitors zagged. The late *New York Times* media columnist David Carr would recollect that in the '90s, "just when tabloid television was beginning to crest and threatened to tip over into a sea of cross-dressing Nazis, [Oprah Winfrey] pulled back, saying that she could build a bigger audience on uplift than on baser instincts." Build she did. In Carr's assessment, "she began proselytizing good books, nagging herself about her own weight and, most of all, listened to her audience. And the money kept rolling in bigger and bigger waves." She became, in short, America's Mother Confessor. Winfrey, acknowledging her own shame, failings, and mistreatment, would coax out overwhelming disclosures from her guests, along with their stories of redemption. Religious scholars, as the professor and columnist Mark Oppenheimer would point out, have made the case that she was drawing on the lessons she'd learned in black churches while growing up in Mississippi and Tennessee, and on the spiritual tutors and self-empowerment guides who would often appear on her program. Kathryn Lofton, a dean at Yale, would assert in her book *Oprah: The Gospel of an Icon* that Winfrey's method—reminiscent of nineteenth-century revival meetings—helped to acclimate her audience to "the familiar ritual turn of daily confession and rejuvenation." By extracting personal admissions of sin or shame or sacrifice (and tales of triumph over adversity), Winfrey served to heal the truth-teller and, by degrees, the viewer. She was preaching to her own electronic megachurch, to what Karlyn Crowley, author of *Feminism's New Age*, would call a nationwide "New Age feminist congregation." Winfrey earned her followers' fealty by propounding that individuals determined their own destiny. She said that women and men, through their beliefs, controlled the means of their own absolution. (Jennifer Eum, "How Oprah Went from Talk Show Host to First African-American Woman Billionaire," Forbes.com, September 29, 2014; David Carr, "A Triumph of Avoiding the Traps," *New York Times*, November 23, 2009, B1, 6; Mark Oppenheimer, "The Church of Oprah Winfrey and a Theology of Suffering," *New York Times*, May 28, 2011, A20; Patricia Sellers, "The

America, always a nation of second chances, was fast becoming a place where the story of temptation, disgrace, public remorse, and personal renewal was a narrative one could *live* by, even *thrive* by. By placing one's trust in the Almighty, a mortal could be cleansed of sin, unburdened of guilt, and freed up for rehabilitation—even for triumph.

In the end, the *60 Minutes* broadcast had been a harbinger. As Gary Hart had warned five years earlier, Kroft's interview with the Clintons had signaled open season on an office-seeker's secrets. If popular culture's most popular TV program was allotting time for a discussion of a politician's love life, then new forces were surely stirring in the bosom of mainstream media. The American press was now asserting the people's "right to know," implying that there might very well be virtue in the argument—even as the electorate pushed back—that one's behavior in his intimate relations was a valid litmus for his likely comportment as a public servant.

Bill and Hillary Clinton, though bloodied, disagreed vehemently—and had won round one. They had diverted attention from the foibles of a private life to the flaws in the system that reported on elected officials and public personalities. Hillary Clinton called for maintaining a threshold of privacy around those in civic life. Bill Clinton, according to Kroft, was asking, on air, "Do we really have a right to know what goes on in somebody's bedroom?"

But this commonsense separation of the public and the personal would not hold for long. As the Web browser was introduced the next year, as tabloid coverage went into overdrive, as sex tapes began to surface, and as the digital camera (soon a national appendage) would make everyone a private eye—the Flowers flare-up faded from memory, and sex scandals would become common diversions, momentarily drenching the media landscape, then dissipating, like summer sun showers.

Business of Being Oprah," *Fortune*, April 1, 2002; Laura B. Randolph, "Oprah Opens Up About Her Weight, Her Wedding, and Why She Withheld the Book," *Ebony*, October 1993; Susan Wise Bauer, *The Art of the Public Grovel: Sexual Sin and Public Confession in America* [Princeton, N.J.: Princeton University, 2008], 121–22.)

CHAPTER 8

A Vagina Travelogue

Let's talk about the '90s vagina.

This is not to imply that the American woman suddenly discovered her vagina during the first (awkward, I know) Bush administration. But a generation after the sexual revolution of the '60s, after the feminist activism of the '70s, and after numerous advances in medicine and public policy related to women's health, social momentum had helped alter American attitudes. By the 1990s there was more widespread candor about the erotic, cultural, and even political power of female sexuality. Women and society were becoming more and more open to all things V.

Exhibit A was Eve Ensler's 1996 play *The Vagina Monologues*, which became a cultural phenomenon. The one-woman show was a direct and defiant meditation on a word uttered 128 times onstage. Groundbreaking theater, *Monologues* was not. Since the '50s, the American stage had been the home for displays intended to inspire sexual debate through provocation. But to its intended audience—the mainstream '90s liberal—the unrelentingly explicit oratory was something of a shock.

For two years, Ensler had been sitting down with women—some two hundred in all—and coaxing out stories about their intimate and often complicated relationships with, as the play puts it, their pussycats, their pookis, their coochi snorchers, their mushmellows.[1] It started as Ensler's own

---

1. The more recent, popular, and playful term "vajayjay" would not make it into modern parlance until 2006, when it was used as a substitute to assuage TV censors monitoring an episode of *Grey's Anatomy*. Soon thereafter, according to the *New York Times*, "The show's most noted fan, Oprah Winfrey, began using it on her show, effectively legitimizing it for some 46 million American

attempt to bridge the disconnect between her own mind and body. "My vagina was something over there, away in the distance," she would write. "I rarely lived inside it, or even visited." Her alienation from her sexual self had been especially fraught: she had been raped in her youth, and that violation had resulted, as she would put it, in feeling deprived of "my motor, my center, my second heart."

By articulating the word "vagina," however, she found that she could reclaim it. When she made it a mantra of a kind, some of its associated shame began to fall away. According to Ensler, "After you say the word the hundredth time or the thousandth time, it occurs to you that it's *your* word, *your* body, *your* most essential place."

The Vagina Monologues was a series of testimonies, humorous lists, and vignettes taken from Ensler's interviews. Some were repeated verbatim, others were composite depictions, many were enlivened through the blender of the playwright's vivid imagination. The play was structured thematically: menstruation; cunnilingus; "My Angry Vagina"; "If Your Vagina Could Talk" ("Don't Stop...Remember me?...Enter at your own risk...Where's Brian?...Yes, there. There"); the aroma ("Earthy meat and musk...Wet garbage...A brand-new morning"). There was a segment entitled "Reclaiming Cunt." There was a survivor's tale from a "rape camp" in Bosnia. There was a story about an elderly woman who had never achieved orgasm, and another about a woman of color from the South who had been sexually exploited as a preteen and teenager. There was a piece called "The Woman Who Loved to Make Vaginas Happy"—a lesbian soliloquy that ended with a valiant attempt at finding the vagina's orgasmic voice by differentiating styles of power moaning.

The labia, the clitoris, the vagina, and their environs were presented in all their guises, from the nub of self-pleasure to the birth canal.

Soon after its premiere in the basement of Manhattan's Cornelia Street Café, *The Vagina Monologues* was playing to packed houses, winning awards, and inspiring theatergoers who would come up to Ensler after performances to offer their own testimonies, sometimes about their recovery from sexual violence. Ensler, with her coal-black 1920s bangs, had a chimerical presence

---

viewers each week. 'I think vajayjay is a nice word, don't you?' she asked her audience." (Stephanie Rosenbloom, "What Did You Call It?," *New York Times*, October 28, 2007.)

that heightened each monologue's impact and a comic timing that helped cut through the audience's angst over the intimacy of the subject matter.

When the production opened in cities outside New York, however, there was pushback. The V-word was sometimes excised from ads and theater vitrines. In certain towns, when ticket buyers phoned the box office, a recorded voice would refer to the play as "Monologues." A publishing house made a financial commitment to print the play in book form, then got cold feet. Even though the play spoke to thousands upon thousands of women, its title alone—regardless of its theatrical merits—was met with community and institutional resistance.

So be it. It was unstoppable. Within two years, notable women would take to the stage in New York (Gloria Steinem, Whoopi Goldberg, Rosie Perez, Susan Sarandon, Lily Tomlin) and London (Christiane Amanpour, Isabella Rossellini, Sophie Dahl, Cate Blanchett, Kate Winslet) and give voice to Ensler's voices. Jane Fonda would participate in a subsequent performance—to cheers that rattled the rafters at Madison Square Garden—reportedly calling the process "one of the most memorable and empowering experiences of my life." Glenn Close persuaded the audience to rise and repeat, in unison, "Cunt...Cunt...Cunt..."

The *Monologues* only grew. The play raised money for causes associated with V-Day (an "empowered" Valentine's Day alternative that was first held in 1998), which would become a global initiative to confront sexual violence. College campuses took up the charge. There was a "sex for one" workshop at Brown, a "cunt workshop" at Wesleyan, a "cunt-fest" at Penn State. In theater lobbies, snacks were sold in the shape of ladyparts. As Ensler would describe it, "Women in Islamabad, Pakistan [staged scenes from the show] for their sisters who were there from Afghanistan—everyone laughing and weeping....[There was] a seven-language performance of the monologues in Brussels....[People were] learning to sign 'clitoris' in a performance by deaf women in Washington, D.C."

The notices weren't universally glowing, by any means. Christina Hoff Sommers, the conservative author, would deem it "atrociously written... viciously anti-male...and, most importantly, it claims to empower women, when in fact it makes us seem desperate and pathetic....One of the many laudable goals of the original women's movement was its *rejection* of the idea that women are reducible to their anatomy." Some of the backlash from feminists was particularly harsh. Betty Dodson, the sexologist and self-described feminist sexual activist, saw the show early on, and then again at two of its star-studded galas. She dubbed it "a bait and switch operation. The ruse is to get everyone excited about hearing famous women saying the words vagina, clitoris, and cunt only to bring us down with statistics about rape and the sexual abuse of women, especially in other countries." Germaine Greer went so far as to chide Ensler for the title, professing a preference for the more "inclusive 'pussy' or 'snatch.'" But this, to be fair, was splitting hairs.[2]

Ensler would win out in the end. *The Vagina Monologues*, through the power of a cathartic theatrical experience, became a campaign against misogyny, exploitation, and discrimination. The play was also making a statement about sexual repression and violence against women in forms that were particularly acute in the 1990s: genital mutilation (in Africa), rape as an instrument of war (in the Balkans, Rwanda, Liberia, Indonesia, and elsewhere), human trafficking (across the globe), forced marriages, honor killings, discrimination against LGBT individuals, spousal abuse, sexual abuse of children, harassment, and the curtailing of reproductive rights.

The play was undeniably *of* the '90s. It placed a long-private word—and all of its functions, fallacies, and mystique—into the very public realm. It tried to explore aspects of female sexuality in front of a mainstream audience. It used celebrity star power to promote its message. But in many ways it sprang from the values of previous decades—and second-wave feminism. One of its stridently un-'90s characters is pro-hair-down-there: "You cannot love a vagina unless you love hair.... Hair is there for a reason—it's the leaf around the flower." She is also anti-thong: "That's the worst.... Who thought that up? Moves around all the time, gets stuck." Another speaker even denounces what might be called genital gentrification, which broke out in the '70s (with the flowering of feminine hygiene products) and by the '90s had gone viral. "My vagina," she says, "doesn't need to be cleaned up. It

---

2. Ensler and others have been accused of adopting a flawed naming convention. While the vagina has become the de facto default word for a woman's sexual locus (at the expense of the overlooked clitoris, which is widely considered far more significant in terms of female arousal), the word actually refers—as Toni Bentley has written (in a review of Naomi Wolf's 2012 book *Vagina: A New Biography*)—"uniquely, and only, to the cylindrical passage that leads from the external world to the internal world of a woman's sexual arena, and why it has now come to mean, erroneously, the entire shebang is beyond me.... [Wolf] simply climbs up on the old Eve Ensler vagina bandwagon." (Toni Bentley, "A Woman's Place" [review of *Vagina*, by Naomi Wolf], *New York Times Book Review*, September 16, 2012, 1, 14–15.)

smells good already.... Don't believe him when he tells you it smells like rose petals when it's supposed to smell like pussy."

———

The Monologues, the culture wars notwithstanding, exemplified the demystification of certain aspects of female anatomy and sexuality. Concurrently, there were diagrams and demonstrations in the media about breast self-exams. On the *Today* show, host Katie Couric underwent an on-air colonoscopy (two years after her husband's death from colon cancer in 1998). There were frank representations of women's health issues—along with increasingly graphic sex advice—in women's magazines. Marketing wizards were pushing sanitary pads that came in a blinding variety of absorbency and size and ergonomics, with or without wings or belts or scent.

There was a matter-of-factness to the culture's verbal references to female anatomy, as if large segments of society had at last matured. While art, music, and pop culture had pushed boundaries in the '70s and '80s, its corresponding '90s creations were sometimes less filtered: informed by everything from third-wave feminism, to LGBT pride, to a new generation intent on asserting its anatomy for its own sake, for the sake of exercising power, or as a sign of self-reliance. Among the most strident female-dominated rock bands was Hole, fronted by Courtney Love. The "I HEART Vagina" logo was inaugurated in 1998,[3] raising awareness about cervical and ovarian cancer. Fiction that focused on female sexuality was tagged with the moniker "clit lit," or "cliterature." In *Cunt: A Declaration of Independence*, activist Inga Muscio encouraged women to take back the long-despised term on their path to empowerment. And academic maverick Camille Paglia, in her bestselling book *Sexual Personae*, reprised the *vagina dentata*—the archetypal depiction of a tooth-bearing vagina, the ultimate symbol of castration anxiety. "Metaphorically," Paglia asserted, "every vagina has secret teeth, for the male exits as less than when he entered." *Yowza*.

Still, the medical community and the largest cosmetics and pharmaceutical firms exerted an outsize influence. "Today every aspect of a woman's life cycle," writes Meika Loe, director of women's studies at Colgate University, "has been medicalized—from birth to menstruation to childbirth

———

3. The charitable organization "I Love Vagina" has been around since 1969 (https://ilovevagina.wordpress.com/ilv-charity/).

to menopause to death—revealing a growing dependence on medicine that some say is risky and excessive." And few procedures in the 1990s were more puzzling than those related to female genital reconstruction, or what came to be known as "designer vaginas."

Women went in for vaginal rejuvenation surgery, which promised to restore a tightness approximating one's younger years.[4] There were labiaplasties (sometimes dubbed the Toronto Trim), which reduced the genital lips to make them look less distended or more symmetrical. There was vaginal liposuction that could plump up the labia, affording the beestung vajayjay. There were labial puffs, vulvar lipo, clitoral hood jobs, "g-shots" (zaps of collagen into the vagina's interior wall, purported to give greater sensitivity), and hymenoplasty (surgically recreating a substitute hymen—popular among women in cultures that, when it came to matrimony, prized the virginal). Certain specialists, according to a 1998 overview in *Harper's Bazaar*, would "perform such surgery only if it is a medical necessity for sexual dysfunction or hygiene problems. Other [surgeons were] happy to cater to cosmetic desires." For women with severe issues, these procedures were a godsend. For those merely hoping for perkier privates, vanity beckoned.

Patients rushed to gynecologists' waiting rooms. Once there, they read the testimonies in women's magazines, such as this post-op accolade in the November 1998 issue of *Cosmopolitan* from a thirty-three-year-old woman with a collapsed uterus. Thanks to surgical intervention, she said, she had reclaimed her physical—and climactic—capabilities. "It's kind of strange and wonderful. I've never been into masturbation before, but pleasuring myself now is fantastic—and triggers really sensational orgasms."[5]

Two growing practices, yoga and Pilates, were drawing women's attention to their "core." Kegel exercises were effective for firming up vaginal muscles. And yet the designer vagina, hardly an au naturel procedure, seemed to vibe with the culture's quick-fix mentality, with an American fixation on new

---

4. A smaller diameter, theoretically, would amplify arousal for both the patient and her sex partner.

5. A sidebar in the same *Cosmo* story, however, would play to readers' worries. Under the headline "Does He Think You're a Labia Loser?," young men such as *Scott, the stockbroker* and *Jack, the golf instructor* were asked to give their take on super-protruding labia lips, which some men were said to consider a turn-off. The best answer came from *Adam, the website designer*: "I can't say I recall ever seeing a vagina that turned me off."(Carrie Havranek, "The New Sex Surgeries," *Cosmopolitan*, November 1998.)

modes of sexual display, and with the Boomer fears of aging (and the effects of childbirth and menopause).

David Matlock of Beverly Hills was, and remains, a pioneering vaginoplasty surgeon, whom some refer to as "the Picasso of vaginas." (He has been featured prominently on the reality-TV series *Dr. 90210.*) Matlock would make the case, according to Fiona J. Green, a professor of women's and gender studies at the University of Winnipeg, that "as women's fashions (such as ever increasingly skimpy swimsuit styles) more readily 'expose large areas of skin in the pubic region,' women are more likely to notice physical differences that were previously hidden." Some would attribute this propensity to porn envy: women would see videos or photos of petite or perfect female genitals—sometimes airbrushed or digitized—and demand unrealistic equivalents. Green, paraphrasing Krista Foss, health reporter for the *Toronto Globe and Mail,* would point out that many patients were "women who experience feelings of insecurity, embarrassment, or fear of losing their male partners to younger, more beautiful and tighter women." Others *were* younger, according to Foss, who in 1998 would write about Dr. Robert Stubbs, some of whose patients were "the 25-to-35-year-old trophy wives of sports figures for whom the sexual and psychological ideal is the price of entry into that world."

Whatever the motivations for such surgery and sculpting, the incongruity was not lost on many feminists. While activists among them were speaking out against the practice of genital mutilation in Africa, North American women were visiting their gynecologists and cosmetic surgeons, electing to undergo vaginal and vulval procedures. Fiona Green, citing Betty Dodson and Leslie Hall, would insist that there was a fallacy inherent in reconstructing the vagina. Female orgasm was mainly related to clitoral response, irrespective of the vagina's circumference. "In trying to modify female genitals to make them conform to the cultural norm," Green notes, "the cultural norm continues to ignore the fact that female genitalia come in an assortment of shapes, sizes, and sensuality."

The designer-vagina trend, from a certain perspective, was partly a Freudian snip—the result of a largely male-run medical community asking, "What do women want?" and imposing a cosmetic or orgasmic myth on the fair sex.

Fate, these days, has got the J Sisters by the short hairs.

For twenty-five years, the mysterious Brazilian siblings who brought the Brazilian bikini wax to America had ruled the cosmetological cosmos. Their Manhattan salon had become a shrine to models, socialites, and Hollywood stars. Their "technique" was featured in beauty magazines and on talk shows—even meriting a full episode of *Sex and the City*. But in the summer of 2016, the master waxers were suddenly on the wane. Workers' commissions and wages allegedly went unpaid. Staffers abandoned ship to work in nearby salons. Some clients were bereft, adrift. Soon the J Sisters faced eviction, unable to afford the rent on tony West 57th Street. They were, in truth, victims of their own success. And having created a clean-shaven craze adopted by a generation of women, they began to realize that theirs were no longer the only tweezers in town.

The woman who had started it all was Janea Padilha, a diminutive sixty-something grandmother from the Bahia region of eastern Brazil—one of seven enterprising sisters (along with Judseia, Jussara, Juracy, Jocely, Joyce, and Jonice). After they opened their own New York salon in 1987, Janea decided three years later to introduce the Brazilian wax: a nude nether region, back and front, topped off by a frontal "landing strip," or by a simple design or triangle, or by nothing at all. Bare Down There proved to be a thunderous success.

That, of course, was in their '90s heyday. The J Sisters salon is now closed. But the spirit of the place remains. So, too, do the questions. What was the actual spark that compelled legions of women to grit their teeth, open their pocketbooks, and begin adopting this extreme fashion statement—to the point where today a *mons sans* (by wax or tweeze, laser or razor, depilatory or electrolysis, topical creams or oral drugs, salon or self-administered) is now as pervasive as a pedicure?[6] And what on earth made Janea Padilha want to foist this primitive ritual on the Western netherworld in the first place? Perhaps the best way to arrive at some answers is to recount Padilha and her sisters' many-threaded tale, which has never been told in full until now. It begins with a visit not long ago to their once-bustling domain.

---

6. Moreover, why do many men now prefer that freer feeling, in layman's parlance, around the "back, crack, and sack"? To wit: journalist Christopher Hitchens, who in 2007, as part of an "extreme makeover" for an article in *Vanity Fair*, surrendered to Ms. Janea Padilha. "You are painted with hot wax," he wrote, "to which strips are successively attached and then torn away. Not once, but many, many times." Later, he admitted, "Nothing would induce me to go through that again. It's even worse than waterboarding!" (Christopher Hitchens, "On the Limits of Self-Improvement, Part II," *Vanity Fair*, December 2007; interview with Hitchens.)

On the main wall in the J Sisters waiting room, clients' headshots are arranged in neat rows: Naomi, Cindy, Kimora Lee, and Tyra...Uma, Cameron, Lindsay, and Avril. A grinning Gwynnie, posing in a swimming pool in the altogether, has scrawled on her photo, "You changed my life." Even Bette ("What a wax!") is here, in an Annie Leibovitz rendering: immersed in a bed of roses. The wall's celebrity pedigree confers on the Brazilian wax a whiff of privilege and exclusivity—gilt by association.

"Gwyneth comes for a mani and a pedi and sits out here," one staffer says, beaming, standing amid more down-to-earth clientele. "Kirstie Alley walks around here in her bare feet." Janea Padilha explains that in the close quarters of the waxing room, anatomically self-conscious patrons sometimes ask her to compare their privates to those of the women on the walls. "This area"—Janea motions to her loins, speaking in charmingly broken English. "If they're blonde: do I look like Gwyneth Paltrow? Brunette ask about celebrity who is brunette." But she always reassures them, "We are *all* the same!"

The waiting area has the feel of a large powder room: brocaded chairs, high-ceilinged chandeliers, faux-gold moldings. A glass display case is arrayed with J-brand waxes. On a wall rack, bikinis are hung like Day-Glo tinsel. And despite the harsh, clinical lighting, the mood is cozy: part East Side sleepover, part girls' dorm, albeit one with stylists and waxers scurrying to and fro. Everyone, it seems, stops to greet Janea, a tiny dynamo who has built a career out of talking intimately with women—literally dozens a day—while they're splayed on her treatment table.

"I meet people on the street," she says, "and don't remember they names. We talk, and I think and think—"

"If only they were naked," a pedicure client interrupts, completing the thought. "And had their legs open!"

Atop the grid of glossies hangs a single faded photo. It shows Pedro Padilha, the patriarch, who died in 2002 at age eighty-six. The family fable is something out of Gabriel García Márquez. A train engineer turned meat-market supplier, the handsome Padilha often lived on the edge of poverty as he sired seven sons and seven daughters. His homebody wife, Judith, would monitor her kids' outdoor group showers, admonishing them to wash themselves quickly but thoroughly. "In Brazil," Janea recalls, "you know your body and your sister body. We were told by our parents, 'Clean yourself.' They show the boy how to clean"—she makes rubbing motions again—"the girl. We have to touch. We have to be comfortable. We have to explore our body. Eating together, sleeping together, taking shower together, and with very good respect for each other."

The warm weather called for less clothing. The beach culture encouraged the adoption of a sexier style than those in other climes. Jonice, the youngest and most sultry sister, describes the custom of strolling up and down, day after day, in a skimpy bikini, a wrap, and stylish shoes. "We expose our bodies more," she says. "A blouse without sleeves. No panty hose, no boots. You have to be in a tropical mind-set. You can be sexy anytime, all the time."

In J Sisters lore, the seven daughters, one by one, left jobs at their local nail-and-hair parlor in Brazil and headed north to join their siblings at the midtown salon. Then, in 1990, Janea had an epiphany. She somehow got it in her head to introduce her maximum wax to her New York beauty clients—a homegrown practice she'd perfected in her homeland, first on herself, and then on a few venturesome spa visitors. Jonice was mortified. "I said, 'Janea, I'm going to kill you.' I was doing public relations for the salon and I didn't think the American woman was ready for that. I thought it could have a negative reaction to the spa. This was 1990!"

But in January of that year, Janea, always disarmingly open and upbeat, persuaded one of her regulars—an executive assistant named Sari Markowitz, then twenty-eight—to go full Brazilian. "I'd had bikini waxes elsewhere," Markowitz admits, "but never a Brazilian. I'd go there every week for a manicure, and Janea, who had just come over from Brazil, said, 'Come, try it,' with all the other sisters coaxing me on, and I kept putting them off. Finally, I said, 'Okay, let's do it.' And I know she wasn't prepared, because they didn't have a room dedicated for waxing—so we did it in the *office*. She pushed everything off the desk: the telephone, papers, pens, the stapler. And I was laying on the desk on my back with one leg over the fax machine and the other she was kind of holding apart. And it took about four to six minutes—all in, from beginning to end." Markowitz didn't realize it then, but she would turn out to be America's Patient Zero of the Brazilian wax.

When she got home that night, she couldn't help examining the results. "I felt, 'Oh, wow.' It was like a new hairdo. You kept looking down: 'No, it's gone. No? It's gone.' It was like: 'Do the cuffs match the collar?'" The next day, over lunch, Markowitz described her new "do" to five friends, including an editor at *Elle*, each of whom went in for their own wax, and in turn told *their* friends.

Elle ran a story. Word spread among models and film stars.[7] "At the time," says Jocely's husband, John Marquis, a sort of company adviser, "the top models were coming from Brazil. They were unbelievably sexy. And AOL started as this was taking off." So, as Marquis explains, he bought a six-month banner ad. "Those little [ads] exploded across the U.S. and the world."

Recalls Chris Napolitano, then an editor at *Playboy*, "Models were showing up and they were getting progressively groomed. It went from the taco or nacho or whatever they called it, to the landing strip in, like, five years." As we talk, Napolitano takes out a chronological collection of *Playboy* centerfolds. Surveying the lot, he insists that Miss December 1991 bears "the first definitive shaping." But the first utterly plucked Playmate, in his estimation, didn't come along until Miss September 2001, long after the depubed had wended their way into all manner of porn.

In 1998, a *New York Observer* story about the waxing craze was passed around by fax and email; its opening line: "It's not your mother's vulva anymore." And then, in a now-famous *Sex and the City* episode—reportedly based on a real-life session by Sarah Jessica Parker—Parker's character, Carrie Bradshaw, goes in for a subtle touch-up at an L.A. spa but emerges, because of the language barrier, thoroughly defurred, and fuming. Quoth Carrie: "I feel like one of those freaking hairless dogs."

"People knew what she was talking about," recalls the curvy, devil-may-care sister Joyce Padilha. "Everybody had tried to hide about this, like [they were in] a secret club. Then, suddenly, 'My God, *she* did it too!' Now everyone *knew* about it." Women descended on their local spas requesting a Brazilian or a thong wax. Elsewhere, it was called the Playboy, the Hollywood, the Smoothie. The hirsute would soon go the way of the pantsuit.

———

The appeal of the whiskerless wax, of course, didn't develop in a vacuum. Larger societal forces in the '80s and '90s had been aligning as well. The

———

7. Eventually, Gwyneth would sing the sisters' praises in *Vogue* and Naomi Campbell would describe them as gurus on *Oprah*. (Christina Shea, "Stop the Hair-Removal Insanity!," *Glamour*, August 2004; George Gurley, "What's New, Pussycat?," *New York Observer*, November 23, 1998.)

go-go economy, dispensing disposable income across new demographics, helped manifest a pampering impulse in the culture (spas and nail parlors abounded) and a neat-freak ethos (evident in everything from the self-storage craze to the neighborhood-beautification boom). New sexual hygiene habits took hold, prompted by the AIDS crisis and the rise in STDs. In addition, the more tailored look was already creeping into porn, just as porn was becoming more accessible, thanks to satellite TV, cable, and the Internet. The body had become a public message board for self-expression (piercings, tattoos, sundry shavings). The thong, the belly shirt, and low-rise jeans were drawing more attention to the midriff and thereabouts. "In the '80s and '90s, you see this exaggerated focus on female genitals," says the sexual-empowerment guru Nicole Daedone. "Here's Madonna, who touches herself onstage and in videos and has published a sex book; she's turned on and in control. There's [newly popular] vibrators. There's women on retreats exploring their genitals with mirrors"—as depicted in the 1991 film *Fried Green Tomatoes*.

In this environment, Janea's breakthrough was also an act of turning back the downstairs clock. Some women were getting in touch with that virgin version of themselves. They were feeling younger, more unencumbered. And many, by extension, were inviting their partners to indulge in what had typically been a forbidden fantasy: a mature bod with the patina of innocence. For Daedone, the artifice and juvenilization pointed to a form of Ken-and-Barbie regression—a "sexual malnourishment," she figures, that had set in among many members of both sexes. "Most men aren't accustomed to a fully mature, sexualized woman with full hair," she says, gesturing down with both hands. "So in order to play by the cultural rules today, most women try to stay prepubescent to keep our bodies small, our genitals small.... It's [a social version of] neoteny—genetic arrested development. The danger is you end up with sex—without sex in it. Everyone's *looking* the part, but you have 'façade to façade.' You're not interacting."[8]

---

8. Female sexuality in the '90s, according to Daedone, was often overdramatized, both in private and in its cultural manifestations, untethered to the deep commitment and spiritual intensity that had long been a part of the ultimate act of human intimacy. "Freud actually said anything that is exaggerated is exaggerated because it hasn't been integrated, and female sexuality often operated in an automatic way—like L.A.," Daedone says, laughing. "The surface of it was out there, the show of it was everywhere apparent, but there wasn't any depth to it. There was this arched-back, moaning sort of sexuality—you had all the symbols of it. But, as is said in semantics, you didn't have the actual

As Daedone suggests, letting nature take its course has served the species just fine since well before the Stone Age. But Janea was into promoting a twenty-first-century look—genitalia 2.0. The bottom line, Janea now says, is that "the sex is better." To her way of thinking, less hair means better friction for both partners, more exposed nerve endings, more skin-on-skin intimacy. Some clients, says Janea, often show up *weeks* early for follow-up appointments, which tend to be about five weeks apart. "They say, 'The wax is aphrodisiac.' Or, 'I need to wax for my new boyfriend.' I say, 'I just *saw* you. Come back in five or six weeks.'"

And oral sex would become the Brazilian wax's killer app. "[A Brazilian] heightens the pleasure and sensuality in every place," insists J Sisters customer Dani, a marketing executive in her fifties, who requests that her real name not be used. "You just have the tongue and the intensity of the movement, without any barrier. And the intensity of the orgasm is definitely longer."

The rest, as they say, is history. The J Sisters, though unsuccessful in trying to trademark the phrase "Brazilian bikini wax" in the early '90s,[9] consider it *their* creation. Indeed, a decade later, Jonice would field the call (she doesn't recall the exact year) when a man telephoned for some background, saying the term "bikini wax" might be added to the *Oxford English Dictionary*. "When they called to ask for the definition"—Jonice hits her head to mimic her stunned reaction—"What can you say? I told him, 'What? Its real *meaning*? It produces a better orgasm!'"

————

A lot has changed since that wax over the fax machine. From the dorm room to the locker room to the bedroom, the young and the active can go for months, even years, without spotting as much as a curl. Mothers and daughters now visit salons to "get done" as a sort of bonding experience. Beauty venues have devised waxing tactics that are more user-friendly (meaning: less painful). But for the J Sisters, the standard preference remained the original, back-to-the-roots basics: 90°F wax applied to the entire business; cloth strips tugged with furious force for ten minutes; $75 a visit.

---

referent. In the '80s and '90s you experienced the liberation of the idea but none of that had been actually integrated into our bodies." (Interview with Daedone.)

9. "It was not a product, it was an action," adviser John Marquis says, shrugging.

The salon, over time, would cut back on requests for freaky designs (a mate's initials, for example) and radical dye jobs, but they welcomed the hardship cases that other spas might refuse: the heavily pierced; the gorilla-like men recommended by their dermatologists. Recently, a bride-to-be, four days before her wedding, arrived from Germany—by limo, straight from JFK— just to have a wax. "She take the car service *back* to the airport," Janea says in disbelief. "Don't even shop!" Clients would range in age from seventeen to eighty-two. And all because of Janea's little brainstorm.

Or was it?

The Brazilian bikini wax, it so happens, wasn't immaculately conjured one night in a bubbling vat. The depilous pudendum, in some form or another, actually dates back to Cleopatra's day, at least, and sculptures from ancient Greece depict females, unlike their male counterparts, without genital hair. "[Many of] the women in cultures around the Mediterranean have been hairless from the neck down," says my Turkish friend Emel, a German-raised marketing executive who has been living in the United States and Europe for over a decade. "Waxing has been practiced in the Middle East for centuries and, later, southern European countries, [through the] expansion of the Ottoman Empire. In Islam, pubic hair is seen as unappealing, dirty, and, furthermore, sinful—a sign of sexual maturity. Millions of Turks have immigrated to Germany since 1960—and they were the ones who introduced waxing to German ladies who, up until the late 1990s, were still completely as Mother Nature created them, with hair *every*where. Strong feminists, they were reluctant at first. But they gave in to the 'clean trend,' which made them look more youthful, attractive, and feminine."

Closer to our age, there has been a rich if checkered history of the southerly tonsured. In the 1950s and '60s, ever-shrinking bathing attire triggered ever more aggressive shapings and shearings. Athletes, male and female, fearful of stray follicles that might impede performance or mar appearance, began to embrace the paste.

Actor George Hamilton says he admired the work of top L.A. hairdressers in the '60s and '70s, such as Gene Shacove, the man who inspired the 1975 movie *Shampoo*.[10] Shacove, recalls Hamilton, would have his female clients

---

10. Some hold that two others may have also influenced screenwriter Robert Towne and Warren Beatty in crafting Beatty's character George Roundy: Jay Sebring (the stylist who was slain in the

(many of them movie stars and showgirls) stand "behind a sheet with a cut-out pattern down below for what they wanted the shape to be—waxing, snipping, and coloring—so the hairdresser didn't see their faces." California waxes were "more modest than those in New York [in the 1960s]," insists Tommy Baratta, the restaurateur (and Jack Nicholson confidant), who started as a shampoo boy for New York hairdresser Larry Mathews—also on 57th Street—before venturing out on his own. "I did models," Baratta remembers, "and dancers and upscale prostitutes—they had the brothels on 72nd [Street] on the West Side—starting with the hair-coloring." Dye jobs saved newly platinum blondes, for instance, from the indignity of appearing two-toned. Baratta claims that for a while he even handed out a business card emblazoned with the phrase "BUSH BARATTA: Double the Batch and We Do Your Snatch." By the '70s, he recalls, "as the costumes for performers got as skimpy as they could...we went to waxing [but] it never was a 'total.' The manicurists mainly did it. I liked to supervise!...I would do [the final] shaping with the razor."

In 1974, gonzo hairstylist Paul Mitchell, creator of the shag, helped produce a story for *Penthouse* publisher Bob Guccione for his new spin-off magazine *Viva*: six pages of lower locks that were fashioned into hearts and flames and arrows. "It was for a spread in the magazine—pun intended," according to Westchester salon owner Joey DelVecchio, who passed away in 2012. "I was twenty-one at the time. I went to a strip club with one of the hairdressers who worked with [Mitchell] and the girls who wanted to be in the article. He practiced trimming designs out of the hair."

And then there was Nance Mitchell.[11] For decades Nance had been a pre-eminent West Coast skincare and grooming expert. Come the '90s, however, she became a waxer to the stars, the porn-star set, and even the high-end working girls. *Glamour* claimed that Mitchell, who died in 2009, had "coerced the pants off more actresses than Jack Nicholson." And her decoiffing offerings ranged from sculpting logo-shaped thatches (Louis Vuitton, Gucci) to strafing unsightly patches from male rock stars' chests to fuzz-busting Chippendales dancers. (By removing the mangle, you accentuate the dangle.)

So Janea Padilha, to be truthful, was not exactly inventing the wheel.

Manson murders) and Barbra Streisand's hairdresser turned blockbuster producer, Jon Peters. (William Stadiem, "Studio Head," *Vanity Fair*, March 2010, 281.)

11. Nance was unrelated to Paul, according to Heidi Fleiss, the former Hollywood Madam.

The J Sisters, truth be told, had first gained their cult following for an even more deliciously illicit reason. Anna Maria Tornaghi, the prominent Brazilian marketing consultant and socialite, points out that the Padilhas were first known in New York not for their wax strips but for their boudoir tips.

On Tornaghi's visits to the salon in the '80s, when it was located on 56th Street, she recalls hearing the sisters "always talking very softly, doing the nails, and almost whispering. I asked, 'What are they doing?' and I was told, 'They are telling their clients all the things to do with their partners in sex.' But it was not just this. It was what we call in Brazil, *simpatia*—in Portuguese, sim-pah-*tee*-a—'secret advice' is how I would classify [it], like grandmothers' recipes passed along. They were teaching this kind of folk wisdom. The clients sit down for a manicure and they would say, 'To keep your boyfriend, use this color—red—and tie a little piece of red material, like a ribbon, on the inside of your skirt or in the underwear.' One client would tell another and another."

At first, Tornaghi says, "The clients were from the neighborhood. They were really good manicurists." Soon, however, Tornaghi—a tastemaker who helped kick-start the lambada trend stateside in the late '80s—would be stopped at social gatherings by people who were curious to know what she, as a Brazilian, knew about the J Sisters. "They would say, 'My friend took me to a place and there I saw five movie stars and the sex tips they tell there! [Does] it really work? Is that *macumba*—or *cambomblé*—black magic?' It's characteristic of that region [where the sisters grew up]. The J Sisters—they started with stories and people *want* stories, so they start *creating* stories. They were giving superstitions.... But, I tell you—it doesn't help *anything*. *That*, I know."

When I relay this story, Janea is initially resistant to such a characterization. But she soon becomes increasingly and engagingly animated. "*Simpatia* is superstition, yes. We know a lot of *simpatia*; Brazil is very mystical country." Her sister Joyce quickly agrees. "It's like tricks, tips. Sometimes we tell them, 'Red underwear is good for passion. Pink underwear is good for love.'"

"Yellow," says Janea, "is good for money, fortune."

"Green underwear and bra is hopeful," Joyce adds. "Lots of women have them in Brazil, yes." Joyce admits that she sometimes convinces women to throw their "ridiculous, awful Hanes underwear" in the trash can, right there in the waxing room. "The boyfriend, the husband must hate it. We advise them to dress for themselves. Many times they leave here naked [under their clothes, and go] from here to the lingerie store!"

Janea's book *Brazilian Sexy* is filled with such advice. Eat plenty of acacia berries to make you "horny." Press down on your lover's prostate ridge just before orgasm. Dip in a finger, occasionally, and sample yourself; otherwise, Janea writes, "It's like serving soup that you haven't tasted yet."[12]

Janea admits that she feels a special burden when sexually unsatisfied clients—and there are many—seek her advice. Should they have an affair? Do they just need a sympathetic ear? "In five minutes," she says, "we can say *every*thing." Janea and her coworkers also field calls from boyfriends who make appointments for their lovers—and then show up in person to pay the bill. "Their previous girlfriends came here," she explains, "and the new one, they send them, and pay first, saying, 'I paid already, so you gotta go.'" If the new, uninitiated girlfriend arrives with first-time butterflies, they reassure her, according to Joyce: "We say, 'We know what your boyfriend likes. Sit back.'"

A final, nagging question naturally arises. Why does Janea harbor this almost missionary obsession with hygiene? Had she gone through some trauma back in Brazil, I ask, that somehow made her feel attuned to this issue?

She nods. She falls silent for a moment. Then she pulls over a low wooden pedicure stool. She squats on it in her snug white outfit, deliberately facing her backside to her listener. She looks over her shoulder as she speaks, and she goes back to a day in 1980.

"I was young and cute. I was on the beach in Brazil with some couples and we were all sitting on stools. And I saw this one brown, beautiful girl [walking to] another table and her back was toward me. She got in the chair

---

12. Then there are the secrets she reserves for her most valued customers. Tip One: "I tell my clients, take a little Vicks [VapoRub], very little, and put it on," she says, making a dabbing motion. "And you're going to feel, already, 'Wooaaoh'"—she actually crosses her eyes—"And when he goes to her, the Vicks goes right to him"—she snaps her fingers—"It's amazing. It's cold fire [on] both of us. It's better than Viagra." Tip Two: "Couples in Brazil, we have sex every day, every day, every day. Sometimes the minimum. But the couple don't need to have orgasm every single day. Love is what's important." (Interview with Janea Padilha.)

with her bikini and I saw her hair in her butt and I thought, 'My God, so ugly!' My mind was sick for the rest of the day. This girl was so disgusting."

Never having considered her *own* appearance in this way, Janea began to wonder about how she looked to others, obsessing all afternoon. "I didn't have this kind of hair with *me*?! And when I got home I went to take shower right away and I put a mirror on the floor and looked up and I thought, 'Oh, my God!'" She felt devastated.

The next day at the salon where she worked, she locked herself into one of the private rooms. She had a mirror, a supply of hot wax, and bits of cloth. Her coworkers kept passing by the door, demanding to know what she was up to. "I did myself. It took me almost two hours. And when I finish and I touch myself, it was unbelievable. So good. I didn't want to stop. So smooth. My husband, he also didn't want to stop to touch me."

And *that*, truth be told, is how the rest of the Western world got to be so spanking clean.

———————

The J Sisters salon has gone out of business and shut its doors. Only Jonice remains. "I closed the location two weeks ago," she tells me in August 2016, her heart heavy. "It's only me. I'm the last J Sister here." For the foreseeable future, she has moved her operations to a colleague's spa on 57th Street where she and a handful of staffers from the old salon cater to faithful clients.

She misses her sisters, including Janea, who recently moved back home to São Paulo, where she is spreading the word about the *sunga*—a Brazilian wax for men. Indeed, both sisters see male hair removal as the next great cosmetics frontier.

Jonice, after decades of runaway success, tries to look at the bright side. "Netflix might do a J Sisters miniseries," she insists. "There's two documentaries [on us] coming out—one in Brazil, one in Britain." And despite downsizing, she keeps her appointment calendar full, scheduling more and more men. "They come here for *sunga*," she says, "which means 'Speedo.' They come here for chest, for brows. It's beautiful...I have here today two men waiting, like women."

CHAPTER 9

The Glory of O

Perhaps the breakthrough came in 1989. That was the year audiences flocked to the Rob Reiner romantic comedy *When Harry Met Sally*, written by Nora Ephron.

In the film, Meg Ryan plays Sally, a wholesome, cheery obsessive-compulsive who has a bouffy perm and wears Days-of-the-Week underwear. The signature scene, set in a deli, shows Sally with Harry (Billy Crystal) as she demonstrates how women fake orgasms. He is convinced he can *always* tell the real McCoy; she insists that most women have phoned in their fair share of phony climaxes.

Her moans pierce across the restaurant ("Oooh, oh, oh God. Oh yeah, right there. Oh, uh, God! Yes yes yes...") and make every patron stop eating, stone-faced, to glare. The kicker is priceless. A prim middle-aged woman sitting nearby turns to her waiter and says, "I'll have what she's having."

I'll have what she's having became a national tagline. An earth-shattering climax—whether genuine or fabricated—had become the province of the girl next door *and* the matronly lady at the next table.

Overdub the pleasant, whirring sound of the all-American vibrator.

Sex toys—which used to be referred to demurely as "marital aids"—were no longer playthings for enlightened feminists (think Betty Dodson's masturbation workshops in the '70s) or the kinky lover or Miss Lonelyhearts. Formerly stowed on a closet shelf or concealed in the lining of a secret throw pillow, vibrators were now right there in the bedside drawer, alongside the lube. Sex toys began doing brisk business by mail order, over the Internet, and through companies like Pure Romance, which in 1993 started the Avon-style living-room demonstrations of sex toys for groups of women (Shtupperware parties, as it were). These onetime novelty items were becoming accepted as instruments that could liberate individuals and couples. When it came out in 1999, tech historian Rachel P. Maines's book *The Technology of Orgasm*—regaled as the first definitive history of the vibrator—was favorably reviewed in the popular press. And many men who in the past might have felt threatened—"How can my tool compete with one that's got a motor?"—were starting to welcome the implements as facilitators. After all, a preponderance of nineties guys were already at ease with gaming devices, intrigued by porn, and increasingly clued in to what their partners were perusing in catalogs and online.

Hilary Howard (in a *New York Times* survey of—what to call it?—Gen V) writes that the sexologist Carol Queen "attributes more-honest discussions about sex and pleasure to fear of H.I.V./AIDS in the early 1990s.... 'There was something of a pendulum swing from the sex conservatism of the '80s to the lively sex publishing of the '90s, zines, anthologies, small presses,' [Queen] said. 'Then people in more-mainstream venues heard about toys. As soon as mainstream culture looks at an issue, it becomes fair game for everyone else.'"

But the Toy Story really hit home with the emergence of the Rabbit, a vibrator fitted with a protruding clitoral stimulator that resembled bunny ears.

Women in the know purchased the gadget discreetly. Then demand got out of hand. *Sex and the City* devoted a whole episode to the device in 1998. Sales exploded, and over the next year, Ann Summers, a U.K. purveyor of sex toys, lingerie, and the like, reported that it shipped a million units. The Rabbit became to the '90s bedroom what the Cuisinart had been to the '70s kitchen. Soon, women (and men) were buying more gel and lube (some even scented or flavored), more dildos, pulsators, Kegel balls, strap-ons, plugs, and special attachments that worked like a G-spot GPS. The Rabbit became the gateway drug for naughtier sex toys and a boon to the industry at large. (In 1976, the famous *Hite Report on Female Sexuality*—as the *Guardian* would later point out—had concluded that 99 percent of American women had never availed themselves of a vibrator. By 2009, according to a later survey, fully half of the country's adult females admitted some familiarity with the device.)

The Rabbit was fruitful and multiplied. Today, of all the treasures on sale at America's sex shops, it is the hutch of Rabbits that typically commands the prime shelf space. During a recent visit to the Pleasure Chest, for instance, I spied three racks with fourteen varieties of vibrator of every imaginable hue and cry—many of Rabbit-style design. Each was double-pronged: one shaft for insertion; a smaller adjacent bulb for outside maneuvers. Some had components shaped like ticklers, petals, or sea creatures. A pleasant sales associate walked over and offered a demonstration. She held up a remote control, adjusting the speed of the stim stem ("These 'ears' flutter externally on the clitoris"), then the other control for the larger tube ("The shaft rotates and you can adjust the swing so it hits the G-spot"). Running her hand along the shaft, she pointed out the internal beads—which rotate independently inside a cylindrical cuff—"that give a different feeling along the walls of the vagina."

And here's the rub. Part of the appeal of sex tech in the '90s, and in the years ever since, has been the fact that masturbation, an act often freighted with shame, was slowly becoming acknowledged as a natural human function.[1] In 1994, in fact, the topic emerged in a very public way. That year, Clinton's surgeon general, Joycelyn Elders, was asked at a U.N. forum on AIDS if masturbation could help curtail the disease from spreading among young people who might otherwise be exposed to potential infection. Her response—"I think [masturbation] is a part of human sexuality and it's a part of something that perhaps should be taught"—led to great tumult in Washington and across the country.

Elders was swiftly dismissed, merely for suggesting the benefits of an open discussion with young people about masturbation. But her opinion resonated. Columnists, physicians, and world health advocates came to her defense and protested her ouster.[2] The Good Vibrations sex-shop franchise, for one, took up the charge.[3] In 1995, one of its advisers, the ubiquitous Carol Queen, helped

---

1. The term "masturbation," in casual conversation, was giving way to the more offhanded "self-pleasuring." Films and television sitcoms routinely referenced the subject. Radio host Howard Stern frequently discussed his own self-pleasuring habits and solicited similar stories from his guests.

2. Pro-life and right-wing groups had already been rallying against her for some of her other controversial stances (calling her the "condom queen," for instance), including her contention that students be given greater access to birth control measures. (Karen Klinka, "Elders' OU Invitation Elicits Doctors' Protest," *Oklahoman*/NewsOK.com, June 3, 1994.)

3. Good Vibrations, founded by Joani Blank in 1977 in San Francisco's Mission District, promoted itself as "the clean, well-lighted vibrator store." Its mission: to act as "a diverse, woman-focused retailer providing high-quality, sex-positive products and non-judgmental, accurate sex information." By

devise a public rebuttal to Elders's firing: National Masturbation Month. To be held every May, M-Month was intended as a way to deflect embarrassment surrounding onanism; encourage safe-sex practices; and, by the by, sell sex toys. (One of the movement's slogans: "Think Globally, Masturbate Locally.")

Then, in 1999, Masturbate-A-Thon arrived. It would become an annual live event—organized by Dr. Queen and her partner, Dr. Robert Lawrence—at which attendees in several cities would get off "solo" in a group setting. During one session in London, Queen would recall, "a lovely matron who'd come down on the train from Coventry came out disappointed that she had not had 50 orgasms, which had been her goal, and said, 'I guess I shouldn't have made love this morning before [boarding the train].'" The holder of the longest-time-spent-masturbating trophy, said Queen, was a Japanese man "sponsored by the Tenga line of men's sex toys [who competed while wearing something] like a Nascar suit with Tenga's logo. And he totally won that title! Nine hours and 58 minutes!"

———

Throughout the '90s, women and men were getting mixed signals about their orgasms. A widely reported University of Wisconsin study, which had sampled the sex habits of 805 nurses, found that two-fifths of them routinely experienced multiple orgasms. A team of U.K. scientists proposed a connection between the female orgasm and potential fertility: according to their research, a woman's climax appears to be accompanied by a vacuuming spasm that suctions male ejaculate into the uterus, theoretically increasing the odds of conception.

Rutgers University, according to *New York Times* science writer William Broad, had become America's "ground zero" for studies in which "female volunteers put their heads into giant machines and focus their attention on erotic fantasies." And in 1992, its researchers came out with a pivotal paper that, by Broad's measure, had sexologists considering a "reassessment of the nature of orgasm." The reason: Drs. Gina Ogden (who is independent of Rutgers), Beverly Whipple, and Barry R. Komisaruk had discovered that women in the Rutgers lab, without the aid of self-stimulation, could spontaneously climax through their imaginations alone.[4] New books and research papers, meanwhile, were

———

the '90s, Good Vibrations had expanded across the country and ran a large mail-order and online business. (www.goodvibes.com.)

4. Ogden had started her research in the 1970s before joining forces with Komisaruk and Whipple. "Psychic coitus," in fact, had been identified as early as 1896, and the phenomenon of

looking at Eastern sexual practices and describing men who routinely experienced multiple orgasms.

So much for the good news.

While some researchers saw every erection as half full, others counseled caution. A newly named disorder—erectile dysfunction—was said to have reached epidemic proportions, supposedly affecting as much as half of the adult male population over age forty. (We'll return to this topic later on.) Many women, meanwhile, weren't faring much better. Surveys in the early and mid-'90s concluded that a quarter of all women had persistent trouble achieving orgasm or exhibited signs of greatly diminished (even nonexistent) sexual desire. A 1999 study published in the *Journal of the American Medical Association* put that number at 43 percent. And yet while statistics suggest that two-thirds of women do not have orgasms through intercourse alone, neither is this a symptom of dysfunction.

The condition was given several overarching designations: female orgasmic disorder, hypoactive desire disorder, and female sexual dysfunction (FSD).[5] Soon the condition was being debated—some say conflated—by physicians, by Big Pharma (which provided increasingly profitable treatments to remedy the slate of dysfunctions), and by the media (which devoted many a headline and morning-show segment to FSD, "America's silent scourge").

Some clinicians had other ideas. In the 1990s, psychiatrist Rosemary Basson would formulate what became known as the Basson Sexual Response Cycle—flow charts that pointed to a new understanding among sex therapists about how to treat female patients who complained of diminished libido. As Daniel Bergner would observe in a retrospective article in the *New York Times Magazine*, many women did not seem to have an "initial hunger,"

---

imagination-induced "spontaneous orgasm" was subsequently described by Havelock Ellis, Alfred Kinsey, and the team of William Masters and Virginia Johnson. (William J. Broad, "I'll Have What She's Thinking," *New York Times*, September 28, 2013.)

5. Related conditions had been identified since at least the nineteenth century. And in 1980 sexual dysfunction had been listed as a category in the American Psychiatric Association's bible, the *Diagnostic and Statistical Manual of Mental Disorders*. But Katherine Angel, who has written extensively on female sexuality, has pointed out that it wasn't until 1987 that the *DSM* included female sexual arousal disorder under the category of sexual dysfunctions. (Katherine Angel, "The History of 'Female Sexual Dysfunction' as a Mental Disorder in the 20th Century," *Current Opinion in Psychiatry* 23, issue 6 [November 2010]: 536–41, http://www.ncbi.nlm.nih.gov/pmc/articles/PMC2978945/; biographical page of Dr. Katherine Angel, Warwick Centre for the History of Medicine: http://www2.warwick.ac.uk/fac/arts/history/chm/people/pdf/katherineangel/.)

or what is often thought of as "lust or craving." For them, desire did not trigger sexual arousal; instead, their responses, Basson posited, were driven by a closed loop of stimulus-response-stimulus—or, in Basson's formula, "Desire follows arousal."

In short, a woman's sexual response (or lack thereof) was frequently misinterpreted by her physician, therapist, or gynecologist. In many cases, it was also misunderstood by her partner or partners, who were not attuned to how to arouse her. Moreover, FSD patients were often at the mercy of doctors and drug firms prescribing medicines to address arousal mechanisms, which in fact had multiple layers and deep psychological roots. (The possibility of a dependable and marketable female Viagra equivalent would not get serious until 2015.)

Nowhere, however, was there a greater sea change in the treatment of sexual health among older women than in the field of hormones. Estrogen supplements, which had fallen out of favor, had come back into general use across an aging population. Michael Mendelsohn is a cardiologist who some consider one of the fathers of estrogen-replacement-therapy science. "In the early '90s," he explains, "the national recommendations strongly supported [the belief] that estrogen, in addition to relieving the symptoms of menopause—hot flashes, sweating, and vaginal dryness—was also good for the heart and bones and cognition." (In 2000, the model and actress Lauren Hutton would appear in ads for Wyeth research institute—Wyeth makes the hormone drug Prempro—discussing the merits of estrogen replacement.)

While such ads and treatments had been around since the '50s, it wasn't until the '90s, says Mendelsohn, that "the stars aligned for estrogen. Molecular and cellular evidence began accruing that showed the hormone could actually be beneficial and important for the heart and blood vessels. When women reached the menopause and stopped having estrogen around, it caused dramatic physiological changes. By giving *back* the estrogen, the [premenopausal] responses and the biology were renewed. They had more vaginal lubrication. They became more comfortable sexually, and sometimes more responsive, and interest in sexual activity was sometimes restored. You basically were making women feel younger by restoring the hormonal milieu that, when lost, made their bodies feel different and older." The payoff for many was a more youthful and invigorated sense of self, a healthier body- and mind-set, and better sex. That is, until the court dockets started filling up.

Within a few short years, findings by the National Institutes of Health would raise the possibility that "combination hormone therapy" might be far more complex than had been previously understood and might even contribute to an increased risk in adverse effects. Hormone regimens were tied to a percentage rise in incidents of breast cancer, and questions arose about whether hormones could prevent or cause heart attack, blood clotting, and stroke. Over the course of the decade, hundreds of patients would file lawsuits against drug makers, contending that the companies' hormone treatments had made them seriously ill. (Later, the scientific consensus would shift again and hormone therapy for postmenopausal women would return to favor in many circles, especially around protection from heart disease, depending on individual risk factors.)

———

Estrogen migrated from medicine and popped up in movie plotlines and TV shows. But its place in pop culture didn't hold a candle to that of the new, improved female orgasm.

The blow-your-socks-off orgasm scene was nothing new to the movies. But come the '90s, it had become a film and cable staple, played for laughs. No episode of *Sex and the City*, for example, seemed complete unless Kim Cattrall's Samantha was shown mid-moan (and then sharing postcoital cock tales with the girls). In the film *American Pie*, the bedroom shrieks of Tara Reid's character—on the receiving end of a predinner snack—almost bring the house down. In *Pleasantville*, a send-up of '50s-era conformity (shot in Ike Age black-and-white), Joan Allen, as the uptight suburban mom, is so enraptured by her first self-induced climax that her bathroom's floral wallpaper turns brilliant colors and the tree in the front yard bursts into flame. If these comic depictions were any indication, Americans recognized great value in—and were validated by—the psychic power and healthy release inherent in better orgasms.

Beyond the onscreen O, though, the true-life celebri-gasm was a bona fide '90s thing. The singer-songwriter Sting almost single-handedly helped set a fire under the Tantric sex craze. In 1990, he spoke of putting off ejaculation at will: "It ends when you choose, it can go on for five hours." In 1993, *Rolling Stone* reported that he and his wife, Trudie Styler, had marathon sessions. "The purpose of sex ideally," Sting professed, "is for the woman to attain orgasm and for the man not to." Over time, their lovemaking was said to stretch to seven or eight hours. (Years later, Sting and Styler did a bit of Tantric recanting, saying that their reputation for enjoying hours in flagrante was merely fallout from a goof started by some drink-fueled talk with a reporter, Sting, and his fellow rocker Bob Geldof.)

Tantra, nevertheless, caught on. By prolonging their encounters, couples professed to tap into one's deeper reservoirs of sexual energy and magnify feelings of connection and ecstasy. On television in the late '80s and early '90s, two attorneys on *L.A. Law* (played by Jill Eikenberry and Michael Tucker—married in real life) would jokingly refer to the Venus Butterfly, a female stimulation technique. But it didn't stop there. As Tucker would recount in a 1996 *Maclean's* magazine story on the Tantric trend, "The [show's] writers made it up and then, years later, we discovered what it was and it has become the center of our life." He and Eikenberry, in fact, had become blissful Tantra practitioners, engaging the human body's "chakras"—from groin to heart to head, and back again. "I always thought the point of sex was my pleasure," he confessed. "But the point is fulfilling my woman in the deepest, most spiritual way, but also in a profoundly sexual way.... When my seven chakras are open and all of Jill's are open and we are connecting, we can damn near levitate off the bed." Eikenberry, equally enthused, would tell the *New York Times*, "I come from a strait-laced Unitarian background and at first I couldn't believe I was going in this direction. We kind of feel we have a calling now." (Just as celebrities' blessings had helped legitimize the Brazilian, these endorsements were shining a light on sex practices that had grown out of Eastern spiritual traditions.)

Whether solo or in tandem, separate or simultaneous, by hand or by machine, orally or genitally or otherwise, Americans were building a better orgasm. And in terms of duration, frequency, and variety, a woman's, by many accounts, made a man's seem rather...anticlimactic. Naomi Wolf in 1991 wrote about this disparity. In her opus *The Beauty Myth*, she would attest, "Capable of multiple orgasm, continual orgasm, a sharp and breathtaking clitoral orgasm, an orgasm seemingly centered in the vagina that is emotionally overwhelming, orgasm from having the breasts stroked, and of endless variations of all those responses combined, women's capacity for genital pleasure is theoretically inexhaustible."

And if there was one inexhaustible and insatiably orgasmic woman in the 1990s, it was Nicole Daedone.

Nicole Daedone was celibate for much of 1997. She had recently navigated a series of complicated relationships with men. She had been buffeted by the death of her estranged father. Daedone—a San Francisco art gallerist who had studied sexual identity in college and semantics in grad school[6]—was looking for answers, having always been a searcher.

When things seemed darkest, she sought guidance from various spiritual teachers, eventually returning to the Buddhism and meditation practices that had grounded her when she was younger. As part of this journey, she renounced sex for a year. And then, finding herself at a personal crossroads, she decided to make a life-changing commitment. She would enter a Zen community in San Francisco and become a monk.

Daedone was not standard monk material. Her body was sinuous, her laugh vigorous, her hungers voracious. She had probing eyes, cocoa-butter skin, and long cinnamon tresses. (She has since gone honey blond.) Part Sicilian, part Romanian, she occasionally wrote steamy prose about her erotic encounters.

With only a week to go before her scheduled move to the monastery, she hesitated, wondering if she really had the will to refrain from earthly temptations. As a test, she now recalls, she decided to "go wild for a week." She had spent a year in abstinence. Now she would roll full-tilt in the other direction.

On her first night out, pursuing what she calls "the six deadly sins" (murder: uncool), she found herself at a party in San Francisco, suddenly drawn to a French-Belgian stranger with black hair, black eyes, and a spiritual vibe. They talked about her pending entry into monastic life. In response, he offered to show her a practice he thought might help her. Intrigued, she joined him the following night in a quiet room at the ashram where he was staying. "Okay," he said, after exchanging pleasantries. "Take off your pants."

Daedone was suspicious, yet game. She did what she was told.

"Lie down," he suggested, though he remained fully clothed. She lay down. "Open your legs," he said.

And as she spread for him, he directed the beam of an adjustable wall lamp toward her widened frame. Frightened and confused, she felt herself descending into a trance state, remaining motionless.

His voice was tender, deliberate, enveloping. "Your inner labia look like a coral," he said. "There is a deep rose color at the edges and it fades into a pearlescent pink at the base. I can see your clitoris peeking out from beneath your hood, which is tilted slightly to the side." For several minutes he went on describing each fold and ridge, his voice washing over her in waves. She felt tears coming, felt time slowing, felt deep compassion emanating from him.

He set a timer—for twenty minutes—and, as she would later write, "He sat at my right side. He wrapped one leg beneath my legs and the other over my belly.... He placed his right hand beneath my behind, and placed his thumb gently into my opening, anchoring me to his palm from the base of my introitus. He slid his left index finger up through my labia and onto the upper left-hand quadrant of my clitoris. He stroked.... He narrated, [explaining] everything that he was doing, everything that he felt in his body." He began to stroke up and up, then down and down, his touch grazing the soft groove just to the left of her clitoris.

After a time, as she would describe it, "Everything in me ignited.... My entire consciousness became that spot.... The center of my body buzzed like a phone wire. I felt each stroke.... I felt him speed up, then slow down, shift direction.... A thought arose: I am home."

Later, when the clock's buzzer signaled that twenty minutes had elapsed, he "grounded her" and gently toweled her off. He arose, smiling, and offered Nicole her pants. "Come back any time you want to do this again."

She would return, and often. She ditched the monastery thing. And she fell in with a set of women and men who, once or twice a day, would prop themselves on pillows, take out containers of lubrication, and engage in female-centric stroking sessions, which Nicole would come to know as "orgasmic meditation"—OM. The idea was to transform both stroker and stroked by concentrating on their point of connection at one special spot on the woman's body.

The strokes would crest toward peaks—the apex of an "up" stroke—or descend to the nadir of a "down." The women would surf these waves, riding, extending their time in meditative suspension. For a while, Daedone, in the undertow, would be consumed by embarrassment, anxiety, and the panic of confronting past trauma. But gradually, she says, she released her urge to repress her fears and came to experience a sense of overpowering humility.

In time, she would learn to find a balanced mode in which she would spend twenty minutes, in her words, "in a state that was simultaneously orgasmic and meditative." Finally, during one stroking session, she now recalls, "Everything flared open. I knew my life was changed. All the tentacles of your sexuality are repositioned, placing the locus inside of you rather than outside of yourself, so you aren't bullied by your sexuality. You can use it, aim it, and direct it. A really deep meditative practice will rock your world."

————

"I got rebellious," says Nicole Daedone. "I went nuts. I got obsessed. I lost myself." She began integrating sex into her life as a way of embracing, not dulling, both her human fears and her deepest spiritual yearnings. She lived in various, usually nameless communal retreats in the Bay Area and near the Oregon border. One community, she says, "was like a yoga ashram based around sexuality." She would learn from Ray Vetterlein, who according to the *New York Times* "achieved fame of sorts in sex circles by claiming to lengthen the average female orgasm to 20 minutes." Vetterlein, says Daedone today, "shifted my perspective of what a relationship with a man could be like. He was willing to be a man in service to opening a woman's orgasm." She would meet the purported father of orgasmic meditation, Victor Baranco, who, in her words, "codified and put the practice together. He's the person who said there's a way that you can have a sexual practice of stroking a woman's clitoris that can have profound implications."

Looking back, she says diplomatically, the overly loose structure of the settings made it impossible "to prevent inevitable problems from arising," and some of the men took advantage of the system and the women. So she decided to branch out on her own. She spread the word of the virtues of orgasms by, for, and about *the woman*. Daedone had found herself. She had found her calling too. Her revelation, first received on a hot night in 1997, had become the foundation for a career and a way of being.

Today, after giving and receiving what she calls "several million strokes in my time," she is America's leading OM advocate. With her book *Slow Sex*, an online business, her erotica blog, various demonstration videos and seminars, as well as her orgasmic centers—called OneTaste[7]—Daedone, now in her

————

7. According to Reese Jones, Daedone's partner for a number of years, "OneTaste comes from the Buddhist term, 'Once you've experienced one taste of the divine, nothing else will do.'" The name

late forties, presides over a growing organization. There is a OneTaste product line: pillows, instructional videos, OneStroke natural nonallergenic beeswax lube. There are workshops, coaching programs, and classes with titles such as "Advanced OM" and "Ignited Man II." (The $1,000-a-month residency programs—and the naked yoga sessions—have been discontinued.) There is a retreat center in the wilds of California's Mendocino County. Press coverage has painted OneTaste as everything from a meditative practice to an erotic fitness craze to a cult.

The faithful come every day for two or three sessions. The most observant practitioners gather in a common room, pair off, and engage in OM—the men (and women) stroking reclining women. They call out their own sensations, reinforcing a synchronous feedback loop as their limbic systems kick in. *SF Weekly* has described the scene this way: "Most pair up as 'research partners' to explore sensuality with one another. That can mean simply sharing a bed, making out, having intercourse, or some level of intimacy in between. Research partnerships can last for as short as a week or for more than a year. While some at OneTaste are monogamous, many are not." Says Daedone, "The men who come to the center don't care if it's female-centric.... They get more than they could ever want. It's *too* much. A woman in that state—she'll want to devour a man."

The rise of a practice devoted to transcendence through orgasm would parallel the rise of yoga in the '90s. Looking back, Nicole considers the '80s women's fitness boom (Jazzercise, the Jane Fonda Workout, homebodies watching aerobics videos) as "a nationwide wave of people alone in their living rooms trying to V-step and grapevine their way to tighter buns, thighs, and abs. By the end of the decade, [that] wave collapses because it can't support itself on a model that's so geared around looks, achievement, and isolation. It's like the McDonald's version of fitness—empty calories. Eventually they need something nourishing and connected. So in the '90s yoga reenters the picture."

Yoga, in its way, opened the door for OM. "Vibrators and Internet porn and...hookups," Daedone notes, were fast becoming "the primary

---

OM is borrowed from the term "om," Sanskrit in origin, that is, according to Merriam-Webster, "a mantra consisting of the sound 'om' and used in contemplation of ultimate reality...a sacred syllable considered the greatest of all mantras." (Interview with Reese Jones.)

portal through which people access[ed] sex in the twenty-first century [in tandem with a corresponding rise in] erectile dysfunction, hypoactive desire disorder in women, and increasing social isolation, [which had] reach[ed] chronic levels.... Enter OM, a 2.0 version of sex that...bring[s] the same level of consciousness and connection that yoga brought to the world of fitness."

According to OneTaste doctrine, "In concrete terms, we define orgasm as the moment the involuntary musculature of the body is activated. One may exist in this state for extended periods of time without 'going over.' More abstractly, we define orgasm as the energy that exists in all living things at all times."[8]

---

8. Is there a serious pitfall in devoting so much of one's raison d'être to sex—and to this narrowly directed technique? One former OM-er told the *New York Times* that she and her partner had left the OneTaste scene because they hoped to embark on new paths that were more "heart-focused rather than genital-focused." To some critics, devoting daily (and arguably obsessive) attention to the mechanics of the female orgasm—instead of developing a more balanced interaction that accommodates both partners' overall needs, sexual and otherwise—poses the risk of encouraging practitioners who might become sexually stuck, literally fixated on one partner's clitoris above all else. Daedone counters this argument. "It's an hour a day for most people in this practice," she insists. What's more, the meditative side of OM, she says, benefits "many other aspects of one's life. You're cultivating attention."

I make the point to Daedone that obsessed strokers can seem like compulsive long-distance runners, some of whom acquire a mental or physical need to put their bodies through high-impact strain, perhaps putting themselves at risk for long-term health problems. Couldn't the practice prove limiting to one's sexuality and, more important, to one's emotional balance? On the contrary, she says, science now suggests that extreme athletes have a way of ascending to an elevated state that provides them with "sustained access" to a higher state of consciousness. She contends that "musicians, artists, extreme athletes" tap into what is sometimes called "flow"—a notion coined in the 1960s and '70s by Hungarian psychologist Mihaly Csikszentmihalyi and then popularized in four of his books published in the 1990s. Says Daedone, "It's that sense of being 'in the zone,' of being so absorbed and consumed by the moment that you lose track of time and even one's own awareness of self."

The science writer Steven Kotler, cofounder of the Flow Genome Project, has also pointed out certain neurochemical similarities between the "flow" experiences of those engaged in orgasmic meditation and extreme sports—indeed, across all altered states of consciousness. "OM-ing on a certain level," he says, "no matter how you slice it, is a form of basic, low-grade masturbation. But Nicole has turned it into a practice thick with flow triggers. There's sexual stimuli. There's also scary, heavy, emotional stuff going on. She's harnessing that attention and using it to serve as a focusing mechanism and turn it into a mindfulness process." (Patricia Leigh Brown and Carol Pogash, "The Pleasure Principle," *New York Times*, March 13, 2009; Mary Spicuzza, "Sex and Sexuality," *SF Weekly*, April 4, 2007; John Geirland, "Go with the Flow" (interview with Csikszentmihalyi), *Wired*, September 1996; interviews with Daedone, Kotler, and Dr. Patrick Carnes.)

When I meet Nicole and her then partner Reese Jones for drinks in New York, they suggest I come out to San Francisco. (Jones is a visionary tech entrepreneur whom I have known for many years.) They insist I'll benefit from witnessing a "demo," a sort of OneTaste graduation. At a typical demo, they explain, a woman who has been in the practice for several years—and who is poised to become a more senior instructor—presents herself to an assembly of OM-ers who observe her being stroked for forty minutes nonstop.[9]

How can I refuse? I immediately invite my wife, Nancy, to join me. If there's *any* research expedition for this book that might benefit both of us, this could be it.

A few months later, we find ourselves crossing the Golden Gate Bridge, then descending through mountainous passes toward Stinson Beach, northwest of Sausalito. It is nighttime. It is raining. Lightning illuminates the way. Reese Jones is behind the wheel, with Nicole beside him. Nancy and I are off to our first demo.

We arrive to thunderclaps. We approach a ranch house, set amid gardens and a lily pond. This is the Chevalier Estate, a retreat that OneTaste uses for what it calls invitation-only experiences. In the 1920s, Jones explains, the basement housed a speakeasy, stocked by local rumrunners. For years it was owned by Haakon Chevalier, a French lit professor at UC Berkeley. Local lore has it that during the '40s, physicist Robert Oppenheimer, also on the Berkeley faculty, used to repair here to plan the Manhattan Project, the program that gave birth to the atomic bomb.

As we enter, the parlor has the feel of a chalet. Trays of vegetables and snacks have been laid out. A few dozen young and middle-aged adults (two-thirds of them women) mill around, many dressed in dark, casual clothes. The vibe is expectant but unsettled, like the lull before a wedding ceremony at which the bride is running late and the bar is not yet open.

A double door swings wide to a large living room with dark wood paneling

---

9. The term "demo" has a techie ring to it—with a dash of '50s and '60s engineering, test-pilot, and studio recording culture (not to mention counterculture "happenings" and peaceful protests, sometimes called "demos"), as well as the long-running "demo days" at MIT's Media Lab and similar facilities.

and a crackling fire. The setting recalls Sherlock Holmes's study, with a touch of Goth: candelabra with flickering tapers, brocaded sofas, bookshelves, and a wall of heavy drapes that muffle the sound of pelting rain. There are Persian carpets, a piano, roses in a vase. A Mac provides the soundtrack: the subtle throbbing of drums. Straight-backed chairs with plush cushions have been set in rows ceremonially on either side of a center aisle, facing a makeshift stage set. This is *Young Frankenstein* meets *Eyes Wide Shut*.

Up front by the closed curtains, in the manner of an altar or a nineteenth-century operating theater, a bed has been rolled in, on risers, next to a stepstool. The end of the bed (more like a massage table fitted with white sheets and pillows) is directly in front of the chairs, its head slightly elevated so that the "audience" will have a clear view of its occupant. Nearby, a video camera is affixed to a tripod; the session will be streamed live to OneTaste staffers unable to attend the demo.

Forty-two "witnesses" take their seats and wait, speaking softly. The sound of a single guitar is piped in. An officiate emerges and stands next to the bed. "Welcome to the demonstration," says Justine, twenty-four, a pale blonde woman dressed in a jet-black blouse and tights. "Everybody, please turn your phones to vibrate." Vibrate it is.

"Tonight we're all here to experience the energy in the room," she says. The evening's designated graduate, Racheli, she explains, has been in practice for three years; her partner-stroker, Ken, for almost ten. "Your job is to experience a woman having an orgasm for forty minutes. Be open to it all. As Racheli's being stroked, she's open to feeling all of us in the room and she's sending back out energy—involuntary energy. This is a dress rehearsal for what women do as a 'coming-out' experience—eventually [experiencing] an hour in orgasm.

"People will be invited to come up to the table [and observe] closely. Speak whatever sensation you're feeling…experiencing: fear, elation, whatever. Look for signs of orgasm: a flushing of her cheeks; dark circles under her eyes…fluttering of her stomach."

Nicole sits in the front row, ready to chime in or assist. A spotter named Robert minds the clock. A young bald techie operates the Web feed, the music, the camera.

Ken walks in, stage left. He is stocky and wears a red plaid flannel shirt. He pulls on latex gloves.

Racheli emerges in a silver robe. A petite, almost frail twenty-nine-year-old redhead, she looks innocently nervous. She has been preparing for this day for nearly a year. She hugs Nicole, then drops the robe. Naked, she climbs onto the bed, lies down, and greets the crowd with a playful Charlie Chaplin wave.

Pillows are arranged under each haunch, along with a white towel. Ken leans over and begins to massage her thighs. "This helps 'ground' her," he says, addressing the audience, though facing his partner. Her legs splay open. "This is her anus. Above the anus, this fold is called the perineum..."

The music shifts to chanting and thumping drums and Ken starts stroking. Almost immediately, Racheli shifts too. She sighs "heh-huh-huh" repeatedly, her toes curling, then her fingers. Nicole advises, aloud, "Start a downstroke to bring her back into her body." Soon comes the sound of maracas, bongos, a bass guitar. Racheli's breathing gets heavier. Her pert breasts rise and fall, in time with the strokes, the thickening bass beat.

Justine, standing off to the side, moderates, "Racheli's belly is starting to really shake. Her lips and her upper torso are quivering."[10] Ken, ever stroking, tells the audience, "Her clit just grabbed on to my finger." Her legs shake and flutter. "The clitoris is like a spinning top," he says, "now spinning by itself." Racheli's hand echoes Ken's, middle finger extended, stroking.

A bearded man in the audience begins a soft shimmy in his seat. Some women near him, in high black boots, keep their legs wide as they watch; others sit cross-legged, hands folded, motionless. Several audience members twitch silently. Others emit reactions: "My whole body's molasses...Warm and cool undulations...Waves of light walking over me."

Nicole gives encouragement: "There we go, Ken, that's a beautiful stroke." Justine offers the play-by-play: "We're thirteen minutes in..." Ken calls for more lube.

The audio switches to trance dance, Gabrielle Roth's New Age song "Flowing": *Each moment giving birth to the next...* Ken's gloves glisten. Racheli grabs his back, occasionally stroking his hunched frame as he strokes. Leaning over her, his face and shoulders bent down, "Ken looks"—says my wife, Nancy, whispering—"like a plumber. And that flannel *shirt.* Is he a lumberjack?" Nancy occasionally rolls her eyes at me. (Translation: *You're not*

---

10. After the session, Racheli, in a bathrobe, gives me a postmortem: "I'd shaken before but not like *that.* That was like being plugged into a light socket. The difference [was that] there were fifty people [in the room]." At an early stage, she says, "I heard a growl, like, *Growl.* And I heard someone in the room do the same growl. And it was like a pitched resonance, like a tuning fork. At one point, tears were rolling down my face."

buying *this, are you?*) She adds, "I find this the height of self-absorption. And it's *tedious.*"

To *this* witness, admittedly, the setting is much more clinical and much less sensual than the hype or the trappings would have led me to believe. But I am drawn to the vibe, resisting my wife's skepticism. There is a distinctive, musky tingle in the air—a corona of fever and danger and animal heat. Perhaps that tingle comes from the instantaneous decay of the Eros across the room, a charge that sizzles out over the crowd like rays from Oppenheimer's unstable atoms.

Nancy aside, the room *is* buying it. The rows of witnesses seem to comprise a closed circuit: here and there, people rock to and fro. Many seem in sync with the couple in a sort of libido feedback.

Robert the spotter signals "twenty minutes" to Justine. And suddenly Nicole has left her seat and is standing beside the bed. She wears a black cocktail dress with a plunging neckline. She tugs on gloves and steps in, as Ken recedes.

Nicole places a latex hand on Racheli's thigh, then sets to it. Nicole's strokes are more rhythmic than Ken's, applied with increasing intensity. This is not the "slow sex" she writes about. This is contact jai alai. Her head bobs, bobs, her own chest shivering. Racheli's breathy moans rise, subside, and rise. Nicole Daedone is a safecracker, placing her ear close in, her face almost brushing Racheli's thigh, as if listening. She's a symphony conductor—in the last movement of Liszt.

Soon Nicole is openmouthed, then she grits her teeth. As she bobs, the black sash of her dress seems entangled in Racheli's moist center. Nicole keeps removing juice from the canal with a flick of a gloved hand. On she strokes, and on, her hips bumping into the bed like a pile driver in slow-mo. The pair seem to undulate, a Picasso canvas come alive.

I walk to the back of the room for a breather and see that a woman in black seems to be pressing herself against the hard-angled edge of a doorframe. The crowd offers up deep breaths or quivers or soft peals of joyous laughter. Occasionally, individuals come up for a closer view. One by one, as if receiving the sacrament or paying respects at a wake, they approach, stand in silence for a moment, and take it all in—radiant flesh and blotchy swellings, the flushing and panting and swollen genitalia—and then return to their seats.

Racheli rises to Nicole's touch. There is shimmying. There is *huhh, unnhh, hunnh.* There is, coming from Racheli, something like rapture.

The spotter motions, "time." And Nicole "grounds" Racheli, patting her own hand as it clasps her there, firmly. Then, after a time, Racheli rises from the table, cheeks flushed, in blissful, dazed relief, and she gives Nicole a hug.

———

Perhaps orgasmic meditators are on to something, a kind of clitoral affirmative action in a culture where sex has too often been weighted toward men's desires. This is a very '90s concept—the sex-positive woman taking charge. During the decade, says Reese Jones, "sex-positive sex or safer sex or militant lesbianism came to the fore because sex became a public-health issue [in the face of] AIDS in the '80s. So you had to talk about the distinction between sex for procreation and sex for pleasure. Sex for pleasure [helped shape] the '60s, but it became key again in the '90s."

But it is time to take a deep breath, collect oneself, and return, clear-headed, to 1992.

CHAPTER 10

Culture Warriors, Man Your Battle Stations

There is a religious war going on in this country. It is a cultural war, as critical to the kind of nation we shall be as the Cold War itself, for this war is for the soul of America. And in that struggle for the soul of America, Clinton and Clinton are on the other side, and George Bush is on our side.

—Patrick Buchanan, GOP presidential candidate and conservative commentator, addressing the Republican National Convention in Houston (August 17, 1992)

In the 1980s, human sexuality in some respects had become not just a matter of left and right but of life and death. Communities began losing legions to AIDS. Protestors took to the streets, promoting the battle cry "Silence = Death." There was an escalation in assaults on individuals because of their sexual orientation. Meanwhile, antiabortion advocates mobilized to defend the rights of "the unborn"—a decade after the medical procedure had gained legal sanction. Operation Rescue and other groups pushed for a pro-life amendment; activists blocked the entrances to family planning clinics, and resorted to death threats, bombing, vandalism—and even murder.

With certain sexual frontiers becoming ever more politicized in public life, factions on both sides of the political, social, and cultural barricades became as polarized as their counterparts had been in the '60s and '70s. And many were primed for a fight.

Now came the word "war," as in "culture war." The phrase, coined by social conservatives, was not meant figuratively—at least not entirely. "War" implied two factions whose competing claims had deteriorated into outright conflict. To call this cultural divide a war, surely, was overreaching. But such was the terminology attached to what many on the right perceived as a precipitous downgrade in "values": a perceived deemphasis in society on so-called family values or traditional values or Judeo-Christian values. This cultural shift, in the view of conservatives and the religious right, had been nurtured for the previous thirty-odd years by the country's more liberal forces and constituted a threat to the moral bedrock of civilized society.

By the 1990s, pop culture had gone crude. Pornography was rampant. Casual sexual encounters were more prevalent and less stigmatized. There was an upsurge in cases of sexually transmitted disease. To compound the matter, "the divorce rate remains, stubbornly, one in two," journalist Joe Klein would calculate in a 1992 *Newsweek* cover story (headlined "Whose Values?"). "The out-of-wedlock birthrate has tripled since 1970....A nauseating buffet of dysfunctions has attended these trends—an explosion in child abuse, crime...name your pathology."

Neither side *sanctioned* any of these developments. But the left and the right laid down a set of cultural demarcation lines, as if to stake out their turf and delineate the three most contentious social issues of the day. First: whether, and in what circumstances, a woman should have the legal and medical means to manage her own reproductive health and, if necessary, terminate an unwanted pregnancy. Second: how to improve the sorry state of marriage and divorce. Finally: whether someone who identified as lesbian or gay should be accorded a wider range of civil rights, including the right to a state-sanctioned same-sex union.

Bill and Hillary Clinton happened to be in the left place at the right time. In the seven months between their *60 Minutes* appearance and the Republican National Convention, the couple became a lightning rod for animosity toward those who would defend one's right to choose—and one's right to love whomever one chose. Despite Clinton's broad appeal in his national debut, he and his wife, proud feminists both, were being widely vilified. They were the dreaded duo of the counterculture, so said Republicans, evangelicals, right-wing radio hosts, policy journals, and secular and religious conservatives. They were viewed as the flightiest of '60s free birds, whose liberal—even sinful—beliefs had finally come home to roost.

If that weren't enough of a cross to bear, they were doubly resented for having voiced the desire to reverse the self-centeredness of the Me-Decade '70s and the Reagan '80s. "[The pair were] trying to turn around the greed of the 1980s, change the values, move the country into a new era, still unknown and still not fully defined," journalist Bob Woodward would note. "They were paying the price of being transitional figures."

Nineteen ninety-two, as we will see shortly, would be punctuated by a series of cultural skirmishes in New Hampshire and Hollywood, San Francisco and New York. Then, in August, came the culture-war war games in Houston, where the far right, at the Republican National Convention, officially put its commandos on a war footing.

Not until November of that year would the smoke clear to reveal that Washington, at long last, had fallen. And in the light of the new dawn, it was instantly apparent: the most divisive battles still lay ahead.

But we return, first, to March madness.

————

First, there had been the Gennifer Flowers flap. Next, the draft-dodging flop. Then Bill Clinton put his foot in his mouth in an altogether new way. "I experimented with marijuana a time or two, and I didn't like it," he remarked at a New York forum. "I didn't inhale, and didn't try it again."[1]

Many scratched their heads. He occasionally smoked weed...but didn't *inhale*? What was the point of doing *that*? Surely he realized that such a comment, like his adultery concession, would come across yet again as dissembling—by a man who wanted to have his doob and smoke it too?[2]

And yet Clinton's experiments with pot, to some voters, may have actually *earned* him points. Here was a candidate who'd hit the Boomer Trifecta. He'd admitted to sexual adventurousness. He'd resisted service in Vietnam, a war he had outspokenly opposed. And now he was copping to the occa-

————

1. The comment about not inhaling would be one of only three Clinton gems to make their way, initially, into *Bartlett's Familiar Quotations*. The other two quotes (described later in this book) also grew out of Clinton mastery of truth's elasticity: "I did not have sexual relations with that woman, Miss Lewinsky," and "It depends on what the definition of the word 'is' is...." (Ellen Warren and Terry Armour, "Clinton Getting Familiar with Bartlett's," *Chicago Tribune*, March 18, 2001; Joe Klein, *The Natural: The Misunderstood Presidency of Bill Clinton* [New York: Doubleday, 2002], 11.)

2. The inhalation part may have been too coy by half. My late friend and colleague Christopher Hitchens, hardly a Clinton fan, had attended Oxford in the late '60s while young Bill was there on a Rhodes Scholarship. Hitchens would contend in his memoir, *Hitch-22*, "[Clinton had] always been allergic to smoke and he preferred, like many another marijuana enthusiast, to take his dope in the form of large handfuls of cookies and brownies." (Christopher Hitchens, *Hitch-22* [New York: Twelve, 2010], 106.)

sional joint—a badge of honor to many (yet something no serious national candidate had ever dared declare). When Bush's campaign director, Mary Matalin, later tarred him as "a pot-smoking, womanizing draft-dodger," the label, in certain quarters, was met with nods of approval.

By the spring, Clinton would lap the rest of the candidates in the primary field, facing his only serious challenge from Jerry Brown, the former governor of California. By June, Clinton would officially claim the nomination—with a big win in Brown's home state. But California, for all its sunshine, also reverberated with the clamor of the culture war's war drums.

Two weeks earlier, Vice President Dan Quayle had visited the state and addressed the Commonwealth Club, up in San Francisco. Quayle was the sandy-haired, rock-ribbed conservative who'd hired the young über-con Bill Kristol as his chief of staff. Quayle relished his role as Bush's attack dog, calling himself the campaign's "pit bull terrier."[3] In a speech entitled "Reflections on Urban America," the former Indiana senator had called out Hollywood for sending mixed and troublesome messages about single parenthood and proper childrearing.

There was considerable bite to his bark. Just before Quayle's speech, CBS happened to have aired an episode of its popular sitcom *Murphy Brown.* The title character, an unmarried TV news reporter played by Candice Bergen, was about to give birth, having become pregnant nine months earlier by her ex-husband. And that evening, on prime-time television, she delivered a baby boy, whom she'd decided to raise on her own. The episode drew more than thirty-eight million viewers.

Quayle was appalled. To the vice president—and to a sizable segment of the American public—the network, the show's writers, and the glamorous actress were glamorizing single motherhood. Quayle, who admitted he'd never watched an episode of the program, went on the warpath. "Bearing babies irresponsibly is simply wrong," said the father of three. "Failing to support children one has fathered is wrong. We must be unequivocal about this. It doesn't help matters when prime-time TV has Murphy Brown, a character who supposedly epitomizes today's intelligent, highly paid professional

3. Clinton's retort: "When asked about it, I said Quayle's claim would strike terror into the heart of every fire hydrant in America." (Bill Clinton, *My Life* [New York: Vintage/Random House, 2004], 412.)

woman, mocking the importance of fathers by bearing a child alone and calling it just another 'lifestyle choice.'"[4]

The reaction was thunderous on all sides. Some bridled at the unavoidable subtext of class war and bigotry. Many asked whether a male politician
should be weighing in so forcefully on an issue best left to a woman and
her physician. Others wondered how a mythical TV mom could be made
the whipping gal for far more complicated social, economic, and familial
issues. "I have an announcement here for the vice president of the United
States," quipped late-night TV host David Letterman. "Murphy Brown is a
fictional character." *Entertainment Weekly* called the attack a "Scud bombing
of Murphy.... Would Quayle be appeased if Murphy gave up her fatherless
child to [TV's] Major Dad, to be raised by a proper sitcom family?" The
show's creator, Diane English, would chime in: "If the vice president thought
a woman was incapable of adequately raising a child without a father, he
ought to make sure that abortion remained safe and legal." English would
later posit that the government's role in women's health care choices would
become "the tipping point in a debate that raged on throughout the summer
[of 1992], pitting liberal ideas of an ever-evolving notion of family against the
traditional concept of mom, dad and 2.5 kids."

It turned out to be a spirited and instructive debate. Many sociologists and family experts defended Quayle. They believed he'd succeeded in
drawing attention to the problems faced by single mothers and their children in a way that was reminiscent of a still-controversial 1965 report by
Daniel Patrick Moynihan, later a distinguished Democratic senator from
New York. Moynihan, then with the Labor Department, had pointed out
a cycle: in many households in which black Americans lived at or below the
poverty line, there was a correlation between the single parent (typically an
unwed mother) and her child's lowered prospects for economic and social
advancement.[5]

---

4. Quayle's use of the term "lifestyle choice" was already politically incorrect, wincingly so.

5. When the report was made public, as columnist Nicholas Kristof would note on its fiftieth
anniversary, "Liberals brutally denounced Moynihan as a racist... [which was] terribly unfair. In fact,
Moynihan emphasized that slavery, discrimination and 'three centuries of injustice' had devastated
the black family. He favored job and education programs to help buttress the family.... [Eventually]
William Julius Wilson, an eminent black sociologist... praised Moynihan's report as 'a prophetic
document,' for evidence is now overwhelming that family structure matters a great deal for

In an influential *Atlantic* article entitled "Dan Quayle Was Right," social historian Barbara Dafoe Whitehead would offer hard data that supported the vice president's premise. She observed that the statistically "increasing numbers of single-parent and stepparent families"—whether by divorce, remarriage, abandonment, unwanted pregnancy, or independent choice—"dramatically weakens and undermines society." Whitehead wrote of a single-parent surge and a silent racial asymmetry in America: "The out-of-wedlock birth rate [had gone] from five percent in 1960 to 27 percent in 1990. In 1990 close to 57 percent of births among black mothers were nonmarital and about 17 percent among white mothers."

Quayle v. Brown dominated news and opinion outlets for weeks.[6] And as the campaign percolated along, an animated Quayle (a year younger than Clinton) cranked up his "commitment to values" shpiel: "The baby boomer generation was not homogenous. A lot of people [in that age bracket] are very concerned with values." At a rally in Louisville, Kentucky, the vice president spoke with a tremble in his voice, according to journalist Mimi Swartz in a profile of Quayle for *Life* magazine. He pronounced the V-word, Swartz recounted, "almost with a lover's gratitude, his vowels grow[ing] long and melodic.... 'I want to thank you for joining me on the crusade for family values,' he declares, fairly seething with righteous indignation. 'No matter what

---

low-income children of any color." (Nicholas Kristof, "When Liberals Blew It," *New York Times*, March 12, 2015, A29.)

6. The subject flared again two months before the election, when Murphy Brown, the ersatz TV newswoman, appeared in the show's season premiere and spoke of Dan Quayle, the actual VP: "Perhaps it's time for the vice president to expand his definition and recognize that whether by choice or circumstance, families come in all shapes and sizes." This time the show drew an audience of between forty and seventy million (sources range widely)—including Quayle, who for a photo op was joined by five single parents.

That sentiment would be echoed a year later, articulated by another popular fictional character: Mrs. Doubtfire, played by Robin Williams. In the film of the same name, Williams's character, a father who loses custody of his children, becomes a nanny in drag in order to spend quality time with his kids. (Talk about a committed '90s dad.) Quoth Mrs. D., "There are all sorts of families, Katie. Some families have one mummy, some families have one daddy, or two families....If there's love, dear, those are the ties that bind, and you'll have a family in your heart forever." (Mark Harris, "'Murphy Brown's' Rebuke," *Entertainment Weekly*, October 2, 1992; Jonah Goldberg, "The Wisdom of Dan Quayle," *Los Angeles Times*, March 26, 2013; Greg Braxton and John M. Broder, "It's Murphy Brown's Turn to Lecture Vice President," *Los Angeles Times*, September 22, 1992; "Life Remembers '92," *Life*, January 1993, 48; Tim Teeman, "How Robin Williams' Mrs. Doubtfire Won the Culture Wars," TheDailyBeast.com, August 13, 2014.)

they say, I will never, never back down from talking about the importance of values.'...It is Quayle's peculiar gift that he can convince a crowd that it takes courage to come out for values."

In truth, what other choice did he have? Quayle could hardly run on his boss's domestic record. The country's economy was adrift. And although Bush had tried radical surgery (putting tax increases in play while negotiating a budget compromise in 1990; hammering out a politically convoluted budget deal with Congress in 1991), everything had fallen short. The sinking recession took a double dip, and the national tide turned against him.

The Democrats smelled fear and panic.

It was all augured in a placard that James Carville, Clinton's field marshal, had posted at their Little Rock campaign headquarters: "The economy, stupid."[7] These became the bywords of the Clinton campaign. America's financial concerns might be better served, they argued, by a man who, in contrast to Bush, had balanced a budget—eleven times.

America, after a dozen years of Ronnie and Poppy, seemed primed for a generational change. And Clinton, mining this vein, picked a running mate who was nineteen months *younger* than he. His name was Al Gore—a Tennessee senator, as his father had been. Gore, like Clinton, was a telegenic southern moderate. Yet he also helped tick off three boxes *outside* the Clinton column: Gore had served in Vietnam, he was straitlaced, and he gave every indication of being a thoroughly devoted husband.[8] The candidates were the A.B.B. twins: Anything But Bush.

They were also a Boomer two-fer. Clinton was the younger, gentler Elvis. He and his wife were inspired to name their daughter Chelsea after hearing Judy Collins's version of Joni Mitchell's "Chelsea Morning." And Gore had not only roomed at Harvard with the actor Tommy Lee Jones, but one of their school acquaintances, the author Erich Segal, had borrowed attributes of Jones and a dollop of Gore when fashioning Oliver Barrett IV, the preppie scion in the novel (and film) *Love Story*. Bill and Al nonetheless positioned

---

7. "It's the economy, stupid"—the Clinton camp's internal slogan for the campaign, coined by Carville—was derived from the sign on the wall at headquarters, which said, in full, "Change vs. more of the same. The economy, stupid. Don't forget health care." (Michael Kelly, "The 1992 Campaign: The Democrats—Clinton and Bush Compete to Be Champion of Change; Democrat Fights Perceptions of Bush Gain," *New York Times*, October 31, 1992.)

8. Twenty-five years later, the Gores lead separate lives.

themselves as forward-thinking populists committed to the salt of the American earth. Clinton, in choosing Gore, was making a clear break with the past and doubling down on tomorrow.

The challenge was clear. The Clinton-Gore camp believed they just might be able to win by pummeling Bush on the economy. But was that alone enough? As they set their sights on July's Democratic National Convention in Manhattan, a secondary strategy arose: could they also find a way to reposition their candidacy and gain the upper hand in the "values" war, thereby beating the Republicans at their own game?

The Democrats descended on Madison Square Garden. Staff passes for convention floor access bore a caricature that, at a glance, looked like Elvis Presley, a riff on a recently designed stamp from the U.S. Postal Service. But instead of displaying the King with a mic in his hand, these tags bore an illustration of the Guv—with a sax. At the same time, buttons were handed out, courtesy of Zenith and AT&T, hawking an as-yet-untested technology: digital high-def TV ("I Saw the Future at the 1992 Democratic National Convention"). These tags and badges graced the proud breasts of a convention crowd as diverse as any in American history. "Separatism is not the American Way," Barbara Jordan, the former Texas congresswoman, would say in her keynote speech. "We must profoundly change from the deleterious environment of the '80s, characterized by greed, selfishness, mega-mergers, and debt... to one characterized by devotion to the public interest and tolerance. And, yes, love." The Dems were feelin' the love.

Two of the Clintons' closest Hollywood pals, Harry Thomason and Linda Bloodworth-Thomason, made a short video, *The Man from Hope*. It painted Bill as the small-town boy made good. And it spent a full minute discussing his father's alcoholism. Elizabeth Glaser, active in the fight against AIDS, would talk of having contracted the disease through a transfusion and unknowingly passing it along to her late daughter, by nursing her, and to her young son, in utero. Al Gore, after striding to the lectern to the strains of Paul Simon's "You Can Call Me Al," would describe the night he held his six-year-old son in his arms after a car crash that almost took the boy's life.

Something was being hatched here that went beyond the rainbow crowd and the Boomer references. The convention's speakers, in offering their own accounts of adversity, were interlacing their life stories with similar strands among those watching at home. Here was a relatively untested way to express a political party's values: let its representatives acknowledge their struggles, thereby creating an appearance of commonality through candor. These New Democrats were developing a new kind of stagecraft to connect with voters. "We live in the age of the personalization of everything," writer Richard Todd would later remark, an age in which "our political life doesn't depend on a direct relationship between the governed and the governing, it depends on the ability of the governing to tell stories about [themselves and] the governed, to speak as if they know us."

On the final night, Clinton accepted his party's nomination—and tried to close the deal. He took Quayle's "family" fight, head-on. "Frankly," he insisted, "I'm fed up with politicians in Washington lecturing the rest of us about family values. Our families have values. But our government doesn't. I want an . . . America that includes every family. Every traditional family and every extended family. Every two-parent family, every single-parent family, and every foster family. Every family."

He spoke of his own upbringing, partly playing off the *Murphy Brown* showdown, and spoke of having been born into a loving single-parent household. "I can still see [my mother] clearly tonight through the eyes of a three-year-old," he said, repeating a story he'd told often that year, "kneeling at the railroad station and weeping as she put me back on the train to Arkansas [to stay] with my grandmother. She endured that pain because she knew her sacrifice was the only way she could support me and give me a better life."

In articulating what he liked to call his New Covenant, Clinton hoped to effectively sweep the Republicans' "values" monopoly off the game board: "The choice we offer is not conservative or liberal. In many ways, it is not even Republican or Democratic. It is different. It is new."[9] Mocking the dichotomy that conservatives were putting forward, he argued that "for too long politicians have told [us] . . . that what's really wrong with America is the rest of us—*them*. Them, the minorities. Them, the liberals. Them, the homeless. Them, the poor. Them, the people with disabilities. Them, the

---

9. Senator Barack Obama would explore the same theme when delivering the keynote address at the DNC in 2004: "Tonight, there is not a liberal America and a conservative America; there is the United States of America."

gays. We've gotten to where we've nearly 'them'd' ourselves to death. Them, and them, and them. But this is America. There is no them. There is only us.... And that's what the New Covenant is all about." Clinton's declaration was the first ever by a party's national candidate to address gay rights from the floor of a convention.

Implicit was the charge that the GOP was waging not just a culture war but a war on women—a constituency that Clinton's minions were counting on in the general election. The party was also making the case that it would govern not from the left but from the center: Democrats saw themselves as the defenders of the out-of-work, the working class, *and* the middle class. (The opposition was nonplussed. "I watched that giant masquerade ball up at Madison Square Garden," conservative firebrand Pat Buchanan would remark a month later at the GOP convention, "where twenty thousand liberals and radicals came dressed up as moderates and centrists—in the greatest single exhibition of cross-dressing in American political history.")

And then, the July surprise. On the last day of the convention, the independent third-party candidate Ross Perot, the Texas billionaire, stunned everyone with an announcement. He was dropping out of the race, and many pundits declared that the beneficiary of his withdrawal would be Clinton, the candidate whom voters seemed to prefer as a more trustworthy change agent. (The unpredictable Perot would then *reenter* the race in October, a month before the general election.)

Change was word one. As the convention came to a close, a single visual was singed into voters' minds. It was the sight of two young wives in gold (Hillary) and electric blue (Tipper), joined by their five children, ranging in age from nine to eighteen—alongside their husbands, who, if elected, would comprise the youngest ticket ever to make it to the White House. All that was missing was the dog and the Suburban. Caught up in the moment, they began dancing. And they started singing along to the campaign theme song, Fleetwood Mac's "Don't Stop (Thinking About Tomorrow)."

This image of vigor and pep and marital felicity took hold. In fact, just a week before the convention, the Clinton and Gore families had stood on the back porch of the governor's mansion in Little Rock. "We all watched that scene on the balcony," Mary Matalin would recount, summarizing the mood in the Bush trenches. "The reaction was, 'Oh, my God.' The Clintons, the Gores, all those beautiful kids in front of that quintessentially American red brick mansion, looking youthful and cheery...It was Nirvana, the pinnacle of political introductions. You couldn't have made up a better visual.... They had a perfect picture for their timely message: change, youth, dynamism....

"We were all awestruck. We were all clutching our stomachs."

————

If the '90s culture war had its death match, it was played out over four hot nights in Houston the week of August 17, 1992. The Republican hoedown, held in the Astrodome, featured a cast of forty-five thousand—all intent on diverting the Clinton-Gore Express.

Bush was pleased to be back in the state where he'd made his political hay. But the Astrodome, to be candid, hardly projected a twenty-first-century vibe. By the early '90s, the facility was already a relic. Erected in 1965 as the world's first domed stadium, it conveyed (as did the GOP itself, said the Democrats) an antiquated vision of what a *Jetsons*-esque future was supposed to look like. And outside and inside the hall, the signage set the trash-the-bastards theme. T-shirts advised: *Blame the Media*. Stickers urged: *Smile if you have had an affair with Bill Clinton*. One placard bore a cannabis logo: *Bill Clinton's smoking gun*. Another: *Woody Allen is Clinton's family values advisor*.

Meanwhile, a rearguard challenge had been mounted by the ultraconservative commentator Patrick Buchanan, who had secured nearly a quarter of all Republican support in the primaries. Bush, who was considered far too moderate for those on his right flank, had had to appease Buchanan's forces (religious conservatives would make up some 40 percent of the delegates) or have his convention implode. So to shore up their base, Bush and the GOP mandarins gave over large swaths of the party platform—and prime-time airtime—to the hard-liners.

The platform would be packed with a slate of provisos related to sexual mores, cultural kashrut, and the supremacy of the nuclear family. Entire passages read like war whoops: "Elements within the media, the entertainment industry, academia, and the Democratic Party are waging a guerrilla war against American values. They deny personal responsibility, disparage traditional morality, denigrate religion, and promote hostility toward the family's way of life." Pro-choice Republican Tanya Melich was on hand as they hammered out the fine print. In her book *The Republican War Against Women*, she remembers a hush falling over the room as the committee took up the "individual rights section, the prelude to the abortion plank." Representative Henry Hyde of Illinois at one session offered a stunning argument when discussing the need to protect the life of the fetus—at all costs. "I can't imagine a more egregious crime than rape," said Mr. Hyde. Even so, he added, "There is honor in having to carry to term, not exterminating the child." And still he went on, "From a great tragedy, goodness can come." A new concept: honor birthing.

Meanwhile, the platform identified the deviant who was hiding under every bed. It sought to ban gay marriage, adoption by gay couples, the sale of porn, and public funding that might be used to "subsidize obscenity and blasphemy masquerading as art." It called for "a human life amendment to the Constitution"; judicial appointments for those "who respect traditional family values and the sanctity of innocent human life"; and state laws that would make it a criminal act to knowingly pass along AIDS. There was even a call to overhaul the entire welfare system, which itself was phrased in sexual terms. (The current system, according to the platform, constituted an "anti-work and anti-marriage" pact with the poor that "taxes families to subsidize illegitimacy.") Instead of allowing public schools to provide birth control or abortion service referrals, the GOP pushed "abstinence education." To combat the spread of AIDS, the platform rejected "the distribution of clean needles and condoms" in favor of education programs that would "stress marital fidelity, abstinence, and a drug-free lifestyle."

Extreme forces had managed to commandeer the party's blueprint at the most critical, self-defining phase in the quadrennial election cycle. According to David Brock, a right-wing investigative reporter in the '90s (and, come the 2000s, a progressive pro-Clinton advocate and media watchdog), "The holy war broke out after four years of conservative disunity, frustration, and disappointment during the Bush presidency, in the midst of an economic downturn, a backlash against the gains of women and minorities, and a resurgent religious revival in what became known as the year of the 'angry white male.'...Through organization and sheer force of numbers, the religious right had won control of the conservative movement, and the movement, in turn, now was dictating Republican Party policy."

———

From hour one on night one, things got nasty. "We are America," Rich Bond, the head of the RNC, proclaimed on NBC. "These other people are not America."

The invocation, by Reverend D. James Kennedy, warned of a "godless trail to destruction" that might await the party faithful should they follow "atheists and secularists here in our midst." Addressing the Almighty, Kennedy drew an apocalyptic picture: "We have turned our back upon Thy laws by every imaginable immorality, perversion, vice, and crime; and even now a hideous plague stalks our land."

That was just an appetizer. The main course was offered up by Pat Buchanan, the conservative standard-bearer. Having roughed up (and then made his peace with) George Bush, Buchanan—a onetime *blusterkind* speechwriter in the Nixon White House—had earned enough delegate support and platform muscle to secure the evening's prize time slot: coming on just in front of the headliner, Ronald Reagan.

When Buchanan took the stage, he was the party's martinet. He wore a somber black suit, gestured with karate-style chops, and spoke with a preacher's cadence as he laid out a declaration of war. "There is a religious war going on in this country," he warned. "It is a cultural war, as critical to the kind of nation we shall be as the Cold War itself, for this war is for the soul of America."

He clearly defined the enemy. They were the Democrats—a collection of "malcontents," "prophets of doom," and "carping critics [who were hawking the] discredited liberalism of the 1960s...no matter how slick the package in 1992." They were Clinton and Gore, "the most pro-lesbian and pro-gay ticket in history." They were "Prince Albert" Gore and "Teddy" Kennedy. ("How many other sixty-year-olds do you know," Buchanan asked, "who still go to Florida for spring break?") They were "Clinton & Clinton," the designation meant to connote a family law firm, whom he accused of promoting an agenda that "would impose on America abortion on demand, a litmus test for the Supreme Court, homosexual rights, discrimination against religious schools, women in combat units—that's change, all right....And it is not the kind of change we can abide in a nation that we still call God's country."

In closing, Buchanan moved the fight to the streets, metaphorically, by juxtaposing his description of a "cultural war" with his depiction of National Guard units with "M-16s at the ready [who] had come to save the city of Los Angeles" during the riots that had convulsed the city and claimed more than sixty lives the previous spring. Just "as those boys took back the streets of Los

Angeles, block by block, my friends, we must take back our cities, and take back our culture, and take back our country."[10]

Buchanan's words played well in the Astrodome. "They walked out of here tonight enthusiastic," ABC's Ted Koppel told viewers at home. "They walked out of here with something that Republicans have not had for quite a few months: a sense of optimism." Buchanan, to many of the conservative faithful, had effectively deflected discussion of the tanking economy and focused instead on Clinton's Achilles' heel: public morals.

But at what price?

Even many Republicans recognized the language of race-baiting. Buchanan had stirred up images of urban riots and then pretended that liberal forces—the Democratic ticket, in particular—were fomenting "a religious war," "a cultural war," "a guerrilla war." But *he* was the one spoiling for a face-off. His brimstone conjured tent-show revivalists, brought to mind Huey Long and George Wallace, and foreshadowed the slurry of slurs issued during Donald Trump's 2016 campaign. (Buchanan, with his hair slicked slightly back and to the side, actually looked like a taller, trimmer version of Old Joe McCarthy.)

Columnist Molly Ivins, the humorist and avowed liberal, went so far as to compare Buchanan's rattled saber to those of the brownshirts: "It probably sounded better in the original German." Rachel Maddow, the liberal commentator, had tuned in that night from Philadelphia. She was nineteen at the time, having publicly identified herself as lesbian two years earlier, in her first year at Stanford. She would later note that Buchanan's appearance "hit her right between the eyes. He was, without euphemism, declaring that my own country was at war with me. I get it intellectually and strategically now, but at [that stage in my life] I only got it emotionally." David Brock, then a muckraker on the right, was watching the Buchanan speech from Provincetown, as a closeted gay man. That evening, as he would write in his memoir *Blinded by the Right*, he headed out for his "nightly tour of Provincetown's gay bars." The

---

10. Buchanan's is the misplaced pugnacity of the bully. Such inflated hostility would become a trusty Republican default position over the next generation. Unable to bully the Democrats? Gingrich shut down the government. Unable to retaliate against Osama bin Laden? George W. Bush attacked Iraq. Unable to articulate a coherent message? Donald J. Trump, donning the cloak of Buchanan and Steve Bannon, struck out at everyone: women and the media, Mexicans and Muslims, POWs ("I like people who weren't captured"), and the pope.

disconnect was jarring. "I could see the [Republican] party was making a tectonic shift, preaching hatred of government on the one hand, and calling for government enforcement of religiously ordained standards of personal conduct on the other.... The proverbial scales were starting to fall from my eyes."

That week, essayist Lance Morrow would file a column for *Time* insisting that the speech's thesis, as well as Buchanan's "bully mode—an appeal to visceral prejudices, not to American ideals"—had been stewing in the Republican cauldron for some twenty years. Buchanan, as a young Nixon speechwriter in the early '70s, had drafted a memo to the president urging him to slice the nation in half "and pick off 'far the larger half.'" Nixon indeed went after the Republican base and the sizable "silent majority" (a term the president himself had effectively used in the late '60s) and was handily reelected, trouncing George McGovern. That long-brewing culture war—dating back to Barry Goldwater, William F. Buckley Jr., and their peers—had finally come of age.

———

George H. W. Bush, on the convention's final night, restored some decorum to the proceedings. In contrasting *his* version of change with the young Arkansas governor's, the president implored, "Sure, we must change, but some values are timeless. I believe in families that stick together, fathers who stick around. I happen to believe very deeply in the worth of each individual human being, born or unborn.... Maybe that's why I've always believed that patriotism is not just another point of view." And indeed, the ticket left Houston with a bit of a bounce in the polls, slightly narrowing the gap with Clinton-Gore, to a slim nine points in some polls.

But the damage had been done. Bush-Quayle would never recover from what *Newsweek* would call "a four-day festival of fear and social antagonism." To the television audience, the Bush "coalition" had come across as fractured, exclusionary, and extremist. Buchanan's cavalry had in effect hijacked the convention—and the Republican Party. "Houston," Bush speechwriter David Frum (chairman of Policy Exchange, the U.K. think tank) would observe, "is now indelibly engraved in America's political memory as a disaster on the order of the Democrats' Chicago convention in 1968 or the Republicans' San Francisco convention of 1964"—not to mention Trump's ragtag rage-fest of 2016. In the end, much of the viewing public felt that the GOP leadership (who seemed out of step with society) and the party's functionaries (which seemed unwilling to accept people of color or of the nonheterosexual persuasion) were either politicized versions of their battier aunts and uncles or exiles from the Planet Wack.

The "Bush men," to use Frum's anthro-lingo, had only themselves to blame. It was not the far-right fringe, he believed, but the moderates—running the RNC, the campaign, and the convention—who had dictated the flow of the game in the Astrodome. "The convention reflected the Bush men's own conception of smart politics," Frum would surmise in his book *Dead Right*, two years after the fiasco. "Like tourists in Paris, they compensated for their lack of a conservative vocabulary and grammar by absurdly and exaggeratedly mimicking the accents and gestures of the people to whom they were trying to communicate."

Bush Men vs. Cultural Savages. The culture war had gone into high gear. And the young guns had the old guard in their crosshairs.

———

Before we move on from Houston to the general election, however, it's time for a side trip—to Silicon Valley.

CHAPTER 11

Wanderlust

Cyberspace—its early-'90s name—was a secret galaxy. Only those in a few bubble worlds were privy to its mysteries. To gain access, you had to be an academic or a scientist. Or someone in the military or the government. Or a computer hobbyist or a hacker. The early Net, like the tech world in general, was insular, elitist, geekcult.

Then, in a flash, in swept the multitudes. With the creation of the World Wide Web and the first Web browser, any fool civilian with dial-up and some cheap software could suddenly teleport to that stratosphere. And a traveler, once hurtled into that vaporous new realm, had to deal inexorably with the old in-out.

For all the pitfalls of an online existence (Handicap #1: massive time suck) and for all its upsides (the unhindered wanderlust, the personal empowerment, the ease of entry for those in search of information and connectivity), the medium would also plunge its users, if they so desired, into a raging ocean of sex. And not just good old garden-variety sex, but sex of such crazy category and range that it made Bosch and de Sade seem tame.

It might be called Tech's First Law of Sex (borrowing from Sir Isaac Newton—and the Book of Genesis). With each novel technology in communications or entertainment, the first app to fall from the tree is the Sex App. And porn, one of the basest expressions of human desire, is often the crowd-pleaser, offering the cheapest thrill and the quickest kick. According to Gerard Van der Leun in *Wired* magazine, it was none other than William Burroughs, the Beat writer and proud subversive, who considered sex to be "a virus that is always on the hunt for a new host—a virus that almost always infects new technology first."

Examples abound. After Gutenberg turned out the first printed Bible in the 1450s, virtually the second title off the movable-type press was a sampling of erotic prose.[1] With the advent of photography in the 1820s and '30s, it took only a few years before Paris photo studios would make a tidy sum selling erotic "art studies." Once Thomas Edison and the Lumière brothers created the earliest "moving" pictures, customers in the late 1800s were soon peering through peepholes at female dancers, nude bathers, and strippers teasing the eye. A century later, when videotape caught on, the VHS format (so legend had it) triumphed over Betamax because the latter neglected—or refused—to accommodate what was then called "porno." (This turned out to be a suburban strip-mall myth. JVC's VHS stole the market from Sony's Betamax not because of porn but primarily because Beta tapes ran for an hour, max, while VHS put out two-hour tapes—long enough to record an entire movie, porno or no.)[2]

Says Jane Metcalfe, cofounder of *Wired*, which was launched in the early '90s, "You see it with Hi8 [the early camcorder] or cable TV or BBS [the computer bulletin board system]. There were all of these virtual worlds evolving, and the anonymity that went along with that freed up a lot of libido.... It's worked for one technology after another, whether it was Betamax or the Minitel" (the French home-terminal service that in the 1980s became an electronic portal for erotic engagement, right in users' living rooms).

In this grand tradition, it would be hard to overstate the importance of sexual commerce as a crucial come-on in attracting the masses to the fledgling Web.

---

1. Or maybe erotica came *third*. "At one major [publishing] house," observes Ken Auletta in the *New Yorker*, "there is a running joke that the second book published on the Gutenberg press was about the death of the publishing business." (Ken Auletta, "Publish or Perish: Can the iPad Topple the Kindle, and Save the Book Business?," *New Yorker*, April 26, 2010, 26.)

2. What's more, the no-porn provision was simply false. "I *had* some tapes back then," says Betamax connoisseur Tony DiSanto, founding partner of DiGa and formerly MTV's head of programming. As a twelve-year-old, DiSanto would lug his bulky recorder to a friend's house to copy VHS movies onto Beta. "Beta's quality was far superior. VHS [ultimately cornered the market] because it licensed the format in partnership deals with everybody—with Panasonic and other companies. But Beta was better." Beta's superiority is still heatedly debated among tapeheads. (Interview with DiSanto; Jack Schofield, "Why VHS Was Better Than Betamax," *Guardian*, January 24, 2003, http://www.guardian.com/technology/2003/jan/25/comment.comment; John C. Dvorak, "Is Porn the Key to the High-Def DVD War?," PCMag.com, April 9, 2007.)

Among digital age savants, Michael Wolff is both a historian and an oracle. Now a well-known media columnist, he spent a long stretch of the 1990s putting out *NetGuide*, a printed road map to the Web. (It sounds utterly anti-quated today—a paper atlas for an electronic universe, updated every couple of weeks!—and yet *NetGuide* was a useful crib sheet for Internet newbies.) In his book *Burn Rate*, Wolff would chronicle his years in this digital dawn. "I remember when there was *no* porn on the Internet," he now says. "I won-dered why. And then suddenly it was everywhere—as if everyone was think-ing the same thought. With the Internet, you had people leading fantasy lives at a new velocity. It was no longer the spirit of the '60s and we're all liberated. Instead, it's private. It's all furtive…and it's *every*where."

Over a long lunch, he lays out a back-of-the-napkin history of the Net's erotic explosion in the '90s. Michael Wolff is an imposing presence, known for his contrarian, categorical pronouncements on media issues, as well as his withering critiques of the grandees of the infotainment industry. With his shaved head, severe brows, and long, coiled frame, which he cloaks in impec-cably tailored suits, he conveys the menace and tenacity of a raptor. Wolff's contention is that "dirty talk" (often referred to at the time as "hot chat") is really what kicked it all off. "AOL was an entire business founded on sex," he insists. "Companies in the early to mid-'90s all knew this and said, 'Our real revenues and Net traffic are about sex. Interactivity is really about sex.'"

Wolff speaks in a present tense that adds a volt of urgency. "In 1992," he says, "the Internet has become this academic network that had been built on the military's ARPANET. If you're on a campus, you have access. It's just text. It has no interface. There are a few specialty, clubby [platforms] like the WELL, ECHO, and MindVox. At the same time, you have these other systems that are consumer-driven: CompuServe and Prodigy…and AOL. These are closed systems—online bulletin boards. You cannot access them through the Internet.

"And AOL's first real competitive advantage is that it doesn't censor. Everybody else is censoring in a fairly heavy-handed way. They have corpo-rate owners; it never occurred to them *not* to censor [because] they don't want dirty stuff. AOL starts to figure out: this sex chat is an incredible driver. And they find out that not only do people like sex chat, but once you start, you cannot stop. And over the course of '92, '93, '94, AOL explodes on the basis of sex chat"—in which individuals flirt or share erotic fantasies or have suggestive conversations in the form of digital exchanges that they type on their keyboards. ("Some say [AOL] was the house that porn built," one ex-AOL manager tells me, requesting anonymity. "At places like Yahoo and elsewhere, monitors were brought in to clear up the chat rooms and take down inappropriate content. Not at AOL. The stance was: these are *private* areas.")

Wolff circles back again to describe those rudimentary networks. "There are parallel systems," he says, that are "not *actually* [part of] the Internet, but Internet-accessible: the newsgroup hierarchies....At its peak there are probably more than one hundred thousand of these. Then, at some point, the 'alt' hierarchy is created. And there grow hundreds and hundreds of essentially sex-related bulletin boards in every possible permutation....The original 'alt' newsgroups were entirely about sex. It suddenly was ushering in the age of the fetish.

"Just to give you an idea of what these alt.sex groups were like, Ben Greenman, now an editor and writer at the *New Yorker*, was one of the guys writing these synopses"—for the *NetGuide* that Wolff was publishing. "At the time he was about twenty-two. He wrote this thing—I fell down laughing when I read it. This is twenty years ago and I remember it perfectly. The group was alt.sex.spanking. I remember Ben wrote to describe it, 'If spankers had a nation, [this] would be their Congress.' So for the first time in human history we are segmenting sexual practice into communities.[3]

"Functionally," Wolff continues, "we have this thing going on on AOL as well as this thing going on on the Internet—still parallel cultures. But it's

---

3. In 1993, Gerard Van der Leun, in the first issue of *Wired*, wrote about new newsgroups that catered to "all sexual persuasions. For a while there was a group on the Internet called, in the technobabble that identified areas on the net, alt.sex.bondage.golden.showers.sheep. Most people thought it was a joke, and maybe it was." A year later Richard Kadrey, an editor at the edgy cybersex magazine *Future Sex*, would explain that within the universe of alt.sex newsgroups, alt.sex itself was the largest, acting as "a sort of stepping-stone to more specific (and adventurous) regions of sexspace." In second place: the S&M mecca alt.sex.bondage, also referred to as "asb." According to Kadrey, asb, in the early '90s, would become "one-stop shopping for both dominants and submissives, as well as general-interest perverts. The discussion topics range from broad questions...to the more specific [such as] 'How long can I safely leave clothespins on a friend's nipples?'" (Gerard Van der Leun, "This Is a Naked Lady," *Wired*, March/April 1993; Richard Kadrey, "Alt.sex.bondage," *Wired*, June 1994.)

contained. AOL is charging a lot. The Internet is accessible through arcane avenues—you jack in through a community college ID. You've got to be able to work UNIX code." Next, he recalls, "two things happen to open the Internet. First was the invention of the browser, in 1993." (The Web itself, created in the early 1990s, was a system of protocols spearheaded by physicist Tim Berners-Lee, who decided to offer them to users for free. Soon, software engineer Marc Andreessen and his colleagues would distribute Mosaic, the first popular Web browser. Shortly afterward came the first search engine and then, over time, the first modern laptop and the first weblog—later called a blog—among a string of other firsts.)

In the mid-'90s, says Wolff, "AOL abandons its hourly fees. This is the single largest development in the new mass appeal of the Internet and in the use of the Internet as a sexual tool: flat-fee pricing. Suddenly, you can spend as much time as you want on AOL pursuing your sexual obsession and it's not going to cost you any money." In short succession, AOL rolled out Instant Messenger. In a separate window on your screen, you could engage in a private conversation. Then came "a searchable database of fellow chatters," as Wolff describes it, "that grew to vast proportions (any interest or kink was immediately searchable)." Buddy lists came along to help keep tabs on people in your personal network.

"At sort of the same time," Wolff recalls, "the Internet goes graphic"—offering dirty *pictures* too—and soon "AOL links to the Internet and AOL becomes the way Main Street taps into the Internet. AOL sends those discs everywhere." Wolff is referring to free-trial CDs that people would use to install AOL software on their home computers and that were distributed in every imaginable manner: packaged with popcorn boxes or Blockbuster video rentals; bundled as floppies—and flash frozen—along with Omaha Steaks; shrink-wrapped on the outside of magazines, neatly sheathed and almost Trojanesque.

In no time, the service took off, and digital media swiftly became mass media. The public's growing attraction to the Web, according to Wolff, was in large part a product of two forces: "Sex chat on AOL—and porn pictures online. And it happens fast. People are generating their own content. The sex thing is the profound thing because it's the accessible thing. It's consumer-friendly. It's this incredibly interesting, frightening form of entrapment. Pornography has always had this habituating aspect. But [historically] it was rate-limited by the fact that pornography had been fairly exclusive, expensive, and embarrassing. You'd get it in brown paper. Now it's plentiful, free, easy to keep—and secret, so you don't have to feel embarrassed about it.

"What's more, pornography had been lonely. But it's not lonely anymore. It's *interactive*. So the fundamental nature of prurience is revolutionized. There's only one thing missing in this revolution, which is speed. Pictures load slowly. Speed starts to come in '97—you went from dial-up to Ethernet. And after '97, you get moving pictures....Fetishists become entrepreneurs....Webcams catch on and they are essentially about voyeurism: a woman walking around naked or masturbating constantly."[4]

In the meantime came the rise of search...and social. At first there were search engines such as Yahoo, AltaVista, Lycos, Excite, and Infoseek.[5] "Then Google starts in '98," Wolff remembers. "Your 'search' is about sex. For a long

---

4. Wolff would write columns for *New York* magazine on such subjects. He visited an erotic novelist and submissive (an avowed spankee), who'd grown her business by running ads in magazines (*Cosmopolitan*, the *New York Review of Books*) *and* on the Web. Wolff devoted another article to the rise of the webcam, an oddity that grew from a single lens in 1991 (trained on a coffee pot in a lab at the University of Cambridge that conveniently let researchers check the pot's liquid level without leaving their workstations) to an out-and-out craze, pioneered by women like Jennifer Ringley, a Dickinson College undergrad who in 1996 started leaving a dorm-room camera trained on her for hours on end, in a sort of pedestrian version of online performance art—a DIY reality show. She eventually progressed to around-the-clock coverage, writes Wolff, "allowing people to peer in and watch her sleep, eat, work, bathe, dress, undress, and (occasionally) have sex....I know people who keep Jenni in the corner of their [computer] screens as they work—she's a background presence, like radio."

At the end of the decade, the social engineering experiment *Quiet: We Live in Public* would become the ultimate webcam moment. Leading into the new millennium, several dozen tech-savvy artist-participants were sealed up in a New York City warren and then webcammed around the clock—in the name of ad hoc anthropology, performance art, surveillance culture, sex, and drugs. Before it was all over, founder Josh Harris would see his human ant colony implode and the cops would be called. (The experiment presaged TV's *Big Brother* reality series, which would launch in 2000.) By the 2000s, "lifecasting" would become a thing: streaming one's everyday true-as-*Truman* existence, 24/7.

(Michael Wolff, "Slap Happy," *New York*, May 8, 2000, 22; Jamie Condliffe, "The World's First Webcam Was Created to Check a Coffee Pot," Gizmodo.com, April 4, 2013; Michael Wolff, "Must-See PC," *New York*, February 22, 1999; Manohla Dargis, "Embracing Life Under Scrutiny," *New York Times*, August 27, 2009; Hugh Hart, "Smart *We Live in Public* Probes Web Genius' Hubris," *Wired*, October 2009; Randall Stross, "A Site Warhol Would Relish," *New York Times*, October 14, 2007; interview with photojournalist Donna Ferrato.)

5. The founders of Google, Sergey Brin and Larry Page, introduced an early version of their search engine in 1996 while they were grad students at Stanford. (John Battelle, "The Birth of Google," *Wired*, August 2013.)

time, the biggest search word was just 'sex.' Then people realized, 'Oh, you could use this to get *exactly* what you want.' So by the end of the decade"—with the advent of social media, popularized by the big online services like AOL, then segmented with focused networks such as Classmates.com and SixDegrees.com—"the Internet is about to become the greatest hookup medium in the history of the world.

"There is a point [to be made]," he concludes, "that the roots of the Internet are grounded in pornography, in a constant need for images and titillation and fetishized behavior. If you work out the implications of pornography, it's always about a steady devaluation. And it devalues because there's always *more* of it. The economic basis of media is scarcity: there are only so many minutes of airtime, for example, that one can buy [on a TV show—to place one's commercials]. What happens, then, to the nature of media when there is no scarcity and there is an infinite amount? That's what the Internet teaches us. It devalues all content."[6]

———

The early Internet had sex appeal, quite literally.

During the mid-1990s, my friend Aidan Sullivan was the director of photography at the London *Sunday Times Magazine*. He was also a co-owner of image.net, an online licensing service that helped Hollywood studios digitize and distribute their film stills to European publications. Sullivan remembers his early 14K Hayes modem and its molasses-slow dial-up connection. "You'd hear this electronic pulsing—'dindle-iddle-ing,' then this under-the-ocean guttural crackle—then the pictures would build horizontally, line by line, like an old wire-service transmission. It took about three to five minutes." And yet the first time he saw an Internet page build itself, he says, "I thought, 'This is limitless. It's enormous.'"

And so it was. Soon image.net's business—and its Web traffic—soared. But their system often crashed, frustrating clients who had to endure significant "downtime" while waiting to access their images. So Sullivan and his colleagues went looking for larger, more reliable servers. "I went to visit the server site in Clerkenwell, in central London, in an open-floor warehouse,"

———

6. Observes digital artist and designer Jonathan Harris, "Just like oil, timber, rubber, sugar, and the other resources that created great fortunes of the late 1800s, [t]oday's most valuable resource is human attention, and, as before, great fortunes are being made by monopolizing this resource before most people understand its value." (Email exchange with Harris.)

Sullivan says. "The servers were big gray-black boxes with lots of cables coming out of them. And as we were walking by, there was one unit that was
bigger than the others. It was going nuts. The lights were flashing. It sounded
like it was alive—sort of buzzing, like it was steaming. And I said to the guy
escorting me around, 'Oh, I'll bet that's one of the banks.' And he said, 'No,
actually, that's the porn industry. And it goes 24/7.' And I just thought, 'Of
course it is!' They were serving porn clients and, like us, were guaranteeing
uptime. Uptime, in this case, was a rather good phrase."[7]

If Sullivan was a relative techno rube, Jane Metcalfe—the cofounder of
Wired magazine—was something of an old soul.

I meet Metcalfe on the Embarcadero in San Francisco. We are soon
walking through the headquarters of TCHO, the high-end chocolate manufacturer that she helped get off the ground in the mid-2000s with her partner, Louis Rossetto, and Timothy Childs, a computer-graphics innovator
(and onetime NASA space shuttle contractor who would become an entrepreneur, sustainability expert, and chocolatier). The overpowering aroma of
cocoa hangs in the air as we survey the factory, set on a waterfront pier the
size of an airplane hangar.

Metcalfe and I go out for coffee. Engaging, candid, and full of youthful idealism, even in her fifties, she shares her perspective on the birth of
Wired magazine—and wired culture. She and Rossetto had conceived and
published *Wired*, which they rolled out in 1993, hoping it might some-
day become an indispensable handbook for understanding the impact of
new technology on society and culture. It was an instant hit. (Now they've

---

7. It may have been fitting, then, that the '90s nicknames for the Internet's two central U.S. server
hubs were MAE West, in San Jose, California, and MAE East, in Reston, Virginia. (MAE stood for
Metropolitan Area Exchange.) Tech writer, novelist, and culture critic Po Bronson once described
the telecom co-op MAE West as the hippest destination in the Valley for after-hours field trips.
"[I]n late 1997 it was a very cool thing to do if you were hosting a party anywhere near downtown
San Jose," he would recount. "[H]op on a shuttle bus with your guests and take them over to walk
through the Mae. Put that on your invitation, and the RSVP rate doubled." There was a sense of
wonder to wander—to trespass—through the MAE maze and see the labyrinthine wiring that made
up the literal sinews of this new virtual world. And it was not lost on visitors that the pulsing bosom
of the western Web took its name from a comedic queen of burlesque, who helped pioneer risqué
camp for the big screen. (Po Bronson, *The Nudist on the Late Shift* [New York: Random House,
1999], xix–xx; Michael Learmonth, "Hubba Hub," *Metro Silicon Valley*, April 22, 1999, http://
www.metroactive.com/papers/metro/04.22.99/slices-9916.html; George Davis, "The Decline of
the West," *Vanity Fair*, May 1934, 48, 82.)

embarked on yet another business with intentions of caffeinating a nation, and the world beyond.)

Metcalfe's compass back in those years was aligned not with New York or London but with the more free-spirited ethos that reigned in Amsterdam and San Francisco. In the '80s she was living in the Netherlands with Rossetto when they began hammering out the template for the new tech magazine they wanted to launch in America. "Amsterdam was all about sex," Metcalfe remembers. "It was an extremely permissive place. And I was forever arriving places and people'd say, 'Boy you should've been here ten years ago.' So to be in Amsterdam in the late '80s and here [in San Francisco] in the '90s was the right place at the right time." Rossetto himself was an interesting case. A libertarian and onetime Young Republican leader as a Columbia undergrad, he became a novelist and journalist—ghostwriting a book called *Ultimate Porno*, documenting the experiences of a first assistant director in the 1970s working the Roman backlots while making the colossal orgiastic flop *Caligula*—before making his name as a writer and editor for tech-oriented publications.

As Metcalfe remembers their life in Amsterdam back then, she and Rossetto worked with a couple of the Oxford-schooled magazine editors who were plugged into "the cyberpunk-rave scene. Party kids would take the ferries over [from England] and continue all night...messaging each other about where the party was going to be. So the connection between the cyber scene and the rave scene—before the Web browser—was really interesting. It was being driven by the music—project[ing] imagery onto a sheet, timed to the beat. The culture was influenced by laser discs, by technological advances. It gave way to a time when people could manipulate art and information." (The drugs, inevitably, helped grease the wheels as well.)

If Europe's scene was dominated by ravers and cyberpunks, as Metcalfe tells it, out in California there was a comparable crowd (also influenced by music and the tech boom) that was tapping into the works of a passel of futurist-fantasist-noir writers deeply steeped in the counterculture.[8]

---

8. In the '80s and '90s, the tales of science-fiction master Philip K. Dick, who died in 1982, were engaging a broader audience. His short stories (written during the 1950s through the '70s) were being spun into movies that whipsawed through popular culture (*Blade Runner*, 1982; *Total Recall*, 1990) and influenced such films as 1999's *The Matrix*. (*Minority Report*, from 2002, was also spun out of a tale crafted by Dick.) Into this mix arrived William Gibson, with a bang. His 1984 novel

It was during this same period, Metcalfe notes, that sex would hijack the so-called MUDs and the MOOs, those virtual-reality multiplayer systems popular among early digital adopters. "These were online fantasy worlds," she explains, in which people communicated via ASCII text, "but perhaps their very numeric limitations were what made it so erotic for people in the first place. It really unleashed your own individual imagination, sitting by yourself at your keyboard late at night, and just that thrill of connecting with another human, live, was so powerful that it really just drove this thing. These multiuser worlds became places where everything that would happen in real-life sexual circumstances played out. Only instead of it being between men and women and humans, it's between, you know, a furry squirrel and a hairy ape, or a ten-foot-tall blue android or whatever else you can come up with. So that added this whole other, very playful dimension that actually started to manifest in the physical world at places like Burning Man"—the annual outdoor art happening and so-called fire party that was first hosted on a San Francisco beach in the mid-'80s and was later reconstituted as a festival-pilgrimage-and-portable-community for thousands in the Nevada desert—where, says Metcalfe, people would actually assume alternate identities. "The sexual fantasies of the online world," she says, "became costumes and behaviors at places like Burning Man."

During the '80s and early '90s, the Northwest Coast, from Santa Cruz up to Seattle, was all about tech erupting, venture capital spouting like a geyser, and hackers making headlines. Computer magazines—nerd journals jammed with gadgets, tips, and the scoop on the latest hardware and software—catered to the faithful. *Wired*, however, would be a new strain of

---

Neuromancer, the cyberpunk bible, jump-started the term "cyberspace." Along with Neal Stephenson (*Snow Crash*, 1992) and a handful of others, Gibson was anticipating and chronicling early hacker and Net culture. Meanwhile, there was Bruce Sterling, whose science fiction, as Metcalfe puts it, "was based on the inevitable [question] of 'How does this all play out?' You take this technology out of the labs and you corrupt it with human dreams and ambitions and shortcomings, and the result is this amazing world that he could just visualize so perfectly. That's where the super-geeky guy always gets the hip chick, and it really started that whole thing." (Interview with Metcalfe; Scott Meslow, "Philip K. Dick's Messy, Mindbending Cinematic Legacy," Atlantic.com, August 2, 2012; Simon Critchley, "Philip K. Dick, Sci-Fi Philosopher, Parts 1 and 3," NewYorkTimes.com *Opinionator*, May 20–23, 2012; Andrew Liptak, "30 Years of William Gibson's *Neuromancer*," *Kirkus Reviews*, July 31, 2014; Tom Bissell, "Neal Stephenson's Novel of Computer Viruses and Welsh Terrorists," *New York Times Book Review*, September 23, 2011.)

publication entirely, a sort of next-level mash-up of the *Whole Earth Review*, *MacWEEK*, the cyberculture glossy *Mondo 2000*, and the many tech-biz mags then flooding the zone. *Wired* assembled a clued-in cabal of digerati: their mission was to enlighten readers about how the cyber revolution would upend the established order, empower nobodies everywhere, blur reality and fantasy, and feed everyone's head. *Wired* had a jarring neon color scheme and radical-sleek layouts that did away with the literal and the linear. The look and feel of the magazine would make it plain that it was speaking in a new digital dialect that was decidedly outside the Frequency, Kenneth.

Metcalfe and Rossetto published their first issue in January 1993. And sex was not incidental to the content or to this new worldview. "One of the pull-quotes in the first issue," Metcalfe recalls, stated that " 'Sex is the Killer App' for new technology." One story in that premiere edition focused on how online erotic networking had stepped up the real-world game of individuals' sex lives ("This Is a Naked Lady," by Gerard Van der Leun, the onetime director of Penthouse.com). Another was an interview with Camille Paglia, whom *Wired* called the "bad girl of feminism." Paglia, in a conversation with Stewart Brand (father of the *Whole Earth Catalog* and The WELL, and formerly one of Ken Kesey's Merry Pranksters), discussed, among other topics, Paglia's recent book *Sexual Personae*; the "healthy" sexualization of American pop culture; and her encounters with Marshall McLuhan, the patron saint of *Wired*. "When you were sitting with McLuhan in the middle of the night," Paglia remarked, "all you would see was the tip of his cigar glowing, and you would hear him making these huge juxtapositions.... [Divergent thoughts] *ssssizzle* when you bring them together." Sometimes a cigar is more than a cigar.

Wired debuted at an auspicious juncture. "The magazine hit the newsstands the week Bill Clinton and Al Gore were inaugurated," Metcalfe says. "Al Gore was talking about the information superhighway before anyone knew about it. It couldn't have been better timed. It ushered in a whole new generation, colored by a different set of values and a different set of references. World War II was way over. Even [the] Vietnam [War] felt distant. We thought: this is a post-Vietnam world and if we have a different set of tools in our hands, we can change the world. It was a giddy time. And there's that A. J. Liebling quote: 'Freedom of the press is guaranteed only to those who own one.' It made *sense*: suddenly everyone would have these tools. They would be owning it."

———

In fact, a different set of values had grown out of (and grown up with) the digital world, values that mirrored the men and women present through its birth and adolescence. Since the earliest phase of the electronic age, counterculture and digital culture—indeed, sex and tech—had shared the same fertile mulch in the Bay Area hothouse.

The Internet's roots, oddly, had first grown from the right, not the left. The Net's forerunner was developed for the military, and its earliest users, as well as many of the earliest evangelists for the computer, were often affiliated with research labs, corporations, or academic institutions that had strong military ties. But as 1960s America splintered politically and socially, the region around San Francisco helped propel the counterculture. And this vocal and sizable amalgam of progressive individuals—espousing free speech, self-empowerment, youthful experimentation, consciousness expansion, and a set of ideals that ranged from libertarian to communal to utopian—deeply influenced the San Francisco–area engineers, programmers, and hackers, along with the nation's wider community of netizens. In ways large and small, the '60s youth rebellion, the mind-set of the so-called New Left, and the attendant sexual revolution had all helped lay the track for the digital revolution.

John Markoff, the Pulitzer Prize–winning technology writer for the *New York Times*, makes this point persuasively in his book *What the Dormouse Said: How the Sixties Counterculture Shaped the Personal Computer Industry*: "The Vietnam war, drugs, sexual liberation, women's liberation, the Black Panthers, the human-potential movement, the back-to-the-land movement—at the end of the 1960s, all of these were concentrating with wicked force on the San Francisco Peninsula." These elements, he says, helped shape the values and priorities of the computer culture vanguard.[9]

———

9. The San Francisco–based science writer and entrepreneur David Ewing Duncan sees these roots as laying the groundwork for the '90s scene in terms of tech innovation—and lifestyle. "There was always an innocence about San Francisco," he tells me during a long lunch, "a strange kind of exciting naïveté. People were indulging in new and experimental things, whether it was sex or new companies or art or music—but there wasn't any sense of danger, that this could all go horribly wrong. I think of the beach movies from the '60s. It was innocent, youthful—some of the smartest

There was a loose but undeniable confederation between various groups in the area: the statistical analysts who assisted the Pentagon during the Vietnam War *and* the antiwar activists; the early acid trippers *and* the pioneering propeller-heads at local electronics companies and research labs; the Merry Pranksters and the participants at clothing-optional parties hosted in the mid-'60s by math professor turned computer wizard Jim Warren (where, according to Markoff, "a whole range of worlds seemed to intersect in the parties at his mountain cabin: hippies, academics, rock and rollers, and people from the nude beach scene... [enticing a BBC film crew to shoot] part of a documentary on the 'Now' generation") and, later that decade, guests at parties thrown by real estate lawyer John Montgomery (which, in Markoff's words, were "attended by many of the Valley's more liberated techies.... There were nude sunbathers, peacocks strolling in the backyard, a PA system playing rock-and-roll music, and a light organ, an electronic device that projected colored lights to accompany music. Inside...there were orgy rooms and a room where everyone could try laughing gas").

As Markoff recalls, some of the region's visionaries believed that the insights derived from mind-altering substances mirrored the nonlinear

---

people in the world [lived there] in the '50s and '60s. You literally had guys like Jack Kerouac and Wallace Stegner, these very liberal, counterculture sort of writers [intermingling with computer pioneers]. Back then Palo Alto, I'm told, was more like Berkeley. Stanford basically started shipping out whole departments from places like Harvard and MIT, and this attracted a new kind of person.

"Then, it really hit its stride in the '80s with Apple and the early IT and the Internet, and then another wave with the dot-coms in the '90s. These were young, incredibly smart people. Whatever they set out to do in life, they would be successful at. And [they wanted] to rock the world and change things—to win at the highest level of the game. Now, that can come with sex. And there is a whole underground world, particularly in San Francisco, [where] people pursue things with an intensity and a kind of innocence and a sense of fun in a way that I don't see elsewhere. That includes sex. It includes underground sex. It includes partying. [This is in contrast to other places, where] there was always something just slightly dirty or dark or edgy. But not [in San Francisco in the '90s]. Women were as aggressive as men. Everybody was kind of empowered to be somebody that [they] normally weren't because you wouldn't have the money or the power to do it until you were much older. But it was also people who were very dedicated to their work. It wasn't a bunch of ne'er-do-wells. They worked very hard. They played very hard. The club scene was a very intense scene. People barely slept. They were on a mission. The whole Internet thing was a mission. And San Francisco is a place where nobody judges you. I wouldn't call it a utopia because there are all the usual problems people have. But this is a culmination of [a movement toward living in a state] of freedom—[without] a sense of evil there. Obviously during the whole [protest period and the murder of] Harvey Milk, San Francisco was quite violent. But by the late '90s, it was a [haven] for libertines." (Interview with Duncan.)

thinking that was central to tech innovation. There was Douglas Engelbart (seer of the modern computer network and personal computing, as well as father of hypertext and the computer mouse), who headed up the Stanford Research Institute in the 1960s—"a tiny band," as Markoff describes them, "distinguished by their long hair and beards, rooms carpeted with oriental rugs, women without bras, jugs of wine, and on occasion the wafting of marijuana smoke." There was the aforementioned Stewart Brand, who, in a no-holds-barred story for *Rolling Stone* in 1972, discussed the use of psychedelics among a key sector of the computer community. (A generation later, he would offer the elegant decree, in a 1995 *Time* essay on the computer boom: "We Owe It All to Hippies.") There was Steve Jobs, the cofounder of Apple, who in 2001 showed Markoff an early demonstration of iTunes, which produced "dancing color patterns that pulsed on the computer's screen in concert with the beat of the music," the author recalls. "Jobs turned to me with a slight smile and said, 'It reminds me of my youth.'... He explained that he still believed that taking LSD [in the early '70s] was one of the two or three most important things he had done in his life."

The makers and shakers of the Silicon Valley—like the information that graced their creations—wanted to be free, and freewheeling.

And in terms of sex, how freewheeling was it?

CHAPTER 12

The Wild Blue Web

It was hard to envision its enormity.

At the Web's inception, few outside the tech world realized it would be seen as one of the signal events in computer science. Or that it would ignite an information revolution. Or that it would make it possible for an individual or a group or a government to communicate with billions.

Even fewer foresaw that the Web would become the largest wank-off machine in creation. Though there were inklings.

People browsing for sexual content, like those searching for illicit love, guarded their anonymity and frequented hard-to-find addresses, often at night. Like those caught up in affairs, they could become obsessive, protective of their time in the zone. Like those donning drag, they assumed new names and created parallel identities. The tech writer (and self-described nethead) J. C. Herz would make the point in her 1995 book *Surfing on the Internet* that the wired universe offered "gender options that don't physically exist. For instance, the LambdaMOO virtual world gives users a choice of male, female, neutral, neither, royal (the royal 'we'), and the natty, insouciant 'splat' (*) option." Women and men would assume cross identities: a member of one sex, disguised as another, would engage in cybersex with Net partners of either gender, or both, depending on the mood and circumstance. This elasticity unleashed a new freedom to experiment, fantasize, and role-play.

As the digital age bloomed, sexual variety reigned. In the late '80s and early '90s, cybersex had a limited connotation: virtual-reality kink. VR sex, theoretically, involved people in proximity or in distant locations donning special suits and/or cybergloves and/or headgear, festooned with wires, and then remotely diddling their partners and sharing a simulated sexual experience, sometimes accompanied by SFX audiovisuals. (CGI—computer-generated imagery—was a huge gaming and cinematic break-through in the 1990s.) Cybersex was sim stim. For a time it went by the cringe-worthy name "teledildonics." And at the time, it was pure hokum. (In 1997, Mike Myers, with a debt to Wilhelm Reich—and to films such as *Barbarella*, *Putney Swope*, *Sleeper*, and *Liquid Sky*—introduced "fembots" to explore the concept of robo-shagging in his Swinging Sixties spoof *Austin Powers: International Man of Mystery*. But for a species that now got its babies from test tubes, why shouldn't a geek try to get his ya-yas out by way of Alpha Centauri?)[1]

Back then, it was called cybersex. Or virtual sex. Or netsex. And much of it, as discussed earlier, was emerging from Usenet and newsgroups. In the fantasy forums called MUDs, it was sometimes called TinySex, as Sherry Turkle would note in her 1995 book *Life on the Screen: Identity in the Age of the Internet*, discussing early "computer-mediated screen communications for sexual encounters. An Internet list of 'Frequently Asked Questions' describes the latter activity…as people typing messages with erotic content to each other, 'sometimes with one hand on the keyset, sometimes with two.'"

Along came CD-ROMs and DVDs—interactive discs that could be slipped into a disk drive or game console—which allowed users to issue simple commands and choose various options or outcomes in their sexual entertainment. There were Internet forums where people could post erotic stories (or add to others' stories)—many of which would evolve into multipart series—that would attract tremendous followings. There were hatchling websites that stole printed porn pictures and posted them as their own; sites that featured virtual strip blackjack; sites where online models popped up in tiny matchbook-size peep-holes, responding to keyboard commands ("How about removing those fish-nets?"). The Internet began to micropander to every type of sexual connoisseur.

In the larval stages of the Web, as *Time*'s Philip Elmer-DeWitt would attest,

---

1. It wasn't until the mid-2010s that robotics and VR had come of age on the cybersex frontier. In 2015, *Wired*, for example, visited VRtube—"a nascent online studio and distribution center for VR porn"—and wrote of the wonders of the coming explosion, reckoning that "no visual technology has ever been so perfectly suited to sexual applications.…[VR] doesn't just change the frame. VR erases it. It allows us to exist *inside* the environment." (Peter Rubin, "Virtual Reality Porn Is Coming, and Your Fantasies May Never Be the Same," Wired.com, February 16, 2015, http://www.wired.com/2015/02/vr-porn/.)

crusaders against cybersmut would infiltrate newsgroups that trafficked in nude photos and type in screeds with subject headings such as YOU WILL ALL BURN IN HELL! And even if websites had entry screens that required users to click on a button to admit they were over eighteen years of age, many minors clicked with abandon. Soon politicians and parents everywhere were talking about ways to filter the content to protect kids, and to punish offending content providers and hosting services.[2]

As the medium welcomed faster modems and less glitchy video, in marched the credit cards. Electronic payments—at the time a new method of consumer, banking, and business transaction—accelerated access to sexual content. At first, the casual browser had trepidations: Do I really want my credit card information out there? Do I trust potentially shady merchants and faceless content providers?[3] Shouldn't I worry about an entry on my statement with the words: *VHS Tape: Bordello of Blood*? In fact, consumers late into the 1990s generally preferred shopping via catalog over shopping online. As hard as it is to conceive of today, many people would compare prices on the Web, then drive to the mall to make their purchases. And when it came time to pay for virtual or mail-order transactions, customers, according to the marketing trade publication *Brandweek*, favored reading their credit card info to telephone salespeople, or sending checks or money orders by mail or express shipping companies.

New e-commerce methods, along with a robust Clinton-era economy, would make the Internet a clearinghouse for products, services, and hard-to-find items (Amazon and eBay launched in 1995, as did Craigslist, which began as a free emailed newsletter. PayPal, the e-commerce service,

---

2. Judge Robert Bork, in his 1996 book on how liberalism has contributed to America's decline, would warn about the truly degenerate areas of the early alt.sex sphere, referencing the writer Simon Winchester: "One day [Winchester] came upon a category called alt.sex, which has fifty-five groups including...alt.sex.intergen (intergenerational: the pedophile bulletin board) [and] alt.sex.snuff (the killing of the victim) which includes subcategories for bestiality, torture, bloodletting, and sadistic injury....It is impossible in short compass to give an adequate idea of the depravity that is being [offered and] sold, apparently profitably." (Robert H. Bork, *Slouching Towards Gomorrah: Modern Liberalism and American Decline* [New York: ReganBooks, 1996], 135–36, citing Simon Winchester, "An Electronic Sink of Depravity," *Spectator*, February 4, 1995, 9.)

3. American Express for a time blocked vendors from pushing porn after bogus charges began to show up on card members' bills. A score of adult websites were cited by the Federal Trade Commission for allegedly asking customers for their card numbers if they wanted a free "trial" peek. In such scams, cardholders' accounts would then be automatically—and fraudulently—charged. ("FTC, Credit-Card Cos. Bump, Grind Web Porn," Forbes.com, August 25, 2000.)

would premiere in 1998.) By increments, consumers saw fewer and fewer downsides to using their credit cards for Web sales, especially when it came to paying extra for adult material. In time, of course, an ever-greater share of the online porn market became free or shared or user-generated—or all three. According to *Forbes*, by the end of the '90s there were half a million sex sites, with one hundred fresh ones popping up each week, many of them very profitable very quickly due to the sales of ads, products, and links to spicier paywall-protected areas. Come 2000, the porn industry's total yearly take was some $2 billion in Web business alone.

––––––––

The pioneers of the computer industry were largely a boys' club, with a few exceptional exceptions.[4] Men dominated the institutions that supported the industry. The teams writing code skewed male. (They were later dubbed "brogrammers.") And while there were significant, accomplished women in tech, up through the '90s dot-com surge, their numbers were small. (As of this writing, the workforces at the most influential tech giants—companies already under fire for a lack of racial diversity, especially in management—remain about two-thirds male, with men dominating the executive ranks.) As a result, gender bias has been coded into the industry, its culture, and, inevitably, the digital media it produces.[5]

––––––––

4. In his book *The Innovators*, historian Walter Isaacson has described the contributions of Ada Lovelace, Lord Byron's daughter, who helped formulate Babbage's basic computational device. Female minds and hands programmed ENIAC (the first electronic computer) as well as UNIVAC (a pivotal commercial computer). Grace Hopper, responsible for COBOL (a machine-readable programming language) became known as "the Queen of Software." (Walter Isaacson, *The Innovators: How a Group of Hackers, Geniuses, and Geeks Created the Digital Revolution* [New York: Simon & Schuster, 2014], 24–31, 88–100, 117, 323; Laura Sydell, "The Forgotten Female Programmers Who Created Modern Tech," NPR, *All Things Considered*, October 6, 2014.)

5. It is difficult to gauge the long-term impact of such bias—or the sea change that could result from gender equity. In 2014, the *New Yorker* would report that a respected global study of "four thousand R&D teams found that gender-diverse teams were considerably better at driving 'radical innovation.'" And yet there is evidence that from the very start, cultural norms and the American educational system have made girls feel uncomfortable enrolling in computer science courses or, later on, pursuing tech careers. According to Eileen Pollack, author of *The Only Woman in the Room: Why Science Is Still a Boys' Club*, a recent University of Washington study headed by Sapna Cheryan has found that "female college students are four times less likely than men to major in computer science or engineering....Women today still are avoiding technical disciplines because, like me, they are afraid they won't fit in." (James Surowiecki, "Valley Boys," *New Yorker*, November 24, 2014, 52; Eileen Pollack, "What Really Keeps Women Out of Tech," *New York Times*, October 11, 2015, SR3.)

During the '80s and '90s, some serious coin had rushed into the world that built the virtual world. Twenty- and thirty-somethings—mainly of the male persuasion—became flush with preferred stock, drove sleek cars, and lived in sprawling, spartan abodes. (A few tech tykes that decade were worth a billion—with a *b*—before they turned thirty-five.) Despite the nerd quotient, the computer industry scene on both seaboards attracted those who were not altogether tethered to conventional norms. Their work hours were ungodly. Their attention to physical fitness was dubious. Their affinity for gadgets was even more pronounced than their nontechie peers. But many were bright, intense, and charmed to their bones with the knowledge that they were apostles of a new medium that would drive the culture.

A not insignificant number of these young men soon became chick magnets. They operated under the laws of sexual physics: a body that has been long at rest will sometimes wobble wildly when suddenly set in motion. "Give a guy a few stock options and a DSL line and suddenly his Asperger-y tendencies become adorable," says Abby Ellin, who in the '90s covered the dot-com boom (and its subsequent bust) for the *New York Times*. "It was the ultimate aphrodisiac. Women suddenly realized that their mothers had been right: that AV guy with the giant key ring, that Dungeons & Dragons–playing geek, really did have a lot of potential—and he would reach it soon. The guys, of course, were well aware of (not to mention thrilled with) their newfound desirability. Talk about revenge of the nerds."

Sian Edwards-Beal, a television and film producer, was drawn to New York City's so-called Silicon Alley in the late '90s, working for a time on a pilot for an unrealized TV series, tentatively titled *In Bed with Manhattan*. She remembers the wilder nights among her friends and colleagues. "The Internet parties were a bunch of geeks who'd never had sex," she says, remembering scenes in the back rooms at soirees thrown by the folks from places like Nerve, the online portal devoted to sex, culture, and human interaction. "It was the first time math-and-science geeks could get fucked insanely they had so much money. And the Net was all about allowing you to meet up—sometimes sexually. The dot-com parties in SoHo, party after party, had this naughty underground feeling to it and the Internet had this *Brave New World* sense of vision in the same way that Kerouac did.

"A close friend of mine went to one party," she recalls, "where people were making out in [pitch] black rooms with cameras [trained on them]. It was voyeuristic. Technology created a new way to see sex—and it was exciting. [I remember being told,] 'You've gotta meet Jack. He's getting laid more than anybody in Manhattan.'" Geeks became, if not sexy, then at least worth the effort—for the mental stimulation...and for a glimpse of the aerie where the future was hatching.

Some guys in tech, of course, exhibited little interest in making sexual connection. These were the e-monks. Many were driven by a nobler hunger than the erotic, one that seemed to derive not from flesh but from quicksilver. Their drives appeared to be neither hormonal nor harmonic but the product of a self-imposed exile from the rhythms of the natural world. They were, essentially, moonchildren. "The engineers at the height of the Web explosion in the 1990s," according to the *New York Times*'s Mark Leibovich, who then covered Silicon Valley, "often worked through several nights straight and never seemed to notice or to mind. They were mostly male and single. The real prodigies appeared to achieve total synergy with the machines."

The earliest adopters of the Net life were guys who set Guy Rules. Games were prized and winners rewarded. Passwords were protected, protocols created, gauntlets laid down. Speed was deified. Piracy was romanticized. The real renegades among them were called hacks and hackers, phreaks and phreakers, black hats and gray hats.

As the online world grew, its discourse evolved (and in many ways devolved). Pranks, quick wit, and rough language were encouraged. Ego was inflated in value; so too was the brute, market-force wisdom of the mob. The Net's waters became a snark-pool, more gaseous than viscous. And nothing in this evanescent medium was worth saying if not said snidely—or chauvinistically.

In this virtual world, actual women were sometimes considered not just a distraction to the business at hand but a class of trespasser, not infrequently belittled or ridiculed. What's more, the cloak of anonymity—and the belief that women who engaged in Web discussion groups or forums were mere online "presences" and not people—gave license to misogyny, which metastasized as the Web grew. By the end of the '90s, even though the gender balance on the Internet was almost equal, incidents of verbal abuse and physical threat against women became so pernicious, dangerous, and epidemic that over time an environment would set in, one that fostered what journalist Amanda Hess would call "the banality of Internet harassment...[in which] the vilest communications are still disproportionately lobbed at women."

Initially, the World Wide Web held vast promise. "The ways by which ordinary men can be of use," James Agee had written, "are tragically limited, even in a democracy." But in one stroke the Web gave solace and meaning to those hoping to be or to feel "of use." The Web was a global stage and the browsing masses newly players. Indeed, those who went online became known as "users," a term emphasizing their utilitarian function (as well as the Internet's). With time, they became "unique visitors" or "uniques," underscoring their specialness, in spite of their anonymity. They "shared" (and sometimes overshared) information with "followers," a word that can have religious connotations. Through email "addresses," they had a destination, a virtual place to go or to be. By building websites they could set up their own "home" page. In joining social networks, they could create new personas and start afresh.

My friend David Kirkpatrick, tech writer and entrepreneur who authored *The Facebook Effect*, is unreservedly sunny on this score, cautioning against those who argue that deep and vital personal connection is being degraded or trivialized in the age of digital interaction and social media. "When billions of people choose to do things in a certain way," he explains, "they are making a grand statement about what they think it means to be human in this era. And they cannot really be wrong. If all those people are choosing to spend their focus and their time in virtual interaction, there must be something genuinely gratifying and useful in it for them, even if sociologists and sexologists et al. may not have fully discerned what it is."

The Web's connective tissue from the get-go was its web of generous users. "Who would have guessed (at least at first)," writes Jaron Lanier, the father of virtual reality and a digital-era seer, "that millions of people would put so much effort into a project without the presence of advertising, commercial motive, threat of punishment, charismatic figures, identity politics, exploitation of the fear of death, or any of the other classic motivators of mankind. In vast numbers people did something cooperatively, solely because it was a good idea, and it was beautiful."

Lanier, however, understood that the Web's recesses, despite this early volunteer spirit, had their own dark fissures. "The way the internet has gone sour since then is truly perverse," he has observed in his bestselling manifesto *You Are Not a Gadget*. "The fad for anonymity has undone the great opening-of-everyone's-windows of the 1990s." In Lanier's view, a "culture of sadism online" has sprung up and, by degree, "has gone mainstream" as individuals have used the medium to take out their aggressions, to demean and humiliate, to flame and defame. "We evolved to be *both* loners *and* pack members," he says of this emerging clan-think. "We are optimized not so much to be one or the other, but to be able to switch between them." (It was not surprising that two of the Internet's popular peepholes early on were sites that were created in large part *to expose.* The *Drudge Report*, which started as an email blast in the mid-'90s, would often post incendiary stories that the mainstream media resisted, ignored, or had not yet fully vetted. The Smoking Gun—a WikiLeaks predecessor, founded in 1997—made it its mandate to unearth and publish "material obtained from government and law enforcement sources, via Freedom of Information requests, and from court files nationwide.")

The Web, by definition, offered virtual sex. Much of it was literally auto-erotic. The solitary online sexual encounter, for many men and women, came to be regarded as noncommittal, less emotionally taxing, and less *trouble.* Why deal with the challenges or rewards of *another's* needs, when one could satisfy one's own—and so efficiently? For many online users, the synthetic actually *replaced* the actual: online sex became not an expression of mutual connection but of selfish release. But this was only half the picture.

For millions of others, the earliest forms of cybersex brought the promise of genuine engagement, not alienation. Strangers typing words to one another—digitally stimulating a partner by *writing* on a keyboard—could experience real-time interaction on an entirely new plane. Online sex brought Insta-Grat. It boosted the ego. It offered a number and variety of potential partners that were theoretically limitless. It allowed for a semisanctioned embrace of new taboos, which was arousing in and of itself. Its virtual nature made "online cheating" arguably more acceptable to one's real-life partner or one's conscience. Its attendant anonymity could be exhilarating and often emancipating. Its seamless utility (from the comfort of one's home) was liberating. Its relative safety, to many users, beat its real-world equivalent hands down, because electronic transmission came with zero risk of STDs.

Lisa Palac, a leader in the so-called sex-positive movement, has written at length about digital Eros in its old covered-wagon days. In the '80s, Palac had gained notoriety as an editor at *On Our Backs* (the seminal journal of feminist lesbian erotica), and she would be celebrated as "the queen of high-tech porn," partly for her stint editing *Future Sex* magazine in the early

'90s. But in 1993, she was a neophyte when, one night, she found herself in her first chat room. In her memoir *On the Edge of the Bed*, she recalls adopting the handle Lisapal (turn-ons: "sushi and red lipstick"), then entering the "Jacuzzi" area of an adults-only online bulletin-board system called Odyssey. She was "overwhelmed," she writes, not so much by the steamy chat that zapped around her but by the number of direct requests from male members to "go private"—to slip away from the others and sex-chat tête-à-tête. The next evening she returned. But she remembers being weirded out when she typed a few rather filthy remarks to a guy named GI Joe and he had the gall to log off, presumably intimidated.

Palac, frustrated but aroused, decided to go to another forum. She tried ECHO, a hip virtual community that was run, salon-style, out of a Greenwich Village apartment. Sitting in San Francisco, she typed in "Lisa Palac." And within minutes, a man who recognized her byline—a doctor who actually knew some people she knew—got into a bit of online repartee about spanking, S&M, and "erotic humiliation." Palac typed, "Maybe you should give me your phone number," thinking it made more sense for her to initiate the follow-up, as she puts it, "in case he's a psychopath masquerading as a normal person."

Palac's description continues:

At 11:30 P.M. West Coast time, I was lying naked on my bed, phone locked against my left shoulder, right hand poised. "How about a story?" I suggested.... His voice was low and sexy and oh man, that British accent. He told me something that went like this:

"You're on a lonely road, somewhere in the Southwest, in the desert. You're hitchhiking and a green Citroen pulls up in a cloud of dust. Inside are two Mexican soap opera stars, a man and a woman. They pick you up, offer you some tequila and orange juice.... Suddenly the car stops. There's a large boulder in the middle of the road.... From behind the boulder steps a gorgeous outlaw cowgirl and soon it's evident that you're all being held up at gunpoint.

"The outlaw handcuffs [all three of you...and] thinks about robbing you all, but realizes there isn't anything to take. So she decides she wants something else...."

I can't remember exactly how the story ended because I was coming so hard.

Palac was hooked. They continued their communication, largely through email, sometimes exchanging three dozen messages a day. "I shouldn't have had cybersex on the first date," she would admit. She was soon "logging on to ECHO every twenty minutes, breathlessly anticipating our next communication. Telnet, log-in ID, password—come on, you stupid slow thing.... How could I be in so deep so fast, without any physical contact?" Palac's reasoning: in reality, the physical cues spur erotic chemistry; online, however, "this process works in reverse: If our sexual interests match up, then we ask to see the body.... Disembodiment, ironically, leads to an immediately greater sense of intimacy... conveyed only with the alphabet.... This is completely unparalleled in the human saga of love."[6]

Not all such encounters were sweetness and light. One of the earliest Net-sex horror stories involved an online skeeve who turned out to be a con artist. Susie Bright remembers it vividly. One of the West Coast leaders of sex-positive feminism, Bright in the early 1990s had left her job editing *On Our Backs*, where she had helped mentor Palac. Bright recalls that she had first gone online because she'd heard that on a computer bulletin board called The WELL[7] a community of people was engaged in a discussion thread labeled "Why I Love Susie Bright."

Bright now says, in a series of interviews and emails, "The WELL was

6. Palac would actually fly out and meet her mystery man ten months later, but only after he'd warned her he had been struggling to lose weight—"I'm working my way down from three hundred and fifty pounds." Their first meeting involved blindfolds, cathedral candles, and a ménage that included a female "friend of a friend" serving as chaperone and who, Palac asserts, resembled "Sharon Stone—only better." (Lisa Palac, *The Edge of the Bed: How Dirty Pictures Changed My Life* [Boston: Little, Brown, 1998], 111–16.)

7. The WELL, launched in the mid-'80s by Stewart Brand and Larry Brilliant, was one of the most significant of the early digital communities. Initially it was based out of the offices of the influential *Whole Earth Review* in Sausalito, California; its name stood (and still stands) for "The Whole Earth 'Lectronic Link." As the Stanford culture and technology historian Fred Turner has noted in his book *From Counterculture to Cyberculture*, The WELL was a free electronic teleconference popular among counterculture cognoscenti, techies, journalists, and Deadheads, which for its era had a sizable percentage of female participants. "To many, these virtual communities—and the WELL prominently among them—seemed to offer alternatives to the hierarchical bureaucracies of a heavily institutionalized material world," writes Turner. "[M]any imagined their movements as the reincarnation of the American frontier, a place where the world could be remade." ("Learn About The Well," WELL.com, The Well Group, Inc., http://www.well.com/aboutwell.html; Fred Turner, *From Counterculture to Cyberculture: Stewart Brand, the Whole Earth Network, and the Rise of Digital Utopianism* [Chicago: University of Chicago Press, 2006], 141–44, 152, 279.)

like the shiny new toy that everyone in the media was fascinated with. Soon, of course, came the con man. The first time there was a sex hoax on the Internet—at least that I am aware of—it happened at The WELL. There was a private women's conference that only [female] members could be part of. There were quite a lot of women on The WELL—for an Internet group, it was a shocking number. That was part of what made The WELL so cool. It didn't even occur to me that computers were supposed to be a guy-only space. [As part of] this private women's conference—it was more gossipy and talking about our private lives and things you didn't necessarily want everyone else to see in public—someone started a topic called 'That Son-of-a-Bitch.'" She laughs. "Sounds promising, right?

"This woman told a story about how she'd met this wonderful man on The WELL and it just all seemed so incredibly touching and poignant and like a match made in heaven. It's hard to capture how innocent we all were. So we were 'listening' to her describe how sexy it was. By the end of the story, as you can imagine, he turned out to be a con artist. He [had seemed] really, sincerely interested in her—'We're going to have dates and so on'—and then he had these emergencies where she had to send him money. That was when the worm turned. But by then she was so in love with him, so infatuated with their virtual affair: they'd had phone sex; they'd done so much [online]. So when he started extorting money from her, she didn't even see it [coming]."

Bright remembers that one of the other WELL participants chimed in. "The woman stopped her and said, 'This same thing is happening to me and I haven't told anyone because I'm so embarrassed and ashamed and I'm starting to feel like a chump. And here we are, we're both these ultra-smarty-pants, computer-genius women—how can this be happening to us?' They compared notes—and it was the same man." When they floated his name to the wider community of The WELL, Bright recalls, "there was complete pandemonium. They outed him. And he had been doing this with so many other chicks, it was just [crazy]."

Bright recalls her reaction: "I'm sitting there at my keyboard and I just dropped my cup of coffee, because I had just fucked this guy in New York City a couple of weeks earlier. In real life. And I felt really embarrassed because, unlike the others, I had not given him money. I had merely had sex with him. I wasn't that attracted to him. I was on a book tour. It was proximity. Yes, he had been a big fanboy and told me how much he just loved-loved-loved the idea of seeing me and he would do anything for me when I came to New York. Then I said, 'Well, we can meet.' He was based in New Jersey. This guy has all these super-brainy women dangling on a string. [He] was, as far as I knew, the first Internet cad."

There were downsides, there were upsides. My friend Stephen Mayes, a respected photo editor and champion of photojournalists, insists that the Web had a largely salutary effect on the sex lives and love lives of many gay men. "I had had an incredible disability in the gay world of never having picked up a man in a bar," Mayes confides over drinks at a speakeasy in Manhattan's East Village. "What the Internet did was give me a new awareness of myself. Previously, the gay bar scene revolved around a body fascism: a prescriptive sense of muscles, tight abs, shoulders that you had to have. And I am less of a physical specimen in that way. So in a bar, my eyes had always been filled with fear—the fear of rejection. Along comes the Web, and I dropped into this world in which I believed my body would be accepted. The Internet released me from all that fear. It suddenly gave me a freedom to meet with men in a way that I'd never experienced before."

Mayes believes that when it came to the stereotypical sexual aesthetic of the gay man, the digital realm had much to recommend it. "The gay world seems to lend itself to this idea of sharing stuff," he insists. "It's open-source, like the Web. It has that reputation: open relationships, sharing partners, etcetera. It has, historically, a sense of being furtive—pushed into the underground for centuries—but once outside social constraints, it was a lot freer within a private, underground context." In many ways, these were also the hallmarks of the early digital space: a private, members-only society with its own language and codes and libertine ethos that existed under the radar.

At the same time, Mayes recalls, the digital photography revolution of the 1990s served to enhance the sex lives of those who were drawn to the visual, to exchanging private pictures, and to creating homespun erotica that might invite and satisfy the fellow male gaze. In previous decades, many gay men, he says, had relied on Polaroids (which required no processing) since they were concerned about bringing their undeveloped film to the corner drugstore or one-hour photo shop. "There was a social stigma," says Mayes, "and, more importantly, legal issues in taking your film to the lab. Sodomy was illegal in places like Texas until the 2000s.[8] So the digital camera freed up people." And those intimate digital photos could be easily traded electronically. In the early days of the Web, Mayes notes, "the digital sexual image is very private—you take it, put it up on your computer, share it just with the people you want to see it. No lab technician! In the late '90s this changed. If you wanted to, you could place an explicit photo online to attract partners, and you felt it was private. You had to register under a screen name. You were addressing members like yourself. But it was a misguided belief that you were addressing a private club. In fact, anyone could register and, more than that, you could download the image—and suddenly your own photo [would be] feral, animal, developing a life of its own. For all the benefits that these websites brought us—gay and straight and otherwise—little did we know the extent to which our personal images would become public commodities that had the potential to spin out of control."

———

The '90s coincided with great shifts in the nature of American romance (remember romance?), long-term relationships of all kinds (including civil unions and marriage itself), and sexually charged socializing (as the practice of "hooking up" became common on college campuses). Accompanying these course corrections, there arose a new phenomenon: online dating. Among the first successful mate-finding sites were Match.com (1995), JDate (1997)—a digital matchmaking service for Jewish singles—and eHarmony .com (2000), a site started by a Pepperdine psychologist active in Christian divinity circles, some of whose books were published by James Dobson's Focus on the Family. eHarmony.com served as a traditional-values counterweight to the Web's more freewheeling alternatives, and the site used a proprietary "Compatibility Matching System" to target those set on more committed relationships. That same year, Salon and Nerve.com (billed as the Web's home for "literate smut") would join forces to launch Salon/Nerve Personals (touted as "the definitive space for online flirting"). Meanwhile, the

———

8. Some antisodomy statutes remain on the books despite their being ruled unconstitutional. (Ashley Alman, "12 States Still Have Anti-Sodomy Laws a Decade After They Were Ruled Unconstitutional," HuffingtonPost.com, April 23, 2014, http://www.huffingtonpost.com/gay-voices/ the-news/2014/04/21/.)

fledgling Craigslist would roll out "Casual Encounters," which the *New York Times* would refer to as "the erotic underbelly of society, where courtship gives way to expediency." Craigslist would eventually become a staging area for escorts, hookers, and those offering other "erotic services," until state and federal law enforcement agencies moved in.

The Internet, for many, was a virtual singles bar. On the largest dating sites, chemistry (both sexual and interpersonal) would be replaced by algebra. Algorithms that had been designed to sift through a voluminous database of attributes listed in members' profiles would sort and rank potential partners' likelihood of attraction and relationship longevity. Individual subscribers would then be presented with a slate of possible dates who, in time, might be possible mates.

Matchmaking services, of course, had been around for decades. But the Web brought a new level of respectability to such artificially induced interaction. Little by little, the fix-up began to lose its total-loser stigma. In the digital age, the unattached, no matter what age, came to see e-dating as socially acceptable, safe, and efficient. In fact, the algorithms and the screening process conferred a certain authority. (At the time, Michael Wolff would describe online dating as a new and rather vanilla way of mating: "a perfectly decent, unremarkable, squaresville thing to do.") By comparison, the singles scene, the bar scene began to be regarded as crass.

Dating sites took off. And this '90s phenomenon so revolutionized the way urbanites coupled up and settled down that today, according to the *New Yorker*'s Nick Paumgarten, "fee-based dating Web sites" take in more than a billion dollars annually and have become "the third most common way for people to meet. (The most common are 'through work/school' and 'through friends/family.')"[9] As the dating dot-coms grew, so did a new set of online meeting places that turned one's wider net of contacts into their own raison d'être. These were the start-up social networks. And in terms

---

9. Come the 2010s, two-thirds of all gay and lesbian couples, as measured in one Stanford study, had made their acquaintance over the Internet. At the same time a third of all newly married Americans would first meet electronically, whether by logging online or by downloading mobile apps. (The comedian Aziz Ansari makes the point that every twenty-four hours OKCupid accounts for forty thousand dates and Tinder for twelve million "matches.") (Laura Blue, "How Couples Meet," *Time*, August 17, 2010; Aziz Ansari and Eric Klinenberg, "How to Make Online Dating Work," *New York Times*, June 14, 2015; John Heilpern, "Take This Tinder Advice from Aziz Ansari," *Vanity Fair*, May 2015.)

of the wider culture they would become far more influential than the dating sites. Social media would not only help define one's persona and sexual expressiveness (shaping one's real-world reputation and online demeanor in the eyes of potential suitors, friends, strangers, and even potential employers), but would also have long-term effects on social interaction, free speech, and political change. Services like TheGlobe.com and SixDegrees.com (well before Friendster or LinkedIn, before MySpace or Facebook) were the online hubs where communities of users gathered to converse and exchange information about shared interests, pastimes, or backgrounds.

Sex, of course, was central to the origin story of social media. "We often forget that social networking, early on, was really all about sexual stereotyping," says my friend Rachel Winter, the film producer. "Facebook was *founded* as a way of rating women's looks. From that nucleus—devised by male students at Harvard—came everything that followed, including the trolling and shaming. At this stage I would say: let's all take a breather and *ban* social media for five years. We'd all be better off."

Much of the Web to this day remains powered by social connection, by sex, and, yes, by porn—a subject that demands a deeper '90s dive.

But we're getting ahead of ourselves. It's time to toggle back to Washington and reenter the political force field.

CHAPTER 13

Don't Ask, Don't Tell

It was all over but the sniping.

In November 1992, Bill Clinton went on to win the White House—illegitimately, many groused. Clinton had garnered only 43 percent of the total ballots cast (3 percent *fewer* than had Mike Dukakis during his loss four years before). But the math cut both ways. Third-party spoiler Ross Perot, it turned out, had siphoned more votes from Bush than he had from Clinton, helping to open the door for the Democrats.

"The old order passeth, a new generation riseth," Reagan speechwriter Peggy Noonan would observe in a *New York Times* column two days after Clinton's win. It was simply time, she said, for the coming of the Boomers, a designation that applied to many members of the press as well: "They want a new story, a new headline, new news. They love their country; they want change; they're sick unto death of Republicans. (Note to the Clinton staff: your new friends have built you up for a steep fall.)"

Clinton, more to the point, had appealed to voters as a new-wave leader, one who, in marketing vernacular, "reflected the electorate." The down-home working-class southern boy with a Rhodes Scholarship appealed to the proles and the progressives, the centrists and the lefties, the LGBT voters and the minority voters, the single moms and the soccer moms and the single soccer moms and dads.[1] "We all live with contradictions," observes legal scholar Joan

---

1. From the perspective of many African Americans, Bill Clinton came to be considered "our first black President," as Toni Morrison wrote in 1998. "After all, Clinton displays almost every trope of blackness: single-parent household, born poor, working-class, saxophone-playing, McDonald's-and-junk-food-loving boy from Arkansas....And when virtually all the African-American Clinton appointees began, one by one, to disappear, when the President's body, his privacy, his unpoliced

Williams, the founding director of the Center for WorkLife Law, at UC Hastings in San Francisco. "In my view, Bill Clinton is still a hard-living, working-class guy. He was bringing that with him [to the general election], including the sleeping around. And then, on top of that, and partially integrated—he's what I call a class migrant. [As] a class migrant, you *present* as 'upper-middle-class, professional-managerial.' [But] there's actually nothing 'middle' about them." Once Clinton and Hillary Rodham became a couple, as Williams sees it, she helped to further integrate Bill's transition into this social stratum.

"He was able to embody these two parts," she says. "That's why he *won*. He was a feminist, but it didn't erase his hard-living, good ol' boy origins. Johnson was a good ol' boy. Carter was a good ol' boy. By the time that Clinton came along, he was not only a good ol' boy—and therefore countered the Republican southern strategy—but he was also a good ol' *working-class* boy."

Good or bad, ol' or new: he was the people's choice. And the cultural and social shifts commenced the very week he became president. "We have heard the trumpets," said the sax-player president upon taking the oath of office. "We have changed the guard."

––––––––

Clinton went to work, pen in hand. On his third day as president—the twentieth anniversary of *Roe v. Wade*—he reversed the moratorium on the use of fetal tissue samples in experiments that many believed would eventually help treat diseases such as Alzheimer's. He struck down a directive that had prohibited government money from going to overseas health groups known to propose abortion as an option when advising women about fertility and family.[2] He threw out "the Bush 'gag' rule" that, as Clinton would later describe

––––––––––––––––––––––––

sexuality became the focus of persecution, when he was metaphorically seized and body-searched, who could gainsay these black men knew whereof they spoke?" In fact, two months before Morrison, in a *Vanity Fair* profile, comedian Chris Rock had ventured, "I view Clinton as the first black president. He's the most scrutinized man in history, just as a black person would be. Everything he's ever brought up has to be second-guessed. He spends a hundred-dollar bill, they hold it up to the light." (Toni Morrison, "Comment," *New Yorker*, October 5, 1998; David Kamp, "The Color of Truth," *Vanity Fair*, August 1998, 167; Susan Wise Bauer, *The Art of the Public Grovel: Sexual Sin and Public Confession in America* [Princeton, N.J.: Princeton University Press, 2008], 176.)

2. His first week in office, Bush II would restore the ban. His first week in office, Obama would lift it again. *His* first week in office, Trump would reverse it. (Peter Baker, "Obama Reverses Rule on U.S. Abortion Aid," *New York Times*, January 23, 2009; Anna Diamond, "Trump Strikes at Abortion with a Revived Foreign-Aid Rule," Atlantic.com, January 23, 2017.)

it, "[barred] abortion counseling at family planning clinics that receive federal funds," a rule that effectively forbade "clinics from telling pregnant women—often frightened, young, and alone—about an option the Supreme Court had declared a constitutional right."

This was Clinton in full battle array, taking command of the culture war.

He diligently and deliberately set the social clock ahead, establishing a parity agenda that, as it turned out, would grant women greater latitude in their health decisions and would begin to create a semblance of equity between the sexes and among various sectors and classes of society. With every passing month, his administration would push plans that curbed everything from sex discrimination to sexual harassment in the workplace to gender equality in schools. Clinton put his own spin on "family values": expanding education reform, slashing the price tag of college loans, opening up "empowerment zones" in low-income communities, granting workers more flexibility to care for loved ones during times of need (the 1993 Family and Medical Leave Act), and attempting to set up a comprehensive health care program (a failed effort spearheaded by Hillary Clinton). The president's influential labor secretary Robert Reich would head up a three-year Glass Ceiling Commission to examine obstacles to advancement faced by female and minority workers. (In the early 1990s, by some accounts, all but 5 to 10 percent of senior management slots in corporate America were held by Caucasian men.)

In perhaps his strongest rebuke of the Christian right, Clinton twice vetoed a law that came to his desk that would have outlawed so-called partial-birth abortion.[3] He also encouraged the FDA to reconsider the U.S. embargo of the French "abortion pill" RU-486, and the agency, on his watch, would end up approving the drug's use.

His agenda dovetailed with decisions in the courts and statutes from the Congress. During Clinton's tenure, key legal rulings would run the gamut from penalizing universities that discriminated against female athletes to helping establish codes that would give workers and employers a system for identifying unwarranted sexual advances or incidents of harassment. Lawmakers would

3. Bush II signed the "partial-birth" abortion ban into law in 2003, and four years later the Supreme Court would uphold that ban. (Julie Rovner, "'Partial-Birth Abortion': Separating Fact from Spin," NPR.com, February 21, 2006; Robert Barnes, "High Court Upholds Curb on Abortion," *Washington Post*, April 19, 2007.)

pass legislation, supported by the president, to aid victims of sexual and domestic violence (the Violence Against Women Act, proposed by Senator Joe Biden).
Clinton signed the so-called Oprah Bill—the National Child Protection Act
of 1993—with Ms. Winfrey (herself abused as a child) leaning over his shoulder. The act would set up a nationwide database listing perpetrators of violent
acts and sex crimes. Initiatives during Clinton's tenure ranged from the Gender
Equity in Education Act to National Pay Inequity Awareness Day, from gar-
nishing the wages of deadbeat dads, to extending benefits for family leave, to
overhauling the adoption and foster-care systems. Clinton signed into law an
act that provided safety at entrances to family planning centers and championed the Hate Crimes Prevention Act to make it easier to prosecute violent acts
against LGBT people. And all the while, the president made it a priority to place
women, minorities, and gay men and women in visible leadership posts.

The shifts were neither subtle nor cosmetic. They were sweeping and
for the most part irradicable. Bill Clinton—who during his campaign had
promised to set up a government that "looks like America"—was doing just
that. He was addressing imbalances in the nation's social, familial, and gender power schemes in ways that were striking and new—and a threat to the
defenders of "traditional values." And as the decade played out, virtually every
cultural calamity that the conservatives had forewarned would come to pass.

————

The changes began almost from the moment Clinton settled into the West
Wing. But that very first week, he was hit with a culture-war broadside. The
confrontation became known by its sound bite: "gays in the military."

Absolutely *no one* in the administration had sought to make such a hot-button
issue a priority, especially during *week one*. If Clinton—considered history's first
gay-rights-prone president—wanted to make points on this score, surely he might
have focused instead on marriage equality. Or violence against members of the
LGBT community.[4] Or increased funding for battling AIDS. But circumstance,

————

4. Anti-LGBT hostility was certainly widespread. Politicians and clergymen excoriated Disneyland
(Disneyland!) for holding its annual Gay Days. Conservative groups backed increasingly high-profile
campaigns to "convert" homosexuals through absurd "reparative therapy" or "sexual *re*-orientation."
Comments like those of Illinois congressman Henry Hyde—"Most people do not approve of
homosexual conduct"—were not uncommon. Some public figures were becoming especially
outspoken against LGBT rights and same-sex partnerships. The steady drumbeat of such talk, and
of hate speech in general, gave quiet cover for a surge in hate crimes. For the first half of the 1990s,

not logic, often dictates the West Wing calendar. The previous November a federal judge had decreed that the military's rules banning LGBT service members violated the Constitution. The ruling, as described by Senator Barney Frank in his memoir, *Frank*, had forced Clinton's hand, ensuring that during his first weeks as president "[his] administration would be required either to appeal the decision, that is, defend the ban, or abolish it by executive order."

At the same time, the fight over homosexuals fighting in the armed forces was part of a synchronous drift that had riled social conservatives and spread through the courts. In the previous year, more and more members of the military were proudly and publicly coming out—and then being sacked because of it. A handful of highly visible cases revolved around lesbian and gay individuals in the uniformed services who had sued after being outed and then dismissed. An antigay propaganda film was passed around like samizdat among key lawmakers, clergy, and military leaders. According

---

according to statistics compiled by Washington's National Gay and Lesbian Task Force, "anti-gay violence...increased 127 percent" in six major American cities. (Attacks of this kind went routinely underreported.) The brutality was particularly abhorrent in the slaughter of members of the trans community. In 1993, the Nebraska killing of Brandon Teena, a young transgender man, was one of the first such incidents, in the words of journalist Buzz Bissinger, to focus "widespread public attention [on] an anti-transgender hate crime." (The murder would inspire the 1999 movie *Boys Don't Cry*.) And after a litany of unconscionable crimes targeting individuals because of their sexual orientation or gender identity, a single slaying in 1998 served to awaken lawmakers in Washington. In Laramie, Wyoming, Matthew Shepard was beaten, burned, and left to die, reportedly trussed up against a fence, as if crucified. The grisly, senseless death of Shepard—coming just four months after white supremacists had abducted an African American man named James Byrd Jr., then chained him to the back of a pickup and dragged him alive for three miles, resulting in his decapitation and death—accelerated the push (already a Clinton administration priority) for passage of the federal Hate Crimes Prevention Act. (Despite such legislation, the menace would continue. In 2016 the FBI would report that when it came to hate crimes, LGBT people were "the most likely targets" of attackers. And among such victims, according to the Human Rights Campaign, "transgender women of color are facing an epidemic of violence that occurs at the intersections of racism, sexism and transphobia.") ("Robertson's Revenge: Gap Flag Flap Leads to Orlando Ban," *Church & State*, September 1998, 15; "What Is Orlando Gay Days?," Gaydays.com/history; Benedict Carey, "Psychiatry Giant Sorry for Backing Gay 'Cure,'" *New York Times*, May 19, 2012, A1, 3; Adam Liptak, "Looking for Time Bombs and Tea Leaves on Gay Marriage," *New York Times*, July 20, 2010; Buzz Bissinger, "The Killing Trail," *Vanity Fair*, February 1995, 85–86, 142; Bissinger, "Across the Ages," *Vanity Fair Special Edition: Trans America*, Fall 2015, 9; Melanie Thernstrom, "The Crucifixion of Matthew Shepard," *Vanity Fair*, March 1999, 210, 271–72; "HRC Condemns Wyoming Hate Crime..." [press release], Human Rights Campaign, October 10, 1998; "Matthew Shepard Act" [editorial], *New York Times*, May 6, 2009, A28; Rick Lyman, "Man Guilty of Murder in Texas Dragging Death," *New York Times*, February 24, 1999; Haeyoun Park and Iaryna Mykhyalyshyn, "Hate Crimes Now Directed at L.G.B.T. People the Most," *New York Times*, June 18, 2016, A12.)

to scholar Nathaniel Frank, in the definitive book on the subject, *Unfriendly Fire: How the Gay Ban Undermines the Military and Weakens America*, dubious antigay research papers were being commissioned, providing statistical fodder for both the Pentagon brass and religious advocates of a gay service ban. Some studies described "typical" homosexuals as antiauthority, sybaritic, and disposed to disease.

To amp things up, there was an effort by right-wing religious leaders "to mobilize social conservatives against gay service," writes Frank. "Even before Clinton's inauguration... [the Reverend Jerry] Falwell began a 'dial-a-lobby' operation, using his *Old-Time Gospel Hour* program to generate 24,000 signatures on a petition against gay service in a matter of hours. As a result, a week after the inauguration, Congress was besieged with 434,000 phone calls in a single day, overwhelmingly against letting gays serve."

The issue, to be sure, was in the air. In the earliest days of the presidential race, Clinton had declared that he disagreed with the policy that barred homosexuals from joining up or that required a soldier's dismissal if he or she later came out or was revealed to be gay or lesbian. "If they want to serve their country," the candidate had said, "they ought to be able to do it openly."[5]

Clinton's stance was political kryptonite. Most of the Pentagon's commanders—not to mention the rank and file—forcefully disapproved. Many congressional leaders, some of them combat vets, did too.

In Clinton's corner, however, were several notables. One was the independent-minded Barry Goldwater, the former Republican senator from Arizona—and the GOP's 1964 presidential nominee—who had helped found the modern conservative movement. "Gays have served honorably in the military since at least the time of Julius Caesar," he asserted in the *Washington Post*. "You don't need to be 'straight' to fight and die for your country. You just need to shoot straight." Other Clinton allies included the incoming

5. "Given the enormous manpower needs of the wartime military," military sociologists Wilbur J. Scott and Sandra Carson Stanley have noted, "many homosexuals served in World War II, often with distinction and without difficulty." It was not until 1950 that a strict policy was instituted to bar homosexuals from serving or to weed out lesbian and gay service members if their sexual orientation came to light. "Congress enacted the Uniform Code of Military Justice (UCMJ), [which forbid] sodomy.... Between 1980 and 1990, the U.S. military expelled an average of about 1,500 service members per year under the separation category 'homosexuality.'" (Wilbur J. Scott and Sandra Carson Stanley, eds., *Gays and Lesbians in the Military: Issues, Concerns, and Contrasts* [Berlin/Boston: Walter de Gruyter/Aldine de Gruyter, 1994], xi.)

senators Dianne Feinstein and Barbara Boxer, as well as Senator John Kerry, the decorated Vietnam veteran who would later run for president and serve as Obama's secretary of state.

If Clinton's culture-clash foes saw a battle they could win, hands down, it was this one. The president, for all the leverage he held on other fronts, had yet to earn a whit of respect on military matters. He was perceived (inaccurately) as being unschooled in foreign affairs. He had strenuously objected to the Vietnam War, a conflict in which many commanding officers had fought with distinction. He had gone to great lengths to avoid the service as a young man—behavior that didn't sit well with troops in an all-volunteer military. And he was the first commander in chief in half a century with no tangible connection to World War II.

It was more than a sore point, then, when he received a request right as he came into office. The Pentagon's Joint Chiefs of Staff (JCS) wanted to air their views on this very matter.[6] It was a showdown Clinton had tried to avoid. Since the November election there had been many prep sessions between the incoming Clinton team and members of Congress and the military to try and reach some form of consensus on the subject. Options had been presented and hashed over. But the state of play remained strained and inconclusive. *Time* reported that the head of the Joint Chiefs, Colin Powell, had signaled he might bolt if his new boss lifted the ban unilaterally; *Newsweek* reported that all of the chiefs might step down.

Clinton's Machiavellian radar detected a setup. Bob Dole, the Kansas Republican, was then the Senate minority leader.[7] In a sign that there would be no Clinton honeymoon, Dole threatened to tack a gays-in-the-military ban onto whatever bill the White House first sent to the Congress. The president had the *authority*, by the powers of his office, to lift the ban. But such a maneuver by Dole would effectively pluck an executive prerogative from the president's grasp. The senator went on *Meet the Press* and issued a shot across Clinton's bow, invoking the separation of powers. Dole cautioned the

---

6. Writes historian Nathaniel Frank, "Although it was their first meeting with Clinton as president, they never even discussed the evolving trouble spots in Iraq, Bosnia, or Somalia. Instead, they focused on whether a certain variety of love—instead of a certain variety of hate—could bring down the world's strongest military." (Nathaniel Frank, *Unfriendly Fire: How the Gay Ban Undermines the Military and Weakens America* [New York: Thomas Dunne/St. Martin's Griffin, 2009], 82.)

7. Dole would go on to face the president four years later as the Republican nominee.

president against forcing the Senate to override him: "There are other things you can do by executive order that wouldn't blow the lid off the Capitol."

Clinton, when looking back on the first cultural incursion of his presidency, said he believed that Dole "clearly wanted this to be the defining issue of my first weeks in office. . . . By raising the issue early, and repeatedly, he guaranteed it so much publicity that it appeared I was working on little else." In that, Dole succeeded. And as the president filled in his postinaugural datebook, legislators worked the phones and took to the airwaves. "Congressional resistance," wrote the *New York Times*, had broken into "open revolt."

––––––––

On January 25—day six of Clinton's first week in office—he called an afternoon meeting with the Joint Chiefs. They were led by General Colin Powell and Clinton's incoming defense secretary, Les Aspin, a supporter of lifting the ban. At precisely 4:30 p.m. the generals took their places in the Roosevelt Room of the White House. Clinton, however, didn't show until around 6:30, according to one of those in attendance, Air Force Chief of Staff Merrill "Tony" McPeak. "We were all on time and got to cool our heels for two hours," McPeak would remember in an interview for *A Complicated Man*, Michael Takiff's oral history of the life and times of Bill Clinton. "It was maddening. I had things to do."

Clinton asked his generals for their frank opinions. And one after the other, the men in uniform spelled out the reasons for their opposition. Privacy concerns were "paramount," according to a report by Eric Schmitt two days later in the *New York Times*. "Unlike civilians who go home after their work is done, many service personnel live together in barracks, ships or in tents." There were worries about everything from unit cohesion, to the deterioration of command structure, to an infusion, as the *Times* put it, of "an element of sexual tension and anxiety [that might] undermine the teamwork necessary for efficient military operations."

Among the most adamant voices in the room was that of Carl Mundy, the commandant of the Marine Corps. As Clinton recounted, "He was concerned about more than appearances and practicalities. He believed that homosexuality was immoral, and that if gays were permitted to serve openly, the military would be condoning immoral behavior." (Servicemen sounded a similar theme, the *Times* noted after the meeting. Writing in that month's edition of the *Marine Corps Gazette*, Sergeant Major S. H. Mellinger went so far as to state, "The Bible has a very clear and specific message towards homosexuals: 'Those that practice such things are worthy of death.'" If the ban were to be lifted, some Marines suggested, it might be better to dissolve the corps altogether than to appear to endorse such dishonor.)

Colin Powell, who had been the JCS chairman during the allies' overwhelming victory in the '91 Gulf War, argued that it would be a grave error to shake things up. A policy reversal, he said, might be "prejudicial to good order and discipline." But then he switched tack and suggested a middle ground, and a plan began to emerge. "[Powell] raised an alternative that he'd been discussing with Aspin," George Stephanopoulos would recall in his memoir. "'Stop asking and stop pursuing,' he called it."

McPeak would remember proposing a notion along the same lines: "I even used the words, 'Let's have a "don't ask, don't tell" policy.' We said we were willing to do that, we recommended it. We could make his political day easy. At the time, to enter the armed forces, there was a form you had to sign at the recruiting station, and one question was, 'Are you a homosexual?' We said, 'We'll stop asking the question.'"[8]

The president seemed genuinely pleased and open to the proposal. This new formula let some air out of the balloon and, in true Clintonian fashion, it accommodated diametrically opposed viewpoints. He assured the Joint Chiefs, however, that he wasn't waffling. One way or another, he said, he was going to open the path for gays and lesbians to have a secure place within the armed forces. They had been fighting and dying for their nation since the War of Independence. They were owed the honor of serving. "I want to

---

8. Nathaniel Frank reports that the phrase "Don't Ask, Don't Tell," as it applied to gay and lesbian members of the armed forces, was first articulated in late 1992 by Professor Charles Moskos, a top military sociologist who, beginning in the 1950s and on through the 2000s, had made a name for himself by advising the uniformed services on their policies and procedures for widening their ranks to include minorities. (During the 1990s debate, Senator Barney Frank had put forth his own middle-ground formula that stopped short of what would become "Don't Ask, Don't Tell"—a policy he opposed. As he describes it in his autobiography, *Frank*, "I publicly proposed allowing LGBT people to serve in a sexually neutral way when performing their military duties, while remaining free to express their sexuality at other times.... As I saw it, refraining from discussing our sexuality with fellow members of the military was a restriction, but not an intolerable one. In fact, it did not greatly differ from how a majority of LGBT people behaved at the time in civilian occupations.") (Nathaniel Frank, *Unfriendly Fire*, xvii–xviii, 26–28; Barney Frank, *Frank: A Life in Politics from the Great Society to Same-Sex Marriage* [New York: Farrar, Straus & Giroux, 2015], 161.)

work with you on this," he said, signaling the inevitable. Powell and the brass agreed to meet him halfway.

As the meeting broke, McPeak would recount to oral historian Michael Takiff, the president "came around the table and grabbed me by the shoulders. He said, 'Tony, you should have been a lawyer'—I guess thinking that was a compliment, which it isn't. But I came out of there feeling ten feet tall, like you always do with Clinton. The guy's so charming, you fall in love. It isn't until the next morning you realize you had too much chocolate."

The Joint Chiefs had expressed not only reservations but firm disfavor. Yet they were duty-bound to follow the dictates of their president. Some of those in the room even believed "Don't Ask, Don't Tell" might actually prove to be workable. As McPeak would later put it, "We left on great terms. Every guy on our side of the table came out of there thinking, 'This is a great guy. Good ol' boy from Arkansas. Hell yes, he understands. He's our kind of guy.' "[9]

But the spirit of compromise was gone in a flash. The next morning, according to Takiff, National Public Radio would report, "White House aides say they're…angry over what they call insubordination by the Joint Chiefs of Staff"—even though their commander had *asked* for their points of view, unfiltered. The JCS, said McPeak, felt blindsided.

The stress level rose as the week wore on. Clinton next held a cabinet room session with Democrats who served on the Senate Armed Services Committee, a formidable group responsible for military oversight. Their perspectives—and backing—would be critical. Clinton canvassed each senator in succession over the course of two hours.

Sam Nunn, the committee chairman, was dead set against Clinton's stand and made the point that lifting the ban too quickly might incite acts of antigay rage within the ranks: "If you did it overnight, I'd fear for the lives of people in the military." In contrast, Senators Edward Kennedy (the brother of a president) and Chuck Robb (the son-in-law of a president) supported *lifting* the ban. But the man who left the most indelible impression that day was West Virginia's Robert Byrd. A Democratic warhorse and the unofficial

---

9. McPeak would remain consistent. In 2010 he wrote an op-ed piece that defended the idea of keeping the provision in place: "I do not see how permitting open homosexuality in these [closed military] communities enhances their prospects of success in battle. Indeed, I believe repealing 'don't ask, don't tell' will weaken the warrior culture at a time when we have a fight on our hands." (Merrill A. McPeak, "Don't Ask, Don't Tell, Don't Change," *New York Times*, March 5, 2010, A27.)

historian of the Senate (as well as a repentant ex-member of the KKK), Byrd would engage with eleven presidents during his career, going on to serve longer than any senator in American history. His opinion held gravitas. He was the last to address the group. And instead of remaining seated, as his colleagues had, he rose and scanned his audience.

"The fingertips of his left hand rested lightly on the table," as George Stephanopoulos would describe the scene in his autobiography, "his right hand clutched the buttons of his jacket—a classic orator's pose. Rome was where he began." Ted Kennedy, in his memoir *True Compass*, would relate how Byrd had opened with a discussion of homosexual conduct in antiquity: "He informed us, with many ornate flourishes, that there had been a terrible problem in ancient Rome with young military boys being turned into sex slaves. I don't remember the exact details, but I think the story involved Tiberius Julius Caesar being captured and abused....And then years later he sought vengeance and killed his captors."

In another account of the meeting, by historian Taylor Branch[10] (reconstructed from audiotapes he had made with Clinton during his presidency), Byrd, according to Clinton, had insisted that "homosexuality was a sin. It was unnatural. God didn't like it. The Army shouldn't want it, and Byrd could never accept such a bargain with the devil. Clinton [recalled that] this classical foray rocked everyone back in their seats....Some senators noted that the Roman emperors won brutal wars for centuries while indulging in every imaginable vice. (Augustus Caesar ravaged both sexes, wrote the gossipy Suetonius, and softened the hair on his legs with red-hot walnut shells.) Byrd invoked Bible passages....There were sharp stabs of tension, leavened with astonishment at such a debate between senators and a brand-new president. 'I couldn't tell,' said Clinton, 'whether Teddy Kennedy was going to start giggling or jump out the window.'"

Byrd's point was not that the ancient Romans had allowed homosexuality. He was arguing that their empire had fallen because their decadent

---

10. Branch, the Pulitzer Prize–winning historian, was a longtime friend of Clinton's and shared living quarters with Clinton and Hillary Rodham when the three of them worked on George McGovern's presidential campaign in 1972. During Clinton's eight years in office, Branch would conduct seventy-nine conversations with the president, which would comprise the backbone of his 2009 book *The Clinton Tapes*. (Wil S. Hylton, "The Bill Clinton Tapes" [Q&A with Branch], GQ.com, September 16, 2009.)

behavior had corrupted the state from within, leading to the civilization's collapse. "Rome fell," said Byrd, "when discipline gave way to luxury and ease."

After a long silence, Clinton rose from his seat. "His response," according to Kennedy's account, was commanding and brusque. " 'Well,' [the president] said, 'Moses went up to the mountain, and he came back with the tablets and there were ten commandments on those tablets. I've read those commandments. I know what they say, just like I know you do. And nowhere in those ten commandments will you find anything about homosexuality. Thank y'all for coming.' He ended the meeting and walked out of the room."

Soldiers...Romans...Countrymen...The so-called gays-in-the-military ban consumed Washington for weeks. And after much back-and-forth, the Congress, the military high command, and the president agreed on a Clintonian compromise: they would *suspend* the decision. The president agreed to delay any plan's implementation for half a year in order to canvass stakeholders' positions and move cautiously toward a final presidential directive.

As Nathaniel Frank would recount the onslaught in *Unfriendly Fire*, the National Association of Evangelicals and a phalanx of military chaplains worked overtime to block any policy shift: "Brigadier General Richard Abel, head of the Campus Crusade of Christ's military ministry...equated homosexuality with selfishness." The Chaplaincy of Full Gospel Churches, according to Frank, drafted a directive to the president decreeing that "homosexuals are notoriously promiscuous...perverted...pedophiles" and wondering about blood-spattered battlefields in the age of AIDS. And on it went.

Alarmist, dire, and ragingly homophobic, these Klaxons rang on deaf ears. Six months to the day after he took office, Clinton began to implement what came to be known as "Don't Ask, Don't Tell." The new arrangement allowed closeted homosexual or bisexual members of the U.S. military to continue to serve. It purported to penalize those who might harass or discriminate against servicemen and -women because of their sexual orientation. And it forbade openly gay, lesbian, or bisexual men and women from serving in or joining the armed forces (or from engaging in homosexual acts, as service members, on or off duty and on or off base), since, according to the statutory language, "the presence in the armed forces of persons who demonstrate a propensity or intent to engage in homosexual acts would create an unacceptable risk to the high standards of morale, good order and discipline, and unit cohesion that are the essence of military capability."

It was convoluted. It was tortured. It was a disaster. It would codify a two-tiered setup that unfairly disadvantaged gays and lesbians, according to a subsequent legal review commissioned by the Center for Sexual Minorities in the Military.[11] The policy, so the study argued, would deny victims of discrimination or abuse from having a legitimate procedure for redress—in effect tabling their constitutional right to equal protection. And it would set in motion, in the words of the center's director, Aaron Belkin, "a system that gives a wink and a nod to anti-gay harassment."

Clinton took flak from virtually all sides, most notably from LGBT activists and opinion-makers. Indeed, in 2014—two decades after the adoption of "Don't Ask, Don't Tell"—the *New York Times'* assessment was that the program was "widely viewed as among the most significant setbacks the gay rights movement has encountered."

"If you look at the history of the gay movement," arts arbiter Ingrid Sischy would tell me, apropos of the policy, "what is at stake when one has to hide and lie? The fact that Clinton's first act when he became president was to put people back in the position of lying? I speak not just for the gay audience but...for the audience in general: this idea was a terrible disappointment, and I think [it signaled] the beginning of a loss of faith in politics. I really believe it. It was also a manifestation of a return to lying—and hiding—about sex...It kind of institutionalized lying about sex."

Clinton, for all the grief he received through the years, had nevertheless managed to take a position. He had been committed to forcing the issue. He had managed to tease out the consensus-building and decision-making process over the course of many months. And to do so he had moved bureaucratic mountains: persuading two recalcitrant, historically hetero, indeed macho, institutions to seriously (if obliquely) address the social ramifications of sexual orientation. He got no credit for these efforts, least of all from leaders of the LGBT community, many of whom came to regard their supposed

---

11. The center is now called the Palm Center and is based at the University of California, Santa Barbara. The writer of the original study was Sharon Terman. (Sharon Terman, "The Practical and Conceptual Problem with Regulating Harassment in a Discriminatory Institution," PalmCenter.org, Palm Center Whitepaper, May 1, 2004; Yoji Cole, "'Don't Pursue, Don't Harass': The Other Half of 'Don't Ask, Don't Tell,'" DiversityInc.com, June 15, 2004.)

advocate as a sellout. Clinton's edict, in the eyes of leading gay and lesbian advocates, was as discriminatory, shameful, and shaming (if not more so) than the framework it was meant to replace.

In '90s America, the bridge to such acceptance and tolerance had been a bridge too far. And it would take a decade or more before two larger truths became evident, at least as far as "Don't Ask, Don't Tell" was concerned. First, when hidebound sectors of society conscientiously object to changes imposed upon them by a transformation in the wider culture, it sometimes takes byzantine means to justify ineluctable ends. Second, discrimination *is* discrimination. Writer Nathaniel Frank would identify a telling comment by Senator Howard Metzenbaum, the Ohio Democrat. When presented with poll numbers suggesting that as many as one-half to three-quarters of American troops did not believe that their openly gay peers should serve among them, the senator had responded, "*So what?*" Metzenbaum's point was simple: no opinion polls were needed when the Pentagon was deciding to freely admit blacks or women. The generals back then had simply decided to do the right thing.

Over the subsequent two decades, new attitudes and new laws regarding sexual orientation would evolve as the culture, the nation's leaders, and the military evolved. In 2008, candidate Barack Obama would make the repeal of "Don't Ask, Don't Tell" a campaign pledge. By then, a majority of Americans supported his call to rescind a system that, all told, had required the dismissal of fourteen thousand servicemen and -women. The cost to the Pentagon (and the American taxpayer) by one estimate: upwards of $364 million—not to mention all the reputations upended, loyalties betrayed, and careers shortchanged.

The policy would be abandoned in 2011. Four years later, the Pentagon would begin to have its first serious discussions about permitting transgender Americans to serve their country.

CHAPTER 14

The Age of the Long Lie

William Jefferson Clinton, while breaking down barriers with his progressive agenda, was also helping to break down society's tolerance for moral absolutism. From a liberal perspective, not all creeds or sects or relationships were perceived as being beholden to an ultimate set of practices and principles. And yet this rejection of a common, fundamental value system also had its troubling downside. It allowed the ethically ambiguous individual—it allowed the president himself—to play fast and loose with the truth. It allowed him to waffle in his public pronouncements and private behavior, and then to recalibrate, reboot, and be redeemed.

Clinton, during one of his first crucial moments on the national stage, had been untruthful. And he would ultimately admit the obvious in his memoir—long after his initial encounter with Ms. Gennifer Flowers: "Six years after my January 1992 appearance on *60 Minutes*, I had to give a deposition in the Paula Jones case, and . . . I acknowledged that, back in the 1970s, I had had a relationship with [Gennifer Flowers] that I should not have had." In reassessing that TV appearance, *60 Minutes*' Steve Kroft now says, with a bit of perspective, "The thing that I was most proud of about the interview: that we put him on record [addressing] what he thought about [the Flowers accusations] and that he was either lying or telling the truth. And, it turned out, he was lying. . . . There was no question he was lying to me."

Many of us had first met Bill Clinton on national television as we watched him lying about sex. His first week in office, he had laid the groundwork for "Don't Ask, Don't Tell," an executive directive that *mandated* lying about sex. Indeed, he had almost lost the presidency by lying about sex *under oath*. But the lies about sex, in the end, didn't seem to faze the nation. For all the pique and wincing and mincing, this tendency to parse the truth was a Clinton habit, a strategy, an ethical tic—and one that the citizenry appeared to be adopting in many facets of modern life. If the president had told a white lie? Big whoop.

The lesson of the Watergate scandal of the 1970s had been that the lie— the *cover-up*—was always worse than the crime. (Corollary: no man, even the president, is above the law.) But modern presidents have long terms and short memories. Clinton, and George W. Bush after him, would elevate lying into spin art. Over the sixteen-year span of their back-to-back administrations, truth, as presented by White House aides and political spinmeisters and news outlets, became rhetorical taffy. News consumers became seasoned skeptics, learning to expect and tolerate a certain level of elastic veracity (a quality later identified by comedian Stephen Colbert as "truthiness").[1]

Apropos of Clinton and Bush, Frank Rich, the columnist and cultural observer, would propose a name for a politician's impulse to pontificate in complete fact-check freedom: "post-fact syndrome." Rich defined the term in 2006 as a collective bargaining agreement between politicians, the media, and the commonwealth in which "anyone on the public stage can make up anything and usually get away with it." Expounding on this thesis in his book *The Greatest Story Ever Sold*, Rich would conduct a granular analysis of the George W. Bush administration's spin machine: "It dramatized its fable to the nation and made it credible to so many, even when it wasn't remotely true.... Only an overheated 24/7 infotainment culture that had trivialized the very idea of reality (and with it, what once was known as 'news') could be so successfully manipulated by those in power.... The very idea of truth is an afterthought and an irrelevancy in a culture where the best story wins."

In the walkup to America's 2003 invasion of Iraq (and then Bush's spuriously advertised "Mission Accomplished"), for example, it would only belatedly dawn on the country, in Rich's view, "that the reasons sold to the public and

---

1. Colbert's catchphrase, according to journalist James Poniewozik, was meant to call into question "the idea that it was more important for a thing to feel true than to actually be true." Indeed, come the new millennium, power figures were tailoring the truth to suit their own purposes. And neologisms were spawned, some of which perfectly characterized the phenomenon. Science-fiction sage Bruce Sterling (in his 2000 novel *Zeitgeist*), for example, came up with the phrase "consensus narrative" to highlight the subjective nature of truth. By his thesis, truth—reality itself, in some respects—was envisioned as a narrative construct. (James Poniewozik, "A Makeover, Populist and Ambitious," *New York Times*, September 10, 2015, C1; [re: Bruce Sterling] Andreas Müller and Lutz Becker, eds., *Narrative and Innovation* [Berlin: Springer Science & Business Media, 2013], 7.)

the world by the administration were decoys.... The real crime was the sending of American men and women to war on fictitious grounds."

In a similar vein, both Hillary Clinton *and* Donald Trump, perhaps the two most distrusted opponents in a modern presidential contest, perpetuated the post-fact syndrome during their 2016 race for the White House. Ms. Clinton, from her tenures as First Lady (Travelgate) up through secretary of state (Emailgate), was considered by many to be an unconscionable obfuscator. Trump, for his part, fairly cultivated the art. "On the PolitiFact website," *New York Times* columnist Nicholas Kristof would report, "53 percent of Trump's [public statements were rated as demonstrably] 'false' or 'pants on fire'—a number that would climb to "71 percent...'mostly false'" on the eve of the election. This endemic fabrication was tactically deceptive in a manner reminiscent of totalitarian leaders—a pattern made all the more ominous, as *Vanity Fair* editor Graydon Carter has pointed out, since Trump would routinely crib his "talking points from the dark corners at the bottom of the Internet."

Trump, to columnist Michael Tomasky's thinking, was "not an occasional liar or accidental liar, but a liar as a matter of course, a liar as strategy." Indeed, Trump would prove to be the ideal candidate for the era of fake news, hate blogs, "agita"-prop, fear-and-ballast news networks, nonstop gossip, and Twitter-feed screeds.[2] And it is no exaggeration to state that the candidacy of Donald Trump would not have been possible, or viable, had it not been for the rhetorical and stylistic precedents set by the ever-parsing Bill Clinton.[3]

---

2. In 2016, a week after Trump was elected president, linguists advising the *Oxford English Dictionary* would select "post-truth" as their international word of the year. The terms "post-fact" and "alternative facts" would also make the rounds. Said Oxford's Casper Grathwohl, "Fueled by the rise of social media as a news source and a growing distrust of facts offered up by the establishment, post-truth as a concept has been finding its linguistic footing for some time." ("'Post-truth' Declared Word of the Year by Oxford Dictionaries," BBC.com, November 16, 2016; John Herrman, "Fixation on Fake News Obscures a Waning Trust in Real Reporting," *New York Times*, November 19, 2016, B1.)

3. Barack Obama, by comparison, served two terms of a largely "fact-based" presidency, unlike those who came before and after him. The Budapest-based media observer Dean Starkman has made the case—as reported by Steve LeVine, the Washington correspondent for Quartz.com—that "[Donald] Trump's brand of lying is rooted in a trend that goes back to the 1980s.... [Since that time, many] elite political and media figures have dispensed with [what Starkman terms] 'fact-based argumentation itself, on everything from supply side-ism to climate-change denial to death panels to birtherism, you name it. In a sense, it's more like never allowing any fact to become established (a practice that's spawned its own field, known as agnotology). And then Trump just turned the knob

Much of this flimflam, of course, predated the 2000s. Elastic veracity in the second half of the twentieth century had been rolled out by Lyndon Johnson's Vietnam advisers and spokesmen, honed by Nixon and his White House aides, and fine-tuned by Reagan—all before the preeminence of cable news and the World Wide Web. (We had traveled light-years from those noble days when Watergate reporter Bob Woodward defined journalism as being "the best obtainable version of the truth.")

But to circle back to the decade at hand. It was William Jefferson Clinton, first and foremost, who turned out to be the Michael Jordan of this craft: deft, cunning, and convincing, a born debater, talker, and persuader. He perfected the spin default at the very moment that truthiness was becoming an acceptable response in human interactions of every kind—on Wall Street and the ballfield, in the boardroom and the bedroom.

"I think we do live in a Clintonized culture," said Arkansas journalist Paul Greenberg, as Clinton was making his second run for the White House. "Just turn on your television set, or read your newspaper, or try to find out what the latest spin is, and you can see what counts is the right sentimental expression, the right style, rather than anything below the surface." (Indeed, columnist William Safire, that same year, would brand First Lady *Hillary* Clinton "a congenital liar.")

It was, in a phrase, the age of the long lie.

———

Bill Clinton, as the '90s progressed, began to incarnate the equivocal. Journalist Joe Klein, in a famous 1994 essay for *Newsweek*, would call it "the politics of promiscuity." In making his case, Klein was describing both Bill and Hillary Clinton, whom he had rather canonized during the early swoon of the '92 campaign. "A clear pattern has emerged—of delay, of obfuscation, of lawyering the truth," he wrote. "With the Clintons, the story always is subject to further revision. The misstatements are always incremental. The 'misunderstandings' are always innocent—casual, irregular, promiscuous. Trust is squandered in dribs and drabs. Does this sort of behavior also infect the president's public life, his formulation of public policy? Clearly, it does. A president's every word, the nuances of each position he takes, must be carefully considered. There is no room for carelessness—or promiscuity."

---

on this practice to 11.'" (Steve LeVine, "New York Times Editor on Trump: 'We Will Call Out Lies,'" Quartz.com, September 20, 2016.)

Klein would see this promiscuity—this compulsion to share or receive affection and admiration indiscriminately—as a deep character flaw when it came to assuming the job of leader of the free world.[4]

Dee Dee Myers is more charitable, if critical nonetheless. "[It] was a tactic that Clinton used more effectively—and I don't mean it in a good way—than anyone I'd ever worked for," she says. "In politics, people lawyer the truth, and Clinton did. That's a fair criticism. Clinton would say things that were technically true but that created a misimpression that kind of intentionally sent people in the wrong direction. Or, more often, I think he tried to leave himself wiggle room and change his mind and say he never said [that].

"Did he do that in his personal life? I tried to make the argument for a long time—to myself and publicly—that there was a [distinction]: a private morality and a public morality. Not that the private morality wasn't important; it is, because it does create trust. But isn't it more important that the public acts—the things that affect the commonweal—are much more [significant] than what affects his marriage? Can you separate those two things? I think, in a way, you can. But it's not a healthy thing to do."

True, Clinton had arrived *into* this shift in American conscience. But he was also subject to laws, judges, and prosecutors that seemed less flexible than in previous eras. "People often lie when interrogated about sex, and American law used to be more sensitive to human frailty than it is now," notes the journalist and legal scholar Jeffrey Rosen in his book *The Unwanted Gaze: The Destruction of Privacy in America*. "For most of American history, courts didn't put people under oath in situations where they might be tempted to perjure themselves."

America, then, had learned an important lesson from the man running for its highest office. If there is anything we *are* given the green light to lie about, it is sexual fidelity. Author and journalist Jonathan Rauch has a refreshing take on it all. Looking back on Clinton's false statements about sex, he recently told me, "I'm a fan of hypocrisy," contending that one's love life is not a fair litmus test for how one will behave in public office. "No,

---

4. Klein would later backtrack on some of his criticisms, while not disavowing the underlying hypothesis. In his book *The Natural*, he would acknowledge that Clinton "gradually became far more disciplined in his statements and public actions." (Joe Klein, *The Natural: The Misunderstood Presidency of Bill Clinton* [New York: Doubleday, 2002], 108.)

lots of estimable politicians have had affairs. [In Clinton's case], he showed ridiculously poor judgment, [eventually] attempted to smear [Monica] Lewinsky, and broke real laws—lying to the grand jury. But that's a function of Clinton, not an expression of decent hypocrisy."

Rauch's thesis, which he would lay out in a series of articles in the *New Republic* beginning in 1997, is that human beings over the course of "two or three millennia of social experimentation" have come up with a code regarding adultery and other ethically sticky behavior, which Rauch dubs "genteel hypocrisy." As he deconstructs it, the code amounts to "a Chinese box of rules.... If you absolutely must fool around, keep it out of sight. Within that rule is a still more subtle one: If you pretend not to do it, we'll pretend not to notice. [And] if the cuckolded spouse either doesn't know or pretends not to know, then no hanky-panky is going on.... Not even James Madison could have invented a better set of checks and balances."

Rauch would go a step further, insisting that our tacit adoption of "hidden law" (outside the legal realm) is "not only hallowed but indispensable" to upholding society's larger ethical scaffolding. "The one sort of lie that a civilized culture not only condones but depends upon [is] a consensual lie about consensual adultery.... The only way to insist that adultery is intolerable while actually tolerating it is by hiding it in the closet."

In other words: "Don't Ask, Don't Tell."

Rauch expounds on the Clintons as a case in point. "In the ancient social compact," he states, "it is up to Hillary to decide whether to accept her husband's behavior. If she pretends to believe him, then we pretend to believe her." The problems would come, in Rauch's view, only when the press pressed on and, come the late 1990s, when political and legal remedies—"the sexual harassment law, the tort law, the independent counsel law"—put Clinton in jeopardy.

That's all well and good if you buy Rauch's argument. Or if you're a die-hard Hill and Bill fan. Or if you have the backbone (or the stomach) to accommodate parsing the truth. William J. Bennett does not. The conservative commentator, who worked in both the Reagan and Bush administrations, would pick apart Rauch's rationale and, in so doing, make a larger culture-war case.[5]

---

5. It is important to note that the lion's share of Rauch's and Bennett's writings on this topic appeared at the time of (or after) the 1998 revelation of the president's relationship with Monica

To Bennett, there is no justification for collectively excusing adultery in an ethically grounded society. "Much, if not most, of the public commentary about President Clinton's adulterous relationships makes them seem unimportant, trivial, of no real concern," he would write in his polemical tour de force *The Death of Outrage: Bill Clinton and the Assault on American Ideals* (published in 1998, as the independent prosecutor was concluding its investigation of the president). "Sex is reduced to a mere riot of the glands," Bennett observes. "Apologists for the president are attempting to tap into a new attitude in the country toward sexual relations, one that has been deeply influenced by the sexual revolution.... [Many believe that] sexual relations between consenting adults...are a personal matter that we ought not judge whatever the context."

Instead, Bennett ventures, civilized societies over the centuries have regarded sex—perhaps the most "special and powerful" human interaction— as "a quintessentially moral activity.... Far from being value-neutral, sex may be the most value-laden of any human activity.... Sexual indiscipline can be a threat to the stability of crucial human affairs. That is one reason why we seek to put it under ritual and marriage vow.

"Adultery," he believes, "is a betrayal of a very high order, the betrayal of a person one has promised to honor. It often shatters fragile, immensely important social networks." For this reason, Bennett denounces Clinton in particular, along with those in the culture who would argue that extramarital sex is a morally relative matter, depending on the sex partner and the circumstance:

> Civilizations understand that we need to construct social guardrails to protect the vulnerable against the rapacious. And these social guardrails are not simply the products of the law; they are built as well by moral codes. Leaders who flout moral codes weaken them....
>
> Chronic indiscipline, compulsion, exploitation, the easy betrayal of vows, all suggest something wrong at a deep level—something habitual and beyond control. The behavior appears to be incorrigible; it does not occasion contrition, a need for absolution or change.... Yes,

---

Lewinsky. But both critics were also addressing moral issues that were roiling in the public mind much earlier.

we are, all of us, sinners. But aren't we at least supposed to struggle to do better and to be better?...If ever there has been a case in which adultery matters because of what it reveals about the corruption of a man's loves and his aims, as well as of his governing character...it is the presidency of William Jefferson Clinton.

In the 1990s, the public wasn't buying Bennett's argument. Even when the president was judged most harshly—during his second-term sexual revelations and his impeachment trial (when an ABC/*Washington Post* poll found that only 28 percent of Americans believed he had "high personal moral and ethical standards")—Clinton's concurrent approval numbers still hovered around 60 percent. They would climb at one point to a whopping 73 percent.

———

Bill Clinton himself, in addressing the results of the 1992 election, would assert in his memoir that voters "usually pick the right leader for the times." He asked rhetorically, "How did Americans come to choose their first baby-boom President, the third youngest in history...[c]arrying more baggage than an ocean liner?"

William Bennett had a ready answer in *The Death of Outrage*: "The history books may describe how a diffident public, when confronted with all the evidence of wrongdoing and all the squalor, simply shrugged its shoulders. And, finally, that William Jefferson Clinton really was the representative man of our time."

In the battle about how we judge others' sexual behavior, Bennett and company were on the losing end. As a culture, we were becoming more and more comfortable excusing sexual indiscretion in our leaders, in our neighbors, and in ourselves. And by living through the age of the long lie—the trail of mistruths that would help typify many of our national leaders, our clay-footed heroes (from Pete Rose to O. J. Simpson), and even our '90s-born information sources (from the *Drudge Report*, to hyper-partisan news outlets, to the rank recesses of social media)—we were finding it easier and easier to live in good conscience with our own dissembling.

We realized that we routinely rely on fiction to leaven the facts as we edit and temporize the story of our lives.

CHAPTER 15

The Oversexed, Underexamined, Media-Soaked *Yadda Yadda* of Everyday Life

Scene 1. **1994.** I am napping in my tent when I hear a howl. I can make out the words distinctly: *I want to fuck you like an AN-I-MAL!*

For a moment I'm muddled by dream and hangover. But the howl persists and it confirms that I'm awake. In a tent. In August. In Saugerties, New York.

I'm at Woodstock '94, a three-day, mud-spattered gathering to mark the twenty-fifth anniversary (Boomer alert) of the original Woodstock festival—the counterculture's crowning hour.[1]

I shamble into the open air to hear the music more clearly. A band is performing on a faraway stage. The lead singer is screeching now. The electronic *hisssss* is unnerving. The lyrics too. And for a moment I can't quite make out the rest of the verse against the feverish beat. But soon the chorus resounds again, and this time the lines are bone clear:

I want to fuck you like an animal
I want to feel you from the inside
I want to fuck you like an an-i-mal
My whole existence is flawed
You get me closer to God

---

1. I was attending in my capacity as *Life* magazine's director of photography, both covering the festival and screening an Apple-sponsored music video I'd produced for the main-stage monitors, contrasting *Life* images of Woodstock performers in 1969 with new portraits from 1994.

"It's Trent Reznor," says Josh Simon, the *Life* reporter standing next to me. The band, he tells me, is Nine Inch Nails. The track, "Closer," is from their new album, *The Downward Spiral.*

There is something unnerving in the howl of this rough beast. Reznor seems to be asserting that sex on the primal level—hot monkey love— reinforces what we all are at root: animals in a single jungle. And perhaps it is our shared carnality that connects all living creatures, reinforcing our deeper, spiritual bonds.

In looking back on that moment, I concede: rock has always been about sex. But in Reznor's splintering cry, it had *become* sex.

***Scene 2.* 1997.** My office at *Life* magazine hangs four floors above midtown Manhattan. At dusk, I relish the picture-window view of the Sixth Avenue bustle. And as the winter holidays approach, life-sized toy soldiers grace the Radio City Music Hall marquee, directly across from me. They emerge from their perches and, at designated hours, go through a mechanized march, set to booming Christmas music. Work in the office stops for a minute or two and we admire the festive procession, then go about our business.

One afternoon, though, I notice a large sign in a storefront window below. A new clothing emporium has just opened, a few doors down from the Radio City entrance. The sign on the storefront reads: F.C.U.K. In big letters. Designating: French Connection U.K. In other words, sort of like F.U.C.K. In the '60s, surely, protestors used the verb plenty—to vent against THE WAR or THE DRAFT or NIXON. So did punks in the '80s, as an antiestablishment adage. But this F.C.U.K. serves a less lofty purpose: to awaken passersby so that they'll veer inside and buy shit.

How many children, I wonder, will now pass this sign on their path to see the toy soldiers?

A Thesis. It was known as Moore's law. In 1965, data-processing wizards were cramming more and more transistors onto smaller and smaller computer chips. And Gordon Moore, a cofounder of Intel, came up with a proposition. He forecast that every two or three years the processing power of these integrated circuits would double, even as their cost declined. In the half century since, Moore's theorem has proved to be fairly accurate.

For the 1990s, then, I propose a new Moore's law. I call it Demi Moore's law. (Apologies to Demi.) *This* thesis holds that every five to ten years the quantity and tolerability of sexually suggestive content in the culture increases exponentially—in inverse relation to its cost. Indeed, well into the new millennium, consumers have not yet reached their sexual saturation point despite an overabundance of stimuli. Which is all a way of saying that countless aspects of our personal and social lives in the '90s, and today, have withstood erotic encroachment, making the significance and sanctity of the individual sex act, along with our general sense of wonder regarding human sexuality, somewhat demystified, devalued, casual.

In a way, the '90s escalation of such stimuli (during the decade when the digital camera began its ascent) was akin to the omnipresence of images of conflict and inhumanity a generation before. As cultural savant Susan Sontag would observe in her pivotal 1977 book *On Photography*, "The vast photographic catalogue of misery and injustice throughout the world has given everyone a certain familiarity with atrocity, making the horrible seem more ordinary. . . . Photographs shock insofar as they show something novel. Unfortunately, the ante keeps getting raised—partly through the very pro-liferation of such images of horror." Not surprisingly, Sontag would com-pare this glut of "photographed atrocities" to the glut of porn, whose novelty, erotic power, and "sense of taboo . . . wear off" after frequent viewing.

Demi Moore's law, then, suggests two corollaries. First, arousal over-load can douse arousal, requiring even greater or more focused (or fetishized) stimuli to arouse. Second, all of the sexual cues and teases and come-ons in social interaction, in ads and pop culture, in media and fashion serve to inspire new behaviors and manners and preoccupations: in dating and mat-ing; in society's sexual tastes and boundaries; in how we express ourselves as sensual creatures; and in the ways the human body is portrayed in high and low culture.

There were new patterns of sexual interaction across the age scale. Estro-gen replacement therapy came back in vogue and helped older women to become more sexually active. Viagra did the same for older men. Anthropol-ogist Helen Fisher saw the rise of a phenomenon she calls protracted middle age. "In past generations, an older woman was expected to stay at home and take care of her grandchildren," Fisher insists. Around the turn of the millen-nium, she says, they discovered "they're divorcing more, and they're expected to go out and find love again—and deep attachments. [Seniors] not only have estrogen replacement but they have testosterone patches and they've got hip replacements and nips and tucks...and Viagra. We're seeing more and more older people who are really expressing their sexuality, staying in the dating game [and] finding new people if a partner dies or deserts them."

A younger demographic was embarking on its own sexual journey. Historian Debby Applegate and her husband, Bruce Tulgan, an expert on young people in the workplace, conducted online interviews with an array of adolescents in the '90s for a project entitled "Generation X-Rated." They found that whatever else the information revolution was providing teenagers, it was also offering a clearinghouse of *sexual* information: advice on sexual health, cautionary tales about high-risk behavior, and warnings about sex offenders and child predators, who, once convicted, now had to register with authorities.

In the meantime, teens were receiving positive social messages about issues surrounding sexual orientation. "Popular awareness and acceptance of homosexuality has increased dramatically on a track which has directly paralleled Xers' lifespan," Applegate and Tulgan wrote in 1997. "When the issue was really coming out of the closet, Xers were in elementary school. By the time [they] went off to college, it was cool to be gay—[students] saw the Harvey Milk documentary during freshman orientation and LUGing (Lesbian Until Graduation) became fashionable." In fact, *Rolling Stone* would note, "At the beginning of this decade, there were no Gay-Straight Alliances in public high schools. By 1997, 400 alliances had registered.... [And] the National Education Association voted to include 'sexual diversity' in sexual-education curriculums."

That said, these same young people were also being afforded new pathways to porn. According to Applegate and Tulgan, "Xers knew more facts, fears, and fantasies about sex at a young age than any generation which came before in the modern era." What's more, many minors were now "latchkey kids," left alone to their own devices "either because their parents didn't stay married, or because both parents worked, or because parents [who had come of age in] the 1960s and 1970s just tended to be more permissive than parents in the past." The result, in Applegate and Tulgan's estimation, were multitudes of unsupervised kids prone to masturbate more, sample porn from cable and the Web, and sexually experiment with partners.

Julian Sancton, an editor at *Departures* magazine, was thirteen in 1993 when his family moved from Bronxville, New York, to Paris, France. He remembers phoning a friend to catch up seven months later, only to learn that kids at parties were now playing spin the bottle and "showing each other their pubic hair—and I didn't have any at the time. I was shocked. I wasn't jealous—I was saddened that [things] had evolved in this direction. I thought it was morally unsavory. From what I sensed, American culture was on overdrive compared to seventh grade in France. When I came back to visit in 1994, some of my old friends were doing drugs, mostly coke, at age thirteen and fourteen.... The language [had coarsened]. When something was good, it was 'the shit' or 'the bomb.' Gangsta rap had started.... Music videos in the U.S. were sexual in a skeevy way. In [contrast], France had boy bands—tame, corny pop music. France was teeming with sexuality. But it all felt forbidden, transgressive; there was never this sense of exploitation."

Journalist Stefanie Cohen, a veteran of the *Wall Street Journal* and the *New York Post*, has her own recollections of her years in public high school in Winter Park, Florida. "The prevailing culture underwent a shift [by the time] I graduated in 1993," she says. "In 1990, the student council scene still ruled the school. It was cool to be a cheerleader, to get good grades, to wear clothes from The Gap, to be good at sports, and to be generally well-behaved, which included some degree of chastity. People had boyfriends, they didn't sleep around. By the time I left—around the time Nirvana and Pearl Jam had trickled all the way over to Florida—being a shiny-faced striver was decidedly not cool. The more alternative, the less earnest—the better. It was cool to not care. It wasn't a function of freshman versus senior year. It was a downshift in values among teens."

For college-age students, few forms of sexual or social behavior had a more profound impact than the practice of "hooking up," which became customary in the 1990s and would later take hold among high school students. In her book *Hooking Up: Sex, Dating, and Relationships on Campus*, Kathleen A. Bogle, a professor of sociology and criminal justice, explains the pliability of the phrase. One large national survey, using heteronormative terminology, would define hooking up as "a girl and a guy [who] get together for a physical encounter and don't necessarily expect anything further." Another study defined it as "a sexual encounter, usually lasting only one night, between two people who are strangers or brief acquaintances [in which] some physical interaction is typical but may or may not include sexual intercourse."

This coupling-sans-commitment experience could be prearranged or random; sexually adventurous or limited to sharing some chaste, overnight companionship; a "one-night stand" or a semiregular rendezvous. Writes Bogle, "the term 'hooking up'"—and presumably the practice—"was being used by college students across the country since at least the mid-1980s. But 'hooking up' is a slang term," which, over time, would overlap, she contends, with terms like "friends with benefits" or the "booty call." (The latter phrase is often attributed to Bill Bellamy, the comedian and actor who went on *Def Comedy Jam* in the early '90s and asked the audience, "[When the guy] calls the honey from the hotel room, two o'clock in the morning—is that or is that not 'a booty call'?")

Whatever the definition, Bogle submits, a new sexual script was emerging as the dating track went into eclipse. The reasons were many. More young people were going to college, where gender ratios began to skew female. More were delaying marriage—or choosing *not* to marry. More perceived themselves as being equal partners in any sexual interplay. More were consuming alcohol, with more frequency, raising the likelihood of disinhibition.[2] More began "socializing in groups, rather than pair dating," Bogle contends, "and 'partying' with large numbers of friends and classmates [in settings that] represented more than just a social outing; they became the setting for potential sexual encounters." More were choosing to maintain what writer and editor Pamela Paul has referred to as "overlapping lovers or, in academic parlance, 'concurrent partners.'" More were the children of divorced parents and thereby (as some conservative observers argued at the time) had had more exposure to "casual" partnering. Whatever the reasons, the college-age students who were hooking up in the '90s were the Leif Eriksons of the liaison game, forerunners of the swipe-right singles of the Tinder/Grindr era.

As social patterns changed, the *definition* of sex was changing too. Americans everywhere were becoming vocal about oral. Researchers, columnists, and daytime talk-show hosts spoke of a marked increase in oral sex among teens and adults, attributable in no small part to the implicit sanction of Bill

---

2. New graphic-design software, mail-order houses, and websites made it easier for minors to create or procure fake IDs. And a public service campaign was launched in 1990 to address driving-related fatalities: "Friends Don't Let Friends Drive Drunk." ("Drunk Driving Prevention [1983–Present]," Advertising Education Foundation, aef.com, http://www.aef.com/exhibits/social_responsibility/ad_council/2399/.)

Clinton, who had testified under oath that he didn't consider oral sex to be *actual* sex.

The president had good company. A paper published in the prestigious *Journal of the American Medical Association* by Dr. June Reinisch, then chief of the Kinsey Institute, showed that in one survey of some six hundred university students, 59 percent viewed mouth-to-genital sex as being outside the bounds of "sex" sex. (The editor of the 116-year-old journal was fired after deciding to run the article during Clinton's impeachment trial.)

In the same time frame, there was a jump in the frequency of cases of oral cancers and STDs across the population. Some experts attributed the increase to the fact that couples, keenly conscious of safe-sex methods during the 1980s, were less inclined to engage in penetrative sex. Moreover, there was broader cultural acceptance of oral sex, which had been on the rise since "the great year of nineteen *soixante-neuf*," in the words of sometime social historian Christopher Hitchens, "when Mario Puzo publishes *The Godfather* and Philip Roth brings out *Portnoy's Complaint*"—two books with oral sex scenes that went down well with readers. (The practice became a full-on craze three years later when the breakout porn film *Deep Throat* hit theaters.)

By the '90s, "oral sex became 'making out,'" says Dr. Drew Pinsky today. Pinsky—the man whom the *New York Times Magazine* once christened "the surgeon general of youth culture"—has spent much of the last three decades advising sexually active young people in his roles as a therapist, lecturer, TV personality, and radio talk-show host. "I watched it happen in real time," he insists. "One day, oral sex…all of a sudden moved over to second base—in, like, a week. It was incredible. [Young people] became very defensive, like, 'What's the big deal? The *president* said it wasn't sex. It's not sex.' Of course, young males *seized* on that. I actually pushed back on it for a long time, thinking, 'It's not really happening.' And it was happening."[3]

---

3. "Blowjobs were fraught in the nineties," according to Megan Carpentier, the editor, columnist, and self-described feminist and political junkie. "They weren't really outré any more.… If anything, they were more of a thing that good girls did to avoid being 'bad' girls by having vaginal sex.… But they were also the ultimate expression of sex that men wanted and women gave: supposedly 'unfeminist,' unreciprocated, gross, uncomfortable, heavy with unspoken power dynamics. Women who gave blowjobs willy-nilly were the ones who made it harder for other women *not* to give blowjobs." Among L.A.'s entertainment industry crowd, the b.j. became such standard fare that in 1996, L. Lou Paget, a rather Junior League–ish ex-Fox studio hand, began to host living room fellatio seminars for groups of "Hollywood wives, ex-wives, actresses, agents, and P.R. women," according to

There was collateral experimentation as well. "Anal sex has become a surrogate for maintaining virginity," Pinsky would argue in a *Playboy* interview, citing those who use the same rationale for having oral sex. "Young women will call [the radio program] and say… 'Me and my boyfriend were doing anal sex, so I'm still a virgin.'…Virginity has become some sort of technicality.…But what's lost is the notion that virginity once implied chastity. Anal sex is not chastity!"

Private acts were one thing. In the semipublic world of party culture, sexual "acting out" became a rite of passage for many young people, facilitated by a boom in binge drinking. When high school and college-age friends, for example, zipped off for spring break, the drinking, drugs, and public debauchery seemed progressively more pronounced, or at least more out in the open than in earlier eras. And an added level of peer-pressure prurience gave these excursions their own virality. Beginning in 1997, producer Joe Francis would send camera crews to breaker beach towns to shoot *Girls Gone Wild* videos. The filmmakers, playing off the pack mentality of the inebriated mob, would come away with pure fool's gold: footage of young women (often utterly blotto, sometimes underage) being persuaded to remove their tops, French-kiss female companions, or perform sexually suggestive acts for the camera. *Girls Gone Wild* tapes, clips, and downloads would make Francis millions before he'd be named in multiple lawsuits (for privacy invasion, among other charges), eventually being convicted and fined for submitting false tax returns.

Many adolescents, of course, were following television's lead. As network audiences shrank and Americans migrated elsewhere for their entertainment and information,[4] the level of flesh and din went into overdrive—to hold eyeballs, eardrums, and market share.

Each week *Baywatch* conjured a beachside paradise where the waves

---

Krista Smith, who wrote about the fad in *Vanity Fair*. During the three-hour sessions, Paget would hand out "instructional products (read 'dildos') affixed to fine-china plates" and participants would learn the fine points of the Basket Weave and the Taffy Pull. (Megan Carpenter, "Monica Lewinsky's Story Is a Scandal of America's Double-Standards," *Guardian*, May 8, 2014; Krista Smith, "Lips Together, Teeth Apart," *Vanity Fair*, March 2000, 146.)

4. From 1982 to 1992 to 2002, the percentage of television households that turned on network shows in prime time shrank from 51 percent to 37 to 22. (James Poniewozik, "Here's to the Death of Broadcast," *Time*, March 26, 2009, 62.)

always beckoned and Pamela Anderson always bounced. On air for the entire decade (actually 1989 through 2001, with one short lapse after its maiden season), *Baywatch* was syndicated to 148 countries and drew a *billion* viewers a week, becoming a global ambassador for nubile sexuality and a triumphalist American assuredness (lifeguards always on duty). Concurrently, ABC broadcast detective drama *NYPD Blue*, which was notorious for its early (1993) use of four-letter words on network TV and for its occasional exposure of actor David Caruso's butt. Leading the pack was the Fox network, launched in 1986, which would provide heaping helpings of raunch sauce, from *Married...with Children* to the nightly tabloid-news program *A Current Affair* (with segments like "Worship of the Flesh" and "Superbowl Hookers").

L. Brent Bozell III, then president of the Parents Television Council, a conservative cultural watchdog group, would release some vexing findings in 1997 after the organization's researchers sat through the February "sweeps" and monitored content during the so-called family hour (from 8 to 9 p.m.). By PTC's count, the networks had aired "60 references to sexual intercourse in 93 hours of programming.... Forty-three of them focused on either premarital or extramarital sex, [making] the overall sex-outside-marriage to sex-within-marriage ratio: 3.6 to 1." Bozell would also lament the preponderance of gay and lesbian characters and plots on prime-time TV. The PTC's statisticians, for good measure, would designate Fox as "the most sex-obsessed network."

To sell products—and to remain relevant to the vital and elusive eighteen- to twenty-four-year-old demo—programmers had to *target* them. Many series featured tribes of adolescents coming of age, or clusters of young adults just chilling. The programs were sometimes family-friendly (*7th Heaven* stands out) but many, too numerous to name, taught questionable, soapy lessons to younger viewers, among them *Beverly Hills 90210*, *Melrose Place*, and *Dawson's Creek*, which the PTC labeled broadcast's "filthiest TV series."

Others were part of the communal grope-and-gripe genre, most notably NBC's *Friends*, which debuted in 1994. Culture editor Amy Paulsen (my sister-in-law, it so happens), who wrote the compendium *True Friends*, recalls the long-running series as "a non-stop pageant of hooking up, breaking up, and making up. If anything, the women on the show seemed much more sexually active than the men. They weren't trollops; it was understood they would sleep with whomever they wanted. There was absolutely no double standard. *Friends* felt groundbreaking because these twenty-somethings didn't dance around the topic of sex. They talked about their encounters openly, matter-of-factly, and *often*. These kids were having a *lot* of sex.

"But because the sex talk was [couched in] well-constructed comedy, the audience was laughing too much to feel shocked or offended. No one was outraged when Jennifer Aniston—as Rachel—sought a penis embargo, or when David Schwimmer, playing Ross, had his horny monkey, Marcel, hump inanimate objects, [prompting Rachel to react], 'I have a Malibu Barbie that will no longer be wearing white to her wedding.' The sole function of the sex was to serve as a great source of witty, wonderful, toss-away lines."

James Wolcott in 1999 would accurately diagnose the teen-and-tween entertainment dynamic in a *Vanity Fair* column: "The 90s teen craze seems more like a marketing bonanza, a precision strike to reach the baby-boomers' affluent offspring." On programs like *Dawson's Creek* and *Party of Five*, he suggested, the serial misbehavior of the New Pubescent was made to feel cool, as if "it's always party time in teenland, where unchaperoned orgies are the weekend norm [and the dawn is punctuated by] bleary-eyed visits to the local convenience store where the gangrene fluorescent lighting represents The Soullessness of Late Capitalism." The "mean girl," meanwhile, became a trope in films like *Heathers* (1989), *Wild Things*, and *Cruel Intentions* (both of late '90s vintage), in which torturous shame games went beyond all established moral boundaries. To young audiences, there was *glamour* in being cruel and bored and sexually numb—just like *adults*.

Of course, there were TV's *young adults* too. *Seinfeld*, created by Jerry Seinfeld and Larry David, aired an hour after *Friends* on NBC's Thursday night lineup. The sitcom followed the angst-laden lives of three Manhattan friends and their pal, Jerry (the actual comedian, playing a comedian). The characters—self-absorption made corporeal—agonized over social gaffes, surface appearances, and sexual hang-ups.[5] And, naturally, some of the program's most popular episodes revolved around Sex and the Single Neurotic:

---

5. "*Seinfeld* signaled the end of Western civilization," my friend Robert Longo, the artist, tells me. In his view, the program "brought in the idea of real selfishness that everyone's adopted very prevalently in the culture. 'I gotta get mine first.'...They all had that quality of not looking out for the fellow man—and finding humor in it. 'Schadenfreude' could have almost been the subtitle of the show." (Interview with Longo.)

a contest to see how long a person could forswear masturbation; a panic over the discontinuation of a favorite prophylactic sponge; a rebuff of homophobia, with an almost snidely delivered refrain, "Not that there's anything *wrong* with that." *Seinfeld* became the most popular show on television, still syndicated to this day.

Which brings to mind an anecdote.

One night in 1993, photojournalist David Turnley called me and urged me to dash uptown. All day, he'd been with Seinfeld, bopping around Manhattan and taking pictures for a story for *Life* (where at the time I served as director of photography). "Jerry's doing a set," Turnley said, and if I could catch a cab, I could catch his stand-up routine and meet him.

I did as I was told, and upon arrival was introduced to Seinfeld. "Jerry," said Turnley, "this is David, from *Life*." I was also introduced to Jerry's young companion, Shoshanna Lonstein. Seinfeld, it turned out, had met her in Central Park (that afternoon or earlier that week). At eighteen, she was twenty-one years his junior.

The text in the *Life* story would provide some background. On a lark, Jerry thought they'd have some fun—and get some lively shots for *Life*—if he walked up to women and asked them to pose for photos with the hottest comedian on network television.[6] *Click.* Amid the innocuous snaps, something clearly clicked between Seinfeld and a smiling stranger. And here she was.

Seinfeld and Lonstein in fact would end up dating for several years, becoming fodder for the gossip pages, which would routinely take digs at Lonstein for her age (the "cradle-robbed...high-school honey") and her figure ("We have called her curvy, well upholstered," admitted Richard Johnson, then the editor of the *New York Post*'s "Page Six" column). The meet-cute meet-up and the ceaseless coverage of their romance made picture-perfect sense in the media's hall of mirrors. Here was the stand-up-comic star of a TV show about the life of a stand-up comic—a show, famously, *about nothing*—meeting a real-life girlfriend as part of a magazine photo op. It was

6. "Sunday In The Park: Jerry is on a mission," Brad Darrach wrote in *Life*. "He and a friend are hunting for pretty girls in Central Park. Whenever they find one, the friend takes a picture of Jerry and the girl. 'It's a prank,' Jerry explains—a way to *ootz* his absent buddy Mario Joyner, the comedian. 'Mario had to be out of town this weekend, and we want to show him pictures of all the gorgeous girls he didn't get to meet.'" The *Life* article points out that Seinfeld procures Lonstein's phone number that day. (Brad Darrach with Judy Ellis, "Jerry Seinfeld Lets It All Hang Out," *Life*, October 1993, 84.)

sheer media kismet in an age before social media or the selfie, the cell phone camera or the reality-TV boom. And it was only a matter of time before Lonstein (an Upper East Side scenester and social presence even prior to meeting Seinfeld) would become a brand in her own right as a successful fashion designer.

But back to *Seinfeld.* The series—socially savvy, sexually sophisticated, and addictive—would set the table for a spate of brainy, urban-ensemble-cast shows on network television and premium cable. In point of fact, cable in the '90s was already programming its share of series that addressed sexual matters in new ways, far beyond the tawdry public-access offerings of the '70s. (The networks, because they broadcast on "free" airwaves, were still subject to the FCC's codes of decency.[7] Not so programs that traveled via cable, satellite, or Internet connection.) In 1990, for instance, HBO rolled out *Real Sex,* purporting to be the *60 Minutes* of Eros. Segments covered Tantric lovemaking, anal-sex workshops, and the delicate art of making plaster molds of porn stars' pudenda. (Other progressive cable series, from *South Park* to *The Sopranos,* are mentioned elsewhere in these pages.)

A bona fide game-changer, however, premiered in 1992: the first contemporary reality-TV show. MTV's *The Real World,*[8] created by Mary-Ellis Bunim and Jonathan Murray, started out as a shrewd anthropological study. The concept: what happens when young professionals are thrown together as roommates, cameras rolling, in a cushy Manhattan apartment? In the first few seasons, according to *Newsweek*'s Abigail Jones, coauthor of *Restless Virgins: Love, Sex, and Survival at a New England Prep School,* "sex was discussed, not seen. Tami got an abortion. David got evicted after pulling a blanket off Tami. Pedro, who was HIV-positive, made the disease relatable to many viewers. By the fifth season, set in Miami, came the first of many

---

7. Well, yes and no. As *Newsweek* would point out, "During the budget crunches of the late '80s, [the] networks pared down their standards-and-practices watchdog departments, giving adventurous producers an unchallenged path to the airwaves. The FCC, meanwhile, has lost its teeth to deregulation-happy courts. Since a 1988 federal court decision, the commission has agreed not to mess with programs running after 8 p.m., as long as they eschew the seven dirty words." (John Leland, Marc Peyser, and Maggie Malone, "The Selling of Sex," *Newsweek,* November 1, 1992.)

8. The genre's roots can be traced back to long-form documentaries such as *An American Family,* the groundbreaking PBS study of members of a Middle American household, the Loud family, in the early 1970s.

sex-in-the-shower scenes. Thereafter, sex invaded the series. In Boston, in 1997, Genesis struggled with her sexuality and the roommates discussed, and allegedly heard, Kameelah's sex life. In Hawaii, in 1999, Kaia was the first roommate to walk around naked throughout the season, and Amaya and Colin had the first 'in-house' relationship."

In hindsight, Jones says today, "what began as a novel and intriguing social experiment became an overly sexual, mostly intoxicated, better-looking shell of its former self. When the show began, cast members were chosen to reflect the lives of young people. It was both a mirror and shaper of youth culture. Everything changed, however, in the late 1990s when the Internet arrived, infecting MTV's audience with uncontrollable—and seemingly attainable—urges for fame. [It became] clear that appearing on *The Real World* meant playing an edited, oftentimes unflattering version of yourself—and embracing it. The show marked the very point at which the fantasy of celebrity began to bleed uncontrollably into everyday life."

––––––––

As pop culture became steeped in sex, high culture was in no way immune. Indeed, artists had blazed the trail. "Art tends to precede mainstream culture by five to ten years," the esteemed arts writer, critic, and editor Ingrid Sischy would tell me in an interview. (Sischy passed away in 2015.) "Shifts in culture have their first steps through art, [as if artists see] what's coming down the pike in terms of collective culture. . . . The art world in general, and gay culture in particular, had heavily explored and expressed sexual themes in a very controversial way the previous decade.

"[Throughout] the various revolutions," she continued, "be it the feminist revolution, the gay revolution, the sexual revolution—the [human] figure had new jobs to do, new things to express. You started seeing the return of the figure into art, but in a completely different way. You're talking about the early performances of Marina Abramovic and Ulay. Or [Robert] Mapplethorpe's work. By the late '70s [and] early '80s, his most radical work is dealing with a totally different kind of figurative art: men together; his famous *Single Fist Fuck* or *Double Fist Fuck*; an image of a man's penis sort of being pinned down. These are images that had never come out from underground before."

In the '70s and '80s, "contemporary art. . . was looking for where the frontier is," she said, citing photographer Cindy Sherman's work about women and role-playing, Vito Acconci's live masturbation performances, and photographer David Wojnarowicz's images confronting AIDS. "AIDS was starting to wreak these unimaginable but very real losses in the art world, in the fashion world, in the creative worlds. That slogan 'Silence = Death' "— the AIDS-awareness initiative by the arts collective Gran Fury—"had enormous meaning because it further emphasized that subjects *not dealt with* really led to massive problems: by not talking about homosexuality; by [treating it as] a secret life, where so much shame existed.

"So by the mid-to-late '80s, you would go to an art fair and you would see, from booth to booth, gay artists, straight artists, really dealing with the subject of sexuality. It became—it's a word I don't like to use—but it truly became a trend. After Robert died [of AIDS in 1989] the show was censored at the Corcoran in Washington. It was a perfect storm because all of these cultural issues were meeting. [Senator] Jesse Helms was arguing about 'decadent [or degenerate] art'—very similar to phrases that Hitler had used—questioning how the NEA was spending money. Hysteria and ignorance about AIDS was still occurring." The Corcoran's cancellation came as a shock to the system, generating widespread publicity and art world condemnation. By April 1990, when the Cincinnati Contemporary Arts Center agreed to display Mapplethorpe's work, there were "lines around the block," Sischy recalled. "It was a watershed moment in terms of the public saying, 'We're going to decide for ourselves what we get to see. We don't need guardians of our culture.'[9] It was everywhere. But it wasn't just the Mapplethorpe show. It was this general subject of sex—I believe, very much because of AIDS.

"By the early '90s, it was no longer a province of the art world or the ACT UP world, which was the great organization formed in the fight against AIDS. It had obviously seeped into the general culture. The most forward-thinking people in advertising"—such as Benetton—"start[ed] to appropriate some of these subjects because the public needed it, wanted it, was hungry for it."

---

9. When the Corcoran caved under public and congressional pressure, retribution was swift, including "months of national protests, artists' boycotts, staff defections, patron withdrawals and more," the *L.A. Times* would report. The museum's director was dismissed, its finances crippled. And yet the art sword was double-edged. When the show traveled to Cincinnati, the institution and director there faced obscenity indictments. (Christopher Knight, "Damage Control at the Beleaguered Corcoran Gallery of Art," *Los Angeles Times*, December 20, 1989; Christopher B. Daly, "Mapplethorpe Exhibit Opens," *Washington Post*, August 2, 1990.)

Then, too, on the fringes of art and theater, there was a wave of experi-mentation in transgressive expression. Karen Finley helped pioneer what some called "shock art." She smeared herself with chocolate or rammed yams up various body openings to protest the violation of women by men and by society in general. She spray-painted velvet canvases with her breast milk to critique how establishment values had sanitized motherhood. Finley and three other performance artists, whose work was being proposed for federal grants—John Fleck, Holly Hughes, and Tim Miller—became known as "the NEA Four" as Congress called for defunding any art that went beyond "general standards of decency and respect."[10] (Imagery depicting minors tested those very standards. Photographer Jock Sturges's studio was raided; he eventually fended off porn charges by arguing that his pictures of children outdoors actually constituted "art." Photographer Sally Mann, meanwhile, withstood her own storm of criticism for continuing to exhibit and publish nude or near-nude images of her three young children.)

In London, Sarah Kane put on the play *Blasted*, replete with cannibalism and rape scenes. The "unstated premise," critic Ben Brantley remarked, was that "people like you and me... are capable... of behavior similar to the Balkan war atrocities that inspired [it]." In California, Ron Athey, the HIV-positive "extreme performance artist"—known for self-mutilation and bloodletting—would pierce his skin until blood gushed from his scalp and body in what one critic would call an expression of "fortitude in the time of AIDS." In New York, Cindy Sherman, who had famously concentrated on self-portraits, began using sex dolls and prostheses to craft grisly images of battered or debased women as a critique of the culture's drift toward banal misogyny and objectification. And Matthew Barney's *The Cremaster Cycle* (five films and companion art-works and installations) was named for the mysterious muscle that raises the testes.[11] These fin de siècle performances and portfolios in many ways mirrored

---

10. In a chilling 1998 decision, the Supreme Court ruled *against* them, saying that Congress had the authority to dispense funds by such criteria. ("Historic Case: Finley V. NEA," Center for Constitutional Rights, http://ccrjustice.org/home/what-we-do/our-cases/finley-v-nea.)

11. *Cremaster* featured satyr and fairy fantasies, erections and fallopian tubes, porn scenes and Isaac Mizrahi costumes—with cameo appearances by Norman Mailer, Ursula Andress, and the Mormon Tabernacle Choir. (Stephen Holden, "It's About a Murderer and Yes, Bees, Houdini...," *New York Times*, October 13, 1999; Jordan Hoffman and Alex Needham, "Matthew Barney's Cremaster Cycle...," Guardian.com, July 14, 2015.)

the paradigm shift at the end of the nineteenth century when "decadent" poets emerged in France, and European art and literature were marked by escapism, ennobled desperation, and a sense of impending apocalypse.

Early in the decade, the artist (and onetime commodities broker) Jeff Koons—engaged at the time to Italian porn star and politician Ilona Staller, a.k.a. Cicciolina—was creating sculptures and huge pointillist canvases of the artist and subject having sex. He depicted anal sex, oral sex, spread-eagled sex, sometimes with glistening ejaculate coating Staller's orifices. The pieces were meant to echo Baroque religious sculpture and porn-movie money shots. John Currin, like Koons, was also creating works that others considered kitsch. He would paint cartoonishly bosomy or disfigured models (in tableaux that referenced soft porn and Italian Renaissance portraiture) as well as elderly women, as he put it, "at the end of the cycle of sex and potential, between the object of desire and the object of loathing."

In the U.K., the group that would come to be known as the YBAs—Young British Artists—was in its heyday. Their installations were often grotesqueries: Damien Hirst's pickled animals; the pornified child mannequins of Jake and Dinos Chapman; and the work of Sarah Lucas, who used vegetables as sexual appendages and took self-portraits that upended gender roles and erotic assumptions. Little of this, of course, sat well with social conservatives— especially when the work traveled to American galleries. Public officials, in fact, were outraged when the British group show "Sensation" was mounted at the Brooklyn Museum in 1999, and civic leaders demanded to know why government coffers were being tapped to subsidize morally destructive messages.

Over lunch, I meet Sunny Mindel, who in the late '90s served as New York mayor Rudy Giuliani's press secretary. "The Brooklyn Museum is a museum that's supposed to be available for everybody in New York to enjoy," she says. When its curators decided to exhibit "Sensation," as Mindel remembers it, "Chris Ofili's piece was *The [Holy] Virgin Mary*, surrounded by dung and pornographic images of a woman's vajayjay. That was art. Another one was a dead shark in a tank—by Damien Hirst. Another one, if I recall correctly, was a celebration of phalluses. And another one was a representation of all of these kids that had been sexually molested and murdered in England."

Her boss, she recalls, was incensed. Giuliani decreed at the time, "The idea of, in the name of art, having a city-subsidized building have so-called works of art in which people are throwing elephant dung at a picture of the Virgin Mary—that's sick."

————

Overt depictions of sex or the human body didn't stop with art installations and performance pieces. Mainstream actors, on stage and screen, were becoming more comfortable simulating sex, performing naked, or taking on roles that only a few years before might have been considered career-killers. In 1993, Madonna played an S&M-inclined wife in *Body of Evidence* and would tell Norman Mailer in *Esquire* about her close encounters with Willem Dafoe: "I did feel that this must be what it feels like to make a porno movie.... There was no penetration or anything like that. But if you're sitting on someone's face, you are sitting on someone's face." Kate Winslet, beginning with 1994's *Heavenly Creatures*, would remove her clothes in eleven films. On Broadway and London's West End, Hollywood A-listers would pop up in the buff (the better to fill all those high-priced seats): Jude Law emerged from a bath in *Indiscretions*; Nicole Kidman stripped down in *The Blue Room*. And in *The Full Monty*—a 1997 film that became a hit musical—laid-off steelworkers (whose wives and girlfriends had managed to hold on to their service-sector jobs) soothed their bruised egos by deciding to embrace their feminine sides and do a group strip-tease show—to the delight (and not the rebuke) of their ladies-in-waiting.

Perhaps the most provocative theatrical performance of all was that of Scottish-born Alan Cumming, who appeared as the seductive, debauched, heroin-shooting Emcee in the hit revival of *Cabaret*. The musical, through the prism of Berlin's bawdy Kit Kat Klub, examined the sexual frisson, gender turbulence, and political precariousness of life in Germany as Hitler rose to power. It touched a '90s nerve.

Part of the appeal of the *Cabaret* revival came from the era's Weimar parallels: sharp economic divisions, fundamentalist clashes, global turmoil. America, for all its economic zest, was clouded by a sense of imminent doom. And both eras, Cumming recalls, shared a creeping hedonism. "People had a lot of images and theories thrown at them in the '90s," says the actor, who meets me for lunch at an Indian curry house in Manhattan's East Village. "*Cabaret* came along and it became more than just a musical on Broadway. It represented [an argument for] sexual freedom, provocation, and a sort of slight deviance. I think the fact it wasn't 'modern' gave people this idea: 'This has gone on for a while—so why aren't *we* doing it? Why are we not as free as *they* seem to be?'"

Cumming expresses pride that the production tried to be "emblematic of the [1930s] in terms of the sexuality aspect. I think people sort of saw, 'Oh, that's real. They're doing it grittier and [in a] kind of provocative [way] as it would have been in the Weimar Republic. It made them more comfortable about it. And it also hit at a time when people were hungry for, or open to, that kind of difference...about gayness or bisexuality or not just straight, sort-of-boring sex."

Cumming, having dated and married members of both sexes, abhors labels about his own sexuality. That said, he acknowledges that while playing *Cabaret*'s nasty Emcee his "personal persona and [stage] persona merged. I came to America and there was an explosion with that show and I was very much perceived...as someone who's the poster boy for deviance or decadence." Indeed, he brought such a degree of sizzling eroticism to the role (for much of his stage time he appeared topless, save suspenders, a bow tie, and some red rouge on his nipples) that the audience had an electric response. "It was really interesting how people got really frisky around me," he says, discussing theatergoers' behavior after the show, or at parties, or when approached by fans out on the town. "Married couples would start telling me about sex or they would touch me in inappropriate ways...and be just dirty with each other. People would get giddy and sort of really touch me in a way that I was, like, *Ewww.*...The show, and I, kind of unleashed something— sort of a comfort with people being more sexually exploratory."

And the nadir of high-gloss debauchery? In July 1999, a month after Cumming left the *Cabaret* stage, filmmaker Stanley Kubrick would release his last feature, *Eyes Wide Shut*, in which Cumming makes an appearance. The linchpin of the movie is the ultimate Gen-Degenerate party scene: filthy rich voyeurs, in masks, nonchalantly and almost clinically observing sex acts and what appears to be a ritual or charade of human sacrifice. Only in the '90s would Hollywood's "It" couple—Tom Cruise and Nicole Kidman—drop out of circulation for *two years* to shoot a *two-and-a-half-hour* movie that basically revolves around their characters' sex lives (*and* around Kidman's naked, double-bass booty, filmed from every conceivable angle). *Eyes Wide Shut* would immerse viewers in a chilly mélange of glorified sadomasochism, cult chic, super-sublimated desire, and stilted attempts at cinematic depravity that, inadvertently, catapult into camp.

———

The impressionable youth of the Me Decade (a '70s conceit of Tom Wolfe's) grew into the egocentric individualists of the Greed Decade (an '80s conceit of Oliver Stone's). By the '90s they had come to rule the roost.[12] They published, and favored, confessional prose—*me*-moirs, which energized book clubs and Web forums. Some memoirs were painfully raw, detailing psychological struggles and debilitating addictions: Susanna Kaysen's *Girl, Interrupted*, Elizabeth Wurtzel's *Prozac Nation*, Caroline Knapp's *Drinking: A Love Story*, and Jerry Stahl's *Permanent Midnight*. But the autobiographies that caused the greatest stir among the cognoscenti were the ones distinguished for their sexual candor. Joyce Maynard wrote about her long-ago love affair (at age nineteen) with the reclusive J. D. Salinger (then fifty-three). In *The Architect of Desire*, Suzannah Lessard went back three generations— to the kinky life and death of her great-granddad Stanford White, the Beaux-Arts architect—to account for some of the sexual fallout in her family. *The Kiss*, by Kathryn Harrison, was a story of incest: about her longtime affair with her father, a preacher.

Then there was the *New Yorker* essay by the critic and belletrist Daphne Merkin. "Unlikely Obsession" dealt with Merkin's longing to be spanked. "I cannot remember a time," she wrote, "when I didn't think about being spanked as a sexually gratifying act, didn't fantasize about being reduced to a craven object of desire by a firm male hand." The *New Yorker*, yes, the staid *New Yorker*, had gotten its groove on with the arrival of a new editor, Tina Brown, who began to tart up Eustace Tilley's old magazine. She brought in Roseanne Barr, the blue-collar darling, as a guest editor; commissioned eye-popping Avedon nudes (of actress Tilda Swinton) and outré covers (such as Barry Blitt's "same-sex union" special, showing two male sailors lip-locked in Times Square); and allowed writers to use words that had never graced the publication's pages: "anal," "asshole," "cunt," "motherfucker," and "pussy."

Columnists, too, got into the sexual trenches at other publications as writers like Candace Bushnell and Amy Sohn reported on New York's real-life folkways and three-ways. Celebrities were publishing tell-all books that oscillated between triumph and train wreck. Drew Barrymore's *Little Girl Lost*

---

12. Culture arbiter Kurt Andersen would affix a tongue-in-cheek moniker to the entire period: "The self-absorbed 'Me' Decade, having expanded during the '80s and '90s from personal life to encompass the political economy, will soon be the 'Me' Half Century." (Kurt Andersen, "The Downside of Liberty," *New York Times*, July 4, 2012.)

recounted her childhood chaos, the drugs, the rehab. Basketball god Wilt Chamberlain's *A View from Above* boasted of his having bedded twenty *thousand* women. Nineties "It Girl" Jenny McCarthy, in *Jen-X*, would chronicle the travails of her youth and then offer comic pearls: "Isn't that the American dream? To purchase fine new breasts on credit?"

Literary fiction was going through its own erotic surge. Kathy Acker and Mary Gaitskill explored the multilayered mind-sets of their characters' sensual frontiers. Carol Shields devoted an entire chapter of *Larry's Party* to the hero's penis. And since the Old Lit chauvinists like Updike, Roth, and Mailer had all off-wacked themselves, their heirs now had to go to extremes to get a rise out of readers and reviewers. Bret Easton Ellis's 1991 novel *American Psycho* was the object of a boycott by the National Organization of Women for its graphic passages about torturing, raping, mutilating, and dismembering female characters. Nicholson Baker weaved an entire 1992 novella, *Vox*, around a single marathon phone-sex conversation. That same year, in Will Self's *Cock & Bull*, the female protagonist sprouted a prick while the male found he'd been endowed with a secret vagina.

Books, at least, could be read in private. But more and more, sex seemed to be in the very ether. MTV was running videos that could have doubled as sex-ed classes. With each passing year, songs were taking naughty up a notch: from 2 Live Crew's "Me So Horny" (1989), to Salt-N-Pepa's "Let's Talk About Sex" (1990), to Naughty by Nature's "O.P.P." (for "Other People's Pussy," 1991). Rock groups were stripping down onstage, from the Barenaked Ladies to the Red Hot Chili Peppers, who liked to come out with their junk sheathed in tube socks. *Rolling Stone*'s covers became a skin parade, with nude portraits of Janet Jackson, the Chili Peppers, and Blind Melon—not to mention a shot of seventeen-year-old Britney Spears, the ex-Mouseketeer, in black bra and short shorts in her Kentwood, Louisiana, bedroom, hugging a Teletubby. Yes, musicians had been playing havoc with conventional notions of sex and gender since rock's cave days. But artists such as Björk and Marilyn Manson were now going the art-house route in their performances, publicity photos, and videos.

While gangsta rappers and their producers were being targeted by cops—and consumed by feuds[13]—lyrics in the rap canon doubled down on

---

13. Within a six-month span, L.A.'s Tupac Shakur and Brooklyn's Notorious B.I.G. would be shot to death.

misogyny, sexual debasement, and calls for violence. Time Warner took special heat for supporting content that, according to critics, normalized sexual and physical injury. The company promoted recording artists such as Nine Inch Nails (whose song "Big Man with a Gun" talked about murder "just for the fuck of it" and holding "a big old dick...against your forehead"). It was also home to Ice-T, whose "Cop Killer" was pointedly and recklessly antiblue in the wake of the 1992 L.A. riots, even if the track had been intended as a statement against police brutality—a generation before the rise of the Black Lives Matter movement.

"The industry rallied round Time Warner," observed conservative jurist Robert Bork in his '90s jeremiad, *Slouching Towards Gomorrah*, declaring that music execs had "lost touch with both logic and morality. To speak of songs about ripping vaginas and licking anuses as necessary to retain the right to make creative choices is a rhetorical obscenity that almost matches what is on the records. There has to be a limit somewhere to what a culture can tolerate and still retain not just creative choice but a vestige of decency."

That said, the 1990s did bring hip-hop to maturity, putting it on such a vaunted perch that it would become the dominant American music form over the course of the next twenty-five years. No small feat, that—and quite a significant yardstick in measuring how the right was flailing and failing in the culture war.

————

Then there was the ether itself. On radio, "Dr. Drew" was appearing nightly on *Loveline*. The phone-in show, which Drew Pinsky had pioneered at Pasadena's KROQ in the '80s, featured callers recounting their bedroom exploits and seeking tips on everything from sexual health to dodgy relationships. The program was revolutionary for its candid and often sobering admonishments about interpersonal behavior—mixed in with shock-jock raunch and repartee, courtesy of cohost Adam Carolla. *Loveline* became a radio phenomenon in 1995 (attracting three million listeners) when it was syndicated nationally, along with a companion cable program on MTV.

In many ways, the show anticipated the Web's role as a tool for dispensing useful information to the sexually inquisitive in the age of AIDS and STDs. Ryan Cook, an actor and model, recalls the invaluable role *Loveline* played many a night as he put on his headphones—and locked his bedroom door—as a junior high school student in Geneva, Illinois. "You would listen to these people's stories," he remembers, "and it would teach you a lot about yourself in terms of your sexual being, your sexual sanity.... You're lying in bed, you have the lights off, and these people would get into graphic detail with Dr. Drew.

"You get sexually aroused," he says. "It came at a time for me when I was questioning everything sexually, my orientation.... It was definitely pushing the envelope for that era. *Loveline* was radio porn. [At the time] I was for the most part straight but I was also humping my Ninja Turtle doll, Raphael. [In puberty] you're at your most vulnerable emotionally and sexually." While comedian Carolla kept things light, Pinsky was the voice of reason, Cook recalls. "[A worried caller would say,] 'I'm having this symptom,' and Dr. Drew was no-bullshit, 'Listen, this is what's going on with you—yadda yadda yadda.' He was a sexual reference [book], the encyclopedia."

The chief impulse behind many of the calls, says Drew Pinsky today, was exhibitionism. "People were sort of humiliating themselves on *Loveline*. People would ask me, 'What would motivate people to get up and say those humiliating things?' Really, it's to be famous." In his view, tabloid talk shows—he cites Jerry Springer and Jenny Jones—started it all. "It was 'anything to be seen in the media, to be heard.' That was the beginning of fame-seeking as an autonomous motivator. That didn't exist before the '80s.... That didn't exist in human history."

The true ruler of the airwaves, however, was a man named Howard Stern.

Stern was, and remains, talk radio's foulmouthed comic genius. His humor could be self-deprecating or self-aggrandizing, puerile or enlightened. He was a master of the confessional interview, with a flair for inveigling highly personal and often sexual admissions from his famous and often notorious guests. He was a radio ringmaster, herding office staffers, chatty listeners, and a regular ensemble of misfit "Wack Packers"—all intent on getting their five minutes of shame. His open mic welcomed a succession of celebrities, has-beens, porn stars, the scandal-scarred—and miscellaneous sexually adventurous stragglers, some of whom would come to the studio to strip, have their butts "bongo-ed," or achieve very public orgasms by straddling the office Sybian—a motorized, *rideable* vibrator.

The effervescence of *The Howard Stern Show*—beyond the wall-to-wall laughs—was the result of four essential ingredients. First was the knowledge that at any moment the real-time riffing on forbidden subjects could carom off into salacious, inane, or gross-out terrain. Second, the troupe of regulars gave the program an extended-family feel: listeners felt they were part of a dysfunctional freak-show community—*years* before social media. Third, Stern devoted ample airtime to *fan*-generated content: listeners recounting sexual exploits, sharing humiliating tales, or even playing audiotapes of themselves as they disrupted public events or media gatherings (where they would mention Stern's name or shout "Baba Booey"—the moniker of Stern's executive producer, Gary Dell'Abate).

The overriding thrill, though, came from *listening in*, from overhearing what in otherwise polite society would have been considered private acts or fantasies. This was an audio peep show. And every day Stern and his on-air partner, Robin Quivers—in perfect alignment with tabloid media, "reality"-era oversharing, and the burgeoning Internet—were breaking down the wall between the personal and the public.

Howard Stern was often accused of sexism, homophobia, racism, and demeaning the disabled—sometimes all before lunchtime. But as a First Amendment trailblazer he stood high in the Sybian saddle, battling the FCC, collecting indecency fines, and testing the patience and pocketbook of his corporate overseers. (Stern declined to comment for this book.)

In hindsight, Stern really broke into the media mesosphere in 1993 with a blockbuster memoir, *Private Parts*. The book traced his life story from his nerdy boyhood, to his days as a studio journeyman, to his rise to radio icon. It also taught readers Stern's preferred methods of masturbating and his rules for a healthier rectum. It listed some of the show's classic cringe-worthy moments: call-in favorite "Celeste" agreeing to have sex with a blind person (on TV); "The Kielbasa Queen" swallowing foot-longs; and uncensored recollections, like the time basketball star Charles Barkley called and, by Stern's account, told him he'd "just shared a hot tub with Donald Trump and some hot babes. I said that after that the water must have looked like egg drop soup!"

The shepherd of the project was Judith Regan, a powerhouse publishing presence in the 1990s, first at Simon & Schuster, then at Rupert Murdoch's HarperCollins. Fearless, shrewd, and legendarily profane, Regan could claim a diverse track record, publishing authors who were erudite (Walter Kirn) or zeitgeist-y (Douglas Coupland) or political (Rush Limbaugh) or decidedly risqué (Toni Bentley's *The Surrender*, detailing her attraction to anal sex). But Regan's literary success—and the sizable revenue she brought to the bottom line—rested on her common gal's gut for titles that anticipated mass-market tastes. Her sweet spot: autobiographies that laid bare a celebrity's every jot and tittle. Without Judith Regan there would have been no *Jen-X* by Jenny McCarthy, no *How to Make Love Like a Porn Star* by Jenna Jameson, and certainly no *If I Did It*—O. J. Simpson's hypothetical nonconfession.

I contact Regan to discuss her role in the '90s and in burnishing the Stern brand. She agrees to meet for breakfast, though she sounds skeptical: "You want to talk about how I single-handedly brought about the decline of Western civilization?" (She's riffing on a jibe from old press accounts—a comment that has also been made about Old Man Murdoch.)

"*Private Parts* made [Howard Stern] a rock star," Regan says. Indeed, the bestseller had helped solidify Stern's influence beyond shock-jockery and cable TV, moving him aggressively into print, pay-per-view, feature films, and eventually the Web.[14] "He really *did* become the King of All Media," insists Regan, validating Stern's pet epithet. "He was one of the originators of this"— meaning expanding the culture's comfort level with discussing and confronting sexuality, and forcing others, through a sort of on-air therapy, to publicly describe and defend their private parts: their values, their fears, their psyches' true colors. "He was the one that broke down those barriers," she says. "He was the one that went over the line, repeatedly. Now there are no lines. But he was coloring outside the box on the radio, and building this audience, and he was saying things that were shocking, that people didn't say."

Regan describes their literary collaboration, and the mutual infatuation

---

14. I ask Regan to spell out the reasoning behind the design she chose for the logo of ReganBooks, the imprint she started in 1994 under Murdoch. It showed a lone woman holding a baby—and a sword. (Regan would leave the company under circumstances both acrimonious and litigious, but that's a story for another decade.) Apropos of the logo, she says, women effectively took over the culture—by default and with defiance—once men neglected their traditional roles and obligations to their families. Men, in her view, "threw out the baby with the bathwater. And the '60s had a lot of damaging effects on family life and children.... Now you have a whole culture of the latchkey kids. Nobody's home. There's no extended families, there's no grandparents, there's no father." It started, Regan says, with the counterculture of the 1960s, when she was coming of age. "After the '60s [men] decided, 'Okay, you know what? We don't have to get married. We don't have to make commitments. We don't have to raise the children—*you* do it.' And they did."

Does she mean, I ask, that women, by the 1990s, held the upper hand in the power play between the sexes, and that "the men became sort of milquetoast and my gender allowed the women to just sort of rule?" She responds, "You didn't allow us to rule. No. You abandoned us. You did not fulfill your obligations to us. You left us at the side of the road with children in our arms. We said, 'Well, since you're not going to help raise these children, we'll do it ourselves.' " (Interview with Regan.)

that developed during long sessions by Stern's pool, on Long Island, where she basically moved into his guesthouse in order to get the manuscript completed. "We were very in sync with each other. He's a really sensitive man, incredibly brilliant.... It was like a high school flirtation. But it was really an intellectual one, even though there were erotic elements because we were on the road together and we were of a certain age. But, like, I never had sex with Howard Stern. We didn't have an affair. We didn't carry on in that way. I think we had a deep affection for each other.

"He was constantly aroused—I'll say that much," she admits, laughing. "He always had erections. [I knew] because he would be sitting there next to me.... He was just a really horny guy. I thought for a while he was wearing something because he loved to shock me." One day, Regan recalls, "I took a pencil, on the eraser, and I poked it—and it was alive!"

Much of Stern's shtick in the '90s centered around the humor and frisson that grew out of his desire to stay faithful to his wife, Alison Berns, his Boston University sweetheart, while living in a sexed-up environment that offered temptation at every turn. (Their marriage ended in 2001.) "It was a time," says Regan, "when he reflected the feelings of those guys who were driving around in the trucks in Manhattan and across America, listening to him. He *was* that character he created on the radio. He *did* go home every night. He was frustrated. He did go down to the basement and jerk off to porn. He did feel guilty about everything. He was that guy.

"In many respects, I actually think that Howard Stern, more than anyone that I've ever worked with, echoed so much of what happened to this country and what happened as a result of all that permissiveness."

CHAPTER 16

Botox, Booties, and Bods

The diatribes were falling on deaf ears. About how women were being commodified. About how girls were being eroticized. About society's fixation on body image. In fact, women (and men) by the tens of millions were more concerned than ever before about their appearance, their personal style, their bods. Americans, seeking methods for feeling better about themselves, more attractive to their mates, and less depleted by the ravages of age, were resetting their clocks to Dorian Graylight Savings.

I call comedian Joan Rivers for her insight. (Our conversation takes place in 2011; she would pass away in 2014, at age eighty-one, from complications related to a surgical procedure on her larynx.)

Rivers had been a trailblazing comic. She'd developed her brash and sassy voice by building on the take-no-prisoners approach of risqué forerunners such as Belle Barth and "Moms" Mabley. She'd made her name by pointing out others' social and physical blunders. But she was equally frank about her own flaws, getting bonus miles out of her Jewish Princess preoccupations; her looks ("My best birth control now is just to leave the lights on"); and her arid love life ("My vagina is like Newark—men know it's there, but they don't want to visit"). Sexual relations were an essential part of her act, and yet she professed to find the sex act highly overrated. (Her take on anal said it all: "You can do other things! You can click on email! You can read a magazine!")[1]

---

1. In her Rivers biography, *Last Girl Before Freeway*, Leslie Bennetts maintains that sexual topics have always been essential to Rivers's act. "Much of Rivers' comedy, from the very first," writes Bennetts, "had its roots in sex: sexual relations, gender battles, and women squaring off against

As the '90s became progressively more synthetic, Rivers *embraced* that drift, waxing genuine about her own artifice. With zingers about her lifts and lipo, cosmetic surgery had found its biggest booster. ("My face," she quipped, "has been tucked in more times than a bedsheet at the Holiday Inn.") Like her predecessor Phyllis Diller, Rivers would demystify the process by discussing the "work" she'd had done—and she'd insist that her sisters in the Plastic Class do the same.

She explained to me that she'd started on this offensive around the time she landed her own late-night talk show on Fox in 1986. "I got very taken to task [in] the early '80s and '90s," she said, recalling an incident she found particularly galling. "I sat at a dinner table with four major movie stars, all of [whom] had such scars behind their ears you could have run the B&O Railroad across them. Each one said to me, 'What was it *like?*'" *Grow up,* she told them—a signature line of hers. "Nobody was telling the truth. I got very angry. I come out of the Gloria Steinem generation, where we worked so hard to get women to be 'a woman on your own' and be a sister to each other.... Either we're together or we're not together. So I decided to advocate—to say, 'I am doing this and you can do this and you *should* do this' and became very vocal about it."

Plastic surgery was, prima facie, a fabrication. But Rivers seized the subterfuge and recast it as an empowerment tool. Sharing knowledge about one another's treatments, she said, was "truly an outgrowth of the women's movement, of saying, 'Here's another truth we can tell each other—to help each other.'" And yet, I asked her, wasn't second-wave feminism built on the authentic? The organic? "Don't give me that," she snapped. "Gloria Steinem always bleached her hair.... I used to say to [fellow feminists], 'Why are you shaving your legs?' In those days you shaved. It was all about 'men like me au naturel.' It was nonsense. Half the bras that were burned were *padded.*"[2]

---

each other. Indeed, she made her name as a sexually liberated single woman. During the early 60s, her stand-up routine often closed with the punch line: 'I'm Joan Rivers, and I put out!'" (Leslie Bennetts, "Joan Rivers' Remarkable Rise [and Devastating Fall] from Comedy's Highest Ranks," Vanityfair.com, November 2016.)

2. Since her earliest years in stand-up, Rivers had understood that women, as feminists, needed to confront the harsh reality that they were competing, living, and loving in a society governed by male rules and biases. "From the nineteen-sixties on," *New Yorker* critic Emily Nussbaum has argued, "Rivers had been the purveyor of a harsh Realpolitik, one based on her experience: looks mattered."

Flash forward to the decade under discussion. Rivers would contend that she finally recognized a change in attitude. "A lot of what happened in the '90s," she believed, "is that we learned you could have *both*. Women said, 'I can be strong and empowered and this-and-that, but I can also use my sex appeal. I've got an extra weapon.' It's great." She added, laughing, "And when all else fails—cry!"[3]

Indeed, the entire cosmetic gamut was destigmatized, from peels to microdermabrasion to breast enhancement surgery. And Rivers was at the center of that shift. Patients, as Sander L. Gilman points out in his book *Making the Body Beautiful*, were being referred to as "clients." Surgeries became "corrections." Operations became "procedures." From 1981 to 1996, writes Gilman, "the total number of all aesthetic surgical procedures" would increase more than sixfold, "exceed[ing] 1.9 million [or] about one procedure for every 150 people in the United States every year." And starting in the '90s, the majority of Americans seeking such surgeries, which had long been the province of the elite, would come from the lower- and middle-class income range.

At the same time, Rivers had also become a connoisseur of celebrity surface. Previously, film fans had watched the Academy Awards telecast out of a fascination with actors, filmmakers, and their craft; to get swept up in the spectacle; and to thrill to the thunder of a great horse race. Come the early '90s, though, that horse had gone to pasture. Moviegoers were less taken

---

And when the comedian made fun of actresses' looks ("What's Liz Taylor's blood type? Ragu!"), she was telling her sisters, as Nussbaum puts it, "how to thrive in a sexist world"—to buck up through a "powerful alloy of girl talk and woman hate, her instinct for how misogyny can double as female bonding.... Rivers is explicit about her aim, which is not just to entertain but to educate: she wants fat girls to know that 'they need to pull it together,' to resist their mothers' dangerous lies about inner beauty." (Emily Nussbaum, "Last Girl in Larchmont," *New Yorker*, February 23, 2015.)

3. Many contemporary feminists have come on board in recent years. A skeptical Jennifer Cognard-Black—who teaches gender and sexuality, and sits on the *Ms.* Committee of Scholars—would remark in 2015, "[In the past,] I would have said that getting your boobs done or your tummy flattened is not feminist, and now I'm really not sure.... From a feminist perspective, putting voice behind one's body-image issues is better than feeling ashamed." What's more, the surgery surge was actually global, altering the appearance of women—and men—from Korea to Argentina, whose president Carlos Menem confessed he'd gone under the knife in 1991. "Brazil [recently] made plastic surgery tax deductible," writes *Time*'s Joel Stein. "And Iran, where women cover their hair and bodies but not their noses, leads the world in rhinoplasty." ("Rugged Machos Turning to Plastic Surgeon's Scalpel," Associated Press via *Southeast Missourian*, August 15, 1995; Joel Stein, "Nip. Tuck. Or Else," *Time*, June 29, 2015, 42–43.)

with screen performances than with the drama of stars' private lives. They became less concerned with critical reviews than with which film won each week at the box office.[4] To many Oscar-night viewers, all that began to matter was *the clothes*.

Beginning in 1994, Joan Rivers, as the harridan of fashion gaffes, almost single-handedly made the "arrivals" sideshow at the Golden Globes and the Academy Awards *more* compelling in some ways than the ceremonies inside. Along with her daughter, Melissa, she carpet-bombed the stars on the red carpet for the E! network, helping turn the mere act of *showing up somewhere* into a pastime, even a profession.[5] "Somebody said that Melissa and I made walking into a building an event," she remarked, "and that's absolutely true. The Academy Awards are very boring. Nobody cared who won Best Cinematographer. Nobody has any more attention span—and that was starting [back] then."

The E! network's executives, Rivers remembered, "said that Melissa and I could ask anything we wanted—just spice it up.... So we began to ask very shallow, funny questions. And one of the questions was, '*Who* are you wearing?' because I figured they *knew* that answer. It became an overnight hit."[6]

And yet, I asked, wasn't the red-carpet cattle call part of a deliberate plan by high-end designers? A way to get the great unswathed at home to go out and buy their clothes? "It wasn't a plot at all," said Rivers. "In the beginning [the stars] were still dressing themselves. And they looked like trailer trash—and it was fabulous. For every chic woman that walked in, you had Demi Moore who made her own bicycle pants one year, and you go, 'It's the

---

4. At the giddy close of the '90s (before the rupture of the dot-com bubble), HSX.com became the site of a popular "futures" market—cinema's version of rotisserie-league baseball, in which players bet on the success or failure of newly released feature films. (Mark Harris, "Shorting Tinseltown," *New York*, August 2, 2010, 16.)

5. Though the style arbiter Mr. Blackwell had been riffing on fashion gaucheries for years, it was the Rivers duo that formalized the riff, creating a sort of fashion rap that they televised vérité. By the twenty-first century, it would come to pass that many celebrities existed *only* to be photographed in front of a step-and-repeat wall in that narrow, flash-dappled span between the limo and the cloakroom.

6. ABC, which broadcast the Academy Awards ceremony, would adopt the fashion-interview format as part of its coverage in the time slot leading into the main event. And by 2011 the arrivals parade would become such an indispensable aspect of the evening that the network would expand its coverage (a short montage segment in the early years) to a full ninety minutes. (Manohla Dargis, "Oscars' Red Carpet (Parallel Universe)," *New York Times*, March 6, 2011, AR10–11.)

Academy Awards, you ass.' That's what made it. People began to watch—
to see this. And then the designers said, 'Wait a second. If they're going to
announce my name on television, let me see if I can dress these people.'"

Not quite. By the late 1980s, according to Patty Fox, in her book *Star
Style at the Academy Awards*, "socially and professionally connected women
were hired to be liaisons between the fashion designers and the film and television industry. A major goal was to get Hollywood stars zipped into designer
clothing on Oscar night." The race to dress the town's top talent really began
in earnest, pre-Rivers—in the late 1980s and early '90s—insists Bronwyn
Cosgrave, whose *Made for Each Other: Fashion and the Academy Awards* is
the definitive study of women's style on that enchanted evening. That's when
designer Giorgio Armani, working with L.A.'s fashion-savvy Wanda McDaniel, led the way in aggressively courting actresses to don their threads for the
traipse down the red carpet. Armani's competitor at the time was Fred Hayman, who at his pioneering boutique on Rodeo Drive stocked a veritable
"Oscar closet" from which the stars could pick and choose.[7] "The competition between Armani and Hayman as they vied to dress Hollywood during
1990's Oscar season," writes Cosgrave, "spared women the expense of buying
dresses, so the practice of commissioning great costume designers to make
them halted. The rivalry between Armani and Hayman also established fashion competition as integral to the buildup heralding the Academy Awards."

In any case, it was Joan Rivers, microphone in hand, who more than
anyone turned celebrities' arrivals *at anything* into sport, commerce, and
theater—a visual mash-up of fashion, flesh, and farce. She had fond memories of her maiden telecast. "The first one I spoke to on the red carpet was
John Travolta," she told me, "because I knew him. I think his words to me
were, 'What the fuck are you doing here?'"

Her response: "I was trying to be nice. 'A girl's got to make a living.'"

And what was *he* wearing that night?

"At that point, just a simple sheath and ballet slippers."

---

7. In 1990, Hayman was named the fashion coordinator for the Oscar ceremony and began
"sending an invitation to each nominee and presenter offering assistance in helping to choose an
outfit for the great night," according to the *New York Times'* William Grimes. "It was a bright idea
[Hayman remarked], because [many of] the stars dressed poorly." (William Grimes, "Fred Hayman,
Whose Giorgio Boutique Led Gilding of Rodeo Drive, Dies at 90" [obituary], *New York Times*, April
15, 2016, A25.)

Unlike some of their forebears in the second-wave feminist movement, '90s women seemed much more comfortable cultivating their appearance, their own signature style.

Lines were out. A syringeful of a new substance, Botox—actually botulinum toxin—was being utilized by doctors-in-the-know to smooth out furrows and other unsightlies. (It would be approved by the FDA in 2002.) Part of the perverse appeal of Botox was that it injected actual poison into a person's face. Curiously, this was less of a turn-off than the procedure's secondary risk: bestowing upon its adopters a blank cyborgean mask.

Brows were sculpted. Through the popular process of "threading," thin fiber cord would be tied to the stalks of a woman's eyebrows, allowing individual hairs to be yanked out in succession. The result, as zoologist and sociobiologist Desmond Morris would explain in *The Naked Woman: A Study of the Female Body*, "Female eyebrows have been made super-female by artificially increasing their thinness and smallness."

Hair was big. In the '80s there had been a close-cropped fever. Many ambitious career women had sought "short, tight hair," which, according to Morris, was "associated with discipline, self-control, efficiency, conformity and assertiveness." But by the '90s, fuller looks were coming back. In 1992, Mattel, sensing this transition, released Totally Hair Barbie, which would turn out to be the hottest-selling Barbie ever.[8] Many women developed codependent relationships with their blow-dryers. They went to stylists to "get blown" (later called "blown out"). Sandra Ballentine, in *W*, would eventually write about what became her biweekly '90s "addiction [to visiting] haute hairstylists.... Things got so bad that I avoided traveling to cities where I didn't have a hair connection."

Women also sought new or rediscovered styles. According to scholar Ingrid Banks, author of *Hair Matters: Beauty, Power, and Black Women's Consciousness*, businesses in the '90s were actually firing women—and schools

---

8. Writer and editor Maggie Paley would report that Mattel, in 1993, came out with a Barbie playmate named Earring Magic Ken: "He wore what looked just like a chrome cock ring on a [necklace]. When questioned by reporters, the Mattel people [reportedly] pleaded innocence—they were simply following fashion. But gay men noticed, and that may be why Earring Magic Ken was, according to Mattel, 'the best-selling Ken doll ever.'" (Maggie Paley, *The Book of the Penis* [New York: Grove/Atlantic, 1999], 197; Brian Galindo, "15 Surprising Things You Didn't Know About Ken," Buzzfeed.com, November 11, 2013.)

were suspending girls—for hairdos ("zigzag parts," for example) that were considered gang-related, too outré, or "too ethnic.... Oprah Winfrey dedicated an entire show to the 'black hair question.'" As hard as it might be to imagine today, tennis star Venus Williams caused consternation among some mainstream observers by wearing beaded hair on center court. She was seen as "exotic to some and threatening to others," according to Banks, because she "display[ed] a black esthetic that is linked to an authentic or radical blackness in the imagination of many whites.... [Her] expression of radicalized gender sent the message to a predominantly white professional women's tennis circuit that mainstream constructions of womanhood are insufficient in understanding black women's relationship to beauty culture."

Hair extensions—sewn on, glued on, or clipped on—were everywhere. The *Wall Street Journal* reported that the market for "human-hair imports surged 72% to $78.5 million [in 1995 alone], according to the U.S. Commerce Department." The bulk of the supplies would come from the scalps of women in China, India, and Southeast Asia, where hair collectors scrambled to meet the demand.[9] This boom in extensions was attributable to various constituencies: from black women seeking bounce or braids or a relief from treatments, to women of all races who were simply tired of fussing, from working-class club kids to stylists pushing the new look on their clients.

Then again, **bald** was big too. Bare-cut Meshell Ndegeocello, as well as Sinéad O'Connor, burst onto the music scene. In 1992, Sigourney Weaver sheared it all off for *Alien 3*. So did Demi Moore for *G.I. Jane*, in which she snarled at her commanding officer, "Suck my dick."

Women chose to shave their heads for any number of reasons. To subvert conventional notions of female beauty by rejecting the hair-equals-femininity equivalency. To confer a kick-ass vibe. To purify or purge themselves following the loss of a lover (or to show solidarity with a friend battling illness). To project "butch," depending on the wearer or the beholder. Finally, as salon owner Dexter Fields told the *Washington Post* in 1999: to gain strength

---

9. The exploitation of exported human hair had colonialist and racist dimensions: to accommodate the vanity of Western women, their sisters from the East were giving up parts of their own bodies. Banks correctly states that "the average woman from Asia growing her hair for profit lives in poverty." (Ingrid Banks, "Hair Still Matters," in *Feminist Frontiers*, ed. Laurel Richardson, Verta Taylor, and Nancy Whittier [New York: McGraw-Hill, 2003], 117.)

through vulnerability. "Once your security blanket is gone, you can be exposed," said Fields, who specialized in relieving women of their hair.

Visits to **salons**—which had soared in the '80s as more working women had more disposable income in the healthier economy—became an all-American ritual in the '90s among all ages, races, and classes. Nail art became ever more elaborate. A mani-pedi became as essential and routine as a gas station fill-up.

My daughter, Molly, then eleven, was obsessed (along with her girlfriends) with Britney Spears, the decade's reigning pop tart, and started wearing Spears-inspired **belly shirts**. Desmond Morris fixes the arrival of the garment to "late 1998 to be precise [when] low-slung jeans [were] combined with unusually short tops." The result, in his estimation, was to redirect the gaze down toward a more focused erogenous zone. Molly, who would go on to become a schoolteacher, would look back as a twenty-seven-year-old: "My friends and I all saw Britney's washboard abs and we *had* to have them. I did a hundred sit-ups a day." Navel rings and chains and studs were soon to follow. (My friend Anne Kent recalls accompanying her daughter when she got her belly button pierced. She was alarmed when the guy in the tattoo parlor told her that **navel rings** dated back to slave days, when women were treated as chattel.)

Piercings, for years, had been a marginal adornment. In the '90s they became signs of defiance and self-expression. Face metal was suddenly a badge, a rite of passage. Tongue studs, nipple rings, and bling for the clitoral hood (typically a ring or a tiny bar with twin studs on the end) added to erotic stimulation, for oneself or one's partner. **Tattoos** of all stylings, sizes, and quantity, while not yet as ubiquitous as they are today, were pervasive, borrowing from an array of subcultures—gang, hip-hop, biker, and more. For many women, barbed-wire patterns showed up on biceps, and the "tramp stamp"—a horizontal and often ornate tattoo—cropped up at the base of the spine.

While we're in the vicinity, **the booty** was huge. The designer jeans craze had kicked things off in the late '70s, but the butt would really take center stage in the '80s and '90s. The columnist and commentator Erin Aubry made waves by writing about the ways commercial culture had previously relegated the female African American physique—the rear in particular—to second-class status. She called for a more expansive view of beauty in "The Butt," her 1997 essay for *L.A. Weekly*. She made the case for the "stubborn, immutable [buttocks] . . . It can't be hot-combed or straightened or bleached into submission. It does not assimilate; it never took a slave name." In the article—for which Aubry posed in snug jeans—she insisted, according to feminist scholars Jennifer Baumgardner and Amy Richards, "that black women's bodies, specifically their butts, have been seen only as sex machines and workhorses to such a profane degree that the simple act of trying to buy a pair of jeans becomes a metaphor for not fitting into the white patriarchy and its notions of feminine bodies."[10]

The social activist and feminist scholar bell hooks has proposed that contemporary culture awakened to the sexualized bottom, specifically the black female bottom, in 1988 when the go-go band Experience Unlimited's recording of "Da Butt"—a.k.a. "(Doin') the Butt"—hit No. 1 in the *Billboard* R&B rankings. The track, she notes, "fostered the promotion of a hot new dance favoring those who could most protrude their buttocks with pride and glee." Doin' da butt and shakin' dat thang took hold. The song, according to hooks, "challenged dominant ways of thinking about the body, which encourage us to ignore asses because they are associated with undesirable and unclean acts. Unmasked, the 'butt' could be once again worshipped as an erotic seat of pleasure and excitement."

Soon, performers like Lil' Kim and Missy Elliott were crooning about the merits of a fuller moon. "Booty rap" became a '90s bumper crop. The group 2 Live Crew came out with "Face Down, Ass Up." Q-Tip and A Tribe Called Quest sang the praises of "Bonita Applebum." Snoop Dogg and Dr. Dre coined the phrase "bootylicious" in 1992, around the time Wreckx-N-Effect released "Rump Shaker." The next year, DJ Jubilee coined the term "twerk" (to booty bounce). Shakin' in their wake came Juvenile's "Back That Azz/ Thang Up," Mos Def's "Ms. Fat Booty," and a trail of others.

The top male booty rapper, however, may well have been Anthony Ray

---

10. Dermatological tweaks were beginning to take hold. Desmond Morris would notice that "Bottom-lifters and bum-boosters were already being built in to certain female garments, but now... cosmetic surgeons [began] reporting a surge in requests for more voluptuous bottoms, both by fat injections and silicone implants." In the even-more-arcane department, there was a parallel trend at the tail end of the '90s: anal bleaching. The cosmetic procedure, which used a cream to adjust the color and tone of the anus to better match the surrounding skin, was the Brazilian bikini wax in extremis. Anal bleaching, part of a culture-wide gentrification-mania and germophobia, sought to spiff up the natural, well-used, and unkempt, and replace it with its ersatz ideal. Which brought up a question. For whose benefit, exactly, was a beautified butthole intended, except for the eye (or another body part) of the beholder—or for the person with her or his head up their arse? (Desmond Morris, *The Naked Woman: A Study of the Female Body* [New York: Thomas Dunne/St. Martin's, 2004], 229; Tristan Taormino, "Britesmile for Bungholes," *Village Voice*, July 5, 2005.)

(a.k.a. Sir Mix-a-Lot). In 1992 he had the nation's No. 1 hit with "Baby Got Back." It was powered by a popular video (in which Mix stood atop a field of giant yellow heinies) with a propulsive beat and cheeky lyrics: "I like big butts and I cannot lie." To move the freight, promoters placed a helium-filled derriere atop the Tower Records store in Los Angeles.

Sir Mix-a-Lot was branded a misogynist *and* a racist *and* a liberator. MTV, alarmed, would only air the video in nocturnal rotation. America, however, was hooked. The track would become, in the view of Vulture.com's Rob Kemp, "our national anthem of ass." Or as the A&R-man-producer-journalist Dan Charnas would say, Mix's was "the loudest voice for this cultural overthrow of the Euro-centric beauty aesthetic."[11]

Three other catalysts contributed. In 1996, designer Alexander McQueen unveiled a line of women's pants that were slung so low that his runway show became a procession of butt cleavage. The "bumster look" caught on and copycats started turning out skimpier slacks. Next, in 1998, Puerto Rican American ingénue Jennifer Lopez appeared opposite George Clooney in Steven Soderbergh's *Out of Sight*. To publicize the film, she agreed to a *Vanity Fair* photo session in which she looked coyly over a bare shoulder and flashed her most prized asset—in lace-up lingerie—at photographer Firooz Zahedi. In that one "revolutionary full-page photo," Camille Paglia would write in the *Hollywood Reporter*, Lopez had sent a shot across the cultural bow. "She fetchingly turned her ample…buttocks to the camera. It was the first time that the traditional eroticization by Latin and black culture of that bulbous part of the anatomy had ever received mainstream recognition in the U.S."

Third and foremost, **the thong** was rising.

---

11. Mix had intended the song as exactly that: a celebration of more rounded women, who had been marginalized by myopic, noninclusive forces in commercial society. "Baby Got Back," in truth, had been written partly in response to the experiences of Mix's longtime partner, Amylia Dorsey-Rivas. As a Seattle-area teen, she'd been passed over for modeling and acting gigs in favor of lanky or waiflike women. "Being a woman of color—I'm half-Mexican, half-black, and have always been curvy," Dorsey-Rivas would tell Vulture.com, "[i]f you were a little more broad at the beam, forget it. That kind of thing that women in my position went through made Mix angry." Mix himself would insist that he'd meant his humor-laced homage as a protest song: "Girls had to look like heroin addicts to be accepted" for ads, videos, photo shoots, or runway jobs. He was saying: Enough. "Bottom line: Black men like curves." (Rob Kemp, "'And I Cannot Lie': The Oral History of Sir Mix-a-Lot's 'Baby Got Back' Video," Vulture.com, December 19, 2013; Patrick S. Pemberton, "Still Liking 'Em Big," *San Luis Obispo Tribune*, June 15, 2006.)

Throughout the decade, as inhibitions and pubic hair diminished, so too did the amount of fabric devoted to skivvies. The thong—naughty, uncomfortable, meant to be noticed yet surreptitiously tucked away—became the default '90s undie. Its whisper-thin frontal panty deftly hid a woman's (or a man's) privates; its strap or tie sides rode high on the hips; its stringy remainder nestled along the perineum and posterior folds, leaving the trunk entirely exposed.

Fans and foes alike would call it "butt floss." Worn with low-ride slacks or shorts or skirts, it would stubbornly peep above the trouser line in what became known as a "whale tail." The thong's avowed purpose was a practical one: to do away with VPL—visible panty line. But its deeper mission was tied to its sex appeal. The thong, an item of respectable beachwear in places like Brazil, was in fact the cousin of the G-string, the stripper's indispensable garment.

The thong was part of a pattern. Some have proposed that as global warming brought on more torrid summers, designers had responded. So, more open-toed sandals, see-through blouses, miniskirts, and short shorts. More and more women in urban centers were taking to the streets wearing less and less—to the point where George Gurley, writing in the *New York Observer*, would pen a much-discussed 1998 column about that annual rite of spring's demise when men would go collectively gaga on "that first or second hot day... when that first woman in that first spaghetti-strap shirt of summer steps out of her building." Thus, wrote Gurley, would women declare open season on onlookers' "joy and agitation" until Labor Day.

Calvin Klein (with his topless and naked models), along with other giants in fashion and fragrance, pushed the nude look throughout the decade. More skin in advertisements meant more sales in the marketplace.

The evenings had their own swelter. Items of **lingerie**, which had only ever been conceived as bedtime clothes, were being worn to parties and clubs. For *Vanity Fair*'s first-ever Hollywood Issue, in 1995, most of the ten actresses depicted—including Angela Bassett, Nicole Kidman, Julianne Moore, Sarah Jessica Parker, and Uma Thurman—donned slinky numbers that could have doubled as boudoir-wear. "The slip dress was an offshoot of grunge," according to Bronwyn Cosgrave. "It was redolent of Courtney Love and her whole *Kinderwhore* thing and it culminated in her going to the 1995 Oscars with

Amanda de Cadenet—with both of them, on Hollywood's chicest evening, showing up in their slips."[12]

Bras suddenly announced themselves. Women were wearing them with the straps deliberately exposed. Or in shades that could be easily displayed through light-colored tops or thin fabrics. Some women were making a sexually charged fashion statement. Others were picking up on the "nothing to hide" aesthetic of the punk, grunge, and Riot Grrrl scenes. Many were just being assertively blasé. They were telegraphing the fact that clothes were clothes and that this was how they worked on a person's body. It was as if the boring hydraulics, hidden from polite company for centuries, were now being consciously exposed in both form and function, regardless of any stray erotic value.

Meanwhile, bras and panties became even *more* eroticized by the unapologetically suggestive **Victoria's Secret**. The company, created in the '70s to appeal to men who'd expressed discomfort shopping for unmentionables, would become by the mid-'90s the hottest intimate apparel brand in the United States. Its formula: liberate lingerie from the shadows (and antiseptic department stores) and make underclothes sexy again. Come 1995, Victoria's Secret—worth $2 billion and boasting 670 retail outlets—was the Valvoline of women's apparel, an indispensable lubricant in the lives of sensually aware women and their partners. Its catalog was more popular than most magazines—and a year-round stocking stuffer for adolescent boys. It helped turn the corset, championed by Gaultier and Versace, from a fetish item into a late-evening staple (albeit with a bit of sci-fi kink). Victoria's Secret's runway shows took off; its stores became anchor tenants at the nation's malls; its models bloomed into megastars.

In the spring of 1994, Playtex rolled out **the Wonderbra**. Its secret, as *Newsweek* revealed: "Padding fills out the sides. Underwire scrunches the rest

---

12. A year later Princess Diana did them one better (or worse) when she showed up at the annual Met Gala in a slip dress: midnight blue with come-hither black lace, one of the maiden creations of John Galliano after he'd taken over as Dior's creative director. "This was important, as it launched Dior," recalls Cosgrave, "and also controversial, as it did not fit. Some felt it was distasteful given her station. The slip-dress mishap was similar to Gwyneth Paltrow [in that] corseted bodice of the pink Lauren she wore in [1999 when] accepting her Best Actress Academy Award" for her gender-bending role in *Shakespeare in Love*. (Interview with Cosgrave.)

of the breasts up and in, creating cleavage." And with it came the miraculous mirage of universal décolletage.

The Wonderbra was backed up by a robust marketing campaign. "Macy's had a fashion show with twin models," reported the *New York Times*, assessing the hoopla, "one natural and one Wonderbra-ed. At Lord & Taylor's flagship Fifth Avenue store, the bra arrived in an armored truck. The most popular sizes quickly sold out." *Ad Age* marveled, "Only last fall, the slight-chested look was in. Now, even waif queen Kate Moss confesses [that when she desires] some comely décolletage, she wears a Wonderbra." Within a few weeks, one New York secretary told the *Times*, "I was at a party and I swear every woman there was pushed up."

The new superbra—actually an American incarnation of popular versions sold in the U.K. and Canada—was not an obvious fit for the wholesome Sara Lee Corporation, the parent company of Playtex. But Sara Lee *did* know how to move the cupcakes. And by the end of year one, the $26 garments were selling at a clip of four pairs a minute, accounting for $120 million in annual revenue.

The Wonderbra (with spokesmodel Eva Herzigová peering down and proclaiming, "Hello Boys") signaled a true loosening of consumer fashion. American women seemed to be saying that an added flash of flesh was no big deal, was *natural*, was not to be marveled at but, if at all, simply acknowledged. Women of all shapes and ages and temperaments began to leave a top button or two undone, to wear lower-cut outfits—to convey more openness and to feel more free. The trend became a prevailing style and in time rather standard.

Sports bras, too, saw record sales. The columnist David Brooks, upon seeing women at a local park in summertime "running around in their underwear in public," sounds altogether fusty today. In the '90s, however, he was astute, imagining that Gibbon, if privy to the same scene, would have begun "speculating about the decline of empires. But look at the bra joggers more closely. It's not wanton hedonism you see on their faces.... [It is] grim determination.... The reason they are practically naked, they will tell you, is that this sort of clothing is most practical, most useful for strenuous exercise. What we see at the park is near nudity, but somehow it's nudity in the service of achievement."

Many were not so edified. **"Shapewear"** of all kinds had become the

'90s girdle. And then in 1998, according to Alexandra Jacobs in the *New Yorker*, a woman named Sara Blakely came upon the bright idea "to chop the feet off a pair of control-top panty hose so that she could get a svelte, seamless look under white slacks without stockings poking out of her sandals." The resulting garment—**Spanx**—would instantly slenderize a nation. These so-called body smoothers were transformative. They were also fashion's antidote to the fact that gravity, as retail expert Alan Millstein would tell *BusinessWeek*, was "taking its toll on the baby-boom generation."

———

While pop culture reinforced these trends, no medium proved more influential than the printed page. Women sought **beauty tips** in such numbers that the fashion, beauty, and "women's" magazine categories expanded. There were personality-centric titles such as *Marie Claire* (launched in the States in 1994), *Jane* (1997), and *O: The Oprah Magazine* (2000). There were a raft of edgier publications that straddled fashion, art, music, and street culture. There were *girl*-focused magazines like *CosmoGirl* (1999) that instilled a style sense in a younger audience (the better to turn them into grown-up *Cosmo* buyers).[13]

Among the most studied faces of all were those of the **supermodels**, a relatively new designation epitomized by the 1980s triumvirate of Christy Turlington, Linda Evangelista, and Naomi Campbell. (John Casablancas, the modeling agency chief, is often cited as having created the supermodel, aiding in the ascent of that trio—and many others, from Cindy to Claudia to Iman.) In 1990, Evangelista would notoriously remark of her rarefied and pampered breed, "We don't wake up for less than $10,000 a day."

It was not all sweetness and glam. The **grunge look** clambered in with Marc Jacobs's 1992 show for Perry Ellis. Fashion writer Cathy Horyn would recall in *New York* magazine that Jacobs's runway show—which would help define his career (and yet get him sacked by Ellis a couple of months

———

13. Teens also consulted makeup artist Kevyn Aucoin's 1996 *The Art of Makeup* and his 1997 bible *Making Faces* to learn about the mysteries of the brush and sponge, liner and stick, and to extract beauty clues from studying the facial contours of their favorite actress or model. Two decades later, Rachel Syme, in the *New York Times*, would describe the influence of *Making Faces* on her fourteen-year-old peer group. "We all trekked to the Borders at Winrock mall in Albuquerque to buy a copy, using the savings we had built up by babysitting," recalls Syme, who says her friends considered the book "a codex, a working syllabus, a kind of 'Joy of Cooking' with kohl." (Rachel Syme, "Kevyn Aucoin's 'Making Faces,'" *New York Times Magazine*, August 21, 2015.)

later)—featured models "stomp[ing] out…in Doc Marten boots and Converse sneakers, with knitted caps and granny glasses and dingy plaid shirts…[making it appear] as if Jacobs had not designed any new clothes so much as raided every thrift shop from here to Seattle."

Along came **heroin chic**. Its dazed and sallow-looking models, shot vérité in rec rooms and motels, emerged partly as an assault on the hyper-gloss of the era's glamazons. But this new aesthetic was expressing something more grave. It was an outgrowth of the fashion houses and modeling agencies that venerated the slender, as if sanctioning anorexia and bulimia. Its tone was bleak, coming from an industry that had been decimated by disease in the 1980s. The harsh lighting, unvarnished settings, and runny mascara reflected the marginalized roots of many of the models depicted—"those," in the words of Philippe Venzano for *Mixte* magazine, who had "suffered from Thatcherism" and were being revealed in ways that "push[ed] aside the codes of fashion and introduce[d] daily life, banal occurrences, imperfection."

The look was espoused by taboo-busting designers, stylists, and especially photographers, including Corinne Day, Craig McDean, and Davide Sorrenti. (Sorrenti would overdose in 1997, at age twenty.) Day—whose style was of a piece with the stark 1980s documentary work of visual artists such as Nan Goldin—was the most assertive champion of this new aesthetic. For *The Face*, Day shot a notorious portfolio in the early 1990s that showed an unknown, reed-thin model named Kate Moss—only fifteen at the time—who was photographed seminude in some of the images. Another of Day's shoots, for British *Vogue*, showed Moss chilling out in a bedroom. It would rankle readers and critics alike. "Because it was shot on a teenage girl, they said it was outrageous, pedophilia," Moss would recall dismissively two decades later. "Ridiculous. I must have been 19. I'm standing in my underwear. Really controversial."

For all its authentic grit, the aesthetic was inexorably grim. Were the images really approaching child-porn terrain? Condoning drug use? At one press conference, President Clinton would accuse fashion houses of "glamoriz[ing] addiction to sell clothes." Some runway shows pushed into ever-darker territory, a fact made bracingly apparent when designer Alexander McQueen in 1995 "dedicated his fall collection to 'the highland rape,' a pointed statement about the ravaging of Scotland by England," as Eric Wilson and Cathy Horyn would recount in McQueen's obituary in the *Times* after his 2010 suicide. "The models appeared to be brutalized...their hair tangled and their eyes blanked out with opaque contact lenses."

But McQueen, come 1997, even as he espoused his signature doom-and-gloom glam, would turn to a more traditionally sexy and full-bodied type when he anointed Gisele Bündchen as "The Body" and featured her prominently in his "Untitled/The Golden Shower" show, at which he introduced his 1998 spring/summer collection.[14] (Gisele had been discovered at a McDonald's in São Paulo in 1995, and her success would trip the switch on the "Brazilian model invasion.")

With Gisele's ascension, the swan and geek and waif parade was effectively declared *so over*. And its death spiral was everywhere apparent. Manhattan's flashy Fashion Café—which had been started in 1995 by supermodels—was unceremoniously shuttered. *Newsweek* mourned the death of the supermodel. *Vogue* featured Gisele on its July 1999 cover, broadcasting "The Return of the Curve."[15]

Fashion's raison d'être, though, was retail sales. And the industry, along with other cultural drivers such as *Sex and the City* (which fetishized Fendi bags and pushed everything from Dolce & Gabbana to Absolut), celebrated and validated **shopping** as its own reward. Individual designers were opening flagship retail locations. The first New York tent shows sprouted in Bryant Park in 1993, drawing big-ticket sponsors, paparazzi—and consumer attention. Given shopping's convenience, its illicit abandon, and its infinite choice, the act of browsing and purchasing—with friends or alone—became a kind of mass hypnosis. For many, shopping would *replace sex*, with the credit card serving as the ultimate stimulant.

More style-conscious women—and men. More easily seduced consumers. More body alterations. More fluid fashions. More body ink and face metal. More skin. At times, women wanted to break down gender stereotypes

---

14. Golden Shower was a none-too-veiled reference—as defined by the Urban Dictionary—to "the act of urinating on another person, usually for sexual gratification." The fashion show sponsor, American Express, objected to the moniker, so McQueen agreed to change it to "Untitled." (EJL, "Golden Shower," UrbanDictionary.com, December 12, 2003; Liz Connor, "5 Things You Might Not Know About Alexander McQueen," GQ-Magazine.co.uk, March 10, 2015.)

15. That said, even the Giseles of the world would soon be brought to high heel. Before the decade ended, fashion-forward actresses, rather than megamodels, would become the new "faces" of beauty products, the new mannequins in designers' ads, and the new fashion magazine cover girls.

via the statements they made through their appearance. At other times, they simply wanted to be more classically feminine. "Of all the projects of second-wave feminism, the project to eliminate femininity in dress is one of the most absolute of failures," Joan Williams would assert at the end of the decade in her book *Unbending Gender*. "If feminism did not kill domesticity, it has had even less effect on feminine norms of dress and carriage. Most feminists today embrace femininity and sexy dressing and offer a variety of rationales."

The thrust of it all was that a woman's physical comportment was becoming a more personal, customized statement, a reflection of her inner beliefs, desires, and moods. To convey her own style, she was mixing and matching the natural and the virtual in new ways that tested or catered to conventional concepts of beauty; shattered, downplayed, or exaggerated categories of gender; or emphasized or deemphasized her sexuality.

Such self-invention did not a political movement make. Some have argued that many women were assuming the stereotypes of consumer culture, albeit ironically. Many were. But women, one by one—by taking serious stock of their outward expression and by adopting looks that might very well be common to members of their peer group—were fortifying their sense of belonging, an act that in itself conferred strength in numbers and social agency.

CHAPTER 17

The Bust Boom

Let's talk about glands.

In the '80s and into the '90s, there was a booming trade in the surgically enhanced breast. Many young women, including a sizable number in their late teens, believed that a more bountiful bust could help boost their self-esteem, reinforce their womanhood (a freighted concept, to be sure), or fortify their presence and essence. Many Boomers joined them. Some breast cancer patients received implants during reconstructive surgery.[1] Others were looking for a sense of renewal after bearing children or for social cachet or for a way to hold back the tides of age. The cosmetics culture promoted the procedure as relatively safe. The popular culture regularly featured unapologetically amplified models and actresses.

And yet thousands of women who had previously received implants were falling ill. Starting in the mid-'80s, the lawsuits mounted. Court cases detailed incidents of ruptured devices, compromised immune systems, connective-tissue disease, and myriad infirmities. In December 1990, a distressing and, as it turned out, highly influential report on *Face to Face with Connie Chung* aired interviews with alarmed patients. On the broadcast, pathologist Douglas Shanklin described the silicone implant as "an unproven, probably unsafe medical device." Congress held hearings. The next year, the FDA requested a nationwide moratorium. Class-action attorneys filed suit. Women in droves had their implants removed, often swapping in saline substitutes. In 1995, the ax fell on Dow Corning, the

---

1. Incidents of breast cancer rose significantly in the 1980s and then leveled off come the 1990s, according to the Susan G. Komen organization, "likely due to increased mammography screening."

nation's main supplier of silicone-gel implants. The company, ravaged by litigation, sought bankruptcy protection, eventually settling with 170,000 claimants.

Then, astoundingly, the implant bounced back. A series of comprehensive studies failed to find demonstrable links between silicone and significant disorders. Between 1992 and 1998, the number of breast enhancements actually *increased* fourfold, with more than half of all recipients ranging in age from nineteen to thirty-four.

In the midst of this ebb and flow, a perplexing photo was published. It appeared in the August 1995 issue of *Texas Monthly*. And it was the centerpiece of a cover story by Mimi Swartz entitled "Silicone City: The Rise and Fall of the Implant—Or How Houston Went from an Oil-Based Economy to a Breast-Based Economy."

The picture showed a Houston-area nurse named Cyndi Lovell with her daughter, Melissa. They posed together, poolside, in bathing suits. Photographed from above, mother and daughter were depicted smiling, showing off their bustlines. Cyndi—possessed of 400cc implants—had recently offered to pay for her daughter's surgery, reportedly asking her one day, "So, do you want your breasts done for high school graduation or college?" (The article did not state Melissa's age, but she took her mom up on the offer.)

When I saw the picture at the time, I did a double take. If American mothers were endorsing their kids' cosmetic surgery, then there'd been some sort of overhaul of the intergenerational mind-set. While researching this book, I came across the photo again. And I was determined to find the surgeon who'd transformed Cyndi and Melissa—and many a Houstonian.

————

His name is Franklin Rose, MD. In the Houston press he is called the Body Baron, the Michelangelo of Plastic Surgery, and, simply, Breast Man. I figure that if anyone can help me understand the reason for the bust boom of the 1980s and '90s it is Dr. Rose, who agrees to meet with me.

A month before my visit, he mails me a DVD: a copy of the 1997 HBO film *Breast Men*. It is a cautionary tale. Actor David Schwimmer plays a cosmetic surgeon who becomes, in a word, obsessed. Schwimmer's character snorts cocaine off a woman's chest. He has bosoms painted on the bottom of his backyard swimming pool.[2] And—*spoiler alert*—he is eventually killed when a truck smashes into his Corvette because he's too busy staring out the window at a busty woman in a convertible. (In one scene in the movie, Dr. Rose gets a shout-out—by name.)

As I drive into Houston from the airport, I see massive storage warehouses. I pass billboards for strip clubs, for a "High-Caliber Gun Show," for Slick Willie's Family Pool Hall. Here and there are signs on no-frills, men-centric stores with two-by-four-letter names: COLD BEER, USED CARS, BAIL BOND, SAM'S CLUB, VALU PAWN, WING•SPOT, SUITMART.

This is a town with a macho, frontier spirit that has long been evinced by its derricks (signifying the oil boom) and its rockets (the aerospace boom). As NASA's home base, Houston was the Southland's capital of the can-do '60s. It became the place where visionaries introduced the ersatz triumphant: indoor stadiums and outer-space gadgetry; artificial turf and the artificial heart. (In the 1990s came the artificial deal: Houston-based Enron would turn creative-accounting fraud into a science, becoming the consummate financial casualty of the early 2000s.)

It was in Houston, in fact, that two surgeons, Thomas Cronin and Frank Gerow, in 1961 first used silicone gel to artificially expand the proportions of the female breast. "They got the idea," writes Alex Kuczynski in her book *Beauty Junkies*, "after gazing at a plastic sack of blood hanging from a pole during a transfusion." Franklin Rose, as it happens, is among a cadre of Houston visionaries, chiefly male, who foresaw vast promise and profit in the bionic breast.

I meet Rose in a rush, at a party. Dark-framed glasses. Blinding white teeth. Bald crown. Strong, finchlike profile. Rose—fifty-nine at the time—is unfailingly convivial, solicitous, and, now and again, genuinely tender. Yet

---

2. Houston surgeon Gerald Johnson—known for clients like Texas-born model Anna Nicole Smith and for his unusual techniques (e.g., implanting a synthetic mesh in some of his patients' mammary glands)—actually owned a swimming pool that was shaped like a giant breast. "Gerald was a genius," says Rose today. "He would do 'Kroger's Specials'—the supermarket. He would get all the Kroger's check-[out] girls in and do them ultra-inexpensively. One day he even tried to do [around] twenty breast implant [patients]. Gerald was a good surgeon, but eccentric." (Mimi Swartz, "Silicone City," *Texas Monthly*, August 1995, 66; Joan Kron, "Implant Nation," *Allure*, February 2010, 111; interview with Franklin Rose; Art Harris, "Anna Nicole Nip Tucker Nipped!," ArtHarris.com, July 10, 2007.)

he presents himself, as do many surgeons, as constitutionally incapable of conveying modesty. Even so, judging from the warmth and the wide respect he receives throughout the evening (and for the next forty-eight hours), I sense that I am in the presence of a good man of goodwill.

Franklin Rose's camera-ready smile defaults to high beam. He speaks with a soft Mr. Rogers cadence, enunciating deliberately. Tonight, though, we are in a hurry. We hustle through Fleming's Prime Steakhouse & Wine Bar. Waiters zip past us and diners stop him to offer compliments. Rose seems to relish seeing and being seen.

We are heading to a banquet room for a benefit dinner. The event has been spearheaded by the doctor's wife, artist Cindi Harwood Rose. Along comes Dr. Michael Ciaravino, a dashing young plastic surgeon. Rose introduces us, lavishing Ciaravino with praise: "Here's the next holder of the big breast record. Go to thebodydoc.com."

"I'm doing close to eight hundred a year," Ciaravino says with pride, and showing great deference to Rose.

"Houston is an implant city," Rose asserts. "More per capita than any city. And Michael puts in more than anyone *in* this city.... He does more than anybody in the *world*."

With Ciaravino out of earshot, I inquire about the percentage of women on the premises who have had that kind of work done. "This crowd is an 80 percent plastic surgery crowd," Rose says. Later, he adds, "In my estimation, Houston is a very overaugmented city. I don't really go to the nightclubs much anymore, thank God, but I go out to the restaurants and sometimes it all looks so overaugmented to *me*. And I've done five *thousand*."

———

The evening is resolutely about breasts. The gala helps support the Rose Ribbon Foundation, a charity established to honor Cindi Rose's sister Holly Harwood Skolkin and others who have battled breast cancer. Each year the group offers reconstructive surgery, at no charge, to recovering cancer patients, many of whom lack adequate health insurance. As guests mill about, I look down at the place settings at our tables. On every plate rests an appetizer of two pert porcini ravioli, each adorned with a small mushroom. Am I simply imagining twin nipples?

I am a bit dizzy from the cocktail hour. In rapid succession, Franklin or Cindi or both have introduced me to society columnists and philanthropists, to a Wildenstein, a teenage beauty pageant winner, and the fashion model Ursaline Hamilton. I meet the Roses' daughter, Erica, twenty-seven—a veteran of *The Bachelor* reality-TV franchise *and* an aspiring entertainment lawyer—who looks fetching in a low-cut spaghetti-strap dress. (All three Roses have made the reality-TV rounds.)[3] In every direction, there are plunging necklines and strategically placed jewels.

At one point during cocktails, Dr. Rose draws my attention to Jessica Stern Meyer, a socially connected artist and jeweler from a wealthy Mexican family. Meyer greets me and, without much prompting, offers a closer look at the pendant on her chest—created from bullets normally used in .357 Magnums and .45 automatics. "My [jewelry] line is called bulletgirl.com," she says. "I get ten thousand blanks at a time—delivered to my door by UPS—that I fashion into rings, earrings, bracelets." (Her grandfather, I learn, manufactured bullets. She takes the ammo and—as the Bullet Girl website puts it—"unearth[s] the beauty in something meant for destruction.")

At dinner I am seated next to Franklin's wife. Cindi Rose is a painter, sculptor, former columnist, and fixture on the Houston social scene. She is vivacious, spiritually attuned, and—not unlike her husband, as I soon discover—unfiltered when it comes to discussing her accomplishments, her professional passions, and her private life. I soon hear about the beauty-pageant titles she collected in her day (Miss Austin Beautiful, Oklahoma University's Miss Venus, Miss Mod Bod, and so on), and I see that she has maintained her striking looks and figure into her late fifties.

Three curious things happen as we dig into our ravioli. First, she tells me, "We were married, then divorced, then married again." (More on this

---

3. That very week, Erica Rose is set to premiere in a new program, *You're Cut Off!*, playing a spoiled-princess type. In 2015, with a law degree and a master's in entertainment and media law, Erica would move to L.A. and become director of business development at Gentry Law Group. That same year, I check in with Cindi Rose, who tells me that she too is about to appear in a reality series, for which she has taped twelve episodes: Bravo's *Married to Medicine Houston*. "He's the established surgeon," she says. "I'm the established wife, with a social background—the socialite of the city." Behind every great man is a great reality show. Even Dr. Rose has put in time on the reality circuit, including a spot on the MTV program *I Want a Famous Face*. (Interviews with Cindi, Erica, and Franklin Rose; Cary Darling, "'Ladies of Dallas' and 'Married to Medicine Houston' Join Bravo Schedule," *Fort Worth Star-Telegram*, March 30, 2015; "Meet the Cast of 'Married to Medicine Houston,'" TVDeets.com, January 8, 2016; http://lalawland.com/about; http://galengentry.com; http://la-divorce-lawyer.com/.)

shortly.) Next, she says, without my asking, "My body's natural"—as if I might assume otherwise given her husband's profession.[4] Third, Cindi describes her lifelong calling: silhouette portraiture.

She suddenly whips out a tiny pair of surgical scissors and a sheet of black silhouette paper. And she begins cutting, freehand, right there at the dinner table as other guests look on. She examines my profile intently, asking me to stare straight ahead. "There's only about twelve people in America," she tells me, snipping away, "who do what I do."[5] In under a minute or so, she produces a disarmingly accurate likeness of my profile, and affixes the jet-black cutting onto textured white paper. I am at once mesmerized and weirded out. While sitting at dinner, I have been elevated (into an artist's model) *and* reduced (to an object, literally to a body image). It dawns on me that both Franklin and Cindi Rose share a specialty: silhouette art.

The evening's mood keeps shifting. A woman named Stacie is introduced to the attendees and approaches the front of the room. She is the daughter of one of the night's guests of honor—a woman who underwent post-mastectomy reconstruction only days before. Stacie tells the crowd, "Just to see [my mom] smile again when she took off the bandages was awesome. 'Cause she's so pretty." The audience is soon tearing up, applauding. At our table, Cindi explains, "We make forty to one hundred thousand dollars with the dinner, [which covers] ten free reconstructions a year."

Things pivot again as Cindi tells me a story over dinner. It is a signature '90s tale that I later explore with her husband and those in the Roses' inner circle.

———

"The divorce was 1990," she says. "We were divorced seven years. Then we got married seven years later." The seven-year cycle, she mentions, echoes those prescribed in the Bible—for crops, for debts, for the term that a servant or a worker can toil.

---

4. According to media accounts of public records, Franklin *did* perform some minor work. When I later ask about the discrepancy, she tells me, "He did this little mini-lift. . . . They put in the tiniest, tiniest little implant there, which I didn't want. . . . I was trying to keep the marriage together. It was something he wanted of me to do, and so I did that." (Lisa Gray, "Image Augmentation," *Houston Press*, December 30, 1989; interview with Cindi Rose.)

5. That night Franklin Rose offers evidence of his own career distinction: "There are maybe twenty, thirty people in history who've done as many breast implants as I have."

The breakup, I learn, occurred largely because the good doctor had been getting overly familiar with one or two of the women he'd been surgically enhancing. One night, says Cindi, "a beautiful friend pulled me aside at a party, with tears in her eyes, and said, 'Your husband is having an affair.' The next day, another friend, a former model with true psychic powers, told me, opening a newspaper [and] showing me a write-up, 'This is your husband's girlfriend.' He was dating a *Penthouse* Pet....My husband was eating the cookies from the cookie jar.

"I made a split-second decision," she says. "I divorced him so fast. People were throwing themselves at him. They thought he was God because he made everyone beautiful."

Franklin Rose later gives me his version. "Cindi and I were apart for a while and at the time I operated on Lynn Johnson, the *Penthouse* 20th Anniversary Pet."[6] Moving the discussion away from Johnson, he continues, "There was a period of time when I was the house plastic surgeon for *Penthouse*. I was kind of like Bob Guccione's guy in the '80s and early '90s. They'd fly girls in. Guccione had this ominous, scary penthouse. It was kind of like a descent into hell. There were Dobermans or mastiffs. It was very lovely, but menacing. There were *a lot* of evil vibrations surrounding many of these patients. People who use their bodies as a conduit to make money—it all kind of merges. If you look into it, there was a lot of sexual abuse. I don't think it brings positive, angelic spirits into your life."

Of the split with Cindi, Dr. Rose reflects, "I guess there were actually two or three girls I sort of dated. [I would call it] more 'dalliances' than anything else....Our offices in those days [were filled with] young, beautiful women. It's hard to describe....When the plastic surgeon does a transformative experience for them that's even more benefiting of their beauty, they fall in love. It's crazy. It's weird how that happens."

Rose confesses that back in the '90s, upon walking into Rick's Cabaret—then the town's leading gentlemen's club—he would be besieged by dancers,

---

6. Lynn Johnson—born in 1969, the same year as *Penthouse*—was selected as the magazine's 20th Anniversary Pet following a nationwide search. The publication described her as a nineteen-year-old from Millerton, Iowa (dimensions 38D-24-36), who settled with her family in Houston. "I'm confident," she told the magazine, "that the 1990's will be our best decade yet." Despite attempts to contact Johnson through former *Penthouse* executives and associates, I was unable to locate her for comment. ("20th Anniversary: Lynn," *Penthouse*, September 1989, 139–52.)

many of them his patients. "I was David Schwimmer," he says, referring to Schwimmer's character from the TV movie *Breast Men*. "I'd walk in and it would be an absolute swarm." Did they offer him private dances? "They would do whatever you wanted them to do. These were women who made money with their body and it wasn't like they drew a line at this, that, or the other thing. They were happy [to oblige]. And I was kind of happy-go-lucky in those days myself.

"There was a period of time when I was the team plastic surgeon for the Houston Rockets"—during their 1990s wonder years—"and I operated on a number of the players' wives and some of the cheerleaders. And so I had front-row seats. I would walk in with some spectacularly beautiful girl and there was kind of more attention placed to her and to me than the basketball game."

The gentlemen's clubs of the era, Rose recalls, "were brand-new, fresh-built.... It was so *accepted*. Now it's a bunch of tacky girls with tattoos and stuff. But back [then] it was [packed with] beautiful girls—[one, for instance,] who might be an SMU girl on college break for the summer. It was a whole different crowd.... And I say that not with a sense of nostalgia or a sense of self-protectiveness. It's true."

Sharon St. Romain-Frank used to run Rose's public relations. She recalls two particularly memorable scenarios from the early '90s. One day, she had a contract that she needed Dr. Rose to sign. Instead of meeting at the office, she says, he asked her to bring the paperwork to Rick's Cabaret. And there, according to St. Romain-Frank, she found her boss seated amid his handiwork: "He was wearing his [surgical] scrubs—blue-green—*in* the strip club."

Another time, she remembers, "We had a party at a high-rise. He came in late. And he had five girls from his shoulders to his fingertips.... He walked in like P. Diddy. Can you imagine? I grabbed his hands. They were so sweaty. I said, 'What are you trying *to do*?'" St. Romain-Frank remained close to both Cindi and Franklin Rose, she says, "during the whole period when he was dating the *Penthouse* Pet. And I prayed for him daily. I am Christian Baptist.... Cindi and I have always been great friends. She would cry to me. She always knew he'd come back. And he did. Dr. Rose is a wonderful, very smart, kindhearted human being. He's driven. He's gentle. [But] Houston became one of the capitals of the country with all these strip clubs...and he was seduced by what was going on because he was so good at what he did. And now he's turned it around."[7]

Rose compares his circumstances to those of another figure from the decade: Bill Clinton. "I had the opportunity to meet and chat with him up in Aspen," he says. "He's a really bright guy. Of course, he was excoriated, as well you know, for his 'lack of values,' if you will. But in my own life, per se, I kind of lost my moral compass in the late '80s, early '90s, personally speaking. You're thirty-five years old. You're surrounded [by] dancers, models, actress-wannabes, people who were gorgeous. You get lost.... But in your heart of hearts, you knew this wasn't a good life."

Was there a moment, I ask him, when he hit rock bottom?

"I don't know," he says haltingly. "Go ask Tiger Woods. Who knows what happens in that environment?... You just get frickin' seduced, you know? Repeatedly. I was doing a lot of what we call the 'virgin augmentation' on the young, beautiful crowd of Houston. And after a while, it's sort of like you fall prey, seduced by the patients and the lifestyle, you're so immersed in it all the time.... When you're younger, the things that seem important to you, [such as] hanging out with the young and beautiful, kind of get revved up. The divorce rate among breast-augment surgeons in their thirties and forties in L.A., Houston, Dallas, or Miami approaches 100 percent"—a statistic I cannot confirm.

––––––––

When I arrive at Utopia Plastic Surgery and MedSpa, in a shopping complex in Houston's upscale Galleria area, I meet the office staff: five fresh-faced women in blue scrubs. One of them is Stacy Tompkins, a friendly, athletic blonde in her forties. Franklin Rose's patient coordinator since 1993, she takes me back in time.

"In the '80s and '90s," she says, "it was adult entertainers and dancers doing their breasts. And by the late '90s it became Sunday school teachers and preachers' wives who wanted to wear big sweaters in the winter so people

––––––––

7. Cindi Rose later talks about their time in the '90s wilderness. While her husband was squiring women around town, she says, she dated three men seriously. "They all had their own jets. They had their own companies. Extremely successful...and younger than me." And yet, she claims, "I was a single parent. I was home every night putting them to bed.... They were four and six years old when I divorced him." (Interview with Cindi Rose.)

wouldn't notice as much and then sort of 'grow into it' by summer.... I was raised in church—Baptist—and I've never come across anybody who's judged plastic surgery [in Houston]. *I've* never felt judged." Stacy takes out her medical chart to tick off her own cosmetic procedures, which she says began in her early twenties and significantly "helped my self-esteem.... I had my nose done in 1995. I did liposuction in '96 *and* '99. I did my breasts in '98. I did my eyes really young. I've had minor skin procedures. I've had tons of injectables too. I was Dr. Rose's first Botox patient... in 1997." Today's patients, she says, range in age from their teens ("usually seventeen-eighteen is okay, it's when they quit growing") to a recent first-timer ("age sixty-eight").

Tompkins gives her perspective on the wilder side of the practice during the 1990s. Their former office, in the heart of the Texas Medical Center, was located close to the gentlemen's clubs, she says. "There would be girls who would come in and want to trade favors for surgeries. That's why he *always* had me in the room. We had one girl do a back bend against the wall and said, 'Look what my breasts do!' And I thought, 'Oh, Lord,' you can't believe that these girls would have the gall.

"He was *known* for the breast. He was always more experienced than other plastic surgeons in town, so we dealt with really beautiful girls—a different class. Back in the '90s [some of] the higher-end dancers had their sugar daddies. They were kind of wild. The [Houston] Rockets were winning and people were running around with the Rockets. It was the appeal of the 'bad girl' lifestyle. Some of the younger socialite daughters... from wealthy families saw that life of nightspots and topless bars as an appealing lifestyle that they wanted to emulate, so society girls would want the procedure. They'd want to look like that, act like that.

"In the '90s," she continues, "everybody wanted big, big breasts. You'd *know* when a woman had it done. Now women are staying in the C sizes, a sporty look. I don't know if it's that Dr. Rose's getting older and maturing [but I think] it's an overall trend."

Part of Tompkins's job at that stage was to lend an ear. "I would spend an hour on a consultation, like a hairdresser, listening to their marital problems. One lady ran her husband's Corvette into his garage, on purpose, because she found out he was cheating. And then [he] paid for her to have the full gamut: breast 'aug,' lipo, tummy tuck, to keep her from leaving him. Back then these people had so much money that if the husband did something wrong, he had a lot to lose. So the wife could pull the strings."

The doctor and I continue our conversation in his office, then over lunch, then in a few follow-up talks and emails. "In the '90s," Rose recalls, "it was just, 'Let's make this girl the hottest, most beautiful girl in the world.... Let's do her nose, her lips, her breasts, and we'll really make her just beyond beautiful.'...In the early '90s, I remember a patient came in, she was Miss Florida Mud Wrestler or some crazy shit. And I put in 1400cc implants, which were *huge*. And, I mean, she said, 'Well, couldn't I have had a little more full-ness here?' It was nuts. It's like two basketballs." (Rose uses silicone and occa-sionally saline for his current procedures. To this day, he says, he considers the FDA's short-lived moratorium "just a pile of shit....I defend the silicone-gel implant immensely. This is the safest biomaterial ever invented for such use.")

The doctor does not apologize for his part in the equation, arguing that one's inner confidence, grace, and "a happier focus in life" often come from one's outward appearance. ("In the Torah," he says, "there are many references to [the virtue of] possessing great beauty.") But he recognizes a deep-seated problem in the culture's "beauty obsession." The cause, he insists, is a decline in values. "The complete emphasis on body versus spirit is accentuated now. It is unhealthy. There is [a concentration] on values that might be superficial instead of values that are more substantive—the values of family, of religion, of morality."

Compared to the 1960s, he asserts, today's "pop culture is more risqué, it's more promiscuous than ever. It's like Rome before the fall. Rome was a very immoral culture. Body image and perfection were revered in those cultures. The culture over the last couple of decades is not far off....We're heading toward an abyss—and I'd say it all started with the early 1960s." The turning point, he says, came with *Playboy* magazine and the ethos it espoused. "I was born in the 1950s," he says. "The *Father Knows Best* and *Ozzie and Harriet* morality was cast aside for a Hugh Hefner morality." That era, he says, was shaken by the approval of the birth control pill in 1960 and the introduction of the implant the following year. "Then, in my estimation, really, the cat got let out of the bag after the JFK assassination....All of a sudden, drugs became popular....To me, at least, it has just been a general decay of moral value ever since."

Franklin Rose, even so, is still suturing while Rome beckons.

He confesses a fear. It is one that all of his peers face: "The inevitable day when every plastic surgeon has to hand over his scalpels." And on that day, I ask, what does he foresee missing most? "It's just so pretty," he responds. "Everything about plastic surgery and wound-healing is so beautiful. And I don't mean that in a vainglorious way. The patients are so nice—at least in my practice. They're so beautiful, kind of, inside and out. And I know: to be one of the biggest plastic surgeons in a very large metropolitan area like this, it's a great blessing. But as you continue to age you know that you can't do it forever and ever. Sometimes I tell Cindi, 'I hope there's a place to practice plastic surgery in heaven.' She gets a kick out of it."

———————

After their years in the '90s wilderness, I wonder, how did the Roses recover their love?

Cindi believes that fate intervened. One night at dinner a man whom Cindi calls the Rose "family astrologer"—also a financial planner and photographer—"said, 'In exactly two months' an old boyfriend would come back in my life.... We consult with him all the time [and he is] never wrong." Two months later, in December 1996, a good friend "who is psychic," she says, informed her, "Tonight is going to be a special night for you."

Sure enough, Cindi returned home from a date that evening with a man who, she says, expressed a desire to settle down. "He kind of wanted the whole program, 'I would love to have a future with you'...and I thought, 'You know, I'm going to give him a chance....I'm tired of being single.'... We were sitting on the couch talking and my phone rang. It was like one in the morning."

It was her ex-husband, of all people—a man who, despite their having been in contact over seven years, had never once kissed her or even held her hand during their time apart. As Cindi recalls, "He said, 'I'm in the emergency room. It's a sign from God.' He [described how he'd been] bringing the children [daughter Erica and son Benjamin] home from the Rockets game. He said he felt pushed by an angel, that he felt pushed on the shoulder, fell over in front of the house...onto the ground, and he dislocated his shoulder." Cindi—who says she had had no clue that *Franklin* would be the one destined to come into her life—followed his instructions. She explained the situation to her date, bid him good-bye, collected Franklin from the ER, and brought him home. "We were intimate that evening." And they woke up the next morning as a couple. They would remarry soon thereafter.[8]

Franklin's account matches Cindi's. "I fell for no apparent reason," he remembers. "It was almost a *Wizard of Oz*–like tumbling." After shoulder surgery, he says, "I could have taken a taxi. For some reason—Cindi and I were cordial [at the time], not warm—I called Cindi, and she said something like, 'I was expecting your call.' . . . I spent the night. And the next morning our little eight- or nine-year-old son, who was forever trying to engineer some way of getting Mom and Dad back together, came bouncing down into the bedroom and said, 'Hi, Dad.'

"It was really weird," Rose continues, attributing their reunion to the Almighty. "It was just meant to be, somehow, through the greater cosmos." (Franklin and Cindi, both descendants of rabbis, have become more observant since their reconciliation.) As for the idea that an angel nudged him, he resists that characterization. "No, no, no. That's not true. I did not mention an angel." Then he retreats, admitting he may not have been in his normal mind-set. "Maybe I *did* say 'an angel.' They gave me Valium and Versed that night—standard-issue protocol in the emergency room for a dislocated shoulder."

---

8. In an email sent ten days after my visit, Cindi stresses, "It is not adultery for a man that is the sin—it is the mistruths that have a domino effect." She goes on to reiterate the importance of family in the Roses' current lives and in life in general. And she declares that there is something extra that has kept them together: the inner nature of the man she reveres. "He is one of the kindest people on this earth. That is why I never quit loving him. I could not stay married to him in 1990 or I would have lost my own self-esteem, and he has apologized over and over. . . . I have never regretted my decision. It was a leap of faith."

CHAPTER 18

Celebrity Sin

There had never been a year so disconcerting for the House of Windsor. In fact, so scandalous was 1992 that Great Britain's Queen Elizabeth II christened it her annus horribilis.

In March, the queen's second son, Prince Andrew, decided to separate from his wife, Sarah Ferguson (the Duchess of York), following revelations that she had been carrying on with a Texas oilman. In April, Elizabeth's daughter, Princess Anne, and Anne's estranged husband, Mark Phillips, were officially granted a divorce. In June, Her Majesty's daughter-in-law Princess Diana of Wales was revealed in a shocking biography to be struggling with Prince Charles's infidelity, her own bulimia, and a depression so deep that she had attempted suicide. (Diana had secretly authorized the book.) In August, "Fergie" was again in the news, photographed in Saint-Tropez— bare-bosomed and having her *bare toes* lovingly sucked upon (*not* by the aforementioned oilman, but by *a different* Texas financier). Meanwhile, the marriage of Charles and Diana continued to unravel. Rumors swirled of an affair between the princess and the polo player James Hewitt. Then clandestine tapes emerged exposing intimate discussions between Diana and her longtime friend James Gilbey—about masturbation, Diana's pregnancy worries, and the travails of married life. (On the recordings, made several years earlier, Gilbey refers to Diana as his "darling" and, cringingly, as "Squidgy.")

In late November, when a damaging blaze raged through Windsor Castle, it seemed a kind of elegy. The dirge sounded before Christmas: an official announcement came down from 10 Downing Street that, yes, Charles and Diana had decided to separate.

Not that 1993 was any great shakes either. Two weeks into the New Year, conversations from Charles's hacked cell phone were leaked, exposing a string of nerd-perv come-ons to his not-so-secret lover, Camilla Parker Bowles (later his wife). On the tapes, the heir to the throne fantasized about how he'd like to "just live inside your trousers" and return to Earth in the next life as "a Tampax." (The public could dial a number and, for a small fee, have a listen.) Next came *Diana's* shaming. The owner of a London fitness center connived to rig up a hidden camera in the ceiling of his gym to spy on the princess while she worked out. The resulting photos—depicting Diana in a leotard on a leg-press machine—were published in the *Sunday Mirror* and *Daily Mirror* and scored the health club operator more than $300,000. For the price of a newspaper, the public could delight in *two* forms of humiliation: seeing a royal at her most plebeian (her face contorted while she worked up a sweat) *and* defrocked (stripped down to her skintight training attire).

There was a corrosive pattern here. The Princess of Wales had perceived her activity as private. So had Charles and Camilla. So had Fergie and her beau. Diana's attorneys, in a stroke of sanity, decided to file suit. And a British court sided with *her*, ruling against both the newspaper group and the owner of the club.

For the moment, decorum and reason prevailed. Or so one might have gathered.

———

The current, however, was too strong. A scandal riptide swept across the U.S. in the 1990s, even more so than in the U.K. And it submerged the reputations of dozens of individuals who in past eras might have ridden it all out.

The popular press had become fixated on celebrities, colorful commoners, and their falls from grace: the steeper the descent, the sweeter. As a result, much of the decade's media coverage would amount to a clown-car cortege of revelations involving sex, scandal, violence, crime, sleaze, or some combination of these, all Cheez-Whizzed across the culture.

The rot in the House of Windsor, then, was merely the drama of the royal enclosure. Theirs was a pox being visited on countless houses, especially in L.A., New York, and Washington, D.C. Herewith—to quickly survey the damage before assessing its causes—is a chronology of some of the decade's nadirs of disgrace, moments that ranged from libidinous to criminal, from the purely prurient to the simply crass.

- Marion Barry, the mayor of Washington, D.C., is snared in an FBI sting while smoking crack with an erstwhile girlfriend, Rasheeda Moore. A videotape records the scene as Barry is placed in handcuffs and declares, "Bitch set me up."

- Donald and Ivana Trump, one of Manhattan's golden couples of '80s excess, announce a public separation after Mrs. T, on the slopes at Aspen, has a tense exchange with her husband's paramour, the model and actress Marla Maples. The *New York Post* soon trumpets an alleged Maples comment about Trump on its front page (twenty-five years before he would ascend to the presidency): BEST SEX I EVER HAD.[1]

- Christian Brando, the eldest child of actor Marlon Brando, is arrested and ultimately found guilty of voluntary manslaughter in the death of Dag Drollet, the lover of his half sister Cheyenne.

- At the start of a San Diego Padres baseball game, comedian Roseanne Barr is drowned out by a jeering crowd during her yowly (and to many disrespectful) rendition of "The Star-Spangled Banner." Barr expresses her appreciation by grabbing hold of her crotch and letting loose a hocker—on live television.

- Med-school student William Kennedy Smith, after venturing out in Palm Beach one evening with his uncle Ted (Massachusetts senator Edward Kennedy), comes back to the nearby Kennedy compound in the company of a young woman. Smith is booked on—and later cleared of—rape charges.

- Comedian Pee-wee Herman (real name: Paul Reubens)—known for his TV and film roles as a mischievous man-child living in a Day-Glo mocktopia—is nabbed in an adult movie theater in Sarasota and charged with indecent exposure. Reubens, claiming his innocence, pleads no contest and avoids a public trial.

- Tennis ace Martina Navratilova is sued by her former partner of seven years, Judy Nelson, for "gal-pal-imony." Nelson nets a bundle, including the $1.3 million house in Aspen.

---

1. In high dudgeon, Maples's spokesperson, Chuck Jones, would cry foul: "Marla is not the cause of the problem between the Trumps." Jones would soon be brought to heel by his *own* scandal after stealing dozens of pairs of Ms. Maples's shoes, acknowledging in court that he had maintained a "sexual relationship" with her footwear. (Elizabeth Sporkin, "Ooh-La-La Marla," *People*, March 5, 1990; Laura Italiano, "Footwear Fetishist Chuck Jones Hit with New Harassment Indictment," *New York Post*, June 27, 2012; Laura Italiano, "Court to Marla's Harasser: Shoo Off!," *New York Post*, September 26, 2001; Karen S. Schneider and Sue Carswell, "Agony of the Feet," *People*, August 3, 1992.)

• Actress Elizabeth Taylor weds her seventh husband, a construction worker named Larry Fortensky, whom she meets while in rehab at the Betty Ford Center. The ceremony takes place at Michael Jackson's Neverland ranch in California, where a paparazzo paraglides from the sky and lands on the lawn, only to be clocked by burly security guards.[2]

• Mia Farrow, while visiting the apartment of her longtime partner, Woody Allen, comes across compromising Polaroids of her adoptive daughter Soon-Yi Previn, who is romantically involved with Allen. A legal battle commences, in which Allen is accused of engaging in sexual behavior with Farrow's daughter Dylan; the State of New York declares, however, that there is "no credible evidence [that Dylan] has been abused or maltreated." Allen is cleared of the charges and denies any misconduct. Allen and Previn marry five years later.

• World heavyweight boxing champion Mike Tyson (who is divorced from actress Robin Givens following charges of domestic abuse) is convicted of raping Desiree Washington, a teenage beauty queen. Released from jail in 1995, Tyson regains his title but, two years later, forfeits his boxing license after a bloody bout in which he takes a chomp out of the ear of his opponent, Evander Holyfield.

• Teenager Amy Fisher, smitten with her married boyfriend—a mechanic named Joey Buttafuoco—shows up at his front door in Massapequa, Long Island, and shoots his wife, Mary Jo, in the head. Mary Jo survives but sustains facial disfigurement. Joey does four months for sleeping with a minor. Amy serves seven years for reckless assault. Their story is regurgitated in *three* quickie TV movies. Over time, Fisher's career path traces a curiously bulbous celebrity bell curve: she pens two memoirs, writes columns for the *Long Island Press*, becomes a prison-rights reformer, performs in strip clubs, appears on *Celebrity Rehab*, and stars in a half dozen porn movies, including *Seduced by a Cougar, Volume 22*. Joey, over the years, is implicated in a fraud scheme, becomes a sometime actor, and agrees to a sparring match with Chyna, the female pro wrestler. Mary Jo, meanwhile, becomes a motivational speaker and advocate for sufferers of facial paralysis, writing a memoir of her own, entitled—wait for it—*Getting It Through My Thick Skull*.

---

2. As the paparazzo makes his descent, my wife and I are among the 160 guests at the Taylor-Fortensky nuptials, sitting at the ceremony with actors Roddy McDowall and George Hamilton.

- In a case that rivets Beverly Hills, brothers Lyle and Erik Menendez go on trial—twice—for killing their parents, Kitty and Jose, in the family mansion. (In discussions with a therapist, the brothers confess to the crimes.) The sons, despite their claims of sexual abuse at the hands of their father, are convicted of first-degree murder and conspiracy, and must spend the rest of their lives behind bars.

- At a practice skating rink, an assailant takes a baton and whacks American Olympic hopeful Nancy Kerrigan above her kneecap, injuring her. It soon emerges that Kerrigan's figure-skating rival, Tonya Harding, along with Harding's husband, Jeff Gillooly, helped set up the "hit" with an accomplice. (The couple later plead guilty, respectively, of conspiracy and racketeering.) Kerrigan and Harding go on to compete on the U.S. Olympic team, finishing second and eighth, behind victor Oksana Baiul. Paydays follow. Kerrigan inks a $1 million cross-platform media deal. A Gillooly-Harding sex tape makes the rounds.

- Michael Jackson, the self-proclaimed King of Pop, eccentric *puer aeternus,* and singer-songwriter-dancer-entrepreneur, agrees to an out-of-court settlement in a child-molestation suit, reportedly paying out $20 million to settle one of a series of sex-abuse charges brought against him. Jackson consents to let authorities take pictures of his genitalia after one of his young accusers describes purported discolorations. The singer calls the photo session "the most humiliating ordeal of my life."

- Anna Nicole Smith, the pillowy *Playboy* and Guess jeans model, marries eighty-nine-year-old J. Howard Marshall II, an oil baron six decades her senior, who is worth half a billion dollars. He dies the next year.

- Actor Hugh Grant—a charming, self-deprecating rogue on the screen, and in real life the significant other of supermodel Elizabeth Hurley—is arrested in Hollywood in the company of a hooker named Divine Brown. Grant redeems himself by going on *The Tonight Show* two weeks later. He addresses the seamy situation rather seamlessly, responding to host Jay Leno's question "What the hell were you thinking?" with a sheepish "I did a bad thing; there you have it."

- Princess Stephanie of Monaco, the principality's resident wild child, marries her ex-bodyguard Daniel Ducruet, already the father of two of her children. Within a year, a paparazzo photographs Ducruet cavorting naked on a chaise with a woman known as Miss Bare Breasts of Belgium. The princess and Ducruet divorce; she eventually weds a circus performer, taking up residence in a caravan.

• On the third day of the 1996 Democratic National Convention, the *Star* tabloid zaps a message to the pager of President Clinton's go-to political strategist Dick Morris. The gist: the tabloid is about to publish a story saying that the married Morris has been spending time in the company of a prostitute, Sherry Rowlands. The *Star* exposé includes photos of the pair on a balcony at the Jefferson Hotel (a power spot a few blocks from the White House) and describes how Morris would occasionally put the telephone receiver to Rowlands's ear so she could hear the voice of the commander in chief. Morris abruptly resigns.[3] (Earlier in the week, he had appeared on the cover of *Time*. The headline: "The Man Who Has Clinton's Ear.")

• The brutal slaying of six-year-old JonBenét Ramsey in Boulder, Colorado, sparks obsessive press coverage and intensifies criticism of the child beauty pageant boom. (The murder remains unsolved.)

• Robert F. Kennedy's son Michael—campaign chief of his brother Joe's run for Massachusetts governor (and his uncle Ted's Senate reelection bid)— is alleged to have been carrying on with his children's underage babysitter. (Michael dies several months later in a skiing accident.)

• Eddie Murphy, after visiting a late-night newsstand in Hollywood, is stopped by authorities in the company of a transsexual prostitute, Atisone Seiuli. The actor-comedian, who is not charged, explains through a spokesperson that he had innocently come to the aid of Seiuli, who appeared to be distressed.

• Popular sportscaster Frank Gifford—married to popular TV talk-show host Kathie Lee Gifford—is caught in the company of flight attendant Suzen Johnson, part of a secretly photographed honey trap that may or may not have been coordinated by the *Globe* tabloid, which denies having set up a "sting."

---

3. The *Star* scoop foreshadowed Morris's career trajectory. Twenty years later he would become the chief political correspondent for none other than the *Star*'s sibling publication, the *National Enquirer*, penning pieces such as "Hill & Bill, THE WORST SHAM MARRIAGE EVER!" Ah, the blackguard calling the kettle black. (Alessandra Stanley, "Dick Morris Takes Aim at Hillary Clinton from a Tabloid Perch," *New York Times*, July 9, 2016.)

• Fashion legend Gianni Versace is murdered outside his villa in South Beach. The assailant turns out to be a twenty-seven-year-old gigolo cum serial killer named Andrew Cunanan.

• Princess Diana of Wales and her companion Dodi Al-Fayed die shortly after their limousine crashes in a Paris tunnel. Their driver, Henri Paul—legally intoxicated at the time, and killed in the accident—is believed to have been speeding to elude a contingent of paparazzi. Nine photographers (some of whom take pictures of Diana in the mangled wreckage) are arrested. Diana's brother, Earl Spencer, remarks, "I always believed the press would kill her in the end. But not even I could imagine that they would take such a direct hand in her death as seems to be the case." Later that week the world tunes in to watch the funeral of Diana, age thirty-six, which becomes one of the most widely viewed events in British history.[4]

• Popular sportscaster Marv Albert is convicted of assault and battery, stemming from an incident with a woman who over the years had occasionally joined him for trysts. In court, a *second* alleged sex partner claims that on two occasions Albert had sunk his teeth into her and that she had escaped his advances by tugging off his toupee. Albert sits down with TV interviewer Barbara Walters to dispute the assertions as fabrications, insisting that all acts were consensual and declaring his hair to be an un-yank-off-able weave. (Dismissed by NBC, Albert resumes his post within two years.)

• At a star-studded industry soiree during Oscar week, Mike De Luca,

---

4. Paris magistrates would clear the paparazzi of manslaughter charges, placing the blame solely on the driver, whose blood-alcohol numbers were shown to have been three times those permitted under French law. A decade later, a British jury would open an inquest and deduce that the photographers had "collectively" contributed to the crash, bearing a level of responsibility with regard to her death.

"The celebrity culture has become a mass psychosis," *New York Times* columnist Maureen Dowd would write the week of Diana's death. "All that the celebrity culture teaches is a counterfeit empathy which mistakes prurience for interest and voyeurism for a genuine human identification....The pictures of the Princess dying—and it is only a matter of time before these scummy photos surface— are not news. They are pornography. And pornography is the natural conclusion of a culture of voyeurism....God rest her soul, because the journalists won't." (Craig R. Whitney, "French Prosecutor Says Pursuers of Diana Did Not Cause Crash," *New York Times*, August 18, 1999; John-Thor Dahlburg, "Charges Dropped Against Paparazzi Implicated in Princess Diana Crash," *Los Angeles Times*, September 4, 1999; Mary Jordan, "Paparazzi and Driver Found Negligent in Princess Diana's Death," *Washington Post*, April 8, 2008; Angela Balakrishnan, "Chauffeur and Paparazzi to Blame for Diana Death, Jury Finds," *Guardian*, April 7, 2008; Maureen Dowd, "Death and the Maiden," *New York Times*, September 3, 1997.)

the thirty-two-year-old bad-boy production honcho at New Line Cinema, as reported in the *Los Angeles Times*, "dropped his pants... and engaged in oral sex with a young woman as several guests looked on. The incident, which took place in the backyard of William Morris Agency President Arnold Rifkin's Pacific Palisades home, elicited tittering as well as outrage from some guests and the host, who had security guards escort De Luca from the property."

———

Kneecaps, honey traps, and penis snaps. No wonder the great American unwashed often felt like they needed a shower.

What common thread connected these '90s scandals? Some had begun as personal encounters that took a criminal or horrific turn. Some involved sexual acts that were considered completely private. Some were the actions of sociopaths. But each, in the end, became spectacles witnessed and then dissected by the thousands—sometimes by the millions—spectacles presented not infrequently in the guise of "public interest." (Indeed, Diana's fatal crash—*while* being pursued by paparazzi—was a moment when contemporary media was knocked off its axis. Then and there, millions of readers and viewers decided to regard the Press-At-Large as a "pack," effectively robbing an entire, vaunted profession of its hard-earned reputation as a defender of the public trust.)

How, then, did such dubious news become a genus of soft porn, diced up in gossip mills, intensified by paparazzi stakeouts, and siphoned through Web portals that would refract the stars' every flicker?

The short answers? Flush with so many brand-new and evanescent media options, news consumers and Web surfers developed a collective ADD, pinballing from story to story, format to format. Average citizens, the beneficiaries of a robust economy, had more leisure time to indulge in the base, disposable pleasures of junk culture.[5] Many viewers were looking for objects of their contempt, for public figures whose social evisceration might assuage their own angst or self-loathing in the face of their own foibles. What's more,

———

5. The "gentleman of leisure," as described by the economist and sociologist Thorstein Veblen during a series of lectures he gave in another Naughty Nineties—the 1890s—was chiefly engaged in the "non-productive consumption of time." (Thorstein Veblen, *The Theory of the Leisure Class* [1899] [Oxford: Oxford University Press, 2007], 28.)

the widening social gap between right and left—between those supporting more conservative values and those bound to a broader definition of ethics and family—upped the national demand for morality tales. Tabloid stories taught lessons about how *not* to behave—and about how society might mete out punishment, or mercy, for such misbehavior.[6]

A final ingredient was a demand for *proof.* A booming visual culture, 24/7 news, and a surge in digital photography had all made Americans more image-savvy at a time when skepticism was rife—the result of countless cons from the political establishment, public authorities, advertisers, and celebrity spinners. People needed to *see* the goods before they believed the stories they were being fed. Mug shots, paparazzi photos, and surveillance videos would become the mother's milk of tabloid culture.

The reality, however, was less lofty than all of this. Media and society, to be blunt, found these narratives to be *lucrative.* Journalist David Kamp said it best in his seminal 1999 essay for *Vanity Fair* in which he bid the '90s adieu. "If the decade must have a name," Kamp wrote, "it might as well be the Tabloid Decade, [which brought about] the tabloidification of American life—of news, of the culture, yea, of human behavior." In his view, two elements set the '90s apart: "advanced technology and increased vulgarity. It's the dance between these factors, the downloadable and the down-and-dirty, that has led to the Tabloid Decade's particularly explicit brand of tabloidism.... That has enabled us... not only to discover that Prince Charles had an affair with Camilla Parker Bowles but also to hear a recording of him stating his wish to be her tampon."

To tweak Kamp's thesis, two forces had conspired to set the stage. First, beginning in the early 1970s, news and information were conveniently trivialized,[7] sensationalized, and sexualized. An entire tabloid industry coalesced around personalities, gossip, voyeurism, sex appeal, crime, and a preoccupation

---

6. There was also the proverbial need to be informed so as to be in a position to gossip. In the age of the tabs, tab TV, and the Internet, it had never been easier to be looped in, especially when the subject was, say, Tonya and not, say, NAFTA. Just *listening* to the experts made *you* conversant. "The most pointless journalism of the year [1994] was the [on-air experts'] effort to lend analytical weight to the froth," Jonathan Alter would write in *Newsweek*—in a time before punditry utterly polluted the airwaves. "Yes, Tonya Harding's behavior raised questions about the pressures of big-time sports.... But that's like saying we eat popcorn for the roughage." (Jonathan Alter, "America Goes Tabloid," *Newsweek*, December 25, 1994, 36.)

7. The board game Trivial Pursuit had become a national phenomenon in the 1980s.

with appearances. Second, a series of electronic advances would alter what we viewed and heard throughout the day. Culture critic Frank Rich would wisely surmise in a 1998 *New York Times* column that *media* had effectively replaced *nature* as "America's backdrop." What Rich was getting at was the fact that the public, thanks to the telecom boom, now had access not only to print, radio, and network TV, but to dozens (and then hundreds) of cable and satellite channels, followed, of course, by the Web and digital devices of all kinds.

When these electronic delivery systems got caught in the downdraft of tabloid culture, it caused a breach in that decorous dividing line that had separated our personal, secret space from our outward, shared space. We didn't really understand where the boundaries were. (We still don't.) And, voyeurs all, we didn't really care.

The public appetite for a more gamey diet of sin, celebs, crime, and innuendo was whetted by three media creations in the mid-to-late '70s. First, press mogul Rupert Murdoch brought his tabloid tastes to the States in 1974 when he started up a paper called the *National Star* (later named merely the *Star*), which would set off a tabloid war with its conjoined twin, the *National Enquirer*.[8] That same year, an entirely new entity would prove to be even more influential: *People Weekly*, the infant divine—or demon seed—of modern celebrity journalism, which would become America's most profitable magazine franchise.[9] Then, in 1976, as Gotham sank into a fiscal funk,

---

8. Working from their respective home offices in mucky, plucky South Florida, muckrakers from the *Star* and *Enquirer* scoured the rap sheets and siphoned off the pond scum from Hollywood's rank Jacuzzi. The *Globe* tabloid also figured into the mix. Director John Waters, the master of cinematic trash, would describe the three thus, to journalist David Kamp. The *Enquirer*: "We hate you because you're famous"; the *Star*: "We hate you because you're on TV"; the *Globe*: "We hate you because you're famous and have sex." Indeed, the "hallelujah days of the supermarket tabloid," according to culture critic James Wolcott, ran from "the mid-70s to the late 90s....At their peak in the early 80s, they had an estimated readership of 43 million per week." Their finest hour—in terms of a nation wading into the muck? Catching *two* candidates in extramarital tangles in successive presidential campaigns: Senator Gary Hart in 1987 and Governor Bill Clinton in 1992. (David Kamp, "The Tabloid Decade," *Vanity Fair*, February 1999; James Wolcott, "U.S. Confidential," *Vanity Fair*, June 2002.)

9. The covers told the tale. *People's* managing editor, Richard Stolley, would formulate a handy scale (called Stolley's Laws) for determining who to feature on the cover so as to maximize newsstand sales: "Young is better than old. Pretty is better than ugly. Rich is better than poor. Television is better than movies. Movies are better than music. Music is better than sports. And *anything* is better than politics." Stolley added a corollary after *People's* sales spiked following the death of Elvis Presley (in 1977) and the murder of John Lennon (in 1980). "And *nothing*," he declared, "is better than

Murdoch purchased the city's oldest paper, the *New York Post*. And overnight the death rattle of the town's vices and bloodlust and financial woes
would resound from the tabloid's front page. A year later, a new section—the
spicy, scandalous, and often anonymously sourced "Page Six"—would ooze
schmutz, gossip, and glitz. (An item from day one: actress-chanteuse Claudine Longet appeared in court in Aspen for the shooting death of her skier
boyfriend Spider Sabich. She would be found guilty of criminally negligent
homicide.)[10]

The *Star*, *People*, and the *Post* were just the tip of the spear. In the '80s
and '90s, the tabloid went steroid with the introduction of a new crossbreed:
tabloid TV. "For most of this century," notes the insightful David Kamp,
"tabloid had been exclusively the preserve of print.... But suddenly tabloid
was suburbanized, ubiquitous, and passively received—not a smudgy read
on the subway ride home, but something that 'more or less comes with the
house, like running water and electricity,' as the novelist Thomas Mallon
wrote in *GQ*."

Why so? First, programmers in the '80s began devoting ever more band-
width to talk TV. The format ran the gamut, filching elements from the
American self-help movement, French opéra bouffe, and the lion-pit blood-

the Celebrity Dead." Looked at in one way, the culture was becoming pop-heavy and postliterate.
One could even extrapolate from Stolley's recipe and suggest the following: trivia was better than
substance; reality was better than fiction (though it was becoming more difficult to distinguish
between the two); visuals were better than text; short texts were better than long (as *USA Today*,
launched in 1982, had proven); scandal was better than "feel-good"; murder was better than scandal.
And *nothing* was better than sex. (Richard Stolley, "Stolley's Laws" [video], Stanford Publishing
Course, Stanford.edu/group/publishing/cgi-bin/courses/blog/stolleys-laws.)

10. The *Post*, as media writer Jonathan Mahler would state in *New York* magazine, became "the
beachhead of [Murdoch's] American conquest. It was there that he perfected the mix of hard
conservative politics and unapologetic tabloid values with which his name would become
synonymous." And it would set the greasy bar for the many daily newspapers that were limboing
across the land. Soon tabloids everywhere were mashing up news and rumor just to keep up with
the saucy Aussie, who bought the *Boston Herald*, then the *Chicago Sun-Times*. Murdoch's prize,
though, was the *Post*—profane, fearless, and hard right. Its distinguishing feature was its front-page
headline, often pun-prone or alliterative. The best of these, naturally, harbored sexual undercurrents:
"Headless Body in Topless Bar"..."I Slept with a Trumpet"..."Wacko Jacko Backo"...and
"Madman Moammar Now a Druggie Drag Queen." (Jonathan Mahler, "What Rupert Wrought,"
New York, April 11, 2005; Garry Wills, "In Cold Type," *Vanity Fair*, May 1984; *Headless Body in
Topless Bar: The Best Headlines from America's Favorite Newspaper*, Staff of the *New York Post* [New
York: HarperEntertainment, 2008]; Niles Lathem and Doug Feiden, "Madman Moammar Now a
Druggie Drag Queen," *New York Post*, June 17, 1986.)

fests of ancient Rome. Talk-show hosts became so popular they were known by their first names: Phil and Oprah and Sally Jessy, Morton and Maury and Montel. Their programs often featured a live studio audience, experts or authors or celebrities with something to hawk, or a collection of guests airing their hang-ups, quirks, or sex habits.

Certain hosts served as referees, presiding over on-air squabbles among feuding families, neighbors, coworkers, lovers, exes, and the psychologically tenuous. (The genre would hit rock bottom when one of the guests from *Jenny Jones* was sentenced to twenty-five-plus years for the 1995 murder of *another* male guest, who, while the cameras rolled, had professed that he had a crush on him.) And yet late into the decade, the frenzied, trash-talking *Jerry Springer Show* would attract eight *million* daily viewers. Springer's program was a whirring Cuisinart of red meat, sexual depravity, dysfunction, and fistfights.

Local news stations were also going lurid, adopting the slogan "If It Bleeds, It Leads." Journalist Michael Winerip, in the *New York Times Magazine*, attributed this switch to one main factor: Reagan-era deregulation that had allowed media owners in the '80s to operate more channels, creating a scramble for local news ratings. This demand was met most easily through coverage that was more tabloid-tinged. Many local stations chose the low road—especially during "sweeps" weeks, when audience numbers were tallied to determine ad rates. One of the low-water marks for Orlando's Channel 2 News, for example, came during one 1995 sweeps period in which the station, according to Winerip, aired " 'Boosting Your Assets,' about the latest bust- and penis-enhancing underwear.... 'I had to go into Mulligan's [restaurant,' reporter Kathy] Marsh recalls, 'carrying penis-enhanced underwear in my hand and ask men at the bar whether they'd wear it. I was ashamed.' "

The networks, for their part, took a while to get on the gravy train. They ran serious news-oriented specials, genuinely believing in their mandate to uphold the public trust. Newsmagazines maintained their gravitas with social exposés, hard news, and law-and-order coverage—exemplified by *60 Minutes* and *20/20*, along with such '80s stalwarts as *West 57th*, *48 Hours*, and *Primetime Live*. But in 1986 the genre began its precipitous slide, thanks to a Murdoch-funded creation called *A Current Affair* (which, in one infamous segment, used stand-ins to "re-create" child-predator claims against Michael Jackson). By 1993, the category would grow to include *Hard Copy*, *Inside Edition*, and *American Journal*. A year later there would be *sixteen* (some perennials, others flashes in the pan;

some concentrating on crime, others decidedly more downmarket). And why the glut? As *Newsweek* would explain, "While a typical half-hour sitcom can cost $1 million an episode, news mags cost less than half that.... Some executives look to the news magazines as money machines for the networks, not the prestigious 'loss leaders' that news programs used to be."[11]

Up jumped TV movies based on each successive scandal. The impulse to ferment docudramas out of epic disgrace was not merely mercenary. There was also a sincere belief on the part of much of the viewing public that fictionalized renderings were a form of "higher art" pulp—as if Tonya vs. Nancy, portrayed in prime time by Hollywood actresses, would magically elevate the original maiming into something within striking distance of *Medea*. The smart "dumb money" migrated to scandal-themed TV movies—and to side projects that could be tacked on to larger package deals. "Simply for being kneecapped," *Entertainment Weekly* would report, "Nancy Kerrigan will be getting a two-hour ABC TV movie...a prime-time ABC special, appearances at Disney theme parks, an exercise video, and a children's book that she'll coauthor for Hyperion."[12]

Things soon went a bit gillooly.

Alongside the TV newsmags and the docudramas came a groundswell of entertainment-news-and-gossip shows. Stations relied on syndicated programming to provide ad-friendly, sponsor-supported content during the dinner hour. And so, in the wake of *Entertainment Tonight* (launched in 1981, back in the Bill-Paley-o-lithic Age), emerged the E! Entertainment Television network (1990), *Extra!* (1994), *Access Hollywood* (1996), and so on. These programs ladled the celebrity cream off of other media and turned it into skim.

A concurrent phenomenon was Court TV, launched in 1991, which allowed audiences not only to see the wheels of justice churning but to become inured to a new form of unscripted entertainment. That same year, cable news triumphed. Though CNN had debuted in 1980 as the first round-the-clock news channel, it wasn't until a decade later, during the network's coverage of

---

11. Meanwhile, new specialties became *career paths*: the media adviser, the handler, the crisis manager, and the "booker" or "wrangler," who corralled fresh guests.

12. Package deals were the new big game. Once the media companies consolidated in the '80s, they were in a position to offer multipronged story venues and spin-offs. And as the talent firms grew in size and sophistication, the agents and publicists upped the stakes and their takes, as did savvy attorneys and crisis managers.

the Gulf War, that it became, in *Time* magazine's assessment, "the common frame of reference for the world's power elite." So significant was CNN's war coverage that *Time*'s 1991 Person of the Year was neither Saddam Hussein, who had invaded Kuwait, nor the military leaders behind the U.S.-led counterinvasion, but *Ted Turner*, whose network televised it all.

Indeed, the *New York Times*' Frank Rich would call CNN's play-by-play of Operation Desert Storm the pilot for a novel kind of news-as-entertainment series: "this new genre could be named the Mediathon," he argued, "a relentless hybrid of media circus, soap opera and tabloid journalism we have come to think of as All Calamity All the Time. 'War in the Gulf' paved the way for the host of breathless sequels that have blanketed the culture ever since: [from] 'The O.J. Simpson Case' [to] . . . the biggest crowd-pleaser of them all, 'Scandal at the White House.' . . . War and assassinations were not required to make the form tick. Sex, celebrity and money would do just fine."[13]

The tabloids, whether printed or televised, were serving as the culture's fleet of "icebreakers," says Art Harris, an investigative reporter, writer, and producer who worked at CNN throughout the '90s. "Whether the stuff was 100 percent true and accurate or not, it didn't matter. Suddenly, what qualified as news or human interest was being redefined. We were heading into areas that the ships—mainstream news—couldn't go because there was no icebreaker there with orders to chop it up. [But together] they could break off bigger chunks and navigate the glaciers—celebs, public figures, etcetera."[14]

---

13. In many ways, the subsequent practice of "binge" watching a batch of TV episodes—adopted by millions of Americans in the 2010s—was derived from the audience's muscle memory of binging on those 1990s scandal sagas. In both cases, the narratives (especially if they involved sex or death or crime) became habit-forming, the contemporary equivalents of potboilers, page-turners, matinee serials.

14. Perhaps the grimiest escalation of all was the shotgun marriage of tabloid journalism *and porn*. That improbable pairing was announced in 1998, courtesy of Larry Flynt, whose flagship skin magazine, *Hustler*, had cornered the market in crude. Two years earlier, the publisher had been lionized as a First Amendment crusader on the big screen in Miloš Forman's 1996 picture *The People vs. Larry Flynt*. Now, in response to what he saw as "sexual McCarthyism" against Bill Clinton and the Democrats, the smut king struck back. Clearly tunneling for Republican dirt, Flynt placed a full-page ad in the *Washington Post* that offered a $1 million reward for information about the extramarital affairs of current congressmen. And after receiving scores of leads, Flynt got his man. Within three months, Newt Gingrich's would-be successor as Speaker-elect of the House, Bob Livingston, the Louisiana Republican, would bow out, having received word that Flynt was ready to publish a bombshell based on supposed accounts from four women. *Hustler* didn't need to publish word one. (William Booth, "Is Larry Flynt a Hero, or Just a Hustler?" *Washington Post*, February 10, 1997; Booth, "How Larry Flynt

All of these media platforms, of course, would pale in comparison with those enabled by the Internet. The tab-mob scramble, in truth, had just been the preamble. Once the Web elbowed in, wagging its social-media tail, anyone could participate in the pile-on: from a scandal's protagonists, to its surrogates and spinners, to the Web's clickering classes, providing death by a thousand keystrokes.

———

In terms of private exposé, there was another odious practice that came of age during the decade—a calculated, strategic move on the part of certain gay activists. The "outing" of public figures became a form of public shaming, a drive-by referendum on personal character and political bona fides, and a next-level parlor game. An individual's sexual orientation—by definition a private matter—was suddenly a commodity that could be exploited by activists or members of the gay or straight press and transformed into another means of tabloid-age unmasking.

Outing had sprung up during a period of radical activism—a history laid out clearly in Larry Gross's 1993 book *Contested Closets: The Politics and Ethics of Outing*. Silence about AIDS had meant death. President Ronald Reagan hadn't uttered the word "AIDS" during his entire first term. Some provocateurs, believing they were on a war footing (a war against a disease, government inaction and intolerance, and societal fear and apathy), rooted out hypocrites, demanding loyalty and action. Desperate times, some argued, justified desperate measures.

Concurrently, there was a strong politics in the '80s and '90s around the idea of stepping up and *claiming* one's lesbian, gay, bisexual, or trans identity, or HIV-positive status. And, as David Tuller would point out in the *San Francisco Chronicle*, if you were actively working *against* the LGBT agenda—and you were closeted—some activists felt they had a right or obligation to out you, especially if you were a public figure, a power broker, a role model. Outing left little room for sympathizing with someone's life path, inner conflicts, or public and private relationships. Instead, it politicized, accelerated,

———

Changed the Picture," *Washington Post*, January 11, 1999; David Cogan, "Larry Flynt Scores," *LA Weekly*, December 23, 1998; Charles McGrath, "Editing Hustler: A Dirty Job Allan MacDonell Just Had to Do," *New York Times*, April 29, 2006; Interview with David Cogan.)

and in certain cases tabloidized[15] the coming-out process, which for many was a profound, protracted, and tumultuous undertaking. Outing, in short, hijacked a personal journey and made it political.

In 1990, Stuart Kellogg, the ex-editor of the *Advocate*, at the time America's largest-circulation publication for the gay community, called outing "philosophical rape." Others used the term "witch hunt." Humorist and essayist Fran Lebowitz referred to the practice as "immoral, it's McCarthyism, it's terrorism, it's cannibalism, it's beneath contempt."

––––––––

The single tabloid-era vocation with arguably the greatest financial upside? The paparazzo—a media species that had been around for half a century.

In the 1990s, a new level of trench warfare broke out, pitting celebrities and their storm troopers against what Evelyn Waugh, sixty years earlier, had dubbed the Daily Beast. On the march were brigades of paparazzi (for photo agencies, tabloids, European publications, celebrity magazines, TV, and websites), whose increasingly predatory behavior had been practically preordained.

The prime motivator? Hollywood's biggest names had accrued unprecedented power, often encircling themselves with a praetorian guard of management teams and PR machines. The stars' talent agencies, attorneys, flacks, and studios started treating the press like the hired help and demanding spotless media coverage. In response, the press—and the public—sought some authenticity, some blemishes, some nasty. "The paparazzi packs began pushing back against the PR hacks," photographer Harry Benson recalls, "trying to fill the void and capture anything *real*." The winners in the fight, needless to say, were the paps and the tabs. And their peekaboo fare suited the tastes of media-stewed Boomers who by then had started to go granular about the unvarnished lives of their heroes.[16]

––––––––

15. In a 1997 *Vanity Fair* column, James Wolcott tagged outing as a mutation of the tabloid press, "the dominant influence on media culture today [which] works from a moralistic takedown mentality. . . . The tabloid foragers assume that each celebrity has a private and public face, like two sides of a trading card, and that when the two sides clash, it's open season. Some of the celebrities who come out may do so less from pride than from battle fatigue." (James Wolcott, "Lover Girls," *Vanity Fair*, June 1997, 67.)

16. Little wonder that one of the enduring film noirs of the decade was 1997 Best Picture nominee *L.A. Confidential.* The adaptation of James Ellroy's novel looks at a morally corrosive city through the eyes of a corrupt '50s tabloid called *Hush-Hush*. One classic line: "You're like Santa Claus with that list, Bud, except everyone on it's been naughty."

A European friend of mine in the photo business has an anecdote he wants to share. Over the second glass of wine, it tumbles out.

"I knew a paparazzo who had many exclusives in the '90s," he says. "He had an unbelievable story.

"It began with a mysterious voice," he recounts. "Every year or two, this photographer would get a call from a stranger. Always the same British voice. Always very polite but direct. The photographer had *no idea* who this guy was. But then the phone would ring and it would be this guy—very specific instructions. 'Go to *this* restaurant at *this* time. Or go to *this* apartment building at *this* address. Wait outside and you will get a surprise.' Then the guy would hang up.

"So the paparazzo would go to the restaurant and wait, and, voilà. Coming out the front door would be a member of some European royal family— with a beautiful woman. Or a celebrity would be meeting a lover in a parking garage. Always, the calls were accurate. Always, the pictures were a *sensation*. The photographer was quite confused, actually. How did this man have [such] good information? And how come the man chose *him* to give the exclusives, never asking for anything [in return]?

"So one time the photographer's phone rings, back in the '90s. It's the voice with the British accent. 'Go *this* Thursday to *this* airport in *this* country'—it is a remote destination where people go on holiday. 'Go to the corporate terminal. Wait for a private plane with *this* tail number. You will get a surprise.' And he hangs up.

"The photographer goes there," my friend says. (He tells me the name of the celebrity involved, but asks me not to publish it, to protect the paparazzo's identity.) "And, voilà, just as the guy predicted, [the celebrity] comes out of the plane, but with a man who is not her husband. They are met by a van. They get in the van and they drive off and disappear. The photographer has *no idea* where to find them. They could be *any*where.

"So he calls a close friend—a business partner of his, who has a vacation house nearby. He is extremely good-looking, this friend. The photographer says, 'Come, you have to help me. So-and-so celebrity is here with a lover. I have to find her.' So his friend comes over. And both of them, together, go to all the rental car places, one by one. At one office, the boss comes out. The two of them ask about the celebrity. The boss is extremely disagreeable. 'How can you *ask* such a question?'

"But they see a secretary off to the side and she is blushing when she looks at the paparazzo's friend. So [the two of them] wait until the boss leaves, and the friend flirts with her. They ask her to go to dinner when she gets off work. Of course, they go out. The friend of the photographer goes back to her place. They make love. And the next morning, bravo, she gives him the address of the celebrity. The photographer and his partner spend a day hiding in the trees, taking photographs. And they are published all over the world. They make a lot—a lot—of money.

"But it doesn't end happily ever after.

"Apparently, there are powerful people close to the celebrity. They want to [punish] the paparazzo. So they plan their revenge."

We pour a third glass of wine.

"Three months later, the photographer's phone rings. This time it is a *different* voice. This time the new voice says, 'I think it would be interesting if you go to the entrance of a hotel near the Gare du Nord'—the Paris train terminal—'at *this* time tomorrow morning. Go to *this* hotel and wait outside.' And he hangs up. The photographer, the next day, does as he's been told.

"And as he is looking through the viewfinder of the camera, he spots her. It is his own wife—*the photographer's wife*. And she's coming out of the hotel with the photographer's handsome partner, the one who had seduced the secretary at the rental car office. The wife kisses the photographer's friend. And they go off in different directions. The photographer is devastated, totally devastated and heartbroken.

"Slowly he begins to realize. *This* is how it feels to be the subject of one of his photographs."

CHAPTER 19

Four Moments That Changed the Narrative

Novelist Virginia Woolf once remarked that "on or about December 1910 human character changed."

Her pronouncement was delivered with the benefit of hindsight—in 1924. But even so, it was shrewd and indisputable. She was describing the dismantling of class, social, and gender barriers as bourgeois society became more urban, global, and cosmopolitan. More to the point, she was addressing how experimental artists were creating what would become known as modernism. "We hear all round us," Woolf asserted—mentioning D. H. Lawrence, James Joyce, and T. S. Eliot, among others—"in poems and novels and biographies, even in newspaper articles and essays, the sound of breaking and falling, crashing and destruction. It is the prevailing sound."

Permit me to borrow from Virginia Woolf a century on. Permit me to put forward the idea that sometime on or about June 1994, American decorum changed.

By a changed *American decorum*, I am referring to the rapt attention that the public paid, then and thereafter, to media coverage of the disgrace of others. By *on or about*, I am referring to a six-week time window. The start: May 6, 1994, the day Paula Jones filed a civil lawsuit against Bill Clinton, alleging that while he was the governor of Arkansas he had made an insulting sexual proposition and later defamed her. (Clinton would deny the charges.) And then: June 17, the day a TV audience of nearly one hundred million watched the former football star O. J. Simpson, in a white Ford Bronco, being pursued by a phalanx of police cars, four days after the brutal murder of his wife and her male companion. Simpson's subsequent trial would draw national headlines for more than a year.

The Jones and Simpson cases—along with two other incidents that served as bookends (the Bobbitt maiming in 1993 and the Pam-and-Tommy sex tape in 1995)—signaled a sea change. Earlier in the century, civilized individuals had come to modulate their baser instincts. Upon encountering a humiliating real-life circumstance, they may have been automatically drawn to it, but they were simultaneously repulsed. They recognized the virtue of turning away from the shameful, and of spurning (or at least taking umbrage against) the busybody, the gossipmonger, the snitch.

No longer. Our predominant impulse amid the rise of the media's tabloid fixation, 24/7 news, and the Internet was to unapologetically eavesdrop, to leer, to pry into the private and often sexual affairs of others, particularly the affairs of the famous, whose desire for renown seemed to somehow justify our intrusion and offer cover for our own deflected shame. Moreover, the decision of the media—in a competitive, attention-fractured, and economically challenging marketplace—to turn every alleged wrongdoing into another excuse for spectacle helped news consumers come to accept *and expect* explicit details about embarrassing, sexually compromising, or criminal events.[1]

Amid this trumped-up coverage of scandal and pseudo-scandal, four particular incidents stand out. Each of them highlights the changing role of media in our lives, along with a new etiquette governing American standards of behavior—and reactions to misbehavior. It is in these four events that the tenor of the times found its guttural timbre.

Two of the incidents pivot around an exposed penis. Two involve alleged spousal abuse. Two involve acts of violence. Two involve vehicles making an escape. Three involve "forbidden" liaisons. All four involve lust, voyeurism, and a media run amok—resulting in the private aspects of an individual's life being exchanged freely as public currency.

I present the events in reverse chronology, as a way of telescoping back to the sordid beginning.

---

1. In the mid-'90s, Christopher Hitchens would point out an important distinction in an article that examined how tabloid culture had made Americans "almost impossible to embarrass": "There is a good reason the words 'shameful' and 'shameless' define the same conduct. You know you've behaved shamefully if you have exposed other people to needless annoyance or embarrassment. You don't know you've behaved shamelessly if you don't get this point." (Christopher Hitchens, "The Death of Shame," *Vanity Fair*, March 1996, 68–72.)

Late October 1995. A locked Browning safe is stolen from the Malibu home of model and actress Pamela Anderson and her rock star husband, Tommy Lee. The contents include a "honeymoon" video showing the recently married couple in various states of connubial union. The thief and his associates take the footage and duplicate it, package it, and sell it off. Despite the lawsuits that follow, a copy of the pirated tape, acquired by an Internet porn mogul, is ultimately sold as a triple-X film and viewed by millions. The video eventually becomes the Citizen Kane *of celebrity sex tapes. And people the world over—some of whom have never before felt compelled to watch porn—find themselves indulging.*

This single "landmark pornographic home video," writes Pamela Paul, "is credited with bringing more users online than any other single event." Paul, now the editor of the *New York Times Book Review*, states in her 2005 book *Pornified* that the Pam-and-Tommy tape, with its "inadvertent combination of professionalism, celebrity, and amateurism," may have also been the catalyst for an exponential rise in "the proliferation of porn."

The details by now are familiar to many. The bride was a frequent *Playboy* cover model, best known as the curvaceous star of *Baywatch*. (Anderson declined invitations to be interviewed for this book.) The groom was the heavily tatted bad-boy drummer from the heavy metal band Mötley Crüe.[2] The tape showed fifty-four minutes of the couple boating, camping, and engaging in sometimes endearing banter—along with scenes of the pair having sex. The filmmakers were none other than the newlyweds themselves.

This mom-and-pop home movie was shocking for three reasons. It was explicit. It was off-limits—clearly intended for the couple's private consumption. And it was among the earliest videos to show *famous* people getting it on, at considerable length. As a result, it was such a pop-culture watershed that it practically defied the chattering masses *not* to watch it.

---

2. Love works in mysterious ways. The Lees would divorce in 1998 but would continue to reconnect or reunite over the years. Prior to marrying Anderson, Lee had been married to model Elaine Starchuk and actress Heather Locklear. Anderson would tie the knot with rocker Kid Rock (once) and Rick Salomon (twice), the latter notorious for orchestrating *another* sex tape, the Paris Hilton video, made public in 2003, that would become *1 Night in Paris*. ("Pamela Anderson Files for Divorce from Rick Salomon," Yahoo! Celebrity News via USmagazine.com, July 9, 2014; "1 Night in Paris" (2004), http://www.imdb.com/title/tt0412260/; Katie McLaughlin, "Paris Hilton on Sex Tape: 'I'll Never Be Able to Erase It,'" CNN.com, June 1, 2011.)

At the time, a celebrity sex tape was a relatively new phenomenon.[3] As confounding as it might seem two decades later, a "leaked" video was virtually a career-killer. (And today, many public personalities have become so unfazed by such depictions that some have purportedly conspired to leak nude snapshots or homemade pornos, hoping that viral exposure might ignite fame's flame.)[4]

But back to 1995. Early one morning as the couple slept—according to an impressively reported account by Amanda Chicago Lewis in *Rolling Stone*—they were paid a visit by an electrician who had done some renovations for Lee.[5] The workman, Rand Gauthier (himself a sometime porn actor), would later reveal a motive, as writer Lewis describes it: he alleged that he'd been shortchanged by Lee for his labors and was once threatened by the rock star with a shotgun. (A case related to the incident would be thrown out of court.)

In *Rolling Stone*'s retelling, it was only after Gauthier had wheeled in a handcart, made off with the couple's steel safe, and got it to a secure location that he discovered the Hi8 videocassette inside. A cohort, as Lewis relates in her article, soon took the initiative to "run off thousands of copies and to hire someone to put up a few websites: pamsex.com, pamlee.com, and pamsextape.com. The sites didn't have the video itself; they merely gave instructions to send a money order"—for $59.95—"to the New York outpost

---

3. The first big sex-tape scandal erupted in 1988, involving twenty-something actor Rob Lowe, who had filmed an encounter with two young women, one of them a minor. (Lowe settled matters quietly with the family of the underage party.) By the millennium, the culture had become so accustomed to news of private pornos ending up on the Web or "in the cloud" that Lowe felt comfortable lampooning his indiscretion by agreeing to appear in the 2014 Cameron Diaz/Jason Segel comedy *Sex Tape*. ("The 25 Biggest Scandals of the Past 25 Years," *Entertainment Weekly*, August 31, 2007, 23; Colin Stutz, "15 Musician Sex-Tape Scandals, from Tommy Lee to Usher," *Billboard*, November 13, 2014; Alexandra Cheney, "Rob Lowe Appears in a New 'Sex Tape,'" *Variety*, July 11, 2014; Marc Malkin, "Rob Lowe: 'Fond Memories' of His Sex Tapes, but Does He Ever Watch Them?," *E! Online*, July 11, 2014.)

4. When Nadya "Octomom" Suleman—mother of fourteen, including octuplets—was offered a cruel million in 2009 to appear in a porn flick, columnist and editor Raina Kelley would observe, "We created Octomom. With our glorification of bizarre behavior, we dare the emotionally needy to shock and appall us. Then we slam them….We are all, each of us, one national scandal away from being offered a million dollars to star in a skin flick." (Raina Kelley, "Octomom Hypocrisy," *Newsweek*, March 16, 2009, 58.)

5. The intruder may have been accompanied by an accomplice or two.

of a Canadian T-shirt company, which then funneled the money to a bank account in Amsterdam."

Despite court filings by Anderson and Lee against an array of defendants, the pilfered tape had already gone full Pandora. Pirates soon made pirated copies, as Lewis recounts; *Penthouse* and *Variety* ran reviews. And, seeking his own piece of the action—and attendant PR—the young porn king Seth Warshavsky decided to crank up the volume. "Warshavsky," writes Lewis, "aired the tape on [his porn site] Club Love on a loop for five hours."

The Lees tried to shut him down, but to no avail. Later that month, Anderson and Lee chose to end the escalating madness by settling their lawsuit against Warshavsky, granting him Web rights, even as copies of the tapes continued to sell briskly. The result, according to the *Independent* newspaper, was that by early 1998—three years after the original taping—"anyone with $35 to spare [could go to a video store, buy the tape,] and . . . gasp as the camera catches [the couple] in graphic close-up in the first flush of conjugal love, groan as they fellate and fish away a four-day boating trip." A year later, the *Wall Street Journal* would report that Warshavsky's company, which continued to stream the movie online, had already "sold an estimated 300,000 copies."

It is hard to overstate the reach of the purloined video. Before the end of the decade, a not-insignificant percentage of the Internet's tens of millions of Web pages (many of them utterly unrelated to porn) would be metatagged with the words "Pam" or "Pamela" or "SexTape"—the websites' owners merely hoping to draw residual clicks; gelt by association. "When the commercial history of the Internet is written, whose names will appear among the chief catalysts?" the *Wall Street Journal's* Thomas E. Weber asked in 1999. "[One could] make a powerful argument for including Pamela Anderson Lee, actress, chronic centerfold and star of what is now perhaps the world's best-known home movie. . . . As Madonna's cultivation of the music video once helped convince viewers that the MTV network was for real, the 31-year-old Ms. Lee—even if unwittingly—has done a huge amount to hammer home the viability of the Web as [an] engine of commercial importance."

But at what price? Ever since the Pam-and-Tommy tape, online marauders have felt emboldened. The penalty for trafficking in someone else's personal nudes or sex clips—disseminated by an ex-lover, extortionist, hacker, or revenge-porn purveyor—rarely seems to match the punishment inflicted on the person whose privacy has been violated. Personalities such as Paris Hilton, Kim Kardashian, Kendra Wilkinson, Jennifer Lawrence, and Leslie Jones would protest—along with others, many of whom would become mired in costly litigation—often to little avail.

June 13–17, 1994. In the affluent Brentwood section of Los Angeles, the blood-ied bodies of Nicole Brown Simpson and her friend Ronald Goldman are discov-ered outside Ms. Brown's condo. The deceased have been slain in grisly fashion. Goldman has been stabbed twenty-two times; Brown's head is almost sliced off, hanging from the spinal column. The prime suspect is Brown's ex-husband, Orenthal James Simpson (a.k.a. O.J.), the football great, rental-car pitchman, and occasional actor.

Five days after the murders, one of Simpson's lawyers tells the press that his client is about to turn himself in to the LAPD. But when authorities move in to arrest him, he is nowhere to be found. Instead, Simpson (possibly suicidal, pos-sibly homicidal, possibly planning to head out of town to elude capture) gets into a white Ford Bronco, brandishing a gun. His friend and ex-teammate Al Cowlings is behind the wheel. The pair—later determined to be carrying $9,000 in hard currency, Simpson's U.S. passport, and a disguise kit (including a false mustache and goatee)—spend more than an hour driving around L.A., pursued by squad cars and a squadron of news-and-traffic helicopters. Their "slow-speed chase," televised live, draws an audience of ninety-five million. Simpson and Cowlings eventually arrive at Simpson's house, where he phones his mom, gulps down a glass of juice, and surrenders.

Many called it the first *real-world* reality-TV show—a serial melodrama about murder and jealousy, race and wealth, sports and Hollywood, bucolic suburbia and domestic violence. And it was, at the most elemental level, a tale of sexual obsession and abuse. Simpson, Brown's ex-husband, had previously beaten her and threatened her life. His history of violent behavior became evi-dent with the release of recorded 911 calls ("He's O. J. Simpson. I think you know his record.... He broke the back door down to get in") and in incrimi-nating letters and Polaroids that Brown had stowed in a safety deposit box. Simpson would harass and stalk his ex-wife, even peering through her window, according to a boyfriend's grand jury testimony, while Brown was having sex.

But from the viewing public's perspective, the saga started with the Bronco ride.

Had the police been poised to take just about any other defendant into custody, the arrest would have been a relatively minor matter. This, however, was qualitatively different. Not only did the pursuit involve a fugitive in flight *and* a police chase *and* a double homicide. It also had, at its center, *a celebrity with a gun* (the barrel sometimes snug to his temple, sometimes lodged under his chin), threatening to take his own life, possibly with video crews recording the scene. What's more, here was a black man in flight—and a famous one, at that—two years after the L.A. riots had enflamed the city. According to the consensus narrative that was being made up on the fly, the forces of law and order were going to nab this dark menace. (Simpson's mug shot would be deliberately darkened on the cover of *Time*'s next issue.) Indeed, a routine apprehension of a murder suspect was being conflated into a scene right out of *Cops*.

But in the age of 24/7 newsbreaks, skyborne cameras, and TV stations flooding the zone with teams of reporters, it was somehow unavoidable that when the gridiron's great running back made the run of his life,[6] we would all be there. We would gather: hundreds of citizens on L.A. roadsides and overpasses,[7] tens of millions of viewers at home. And we would wonder how a live TV feed of the incident could become an extravaganza, a prime example of what novelist Saul Bellow had previously called "event glamour."

There could be no hoarier exercise in '90s pop-psych: revisiting the social lessons and cultural inanities of the O.J. fiasco. But in this context a few points are worth restating. First, the Bronco chase turned out to be a new incarnation of must-see TV: saturation coverage of spontaneous celebrity combustion. And because the story was soaked in the kerosene of double homicide, interracial marriage, sports fame, Hollywood sizzle, and a real-time LAPD showdown, the nation's business stopped, plans were canceled, pizzas were ordered in. (That day Domino's sold a then-record number of pies.) CNN, ESPN, and the networks broke from their regu-

---

6. The title of the 1996 book about the case by *New Yorker* staff writer Jeffrey Toobin was *The Run of His Life: The People v. O. J. Simpson.*

7. Spectators lined local streets, hauled out lawn chairs, and held up signs with slogans such as GO OJ GO and SAVE THE JUICE. (Bill Turque, Andrew Murr et al., "He Could Run...but He Couldn't Hide," *Newsweek*, June 27, 1994, 14–27; Nancy Gibbs, "End of the Run," *Time*, June 27, 1994, 28–35.)

larly scheduled programming, and all eyes turned westward, like a field of sunflowers.

What's more, the Bronco ride was merely the O.J. Show's "cold open." Throughout 1994 and into the next year's trial—which dragged on for a staggering 372 days—the crime would become a daily staple of the news cycle, a nightly fixture of cable TV, and a weekly raison d'être of magazines and tabloids. (The *National Enquirer* became the crime's house organ.) The O.J. saga turned into a '90s craze, like bandanas, JNCO jeans, and *Doom*. Part of its appeal came from the case's pu pu platter of celebrity dish, domestic minutiae, and colorful bit players. Part of it was the gladiatorial aspect: two high-profile legal teams jousting all the way to a final verdict. Part of it was the fact that so much of it seemed to demand an audience: the initial chase; Simpson's "Dream Team" of lawyers; the presiding judge, Lance Ito, who fairly preened for the cameras; the legal experts who, like a colony of bats, would sweep into the cable news green rooms every night, smelling blood and rot and money; the fetishized evidence (the knife, the Bruno Maglis, the bloody glove); the bureaucratic pageantry of Court TV and CNN, with their clinical but hypnotizing parade of natty suits and scuffed briefcases, their appearances and hearings and motions and press conferences. Novelist James Ellroy would call it, hands down, "the most publicized crime of all time."

The case coincided with a curious cultural moment. The Internet and early reality TV were beginning to democratize fame. The media's unremitting data dump about celebrities' lives had made the stars, whether lowly or lofty, seem somehow "familiar." The Boomer-next-door had started to buy into the illusion of *belonging*, of procured privilege. One could upgrade his or her social status, for example, by paying for splurge experiences or party invitations or luxury-box admission to rub shlubby shoulders with real VIPs. In this age of me-too celebrity, many Americans—like the citizens of Brentwood and Beverly Hills—began to sense a macabre connection to the trial and to the members of its ensemble cast.[8]

---

8. It was the talk of the town. "At dinner parties and in restaurants, whole evenings are spent discussing the case," Dominick Dunne would note, reporting from the West Coast for *Vanity Fair*. "Everyone has a topper to everyone else's piece of information.... 'I saw Nicole jogging in Brentwood just the day before,' said a man at a screening, to which another man immediately replied, 'Craig Baumgarten played golf with O.J. that Sunday morning at Riviera.'" (Dominick Dunne, "L.A. in the Age of O.J.," *Vanity Fair*, February 1995.)

On an entirely different level, the case raised chilling questions about spousal abuse and domestic assault, which proved invaluable in forcing legislative action. "Within days of Simpson's arrest," sociologist Andrew Cherlin has recounted, lawmakers in New York voted to make it mandatory that cops "arrest suspected perpetrators of domestic violence whether or not the victim was willing to press charges. Los Angeles County immediately allocated millions of dollars of additional aid for shelters for battered women. Within two months, the House of Representatives had approved nearly all the provisions of the Violence Against Women Act, which had first been introduced, without success, six years earlier."

For all this, the issues at the center of the case revolved around race.

Writer Toni Morrison would call into question the overarching establishment narrative. "The Simpson spectacle has become an enunciation of post–Civil Rights discourse on black deviance," she would argue in her introduction to the essay collection *Birth of a Nation'hood: Gaze, Script, and Spectacle in the O.J. Simpson Case*. That "national narrative of racial supremacy"—which prejudged Simpson as guilty in the murder of two Caucasians and conferred credibility on his accusers (the LAPD and the prosecutors)—"is still the old sham white supremacy forever wedded to and dependent upon faux black inferiority." The press, the tabloids, and TV news outlets, in Morrison's view, actively promoted this narrative from the start, "arous[ing] immediate suspicion" and making many believe that some kind of "white mischief" was at play. "One is struck by how quickly guilt was the popular verdict," she wrote. "The narrative of the entertainment media and their 'breaking story' confederates was so powerfully insistent on guilt, so uninterested in any other scenario, it began to look like a media pogrom, a lynching with its iconography intact: a chase, a cuffing, a mob, name calling, a white female victim." As a result, Morrison stated, the outsize play that the case received in the news and in popular culture "made Mr. Simpson's guilt increasingly remote to some African Americans."

The other subtext, of course, was the sex. There were whispered tales of drug-and-sex parties involving Nicole and her buds. There were rumors about the Simpsons' sex life and infidelities (while married) as well as O.J.'s fixation on Nicole after they were divorced. A porn-star pal of Al Cowlings would testify before a grand jury. Simpson's girlfriend Paula Barbieri would appear in *Playboy*—four months after the murders. Nicole Brown's gal-pal Faye Resnick would do her own *Playboy* spread *and* write a quickie memoir (*Nicole Brown Simpson: The Private Diary of a Life Interrupted*), divulging their sexual antics and disclosing the practice of what locals called "a Brentwood hello"—a blowjob administered to a sleeping, unsuspecting friend. Even a member of the *jury* agreed to pose naked in *Playboy*.

Amid this carny show the murder victims were marginalized. (Even the name of the saga—"the O.J. case" or "the Simpson trial"—left the deceased on the sidelines.) And still America was spellbound. Art Harris, who broke many of CNN's exclusives, today has his own formula for America's fatal attraction to the case:

(fame + tabloid media + sex + race + drugs + murder) × daily exposure = public addiction

"The intimate details of domestic violence and double murder," says Harris, "along with the much-debated police investigation, would likely never have come out in an earlier time period before 24/7 cable or if the protagonist had not been as famous. But when celebrity met the media hydrogen bomb—POW."

And all of it hurtling to a cliff-hanger finish.

———

An estimated audience of 150 million tuned in for the verdict, to be rendered by a jury consisting of nine African Americans, two Caucasians, and one person of Hispanic descent, ten of them female. The broadcast, according to a 2012 Nielsen poll, would become the country's third most "universally impactful" televised news event in the past few decades, ranking just behind the September 11 attacks and Hurricane Katrina.

As Simpson stood and faced the jury box, a courtroom and a nation heard the following statement, read by the court clerk, as the camera kept its focus on the defendant and his legal team: "In the matter of *The People of the State of California v. Orenthal James Simpson*, case number BA097211, we, the jury in the above-entitled action, find the defendant Orenthal James Simpson not guilty of murder."

Not guilty. The verdict was instantaneously polarizing. The jurors, as well as much of the public, had come to believe that the LAPD had bungled the handling of the blood samples. Moreover, some of the police who testified had not come across as credible, which cast doubt on their evidence. In addition, the prosecution had spent too much time discussing forensics and had failed to clearly establish the level and frequency of Simpson's acts of violence against Brown. Finally, the testimony of detective Mark Fuhrman, who had made racist statements in the past, became suspect, according to juror Carrie Bess, who would state, "Fuhrman found the glove. Fuhrman found the blood. Fuhrman did everything. When you throw [such potentially discredited evidence] out, what case did you have? You've got reasonable doubt." In short, the LAPD and the prosecution team had botched the thing.[9]

The jury's decision remains a matter of intense debate. In 2014, Harvard law professor Charles Ogletree observed, "When you ask people today, African-Americans will overwhelmingly say...not that he's not guilty, but the government didn't prove that he was guilty. White people will say that he killed two white people and got away with it." Critic James Poniewozik would make the case that the prosecution and the defense "were presenting the jury a choice of two questions: 'Is O.J. guilty?' versus 'Are you going to stand up to racist cops?' The [opposing] lawyers—and the black and white audiences reacting to the verdict...might as well have been in different dimensions."

All this time later, two other aspects of the case also resonate powerfully. First is the notion that Simpson's attorneys were presenting—and the 24/7 newshounds were regurgitating—a new dialect of the lie: the utter whopper solemnly conveyed as credible. The DNA evidence against Simpson was *invalid* because it had been tainted by investigators. The bloody glove, introduced in evidence, *was not* Simpson's because it fit him too snugly—no matter that the murder victim's blood, presumably, had caused it to shrink.

---

9. In 1997, Simpson would lose a civil suit in which he was ultimately found liable for the "wrongful death" of Brown and Goldman and ordered to pay $33.5 million, only a fraction of which has ever made it to the victims' families. Simpson was later jailed "on kidnapping, robbery and conspiracy charges, related to a confrontation with two sports memorabilia dealers in a Las Vegas hotel room [in 2007]." (B. Drummond Ayres Jr., "Jury Decides Simpson Must Pay $25 Million in Punitive Award," *New York Times*, February 11, 1997; Jane Wells, "20 Years Later, Winning OJ Civil Suit Was Never a 'Pot of Gold,'" CNBC.com, June 11, 2014; "Victim's Family Still Holds O.J. Simpson Accountable," Associated Press via *Las Vegas Review-Journal*, June 9, 2014; Jennifer Steinhauer, "Simpson Attire Goes to Storage in Court Fight," *New York Times*, June 16, 2009, A14.)

Straight-faced falsehood and pseudo-narrative—the vernacular used by autocrats and cheating spouses—would become the common idiom for defending oneself in a scandal; for TV spinmeisters and crisis managers; and (as discussed earlier) for national political discourse, from Clinton I to Bush II to Trump I. When fighting charges of criminal wrongdoing, sexual misconduct, or scandal, why be beholden to rules or facts or—as Al Gore dubbed it in another context—the "inconvenient truth"? (Until, of course, one was caught red-handed. Only then would one be obliged to issue a cleansing public apology.)

Second, the Simpson affair seemed to usher in a new sort of American citizen—a person who is largely a member of an audience. During the newly wired '90s, America was coalescing into a nation in which watchers outnumbered doers, in which individuals were valued as members of their demographic or, in time, their social-media community. This was the body politic as fan base, as an amalgam of market niches.

On the twentieth anniversary of the Bronco ride, Lili Anolik, writing in *Vanity Fair*, would explore this terrain, developing her own hypothesis. The murder and trial, she asserted, comprised not only the first real-world reality show, it was also the miniseries that launched the serial reality genre: "That wasn't a car chase, it was a test run, a pilot episode, the taste that got us hooked."

Anolik's theory would brine nicely with time. "It's the children of the O.J. people," she observed, "who've really caught fire reality-TV-wise. Because if the Simpson case was the daddy of reality TV, it was every bit as much the baby daddy." Her point? Various members of the O.J. pilot would try their luck as reality-TV participants (Faye Resnick, notably, and Kato Kaelin, the part-time actor who inhabited a guesthouse on Simpson's property). More significantly, by Anolik's calculus, three of reality TV's true superstars emerged from Brentwood's murky Petri dish: Kim Kardashian, the daughter of attorney Robert Kardashian, Simpson's friend of three decades; Brody Jenner, the "son of Linda Thompson, Elvis's old flame" (who herself happened to be the ex of Caitlyn Jenner, the former "Olympic gold medalist who married Kris [Jenner] after she split from Robert [Kardashian]"); and the one and only Paris Hilton, for years a pal in good standing of Kimmie's, and whose "sister Nicky," Anolik wrote, "is also the goddaughter of Faye Resnick." Got that?

Anolik was making a more salient point. During the 1990s, viewers "at least had the sense to be embarrassed by [their fascination with the O.J. saga as] a tabloid story. . . . It was trashy, and they knew that it was trashy, and that to give in to the trashiness was to give in to their worst selves." Not anymore. Since that era, she believed, "the feelings of shame . . . vanished." America refined its taste for tastelessness, a nightcap that we took neat, without the old chaser of guilt. Indeed, the audience had lost its ability, says Anolik, to *distinguish* high from low. "The standards and mores and customs of Nicole and Ron," she concludes, "of Kato and Faye and Paula and Kris, of O.J., too—have turned into the standards and mores and customs of a nation. So, O.J., regardless of whether the jury got it right or the jury got it wrong, you have blood on your hands. You killed popular culture."

———

May 6, 1994. Paula Corbin Jones files a lawsuit against President William Jefferson Clinton for violating her constitutional rights through sexual harassment and assault, for intentional infliction of emotional distress, and for defamation.

The civil case stems from a 1991 encounter in a Little Rock hotel suite. Jones claims that at the time, while she was an Arkansas employee working the registration desk at a conference, she was flattered when Governor Clinton dispatched a state trooper to invite her to a private meeting, supposedly believing it might result in a better administrative position. Jones, aged twenty-four, accepted the invitation and was escorted upstairs by the trooper.

But once she was alone with Clinton, so Jones contends, he shocked her by trying to kiss her, touch her inappropriately in the area of her culottes, and then, after making a few passes, literally dropped his trousers, asking her to "kiss it." (Clinton would deny all of Jones's accusations.) Her suit—seeking $700,000 in damages—alleges that she told the governor, "I'm not that kind of girl. . . . I've got to get back to my registration desk." She claims to have swiftly departed, flustered and offended, telling several close associates about the incident. As part of her affidavit, Jones would declare that Clinton's penis had had a "distinguishing characteristic"; it was, she would recall, "bent or 'crooked' from Mr. Clinton's right to left." (An affidavit later prepared by Clinton's urologist would attest that, to the contrary, the president's penis "was perfectly normal.")

Initially, Paula Jones had zero intention of taking Clinton to court. She told intimates that she was embarrassed by the encounter and nervous about losing her job. (The governor had been her nominal boss at the time.) Even when the news broke about Clinton's affair with Gennifer Flowers, Jones had resisted calls to step forward, reportedly telling her friend Debra Ballentine, "No, no, no. I don't ever want anybody to know."

Jones's reluctance was understandable, even more so given her devout upbringing in Lonoke, Arkansas (population 4,000). Her family, as described in a *Washington Post* story by Howard Schneider at the time of the lawsuit, was accustomed to "nightly Bible lessons and church three times a week.... No jewelry. No television. No stylish haircuts." In Jones's early years, as legal scholar Ken Gormley would explain in his book *The Death of American Virtue: Clinton vs. Starr*, Paula was very much the daughter of Bobby Corbin, "a lay Nazarene preacher" and factory worker who had died suddenly at sixty, shortly after being "stricken while playing the piano at church." (The family's strict rules were reportedly relaxed as she and her sisters grew up.)

Was Jones an angel? Her brother-in-law Mark Brown tallied her sexual encounters in *Penthouse* and, according to the *Washington Post*, would give "hints that there are other instances of alleged harassment that she discussed but never pursued, and a history of financial interest in men." (According to a subsequent piece in *Newsweek*, "Brown was recovering from brain surgery at the time [he made his accusatory statements]. Later, he updated his stance, saying that he believed Jones 'absolutely.' ") According to Gormley, Judge Susan Webber Wright would state, "It is hard to see how [the hotel-room encounter] could cause emotional distress, the single incident she was talking about, even if you assumed it happened"; moreover, Wright would reportedly say to Jones's attorneys in a closed-door conference, "Don't tell me, counselor, that she's some blushing magnolia."

To be fair, much of the above amounts to blaming the victim. *Jones* was the allegedly aggrieved party. *She* was invited upstairs by Clinton. *She* hurriedly departed. *She* remained silent—for three years—about whatever did or did not occur in that hotel room.

That is, until a sleaze-laden story in 1994 by journalist David Brock came out in the conservative *American Spectator*. The article dissected Clinton's extramarital affairs, making a series of scandalous charges (some demonstrably false). One sentence spoke of a woman—simply called "Paula"—who after meeting the Arkansas governor in his hotel room had allegedly told a state trooper that "she was available to be Clinton's regular girlfriend if he so desired." Had that sentence not appeared in Brock's controversial exposé, Jones's name and tale, in all likelihood, would have slipped into oblivion.

But the sentence incensed Paula Jones. So on May 6, 1994, with forty-eight hours to go before the statute-of-limitations deadline, she decided to file. And from that instant, nothing seemed to break Bill Clinton's way.

At the time, an independent prosecutor, Robert Fiske, had been appointed by Attorney General Janet Reno to look into the Clintons' real estate transactions, in what would come to be known as the Whitewater scandal. (In the end, the Clintons would be cleared of all charges.) But by August, Fiske had been replaced, due to a conflict of interest, by Kenneth Starr, the man who would become Clinton's chief legal nemesis. As the months passed, *Newsweek*'s dogged Michael Isikoff would pursue the Jones accusations with little letup, having been given wide berth by his colleagues, some of whom (after their zeal during the Gennifer Flowers melee) were disinclined to report on purported high-level indiscretion. "*Newsweek*, frankly, had become almost a sponsoring media outlet for the Paula Jones case," Clinton would later testify, "and [the magazine] had a journalist who had been trying, so far fruitlessly, to find me in some sort of wrongdoing."

I would even go so far as to say that the initial litigation in May 1994 was the catalytic event that would drive a decade of sexual hazing in American politics and, to some degree, wider society. Had Jones not filed her case, it is almost a certainty that Clinton would never have been impeached. But as Ken Gormley would map out in *The Death of American Virtue*, there was a many-branched decision tree that grew out of Jones's decision to sue. And each branch could have led to a different outcome had circumstances at any point broken the opposite way. A close reading of Gormley's book suggests at least sixteen instances when history's arc might have safely shifted from the path toward impeachment:

- If the overly politicized special prosecutor law (the Ethics in Government Act), established in 1978 after the Watergate crisis, had not been on the books.
- If journalist David Brock had not published his story in the *American Spectator* in the first place.

- If Jones had agreed to accept a $700,000 settlement that had been offered by Clinton's attorney.

- If the arguably biased special prosecutor, Ken Starr, a man with staunch conservative bona fides, and interactions with Jones's legal team, had not been assigned to head up the investigation of the Clintons.[10]

- If Starr, as the independent counsel, had confined his investigation to financial matters and not ventured into sexual terrain.

- If a government shutdown had not occurred in 1995, creating an ad hoc workplace environment in the White House—one that allowed Bill Clinton and Monica Lewinsky to interact after hours.

- If Clinton and Lewinsky had never started their affair to begin with.

- If Lewinsky's Pentagon officemate Linda Tripp had not secretly tape-recorded their private conversations or encouraged Lewinsky to hold onto a dress with traces of Clinton's DNA.

- If the Eighth Circuit Court of Appeals had not overturned Judge Susan Webber Wright's 1998 ruling to dismiss the Jones matter (on the grounds that the case was without merit).

- If the Supreme Court had not decided to let the lawsuit move forward.

- If *Newsweek* and the *Drudge Report* had not decided to aggressively pursue and expose Clinton and Lewinsky's affair.

- If the FBI and Starr's prosecutors had not threatened and coerced Lewinsky to make statements against her will.

- If Clinton had given different answers at his deposition.

- If the special prosecutor had not determined that there were sufficient grounds for the House of Representatives to consider impeaching the president.

- If the House had not approved impeachment hearings.

- If the House had not voted to impeach the president on charges of perjury and obstruction of justice.

---

10. Prior to accepting the position, Starr, according to Gormley, "had appeared on national television arguing that Jones could sue the president; he had consulted directly with Jones's lawyer Gil Davis; he had planned to file an amicus brief in the *Jones* case on behalf of the conservative Independent Women's Forum.... Ken Starr was arguably the last person in the world suited for this explosive new Lewinsky [investigation] assignment." (Ken Gormley, *The Death of American Virtue* [New York: Random House/Broadway, 2010], 329–30.)

But the Fates, in the end, had gone against Bill Clinton's interests all six-teen times. And the original he said/she said episode in a suite in Little Rock's Excelsior Hotel would turn into the basis of yet another Trial of the Decade.

Behind all the headlines was Paula Jones, with her scarlet lip gloss, swooping mane, and legal team that swung wide right. Her image was not helped by her shifting cast of conservative backers and advisers; her unpol-ished performances at her occasional press conferences or in TV interviews; her decision to appear in ads for No Excuses jeans (as the "scandalized" Donna Rice and Marla Maples had done before her). Her choices, moreover, were caught in the undertow of a comment that James Carville had made in reference to previous Clinton accusers: "If you drag a hundred-dollar bill through a trailer park, you never know what you'll find." Most damaging of all were Jones's appearances in *Penthouse*: first, when private, unauthorized photos emerged in 1995 and 1998; then again in 2000, once the dust (and the lawsuit itself) was settled, and she decided to pose nude, which would send some of her former supporters running for the hills.

Yet Jones, from the very start, was never given a fair shot at defining herself. Her advisers did. The right did. The White House surrogates did. Worst of all, the press did. Indeed, the media's initial avoidance of her story (and its rush to doubt her or to shame her) helped discredit her. *Newsweek*'s Evan Thomas would hang his head and write an apologia for having chas-tised Jones. *Chicago Tribune* columnist Mike Royko, a perennial defender of working-class readers, would point out that "members of the 'mainstream' press brigade" were too often following the spin of the Clinton infantry and proved to be "willing, even eager, participants in the kick-Paula campaign."

I contact Paula Jones, hoping to hear her side of things. She agrees to have lunch in Little Rock, Arkansas. "I'm not a fancy person," she says. "Let's go to the Olive Garden."

On the drive there, passing countless steeples, I realize I am on church-going turf. (The sign on the local shrimp shack says "Lent Central," inducing the faithful to come in for catfish and oysters.) This is also serious Clinton country, where the Clinton Museum Store, just up the road from the presi-dential library, sells "I Miss Bill" T-shirts and Madeleine Albright brooches.

Jones arrives in a leather rock-and-roll jacket and a spangled aqua top. She wears sequined designer jeans, pear-shaped hoop earrings, and deep pink lipstick. Her hair shimmers chestnut. Jones, a part-time teacher, explains that she has left the real estate business and is going to night classes to train to be a doctor's assistant.[11] Her husband, she tells me, is out bass fishing that day.

Jones, wary at first, soon opens up and turns out to be great company, good-humored, and game for all questions. Early on in the conversation, for instance, she readily offers that she'd decided to get her nose fixed after braving a nightly television barrage of jokes about her appearance. ("Jay Leno." She shakes her head. "Like *he's* got some[thing] to make fun of.") Back in the mid-'90s, she says, she "started getting calls from plastic surgeons all over the country, wanting to give me anything I wanted done because they thought I was being unfair[ly treated] and it wasn't right." She selected a New York doctor, she remembers, who also offered her a "boob job [but I] decided not to. I was scared to—because it was a foreign object." She insists, "I *swear* they're mine! I bet you think they're not."

"*You* brought it up," I protest good-naturedly.

"I know," she says. "I get that all the time.... They are *mine*. I've even had people squish them [and say,] 'Okay, they're normal—they're real.'"

Right off the bat, she wants advice for her own book, which she hopes to publish to set the record straight about the real Paula Jones. "I'm very conservative—*very* conservative," she says. She identifies herself as Southern Baptist, adding, "I grew up in a strict, *strict* religious family. Kind of like old Pentecostal—the bones, and no makeup, no cutting your hair, long dresses. Never have been a wild child or anything. That's why I want to do a book. Because there's so much to be told about me and my upbringing and how people have tried to portray me, as though this is why Bill Clinton did what he did to me. They tried to find the people who would make me look bad— as though I deserved what I got, you know what I'm saying?"

She has approached book editors, she explains, but has been continually shut out by the publishing community. "Nobody gives me an opportunity," she says. "I've had people do several [outlines] for me, actually, and they never get anywhere."

I wonder, aloud, if she's ever considered doing an e-book (an option she dismisses), and inquire if she feels she may be dealing with people who are more concerned with their own interests than hers. "Where are the right people?" she

---

11. In 2015, during a follow-up phone conversation, she says she prefers to call herself a homemaker.

asks. "Why are they not interested? I feel like I've got some kind of plague or something. Everybody who's had any kind of scandal or anything ever come their direction—we're talking murder, rape, molestation, it doesn't matter what it is—they eventually end up as a Lifetime movie or they do a book. I have not been allowed—by some force—to ever do a book." She says she can't understand why she's been stiff-armed while others with "notoriety"—such as "the Bobbitt guy"—still get publicity.

The subject turns to the instigator of it all: David Brock, the man whose article set her on this course. "That's what got it started," Jones claims. "I would have *never* told anybody. That's not me. That's not my personality." Even so, she chose to move forward, she says, because of Brock's initial assertions and the encouragement of "the attorneys that got involved. It had been three years. He'd already made the president. If I was going to come out and wanted to make him pay or hurt him, I would have done it during the election."

Mindful of her initial reluctance, I ask, if Jones had to do it all over again, would she have gone through with the lawsuit?

"Yes," she says. "Because I'm who I am today because of it. I'm a stronger person. I was a very, very introverted, shy, quiet, submissive type person before all this. [In addition,] it has made a lot of key laws. Like, for instance, if somebody files a lawsuit about sexual harassment in the workplace, they're going to go get my case. I think it's probably made it a lot better for women in the workplace because of what happened with my case."

Regrets, she's had a few—especially about the "bickering" among her legal and support team. "My lawyers," she says, spurred her "to do certain things that they wanted me to do and it's almost like they were pushing me. They were using me for their own agenda.... Both sides were using me.

"Then, when I posed for *Penthouse*—Lord, I was a heathen! Oh, I *couldn't* have been a Christian—that's what so many people thought." Today, she says, things have changed: young women take selfies and make sex tapes. "The world's going to hell in a handbag," she says, laughing. But back in 2000, she maintains, her *Penthouse* appearance was not about vanity but about cash, plain and simple. "I needed the money," she says. "I was going through a separation at the time, a divorce.... I had to pay taxes [on earnings from the settlement]. I had to buy a home for me and my boys.... The IRS was after me."

Did she recognize, I ask, why people might find the act of posing naked to be exploiting the situation, given the fact that she had been the victim of sexual harassment? "But why?" she asks. "It had nothing to do with a man harassing me. Nothing. Two different things. *That* was a decision I made as an adult. And *that*, over here, was a decision I did *not* make, when he first forced himself on me."

She admits to having felt "used" and then discarded—not by the *Penthouse* editors but by her own former backers. "People that were supposed to be my friends and people that were supposed to help me [while] I'm over here in financial straits," she recalls, echoing comments she has made elsewhere. "When I posed for *Penthouse*, those same people were like—they just squished me. It's like I was a nobody. They just ignored me and dropped me like a hot potato. I never heard from them again." She says she feels particularly betrayed by conservative pundit Ann Coulter, one of the supporters who pitched in to assist her legal case. "I was her Rosa Parks," she claims. "Now I'm no better than—what did she say that I was? You can find it out on the Internet. It was horrible what she said about me." Coulter would write the following after Jones's *Penthouse* appearance: "She used to have dignity and nobility and tremendous courage. Now she's just the trailer-park trash they said she was." (Jones would continue to bash both the Clintons *and* traditional conservatives, agreeing in 2016—on the eve of one of the presidential debates between Hillary Clinton and Donald Trump—to appear as part of a Trump-hosted panel of Bill Clinton accusers.)[12]

I bring up one last sore subject: "You obviously never intended—in exercising your legal right to prove sexual harassment—to trigger the invasion of privacy of Monica Lewinsky, who was in a private, consensual relationship with the same man who you believe [had] harassed you. Her life, like yours, was turned upside down and tarnished, and she became a household name. How do you feel about what *she* had to go through in order for you to prove your case?"

---

12. During a cable TV interview at the time of the Clinton-Lewinsky revelations, according to *Newsweek*, "Trump weighed in, seemingly scorning [Paula] Jones by calling her a 'loser.'...When Trump was asked about whether he would run for public office, he compared himself to Clinton, saying, 'Can you imagine how controversial I'd be? You think about him with the women. How about me with the women?'" (Michele Gorman, "A Brief History of Donald Trump and Bill Clinton's Friendship," Newsweek.com, May 27, 2016.)

"But that's what we had to do," she says, without a hint of remorse. "That was my lawyers' job. That's the way I look at it. She shouldn't have done it [in the first place]. He was the president of the United States. He was a married man.... He sure didn't have no business doing it. So why should I feel bad?... I didn't expose her. Linda Tripp did."

"Do you regret the damage it did to her?"

"I think she's just fine," Jones replies. "I don't think she's a basket case tied up somewhere in a padded room. I think she's fine."

Jones v. Clinton *would make its way to the Supreme Court, which decided—9 to 0—in Jones's favor, allowing her case to proceed. The suit would eventually be settled for $850,000, seven years after the initial encounter, with no admission of wrongdoing on Clinton's part. But before it was all over, the Jones matter would:*

- Uphold the principle, reestablished when Richard Nixon was forced out of office, that no sitting president is above the law.
- Reinforce the idea that no woman should be denied the right to seek damages if a workplace superior puts her in a sexually compromising position.
- Expand the level of explicit detail that average citizens and the press would use in discussions about sexual matters involving government officials.
- Prompt the public exposure of the private affair of a government employee, Monica Lewinsky, whose name was revealed in depositions taken in the case and in testimony demanded by the independent prosecutor.
- Lay the groundwork for the second presidential impeachment in the history of the republic, based in part on charges that Clinton, while under oath in the Jones matter, had committed perjury when discussing his relationship with Lewinsky.

June 22, 1993. In Manassas, Virginia, ex-Marine John Wayne Bobbitt goes out for a night on the town. Upon returning home inebriated, he has sex with his wife, Lorena, a nail-salon employee from Ecuador and Venezuela who has suffered from clinical depression. (He claims in court that his wife initiated their lovemaking that night but that he was "too exhausted to perform." She, unequivocally, calls it rape.) At about 3 a.m., while he is passed out in bed, she goes into the kitchen, finds a filet knife and, in a single motion, slices off his penis. She then gets in her car and drives away, the lopped-off object in hand, stopping briefly to hurl it to the side of the road. In the morning, a member of the local fire department, as part of a search team, discovers the fleshy mass in a grassy area near a 7-Eleven, slips it into a baggie, and puts it on ice. It takes a medical team nine hours to reattach it.

Domestic violence. Spousal abuse. Mental illness. They take their insidious toll. Evidence of such suffering usually occurs behind closed doors. But a single rash act involving an eight-inch kitchen utensil turned a wife and husband's private anguish into a cause célèbre. And before their separate trials were over, their relationship would be thoroughly scrutinized, the subject of marital rape would became part of a national debate, and many advocates for victims of domestic violence would find common ground.

The Wife with the Knife would be heralded as a women's rights renegade. Camille Paglia affirmed that "in some sense, Lorena Bobbitt has committed the ultimate revolutionary act of contemporary feminism." According to Katie Roiphe, "Lorena Bobbitt has become a symbol of female rage." After the Bobbitt verdict, Kim Gandy of the National Organization for Women would note, "This whole saga drives home the need for swift passage of a comprehensive version of the Violence Against Women Act." (The law, in fact, would be adopted later that year.)

And what of John Wayne Bobbitt? He would appear on a Howard Stern radio-thon. He would start a medical and legal defense fund. And, most memorably, he would become the country's least likely porn star, appearing in adult features such as *Frankenpenis* and *John Wayne Bobbitt Uncut*.[13]

What made the Bobbitt case resound across American society quite simply was the primitive nature of the violation. The deliberate severing of a male member is an act so rare in contemporary Western society that one has to go back to Freud, *Grimm's Fairy Tales*, or Greek tragedies to find cultural precedents.[14] "My first reaction when I heard the Bobbitt story," anthropologist

---

13. During the height of his acting career, such as it was, Bobbitt was represented by Paul Erickson, who had been the political director of the 1992 presidential campaign of Pat Buchanan, Mr. Family Values. (Tim Purtell, "The Shock Troops," *Entertainment Weekly*, March 4, 1994, 22.)

14. Such severe severing, however, seems to be part of a microclimate of retribution in certain regions of Southeast Asia. "There have been a few incidents of penile amputation in other parts of the world, such as Singapore and Hong Kong," *People* magazine would point out on the eve of

Helen Fisher would tell *People* at the time, "was amazement that it has not happened more often. We're playing with very strong emotions."

People responded viscerally. Castration as comeuppance became a female-empowerment meme, drawn from a reservoir of anger that was similar to the one that, two summers before, had been tapped by the film *Thelma & Louise*. "This was a watershed act," said pop psychologist Dr. Joyce Brothers, "dividing men and women." And even as the ensuing crop of Bobbitt jokes punctuated comedians' monologues, the incident was uneasily rehashed in households across the country. The Bobbitt case was an opening to address inadequate laws, the silent fury experienced by abused partners, and the larger questions of female subjugation in male-dominant relationships. Others used it as an opportunity to lash out at feminism's excesses, asking why the battle of the sexes seemed to disproportionately penalize men (an apt word here). This unkindest cut, journalist Kim Masters would state in *Vanity Fair*, was merely "the latest, and perhaps the ultimate, escalation."

The underlying message was twofold. First, many American women considered Lorena Bobbitt's action a call to arms: they were going to stand up against abuse, once and for all. Second, on an entirely less profound level: when someone's dick made the nightly news (whether Bobbitt's or Michael Jackson's, whether Pee-wee's or the president's), the country was going to discuss it incessantly around the beverage dispensers. The American penis was no longer a topic reserved for the tabloids or edgy art shows or porn films. Gossip about the Bobbitts, like crude utterances two years before at the Clarence Thomas hearings—with senators muttering about dongs and pubes—had seen to that.

I invite Lorena Gallo Bobbitt, who lives near Washington, D.C., for a quiet dinner in Georgetown. She arrives with a female confidante.

Lorena tells me about her four-year-old daughter and says she's been happily involved with a man for fourteen years. She talks about her life in Virginia, her long road back to equanimity, her work involving a shelter

---

Lorena Bobbitt's trial. "And in Thailand in the mid-'70s, according to an article in the *American Journal of Surgery*, at least 100 women foreshortened their unfaithful husbands and tossed the offending organs out the window—an act known locally as 'feeding the ducks.'" (Elizabeth Gleick, "Severance Pay," *People*, December 13, 1993.)

for victims of domestic violence and her related foundation, Lorena's Red Wagon. She also brings up her jobs as a Realtor and licensed hairstylist who provides skincare, facials, and bikini waxes.

Before I get into conversation, however, let me recount the Bobbitts' claims and counterclaims.

The Bobbitts had had a rocky marriage. They had gone through a prolonged separation or two. John, as Kim Masters would report, liked to party, often without his wife. He would invite friends or relatives to live in their small apartment. Lorena, who had taken a while to master English, often felt alienated. Though she expressed a desire to start a family, she claimed to have allowed John to persuade her to have an abortion. She would insist that John beat her and pressured her to have sex, including anal sex, against her will—charges he would dispute in court. At John's trial, various witnesses described his behavior as being consistent with that of a batterer, a characterization he has continued to object to. At one stage, Lorena filed a police report about an alleged choking incident; John accused her of kneeing him in the balls. Two days before the maiming, she said, she had made moves to file a protection order against him, executing the proper forms. Bobbitt, meanwhile, said he was in the process of removing his belongings from the house, intending to leave her for good.

When I meet Lorena (on Mother's Day weekend 2010) I find her compact, feisty, intense—almost coiled. Gone is the wallflower persona. Gone too is the dark hair; she's now a strawberry blonde. Although she is quick-witted and focused, the tears do well up in her eyes now and again. She can display a guarded, haunted look, her attention seeming to drift.

I tell her that many women, including my friend Donna Ferrato—the premier photographic chronicler of domestic violence—have described her as a trailblazer.[15] Ferrato, whose charitable work has raised hundreds of thousands of dollars for victims of sexual assault and partner and spousal violence, had recently told me that Lorena Bobbitt's action was bold and, in her case, long

---

15. In 1991, Ferrato would publish the first photographic book to directly and systematically address domestic violence, *Living with the Enemy*, leading to a shift in attitudes, funding, and legislative action. (Paul Moakley interview with Donna Ferrato, "*Time* 100 Photos: The Most Influential Images of All Time," New York, NY, November 16, 2016.)

overdue. "She had to disarm him," Ferrato says. "He was using his cock as a weapon."

Does Lorena consider herself a pioneer? "I do," she says. "Before my case, nobody really cared as much [about] domestic violence. After what happened, laws have been changed, the police have a [justification] to put a man in jail, if necessary.... Because of what happened to me, because it was such a circus—and it was worldwide known that domestic violence come up to the surface and everybody have to say, 'That happened to me.' Millions of women *felt* like me."

The adulation, however, went only so far. "It was horrible," she continues, explaining her private torment. "At a personal level, I experienced all the physical abuse, the psychological abuse, the economical abuse, and emotional abuse.... I was not talking to anybody [about it]. I felt ashamed of saying my husband was abusing me. It is very common [among women trapped by domestic violence]."

In the 1980s and '90s, she says, more and more women began to set up shelters and treatment centers and call for legal changes, realizing that they had to take matters into their own hands. "I look at it like a sisterhood type of thing. A lot of women felt it was important to help other women. [The women's movement of the '70s] opened their eyes a little bit more [and made them] say, 'Look, we have to stick together because we don't want these things to happen anymore.'"

She remembers this sense of solidarity at her trial and at rallies on her behalf. Some protestors would raise their hands in a "V" and make a scissors-snipping gesture. "The women who came to my trial in support," she recalls, made her feel "more confident. I wasn't alone." Describing her foundation, set up in 2007 to educate women about the remedies for escaping domestic violence, Lorena explains that it took her almost fifteen years to gain the strength and equilibrium to become a public advocate. "I wasn't mentally ready to help others," she contends. "People were dying [for me] to write books and I said, 'You know what? I don't want to talk about the incident. All I did was cry and remember."

Her ex-husband, in contrast, took a different path. "He made hundreds of thousands of dollars," she says. "He is an adult. He can choose whatever he wants to.... Doing the porno movies. I have never seen [them. But] he took advantage. He could have [used his earnings from the films] to help others."

On balance, however, she says she doesn't resent his having profited from the incident, allowing that others may have taken advantage of him and led him astray. What galls her the most, she says, is that her husband was found innocent of marital sexual assault.

Did John get what he deserved?

"I don't think he has what he deserved because I would have like to seen him in jail for what he did—not because of what I did to him. That's not right."

And what you did to *him*?

"Was wrong," she tells me.

If you had to go back, you wouldn't do it again?

"No. No. No, no. No, no, no, no." Later she adds, "Yes, I did wrong. But I wish people would stop judging me."

But *why* did she do it in the first place?

When Lorena was taken into custody and was asked to recount the incident, she gave this statement, which sounded to many like an attempt to explain her motivation: "He always have orgasm and he doesn't wait for me to have orgasm. He's selfish. I don't think it's fair. So I pulled back the sheets then and I did it." In hindsight, she insists, "I didn't make [the statement to the police] in my right state of mind. What I tried to say is that he raped me. And I couldn't say it, that he was raping me. So my way of saying that: '[We] don't finish [to] have an orgasm' or something, like you enjoy as a couple with your wife, in a couple, intimacy. I was not able to communicate in English."

There is another question I want to ask her, though. From where in the depths of her despair did such a primal impulse emerge? How is it that she even conceived of the idea of an act so rare in contemporary society that it seemed both historic—and *pre*historic?

"I don't remember anything what happened," she contends. "It was more like a bad dream, from the abuse that happened. . . . A lot of people thought it was premeditation. It was nothing 'premeditation.' . . . I don't know [where the impulse came from]. I don't know. I honestly [don't]."

At one point I ask about John, gingerly. "Do you ever hear from him or talk to him?"

"Oh yeah," she says, taking out her BlackBerry. "He just texted me he loves me. You want to see the text? It's crazy. He texted me on Valentine's Day: he loves me, he wants to marry me."

Dumbfounded, I look at her smartphone and see a string of messages from the same number—a 716 area code, in upstate New York. One is from two days before. *Good morning. Happy Cinco de Mayo, cha-cha-cha. XXX's and OOO's, JB.* There's another from April 21: *Lorena, We have to love. It's the greatest force the world has ever known. Love is God. Do you feel it.* The texts, back in April, appear to have come in bursts, several sent in a matter of minutes, then every hour or two. *Love never dies and it's never too late. I can teach you. Do you think it's too late for all that? Please, be nice. What life would be like for us if we got back together and you got pregnant?*

Lorena says she considers the text barrage—along with the cards she claims he sends on holidays—to be harassment, especially since John knows that she has a child and has been in a serious relationship for years. "It's just ridiculous, really," she says, brushing it off and explaining that she rarely responds, usually deleting the messages in batches. "I'm above that. I'm above the person who had caused so much damage to me. . . . This is reality. This is what happens to women. . . . It's just sickening."

Another message says, *Please forgive me.* And then, *LOL.*

I copy the phone number and, with Lorena's permission, call John Bobbitt a while later.

He answers and says that he is, indeed, *the* John Wayne Bobbitt. He tells me that he works as a carpenter and limo driver. He says he goes on dates but finds it challenging to be in his forties and meet the right partner. He is forthcoming about his former porn career and claims he was supposed to have been paid $10 million for his appearances but that he never saw much of it. "I got ripped off," he says. "Somebody else got it—agents, the production company. . . . There was a lot of negativity involved in the adult entertainment business."

He contends that his private parts still function. "I did the films to prove myself," he says. "To prove I had my penis cut off"—but that he was subsequently repaired.[16]

When I ask about his incessant texting, he responds that, yes, he does

---

16. Susan Faludi, in the *New Yorker*, would describe the filming of *John Wayne Bobbitt Uncut.* "Bobbitt could barely get it up, much less keep it there," she would report, stating that he relied on syringe shots of a miracle substance called prostaglandin to keep him going. (Susan Faludi, "The Money Shot," *New Yorker*, October 30, 1995, 82–83.)

send Lorena messages saying how much he loves her and wishes they could get back together. "Yeah, I do. But she almost killed me, but I realize now, looking back"—he tries to explain how things might be better if they reconnected *now*—"we got married and we never lived alone. We always had somebody with us [in our apartment]."

But why, I ask, would you send affectionate text messages if she cut your dick off?

"Yeah, but..."

"Why?" I ask.

"Well, Benjamin Franklin said that a lot of people criticized him and complained, and most people do, but it takes character and self-control to be understanding and forgiving. I was the cause of her pain. She needed me to be [in] as much pain as she was in. Then, knowing that I was leaving her, she didn't want anybody else to have me, if she couldn't have me.... That's the way she was. When she didn't get what she wanted, she would get really mad."

The attack, he says, was not a reaction to a sexual assault but to the fact that he was moving out and abandoning her. "She was charged with malicious wounding." For a moment he sounds like he is reading from a script. "Malicious means—it's a deep-seated, often unexplainable desire to see another person suffer harm, injury, or distress, or even death.... This make-believe thing that I raped her or beat her had nothing to do with that at all. The important thing to know of this whole case was that she did what she did because she was heartbroken. She was jealous. She was angry. You should have seen the expression on her face when my best friend arrived [to help me pack up] and I told her, 'See you, Lorena. I'm leaving. We're getting a divorce.' We went through this tumultuous relationship, back-and-forth fighting, and going to court. The judge told us, 'If you can't work your marriage out, get a divorce.' I said, 'Damn, you're right.'"

Were there any incidents, I ask, in which you were trying to do things sexually when she didn't want to do?

"No, that's what she wants you to believe," he says. "We experimented one time with anal sex—it was a failed attempt.... But there's no evidence. She's never been hospitalized for repeated anal sex or rape. If I did, wouldn't she go to the hospital? The only sign of violence—that night when I had my penis cut off—was me, in the hospital, bleeding to death." After a pause, he reflects, "Okay, yes, I was a bad husband. I wasn't there for her. I was out—with my friends. I wanted a divorce. Neglect. I stopped communicating with her. That's why [she did it]. I wish I would have been a better husband."

Both partners, at one time or another, had said that they'd had sex that evening. True?

"As soon as [I] got home, I fell asleep. I went into a deep sleep, and she was trying to have sex with me. I didn't respond to her. I couldn't. I was too tired. And she was trying to talk to me but I couldn't understand what she was saying. She said, 'You hurt me. You do it again and again and again. Are you happy?' That was the statement. Basically, she was referring to the three times I left her. This was the third and final time. People don't understand. People are so shallow-minded that they don't know the real reason why. There it is."

John Bobbitt admits that he did hit her on occasion. "A lot of times we'd fight. We'd throw things. We'd yell, pushing and shoving or whatever. But no battery."

Obviously, I stress to him, she's now in a serious relationship. She has a family, a new life. So why would you send her texts?

"I'm trying to look for some closure," he says.

The number and type of texts, I tell him, might arguably verge on harassment. What drives you to send them?

"That's me trying to make amends or trying to say I forgive her. I wasn't ready to be married then. I'm ready to be married now."

Do you feel you're fixated on her?

"I know," he agrees. Then he asks for advice. "Is our relationship unrepairable [sic]? That's just a question. She wanted to have this dream [marriage], and I wasn't ready to fulfill her dream."

I explain that Lorena has been distressed by his texts, which is why she didn't respond. I say that she has moved on.

"Oh," he says, taking it in. Then he wonders aloud, "You're basically saying to me that it's foolish for me to get involved with a woman who cut my penis off."

"That's what I'm asking," I respond.

"You're *asking* now?"

"What do *you* think?"

"I think it went beyond that. It went deeper than that. It's about love.... [About] transforming an enemy into a friend."

At their trials, each had faced twenty years in prison. John Bobbitt would be cleared of marital sexual assault charges. Lorena Bobbitt would be found not guilty of malicious wounding due to temporary insanity and would spend a month in a psychiatric unit.

CHAPTER 20

The Boomsie Twins

In the mid-'90s, they were the nation's two most powerful politicians—and America's favorite frenemies. They were President William Jefferson Clinton and Newton "Newt" Gingrich, the Georgia Republican who would lead a conservative groundswell while serving as Speaker of the House.

The disparity in their core convictions reflected those of a bipolar electorate: blue vs. red, left vs. right, consensus vs. orthodoxy. One man, who'd been baptized at age nine, espoused a moral relativism that encouraged tolerance of diverse worldviews and belief systems. The other, a longtime Southern Baptist raised in a Lutheran home, would later convert to Catholicism. He believed in a universal morality for humanity at large. The two men were nothing less than the "leaders [of two] cultural armies fighting over the legacy of the decade," in the words of Steven M. Gillon, author of *The Pact*, the definitive book on the Clinton-Gingrich rivalry.

Clinton we have already met in these pages. Gingrich, by way of introduction, was the man credited with coming to Capitol Hill and deliberately avoiding compromise *as a tactic*: a method for upholding one's conservative principles, ramming through legislation, and provoking concessions from one's opponents, even if it led to governmental paralysis. The 1990s, in fact, marked the beginning of "the Gingrich era of hyperbolic partisanship," according to historian Geoffrey Kabaservice. "It was Mr. Gingrich who pioneered the political dysfunction we still live with…usher[ing] in the present political era of confrontation and obstruction."

Gingrich was erudite, a history buff, and a blue-sky futurist. With his cherubic presence and silvery shock of hair, he evoked both the college professor of his early career and a right-wing Phil Donahue. And yet his playbook favored hard tackles and end runs. Gingrich was prone to bombast, to moralizing, to demonizing his foes—"a politics of anger," in *Time*'s terminology. He was also, in the primeval days of reality TV, a master of the synthetic narrative. Sheryl Gay Stolberg would note in the *New York Times* that Gingrich's ascension in the '80s "coincided with the rise of C-SPAN, the cable channel that televised House proceedings.... Night after night, he would lambaste Democrats, speaking in an empty House chamber after the day's legislative business was done. Mr. Gingrich would needle Democrats, challenging them to come forward and defend themselves. No one did, because no one was there."

Then came 1990. That year, as part of a controversial budget deal, President George H. W. Bush broke his long-standing vow never to raise taxes—pure anathema to Reagan conservatives. This concession gave Gingrich and his band of mutineers an opening to wrest control of the party. And over the next several years they all but neutered the GOP establishment as they forged a new style of Republican: rebellious, contrarian, and partial to brinkmanship.

Newt Gingrich in short order became a quantum force in American conservatism. During his shining hour—September 27, 1994—he enlisted 367 men and women, all running in that year's midterm elections, and assembled them as one battalion on the Capitol steps. As the cameras rolled, he made sure that each candidate affixed a John or Jane Hancock to a so-called Contract with America, its preamble purporting to install "a Congress that respects the values and shares the faith of the American family."

To that end, Newt's contract—beyond addressing popular bread-and-butter issues (tax breaks, street crime, an invigorated military, and the holy grail of a balanced budget)—focused on some of the same culture-war priorities that had been laid out at the 1992 Republican National Convention. The Personal Responsibility Act "discourage[d] illegitimacy and teen pregnancy" by revamping welfare and barring teen moms from getting federal funds. The Family Reinforcement Act dealt with adoption, child support, parents' rights, and child-porn statutes.

The signing made for great political theater, even if opinion polls revealed that two-thirds of the country didn't have a clue what was in it. But Gingrich had animated and unified the party. The fact that legions of potential legislators were in lockstep, as historian Gillon has observed, effectively "nationalized 435 local races... turn[ing] the election into a choice between the Republican agenda and the failures of the Clinton administration." The contract prized Newt's gravity over Bill's perpetual motion.[1]

The Boomsie twins, differences aside, were cut from the same bolt of tie-dye. "The evidence keeps mounting that Bill Clinton and Newt Gingrich were separated at birth," ventured columnist Frank Rich. "Both men are self-invented American archetypes, presenting a persona more at odds with their origins than Mark Twain was from Samuel Clemens.... [Both] were favored eldest children, brought up by tough mothers who survived spouse abuse. As boys, neither knew his biological father and both had difficult relationships with their adoptive fathers[2]... These two ambitious boomers both smoked dope and ducked Vietnam."

The Boomsies, in the '60s, supported the civil rights movement. They made their maiden runs for office in the '70s—as southern populists. They were insufferable wonks who came to relish the Beltway rumble. They were self-involved, surely, but worked hard for working- and middle-class Americans. They were temperamental tricksters, passably handsome devils in their day, and, on occasion, hot pockets of hot air.[3] And both politicians were sexually adventurous, sometimes devastatingly so.

We have read herein about the president's past. But Gingrich too was a man of appetites. *Mother Jones* in 1984 would report on an incident from the '70s, citing a former campaign aide who insisted that one day while he was escorting Gingrich's daughters through a parking lot, he had passed a car and saw the candidate sitting inside "with a woman, her head buried in his lap." (The aide would later clarify, "Newt kind of turned and gave me this little-boy

---

1. Newt's gravity would again come tugging in 2016 when he would serve as an adviser to President-elect Donald Trump, who, as if starring in the premiere episode of *That '90s Show*, would introduce his own "Contract with the American Voter." (Reena Flores, "What Do Donald Trump's First 100 Days in Office Look Like?," CBSNews.com, November 11, 2016.)

2. Each would acquire his name later on in life: Clinton was born William Jefferson Blythe III; Gingrich was born Newton Leroy McPherson.

3. They were, in the words of columnist Lance Morrow, the "famous fraternal twins of American power, yin and yang of the Baby Boom....A generation or two ago, leaders were father figures. For better and for worse, Clinton and Gingrich—powerful yet indefinably immature—give off a bright, undisciplined energy, a vibration of adolescent recklessness." (Lance Morrow, "Newt Gingrich's World: How One Man Changed the Way Washington Sees Reality," *Time*, Man of the Year, December 25, 1995, 50–51.)

smile. Fortunately [the daughters] were a lot younger and shorter then.") In a 1995 *Vanity Fair* profile by Gail Sheehy, Gingrich had allegedly prefigured the president in appearing to treat fellatio as Sex Lite. A former campaign volunteer, according to Sheehy, claimed that she and the congressman began a relationship while both of them were married: " 'We had oral sex,' she says. 'He prefers that modus operandi because then he can say, 'I never slept with her.' "[4]

The *Times*' Maureen Dowd—a serial skewerer of Newt—would reduce his marital history to a single scathing paragraph: "His first wife, Jackie, was his former high school geometry teacher. The family-values pol cheated on her and left her when she was fighting uterine cancer. He then married his mistress, Marianne, and worked on books and politics with her until he cheated on her and left her when she was fighting multiple sclerosis. He then married his mistress, Callista, and now he produces agitprop with her."[5]

Clinton and Gingrich. Exemplars of public service. Defenders of their parties' bedrock principles. Creatures of the flesh.

These were the two men in whose hands lay the fate of a nation.

But before moving on to the great Clinton-Gingrich clashes, a question arises. Why, in the '90s, was there a sudden surge in the sex appeal of politics and politicians?

———

Power in twentieth-century Washington, with a handful of exceptions, had always been about as sexy as contract bridge. Yet Clinton and Gingrich came

---

4. When Gingrich eventually ran for president, he appeared on the Christian Broadcasting Network in 2011, and attributed his straying ways in some measure to his patriotism: "There's no question that at times in my life, partially driven by how passionately I felt about this country, that I worked far too hard and that things happened in my life that were not appropriate.... [I]t may make me more normal than somebody who wanders around seeming perfect and maybe not understanding the human condition." (Gail Collins, "Eye of the Newt," *New York Times*, March 12, 2011, A3; Collins, "Newt's Real Legacy," *New York Times*, January 29, 2012, SR1, 7.)

5. It was sex, curiously enough, that had first immersed Gingrich in politics. In 1968, during his grad school days, administrators at Tulane banned two photographs that reportedly showed a naked art teacher and nude sculptures with "enlarged organs." University officials dubbed the pictures obscene and forbade their publication in *Sophia*, an arts-and-literary supplement to the school paper, the *Tulane Hullabaloo*. In response, classmates held demonstrations. Gingrich was among a small group— the Mobilization of Responsible Tulane Students (MORTS)—who staged protests, drafted a platform calling for a "free press on campus," and met with the university's president to discuss key demands. (Bruce W. Eggler, "Student Demonstrations Subside but Protest Leaders Still Dissatisfied," *Tulane Hullabaloo*, March 15, 1968, 1, 15, 19; "MORTS Issues Election 'Platform'," *Tulane Hullabaloo*, April 5, 1968; "Anniversary of the Newt," *Washington City Paper*, March 25–31, 1988.)

along at a time when high office was beginning to acquire an added allure. And no one recognized this as intuitively as a lawyer and editor named John F. Kennedy Jr.

The photogenic son of a perpetually photographed First Couple, Kennedy was a bachelor in 1988 when *People* magazine christened the twenty-seven-year-old "The Sexiest Man Alive." Three years later, he began toying with the idea of putting out a magazine focused on the intersection of politics, personality, and popular culture. Its mission was simple, cooked up by his friend Michael Berman: why not make politics more relevant to the masses at a time when other such publications (the *National Review*, the *New Republic* et al.) were stiff as a starched shirt? Kennedy and Berman hoped their magazine would apply a glossy brush to individuals in and around Washington power in much the same way that *Manhattan, inc.* in the '80s had seductively portrayed the business elite as mighty titans.

"John and I began talking about it as early as the campaign of '92," recalls attorney Gary Ginsberg, a White House staffer under Bill Clinton who'd known Kennedy when they attended Brown and who joined the magazine's start-up team in the mid-'90s. (Ginsberg would go on to lofty corporate communications posts with News Corp and Time Warner.) "[John] was particularly fascinated by how Clinton used the leverage of popular culture to promote his campaign and how, in his mind, there was a real confluence of politics and entertainment: [appearing on the] Arsenio Hall [talk show on] late-night television and playing the saxophone. [Courting] Hollywood. He'd seen vestiges of this in his father's relationship to Hollywood, but you really hadn't seen it flourish in the thirty years since."[6]

Clinton and Gore's 1992 victory cinched the deal. "By '93," Ginsberg remembers, "he began writing his business plan"—securing financial backing from the French publishing company Hachette. And when the first issue of Kennedy and Berman's magazine, *George* (as in Washington), was unveiled at a 1995 news conference, the cover, shot by Herb Ritts, featured supermodel Cindy Crawford as Washington, in a powdered wig and an open waistcoat, showing off her abs. Subsequent covers had Drew Barrymore playing Marilyn (cover line: "Happy Birthday, Mr. President"); Claudia Schiffer wearing

---

6. Indeed, JFK Jr.'s grandfather Joe Kennedy had run Hollywood studios in the 1920s and was the sometime lover of Gloria Swanson.

a Clinton-Gore banner (and nothing else); and a naked Christy Turlington straddling a TV set (for the Media Issue). Even Kennedy himself, for an editor's letter on the subject of temptation, decided to pose nude—with an Eden-esque apple. In the accompanying column, he disparaged his romantically entangled cousins Joe and Michael Kennedy as "poster boys for bad behavior."

George attracted a sizable dual audience—for a time drawing more female than male readers, a rarity for a journal covering politics. But the magazine failed, if not spectacularly, then consistently. Its nose was too close to the glass. Its mix of stories was confounding ("Top 10 Hunks in History"—by Arthur Schlesinger Jr.; "Why Hillary Won't Be Senator"). To those in the media and at other political publications, *George* seemed flyweight. "[Our competitors] viewed politics as an intensely serious affair," Ginsberg avers. "They thought we were silly, simplistic, we dumbed it down, that we were doing a disservice to the electorate by focusing not on the issues that were important but on the personalities and the process. And they were ruthless."

What *George* had gotten right, though, was the premise that the world of politics had a new mystique—right, left, and center.[7] The attraction was a result of more media play being devoted to political personalities; younger people on the stump, in field operations, and working for consultants and the press; and the seamless and often shameless way that politicians were publicly trading on their personal lives. There was also a sense that the countless scandals involving unbuckled belts in the Beltway implied that "everybody's getting it—Democrats, Republicans," recalls journalist Judy Bachrach. "It was all about the sex appeal of power." Washington, she says, quoting a local adage, had come to be referred to as "Hollywood for the ugly."

One sign of the more intimate D.C.-L.A. tango was the annual White House Correspondents' Association Dinner. For years the gathering had been a staid affair. Members of news organizations that covered the Washington scene would don formal attire and listen politely (seated beside their invited sources—elected officials, power brokers, and their aides) as the president and an emcee delivered comic monologues. Then, in 1987, journalists began competing to invite what *Vanity Fair* editor Graydon Carter would call "novelty

---

7. For *George's* March 2000 cover, a dreamy, blue-eyed Donald Trump (called "The Trumpster," in small type) was photographed being kissed by an anonymous female model. The cover line: "The Secret Behind Trump's Political Fling." That fling would turn into a tease and, finally, a love affair.

guests." At first the most notorious of these tablemates were women made famous by scandal or romance: Fawn Hall, the assistant to Lieutenant Colonel Oliver North at the center of the Iran-Contra mess; Gary Hart's honey Donna Rice; model and actress Marla Maples, the year America learned of her relationship with Donald Trump.[8] But by the mid-'90s, film and TV figures, from Warren Beatty to Ellen DeGeneres, were crowding the ballroom of the Washington Hilton. And Hollywood, D.C., and the media, trading off one another's cachet, began to call it what it was: The Nerd Prom.[9]

Jennifer Rider, a respected consultant and adviser to CEOs, helped handle communications for Republican candidates like Bob Dole and Christie Whitman in the '90s. (She has since become a Democrat.) Rider considers the decade a political game-changer. "The people running for office, the pundits, the campaign staff were younger and more charismatic," she says. "There was a buzz. Bill Clinton was this dynamo—brilliant, articulate, a babe—after twelve years of Reagan, Bush, and Quayle, apple pie and the boy next door. Both parties needed 'youthful and sexy' on their bench.

"It was a point in time before blogs [or] social media," she recalls. "You had to be on TV, and the '90s changed everything: Fox News and MSNBC launched"—more on this shortly—"so there were more chances to be 'on air.' The entire country was suddenly hot and heavy for political news. And you had this wave of smart, sexy, badass women—Dee Dee Myers, Lisa Caputo, Susan Estrich, Mandy Grunwald, Laura Ingraham, Monica Crowley, Ann Coulter, and Arianna Huffington" (then a formidable presence on the right) "rising up as strategists and TV [commentators], which used to be mainly balding-guy territory.[10]

---

8. During the cocktail hour before the 1998 Correspondents' Dinner, I encountered one Ms. Paula Jones braving the pre-party scrum in the inner courtyards of the Washington Hilton. If recollection serves, she was in the company of the Web's new bad boy, Matt Drudge. (Felicity Barringer, "Media Glamourfest; The Dinner, the Heartburn," *New York Times*, May 3, 1998, WK5.)

9. One of the most memorable after-parties was held in May 1999, hosted by *Vanity Fair*. On that night, I remember being taken aback as I watched a collection of VIPs staring out onto the lawn at a particularly stylish couple cuddling in a white chair. The celebrities' collective gaze, for a lingering instant, was fixed on none other than JFK Jr. and his wife, Carolyn Bessette. (Three months later, Kennedy, Bessette, and her sister Lauren would perish when the small plane that Kennedy was piloting crashed off the coast of Martha's Vineyard.)

10. George H. W. Bush had his own youth squad. Mary Matalin occasionally went the Annie Hall route, wearing men's ties to "spunk up" her ensemble, as she put it. In her campaign memoir,

"Young women—age twenty-five, twenty-six," Rider explains, "came to D.C. thinking that it was sexy to be young and Republican. I remember being around that age [when I arrived, and] years later the first guy who hired me for a political position admitted that one of the two main reasons he did was because of my legs. It's always about the legs." Looking back, Rider admits to having gotten the bug after seeing a thatch of premature gray. "I became a Republican *because* of Jack Kemp. He was an ex-football star—big on tax reform but also a can-do social activist who was into urban renewal. His story made me feel Republicans were suddenly cool and relevant.

"Even Newt Gingrich found a way to appeal to the rebel-chick and surly-guy types. His Contract with America connected with independents and Republicans and young people and libertarians who saw big government as the enemy. The GOP wasn't as hard right [as it is now], so moderates like me could still join in, and it felt like something huge was happening."[11]

Matalin would write about how her colleague Torie Clarke donned "lime-green and hot-pink suede miniskirts, which she wore with matching tights. She had a blond-red spiked hairdo. This was not your mother's Republican."

In Matalin's view, in fact, the media's obsession with youth began not with Clinton's first presidential run but one election cycle earlier, when Boomers entered the press corps in large enough numbers to make their mark covering Boomer candidates, consultants, and staffers. "The prominence of the Boomers on the national political scene," she posits, "was the 1988 campaign.... The Boomer press covered us as personalities because of their own narcissism—not as individuals, but as a generational characteristic. To this day there is nothing the press of that era likes to cover more than *themselves*. The younger guys appear in their own media because it is now intrinsic to the [digital news] business, but they are less 'center of their own universe' than the Boomer generation." The 1988 race, Matalin asserts, "was the first time it was tentatively permissible for operatives to be on the record and visible in their own right. Prior to that, at least on the GOP side, it was close to a fireable offense to be quoted in a story unauthorized, and unthinkable to be the topic of a story, à la [Lee] Atwater and the other personalities that emerged in 1988." Former Clinton strategist Dick Morris would make a similar point, contending that the Clintons saw the press's relentless animus, in part, as a function of affinity breeding enmity. "They resent us," the president once remarked, according to Morris, "because we are the same age as they are, we're all baby boomers, and they're just jealous and envious." This quote has been variously attributed to Bill and to Hillary Clinton. (Mary Matalin and James Carville with Peter Knobler, *All's Fair: Love, War, and Running for President* [New York: Random House/Touchstone, 1994], 264, 336; Interview with Matalin; Dick Morris, *Behind the Oval Office: Getting Reelected Against All Odds* [New York: St. Martin's, 1999], xxv; Howard Kurtz, *Spin Cycle: Inside the Clinton Propaganda Machine* [New York: Simon & Schuster/Free Press, 1998], 85.)

11. In *Vanity Fair*, Sam Tanenhaus suggested there was "a genuine conservative chic." Under the headline "Damsels in Dissent," he profiled "a new breed of female conservatives" (ages twenty-four to forty-three), whom the magazine rendered in chic and striking studio portraits. Among them: Lynn Chu, Danielle Crittenden, Pia Nordlinger, Virginia Postrel, Wendy Shalit, and Amity

Lisa Baron is the author of the political tell-all *Life of the Party*, who worked for Republican operations, including Dole's, during the '90s. She would ascend to the role of spokesperson for Ralph Reed, the head of the Christian Coalition.[12] "Girls like me," she says, "were called 'press tarts.' You have to think about men like Newt Gingrich, Henry Hyde et al. as struggling musicians. Then, when they hit the big time—becoming the party of power—they become rock stars. And we—the staffers—were groupies. The [political] conventions were like Woodstock for wonks."

Baron remembers an evening during her first year in Washington when, after countless rounds of drinks with a male political coordinator from the Republican National Committee, she says she ended up naked, along with her new friend, on the front lawn of the Capitol. For a young politico, she recalls, "It was just a big party. It was like being in college almost. Everybody's running around with everybody—not necessarily having sex [because then] you're deemed a slut and written off."

Manhattan had its own young conservative scene, and for a time, its nexus was a monthly salon. The so-called Vile Body parties of the '80s and early '90s were started by writer Terry Teachout and a few cohorts. The soirees were held in the library of an Upper East Side town house that had once belonged to songwriter Alan Jay Lerner. The first Wednesday of each month, attendees were served popcorn, libations (from a cash bar), and right-of-center discourse. Its members were chiefly younger Boomers, sired too recently to have been on Kesey's bus. They believed that the free-radical values of their older, liberal sibs had sunk the blinking country. "We definitely saw ourselves as representatives of an ideological break with the older Boomers," Teachout

---

Shlaes—at thirty-nine, the youngest member of the *Wall Street Journal*'s editorial board. Similarly splashy treatment would be given to their peers (David Brock, Bill Kristol, and Lisa Schiffren among them) in the *New York Times Magazine*, though the accompanying photos were criticized as being more "ghouls gallery" than glam. (Sam Tanenhaus, "Damsels in Dissent," *Vanity Fair*, November 1999, 144–58; James Atlas, "The Counter Counterculture," *New York Times Magazine*, February 12, 1995; Christopher Buckley, Letter, *New York Times Magazine*, March 12, 1995.)

12. Baron earned a bit of notoriety for writing about how and why she administered a blowjob to a man who would become a presidential press secretary. She would also give Ralph Reed's staff agita because while in his employ she penned a column for an Atlanta alternative weekly called the *Sunday Paper* that contained gems of this caliber: "I swear I don't have a big vagina, but over the Thanksgiving holiday I told my father-in-law I did." (Interview with Lisa Baron; Baron, *Life of the Party: A Political Press Tart Bares All* [New York: Citadel, 2011], 5, 10–11, 153, 192; Amy Argetsinger and Roxanne Roberts, "Thou Shalt What??," *Washington Post*, December 22, 2005.)

says today. "Young conservatives, neoconservatives, and libertarians…felt a bit isolated in the sea of Manhattan liberalism, and found that we enjoyed spending time with and talking to politically and culturally like-minded writers and intellectuals our own age."

Participants were Brainy Young Things such as David Brooks, Richard Brookhiser, Andrew Ferguson, Maggie Gallagher, and John Podhoretz, along with Wall Street types and editors and writers from conservative journals. The Vile Body had "a vaguely Oxbridge-ish sense," recalls Sam Tanenhaus. (Its name referenced the party-mad crowd of Evelyn Waugh's 1930 novel of the same name.) "This was the New York beachhead of the [conservative] movement [that had won] three presidential victories in the 1980s.…The Young Right had recomposed itself in frothing hatred of Bill Clinton."

Not entirely. The soirees in fact began in the mid-'80s, a period when Clinton was on no one's radar. And when it came to the newfound allure surrounding political power and opinion, Teachout attributes that change not to the bright-eyed Boomer from Arkansas but to an ex-actor from Hollywood. "That transformation," he tells me, "I connect directly to Reagan's presidency. To be sure, it got glossier later on, as evidenced by *George* magazine. But it had already happened."

Another reason for the sizzle, especially on the right, was the press itself. And the four most distinctive and politically influential media voices to emerge in the '90s were all angry, tough-talking, and staunchly conservative.

First in line was talk radio's high priest of the right, Rush Limbaugh. A looming presence during the Reagan years, Limbaugh by the '90s was reaching twenty million listeners a week. He was hardly a hottie: physically imposing, fond of cigars, and a pro-abstinence promoter. But he talked *muy macho* as he bitch-slapped the Clintons. He liked to segue into snippets from Steppenwolf and the Pretenders. And he amassed a loyal fan base, becoming a bestselling author, a late-night TV host—and an overnight guest at the White House. (George H. W. Bush is said to have personally schlepped Limbaugh's bag to the Lincoln Bedroom.)

Limbaugh's program mainly consisted of Angry White El Rushbo, alone in a room. Yet he delivered his color commentary on the culture war with a peculiar urgency and gloom, as if he were the last man alive in the press box, covering Doomsday. His secret sauce was his comedy, into which he sprinkled a spice cabinet of biting insight and outrage. In a 1992 Limbaugh profile for *Vanity Fair*, political journalist Jeff Greenfield would tell Peter J. Boyer that the broadcaster had grown his audience by opening the conservative tent to include listeners who were "working-class, younger, humorous. They love satire, they love rock 'n' roll music.... It's generational."

Limbaugh expressed pride in having coined the term "femi-Nazi." He railed against educators who would read books such as *Heather Has Two Mommies* to first graders, thereby "indoctrinating students with the false notion that homosexuality is as normal as heterosexuality [despite] overwhelming evidence that homosexual behavior statistically reduces one's life span." Such incendiary speech, along with his race-baiting, earned him entire zip codes of detractors. It also attracted a following sizable enough to land him on the cover of *Time*.

Limbaugh, stridently un-PC—and presaging the twenty-first-century rise of the Tea Party and, later, Donald Trump—emerged as a sort of Republican id, to the consternation of many of the party faithful. Michael Lind, for one, would observe in a 1995 *Dissent* article that Limbaugh personified the "collapse of intellectual conservatism" and, quite possibly, of the public intellectual. Lind, a political writer and editor, would declare, "In 1984, the leading conservative spokesman in the media was George Will; by 1994, it was Rush Limbaugh. The basic concerns of intellectual conservatives in the eighties were foreign policy and economics; by the early nineties they had become dirty pictures and deviant sex."

The media's second booming voice on the right was that of journalist David Brock. He would make his mark writing books as well as articles for conservative journals, capitalizing on a new kind of "ideological publishing," as he would put it, "that became very hot in the late '80s and early '90s." To leaders and readers on the right, Brock was the decade's fair-haired hatchet man. He helped dispense, in his own words, "hypocrisy, smears, [and] falsehoods... abandon[ing] the conservative traditions of restraint and civility for Gingrichian ends-justify-the-means radicalism."

It was Brock, funded by conservative backers in the shadows, who flushed out political sex scandals for vindication and profit. Brock slimed Anita Hill; spread slanderous and unproven stories that Governor Clinton had used state troopers to escort him to trysts; and outed a former Arkansas state employee, Paula Jones, as the object of the president's alleged advances, triggering what would become Jones's pivotal lawsuit. Brock was not just a soldier but a dead-eye sniper taking aim from his perch in the "vast right-wing conspiracy" that Hillary Clinton would quite accurately describe. He became the New Right's media pet. "My friend Ann Coulter," Brock would recall, "told me that when I walked into a room full of conservatives, it was like Mick Jagger had arrived. Ann was joking, but I believed her."

An evening hang at Brock's town house, in the company of the haut monde of conservative Washington, would become one of Georgetown's most coveted invites. Indeed, in 1995—on the night Gingrich's congressional class first convened—many of the movement's young turks (from humorist P. J. O'Rourke to Andrew Ferguson, from Danielle Crittenden to David Frum) would share cocktails Chez Brock "to the strains of Smashing Pumpkins and 10,000 Maniacs," according to James Atlas in a *New York Times Magazine* story, "drinking and laughing and comparing Newt sightings." They were, said Atlas, the Counter Counterculture. (Brock, as stated previously, would eventually abandon the movement, join the enemy camp, create a journalism-watchdog group and Democratic strategy organization, and become a key fund-raiser for Hillary Clinton.)[13]

If Limbaugh and Brock, playing Elvis and Mick, were the right's old-media rock stars of the '90s, they had nothing on the decade's most transformative conservative voice: Fox News. The right-of-center cable network, devised by Rupert Murdoch and developed by Roger Ailes, premiered in 1996. At the time, CNN was being derided on the right as unapologetically leftist; some called it the Clinton News Network. (CNN in fact had been the '70s brainchild of a Murdoch bête noire, billionaire Ted Turner, the left-leaning mogul and then-husband of Hollywood icon Jane Fonda, an über-liberal in her heyday. "I thought about killing him," Ted would say of

---

13. James Warren, the *Chicago Tribune*'s Washington bureau chief at the time, recalls attending one memorable Brock fete. On hand, Warren says, was "a star-studded troupe of the new-conservative media elite. Matt Drudge answered the door. Mark Foley was there—the Florida representative later alleged to have sent come-on emails to young congressional pages. So was Laura Ingraham. And *Michael* Huffington, wearing a loosely buttoned cotton Hawaiian shirt. As I recall, this was the evening before the *Washington Post*'s 'Reliable Source' gossip column would reveal that Michael and Arianna were getting divorced. The column stated that Huffington 'has said he has dreams of becoming a priest.'" Subsequently, after losing his California Senate bid, he would come out as gay in an *Esquire* story— by David Brock. (Interview with Warren and confirmation from an anonymous source; Annie Groer and Ann Gerhart, "Reliable Source" [column], *Washington Post*, June 27, 1997; "Michael Huffington Secret Unveiled: He's Gay," *San Francisco Examiner* via sfgate.com, December 6, 1998.)

Rupert, shortly after Fox News debuted. "In his [news]papers, he said…I'm insane. [So] if I did shoot him, I'd get off.")[14]

Fox News was formulated during the GOP's stunning Gingrich-led resurgence. It went on air as Bill Clinton ran for reelection. And Roger Ailes would prove to be its ideal architect: a TV sage with McLuhanesque instincts; a political strategist who had helped shape hard-right "brands" such as Nixon, Limbaugh, and, in time, Donald Trump. Ailes recognized Turner's genius for turning a traditional money loser (TV news) into a cash cow. But he envisioned cable news with a twist. Headlines, truth be told, were bland. The real heat and throb and tang, Ailes believed, came from analysis of the news, as evidenced by the success of right-wing radio. If at times the debates turned into verbal cock-fights, all the better. (From day one, the channel featured alpha-dog hosts Sean Hannity and Bill O'Reilly on evening shows.) The channel would build its head of steam on the rancor of the disenfranchised, a public itch for tabloid stories, and a moral seething about the Clintons and the culture's progressive drift.

To many, Fox News, despite its tabloid-TV production values and occasional wingnut commentators, was a breath of fresh air, with earthy notes of blood and musk. The above-mentioned Lisa Baron believed the network was essential, she says, in having brought "a new, sexier image to the face of the party and what a Republican can look like. Women on Fox were generally foxier than those on other cable networks. Viewers watched and thought about lower taxes—and Brazilian waxes.… The stereotype was always: Republicans have hotter women than Democrats. Because a woman encountering a Democrat would think: tree-hugger, they don't shave, they don't shower, they're wearing clothes for the third day in a row. I one hundred percent think Fox helped that."[15] (Not so, says a left-leaning colleague of mine who requests anonymity. "You've got to wonder," he translates, "what most

---

14. Turner, at the time, was known for spouting off and had a habit of sparring with Gerald Levin, his new boss at Time Warner, which had acquired CNN and effectively demoted him. "You talk about barbaric mutilation," he complained. "I'm being clitorized by Time Warner!" (Ken Auletta, *Media Man: Ted Turner's Improbable Empire* [New York: Norton, 2004], 66; Kim Masters and Bryan Burrough, "Cable Guys," *Vanity Fair*, January 1997, 129.)

15. Over time, the reportedly hostile and intimidating working conditions for women at Ailes's Fox News would become toxic. In 2016 an ex-cohost would file a lawsuit accusing Ailes of sexual harassment and alleging that the network "masquerades as a defender of traditional family values, but behind the scenes, it operates like a sex-fueled, Playboy Mansion–like cult, steeped in intimidation, indecency and misogyny." Other network employees would come forward to make supporting

viewers think when they watch these dweebs. Everyone knows: it's always someone too well coiffed and too well tanned who has a secret to hide.")

In time, the channel—tempestuous and incestuous (many of its commentators were GOP stars)—would become the party's 24/7 infomercial, a handmaiden of the right's sustained successes into the next century.[16] And all the while the network would advertise itself as politically evenhanded—what Sam Tanenhaus, the conservative historian, would describe as a "sardonic parody ('fair and balanced') of a mainstream media [that] it assumes to be rife with contempt."

The fourth horseman in this posse was a man named Drudge. He grew up as a Beltway boy who delivered the *Washington Star*. He moved to Hollywood, settled into a job managing the trinket shop at the CBS Studio Center, and in 1995 started a gossipy email blast. Matt Drudge, age twenty-nine, had a nose for scandal and hewed to libertarian views. He called his creation the *Drudge Report*—the first comprehensive online aggregator of opinion, headlines, and celebrity and political poop. For a while, his target audience was the rumorati within Washington, Hollywood, and the media itself. But by June 1997, once AOL started cohosting his site, Drudge had become a Web-wide phenomenon and the darling of American conservatives.

---

claims, even as Ailes, dismissed by Fox after an internal investigation, vigorously denied the charges. (Gabriel Sherman, "The Revenge of Roger's Angels," *New York*, September 5, 2016.)

16. Fox News would find its voice through Clinton's second-term scandals and impeachment, then come of age at the decade's final curtain: on election night 2000. As the networks, one by one, predicted Al Gore would be the likely victor in the presidential sweepstakes, Fox poll consultant John Ellis—a first cousin of George W. Bush and his brother Jeb, then Florida's governor—phoned his relatives from the network's New York decision room at 2 a.m. to inform them that, miraculously, "our projection shows that it is statistically impossible for Gore to win Florida." As Ellis would tell the *New Yorker's* Jane Mayer, "It was just the three of us guys handing the phone back and forth—me with the numbers, one of them a governor, the other the President-elect. Now *that* was cool." Fox alone would declare Bush the next president of the United States. The numbers, however, proved too close to call, and it would take a ruling by the Supreme Court to award Florida—and the election—to Bush II. The coup de grâce, in 2016: Roger Ailes, after being let go by Fox, would go on to advise Donald Trump's presidential bid. And speaking of connections, who was revealed to have served (while Fox News was covering Trump's presidential campaign) as one of the five trustees "for a large bloc of shares in 21st Century Fox and News Corp that belongs to Rupert Murdoch's two youngest daughters"? According to the *Financial Times*: none other than Trump's older daughter, Ivanka, a friend of Wendi Deng Murdoch, the News Corp executive chairman's ex. Ms. Trump reportedly "stepped down from the board" seven weeks after her father won the election. (Jane Mayer, "George W.'s Cousin," *New Yorker*, November 20, 2000, 38; Caitlin MacNeal, "Trump Complains That Only Fox News Covered His CIA Speech Fairly," TalkingPointsMemo.com, January 26, 2017; Matthew Garrahan, "Ivanka Trump Oversaw Murdoch Daughters' Trust," *Financial Times*, February 8, 2017.)

With his Web links and gossip droppings, Matt Drudge was a national nemesis and a guilty pleasure. He linked to far-right columns and home pages, some of them borderline batshit—and gave their rants and rumors equal weight with wire-service items. He reported on other reporters' reporting-in-progress—and got the biggest political newsbreak of the decade. (More on this later.) Drudge became the model of the gallant ruffian to which other young geeks aspired. "For seven premillennial years, I've covered the world from my Hollywood apartment, dressed in my drawers," he would write in his 2000 book *Drudge Manifesto.* "There's been no editor, no lawyer, no judge, no president to tell me I can't. And there never will be. Technology has finally caught up with individual liberty.... The Elites, fearing loss of power, see chaos and anarchy."

A notorious recluse, Drudge was a walking, blogging paradox. "In his own life, Drudge maintains ironbound privacy," Philip Weiss would note in *New York* magazine, "but his Website has grown by seizing on incidental, personal actions of public figures and blowing them up, at times viciously." Even as Drudge pioneered a new news medium, he was a throwback to the days of hot type (press arbiter Gabriel Snyder has called him "the best wire editor on the planet"), adopting as his trademark the bygone fedora, years before it became a hipster accessory.

In short, Limbaugh, Brock, Ailes, and Drudge, respectively, ruled right-wing radio, print, cable, and the Web. Together, Rush and Roger would mobilize literally millions against the Clinton agenda and the Clintons themselves. Brock and Drudge, for their part, would become the young sensei of conservative crypto-journalism, scandal-mongering, and innuendo inflation—nearly torpedoing Bill Clinton's presidency.

In the '90s, media types would debate whether the ethical standards of mainstream newsmen and -women applied to bloggers and their ilk. But within a decade, that question was moot. Journalism was journalism, whether delivered traditionally or electronically. And thanks in part to this rogues' quartet, the dividing lines were ever less distinct between news and rumor, between information and entertainment, between the media's treatment of one's public and private behavior.

A clean line can be drawn, attests Sam Tanenhaus, from Matt Drudge in the 1990s to Donald Trump twenty-five years later. "It all goes back to Drudge in Hollywood," Tanenhaus says, in an assessment of Trump's brain trust: "From Drudge to the late alt-right news pioneer Andrew Breitbart and then to Steve Bannon, President Trump's chief strategist. It's not just the alt-right. It's alt-politics—outside the two parties, all via sensationalist media." Over the course of a generation, these new-media, ultra-right conspirators were complicit in disseminating rumor, agenda-bent "alternative facts," and the long and gnarly anti-Bill-and-Hillary thread. Also in the cauldron: the late Roger Ailes, godfather of the whole Fox brood and a media mentor to GOP presidents and to Bannon, former overseer of Breitbart News.

That blurring, and the far right's accusations of a "liberal bias" by a supposedly monolithic mainstream media, turned much of the public myopic. Many saw the press as the problem. They demonized an entire profession that since the time of Edmund Burke had been valued as an essential Fourth Estate (that looked after the public interest) and served as a necessary check on government (that was often prone to overreach). In the digital age, print publications began folding their tents. Traditional media companies shed staffers by the thousands. And despite the invaluable journalism still being practiced in valiant quarters, many members of the cut-and-paste press, along with all the blow-dried bloves, became mired in the rant and pant and shame game.

————

But back to the conflict in question.

It was Fight Night, midterm elections 1994, as America went to the polls to elect the incoming congressional class. In the right corner: Gingrich and his shock troops. In the left: Clinton, who would soon be on the ropes.

As the early results came in, the president, by his own account, was "profoundly distressed." In state after state, GOP candidates were projected to win big. By evening's end, it was a rout. "Nowhere," historian Taylor Branch would put it, "did a Republican incumbent lose for Congress or governor, while Democrats across the country lost eight senators, eight governors, and fifty-four representatives. Republicans gained control of both legislative chambers in the biggest midterm shift since 1946, the year Clinton was born." It would come to be called the Gingrich Revolution.

And a revolt it was—as well as a harbinger of populist resurgence and anti-Clinton anger that would lead to Trump's Electoral College triumph twenty-two years later. "We got the living daylights beat out of us," Bill Clinton would write in his autobiography. "I had contributed to the demise by allowing my first weeks to be defined by gays in the military…and by trying to do too much too fast in a news climate in which my victories were minimized, my losses were magnified." His party's outlook seemed particularly bleak below the

Mason-Dixon line. "Democrats had held the majority of House seats, Senate seats and governorships in the South—all the way back to Reconstruction," NPR correspondent Ron Elving would observe. "All that changed in one day."[17]

Clinton's political future was suddenly in play. Many wondered how he could be an effective executive—let alone win a second term—with a Congress dead set against his agenda. Gingrich, the new Speaker, and his incoming freshman class of disrupters were "going to force change, not make deals," wrote American history scholar Steven Gillon. The insurgents, he observed, were soon referred to as "'Gingrich's children,' and they reflected his combative style of politics. They were young—over half were under the age of 45. They viewed themselves as outsiders, not professional politicians." And they swiftly implemented most of the provisions of their family-values contract in an attempt to roll back big-government policies, some begun under FDR's New Deal.

Gingrich was hailed as the party's savior. His program was heralded by conservative Jeffrey Gayner, of the Heritage Foundation think tank, as the third great revolutionary "transformation of [postwar] American politics" (after Barry Goldwater's creation of "the modern conservative political movement" and the solidification of conservative power under Ronald Reagan). For the moment, Gingrich ruled Washington. He pushed bills through Congress with a fury. He dominated the news cycle, even as the public cooled to his brusque and haughty manner. (His *dis*approval index nearly doubled, from 29 to 56 percent.) But he would go on to hold the Speaker's gavel from 1995 to 1998 as the culture-war battle lines would become ever more firmly drawn.

After the midterms, the president went into a months-long funk. Robert Reich, Clinton's secretary of labor, commented on his boss's state of mind, telling the *New York Times*, "He was lost, he was completely lost. He just didn't know what to do. It was a real crisis." Clinton during this rough patch was inadvertently reflecting the condition of countless American men who in many ways considered themselves lost in the woods.

---

17. Consider this assessment in the *New York Times* a week after Trump's victory: "It is the stunning paradox of American politics. In a bitterly divided nation, where Tuesday's vote once again showed a country almost evenly split between Democrats and Republicans, one party now dominates almost everything in American governance. With Donald J. Trump's win, Republicans will soon control the White House, both chambers of Congress, the tilt of the Supreme Court, more state legislative chambers than [at] any time in history, and more governor's offices than they have held in nearly a century." (Julie Bosman and Monica Davey, "U.S. Divided, but G.O.P. Dominates," *New York Times*, November 12, 2016, A9.)

CHAPTER 21

Objects in Mirror Are Tinier
Than They Appear

Since emerging from the wilderness of the 1970s, the American male has endured his share of growing pains—the acting out, the boorish backlash, the protracted adolescence. But no matter how wayward he has seemed over the past few decades, no matter how voluminous his disorders, he has managed to *evolve*, not devolve.

American men have become better fathers through more active engagement in childrearing. They have been forced to confront the dire consequences of domestic violence. They have become more conscious of sexual discrimination and harassment as a result of a social awakening and a slate of progressive laws. Their attitudes have been recalibrated by empowered women (who've been transforming society and their place in it) and by exemplary male peers. The "sensitive '90s guy," which quickly calcified into a type, was beginning to gain traction as he tried to get a grip.

Historically, American society has asked men to honor a set of principles for upholding the common good. Among them were loyalty and sacrifice, courage and team spirit, hard work and fair play. But the mass of men, especially in the '90s and onward, embraced an expanded set of values that also incorporated concern and sympathy, identification and understanding, justice and love. As a result they became more grounded individuals, more empathetic souls.

Whatever the case, the net effect has been an American male who is better connected to himself, to his fellow men, to women, to his children, coworkers, and community—to what matters in life and in the world at large. But the path has been a sometimes tortured one. And for much of the decade, many men felt that they were being run off the road.

At first it was adopted gingerly, miserly. On greeting or departing, straight men would often lean in, wrap arms around each other, and...hug.

Starting around the mid-'90s, there was a split second of apprehension that hung above the hug. The social hiccup sprang from two questions: *Do both of us feel comfortable expressing camaraderie so physically? And does the hug imply a transition to a new level of trust?*

After a time, that hesitancy dropped away. The gesture became second nature among acquaintances who were becoming friends. For many American males it was part of a new-macho repertoire, as routine as the handshake or the high five. Men, it turned out, needed a hug—from other men.

It wasn't until 1998 that I processed how widely accepted the male embrace was becoming—after I heard a story from a longtime family friend, Scott Turow, the novelist and lawyer. Turow described how he'd recently spent a sociable evening in the company of a new acquaintance, Steve Javie, a pro basketball referee known for his no-nonsense style on court. "We'd just met for the second time, had dinner, shaken hands, and said good-bye," Turow recounted. "But that was not enough." A moment later, he recalled, the hulking figure, in a dark parking lot, "stooped far to reach me [because] a hug was required to establish that we had crossed the borderland to sincere friendship."

The man hug. Turow and I had each shared in the double clutch ourselves, with schoolmates and family members, or witnessed it among open and expressive associates. Our gay or bi relatives and friends had led the way, as did the actors, fashionistas, and artists we knew, many comfortable with the demonstrative squeeze. The man hug, often accompanied by a special grip or handshake, had also become de rigueur in team sports, where athletes took to grabbing and patting in the heat of the game. Turow and I, as Chicago Bulls fans, remarked on the classic 1997 NBA Finals game in which superstar Michael Jordan, battling the flu and a hundred-plus-degree fever, scored 38 points and then fell into the arms of his main man, Scottie Pippen, who escorted him off the court in a tender B-ball tango.[1]

---

1. Sports sleuths have tried to attribute Jordan's symptoms in the famous "Flu Game" to food poisoning or, as has been proposed, a wicked hangover. But journalists' accounts—and video footage—suggest he was, in fact, fighting the flu. (Emmanuel Godina, "MJ's 'Flu Game,'" NBALead. com, June 7, 2016; Jesse Dorsey, "Jalen Rose Reportedly Claims Michael Jordan's 'Flu Game' Was a Hangover Game," BleacherReport.com, February 5, 2013; Rick Weinberg, "Jordan Battles Flu, Makes Jazz Sick," ESPN.com, June 23, 2004.)

But what was it that had set off this flurry of Arms and the Man? Turow agreed to write a column for *Vanity Fair* exploring just that.

He canvassed producer Norman Lear. The creator of *All in the Family*, the most popular prime-time sitcom of the 1970s attributed the ritual to the fact that as more individuals of diverse backgrounds climbed the social ladder, the establishment had begun to adopt their modes of displaying affection, which were sometimes more overt. Lear, according to Turow, believed that "male hugging was characteristic of many American immigrant communities—groups that generally abandoned the gesture as part of their Americanization but chose to perpetuate it in certain enclaves, such as Hollywood. There, it gradually grew into an almost rote greeting, manifest most notably on late-night talk shows, whose example many TV viewers freely emulate."

Turow also observed that in the '80s and '90s "young African-American males began to engage in a stylized hug as a form of personal greeting." And Margot Magowan, cofounder of the feminist Woodhull Institute, told Turow that she saw the loose, close hug (among both young men and women) as a sign of the more relaxed and casual styles of Generation X: "As Gen Xers become more economically dominant, they become more comfortable in using their private gestures in the workplace."

American men seemed less reserved in general—but also more needy. "Bill Clinton," Turow concluded, "seems to crave a hug from everybody."

There was a larger gravitational force, of course. Many men were realizing how distant they'd become from trustworthy figures in their lives, from their partners, even from themselves. An embrace was a sort of welcome grounding, a shorthand for receiving warmth and showing affinity. With more fatherhood responsibilities, less free time, and fewer opportunities allotted for all-male activities at work, in the neighborhood, or at the club ("fraternal orders" were on the outs and new laws doomed many single-sex, members-only bastions), men at every age and stage in life were looking for rituals to promote male bonding: the tailgate; the weekly game of hoops or poker; the fishing trip; the guys' weekend of golf, cigars, and surf-and-turf. Two Bros Embracing was an outward expression of that bond.[2]

---

2. In the 1960s, anthropologist Lionel Tiger pointed out that this mind-set had its roots in prehistory. (The concept of "male bonding" is sometimes attributed to Tiger and his 1969 book *Men in Groups*.) Instinctively, male hunter-gatherers used to break off in insular bands that purposely kept women

Bud Light capitalized on the sentiment with a series of beer commercials. The debut spot featured a middle-aged guy on a fishing pier, choking back tears and telling his father, "I love you, man." The catchphrase had its meme moment in 1995.

It was during this same period that the word "bromance" came into favor, denoting a nonsexual friendship between males who shared a special devotion. "Apparently the term was coined in the late 1990s by Davie Carnie, editor of *Big Brother*, an American skateboarding magazine," according to journalist Tim Elliott, writing for the Australian paper *The Age*. "Bromance specifically described the relationship between skate-buddies who spent lots of time together and/or shared hotel rooms on road trips." (Of more recent coinage: the phrase "man crush," which scholars at the *Oxford English Dictionary*'s New York branch can trace to 1998.)

More important, guys were actually sitting around and talking out their problems—with a choice group of guys. And in between the barbs, the trash talk, and the guy talk, they began to share their anxieties, trade self-deprecating tales, admit a few faults. They allowed themselves to be, in a word, vulnerable.

————

The front door swings wide. His eyes are narrow. It is late morning and the Reverend Jesse Jackson, whom I appear to have awakened, greets me in a white T-shirt. He has heavy lids and graying temples. He ushers me in with a clipped "Good morning."

"How are you?" I ask.

"I'm the last to know."

Jackson parks me alone for a while in the parlor of his Washington, D.C., town house—a place he has maintained, so an aide later tells me, since his early days as a "shadow senator." I notice that this sitting room, the front hall, and the kitchen entryway are lovingly cluttered, as if by a woman's hand. There are doll collections in glass cases, quilts and throw pillows, ornate

———

at bay. "Men courted and chose other men as working and fighting partners, and as recreational companions," Tiger notes. Eons later, male cooperatives became institutionalized, as evidenced by "the extraordinary predominance of men in forms of public life ranging from church to army to sport to legislature to business to law enforcement. It also prospered in secret societies, mysterious social groups cutting across all sectors of social life." (Lionel Tiger, *The Decline of Males: The First Look at an Unexpected New World for Men and Women* [New York: St. Martin's Griffin, 1999], 244.)

lamps, and sashes with fringes. One wall is lined with African masks. There are flowering plants and Christmas decorations, smack in the middle of July.

We are here to discuss men's roles in the '90s. We are here, specifically, to explore Jackson's take on the Million Man March of 1995, that enormous ingathering of African American males to the nation's capital.

The march had been meant as a clarion call. The individual black man, in community with his peers and exhibiting unity and self-sufficiency, had vowed to redouble his personal commitments as a responsible father and partner, as a member of society, as a man of spiritual backbone. By standing with other men of color—indeed, hand in hand, as men did throughout the vast assembly—he sought to show the country and the world his strength in numbers and character. Organized by the Reverend Louis Farrakhan and his followers from the Nation of Islam, in consort with clergy and civil rights activists, the conclave appealed to members of all denominations, ages, and social classes. Among the participants: a thirty-four-year-old former law professor (and a soon-to-be legislator in the Illinois Senate) named Barack Hussein Obama.[3]

Reverend Jackson returns in a lavender open-collared shirt. I bring out a pocket-sized digital tape recorder and suggest it might make sense for him to hold it while we speak. He grabs it, and without a word, drops the device, *swoomph*, into his breast pocket, close to his heart and his vocal cords. It is clear who is in command of the conversation.

I characterize the Million Man March as a civil rights march, one that was politically motivated. He corrects me. "It was not really a political march," he says. "It was a gathering. Farrakhan's basic theme, contrary to the image of it, was a conservative one. Atonement. Self-analysis. Being a better, stronger person. Politically, it was not a very public-policy-oriented march.... We marched on personal issues.... Private, flesh-and-blood issues."

What distinguished it from Martin Luther King's 1963 March on Washington, he elaborates, was that the former protest "was a march for public accommodations, workers' rights, and the right to vote—and a very

---

3. The march's legacy will always be tainted by the racist and anti-Semitic pronouncements, and politics of exclusion, espoused by Farrakhan. But in the African American community, Farrakhan the man was beside the point. "The discussion of Farrakhan is a side issue for us," political scientist Ronald Walters remarked at the time. "For most blacks, this is about pain." (Charles M. Blow, "The Million Man March, 20 Years On," *New York Times*, October 12, 2015.)

integrated march because [of that]. The march of '95 had to do with ethnic pride and solidarity.... We were saying that the gains that we had made were being eroded. EOC [equality opportunity] contract compliance. Affirmative action. Issues of equality. We were *free*, but not equal.

"Among other things, we experienced this extreme alienation because of the impact in '94 of [House Speaker Newt] Gingrich. All the gains that we'd made were being rolled back.... The same week of the Million Man March, Gingrich [and the House of Representatives] passed two or three pieces of utterly right-wing legislation—and there was no response to it, there was no preparation for it."

What Jackson remembers best was the sheer size of the crowd (estimates ranged from four hundred thousand to just under a million), adding that "the *idea* of blacks coming together, displaying the strength of our numbers, was an exciting idea." But the event had another takeaway. Many attendees, he says, returned home with a new perspective. They understood that no man could get his due unless he could *see* the benefits just beyond his grasp and until he had the *means* to do so. The march had been a way to publicly assert the dignity and consequence of those assembled, while acknowledging that many individual setbacks were not self-inflicted but often imposed by society and by policy.

"Dr. King's marches changed our legal options—and our behavior options," Jackson insists. "If you're going to, in fact, get on the bus, attitudinally you may think, 'I don't have the right to sit there.' [But] because the law changed—'You can't *make* me move'—it affects your behavior. When the cookie cutter changes, the shape of the cookie changes. So, legally, we changed the cookie cutter with the '64 Civil Rights Acts. [By 1995,] I am convinced that many men assumed our problem was personal when it was structural."

Many men, he says, thought that *they themselves* had brought on many of their larger social ills—"plants closing, jobs leaving, drugs and guns coming"—when in fact trade policies, for example, had pushed untold thousands of jobs overseas. And in houses of worship—"you had the megachurches exploding during that period," Jackson recalls[4]—men were being

---

4. "By some estimates," according to historian Steve Gillon in his book *Boomer Nation*, "over 100 megachurches were springing up every year by the 1990s...'Baby Boomers think of churches like they think of supermarkets,' noted a church marketing consultant. 'They want options, choices, and convenience. Imagine if Safeway was only open one hour a week, had only one product, and didn't explain it in English." (Steve Gillon, *Boomer Nation: The Largest and Richest Generation Ever and How It Changed America* [New York: Simon & Schuster/Free Press, 2004], 111–12.)

asked to face their problems squarely, "to look at yourself in the mirror [but] the mirror is limited to self-analysis."

Even though Jackson says these words in his home and not in a house of worship, he speaks with the reassuring certainty of a cleric. "I often say, if you have a size-ten foot and a size-eight shoe, you can be a good person, you can be drunk or sober—you've got a corn coming your way on your toe. Because of the *structure* of things. That's why Paul [Ephesians 6:12] said, 'This issue is not about flesh and blood. It's about powers and principalities, and wickedness in high places.' And [those who blame themselves alone] cannot get beyond flesh-and-blood private behavior. You can have all kinds of high morals. But until the Thirteenth Amendment, you couldn't walk off that plantation. You were a good person, an intelligent person, a strong person—but the cookie cutter hadn't changed.

"Change the structure...and out of that comes freedom of expression. You have the right, now, to dance in the end zone. You have the right to express yourself."

The notion that men in the 1990s were feeling besieged, regardless of their race, class, belief system, or sexual orientation, is hardly an unfamiliar one to introduce all these years later. Men, individually and collectively, were often lost in the woods. But it stands repeating that after the women's movement had erupted in the '70s and shook up the social, legal, and political landscape, all manner of American men were merely trying to find their footing on a rocky path. Many were facing the personal turmoil that Jesse Jackson describes. And while men of color were gathering in Washington, large groups were also filing into stadiums in Boulder and Anaheim and Jacksonville.

I telephone Bill McCartney, who had helped turn his University of Colorado Buffaloes into the nation's top-ranked college football team (a distinction Colorado shared in 1990 with Georgia Tech). That same year, McCartney—who had followed a calling to spread God's Word—had founded Promise Keepers, which encouraged Christian men to reclaim responsibility for their lives. It would become one of the most influential outreach organizations in the larger sphere of the men's movement.

Men were asked to make "Seven Promises": from honoring Jesus Christ, to "practicing spiritual, moral, ethical, and sexual purity," to "building strong marriages and families through love, protection, and Biblical values." Participants at

McCartney's conclaves were also urged to adopt this crucial precept: "A Promise Keeper is committed to pursuing vital relationships with a few other men, understanding that he needs brothers to help him keep his promises." Men needed support, and who better than a small circle of similarly minded men?

What, in fact, had motivated McCartney? "I'm a football coach and I'm a guy spending a lot of time with men—young men," he answers, describing that first core group of seventy-two men who convened in 1990. "A real man, a man's man—he's a godly man. What the culture defines as a man is not a real man. A real man is tenderhearted. He's loved by the Spirit. So what Promise Keepers was about was bringing guys together."

In 1991, at Promise Keepers' first large assembly, held at a Boulder basketball arena, forty-two hundred men showed up. McCartney lit a candle that would be passed from hand to hand among every male in attendance. The next year's rally pulled in twenty-two thousand at Boulder's Folsom Field. "These great preachers started coming," says McCartney (who calls himself a "reacher, not a preacher"). "When they would preach, I would be sitting in the front row and I would be weeping, because I was under conviction. The Lord didn't use me to start Promise Keepers because I 'had my act together.' I was a classic example of a type-A guy that needed to get more balance in his life." Come the summer of 1996, McCartney's call to worship and commitment had filled twenty-two stadiums across the nation—on a single Sunday.[5] "When we would meet," he recalls, "women would gather at the gates of the stadiums and they would protest because they thought that we were deemphasizing them, when in fact we were telling these guys, 'A real man lays down his life for his wife. He serves his wife. He dates his daughters—he takes her out and treats her like a real man treats a woman, and he shows her what to look for in a real man.'"

Today, McCartney, in his seventies, is under no illusions that he has altered the life of every man who attended those gatherings or workshops, or who bought Promise Keepers books or audiotapes. That was never his intention. Figuratively, he was merely trying to get the best out of the players on the field.

5. On hand at that very first Promise Keepers conclave was Dr. Jack Hayford, who addressed the crowd. An early leader of the megachurch movement (the founding pastor of the Church on the Way, in Van Nuys, California), he tells me, "It was a stunning sight. These things that were happening are not like anything in [the] history of our country, where men came together for such purposes in such size groups. There's been men crusades, [but] this was unprecedented." (Interview with Hayford.)

"Back then in the '90s," he continues, "the churches were predominantly being filled with women. There would be men in church, but it was the women that were singing the loudest and who were filling the pews. So this became the rage. For a pastor, it was a way to rally the men. It was a way to challenge the men. In many churches, men's groups surfaced.... It was a bonanza. It became acceptable to get into one of these stadiums and attend something like that. The pastors in these churches would rent buses and airplanes.... In 1997, we had 1.4 million men in Washington, D.C. [on the National Mall]"—news accounts estimated the crowd to be half that size. "We all got down on our knees and our faces, and cried out to God. As I look back on that, on the whole Promise Keepers time frame, [I realize that] there is something in the heart of men that longs to be right with God." Being with other men was energizing, surely, but the drive, McCartney is convinced, came from men's need to feed a deeper, spiritual hunger.

And yet, he says, "the reality of it is: most of [the men] have fallen off the wayside." Quoting Matthew 13:3–9, McCartney describes a farmer planting seeds, some of which take root, but most of which are scattered on the footpath or the rocky soil. He discusses committed Christians the way the disciples discussed those seedlings: "The last group, the good soil—thirty-, sixty-, a hundredfold—they hear and obey the Word of God and the power of the Holy Spirit. They wholeheartedly embrace the truth of Gospel. See, we had over six million men attend our events. But in my opinion, after all this time—as the Lord has kept me up and about and traveling and everything—just a percentage of those guys have a good soil."

However grateful he is for that renewal of faith among the Promise Keepers, McCartney knows that that first flush has long since dimmed. "If you don't take anything away from this conversation, [let it be nothing] other than this: *That* was a season that came and gone. It didn't *sustain*. It didn't take hold. The only ones it took hold with were the ones that stayed in the Word. The rest of them got picked off.... The stark raving reality is they're getting picked off.

"If you're not in the Word every day, you're in the *world*, [and] if you're not in the Word every day, the world has got a piece of you."

———

What made the '90s male a different breed? Some context might help.

The modern American man had been trying to find his bearings since he'd come back from the battlefronts of World War II. In 1950, sociologist

David Riesman saw the social animal of the Eisenhower era as largely con-formist, a member of a "lonely crowd." His colleague C. Wright Mills in 1951 wrote of society's "New Little Men," the white-collar slaves of bureaucracy who resembled "political eunuchs." Ralph Ellison in 1952 had labeled the African American male *The Invisible Man*. Britain's 1950s brood of writers who spoke for the disaffected working class became known as the "Angry Young Men." Sloan Wilson in 1955 designated the disillusioned business-man as *The Man in the Gray Flannel Suit*. William H. Whyte in 1956 called the work-world masses *The Organization Man*. In the 1960s, James Baldwin wrote of a "New Lost Generation," referring to many alienated Americans, some of whom would seek acceptance as expats after the war. Herbert Mar-cuse described the *One-Dimensional Man* as being oppressed by the forces of technologized society. And authority itself was given a two-word indictment: The Man. Long before the men's movement, then, many saw the established social hierarchy as a suppressive, dehumanizing, and emasculating system that needed to be overhauled or at least taken down a couple of Oedipal notches.

The '60s, as discussed elsewhere in these pages, saw the flowering of the civil rights movement, individual empowerment, the counterculture, and popular culture, even as it rewrote the dynamics of sex and power, sex and commitment, sex and procreation. By the 1970s, the feminist movement was helping to secure long-sought legal guarantees for American women. Most auspiciously, the Equal Rights Amendment established, once and for all, the constitutional promise that equal treatment under the law, for any woman, could never be rescinded or whittled away because of her sex.

In ways large and small, the New Woman was gaining the high ground. She asserted newfound sexual freedom. She discovered new avenues for cultural expression and social acceptance. She was more often a healer and consensus-forger, more community- and family-oriented than her male counterpart. She also had the means to control pregnancy: she could bear children through new fertilization procedures, none of which required a consenting male.

From a purely psychosocial point of view, then, many men were wonder-ing: who exactly wears the loincloth in this family? "Our species seems to be leaping back in time to the more basic mammalian system that was the core of our evolutionary history," anthropologist Lionel Tiger would note in his '90s treatise *The Decline of Males*. "More and more we appear to resemble the other primate species whose communities are focused on *females and their young*, with males scuffling for reproductive access to females and a place in the political sun." In 1991, Camille Paglia would pose an even more emasculating proposition, noting that young men had only a "brief season of exhilarating liberty between control by their mothers and control by their wives. The agon [struggle] of male identity springs from men's humiliating sense of dependence upon women. It is women who control the emotional and sexual realms, and men know it."

To top it off, women were encroaching on—and in some professions dominating—the workplace. From the 1970s onward, women entered the job market in droves. And by the '90s nearly half of all working Americans were female, a fact that seemed to validate the job-displacement fears that many men had voiced in the early days of "women's lib."[6]

Many men, of course, got the blowback. Many began to feel like social collateral. Many saw their jobs evaporate or their parenting responsibilities made

---

6. Small wonder, then, that as the country's financial straits became more uncertain in the twenty-first century and industrial-sector businesses continued their decline, the "Make America Great Again" message would appeal to disaffected males. The morning after Donald Trump was elected president in 2016, *New York Times* columnist Nicholas Kristof would frame it this way: "Trump was absolutely right that the economic system is broken for ordinary Americans, especially working-class men. Since 1979, real hourly wages for men have essentially been unchanged for the bottom half of Americans by income." ("Unfortunately," Kristof would go on, "Trump's proposed policies would exacerbate the inequity that he campaigned on.")

The trend would not abate. Hanna Rosin identified the "alpha female" and would state in an *Atlantic* article called "The End of Men" (which she would expand into an influential book) that by the 2010s "for the first time in American history, the balance of the workforce tipped toward women, who now hold a majority of the nation's jobs. The working class, which has long defined our notions of masculinity, is slowly turning into a matriarchy, with men increasingly absent from the home and women making all the decisions. Women dominate today's colleges and professional schools—for every two men who receive a B.A. this year, three women will do the same." Indeed, if one contrasts current male wages with those at the beginning of the women's movement—according to David Brooks, citing figures presented by Michael Greenstone and Adam Looney of the Hamilton Project—"median incomes of men have dropped 28 percent and male labor force participation rates are down 16 percent." That said, the gender salary lag would persist. Some fifteen years into the new millennium, American women, writes *New York Times* personal finance reporter Tara Siegel Bernard, would "continue to make less than men for the same work." (Nicholas Kristof, "Gritting Our Teeth and Giving President Trump a Chance," *New York Times*, November 9, 2016; Hanna Rosin, "The End of Men: How Women Are Taking Control—of Everything," *Atlantic*, July–August 2010, 12, 60; David Brooks, "Free-Market Socialism," *New York Times*, January 24, 2012, A27; Tara Siegel Bernard, "Vigilant Eye on Gender Pay Gap," *New York Times*, November 15, 2014, B1.)

more murky or demanding (even if their lives were, in countless cases, *more rewarding*). A caveat here. Many men welcomed women's progress and, in their own households, a second revenue stream. Many took the opportunity, the "flex time," and the convenience of new technologies (PCs, fax machines, cell phones) to become work-at-home or full-time dads. Yet males in growing numbers felt their manly duties challenged, their traditional roles upended.

Many believed that it wasn't society that was shifting. It was *them*. Some became morose, despondent. The most damaged among them felt unworthy and burdensome. Many took refuge in a state of suspended adolescence.[7] Many turned inward, turned desperate, turned violent. Many feared they were broken beyond repair.

Displays of male rage, often of a criminal nature, were becoming all too common. Incidents of domestic violence and spousal or partner abuse rose to epidemic levels. And increasingly, men of otherwise upstanding repute in their professions and their communities were out there jostling the crockery. Courts were ordering "anger management" classes in domestic disputes. Counselors were recommending cognitive therapy programs.

Steven Gillon, who has studied the Baby Boom extensively, has discussed how the "Angry White Male" became a trope. "By the 1990s," he contends, "Boomer men, especially white heterosexual men, found themselves under assault from assertive women, gay men who openly mocked traditional notions of masculinity, and African Americans who benefited from affirmative action policies that threatened their dominance in the workplace." African American men, of course, did not comprise the nation's only marginalized community. Nor had Caucasian Dude cornered the market on anger, as Jesse Jackson herein has made abundantly clear.

Lucia Brawley, an activist, communications strategist, and woman of mixed heritage, makes the point that the societal pressures contributing to black male anger in the '90s were for the most part qualitatively different than the forces affecting most white men. "Shared parenting roles, constrictive notions of masculinity, and the emerging role of women in the work-

---

7. Millions of men were retreating into their shell and lashing out *virtually*. At the core of a new generation of video games—especially "first-person shooter" games—were remote-control massacres that would trigger what experts began to call a "lower empathy" threshold, a generational desensitization to the real-world carnage wrought by guns, bombs, and laser-guided armaments. These were worlds away from the pokey video arcade games of the 1970s.

place took a similar toll on men, across racial lines. But anger among men of color in general was often a result of oppression, while white anger often emerged from losing a modicum of privilege in a persistently oppressive hierarchy. It's not to say that white men didn't have valid reasons for their rage and outrage, but to compare the two is to set up a false equivalency. Think Michael Douglas in *Falling Down*, from 1993, versus John Singleton's *Boyz n the Hood*, from 1991. Douglas's marginalized California defense-industry worker is violent because he's losing his favored place in society. Singleton's marginalized characters from South Central L.A. are violent because they are the scapegoats of a society they perceive to be set up to keep them down."

There was also the anger of *young* Americans, male and female, who resented being sidelined by material culture, outmoded values, and stereotypes that were based on race, faith, gender, class, or social affiliation. The grunge icon of '90s youth, Kurt Cobain, Nirvana's frontman, was a figure whose beliefs synced up with many of those in his generation. Cobain was angsty and intense and defiantly *un*committed. He felt angry—about his sense of alienation and about his confusion when confronting the human condition. He was withdrawn and often suicidal. (He would take his own life in 1994.) Cobain rejected social artifice, conformity, and "commercial shit," as he put it, contrasting Nirvana's ethos with that of Pearl Jam, a band he slighted (unfairly, many said) as being part of the "corporate, alternative and cock-rock fusion" machine. And he tended to dispense with standard sex roles altogether. "I definitely have a problem with the average macho man— the strong-oxen, working-class type," he told Michael Azerrad in *Rolling Stone*, "because they have always been a threat to me. [I've been] taunted and beaten up by them…I definitely feel closer to the feminine side of the human being than I do the male—or the American idea of what a male is supposed to be.'"[8]

---

8. In a 1999 article for the *New York Observer*, George Gurley asked readers, "What's Your Gay Quotient?" as a way of addressing men's identity along the decade's more flexible gay-bi-straight spectrum. "Let us look upon our own [age]," observed Gurley, referencing Henry James, "and declare it the Ambiguous Age. Even the greatest, most solid American historical personage of all, Abraham Lincoln, the rail-splitter himself, is entering the terrain of sexual uncertainty [as] two upcoming biographies…argue that Lincoln had a homosexual bond with his dear Illinois friend, Joshua Speed." (George Gurley, "…What's Your Gay Quotient?" *New York Observer*, June 28, 1999.)

Modern man first got his back up in 1970, writer Nick Tosches has noted, with the kickoff of Men's Liberation, Inc. At a conference in New York City, this small contingent expressed the desire to escape the strain of "having to prove our masculinity 24 hours a day." If the name—Men's Liberation—reeked of irony, it was hardly lost on members of the nascent women's movement. Just as feminists felt the need to make a radical break with society's male power structure, Men's Libbers were arguing that society had unfairly victimized *men* too, who deserved to be emancipated from the bonds imposed upon them by the state, their employers, and centuries of rigid patriarchy.

Males joined forces. *Farewell*, fraternal orders. Hel-*lo*, men's support groups.

Several organizations took their cues from "fathers' rights" associations (first formed in the '60s): small bands of legal advocates in Maryland, California, and the Midwest that were trying to counsel men caught in the middle of divorce trials and who felt mired in a court system that greatly favored wives over husbands. Some coalitions cribbed directly from feminists; others from evangelical outreach, civil rights groups, the Stonewall-energized gay rights movement, and twelve-step programs. Still others accused the women's movement of applying a sort of female affirmative action to the gender equation. Many were defiantly antifeminist.

At the time, according to sociologist Michael A. Messner in his book *Politics of Masculinities*, "Men's liberation was especially focused on the ways in which socialization oriented boys and men toward competition and public success, while stunting their emotional and relational capacities. Thus, [one of the movement's] major attraction[s] was the permission it gave to men to expand their definitions of manhood to include the emotional expression, 'It's okay to cry.'"

Soon, the '80s and '90s guy was finding drums to pound and sweat lodges in which to *shvitz* out rivulets of shame. He was diving down to meet his deeper self, asleep in the mangroves. "All across the country in the first few years of the 1990s," Michael Kimmel would write in his groundbreaking 1996 book *Manhood in America*, "men have been in full-scale retreat, heading off to the woods to rediscover their wild, hairy, deep manhood.... [Many men have felt the] need to be rescued from the clutches of overprotective mothers, absent fathers, and an enervating workplace and need to rediscover themselves through a manly quest against a pitiless environment."[9]

Initially the men's empowerment wave had predominantly been the province of white, straight, and rather irate guys, who were generally well-off or middle-class.[10] But it blew up by the late '80s across class and ethnicity. Come the early '90s many bookstores kept a well-stocked larder of men's self-help volumes. Newt Gingrich would tell the *Washington Post* that for a stretch in 1988 he found himself crying about three or four times a week. "I spent a fair length of time trying to come to grips with who I was and the habits I had," he disclosed. "I read *Men Who Hate Women and the Women Who Love Them* and I found frightening pieces that related to . . . my own life."

Men's handbooks and manifestos were rife. Sam Keen's *Fire in the Belly* offered "an alternate vision of virtue and virility." In *Against the Wall*, Marshall Hardy and John Hough outlined "men's reality in a co-dependent culture." Aaron Kipnis synthesized the different strands of the "masculine soul" in *Knights Without Armor*. There was *Cool Pose* (about "the dilemmas of black manhood") as well as *Manhood in the Making*, *What Men Really Want*, *Naked at the Gender Gap*, and *The Prince and the King: Healing the Father-Son Wound*. Even the well-regarded memoir of Howell Raines (later the executive editor of the *New York Times*) bore the prescriptive title *Fly Fishing Through the Midlife Crisis*. Men were evidently in crisis while casting for smallmouth bass in pristine Ontario.

"Daddy, daddy, daddy. Wounds, wounds, wounds," Nick Tosches opined—in *Penthouse*, in 1992. "From John Lee, a founder of the Austin Men's Center, came *The Flying Boy: Healing the Wounded Man*"—which, in Tosches's view, at least, espoused that "nothing short of spiritual patricide

---

9. Kimmel would go on to set up SUNY Stony Brook's Center for the Study of Men and Masculinities.

10. In time, the "angry white male" would become a sanctimonious construct steeped in its own liberal bias. After Trump won the presidency, humanities professor Mark Lilla would lay out the so-called "whitelash theory": a perceived white backlash to the growing clout of women and minorities. "The media's newfound, almost anthropological, interest in the angry white male," in Lilla's view, "reveals as much about the state of our liberalism as it does about this much maligned, and previously ignored, figure." Many liberals, according to Lilla, believed that Trump had succeeded by "transform[ing] economic disadvantage into racial rage." But they were deluding themselves. This sort of thinking "sanctions a conviction of moral superiority and allows liberals to ignore what those voters said were their overriding concerns. It also encourages the fantasy that the Republican right is doomed to demographic extinction in the long run." (Mark Lilla, "The End of Identity Liberalism," *New York Times*, November 20, 2016, SR6.)

would do. 'Each man,' wrote Lee, 'must find the manner that suits him to kill off the father who lives in his muscles, brain, soul, and dreams.' "[11]

One book that dogged the bestseller lists week after week was *Men Are from Mars, Women Are from Venus*. The guide, by psychotherapist John Gray, counseled the sexes on how to better interact by appreciating their elemental differences. "Martians tend to pull away and silently think about what's bothering them," read one rule of thumb. "Venusians feel an instinctive need to talk." Gray's postulates on Mars and Venus were clearly intended for mass-market Earthlings.

Finally, there was the intellectual granddaddy of them all: *Iron John: A Book About Men*. Written by Robert Bly, the poet, lecturer, and men's movement guru, *Iron John* generated its own force field, clinging for sixty-two weeks to the *New York Times* list. Many men *lived* by the book. They tapped into their subterranean Wild Man by divining wisdom from Bly's parable about a hirsute Yoda who mentors a boy. The youngster, after swiping a magical "key" from Mother, goes to the forest and springs the Wild Man from his cage. Not the worst idea, actually.

"The Wild Man encourages and amounts to a trust in what is below," Bly states, "the lower half of our body, our genitals, our legs and ankles, our inadequacies...the animal ancestors, the earth itself [and] the dead long buried there." Bly is not explaining the noble savage, the contemporary Caliban. Instead, he is talking about a man who has reached out to a father figure, found and bound his own psychic wounds, and mingled with other men, ultimately to have been initiated into a "second birth." (Being wounded, Bly notes, has been interpreted as akin to receiving a male vulva.) Bly is talking about a man who has made a separate peace with his instinctual self and at middle age has become more spiritual, even mystical, a man attuned to the dark, wet forest of the soul.

In his writings and workshops, Bly preached the profound power of myth. Since humans first rubbed two words together, compelling narratives have provided guidelines for heroic behavior, the framework for the dreams we dream collectively. Bly's stories of hunters and kings and men in bogs have roots in tribal and Bible tales, in Homer and Sophocles, in the Brothers Grimm and *Star Wars*. The main fable of *Iron John* was meant to instruct what Bly calls "father-hungry" men, whether gay, bi, straight, or undeclared. The story, Bly

---

11. Alfred Gingold would lampoon these epistles in his 1991 book *Fire in the John*, intended as a manly twelve-step manual for the "mid-life soft male." (Alfred Gingold, *Fire in the John: The Manly Man in the Age of Sissification* [New York: St. Martin's/Cader, 1991], 67, 119–21.)

notes, "could be ten or twenty thousand years old." And yet he wrote the book directly for his audience—for '90s men who were searching, often with low self-esteem, to find a connection with men who might have lessons to impart.

In Bly's telling, men had been softening since the end of agrarian times. With the coming of the factory, the machine, the skyscraper, the office park, and the sprawling bureaucracies of modern industry and government, they had had to leave their homes in order to labor. As a result, their daughters and sons had been cheated out of the chance to witness the workaday activities of their most direct and trustworthy role models.

Boomers, especially, were at a disadvantage. Come the 1960s, Bly posits, "men have been asked to learn how to go with the flow, how to follow rather than lead...how to be vulnerable." In American households, Bly says, many women began to telegraph the message that it is *mothers* who place more value on "feeling and relationships" than fathers do, and therefore mothers sustain more reliable emotional bonds with their kids. "Whereas the father," insists Bly, "stands for and embodies what is stiff, maybe brutal, what is unfeeling, obsessed, rationalistic: money-mad, uncompassionate. 'Your father can't help it.' So the son often grows up with a wounded image of his father."

Much of this assessment might seem alarmist. But Bly backs it up by examining the men in his seminars and retreats,[12] many of whom had been dealing with the sobering issues tearing at the family and social fabric: economic strain, office stress, divorce, domestic violence, and sexual abuse, along with what Bly calls "the workaholism of fathers, their alcoholism, wife-beating, and abandonment." As the 1990s commenced, Bly predicted, "We can expect [modern man's] demons of suspicion to cause more and more damage to men's vision of what a man is, or what the masculine is. Between twenty and thirty percent of American boys now live in a house with no father present, and the demons there have full permission to rage...."

"Making contact with this Wild Man [inside of us] is the step the Eighties male or the Nineties male has yet to make," wrote Bly. And in that tangled forest the truly evolved creature was the man who, in plumbing his depths, also

---

12. "When I taught *Iron John* at Berkeley in the 1990s," recalls Michael Kimmel, "the young male students didn't get it at all. They saw masculinity as 'aspirational' and anticipatory, whereas Bly was nostalgic about what was lost....At the Bly events I went to it was the *older* men who were weeping and the younger men were always looking around puzzled." (Correspondence with Kimmel.)

recognized his proper limits and his manly potential. He was a man, in short, "open to new visions of what a man could be." Where there was open-mindedness, there was promise—the promise of renewal, vitality, and strength.

———

I admit it. In my efforts to come to grips with my Deeper Male, I've never marched or assembled or broken a sweat in a sweat lodge. But in the interest of full disclosure I should point out that I have made my own modest contribution to the subspecies of the put-upon American man.

In 1988, my wife and I became the parents of boy-and-girl twins. With their jubilant arrival came several years of sleep deprivation and tag-team childrearing. (We both held down full-time jobs in New York publishing—my wife in children's books, myself in magazines.) We were shocked at first by our sudden, irreversible domesticity. How could we party all night, we wondered, when there were *two* of them, count 'em, partying at daybreak? We had new and cryptic parental responsibilities. We had financial pressures. We would eventually have the weekly trials of the kids' soccer games and dance recitals, experienced through a three-aspirin hangover. The finishing touch was the need to schedule or steal every act of shared intimacy, a.k.a. Saturday morning.

One morning, when a man in our neighborhood, *also* a father of twins, was said to have been taken away by paramedics—in a straitjacket—I could heartily identify. I was beginning to feel my life shrink-wrap around me. On some nights, I'd burst from the membrane of a dream, gasping for breath. I needed a release. To this day, I have no idea what set me off.

One night in 1990, I couldn't take it any longer. I felt compelled—propelled, actually, with an almost blinding clarity—to smash my fist into the dining room wall of our New York City apartment. Three or four times. I remember all of my attention focused on that fist and on that wall, the rest of the world having gone white and silent.

Luckily, the wall, and not my hand, registered the crack.

Some time passed. Until one night I did the same, at our new house in suburban Westchester. This time, angered by what I viewed as my wife's laissez-faire attitude toward our daughter's behavior, I chose to pound the less forgiving doorjamb of the upstairs bathroom. More than a few times. For good measure, I also opened and slammed the door four or five slams, back and forth on its sorry hinges, whacking it against an abutting chest of drawers, until I was satisfied that I'd splintered the blasted door and vented sufficient steam. A couple of my knuckles took the brunt and I iced them. I considered an X-ray, then thought better of it. My reasoning: better to let the ache nestle into the old bones. My hand, in time, healed.

Twice I'd come to the edge. Twice I'd reached a breaking point. My kids were uncontrollable. My life and world were too. My warped logic, in hind-sight, was that I felt hedged in by circumstance and by my loving, if frustrat-ing, family. And instead of purging myself by directly hurting my person or my cherished loved ones, I would strike out at a convenient signifier of the intractable world, knowing, masochistically, that the wall would impart a louder message: it's *your* fault, you clod.

Coiled within my anger, of course, I had a secret wish: perhaps my wife and kids would now see how damaged I was inside. And maybe, some-how, they'd empathize or, at the very least, pity me for punishing myself so. "Something there is," wrote Robert Frost one hundred years ago, "that doesn't love a wall." He had a point. But my pummeling the wall (or, more accurately, pummeling my clenched fist) had a point too: something there is that doesn't love me.

In August 1992, I read an "About Men" column in the *New York Times Magazine.* In it, the writer recounted a recent trip to the emergency room after *he'd* punched a wall, breaking his fifth metacarpal. "On the way to the hospi-tal, gloriously revved on adrenaline," he wrote, "I thought I must have done something terribly original. It turned out I hadn't—practically every man in my circle of friends had done the same thing. One shattered his hand against a concrete block after missing a shot in a volleyball game; another brutalized a bathroom door for 15 minutes until his knuckles were blue."

The essayist—described as a Boston-based freelance journalist—suffered a fracture. His first doctor straightened it some twenty degrees. Once the cast came off, a second doctor recommended surgery, remarking, "In my experi-ence, the wall always wins."

The writer offered his own diagnosis. Unlike women, whom soci-ety granted what he called socially acceptable "spillways" for their extreme anxiety—"they cry, they break dishes (or at least my girlfriend does), they yell and then they feel a lot better"—the most macho of men have been con-ditioned to buck up and hold it all in. "Exploding is risky around someone

you love," he reasoned, "so I hurt myself. It's the one way a man has of showing anger without harming someone or appearing weak. It communicates
clearly that things must change.... Remember that the point of all this isn't
property damage or injury, it's to show the other person how upset you are."
Yes, and to proclaim to the stone-deaf world the torment of feeling so utterly
boxed in.

Five years later, my wife and I would be invited to a book party in an
apartment in TriBeCa. The guest of honor was a first-time author we'd
never met, a ruggedly handsome young man who was represented by our
friend Stuart, his literary agent. The party was crowded and casual. The
guests streamed upward into a tiered, exposed-brick kitchen. Stuart had
explained that the book was a reconstruction of the events surrounding a
deadly Gloucester fishing-boat disaster during the infamous 1991 nor'easter.
Six crewmen had died in the shipwreck; a second man had perished when
a rescue helicopter went down in rough weather. The book was called *The
Perfect Storm*. I was intrigued by the title, but I was skeptical. How could a
self-respecting journalist, I wondered, actually craft a credible account of an
incident in which all the main characters were dead?

The author whose book we were celebrating was Sebastian Junger. And
he turned out to have been the essayist who'd written about smashing the
wall. (We would later become friends and colleagues.) His book, published
that week, was one of a rash of true adventure sagas by new young voices in
American nonfiction, writers who concentrated on the travails of men-at-risk.
Their works would become bestsellers in the 1990s: from Jon Krakauer's *Into
the Wild* (about death in the wilderness) and *Into Thin Air* (about death on
an Everest climb), to Mark Bowden's *Black Hawk Down* (about the ill-fated
1993 U.S. military rescue operation in war-torn Somalia).

Junger, Krakauer, and Bowden would be compared to the likes of
Conrad, Hemingway, and, at times, Jack London. Their works slaked a common thirst in their audience: the need to read about other men facing death
in dire situations; men dwarfed by destiny, the elements, and their sense of
their own limits; men who strive to prove their mettle through their need to
overcome these obstacles—despite the risks and, in many cases, compelled
by those risks.

Thinking back to that long-ago book party (and remembering the sprawling redbrick kitchen walls), I recall the good counsel Junger had offered at

the close of his column: "If you're going to punch a wall, here's a suggestion: Don't. It simply takes too long to recover. As a substitute, I recommend using sledgehammers, baseball bats, tire irons, anything unyielding brought down on things that break. It gets the same message across.... If you absolutely have to punch something... [at least] try to hit the wall square-on. That way the impact will be spread across all the knuckles.... If you're lucky you'll go through the wallboard and create a handsome testimony to your manhood."

———

If there was a five-alarm moment when American males realized that they might need to take a collective time-out, it came on February 8, 1994. On that day, actor Jack Nicholson was stopped at a red light in Studio City, California. He emerged from his car with a trusty two-iron, walked over to a Mercedes that he believed had cut him off in traffic, and took a few well-apportioned whacks at the driver's windshield. With that bashing, the country became instantly conversant with the terms "anger management" and "road rage."

Road rage had only recently entered the lexicon. According to Michael Fumento in an essay in the *Atlantic Monthly*, the phrase was "presumably based on [the term] 'roid rage," which denoted "sudden violent activity by people on steroids." The term crept into news stories throughout the mid-'90s. Federal highway records were reporting an "epidemic" of irate drivers, flare-ups in snarled traffic, and deliberately aggressive driving. (Police records at the time actually suggested a *decline* in such episodes. "There has always been a degree of aggression while driving," the analyst David Murray, director of research at Washington's Statistical Assessment Service, told Fumento. "Now that we have a name, we look for things that seem to be similar and build a pathology.")

If much of this built-up anger and spiritual drought sounds negative and unredeeming, that's partially the fault of this observer, recounting those whose opinions were offered *during* the '90s. The period's culture critics and sociologists and shrinks made their living from diagnosing woe. They Dopplered the decade by observing it so often that it had shifted a few Pantones, into Hypertension Red. Yours truly, in turn, may have taken on too much of their taint and tone. Which is to say: every male retreat or advance is not merely compensation for some deficiency.

Objects in the mirror may be much less damaged than they appear.

CHAPTER 22

Shadows on the Wall of the Man Cave

Many '90s men were exercising their unalienable right to artificial expansion. They popped Viagra like Tic Tacs. They slapped on Androderm—the first-ever T-patch—to help boost their flagging testosterone levels. They added enclosed porches and immense decks to their '80s McMansions. They pulled up to the fast-food drive-through windows (for their "supersized" meals) behind the wheels of vehicular monstrosities: SUVs, Jeeps, and all-terrain gas guzzlers.

The next logical step, of course, was the Hummer. A year after the 1991 Gulf War, the "civilian truck" rolled into showrooms. Marketed as a noncombat version of the military's Humvee, the wide-bodied, tank-tough, ominously boxy Hummer was the most muscular and martial presence on four American wheels.[1] It barreled down country lanes and literally threatened any passenger vehicle in its path. The Hummer had all the grace of a Panzer division. And its absurdly inefficient fuel economy was an abomination in an environmentally conscious era.

Men, for a variety of reasons, needed to feel enviriled. Postmodern man, Freud might have argued, was becoming obsessed not only with the smooth functioning of his phallus but with the heft and loft and status of his phallic *symbols*.

---

1. Actor (later California governor) Arnold Schwarzenegger helped persuade the manufacturer, AM General, to produce the civilian version after he'd encountered some Humvees driving along the road while he was shooting a movie. In October 1992, he would take possession of the first such vehicle to come off the assembly line. (Joe Mathews, "The Hummer and Schwarzenegger," *Washington Post*, February 28, 2010; *The 90's: The Last Great Decade?*, Nutopia and National Geographic Channel, July 2014.)

The Hummer said Huge. It said American and Ready-for-Combat. It said Me. But when that colossus pulled into country club parking lots—and valets and caddies began to extract the golf bags—they encountered a boy toy even more coveted than the Hummer. Big Bertha, the steelhead driver, was the ne plus ultra in performance enhancement. Every scratch golfer, every weekend duffer, every man jack who'd ever swung a club felt he *had* to have a Big B or a Big B knockoff.

Introduced by Callaway in 1991, the outsize driver had a head the size of a casaba melon. (Bertha, so the story goes, had borrowed its name from the old German howitzer.) A tee shot made with a Big Bertha, even if the golfer hadn't smacked it on the sweet spot, was suddenly monster-grade—and sometimes even accurate. Callaway could barely keep the clubs in stock. Within two years, the company's annual revenues hit $255 million, leapfrogging to the front of the sporting goods queue.

Obsessive-compulsive golfing equipment became standardized. More expensive shafts, made of graphite, appeared. New balls offered "extreme distance." Large golf-gear warehouses (forerunners to golf superstores) opened. And by 1995, Callaway came out with its Great Big Bertha, made of titanium and measuring 250ccs in volume, the size of a moderate breast implant. Bertha implied a siliconed partner, eighteen-hole arm candy.

Next came Cohibas and Montecristos. As larger cars and clubs were to roadways and fairways, *cigars* became the most predictable manifestation of men's need to overcompensate. From trucker to bond trader, guys became cigar snobs. Cigars were the new, nasty after-dinner mint. Cigar bars opened in major U.S. cities. Traffic in humidors rivaled traffic in Hummers.[2]

The cigar served different masters. To impress other men, the he-man needed his to go big-and-long. Others used the smoke itself to delineate their turf. For the whiny infantile, the old stogie supplanted the old nip. But the cigar's appeal, most of all, came down to the fact that men puffing in groups

---

2. Bill Clinton, Mr. Un-Inhale, often liked to faux-smoke his unlit stogie. Shortly after the Clintons took up residence at 1600 Pennsylvania Avenue, in fact, *Cigar Aficionado* magazine would report that while George and Barbara Bush had discouraged smoking on the premises, "Hillary Rodham Clinton took the next step and removed the ashtrays [and] specifically prohibit[ed] smoking in the White House." (Carl Sferrzza Anthony, "Our Presidents and Cigars," *Cigar Aficionado*, Autumn 1993.)

almost invariably turned off the womenfolk, assuring some unbreachable guy time.

A patron of the Grand Havana Room in Beverly Hills told writer Kim Masters, for a 1996 *Vanity Fair* story on that year's turmoil in the film industry, "Cigars are the drug of the 90s." As Masters put it, "Cigars represent security and sharkdom, lascivious abandon and moderation, oral gratification...and the kind of past when it was the boss—not the kid agent, not the $20 million schmuck with his name above the title—who called the shots."

––––––––

Since humans started walking upright, man's appearance and deportment, like woman's, had been the foundation of his sex appeal. And to that end, new folkways began to accent how American men chose to display themselves in the 1990s.

Men of all classes and kinds were spending serious hang time at the mirror and adopting new tricks to alter their looks. Everywhere, guys were playing the angles. Everywhere, guys were enhancing.

Men who had rarely lifted a toothbrush, let alone a hairbrush, were using skin creams (antioxidants! beta-carotene!). They were scheduling discreet visits to the plastic surgeon. They were splashing on cologne with names like Égoïste, Polo Sport, and Swiss Army (yes, a fragrance named after a pocket-knife). They were getting manicures and—unheard of!—tweezing their craggy brows. They were dyeing their temples and planting tidy rows of hair plugs. They were shaving their pates (a convenient "cover" for hair loss) or aping their girlfriends' habits: dabbing in hair gel or calling down to the hotel's front desk to borrow the blow dryer. They began *grooming*.

Men were dressing, as if for the first time in their lives, to be *seen*. They took up accessories (the return of the man bag!). They underwent wardrobe overhauls and tried odd combos of casual and formal. Some execs even hired fashion consultants to help them modulate to business casual (pronounced "biz caj"). They snapped up catalogs and men's magazines to study how other men dressed. These were not the Mod guys of the '60s or the lapels-and-bells guys of the '70s. They were, instead, Men De-crassified, with a respect for hygiene (the grunge movement notwithstanding) and a sense of personal style.

"As a gay man, I feel that fashion for men changed," says Joel Paul, a friend who teaches law in San Francisco. He recalls his surprise at seeing billboards in the '80s and '90s that showcased pictures of buff male underwear models, often assiduously disrobed. "Previously you wouldn't think that a man would look at an image of another man and say, 'Oh, I want to look like him'—and then go out and buy that. We looked at the Arrow shirt guy in the '60s and said, 'That's a nice shirt.' I don't remember in college in the '70s ever talking to another man about where I bought my shoes—all that seemed to have happened in the '90s.

"There was a shift in the way in which men, gay or straight, responded to images of other men," he notes. "Suddenly we aspired, in a self-conscious way, to look like other men look. Some of it was the cross between advertising, fashion, and Hollywood: homoeroticism became acceptable—and not off-putting, but appealing. Having a virile guy like Marky Mark, standing in Times Square in his undergarments, made it safer for heterosexual men to acknowledge that."

Or not. Sports-culture arbiter Brett Forrest holds an opposing view: "I would counter this by saying these images were engineered by women and gay men in ad firms. And they were foisted on straight guys, who were repulsed by them. However, while most guys didn't find this homoeroticism appealing, the images *did* make them realize they had to start [getting buff and] lifting weights to keep up with the competition."

Stay-at-home dads achieved critical mass in the 1980s. But as sex roles continued shifting, even fatherhood began to adopt its own style. The '90s were a period, after all, when Everydad began attending Lamaze class, sharing carpool duty, slaving in the kitchen, and taking his daughter to "Y-Indian Princess" functions. Being the Perfect Dad was an aspiration. And given the healthy economy, it seemed an achievable ideal—if only Pops had the right *equipment*. Fathers were suddenly carrying infants in Snuglis and pouches. They were strapping kids into car seats and conveyances and jogging strollers.

One 1997 ad, for a Lauder cologne called Pleasures for Men, tapped into the fatherhood frenzy. It showed a man in a mesh sweater snoozing in a hammock and cradling a small boy to his chest. This was not your standard advertising fare: a perfectly lit photo of a sleeping man hugging a sleeping child. In fact, it furrowed many a brow. But the tip-off—that he was wearing a wedding band—removed any hint of impropriety.[3] It also gave the ad a

3. The original ad was published without the wedding ring; the telling detail was added a few months later. "The only difference between the old and new versions," writes Anne Higonett, "was

tenderness that emerged with a wave of recognition. The ad became iconic, a new way of conveying "male wholesome." And it sold boatloads of cologne.

Then there was the man bod. Even the most idle of shlemiels was now an out-and-proud gym rat, obsessed with chiseled pecs and toothsome flanks. Men stashed the Discman in the gym bag and hit the elliptical trainer. Men and women began pushing their bodies to places somewhere between unsafe and insane. Marathons segued into ultra-marathons. Triathlons were lapped by Ironman Triathlons. Men spent so much time on their bicycles that many were complaining of "numb nuts," prostate problems, and even erectile dysfunction. So designers came up with contoured seats—big sellers in the late '90s—to limit the wear and tear on a cyclist's perineum.

If a fitness freak couldn't control his lot in life, at least he could control his physical being. And so emerged the new Six-Pack Men, to whom abs were all. And so emerged the new "Step" Aerobics Mamas (a step up from the '80s ladies who'd sworn by Jane Fonda and Richard Simmons) in tank tops and Lycra and spandex. And so emerged new temples to the body temple. There was a boomlet in fitness centers as corporations sweetened their programs to pay for part of their employees' gym memberships—around the time that the surgeon general, in 1990, began an initiative to promote regular exercise among older adults. Over a six-year span, beginning in 1989, there was a franchise explosion of new megaclubs: Crunch, Equinox, David Barton, Life Time Fitness, Curves for Women.

The new temples beckoned the faithful, from the Boomers to the club kids. The regular grind, the weight training, the intense focus on an exercise regimen brought nobility through self-discipline. The workout built up stamina and recharged one's sexual appetites (except, of course, when it depleted them). And it made the gym rat progressively more appealing as a physical specimen, despite the fanny pack.

The acid-tongued movie producer Julia Phillips, in her early-'90s takedown of Hollywood's most egregious egos, *You'll Never Eat Lunch in This*

---

the addition of a tiny but densely symbolic detail: a wedding band on the man's ring finger. Today, all photographs of children hinting at 'pleasure' are suspect, let alone photographs of children explicitly titled 'pleasures for men.'" (Anne Higonett, *Pictures of Innocence: The History and Crisis of Ideal Childhood* [London: Thames & Hudson, 1998], cited in Sara Bragg and Mary Jane Kehily, *Children's and Young People's Cultural Worlds* [Bristol, U.K.: Policy Press, 2013], 45.)

Town Again, addressed the vanity fair of the fitness scene, commenting on the constant cruising among health club clientele:

> After the tenth person gives [her male friend] Brooke the eye, he says, "People fuck you with just a glance, don't they?"
> "Welcome to the '90s," I reply.
> "No, in the '90s they'll fuck themselves in the mirror," he says.
> Well, he should know.

———

Men were pampering and styling and toning and remaking themselves *because they could*. The frisky financial markets and an economy on autopilot boosted discretionary spending. Advertisers treated the male-consumer marketplace (along with all sports-related media) as perpetual trade shows. And all of the dollar signs aligned. If women were shelling out billions in the name of beauty, then what of men, in the name of vanity?

In 1994, a U.K. writer named Mark Simpson, in the *Independent*, came up with a label for the surge, mixing pop psychology, sexual nuance, and linguistic flourish. For an article about a men's fashion-and-style installation in London, curated by *GQ* magazine, Simpson visited the five pavilions that made up what organizers called "It's a Man's World—Britain's first style exhibition for men." And there, undeniably evinced, was a new cult in full flower. He dubbed it the cult of the "metrosexual."

Simpson defined the metrosexual as "the single young man with a high disposable income, living or working in the city [and constituting] perhaps the most promising consumer market of the decade.... Metrosexual man is a commodity fetishist: a collector of fantasies about the male sold to him by advertising." In the previous decade, in Simpson's estimation, the metrosexual "was only to be found inside fashion magazines such as *GQ*, in television advertisements for Levis jeans or in gay bars. In the Nineties, he's everywhere and he's going shopping."[4]

———

4. By now the term has passed its shelf life. "The metrosexual," culture critic Teddy Wayne declared recently, is "a term that's already become obsolete because it applies to such a broad spectrum [and nowadays refers to an urban male] who tends to his appearance as obsessively as does Patrick Bateman in *American Psycho*." (Teddy Wayne, "Let's Call a Yuppie a Yuppie," *New York Times*, May 10, 2015.)

GQ, as it turned out, was the ideal host for the exhibit. Like many of its British-bred mates (*The Face, Arena, FHM,* and, to some degree, *Dazed & Confused,* as well as *Esquire* and *Details* in the States),[5] every ad and editorial page communicated a crucial subtext. "The 'heterosexual' address of these magazines is a convention," Simpson believed. "[It was] there to reassure the readership and their advertisers that their 'unmanly' passions are in fact manly." And these publications were rewriting the book on the male gaze: "The metrosexual man contradicts the basic premise of traditional heterosexuality—that only women are looked at and only men do the looking. Metrosexual man might prefer women, he might prefer men, but when all's said and done nothing comes between him and his reflection."

Men were becoming more discerning in their material choices. They were becoming more attuned to consumer cues. They were becoming more conscious of how they arrayed themselves publicly and how that display prompted a reaction in terms of social radar, peer envy or allegiance, workplace respect, and sexual allure. And many of them sounded nuts when fussing about all of this in public places. The zenith of consumer parsing to impress one's peers, West Coast Division? Steve Martin's character ordering coffee in a chichi eatery in the 1991 film *L.A. Story*: "I'll have a half double decaffeinated half-caf, with a twist of lemon."[6]

———————

And the virility gods said: Let there be Rogaine.

Just as men were going on a shopping binge, pharmacies were beginning to stock the miracle of miracles. Minoxidil, the vital ingredient in

———————

5. *Sports Illustrated* and *ESPN The Magazine,* along with ESPN-TV, would contribute in their own way to a "new jock vanity," according to the *New York Times.* So too the tandem explosion of the "lad" magazines in the 1990s, such as *Loaded* and *Maxim.* Mark Simpson announced in his essay in the *Independent,* "The New Lad bible 'Loaded' magazine, for all its features on...babes and sport is (closeted) metrosexual. Just as its anti-style is style...its heterosexuality is so self-conscious, so studied, that it's actually rather camp. New Lads, for all their burping bloke-ishness, are just as much in love with their own image as any metrosexual, they just haven't come to terms yet." (Bruce Feiler, "Dominating the Man Cave," *New York Times,* February 6, 2011, ST2; Mark Simpson, "Here Come the Mirror Men: Why the Future Is Metrosexual," *Independent,* November 15, 1994.)

6. One sign of the lengths to which Hollywood actors would go? The '90s saw "the dawn of 'male celebrity groomers,'" according to the *New York Times,* which designates Diana Schmidtke as one of the forerunners of this breed. Her clients in recent years: George Clooney, Viggo Mortensen, and Jon Hamm. Guyliner, anyone? (Bee Shapiro, "Sometimes a Guy Just Likes to Feel Pretty," *New York Times,* September 19, 2013, E3.)

Rogaine, had been created to help control high blood pressure. But many men in the early trials for the drug began to go Rapunzel. Soon there was an FDA-approved topical solution for slowing down hair loss and spurring hair growth. Rogaine, with a major marketing infusion in 1989, began to take the nation by scalp. Here was the follicular parallel to the bodybuilding crazes of the Depression (thank you, Charles Atlas) and the 1950s (ditto, Jack La-Lanne). Men whose thinning manes and comb-overs had somehow shunted them to the social sidelines were now out and about with unbridled vim.

In Hollywood, meanwhile, beards and bellicosity were to '90s moguls what mustaches had been to '70s macho men. "In the early Nineties," producer Brian Grazer has noted, "there was a group of young, successful producers doing loud, aggressive movies. They were themselves loud and aggressive—they were 'yellers.'...And many in this same group wore beards. Bearded, aggressive men, producing aggressive movies."[7]

Some men went the other way entirely: full cue ball. In the 1980s, according to the *Independent*, "a shaven head became part of the new gay code, a rejection of the old moustache-and-leather look." Straight culture followed suit. The undressed skull implied a manly security—a comfort with a form of public nakedness. It conjured *emperor*. It conjured *monk*. It said: I am such a singular and pure presence—such a manly man—that I don't need hair to prove it. (Remarked Michael Rooney, the first publisher of *ESPN The Magazine*—launched in 1998—apropos of his buff chest, "Hair, after all, doesn't grow on iron.") The bullethead became a chapeau for the tycoon, the banker, and, most visibly of all, the athlete (e.g., MJ, Shaq, and Sir Charles, not to mention Mark Messier and, in time, Cal Ripken Jr., Barry Bonds—and Andre Agassi, who got tired of futzing around with his wig). It also compensated for the dreaded Boomer yarmulke: the receding hairline and male pattern baldness.

And oh how they futzed with the locks they *did* have.

---

7. L.A. was also the locale of the "Hair to the Chief" incident. Only in the 1990s could the president of the United States have been accused of sitting on Air Force One and delaying air traffic on two runways at LAX while a pricey hairstylist gave him a tarmac trim. The Secret Service and the White House would assert—and the FAA would later prove—that the reports about air congestion had been erroneous. True, "Cristophe of Beverly Hills" had been giving Bill Clinton a clip job. But the appointment had caused hardly a ripple: *one* other aircraft was reportedly delayed two minutes before taking off. (Thomas Friedman, "Haircut Grounded Clinton While the Price Took Off," *New York Times*, May 21, 1993; "Clinton's Runway Haircut Caused No Big Delays," *Newsday* via *Baltimore Sun*, June 30, 1993; Katy Steinmetz, "Top 10 Expensive Haircuts," *Time*, April 2, 2010.)

When rap star Snoop Dogg showed up at the MTV Music Awards with straightened hair (one year with curls, one year shoulder-length), "his 'manhood' and sexuality [were] not called into question," observed Ingrid Banks, the author of *Hair Matters*. "Like other younger black males who are straightening their hair, wearing braids and cornrows, and barrettes and rubber bands…Snoop's image is still seen as masculine." In many rap videos, beaded or braided hairdos that previously might have been considered feminine passed, instead, as masculine. Banks writes, "[Rap video] characters' masculinity and sexuality…are never questioned because they are gangstas and thugs."[8] ("With the violent slayings of rappers Biggie Smalls and Tupac Shakur," says writer Lucia Brawley, executive producer of the World Cup of Hip Hop competition, "so too died the notion that 'thug life' was the only avenue to express masculinity in hip-hop. In 1997, Sean Combs—then known as Puff Daddy—instantaneously transformed hip-hop's image from gangsta to entrepreneur, wearing debonair attire and ultimately creating his own fashion line, Sean John.")

―――――

Male peacocks strutted their stuff in the '70s. Wall Street titans in the greed-fueled '80s were known as "masters of the universe" (Tom Wolfe's phrase, from 1987's *The Bonfire of the Vanities*) and "Big Swinging Dicks" (chronicled in Michael Lewis's 1989 exposé *Liar's Poker*). By the '90s, the hankering for the big stick and the long ball was nowhere more apparent than in the realm of spectator sports. And a captivated audience became enamored of a burgeoning television network. ESPN, launched in 1979, had grown into an entertainment and sports-news powerhouse. Sport—and sports *talk*—could now be consumed twenty-four hours a day, turning what had essentially been radio chat or water-cooler bull into a continental conversation.

The network became the nation's male bonding frequency. Once or twice a day—especially when *SportsCenter*'s nighttime hosts occupied their anchor chairs—guys' biotic clocks turned to ESPN. So essential was the net-

―――――

8. "This was true in the 1970s as well within the urban pimp culture scene," Banks continues. "No one challenged Ron O'Neal's masculinity in the blaxploitation film *Super Fly*. If anything, he was hypermasculinized and seen as the perfect example of a 'brother's brother.' That is, a man's man. He had women, money…a fancy car. And he had straightened ('fly') hair." (Ingrid Banks, "Hair Still Matters," from *Feminist Frontiers*, ed. Laurel Richardson, Verta Taylor, and Nancy Whittier [New York: McGraw-Hill, 2004], 116.)

work to a plurality of American men that it actually exerted a more compulsive tug than porn. According to Bruce Feiler in an essay for the *New York Times*, ESPN and its ancillary units were "a 3D juggernaut of television, radio, print and digital [assets, under the Disney corporate umbrella] that arguably constitutes the single greatest cultural force in male identity today."

All sports, like all politics, had forever been local-local. You played against guys in the 'hood; you rooted for hometown teams. But ESPN and ESPN2 (along with large regional networks like Chicago's WGN and Atlanta's TBS and TNT) made pro sports part of a *national* backdrop. With more men feeling more isolated, they could at least forge a gender-wide connection through the ebb and flow of the American sports calendar. (*Female* sports fans would join in too.) No matter which beer tap you drank from, no matter where things stood in the standings or the cycle of a sports season, you knew about the big play, the big game, and the changing fortunes of the big-name gladiators who numbered in the hundreds. "You knew the drift," says marketing analyst Tim Zahner, "so you could connect with another guy—a total stranger. Sport has *narratives* and you can plug into the conversation. You'd watch the analysis on ESPN and you pretty much knew what you were talking about."

True enough. But ESPN's ulterior allure, insiders insist, was gambling. With the rise of rotisserie leagues and fantasy sports and round-the-clock betting, fans were tuning in for one reason above all: to see if they were up or down on the day.[9]

For many viewers ESPN became a nightly event because of one man: Keith Olbermann, on *SportsCenter*. Every evening at 11 sharp (10 Central), while cohost Dan Patrick riffed on the events of the day, Olbermann could be seen venting the antiestablishment anger that was simmering inside his audience. His presence was dark, vituperative, and irresistible. He bit the hand of all three institutions that fed him: professional sports, the medium of television, and ESPN itself (along with its executives). According to one of the network's former producers, Bill Wolff, "The guy who made ESPN a

---

9. Gen X and, later, Gen Y, were often following sports for *virtual* reasons: to root for particular athletes who might round out their fantasy-league teams. Today many a millennial sports nut has never set foot in a stadium or rooted for a "home team." Instead, having been brought up almost exclusively on televised sports and Web highlights—and beholden to players and personalities rather than to sports franchises—he or she tracks the stats of players so as to field and trade them in a digital fantasyland.

household word, the guy who made ESPN mean something in the market to everyone, was Keith Olbermann.... Watching him in the mid-'90s was... appointment viewing: What was Olbermann going to say that night?"[10]

In terms of casual apparel, the audience was already cribbing a lot of its sartorial advice from the sports world. Guys wore basketball shoes at all hours. They wore sweats or tracksuits or team jerseys when they were out running errands. They wore T-shirts with...anything. Their style, such as it was, often matched that of teens in the street. Adolescents and twenty-somethings during the '90s favored ballcaps turned sideways or backwards. And in line with late-'70s and '80s trends in rap and hip-hop, they added heavy chains and bracelets, earrings and studs, even dental grills. Jeans continued to sag so baggily that underwear became outerwear, prompting politicians to call for an outright ban on low-hanging pants.[11]

There was a rash of incidents, beginning in the late '80s, in which teens killed other teens merely to take possession of their high-end clothes or high-top sneakers. Kids were committing murder over *jackets* and *shoes*. Certain sneakers, for example—Air Jordans, most of all—conferred status and therefore power. And teens, to be accepted or revered or feared, were making fashion statements that were entangled with greed, desperate need (for signs of economic aspiration and personal expression), and the unrealistic material aspirations that were being peddled to them in ads. By 1996, Bill Clinton in his State of the Union address would go so far as to throw his support behind

10. Some of the network's influence also extended to the *look* of the on-air talent as well. For the most part, the channel's commentators and hosts, some of them former athletes, dressed conservatively, if nattily, in the '90s. But many were primping, more or less, as they screened the day's highlight reels—for other men. "ESPN has an unmistakable obsession with the male body, clothed and unclothed," writes Bruce Feiler. "'The proper man dresses properly' is the prevailing message of a parade of handmade suits, wide-knotted ties...[down to] the ultimate sports accessory, 'the ring'"—as in: the championship ring, the most exclusive bauble in professional sport. (Bruce Feiler, "Dominating the Man Cave," *New York Times*, February 3, 2011.)

11. Saggy pants and laceless gym shoes originated as a jailhouse style (or a counter-embrace of the jailer's rules), Brooklyn borough president Eric Adams would contend. "All this is born out of prison," noted Adams. "We took the shoestrings and the belts from prisoners....The first indicator that your child is having problems is the dress code." Presidential candidate Barack Obama would pick up the thread in 2008, while fielding a question during an MTV interview: "Brothers should pull up your pants. You are walking by your mother, your grandmother, your underwear is showing. What's wrong with that? Come on....Some people might not want to see your underwear. I'm one of them." (Clyde Haberman, "Put This on a Billboard: Droopy Pants Can Kill," *New York Times*, April 2, 2010, A19; Geoff Earle, "Kick in the Pants from O," *New York Post*, November 4, 2008.)

school uniforms "if it means that teenagers will stop killing each other over designer jackets."

Many young men who had never been to a tattoo parlor in their lives began displaying ink openly and expansively. Tattoos were partially an attempt to brand oneself, literally. The tat became a '90s statement of commitment and permanence in a world where everything was in flux. It displayed one's distinction from the established order, marking him or her as "apart," or, in fact, "belonging" to a cohesive group of "others." By decade's end, though, so many men and women had tattoos that they would become played out as a sign of rebellion.

Among the most visible full-bod tat adopters were pro basketball stars. The Philadelphia 76ers' Allen Iverson, for one, excelled at body art and helped infuse hoops with hip-hop style. Then there was the sport's clown prince, Dennis Rodman, a defensive standout for the Detroit Pistons and the Chicago Bulls, whose tats and dye jobs were signatures. By the end of the decade, more than a third of the NBA's players were reportedly sporting ink.[12]

Though Rodman was the most outré example, the athlete-as-exhibitionist and nonconformist had begun to replace the strong, silent sportsman (an attitude that persists to this day). More jocks were less reluctant to express unpopular opinions, indulge their vanity, or display their emotions—joy, defeat, anger, swagger—on the field or off.

At the same time, when star athletes stepped out at night, many of them were tricked out, their raiment a reflection of their escalating salaries, endorsement contracts, and cross-media deals. "The '80s and '90s were a low point in sports style," men's fashion authority Jon Patrick, founder of *The Selvedge Yard* blog, would tell Forbes.com. "Players wore over-the-top six-button

---

12. Rodman broke the sports-star mold. He would offer synopses of his sexual encounters and admit to having his scrotum pierced. He would talk openly about his homosexual fantasies. ("I wouldn't be ashamed to say I was gay," he told *Playboy* in 1997. "I'm the first to say I would fuck a man's brains out.... We all have a little homosexual in us.") He would frequent strip clubs *and* gay bars. Like an X-rated Ali, he would brag, "I am the reality. I'm Elvis, Jimi Hendrix and the Grateful Dead all wrapped into one. The president of the United States gets a hard-on just thinking about me." Prone to stunts, Rodman—who was not averse to appearing in public in drag—would appear on the court sporting different hairdos, dyed a new shade one night or patterned into a "text message" the next. ("Dennis Rodman: The Playboy Interview," *Playboy*, June 1997, 62, 171; "Dennis' Biography," DennisRodman.com/bio; Michael Silver, "Rodman Unchained," *Sports Illustrated*, May 29, 1995; Chris Heath, "Wherever He Goes, There He Is," *Rolling Stone*, December 12, 1996; Mike Puma, "Rodman, King or Queen of Rebounds?" ESPN.com, October 9, 2003; Vincent M. Mallozzi, "Rodman, Heading to Hall of Fame, Is Already Back on 'A' List," *New York Times*, May 15, 2011, SP5.)

suits, big jewelry. It was very gangster, not in good taste." And yet. For many an influential sports icon, taste mattered—especially as the lines began to blur between the worlds of sport, music, and fashion. Nightclubbing models and starlets in the '90s would never have shown up on the arms of certain players (baseball's Derek Jeter or basketball's Shaquille O'Neal, for starters) had these gents not stepped up their style game.[13]

Soon all hell broke loose. Casual Friday seemed to come out of nowhere... or, more accurately, out of the Pacific Northwest. The trend was partly a manifestation of the Silicon Valley youthquake that was powering the dot-com economy. Adults, subconsciously, were aping slovenly-chic Gen Xers—some of them the underlings who were writing code or the pimply-faced CEOs who were raking in VC funding for their digital start-ups.[14] The casual look was an offshoot of grunge culture and the Seattle alt-rock scene that was echoing out across the land on serious reverb. Everywhere, young people, turned off by the pretension and pandering of material culture, were donning wool and cotton, often outsized or ragged or mismatched: super-long shorts, lumberjack shirts, alt-band Ts, ironically patterned skirts and dresses collected from thrift shops—paired with shit-kickers (work boots for the out-of-work). Marc Andreessen, who had conceived of the Internet browser while a student making $6.85 an hour—and then made a nifty fifty mil the day Netscape went public in 1995—would crack, in rascal fashion, "Got my Armani suit on today." Translation: "I'm in jeans, a sport shirt, and hiking boots."

"By the mid-'90s you had the high-tech boom and investment bankers [along with] Wall Street coming back from the setback [of the late '80s] and you had dress-down Fridays," says Ken Aretsky, who at the time was running New York's '21' Club, where a jacket was required. "It became dress-down *every* day. Suddenly guys were coming in like they'd just taken out the garbage. You had

---

13. Pro athletes had always drawn their share of groupies. But with the rise in sports stars' salaries and media exposure, these admirers stepped up *their* game. In 1992, a female writer for *Esquire* memorably embedded with a coterie of NBA companions, who would rank and rate players like wines. At this level of play, the athlete and his partner, if both were stylish and smoking hot, enhanced each other's public wattage. (E. Jean Carroll, "Risk and Romance Among NBA Groupies: An Embed's Report," *Esquire*, April 1992, via Deadspin.com.)

14. In his mid-'90s novel, *Microserfs*, tech-age sage Douglas Coupland would describe some of these programmers as people who ate "flat" foods—snacks that could be slid to them under their closed office doors as they pulled yet another all-nighter. (Douglas Coupland, *Microserfs* [New York: HarperCollins, 1995], excerpted in *Wired*, January 1994.)

a generation of twenty-five- to thirty-year-olds making millions of dollars— guys who looked like shlumps [buying] $10,000 bottles of wine.... *Pishers*. You have this generation [that] think[s] every woman is available to them. [For these young] guys in '96, '97, it was all about money: 'If I had money and I wanted to be with *that* woman,' they felt they had that right, that access, that power.... It was always more of a transaction. You were giving something to get something."

Older Boomers, moreover, were looking for any way to bond with kids like their young coworkers (not to mention their own kids)—and personal style provided a shortcut. Many were mimicking the man-boys now calling the shots at Hollywood production companies, the junior account execs in advertising, and all their crunchy cousins out west. Men at Work, in short, were dressing like Boys at Play. I remember "taking a meeting" one afternoon in the '90s and pitching a TV-show idea to a young-geek producer. He wore a T-shirt, pressed blue jeans, and pricey kicks. And for thirty minutes he sat on a couch hugging a pillow and rocking rhythmically. I felt like I'd been teleported to middle school, blazed on Red Bull and Ritalin.

———

ESPN was symptomatic of another cultural shift: the era of the Male Spectator. More and more guys liked to *watch*.

Battalions of men in the '90s would set up media rooms in their homes to accommodate their larger TVs with their growing smorgasbord of satellite and cable channels. Armed with multiple remote controls, guys would install killer sound systems and gaming consoles and personal computers. On nearby shelves sprouted whole libraries of VHS tapes, music CDs, and CD-ROMs. Such entertainment centers became more generally known as "man caves."

The term "man cave," in fact, was coined in 1992 by Joanne Lovering in a column for the *Toronto Star*. (Coining pop-cult phrases, by the way, became a nervous tic among 1990s culture critics.) Lovering had originally applied the term to a basement or garage with a workbench where a man could tinker for hours among his power tools, a "cave of solitude secured against wife intrusion by cold floors, musty smells and a few strategic cobwebs." In many cultures, men had traditionally been granted a retreat where they could decompress, recharge, and gain perspective. But in the entertainment age, the man cave soon came to designate a multimedia hovel where a household's papa bear could hibernate with a few bros and a few brews, switching back and forth between games.

And what were these cave dwellers watching? They were watching the

World Wrestling Federation. They were watching motocross and monster trucks and what would become the leading U.S. spectator sport, NASCAR, a riot of speed, noise, burning rubber, and logos. They were watching pro football and hoops and college sports of all kinds, with audiences that seemed to grow exponentially. They were watching, on any given weekend, a dozen or more professional or amateur sports, whose seasons, as if goosed along by global warming, seemed to lengthen a little bit each year.[15]

Part of the reason for the audience upsurge was the tech boom. Production values had gone through the roof. Slo-mo. Dazzling graphics. A surfeit of stat-men whispering in commentators' ears. Added cameras covering each play in parallax. And on-field correspondents with greater access to players and coaches. "A lot of people would have previously planned to attend a game with friends," recalls Brett Forrest, a senior writer at *ESPN The Magazine*. Come the '90s, they often preferred buddies and beers at home "because it was more convenient and, ultimately, a fuller experience. At the game— before the age of handheld devices—they missed out on all the replays, stats, and analysis, feeling a bit empty."

On the other extreme, there was . . . *extreme*. As if to take enhanced behavior to its loftiest level, males found refuge in a broad category called extreme sports. Many of the men and boys who gravitated to it were avowed couch jockeys. But countless others, in their free time, were whitewater rafting. They were snowboarding and rock climbing, inline skating and mountain biking. They were playing paintball. Or they were getting their serotonin surges through a new slate of truly out-there outdoor activities: paragliding and big-mountain skiing, street luge and spelunking and bungee. ESPN was covering all of this and more. The network would begin televising its X Games in 1995 after network execs, as *Time* magazine would note, realized they were "missing out on ad dollars that could be coaxed from finicky flannel-wearing Gen Xers." Pushing the limits and breaking the norm had become the norm.[16]

---

15. The man in the man cave was also watching, oddly enough, *recycled* games. The Classic Sports Network, launched in 1995, allowed Boomer viewers to relive "oldies" games whose outcomes they already knew.

16. One sports genre that also broke out around this time was mixed martial arts (MMA), a national phenomenon at venues across North America. Competitors went at each other in cages in a sort of Brazilian-Greco-Roman (s)mash-up of feet and fists. The Ultimate Fighting Championship was incorporated in 1993 to promote MMA. But the violence, not to mention the barbaric behavior

Through it all, sports fans, as in years past, were imagining themselves in their idols' cleats. But they were taking it further. They were wearing uniforms with the names and numbers of their favorites. They were paying large sums to go on golf outings where they could tee up with genuine jocks. They were attending baseball fantasy camps (which first became popular in the '80s among nostalgia-prone Boomers) and actually taking the field with former stars. They were *emulating.* And they were not just identifying with the undisputed icons (the lyrics of Michael Jordan's 1991 Gatorade commercial insisted that every kid wanted to "Be Like Mike") but with heroes whose legacies would be tarnished, not burnished, by the passage of years.

Bill Clinton, the First Golfer, was caught taking extra mulligans (and lots of 'em).[17] Slugger Pete Rose was caught cheating on his taxes (and went to prison for it, having already been banned from baseball for gambling). Boxer Mike Tyson took to fighting dirty, famously removing his mouth guard and taking a chomp out of the ear of his opponent Evander Holyfield (not once, but twice). Basketball's Latrell Sprewell put his coach P. J. Carlesimo in a chokehold (and was banned from the NBA for much of 1998).

Then, too, more athletes were using banned substances. And in increasing numbers they were arrested for spousal abuse, bar brawls, drunk driving. College recruitment scandals mounted, along with revelations that mystery donors were providing gifts and money to teen athletes. Even the betting habits of Michael Jordan himself would become the object of journalists' speculation. Men were seeing a pattern: many superjocks were really their fans' larger selves, forever playing the angles, gaming the system, and trying to find an edge. Men were struggling to understand how their old, out-of-phase lives fit in with all the new rules, the lax limits, the shifting moral playing field.

———

It was going to be one of the biggest days of my son's young life.

Early that morning, in September 1998, I roused him from sleep, told him I'd already packed his bag, and explained we were heading for the airport.

---

among some of the fans, was considered too extreme for TV, and sustained coverage would not make it onto cable until the next decade. (Amy Chozick, "The Slugfest in the Executive Suite," *New York Times,* February 17, 2013, BU1, 6; Barry Bearak, "A Toehold in the Mainstream," *New York Times,* November 12, 2011, D1, 4–5.)

17. It was the age of the preferred lie—a golf term that was virtually *invented* for Bill Clinton, denoting the act of moving one's ball to a less encumbered position.

"To Chicago?" he asked, sleepy-eyed but smiling. "To see Grandma and Grandpa?"

"Yes," I said, "and not only them."

"To a Cubs game?"

Sam, age ten, was a Chicago Cubs fan, like his dad. His idol was his namesake, Sammy Sosa, the Cubs' Dominican-born outfielder. Sosa at the time was locked in a heated home run derby with Mark McGwire of the St. Louis Cardinals. For months they'd been racing to overtake Babe Ruth's mark of 60 homers in a single season (set in 1927) and Roger Maris's 61 (the gold standard that had stood unchallenged for thirty-seven summers). Now both Sosa and McGwire were on the threshold of sports history.

For years, Major League Baseball had been in a funk. Its fan base had gone gray as young people were flocking to basketball and football. A strike-shortened 1994 season had disillusioned millions. A general malaise had set in due to many factors, including stratospheric ticket prices, scalpers' markups, games televised way past kids' bedtimes, and the owners' shift to stadium skyboxes (to accommodate corporate profligacy). Yet earlier that week—on September 7 and 8—the Cubs and Cardinals had met head-to-head. And the nation tuned in, via TV and radio, to catch the buzz. The daily drama of a pair of bulked-up hulks tearing the stitching off the Rawlings had added a nostalgic crackle to the national pastime.

Throughout August and into September, McGwire vs. Sosa caught on as one of the classic rivalries in American sports, with echoes of Palmer vs. Nicklaus, Ali vs. Frazier, Bird vs. Magic. The race got giddy. Fans began to wonder if the men had secretly corked their bats—or if the league, in a bid to enliven the game, had "juiced up" the balls. All the more remarkable was the fraternal tenor of the contest. As the press covered each game, each brute went out of his way, day after day, to be deferential. They genuinely seemed to *like* each other.

On September 7, McGwire had tied Maris's record. On the eighth, he'd stormed into the record books with his sixty-second four-bagger. Sosa, however, was nipping at his heels. The twenty-nine-year-old Cub—two parts cheery mascot, three parts cocky—had inspired the city of Chicago, and his native Dominican Republic. Fans took to plastering Dominican flags on cars, in bars, in classrooms. My son, Sam, had a Sammy poster on his bedroom wall, a Sosa action figure, and three Cubs caps.

But now had come the coup de grâce, as far as my son was concerned. As a *Vanity Fair* editor, I had arranged to have Sosa and McGwire photographed, separately, for the magazine's annual Hall of Fame portfolio, a collection of portraits of American culture's yearlings. And on September 13, Sam would be on hand at the ballpark for the Sosa photo shoot.

We arrived that Sunday morning and walked up the box-seat ramp into the wide basin of Wrigley Field. Even from the darkened tunnel, below field level, we were beckoned by green: the emerald outfield, the walls clad in ivy. The place was empty, save for the grounds crew, some ushers, two members of the Cubs' PR staff, and photographer Peggy Sirota, along with her two assistants.

Sammy Sosa arrived in a white muscle shirt, cut off at the rib cage, the better to expose his abs. Like the day itself, he was all sunshine and blue sky. He signed a baseball for the younger Sammy and kibbitzed a bit (preferring Spanish to English): "Winning games is more important," he declared, insisting that a World Series for the snakebitten Cubs was a far grander prospect than a home run title. Then he got in his batter's stance, in the gleam of the morning, and, *click*, flexed his bare biceps for the camera, *click*.

That Sunday in September turned out to be not only one of my son's childhood highlights, but the most charmed afternoon of Sosa's career. With two strokes, he hit numbers 61 and 62, surpassing Ruth, then Maris, as the Cubs edged the Brewers in a ten-inning nail-biter, 11–10. "Goodbye Babe, so long Roger," read that night's posting on the Associated Press wire (remember newswires?). "With tears and sweat running down his face as he sat in the dugout after his second triumphant tour around the bases, Sosa came out for three emotional curtain calls, [later saying,] 'I don't usually cry, but I cry inside. I was blowing kisses to my mother.'" (She was watching the game in the DR.)

The season would close with McGwire on top, having logged an astonishing 70 home runs, to Sosa's 66. Heralded as *Sports Illustrated's* twin Sportsmen of the Year, they would appear on the magazine's cover, their heads wreathed in garlands, like Greek gods.

Then the dark mass descended, as though a shadow on an X-ray.

In 2003 Sosa was ejected from a game for using a corked bat. That same year, he would test positive in a league-mandated drug screening. In time, he and McGwire would appear before Congress during an investigation of doping in Major League Baseball. And come 2010, an apologetic McGwire, his voice cracking at times, would admit he'd used steroids during that storybook summer of '98—and had done so intermittently for a decade. He confessed to taking human growth hormone as well.[18] (Sosa denied he had ever "taken illegal performance-enhancing drugs" and to this day has never admitted doing so.)

The bomber boys of '98 would now be branded with one of the most damning asterisks of all sports records. And by the time the dust and rosin settled, their reputations had tanked. When tallying up the twenty-five leading home run hitters in baseball history, the two of them—and a handful of others, including Barry Bonds—would be dogged by accusations of doping in the '90s and 2000s.

My son, now twenty-eight, renders his verdict, with benefit of hindsight: "I remember looking at Sammy Sosa's rookie [baseball] card and thinking, 'How did this skinny little kid become this muscle-bound guy?' I'm sure some people thought all these guys entering the MLB were suddenly 'blowing up' to three times their normal size. But to most of us, the objects of public concern lag by four or five years. We see that in hindsight.

"At this point in my life, I basically assume that success and power drive the world. I fully recognize that we live in a competitive society and that when we get to the highest levels, all the mechanisms we have to check our competitiveness are self-imposed."

For two of the great sports figures of the '90s, evidently, raw talent somehow hadn't been enough. Their manhood had required amplification—one that would appear genuine at the moment but would end up proving, in its way, artificially magnified. Performance, enhanced.

McGwire's disclosures, while unsettling, were hardly staggering. Complicit trainers, teammates, and wingmen had long been suspected of providing athletes with steroids. Nor was it a shock that pro sports produced superheroes with biceps of clay. When a system is ingrained with owners,

---

18. HGH—human growth hormone—took off in the '90s as "the love child of Viagra and Botox," wrote Ned Zeman in *Vanity Fair*. "*The New England Journal of Medicine*, circa 1990, [reported] the results of a study in which a dozen men between the ages of 61 and 81, received large doses of H.G.H. for six straight months." The result: diminished body fat and a boost in lean muscle mass. "The treatment, in the authors' view, essentially reversed '10 to 20 years of aging.'" (Ned Zeman, "Hollywood's Vial Bodies," *Vanity Fair*, March 2012.)

teams, and players who are committed to eking out every last competitive edge, what other outcome might one have expected?

Most deflating, though, was the fact that the McGwire-and-Sosa Show, now tainted, was a metaphor for a win-at-any-cost culture.[19] America had arrived at a juncture where fair play was devalued. As with the all-too-popular junk bonds from the decade before (really risky, burdened with debt, and offering potentially high yields), junk power—if it contributed to victory—had turned into a reliable yardstick of success. Why not gin up the game, so the reasoning went, if it made the contest more entertaining for the fans and more lucrative for the players and profiteers? Performance, enhanced. Ends justifying means.[20]

American sport, we had learned, was for winners. And integrity in sport, like chivalry or chastity, soon became an archaic ideal. The '90s, after all, was the Amplified Age. It was the age of implants and avatars...Cialis and cyborgs...tribute bands and Civil War reenactors...securities fraud and "creative accounting"...counterfeit products and antique reproductions... stop-action animation and CGI...reality TV and virtual reality. Who knew that just weeks into the new decade—in February 1990—Adobe would roll out Photoshop 1.0, inaugurating the era of computer-manipulated imagery and forever nixing the notion of a photo as a rendering of an actual place in a lost slice of time?

Despite the fiction explosion in the Amplified Age, the depreciation of that home run race had been especially hard to swallow. American memory had looked kindly on a contest that evoked earlier summers of streetcars and

---

19. Deflating is an apt metaphor for how this mind-set would persist among certain sports teams. In the 2015 AFC Championship Game, the New England Patriots would be accused—then exonerated, then not so exonerated of secretly deflating their game balls, ever so slightly, in order to make them easier to grip, thus giving them an edge. (The jokes that followed, about shriveled balls, were reminiscent of those from the '90s, about corked bats.)

20. Over time this reasoning would extend to the public's perception of America's ultimate contest of all: the political system. And by the next millennium, there was ample irony to go around when the nation elected Donald Trump as president, embracing his campaign contention that "Our system is rigged"—this from a man who for years had buttressed his fortune by using the tax code to his advantage. Trump, in fact, was a master rigger. In the world of reality TV, where he had expanded his renown, "truth has a low priority," asserts longtime *Boston Globe* journalist Martin Nolan. "Rules are for losers." (Ashley Martin, "Donald Trump, Slipping in Polls, Warns of 'Stolen Election,'" *New York Times*, October 13, 2016; Jonathan Martin, "Donald Trump's Anything-Goes Campaign Sets an Alarming Political Precedent," *New York Times*, September 17, 2016.)

Cracker Jack and the parable of he-men swatting homers. How could something that had seemed so apple-pie pure prove to have been so half-baked, microwaved, and laced with additives?

My son, Sam, takes it all in stride. He now insists that these later revelations "have not diminished *at all* my enjoyment of the day—or the era. Like many childhood memories, it wasn't what it was." His conclusion: "I learned a lot from the disillusionment of the steroid era. Now, when the squeaky-clean Disney character Hannah Montana becomes the sexualized performer Miley Cyrus, I'm not surprised. I'm rarely surprised. The lesson is: look deeper. If it *looks* like a pig, it's a pig."

———

It was only a matter of time.

Along with Michael Jordan, two other megastars ascended in the '90s, soon to dominate their sports. Cyclist Lance Armstrong would earn his first of seven consecutive Tour de France victories after battling back from testicular cancer. And Tiger Woods, at twenty-one, would become the youngest golfer to win a modern major,[21] taking the 1997 Masters by a record twelve strokes.

We all know, alas, how *those* high-flying Icarus boys fell to earth.

Armstrong would be exposed in a doping scandal that would forever shatter his reputation. And golfers everywhere would watch the news reports, slack-jawed, to learn how Woods's darkest hour would play out: on a driveway in front of his house in a tony subdivision of Windermere, Florida.

Tiger Woods and his wife, Elin Nordegren, sometime before or during the groggy morning in question, had some kind of confrontation. (It may or may not have had to do with the fact that Woods would soon be linked to an array of women, some bearing voicemails and text messages from him.) That morning, for whatever reason, Woods would slide behind the wheel of his Cadillac Escalade and travel no more than a five-iron's distance from his front door, after plowing into a median strip, some hedges, a fire hydrant, and, at last, a tree.

Nordegren would smash in the windows of the vehicle. Police would be summoned. She would tell authorities that the car doors had been locked and that she'd wanted to extract her husband, who was trapped inside, semicon-

———

21. Twenty-one-year-old Jordan Spieth would don the green jacket in 2015.

scious. One or more paramedics on the scene were described in police-released reports as suspecting some kind of domestic dispute, yet neither Woods nor Nordegren has ever been accused of domestic violence.[22]

Whichever, whatever. Her instrument of choice that night was a golf club. And Poor Tiger got the shaft.

---

22. The couple would divorce in 2010. By the middle of the decade Woods would tell *Time* magazine, "She is one of my best friends now." (Associated Press via ESPN.com, "Woods Ambulance Crew Had Concerns," March 13, 2010; "Tiger's Private Struggles," *Time*, December 3, 2015.)

CHAPTER 23

Dudes and Subdudes

I'd like to propose that American pop culture had a prototypical '90s man.

It came down, in many ways, to mojo—a term repopularized that decade by Mike Myers, playing the mock-macho secret agent Austin Powers. Will Smith and Tommy Lee Jones had mojo in the '90s. So did Denzel Washington, a sort of fin de siècle Gary Cooper: the aspirational, heroic, and sexually confident protagonist. Kevin Costner had it, as did Mel Gibson and the two Toms (Hanks and Cruise). The same with George Clooney, who was making the move from TV to movies. And all eyes were being drawn to Clooney's homie, Brad Pitt, who would soon become a mega sex symbol. (We got to know Pitt in '90s movies like *Thelma & Louise, Se7en, Twelve Monkeys*, and, rather notably, *Fight Club*, in which he and other flat-bellied hunks—while critiquing consumer culture—got out their aggression in clandestine sparring matches.) So, too, Laurence Fishburne and Samuel L. Jackson, and Sean Penn and Johnny Depp.

But if there was one actor who was attuned to the times, especially when it came to the subject of men's counterreaction to female empowerment, it was the son of a Hollywood legend.

———

"What about *Basic Instinct*?" Michael Douglas asks, insistent and smiling. "*There's* your sex in the '90s."

We are at a cocktail party and I'm explaining the subject of this book. I've always found Douglas to be a genial and generous conversationalist whenever we've crossed paths at such events, as we have in New York, L.A., and D.C. But something sounds a little off. Isn't he getting his dates wrong? "*Basic Instinct* was '87, right?" I ask. "Glenn Close, and the stalking?"

"No, no." Douglas shakes his head, smiling wider now. "You're talking about *Fatal Attraction*. *Basic Instinct* was '92. Sharon Stone. Paul Verhoeven directing."

What an omission, of course. "Yes, and Joe Eszterhas—a wild script," I say, recovering quickly. "We've *got* to talk."

Right he is. Not only is *Basic Instinct* smack in the Naughty Nineties wheelhouse, but I soon realize that the cut and thrust of Douglas's films during this span makes him the cinematic archetype of the decade's Angry Beleaguered Male. He agrees to an interview.

In his late-'80s films and throughout the '90s, Michael Douglas would become the icon of the rattled renegade who was forever being tripped up by his urges. Douglas's offscreen CV fit some of that script too. His father, Kirk, epitomized movie-colony royalty in films like *Paths of Glory*, *Spartacus*, and *Lust for Life*; his mother was actress Diana Dill. Young Michael would inherit his parents' captivating looks, his father's famous cleft chin. At fourteen, he was such a "lothario" at his junior high in Westport, Connecticut—as his mother would describe him in her 1999 memoir, *In the Wings*—that he was sent off to boarding school. "He was being subjected, according to the guidance counselor, to a lot of aggressive female attention," she writes. "She said he was like catnip to the girls, and she thought he would do better in an all-male atmosphere." At sixteen, Michael was reportedly seduced by two of his mother's friends, Mrs. Robinson–style.

He went through his tough-punk stage, his hippie stage. Then, early in his career, he cut an enviable Hollywood figure: bachelor, actor, gutsy producer (who won his first Oscar at age thirty when *One Flew over the Cuckoo's Nest* was named 1975's Best Picture). He would marry Diandra Luker, then Catherine Zeta-Jones.

Over the years, Douglas's frankness in sexual matters would famously make the gossip columns. He was that rare A-list star who spoke about Viagra. To be clear: during an interview with *AARP* magazine, of all places, Douglas sang the praises of the drug—from a theoretical user's point of view. "God bless [Catherine] that she likes older guys," the magazine quoted him as saying. "Some wonderful enhancements have happened in the last few years—Viagra, Cialis—that can make us all feel younger."

He also spoke out, starting in 2010, about his ordeal with oral cancer. After successfully beating the disease, Douglas three years later would tell the *Guardian* that his test results suggested his particular cancer may have been "caused by HPV, which actually comes about from cunnilingus." That one broke the buzz meter. Was the actor really implying that he'd been put at risk not by alcohol or tobacco but by eating too much pussy? Douglas swiftly and publicly backtracked on the quote. And yet during the height of the press storm that followed, he was unflinching as he told the crowd at an American Cancer Society gala, "I never expected to become a poster boy for head and neck cancer, but if what started out as trying to answer a couple of questions about the suspected sources of this disease results in opening up discussion and furthering public awareness, then I'll stand by that." (Douglas, as of this writing, is in remission. He has elsewhere identified his ailment as tongue cancer.)

If there was one albatross, though, that the actor had acquired in the 1990s, it had to do with unfounded rumors about his sexual habits. Early in the decade, he went in for substance abuse counseling at an Arizona treatment center. Press coverage, however, suggested he was battling sex addiction. The assertion, which he has often denied—and denies again when I raise it—made him one of the first prominent actors whose name would surface in such a context.

How, I ask, does a public person shake a false rumor like that?

"Well, you don't," he says, with a sense of resignation. "It hit a zeitgeist [moment]. It was a very smart play by one of those London tabloid editors to turn an alcohol-drug rehab story around. It timed out pretty well, as I remember. I can't remember the exact order of events—from after *Fatal Attraction* and *Basic Instinct*, and there was *Disclosure* in there. So I was known for that trilogy of [sexually charged] pictures, and was in the last gasps of a marriage [to Diandra] that wasn't working out.

"So you don't [escape the rumor]," he says, bristling. "That got a lot of mileage. It's been kept alive. You're mentioning it now."

But how do public personalities get their narratives back, I wonder—especially in an era when we have the ability to widely disseminate stories full of sexual innuendo?

"They don't. [You think] time will take care of it, but it will pop its head up. . . . My heart goes out to a lot of people who are recognized today because it's impossible [to suppress,] with the video cameras and i-cams. It's immediately shot and passed down, sent on, and there it is. It's part of your legacy."

We return to the subject at hand: men's roles in the 1990s—and, in Douglas's case, movie roles.

To a large degree, the era's male-female divide was about power. As women were amassing more, men saw theirs eroding. In the teeth of it, Douglas recognized that for big-screen audiences what the Battle of the Sexes needed was a new twist: *more* sex. He began playing flawed characters who, in a moment of weakness, or as a result of a toxic relationship, end up living a nightmare in which Eros is inextricably entwined with Thanatos. Five of his films in this genre amounted to libido noir, sexual cage matches that played up the more forbidden passions of the gender wars.

Douglas is under no illusions as to why he chose roles and scripts that pushed the envelope about men confronting willful women—and sexual temptation. "I like the gray area," he says, "the idea that you could do things—you could make mistakes, you could sin—and then try to redeem yourself. I've put myself in movies in very, very difficult situations. And audiences enjoyed watching how you're going to get yourself out of them—and combining that with several situations involving women who were proactive....So to be able to portray a man vulnerable enough or weak enough that he is controlled by a woman, I guess, was kind of unique."

And it was pitch-perfect for the time. Male audiences, having had their fill of '80s action heroes, were open to watching an elevated version of themselves on the screen: a ruggedly handsome, fifty-something man who had trouble keeping up with advances in women's rights, keeping his own commitments, and keeping it in his pants.

Douglas's formative dramatic roles were distinctly his own: Richard Adams in *The China Syndrome*; Gordon Gekko in *Wall Street*; and D-Fens in *Falling Down*. But so too were those of his female costars in a quintet of films. His counterparts were, respectively: a homicidal mystery date gone bonkers (*Fatal Attraction*); a conniving, money-grubbing shrew gone homicidal (*The War of the Roses*); a cerebral, homicidal seductress (*Basic Instinct*); a conniving, power-mad seductress (*Disclosure*); and a conniving, duplicitous cheat (*A Perfect Murder*). Critics began to see a pattern, not only in Douglas's choice of parts but in the femmes fatales who were trying to ensnare his characters. Women, these films seemed to be saying, were the true root of men's ills. Women, as in fables from antiquity, were being portrayed as sirens: controlling and sex-obsessed, calculating and untamable. Inevitably, cries of misogyny followed. "Douglas was now the National Dick," *Vanity Fair*'s Evgenia Peretz would suggest, describing how the actor appeared in a sequence of movies "in which he got poisoned, stabbed, stalked, tortured, and virtually raped by beautiful women."

But Douglas wasn't buying it. His focus, he has insisted, was on the silent cost of the women's movement—from the point of view of men who felt that their stature and social options had been greatly diminished. When his blockbuster *Wall Street* was about to open, and *Fatal Attraction* was still very much on the public mind, Douglas would remark in an interview with Val Hennessy for *You*, an Australian publication:

> If you want to know, I'm really tired of feminists, sick of them. They've really dug themselves into their own grave. Any man would be a fool who didn't agree with equal rights and pay but some women, now, juggling with career, lover, children, wifehood, have spread themselves too thin and are very unhappy. It's time they looked at *themselves* and stopped attacking men. Guys are going through a terrible crisis right now because of women's unreasonable demands. In my case I made *Fatal Attraction*, and the next thing is the feminists are ripping me apart and have interpreted it as a metaphor for all single women. My mind boggles at their arrogance.

———

Let's go to the highlight reel.

Film 1 was *Fatal Attraction* (1987). It featured a gorgon-tressed Glenn Close as an unmarried career woman who shares a passionate weekend with the married Douglas. When the mist clears, he rebuffs her, choosing his role as a husband over their roll in the hay. Feeling discarded, Glenn Close's character slits her wrists—and survives. She claims she's bearing his baby. As the movie unfolds, she becomes a full-tilt stalker. She pours acid on his car. She cooks the family pet. She absconds with his daughter. When she finally shows up at the family's home, kitchen knife in tow, it falls to the faithful wife—played by Anne Archer—to take her down. (Murder by her own hand, or at the hands of the male protagonist, would have been too much for the audience; best to leave the job to the morally grounded character, the Good Wife.)

Many women went ballistic. Though the film had been coproduced by Hollywood's most formidable female power player, Sherry Lansing, and had attracted a large female audience, it ended up sensationalizing a new type: the contemporary careerist cum predator. Susan Faludi, in her book *Backlash*, would bemoan how the press used the movie as a way to play up a false "phenomenon," as if the American heartland had been infested with closet Glenn Closes. "Seven-page cover stories [ran] in both *Time* and *People*," Faludi would note. "A headline in one supermarket tabloid even dubbed the film's single-woman character the MOST HATED WOMAN IN AMERICA. Magazine articles applauded the movie for starting a monogamy trend; the film was supposedly reinvigorating marriages, slowing the adultery rate."

Faludi, a Pulitzer Prize–winning journalist and Guggenheim fellow, opens a chapter of her book by describing filmgoers at an evening showing of *Fatal Attraction* in a theater in San Jose. During the last twenty minutes of the picture, as Close closes in, males in the audience begin to scream at the screen: "Punch the bitch's face in.... Do it, Michael.... Kill the bitch." All the while, the females in the crowd sit by silently. Faludi (who singles out Douglas and the film's director, Adrian Lyne, for special scorn) contends that because Hollywood has a longer turnaround time than most media outlets, it took the studios more time "to absorb the 'trends' the '80s media flashed at independent women—and [then] reflect them back at American moviegoers at twice their size."[1]

Douglas today has a different take. "*Fatal Attraction* was a perfect 'what-if' situation," he says. "What if a married man has an affair, and the worst-possible-situation case happens?... It hit a moment [in the culture]." He mentions the '70s for perspective, recalling the dearth of darker roles for actresses during the era of women's liberation. "When we were trying to cast *One Flew over the Cuckoo's Nest*, we couldn't get any woman to play [Ken Kesey's classic character] Nurse Ratched. Because she was a villain. And that was a politically correct time. Women did not politically perceive themselves as being correct to play a villain. Whereas most men—that's made their

---

1. *New York Times* critic Alessandra Stanley would later remark, in a comparable vein, "Despite what many conservatives maintain, Hollywood doesn't set the social agenda. More often it timidly trails the culture, then belatedly buys in and turns up the music." (Alessandra Stanley, "Staking a Claim on Social Causes," *New York Times*, March 3, 2014, C1, 5.)

careers, playing a good villain." By the late '80s, in his view, Hollywood's top actresses, like their contemporaries on the stage, felt comfortable with parts that extended their range through an exploration of the depths of a damaged psyche. "Glenn Close certainly was [comfortable] playing a good villain. *Fatal Attraction* stands out as one of her great roles." Douglas says that as Close's costar, he was embodying a sexy but vulnerable man who was making mistakes and yet "hoping for redemption—a man who was attracted on a sexual level to women, but might pay the price. There was a responsibility. A lot of this all comes out of all the [fear of disease, connected with] AIDS that was going on too. The cautionary tales."

The underlying lesson of the film? Every affair has the potential to drive the straying lover to ruin. The karmic subtext: ultimately, we will be punished for our transgressions.

Film 2 was *The War of the Roses* (1989), a black comedy. It cast Kathleen Turner as Barbara Rose, a woman who harbors a death wish for Douglas, her moneybags husband. When she decides to engage in a scorched-earth divorce—"I was sexually harassed," says Douglas today, summing up his character's predicament—their lives are drawn into a black hole that consumes every last shred of material gain and moral decorum. Its lesson: a soured relationship, given human nature, can turn positively cataclysmic. The karmic subtext: absolute vengeance destroys both parties absolutely.

In **Film 3**, *Basic Instinct* (1992), Douglas plays a detective in recovery from coke and alcohol who begins to fight an addiction of a different sort. He becomes fixated on a crime novelist and murder suspect, played by Sharon Stone as a bisexual succubus.

The movie presents two of the most talked-about sex scenes of the decade. In its opening sequence, a naked man, his wrists bound with an Hermès scarf, is ridden furiously by a naked woman (possibly Stone, possibly not). At the point of climax, she whips out an ice pick and repeatedly plunges it into him—a chilling gender-bent symbol of phallic just deserts. Next, in the film's signature scene, Stone's character, in a skimpy white dress sans panties, drives an interrogation room full of cops (and the audience) to distraction as she crosses and uncrosses her milky gams. Director Paul Verhoeven has stated that it is Stone, not the detectives, who holds the reins; she is a woman who is "brilliant, powerful, in complete control, not a victim." (And by the way, she may *also* be a serial killer.)

Douglas's character is moth flambé. He finds thrill in sexual peril and is devoured by his attraction to a partner so bedeviling. Again, according to Douglas, an actress is cast as "a good villain. Sharon Stone—I would certainly say that made her career. *Basic Instinct* was a real sexual-reactionary thing. We really wanted to do a slam dance, to try to just break the boundaries, do something outrageous.... *Basic Instinct* was just more raw, more carnal. We were doing things in movies that were more in-your-face....And I think we succeeded."

As the *New York Times'* Bernard Weinraub would note the week of the film's release, "If *Fatal Attraction* served as a metaphor for the 1980's, with its theme of the dangers of extramarital sex and one-night stands, then *Basic Instinct*, to be released Friday, is a movie of the 1990's. Its underlying theme seems to be the dangers of sex, period." The film was incendiary even before it hit theaters. Screenwriter Joe Eszterhas was pilloried for his on-set blowups—and his sexist scripts. To avoid the censor's wrath, a minute's worth of violence and explicit sex had to be snipped. During filming, demonstrators railed against what they considered to be the movie's homophobic depiction of lesbians. (Indeed, in her review in the *Times*, Janet Maslin would point out that the picture "incorporates four apparently homicidal women, at least three of whom are bisexual.")[2] Says Douglas, "We were severely attacked by the gay-lesbian community for having a lesbian be a murderer.... We had to shoot scenes in San Francisco with forty riot police in full gear standing around us. It was an easy target. It was a way to bring attention to their cause. It ultimately kind of fizzled out once the movie came out because the movie *worked*."

Basic Instinct's primary lesson (arguably borderline misogynistic): in sexual conquest, the woman has the ultimate power. Lesson No. 2: one's obsession with a love object may easily drift past the point of no return. The karmic subtext: there is a thin filament between sexual ecstasy and violence.

Film 4 was *Disclosure* (1994). Douglas plays an underling at a tech firm called DigiCom (DigiCom?) who refuses the overtures of a newly promoted

---

2. The groping scenes between Stone's character and her live-in female lover are shot and sequenced so as to play to the male gaze: we watch as a clench-jawed Douglas watches, agog. At Stone's sprawling house, and later on the disco floor, the lovers tongue one another or bump and grind as if to rattle Douglas by forcing him to witness something he's being denied. The sequences, to some, represent a warped hetero-male vision of lesbo lust.

exec, portrayed by Demi Moore. Enraged at his insubordination, she lashes out and tries to sabotage his career. It is a role-reversal parable (based on the Michael Crichton novel) with its own beguiling revenge-fantasy kicker in which Douglas's middle manager seeks to take down his boss. The slogan on the movie poster: "Sex is power."

Terrence Rafferty, reviewing the film for the *New Yorker*, seems to castigate the actor and the whole enterprise: "[Douglas is] the beleaguered object of desire—the poster boy for male fear of aggressive female sexuality." In Rafferty's view, Douglas, over time, has perfected this part, portraying "the masculine equivalent of... maidenly modesty. His flushed face and strained sinews tell us that [his character] Tom is spurning [Demi Moore's character] Meredith not because he doesn't want her but because he wants her so bad it *hurts*. He enjoys the thrill of moral victory only after suffering the agony of tumescence."

In *Basic Instinct*, temptation had hurt so good that Douglas's protagonist was willing to risk *every*thing for a demon romp. His character in *Disclosure*, by contrast, chooses the high road over the dirty lowdown—and suffers the same consequences. In both instances, as in all of these films, the cause of man's downfall is enchanting female guile as much as male dickheadedness. In fact, what Douglas says about *Basic Instinct* sounds even more to the point regarding *Disclosure*: "Overall, in these two decades, there's a very uncomfortable relationship between men and women. The women's movement had sprung up. We were much more conscious about being politically correct. There were people having to make their adjustments in the workplace in how they conducted themselves to women.... There had been harassment going on. [But] then there were other areas where it could be abused by women in a controlling manner. So everybody was becoming cautious."

The result, he says, was that "things calmed down. The libidos crawled away. There was a price to be paid for acting on your sexuality, on letting your libido run wild. I mean, there was a legal [framework], lawsuits. And [the cautionary tale of retribution] was pretty common in the [news]papers. We certainly saw it—to what many of us thought was an absurd extent— with the president." In terms of workplace misconduct, Douglas insists, a lot of attitudes, both male and female, were changed by the sexual harassment discussion spurred by the confirmation hearings of Clarence Thomas. "There were a lot of abuses," Douglas says, "[and] I think that turned the tide, and certainly has enhanced the ability for women to rise in a work environment, and in the military, and in a number of places, with more success now. But it might be a little less fun."

Disclosure's lesson and karmic subtext: the dynamics of sexual harassment can favor a female so asymmetrically that the imbalance has made a mockery of how men and women interact in the workplace.

A Perfect Murder (1998) is **Film 5**. Douglas, radioactive with wealth, plots to murder his wife (Gwyneth Paltrow) and blackmail her lover (Viggo Mortensen) to get back at her philandering. The film's lesson *is* the karma of deceit. The picture's vision—"late-90's Manhattan as a luxurious shark tank filled with chic cold fish," according to *New York Times* reviewer Stephen Holden—reveals a dastardly moral: "There really is no contest between love and money. The movie is right in tune with the icy Darwinian mood fostered by the booming late-90s economy. In a climate like this, the hottest sex in the world doesn't stand a chance against the possibility of raking in a quick half-million."

All of these films, like Hollywood itself, were high on glamour, copulation, and paranoia. All swerved toward noir, even parody. But the central character in each movie made one or two clear statements through all the fogged-up windows. First: unchecked libido, greed, and hubris have always been a male's undoing. Second: men were losing their grip on power and on their understanding of the rules governing the male-female dynamic because women in many ways now dictated the social narrative.[3]

---

3. Dovetailed into this sequence of screen roles were three others—arguably among Douglas's best—that addressed similar, if less sexualized, truths about male failings. Douglas's character in *Wall Street* (1987) was his most memorable. So masterfully did he play the part of a cutthroat broker touting the Reagan-era motto that "Greed is good" that for three decades people would approach him, professing that they'd chosen a career in finance because they'd been inspired in part by his character—a role that had been meant to *demonize*, not glamorize, what one of the film's screenwriters, Stanley Weiser, called "the hyper-materialism of the culture."

Then, in *Falling Down* (1993), Douglas would play a laid-off defense contractor. Trapped on a California freeway, his character begins to unravel before going on a rampage. "*Falling Down*," in Douglas's view, was meant to address the impact of "a whole phenomenon. After the war [in the Persian Gulf] and after Vietnam, we had a feeling that a mission was accomplished. At one time, Southern California was known for its defense industry, not for show business. So the idea [was] that these guys—the military—had achieved the end of the Cold War and had achieved their ends, their justice. And now...there was this complete disillusionment about, 'Well, I tried so hard and I worked so hard for my country, and now they're giving me a pink slip.'"

Douglas hadn't set out, with his choice of films, to call into question the goals of the women's movement. Nor did he systematically choose roles that he hoped might help him embody the male ethos of the era. It just turned out that way.

"None of this is self-conscious," he says. "You pick your parts kind of viscerally, because you think they have a really good story."

The male psyche was portrayed in '90s psychodramas and thrillers and romantic comedies. But it surfaced most plainly in the "buddy movie" and its trusty subgenres.[4]

There was the moron comedy (*Dumb and Dumber, Wayne's World*); the quip-and-kill sci-fi (*Men in Black*); the unlikely-pairing picture (*White Men Can't Jump, Rush Hour*); the intense weekend encounter session (*City Slickers, Swingers, The Best Man*); and lest we forget, *The Adventures of Priscilla, Queen of the Desert*. There were influential black urban dramas such as *Menace II Society, New Jack City*, and John Singleton's landmark *Boyz n the Hood*. There were takes on the suddenly ubiquitous slacker, from *Clerks* to *Reality Bites* to *Mallrats*.

But there was one buddy movie that stood stoop-shouldered above the rest in tapping into the fears and dreams of men who were looking to recover their cojones. The Coen brothers' cult classic *The Big Lebowski*, from 1998, would build upon the gravitas of two earlier après-buddy films—*The Fisher*

The American President (1995) was a romantic comedy in which Douglas, as commander in chief (opposite Annette Bening), anticipates the scandal that would erupt three years later: a West Wing love affair, a young daughter, a 60-plus approval rating, and an order to bomb targets in North Africa. Like the aforementioned films, there was a similar underlying theme, Douglas says: "[Writer] Aaron Sorkin was going for 'Is anybody worth redemption?' "—a phrase Douglas has used elsewhere to describe *Basic Instinct*. And in an added bit of meta-mischief surrounding that feature, there was one press organization, Douglas claims, that tried to square the circle. "I'm not going to mention their names," he says, but "one magazine did a follow-up article about the movie, and supposedly liked it, and sent in a writer, and the writer came to my office with a dress split up to her, you know, her waist on the sides and kind of flopped across the middle. And basically the seduction aspect was going on in this interview. I realized what they were [doing], going to try to make a comparison and try to get me in a situation similar to Clinton, to show art imitates life, you know. Well, I'm a gentleman, and the last thing I'm going to do is mess around with a reporter!" (Interview with Douglas; Michael Lewis, "Greed Never Left," *Vanity Fair*, April 2010; Bernard Weinraub, " 'Basic Instinct': The Suspect Is Attractive, and May Be Fatal," *New York Times*, March 15, 1992.)

4. *Thelma & Louise*, discussed elsewhere, would virtually create its own genre.

King (1991) and *The Shawshank Redemption* (1994)—and would end up practically deifying the American slacker.

Jeff Bridges, as the Dude,[5] self-identifies as "deadbeat." He is unemployed and apostolically idle. He partakes of substances with a monastic devotion: weed, White Russians, Miller draft, more weed. When we meet the Dude, he is shuffling through the local grocery in full beard, unkempt mane, open robe, and sandals: savior regalia.

It is the Dude's misfortune, we soon learn, to possess the same name as a rich con artist named Lebowski. And the stage is darkly set. In a case of mistaken identity, the Dude is forced to undergo the twelve sado-stations of the cross. He is pummeled by gangs of thugs; accused of stealing a million dollars; drugged by a smut-film kingpin; set upon by a Malibu sheriff; ensnared in a bloody fracas in a parking lot; bemused as his home is trashed with clubs and cricket mallets; upended when he stumbles on a plank embedded with nails (the Gospels, anyone?). And all of this transpires as he strives to salvage his car—a beat-up Ford Gran Torino, an extension of his pummeled body—which is stolen, vandalized, smashed with a crowbar, crashed several times, and set aflame. Jeff Bridges's character is a satiric stand-in for the downgraded male.

Lebowski is peopled by marginalized men who, as my friend Donald Liebenson, the critic, notes, "have either rejected the American dream or watched as it passed them by." The Dude's favorite bowling partner is a trip-wired Vietnam vet, played by John Goodman as henpecked *ad absurdum*.[6] Bowler No. 2 is Steve Buscemi's docile über-cipher. The ultimate *shlimazel*, he responds to a sword-and-knife fight by collapsing and dying of cardiac

---

5. In the 1800s, "dude" connoted "dandy." By the 1960s, a dude was a hang-loose surfer. A generation later, Sean Penn updated the surfer-dude archetype as stoner Jeff Spicoli in *Fast Times at Ridgemont High* (1982). Since then, according to linguistics professor Scott F. Kiesling, as cited in the *Atlantic*, "The term has long implied a particular understanding of fellowship among guys. Its dominant linguistic function, Kiesling argues, has been to enable men, mainly young men, to address one another in a conspicuously straight mode of laid-back camaraderie [that, as Kiesling states, offers a sign] 'of closeness with other men (satisfying masculine solidarity) that also maintains a casual...distance (thus satisfying heterosexism).'" (J. J. Gould, "A Brief History of *Dude*," *Atlantic*, November, 2013; Mike McPadden, "Awesome-Splaining *Fast Times at Ridgemont High* for Millennials," VH1.com, January 26, 2016.)

6. Divorced for five years, and raised Irish Catholic, he continues to observe his ex-wife's faith: Orthodox Judaism. At one point he agrees to dogsit her Pomeranian—so she can go with her new beau on a Hawaiian vacation.

arrest. Then, when Bridges and Goodman scatter his ashes over the Pacific, the shifting winds blow his remains *back onto them*.

Even the Dude himself is wussified. Julianne Moore, who appears as the avant-garde artist Maude, dupes him into being her unwitting and expendable sperm donor. In Maude's mind, he's the perfect post-male foil: no slacker of his caliber would ever want a hand in the upbringing of the spawn she considers hers alone.

The film depicts its men as part of a larger Castration Nation. Almost every ten minutes a new scene hints at pending dismemberment, some involving threats or fantasies of male rape. A live marmot is tossed into a bathtub and goes straight for a groin. A kidnap victim's toe is severed. An ear is chewed off. Several dream sequences feature bowling pins as gleaming penises, mowed down by humongoid balls.

On balance, the Dude and his bowling buddies embody the man-cave ethos: I grunt, therefore I am. Of cavemen, not much is *required*. In the end, however, the Dude is revered by almost everyone he encounters. He is admired for his stoner equanimity and his Zen-koan counsel. An antiwar activist in his youth, he is now the ultimate pacifist, gliding blithely through a gauntlet of assaults as men with brickbats routinely have at him.[7] As the rest of the Dude's friends rail or sweat or cower, he is the One among men who transcends his misfortune through his shambling calm. "The Dude abides," says the neo-cowpoke narrator, in the film's finale. "It's good knowin' he's out there, the Dude. Takin' 'er easy for all us sinners."

The *Lebowski* boys embody a Boomer gloom. They feel entitled but shortchanged. They feel noble but battered. They feel downsized by women and circumstance. They are Little Big Men.

———

There is a larger theme that supersedes all of these. In the '90s, there emerged a relatively new ethical code for the age of infidelity, brutish cruelty, greed, and corporate conflict of interest: postmoral cinema.

American film had always maintained an ethical grounding. Even in the darkest days of noir—in the pre-production-code 1930s that reveled in the

———

7. The Dude's character also borrows a soupçon of Job, Meursault (from Camus's *The Stranger*), and Jules Feiffer's Alfred, who, in *Little Murders*, uses daydreams as a coping mechanism when a succession of muggers batter him mercilessly.

subversive—it was the good guy who triumphed by the final reel. A lesson would surface. The center held.

All of that began to change in the 1980s. During the Reagan-*Rocky-Rambo* '80s (a period when the American president referred to the U.S.S.R. as the Evil Empire—a phrase borrowed from 1977's *Star Wars*), the studios were producing big-budget films distinguished for their violence and pyrotechnics, and sometimes featuring superheroes squaring off against a daunting menace.[8] Then, around 1989, cinema really took a turn. America—into the third term of Reagan-Bush—was rocked by a series of morality battles over abortion, the AIDS crisis, the frayed socioeconomic "safety net," the surge in sex and violence in society at large—and of their graphic portrayals in the arts, especially in Hollywood. Lines were drawn in Washington, in far-flung communities, and in houses of worship (as mentioned elsewhere in these pages) between those who believed that humanity should live by a common set of ethical standards and those who adopted, often by default, what came to be called moral relativism.

Amid this standoff arose a new kind of movie, sometimes produced through the studio system but more often an "indie" picture. The postmoral movie tacked toward gristle, gangster, or narco noir—*GoodFellas* (1990),

---

8. Bruce Feirstein, the humorist and screenwriter (with several James Bond pictures to his credit), has devised his own Grand Unified Theory about why the creativity of the studio system devolved so drastically. "In the 1980s, when I first started selling scripts," he tells me, "the executives were political, even if they went to film school, and got into the business to 'change the world.' Their ideals and hopes were reflected in films like *M*A*S*H, Five Easy Pieces, Chinatown, Full Metal Jacket, The Deer Hunter*. By the mid-1990s, the lower-ranked executives—the first gatekeepers, if you will—seemed to be less political, less well informed, and more about the spectacle at the box office. The scripts I was getting asked to write or rewrite seemed to have no worldview beyond what the executives or screenwriters had seen in other movies. . . . Over the decade that followed [the mandate] from studios was to make things 'edgier' and 'darker.' And a sense of derivativeness began to creep into the pictures. The 'water cooler' aspect of movies began to evaporate.

"My theory is that starting around 1995, at the dawn of AOL, Netscape, and Internet 1.0, the so-called 'best and the brightest'—those who wanted to change the world—shifted their interest from Hollywood to the Internet. *Northern* California was where the future was being invented; there were less rules, less structure, and it was more like Hollywood itself was in the 1920s. If you were really smart and wanted to make a difference in the world, you went into what was then called cyberspace.

"[It was] a brain drain," he concludes. "I'm mainly talking about big studio releases, but . . . consider this: between 1995 and 2015, Hollywood gave us endless sequels, remakes, TV-shows-into-movies, and superheroes, while the IT world gave us Google, Facebook, eBay, Amazon, the iPhone, the iPad, and Twitter." (Interview with Feirstein.)

Reservoir Dogs (1992), *Bad Lieutenant* (1992), *Fargo* (1996), and *Trainspotting* (1996) stand out. But there were scores of others.[9] These were neutered morality tales, often with a freak-show element. These were films that let the guilty go largely unpunished even as the body count, the drug deals, and the depravity mounted.[10]

The whole genre might just as well have been pared down to two scenes that appeared in the quintessential indie megahit, Quentin Tarantino's 1994 *Pulp Fiction*.[11] When a couple of thugs in a car (John Travolta and Samuel L. Jackson) hit a bump in the road, Travolta's gun discharges and accidentally decapitates the passenger in the backseat (Phil LaMarr), spattering the car's interior with blood and skull and offal. The startling randomness of the slaying, while bone-chilling, is also overpoweringly comic. The audience is unnerved, not only by the cartoonish depiction of sudden death, but by this new kind of delight they feel in their own fright and shock.[12]

In a follow-up sequence, Harvey Keitel's "fixer" character, a sort of wise-guy concierge, saunters in to clean up the mess. "I'm Winston Wolf—I solve

9. Representative of the wider genre: *Wild at Heart* (1990), *The Silence of the Lambs* (1991), *Poison* (1991), *Terminator 2* (1991), *Thelma & Louise* (1991), *Unforgiven* (1992), *Man Bites Dog* (1992), *Love and a .45* (1994), *The Usual Suspects* (1995), *Things to Do in Denver When You're Dead* (1995), *Se7en* (1995), *Sling Blade* (1996), *L.A. Confidential* (1997), *Grosse Point Blank* (1997), *Lock, Stock, and Two Smoking Barrels* (1998), *American History X* (1998), *Fight Club* (1999), and *Ghost Dog* (1999).

10. Moira Weigel, who writes about gender, media, and culture, has discussed such films as part of a continuum, including a cinematic movement coming out of Europe: sadomodernism. Certain European directors such as Michael Haneke, observes Weigel in the journal *n+1*, were attempting in the 1990s to use the depictions of suffering and death to wake up viewers to their own violations and to indict white bourgeois culture and its "spectatorship as violence." In contrast, writes Weigel, "Haneke seems the opposite of Quentin Tarantino, another director whose obsession with violence has become his signature. Tarantino knowingly parodies genre clichés in order to repurpose the intense feelings that they inspire." (Moira Weigel, "Sadomodernism," *n+1*, Spring 2013, 136–40.)

11. *Pulp Fiction* possessed a knowingly ironic nastiness: the heroin OD; the gangland-style slayings; the anal-rape scene replete with ball gag and samurai sword. The moral quandary would be summed up in the cover line of the September 1995 issue of the *Washington Monthly* (picturing the film's female lead, Uma Thurman): "PULP AFFLICTION: Are Today's Hipsters Cool or Cruel?" (Gareth G. Cook, "The Dark Side of Camp: Why Irony and Detachment Sometimes Add Up to Nastiness and Snobbery," *Washington Monthly*, September 1995; Gavin Edwards, " 'Get the Gimp': Breaking Down *Pulp Fiction*'s Most Notorious Scene," RollingStone.com, May 21, 2014.)

12. Jim Windolf, the culture critic and editor, argues for a sort of poetic justice (which others might view as yet more indiscriminate camp): "The Travolta character is killed in the end while taking a dump. A more ignominious ending could not be imagined." (Interview with Windolf.)

problems," he declares. "Now, you got a corpse in a car, minus a head, in a garage. Take me to it." Another house call, another homicide.

Pulp Fiction and its ilk were using the desensitizing effects of ultra-violence (to borrow the Anthony Burgess term), frosty detachment, and decadence as a way of commenting on a society that was swiftly losing its ethical center. Most indie films in this mix were sardonic, antiestablishment (sometimes anarchic), and morally tube-tied.[13] These pictures were largely male-dominated, rich in black humor, and at times malevolent. There was an element of camp to it all: as if the characters were playing out a drag reality that flaunted the vulgar, the morbid, the sordid—along with the destructive impulses and motivations that can haunt the underside of every soul alive.[14]

Politicians, clergymen, and parents' groups began to fulminate against the heads of the studios, accusing them of the culture-war equivalent of appeasement. Every morally bankrupt film that came out of Hollywood, these critics charged, weakened society's ethical firewalls. There were examples by the score.

In Martin Scorsese's Mob classic *GoodFellas* (1990), for instance, the F-bomb is dropped three hundred times and rigor mortis becomes de rigueur,

---

13. Other films of the era, more traditional in spirit, used the backdrop of violence and civil strife to stiffen the moral spine. Spike Lee's 1989 classic, *Do the Right Thing*, for example—about racially inflamed incidents in Brooklyn's Bed-Stuy, on the hottest day of the year—concludes with two contradictory (some say complementary) quotes that flash on the screen. The first, from Martin Luther King Jr., counsels, "That old law about 'an eye for an eye' leaves everybody blind." The second, from Malcolm X, advises, "I don't even call it violence, when it's self-defense. I call it intelligence." While the film appears to be ambivalent, it is actually urging the moviegoer to hew to an ethical middle path. (The irony of it all: while critics warned that Spike Lee's film might actually *incite* riots, it did nothing of the sort. Overall, it sent a life- and neighborhood-affirming message. One might even call the movie conservative, in its way.)

14. The films became forerunners, surely, to the most successful cable-TV dramas of the 2000s— serial sagas that writer David Kamp has described as focused on "slow-burning despair and moral ambiguity [centered around] people who succumb to the darkest, most transgressive aspects of their nature." *The Sopranos*, which premiered in 1999, "gave lie to the notions that...there had to be so-called closure," director Allen Coulter has said, "that there was a moral at the center that you should carry away from the show." Indeed, the ethically neutered character would come to dominate high-end cable over the next generation, epitomized, perhaps, by Walter White, *Breaking Bad*'s schoolteacher/meth dealer, "a protagonist who made a conscious decision," writes *New York Times* columnist Ross Douthat, "to step permanently outside our civilization's moral norms." (David Kamp, "The Most Happy Fellowes," *Vanity Fair*, December 2012, 173; Sam Kashner and Jim Kelly, "The Family Hour: An Oral History of *The Sopranos*," *Vanity Fair*, April 2012, 222; Ross Douthat, "The World According to Team Walt," *New York Times*, September 29, 2013.)

shorn of any emotional valence. In Oliver Stone's *Natural Born Killers* (1994), two fugitives, played by Woody Harrelson and Juliette Lewis, execute unsuspecting strangers in cold blood, often for the benefit of nearby security cameras. The grisly videos of the crimes turn them into folk heroes. And in the final scene, after they shoot Robert Downey Jr.'s journalist character and leave him bleeding at the side of the road, his own camera videotapes him bullet-ridden and howling as the murderers depart, scot-free. Director Stone and Tarantino, who wrote the story, seem to be giving the sociopaths a bye and laying much of the blame for the culture's cruelty at the feet of a bloodthirsty media. (Bloodthirsty indeed. "Copycat killers" in Texas, Utah, Georgia, Louisiana, Mississippi—and Paris, France—all claimed to have been influenced in part by having seen the movie.)

The narratives weren't confined to film. Earlier in the decade, director David Lynch's groundbreaking TV serial *Twin Peaks* (1990–91) would suggest that beneath the veneer of every American community is a violent, eroticized underworld. In Lynch's universe (cue the haunting soundtrack), we all have our eerily stolid public persona...and our eerily secret self, a rivulet coursing sub rosa. Jim Windolf, editor of the *New York Times'* Men's Style section, maintains that *Twin Peaks* ushered in the entire cavalcade of queasy neo-noir. From the show's very first scene, Windolf says, the tone and message disturb the viewer in a new way: "The Laura Palmer character, who is the all-American girl—her naked body is discovered, wrapped in a plastic sheet. Then you realize that this kind of iconic cheerleader type was involved with drug dealers and other stuff and had a secret life that was really dark. As in [Lynch's 1986 feature] *Blue Velvet*, you discover that in every all-American town there's this dark thing happening beneath the surface.

"*Twin Peaks* really created an aesthetic that got ripped off all decade long. You see it in Tarantino, in the Coen brothers. In *Fargo*, Bill Macy's character couldn't be more of an average guy—a car salesman—who hires guys to kidnap his wife, and it all goes horribly wrong. They end up killing her. They're putting a body into a wood-chipper. In many of these films [the takeaway is]: in wholesome-seeming small-town America, something evil lurks.[15]

---

15. It got even more down and dirty. Critic and essayist James Wolcott, one of the great pop-culture synthesizers of our time, identified a substratum within this breed of film, which he dubbed scuzz cinema: "The Big Three [elements] of scuzz film: sex, sadism, and greasy appetite—the white-trash combination platter." (James Wolcott, "Live Fast, Die Young, and Leave a Big Stain," *Vanity Fair*, April 1998, 148, 152.)

"What we learned about Clinton," Windolf adds, "kind of mirrored what was going on in these stories that were popular narratives at the time. We were learning more than we wanted to know about people who, on the surface, appeared to be perfect Americans." In this regard, Thrill Bill made for an ideal post-*Peaks* prez—and a fitting leader to preside during the rise of sin-soaked cinema, tabloid TV, and the Internet.

Something fundamental was at work here. Morality, in these movies, had become dependent on one's perspective, not on fundamental human values. Society's pang of conscience had been fitted with a dimmer switch so that the good and the bad began to merge, and a variety of crimes and misdemeanors (especially four of the Big Ten: adultery and murder, coveting and blaspheming) appeared to level little punitive consequence.

This disquieting construct may have all begun in 1989. That's the year Woody Allen released *Crimes and Misdemeanors*, in which a man orders the contract murder of his lover and then walks free, and *prospers*. In Allen's view, the idea of a just universe (that metes out punishment on unrepentant sinners and rewards the faithful with paradise) has either been cosmically annulled or, from day one, had been an invalid premise. The message of the film, Allen conveys in a conversation in his private Manhattan screening room: "There's no question that there's nobody out there to punish you...if you commit an immoral act like murder. If nobody catches you, you know, then you're fine, if you're fine with yourself. If it doesn't bother you—such a horrible act—there are no consequences from any karmic spirit.... That's just the ugly way life is."

Late-'90s cinema was another animal altogether.

Circa 1997, the creative class was chiefly a Boomer's game, and a *marketing* game at that. And young-at-heart Boomers greenlighting Hollywood pictures were trying to devise entertainment that would appeal to the prized eighteen-to-thirty-four male demo (not the most acquisitive nor reliably predictable consumers).

Kay S. Hymowitz, an expert on American families and cultural change, has examined this hot pursuit of SYMs (single young males) on the part of studio and ad executives. In her probing book *Manning Up: How the Rise of Women Has Turned Men Into Boys*, she recalls that "the word 'elusive' seemed permanently affixed to the phrase 'men between 18 and 34' among advertisers. But by the mid-1990s, two things occurred that helped change that: first, cable television and the Internet fragmented the media audience, and second, with increasing media competition, the last vestiges of bourgeois reticence in entertainment began to give way."

Hymowitz ticks off some of the media convulsions. The lad mag *Maxim* ventured west from the U.K. in 1997 and celebrated the sophomoric, the lewd, the crude. Its pages created a frat-boy paradise in which it was cool to covet or fetishize games, gadgets, and "girls." (*Maxim* would be famously denigrated by Art Cooper, *GQ*'s editor in chief, as a magazine for "men who not only move their lips but drool when they read.") Animated cable shows with a man-child sensibility—including the comic masterpiece *The Simpsons* (1989) as well as *Beavis and Butt-head* (1993)—had already tilled some of this ground. "But it was in 1997," recalls Hymowitz, that Comedy Central "struck gold after it launched a cartoon series starring a group of foul-mouthed eight-year-old boys. With its relentlessly foul subversion of politesse, *South Park*,[16] as the series was called, was like a dog whistle that only SYMs could hear."[17]

Then, too, the gross-out movie arrived, featuring characters (mainly male, white, and weird) living in a state of arrested development. Critic Dave Itzkoff believes the genre started with "a single movie released in 1998 [which intro-

---

16. My Boomer friend Lester points out that *South Park* pioneered the use of puerile and excruciatingly un-PC comedy (sexist, racist, the works) to educate viewers about the perils of bigoted behavior and attitudes. "By the end of each episode," he insists, "the lesson is fundamentally good-spirited, reinforcing more positive social 'values,' than, say, *Family Guy*" (which premiered in 1999). My millennial son, Sam, disagrees. "Elites and liberals would see *South Park* as ironic," he says. "But the deeper intention of the comedy backfires. Many viewers believe it lines up with their actual beliefs. It's entertaining because they see *nothing* as sacred." Sam's millennial cousin, Rosie, goes further: "I was ten years old watching it and the boys [in my class] loved it and then said nasty things, quoting offensive, ironic comedy before they *knew* what irony was." As she grew older she realized, "You don't need an entire episode of abusive humor, written by white guys, to show that misogyny [or racism] exists. Hire more women to write more shows with positive messages."

17. Meanwhile, on Canadian television and then on MTV, *The Tom Green Show* brought prank-shock comedy to a new level of puerility. Green performed unthinkable acts in broad daylight: sucking a cow's teat, humping a dead moose ("Bullwinkle's Last Stand"), and mortifying his parents by defacing the hood of the family car with a huge porn decal. *The Man Show*, premiering on Comedy Central in 1999, encouraged viewers to settle into their man caves, hold on to their puds, and follow the bouncing babes. Recurring gags revolved around scatology, beer chugging, and lingerie-clad models on trampolines. Its audience didn't seem merely fixated but *regressing* through Freud's psychosexual stages, from phallic back to anal and oral. (Charisse L'Pree, "One World, One Image, One Channel: A History of MTV," May 1, 2002, https://charisselpree.com/2002/05/01/history-of-mtv/; Ariel Levy, *Female Chauvinist Pigs: Women and the Rise of Raunch Culture* [New York: Free Press, 2006], 122.)

duced] the refined art of tastelessness." That film: the Farrelly brothers' classic *There's Something About Mary*, starring Ben Stiller and Cameron Diaz.[18]

Mary was seminal, quite literally. In its most memorable scene, Stiller's Ted has jerked off in the bathroom and cannot determine where his gob of shplooey flew. Diaz, playing Mary, pops in and asks innocently, "What is that? On your ear?...Is that hair gel?...I just ran out." She borrows a dab and improvises a spit curl—and the audience winces *and* cackles.

The film—part rom com,[19] part stalker flick—is filled with such cringe-worthy gems. Mary's terrier goes for Ted's crotch. Ted, fearing he'll be caught mid-masturbation, quickly zips up his fly and almost castrates himself. Echoing *The Big Lebowski*, Ted's ever-imperiled member—bloodied but unbowed—is the Farrellys' metaphor for the state of American manhood.

What *Mary* and similar films did was to ridicule and yet ultimately romanticize the clueless '90s male and his "dumbstick" (the nickname favored by Lucy Liu's character on *Ally McBeal*). In a swarm, comedians and filmmakers would serpentine onto the screen, out-grossing one another. Their ranks included Jim Carrey and Ben Stiller but also Adam Sandler and Mike Myers, with a supporting cast that featured Woody Harrelson, Jeff Daniels, Owen Wilson, Chris Kattan, Cameron Diaz, Leslie Mann, Drew Barrymore, and the early Will Ferrell. In these films, diversity was sorely lacking, verging on invisibility. And the movies' depictions of women, while not incidental, were largely secondary and often romanticized, clichéd, or objectified. As for the doofus protagonists, moviegoers were meant to laugh *at* them, not *with* them—though many a character, by the closing credits, would end up revealing his inner teddy bear.

At the crux of many such films was the need to assert one's manhood by parading or inflating the little man. Nineteen ninety-nine alone saw the release of *South Park: Bigger, Longer & Uncut* (the title told the tale), Mike

18. Critic David Kehr fingers 1996 as the watershed year. Jim Carrey's *The Cable Guy*, Kehr contends, "was one of the first 'cringe comedies,' in which the humor is grounded in the painful humiliation experienced by its protagonist." (David Kehr, "Jim Carrey as the Id Unleashed a Bit Before Its Time," *New York Times*, February 21, 2011.)

19. The Farrellys spike the film with so many moments of social discomfort (every misunderstanding leads to a deeper morass, mirroring the *Seinfeld*/Larry David playbook)—and, at the same time, so many layers of schmaltz—that they seem to be declaring that *any* intimation of innocence is virtually impossible in these adulterated times.

Myers's *Austin Powers: The Spy Who Shagged Me*,[20] and *American Pie* (in which Jason Biggs's character, in the ultimate Freudian defilement of MILF and country, violates a warm apple pie). It didn't take a focus group to foresee: movies like these couldn't help but resonate in a year when so much ink was being spilled about the president's privates.

Producers and filmmakers had hit a nerve. Their audience of Gen-X and millennial males had been untethered from reliable role models at home, in their communities, and in popular culture. Many felt socially disoriented, personally alienated, and sexually befuddled. Large segments of this cohort, virtually nursed on media, found simpatico, release, and succor in narratives that used humor to acknowledge their insecurities. These films—salacious, immature, and liberating—gave them a common language with which to bond with buddies. These films gave young men sanction to shame others and thereby deflect their own shortcomings. These films provided a sense of belonging in a world divested of grown-ups, a world that encouraged misbehavior, debauchery, and borderline misanthropy.

Critic David Ansen, looking back at the gross-out canon from the perspective of the Apatow era, would come up with a pat formula for the genre: "scrotums + swear words + third-act saccharin = success." And over time, the gross-out genre, odd as it sounds, became mainstream, feel-good, and, most surprising of all, safe.[21]

————

No American movie, however, would tackle more '90s themes more perceptively than *American Beauty*.

————

20. Austin Powers was the overcompensating, clueless, and unapologetically sexist spy from the "Swingin' Sixties," created by comedian Mike Myers in the 1997 film comedy *Austin Powers: International Man of Mystery*. Powers became a '90s mascot. And he would spend much of the 1999 sequel searching for his mojo—lost in a time-machine mishap that leaves him unable to "shag." (Some of the memorable characters in the Powers harem: Alotta Fagina, Felicity Shagwell, and Ivana Humpalot.)

21. In many ways, they were Woody Allen's comedic descendants, a group that included everyone from the slackers, gearheads, and weirdos of these '90s comedies to Chris Rock (who acknowledges a debt to Allen, insisting, "I've checked into hotels under [Allen's character's name] Alvy Singer") to the alumni of Paul Feig and Judd Apatow's seminal 1999 TV series *Freaks and Geeks*. These latter comedians—Jonah Hill and Seth Rogen among their ranks—took Allen's odd duck and reinvented him as the all-American man-boy. Writer Stephen Rodrick, for one, has specified Apatow & Co.'s "brand of 'dude humor' [as] bumbling young guys who behave badly but have hearts of plated gold." (Frank Rich, "In Conversation: Chris Rock," *New York*, November 30, 2014; Stephen Rodrick, "The Nerd Hunter," *New Yorker*, April 6, 2015, 38.)

Here was voyeurism, materialism, homophobia, antigay violence, sexual craving, contrived ideals of beauty, the pitiable Boomer, and a preoccupation with one's own virility and appearance. Indeed, it is hard to imagine how a movie that opens with its protagonist masturbating in the shower—then quitting his job, blackmailing his boss, and virtually stalking his teenage daughter's schoolmate—could be awarded the Oscar for Best Picture. But Sam Mendes's *American Beauty*, in 1999, did this, and much more, distinguishing itself as the decade's most trenchant film about the male psyche in midlife meltdown.

Lester, played by Kevin Spacey, is so fixated on teenager Angela (Mena Suvari) that he eavesdrops on her while she's chatting with his daughter. When he hears her say, "Your dad's actually kinda cute, he is. If he just worked out, he'd be hot.... I would totally fuck him," he begins lifting weights that very night, hoping to impress her—and to boost his deflated ego. Lester has a career that has been vaporized, with much of the damage self-inflicted. His Realtor wife (played by Annette Bening) is hot and heavy with the local "real estate king." His next-door neighbor is a homophobic and potentially homicidal Marine Corps kook named Fitts (played by Chris Cooper), who turns out to have fixations of his own. And Fitts's son, Ricky, the local drug dealer, becomes a sort of slacker role model in Lester's eyes. Loner Ricky, meanwhile, compulsively videotapes his surroundings, including Lester's daughter, Jane. Ricky appears to be so out of sync with reality that he relies on real-life scenes captured on camera to help him get in touch with the powers that animate the real world and to validate the deeper forces that give life its beauty and meaning.

The movie (spoiler alert) concludes in a series of twists. Jane and Ricky end up expressing the one bona fide loving relationship in the film. Lester, when he finally gets together with young Angela, comes to his senses—and backs off. And yet Lester, despite this confounding act of sanity, has been doomed from the film's opening voice-over, destined to be murdered by the raging Fitts, who imagines Lester has sexually spurned him.

American Beauty, premiering the year of Bill Clinton's impeachment, overlapped thematically with events in Washington. The film touched on the blurring of public and private life, clandestine taping, a clash of community values, and an aging Boomer's obsession with an underage love object—and his own lost youth. There were L.A.-D.C. parallels as well. At the end of Clinton's second term, there had been persistent, unfounded rumors that the president might move out west to work in some capacity with his pals Steven

Spielberg, David Geffen, and Jeffrey Katzenberg, whose then-fledgling studio, DreamWorks SKG, happened to have released *American Beauty*.[22] Kevin Spacey, moreover, was a friend of the Clinton family. (Spacey would later portray the fictional commander in chief Frank Underwood in the Netflix series *House of Cards*—which Hillary Clinton has confessed to having "totally binge-watched" with her husband.)

But none of these back stories mattered. It was the bleak comedy on the screen that captivated the nation as well as Academy voters, who honored the film with five Oscars. *American Beauty* chillingly illustrated two of the darkest real-life pantomimes being performed by too many American males. "In order to be successful," says sleazy real estate mogul Buddy Kane—played by Peter Gallagher—"one must project an image of success at all times." (Back story? Gallagher in 2016 would tweet that he had modeled his portrayal of Kane on none other than...Donald Trump, whose favorite film, it so happens, is *Citizen Kane*.)

Buddy Kane's mantra was the flip side of Lester's equally pathetic and repellent motto: "My job consists of basically masking my contempt for the assholes in charge and at least once a day retiring to the men's room so I can jerk off while I fantasize about a life that doesn't so closely resemble hell."

---

22. At a 2000 benefit dinner in Beverly Hills, Bill Clinton called out the film's producers by name ("David and Steven and Jeffrey...and all the DreamWorks folks and all of you who are here tonight"), and jokingly told the audience that he was an unabashed fan of the film: "I loved *American Beauty*. I love Kevin Spacey." (*Public Papers of the Presidents of the United States, William J. Clinton, 2000–2001, Book 1* [Washington, DC: Government Printing Office, 2001], 725.)

CHAPTER 24

Porn Goes Pop

"Do you mind if I edit pictures while we talk?"

I have just entered the office of Dian Hanson, in downtown Los Angeles, when she poses the question.

I'm here to interview her about porn's ubiquity in the 1990s, a period when Hanson was editing a slate of softcore men's magazines. I'm also here to discuss her current role as an arbiter of modern erotica: she serves as the "Sexy Book Editor"—her official title—for Taschen, the high-end art-book publisher.

Hanson, with her signature blonde bangs, wears a red sweater and sits in a swivel chair in front of a computer, her black boots elongating her six-foot-plus frame. She projects a formidable, almost professorial presence. She apologizes, explaining that she's up against a deadline; her boss, the publisher Benedikt Taschen, is due to review the layouts of a forthcoming coffee-table book—two hours from now. And she's *also* trying to keep on schedule with the *next* photo book she's editing.

"What's the subject of the book you're showing Benedikt?" I ask.

"*The Butt Book*," she says, sliding over to a side table to flip through a book dummy. This is well-trodden terrain for Hanson. She established her reputation editing *Puritan*, the '70s skin mag, and then shepherded a passel of men's titles, adult-video guides, and biker rags during the '80s and '90s—publications such as *Juggs*, *Leg Show*, *Big Butt*, and *Tight*.

I swallow hard and pose the next, logical question. What, I ask, is the *other* title she's working on—the one requiring her to picture edit as we do our interview?

"*The Pussy Book*," Hanson remarks. (It will later be retitled *The Big Book of Pussy*.) And with that, we go to her computer screen, which reveals a cache of snatches: two dozen color pictures of spread legs and vulvas, the images arranged in neat furry rows. "This book is going to have a lot of pubic hair," she says, emphasizing the nostalgic appeal of pre-'90s porn. "American young men can't deal with pubic hair [today]. They find that repulsive. A lot of that came out of the '80s, when sex was made dangerously dirty—pubic hair signaled uncleanliness."

Taschen's L.A. offices, on Sunset Boulevard, occupy a kitschy 1930s complex—once the city's first outdoor shopping mall—originally designed to resemble a cruise ship. The building's sixty-foot mast hoists a rotating globe that bears the words "Crossroads of the World." And an inviting world it is. Hanson's office has the feel of a spacious study in a ranch home; its white curtains, drawn to block the morning sun, reinforce a sense of illicit activity.

In the '80s and '90s, Benedikt Taschen had taken the visual book trade by storm. According to *Vanity Fair*'s Matt Tyrnauer, Benedikt had scaled up his Cologne-based publishing company to such a degree that "every two seconds worldwide," somewhere, someone was buying a Taschen book. His formula: art and photo tomes shaped like bricks. Some books were as large as tombstones, some explored sexual themes, and all were printed in multiple languages. Taschen would charge hundreds, sometimes thousands of dollars for some titles, such as Helmut Newton's *Sumo*—a collection of nudes reproduced in a bound volume the size of a car door.

Taschen made the leap to hardcore in 1998 with his anthology celebrating the gay-porn illustrator Tom of Finland. And in the process he created a new genre: the fun and filthy coffee-table book. (In some cases, the books came packaged *with* a bookstand.) These were smut books as covetable objets d'art, intended for a prime position in one's living room. Indeed, no one at the turn of the millennium did more to gentrify erotica than Benedikt Taschen. And he soon conscripted Hanson to be his chief emissary in this area, gamely turning out collections ranging from an encyclopedic study of porn star Vanessa del Rio to the splashy picture anthology *The Big Penis Book* (also available in a 3-D edition).

This morning, Hanson's manner is meticulous and matter-of-fact. As we talk, she faces me on an angle, dividing her attention between yours truly and the screen in front of her. Her hand rests on the computer mouse and occasionally she clicks on a "select" to enlarge it and save it, then swiftly moves on to the next patch of rosebud. She stops to narrate: "Now I'm looking for pictures of pussies and women holding objects that look like pussies in front of their pussies." Ah, how good to be back in sunny Southern California.

Our topic du jour: how porn became a popular and even mundane commodity in the 1990s—heady years, she explains, to be in the business. "There wasn't one pornography conviction in the U.S. during the entire eight years Clinton was in office," Hanson declares. "We love him. Even postal service threats [to halt the distribution of porn] declined. And when [the cases] went up to higher courts, they were always thrown out. Clinton had a liberal staff. He didn't declare a 'war on porn,' as everyone before him [had done]."

Some tectonic plate in the culture had shifted. Porn was seeping into the crevices of art, entertainment, and the Internet in ways that made it seem hip and transgressive to many viewers, a shift that was interpreted by some, paradoxically, as edifying women instead of exploiting them. To others, still and all, porn was porn: an insidious way to codify oppressive sexual practices, profit from the subjugation of others, and eroticize humiliation itself. What is it, I wonder aloud, that made porn more pervasive—and also more perverse?

"It became more acceptable as it became less aesthetic," Hanson muses. "Because it became more acceptable, porn became more extreme. Because there were no cautionary tales for anyone—since there were no arrests for porn in the '90s—it led producers of porn to get ever more extreme in the acts they would allow actors to perform. Anal gangbangs weren't good or healthy for anyone involved.

"The '90s was the decade of the extreme," she says. "And directors could *always* find women willing to do extreme acts. Once risky behavior was standard, you couldn't go back to blowjobs. You had to keep pushing. And that's what we have in the 2000s."

So-called gonzo porn blew up in the 1990s, championed by filmmakers like John Stagliano (known as Buttman), Paul F. Little (known as Max Hardcore or Max Steiner), and Matt Zane, who created the rock-porn *Backstage Slut* series. Seth Warshavsky, who had started out in the phone-sex trade and then created a wildly successful website called Club Love, made his biggest splash selling pirated porn tapes that showed celebrities doing the deed. Meanwhile, a parade of producers would concoct ever more vile ways to degrade their performers and, in turn, turn on and/or degrade their audiences—to the point where nothing seemed so repugnant that *some* director wouldn't chance it.

Anthony Haden-Guest, the journalist and itinerant night owl, remembers covering the record-breaking feat of a porn star named Jasmin St. Claire (documented in the 1996 picture *World's Biggest Gang Bang 2*) in which she got it on with three hundred men, each of whom had to submit proof that he was HIV-free. Haden-Guest recalls that blue and red condoms were provided, in barrels, and the men—overweight, scrawny, young, elderly, pierced, tattooed—lined up, slipped on a wristband (like a hospital bracelet), only to be summoned in fuck-clusters, sometimes five at a time, to assume their positions around her and inside her. "Fluffers" were on hand to assist the performance-challenged.

"I was covering it for *Penthouse*," Haden-Guest says. "And I was impressed. Jasmin St. Claire may have been part of a gangbang, but she was clearly in charge. Porn stars of an earlier age—Linda Lovelace and Marilyn Chambers—had their careers shaped by men. But this was all orchestrated and marketed by Jasmin herself. She had been an investment banker, living on Water Street [in downtown Manhattan]. Then she got into dancing and acting."[1] St. Claire would be outdone, as it were, on the last night of the 1990s, as reported by porn historian Robert Rosen: "The new millennium dawned as [XXX star] Sabrina Johnson, over a two-day period beginning on New Year's Eve 1999, had sex with 2,000 people for [the video] *Gangbang 2000*." Anything for attention.

As the decade waned, things got simply excruciating. Khan Tusion—the very name implying physical harm—would put out the first in his Rough Sex line of videos. Only in a free-market porn world (one that was often disengaged from the ethical forces of the real world) could the labels "Rough Sex" and "Meat Hole" gain a toehold *as brands*. "There is a trend in misogynistic porn, and it's upsetting," the high-powered adult-film producer Veronica Hart—a former porn star herself—would tell the *New York Times*. "There are little pipsqueaks who get their disgusting little videos out there. . . . I don't

---

1. St. Claire was a Columbia grad who, after paying her dues as a Wall Street consultant, would become a stripper and porn star. She would eventually flower as a successful actress, entrepreneur, pro wrestler, pro-wrestling manager and promoter, VJ, and rock journalist. (Jasmin St. Claire, *What the Hell Was I Thinking?!!* [Albany, GA/Duncan, OK: BearManor Media, 2010], 15–40; interview with Anthony Haden-Guest; notes from Haden-Guest 1996 interview with St. Claire; "Jasmin St. Claire: Biography," Internet Movie Database, IMDb.com, 2015.)

believe that's what America wants to see." But *see* and *buy*—anything short of snuff films—were precisely what America did.

"I consider men born from 1985 on[ward] as being in the post-porn era," says Dian Hanson as our meeting winds down. "By the time they were interested and aware, porn was everywhere available. As soon as the Internet was born, [boys] were jaded by [age] ten or twelve. They [began to] accept very hardcore stuff. They get the idea that everything is attainable, everything is available. They idealize and look for the unattainable girl—the beautiful fantasy, the romance fantasy. It's very exciting to yearn for something." But this superfluity began to inspire fantasists: men and women who held infeasible expectations about potential partners, mating behavior, or their own desirability and sexual compatibility. They were at a loss in many cases when it came to issues like devotion, respect, and love.

For much of the twentieth century, American society tended to consider pornography disreputable. No matter that Hugh Hefner's *Playboy*, in the '50s, had managed to steam the grime off dirty pictures. Or that hardcore films had broken into the public square in the '70s. Or that the President's Commission on Obscenity and Pornography, convened on the orders of Richard Nixon, had made the case that porn was generally *not* harmful and, to many, might even prove "beneficial...in allowing for a release of sexual tension." By the '80s, Attorney General Edwin Meese was on the warpath, finding links between porn and incidents of sexual assault, and between organized crime and many corners of the sex trade. Meanwhile, an alliance of sorts was developing between the religious right and certain feminists (most notably Catharine MacKinnon and Andrea Dworkin, who pushed censorship laws that branded many forms of porn an affront to the civil rights of American women).

By the '90s, however, many women's rights activists had turned their attention to other pressing causes such as reproductive choice, rape, domestic abuse, gender violence, and issues surrounding everything from sexual harassment to equitable workplace compensation. The antiporn "crusade," as a result, became something of an afterthought.[2]

---

2. "The antipornography movement among feminists lost steam in the 1990s," says Fordham University's Kirsten Swinth, an expert in gender and cultural history in America. Instead, she contends, "feminist energies went in a series of important directions to address reproductive

Indeed, porn was shedding much of its onus. There were messy paw-prints across the culture. Out west, porn was literally part of the landscape. The San Fernando Valley was home to Bally-wood, where the bulk of America's triple-X videos were shot. In downtown L.A., porn companies like Vivid Entertainment would advertise on billboards (contributing to occasional fender benders). And one couldn't drive through Beverly Hills without passing the ten-story building emblazoned with FLYNT PUBLICATIONS, in blocky silver letters. The smoked-glass headquarters of the Larry Flynt pornography empire jutted up over Wilshire Boulevard like some massive electric razor.[3]

Christie Hefner, whose father had handed her the keys to the Playboy kingdom in 1988 (making her chairman and CEO), became the corporate face of a softcore dynasty. With a college-dean demeanor, she launched twenty-four-hour TV channels and spearheaded Playboy.com, one of the first websites created by a national magazine. At the other end of the respectability chart, the publisher of *Hustler* was heralded as a vital First Amendment advocate in the 1996 movie *The People vs. Larry Flynt*, with Woody Harrelson and Courtney Love playing the smut mogul and his Ms. The movie drew raves and two Academy Award nominations. The next year, three Oscar nods went

---

freedom and sexual vulnerability and violence. This included defending abortion rights in the face of mounting challenges from the right. It included supporting queer sexualities and the development of queer studies.... In my judgment, [the decade's so-called] preoccupation with sexuality was not a simple triumph of the sexual revolution, but a complex mix of (1) the deepening sexualization of commercial culture and (2) ongoing campaigns to change policy, law, and practice to end sexual violence and protect reproductive freedom." (Interview with Swinth.)

3. During this period, sales of porn magazines were being trampled by the boom in videos, CD-ROMs, and DVDs. Professor Samir Husni, who teaches journalism at the University of Mississippi, in Oxford, is the country's leading expert on the history of the American periodical. "From the late '80s until, like, 1997, there were more new sex magazines published than any other genre. One year in the '90s—I still remember the number vividly—one-seventh of all new publications were sex magazines [often devoted to special interests]. You could dissect the human body—name any part—and you will have five magazines for it. There was actually a magazine called *Foreskin Quarterly*. That's how specific it got.... Tattooing on naked bodies... Titles devoted to black ass or Hispanic ass. And so the established magazines like *Hustler* and *Penthouse*, to compete in that market, started to go completely pornographic. They left nothing to the imagination. With the advent of the Internet, they figured the definition of obscenity is no longer applicable to communities that are literally unbounded." Though porn magazines earned revenue for a time by loading up on ads for dial-in phone sex and DVD inserts, it was too little, too late. Online porn, Husni explains, would sound the skin mag's death knell. "When pornography became disseminated on [cable] and on your laptops," says Husni, "you can't compete in print. I mean, no matter how much you shake the magazine, it will never move the same way." (Interview with Husni.)

to *Boogie Nights*, a picture about the '70s and '80s porn business. The film had both commercial *and* critical chops, and marked model Mark Wahlberg's breakout screen role, in which he played a character partly inspired by the legendary XXX star John Holmes.

The raunch of earlier decades was now being repurposed as retro-chic. In a manner reminiscent of the court fights over "censored" novels and memoirs earlier in the century, pornographers Flynt and Hugh Hefner were being glamorized as free-speech pioneers and éminences grises of publishing.[4] To say nothing of porn-star glam. Traci Lords, the hardcore It Girl of the '80s—who was later found to have been underage while shooting dozens of pornos—began appearing in television shows and Hollywood films. Adult-movie giants like Jenna Jameson and Ron Jeremy were becoming household names. (Jeremy appeared in wink-wink cameos in mainstream movies throughout the decade.) Koo Stark, the onetime softcore star, and frequent companion of Britain's Prince Andrew, was a tablemate of art mega-dealer Leo Castelli at his gallery's thirty-fifth anniversary. And hardcore fixture Jeff Stryker, who divided his time equally between gay and straight videos, appeared on the Paris runway for the designer Thierry Mugler.

Porn terms, too, were being casually bandied about. When '90s pitching ace Kerry Wood began posting monster strikeout totals for the Chicago Cubs, fans in the bleachers began sporting "We Got Wood" T-shirts. Top sales execs were said to "give good meeting," in a nod to blowjob jargon. And the term "money shot," a phrase popularized in the '70s to connote a porn actor's full-splat climax, was starting to circulate in public discourse about politics and economics.[5] Quoth the *New Yorker*, yes, the *New Yorker*, "The on-command male orgasm is the central convention of the industry: all porn scenes should end with a visible ejaculation. There are various names for

---

4. By 1998 Hef had become so respectable in the publishing world that he was inducted into the pantheon: the American Society of Magazine Editors' "Hall of Fame," alongside no less than Byron Dobell (ex-editor of *American Heritage*) and Gloria Steinem (founding editor of *Ms.*). ("Magazine Editors' Hall of Fame," National Magazine Awards/American Society of Magazine Editors, magazine.org/asme/national-magazine-awards/magazine-editors-hall-fame.)

5. In the run-up to the 2000 presidential election, for example, *Time*'s Margaret Carlson contended that George W. Bush's "money shot was a tear in his eye, better even than Clinton's lip biting." (From an October 2, 2000, *Time* column, "The Oprah Primary," collected in Margaret Carlson, *Anyone Can Grow Up: How George Bush and I Made It to the White House* [New York: Simon & Schuster, 1999], 122–23.)

it—'the pop shot,' 'the payoff shot,' 'the cum shot'—but the most resonant is 'the money shot.' It is a money shot for all concerned: for the distributors and filmmakers [and] for the male actors themselves." Talk about filthy lucre.

Porn itself became, in its way, no biggie. In her book *Female Chauvinist Pigs: Women and the Rise of Raunch Culture*, Ariel Levy would recount how young women would flaunt PORN STAR T-shirts, worn snugly, and smugly. Also making the rounds were tees emblazoned with the *Hustler* logo or the *Playboy* bunny. Certain actors and pro athletes saw zero social fallout—and a flash of hellion cachet—from having the press write about their goings-about-town with porn actresses, escorts, and strippers. And many stars were routinely doing their own nude scenes. MrSkin.com, launched in 1999, made a killing by creating a website that offered a database of thousands of feature films, clocking the exact instant (12:29!) when an actor (typically early in his or her career) was doing the nasty (or merely flashing some side boob).

Recording artists, too, were the ones who were taking the sting out of porn. Rap was already preoccupied with porn themes in the '80s. By 1992, when two members of the alternative band Jane's Addiction formed a group called Porno for Pyros, DJs didn't blink. The next year, Snoop Dogg released his sodomistically named gangsta rap album, *Doggystyle* (which later became the title of a Snoop porn video, coproduced with *Hustler*). A year later, as Pamela Paul has noted in her book *Pornified*, NWA's DJ Yella turned out his own porn film, asserting, "By putting my name on it and associating it with rap, I'm bringing porn to the mainstream."

Paul would also address the impact of hardcore and its value system on the wider culture, making the point that "today's pop stars embrace and exalt the joys of porn. Eminem, Kid Rock, Blink 182, Metallica, Everclear, and Bon Jovi have all featured porn performers in their music videos.... Britney Spears, Lil' Kim, and Christina Aguilera emulate porn star moves in their videos and live concerts." In this way, the era conferred upon hardcore a certain street-and-sheet cred. The porn-savvy celebrity was announcing: I'm badass, I'm sexed up, I *party*, and "I set the rules"—with all of the chauvinism and will- ful subordination of women that one might unpack from that last, weighted phrase. Discography recapitulates misogyny.

———

Hardcore became so prevalent so fast that softcore became norm core. *News- week* in 1992 identified the trend in a cover story, describing it as "The New Voyeurism" and remarking on "the middlebrow embrace, in the age of AIDS, of explicit erotic material for its own sake. From [photographer Robert] Mapplethorpe to MTV, from the Fox network to fashion advertising, looking at sex is creeping out of the private sphere and into the public, gentrified by artsy pretension and destigmatized out of viral necessity."[6]

Porn was becoming a low-cal garnish to the cultural smorgasbord. "It's in women's magazines," notes Pamela Paul, "where articles explain how to work your sex moves after those displayed in pornos. . . . It's on *Maxim* magazine covers, where even women who ostensibly want to be taken seriously as actresses pose like *Penthouse* pinups." In the *New York Times* in 1999, William L. Hamilton would identify "pornography chic," discussing how filmmakers, designers, and ad agency creatives had become caught up in the *look* of porn. He cited "the appropriation of the conventions of pornography—its stock heroes, its story lines, its low-budget lighting and motel-room sets— by the mainstream entertainment industry, the fashion and fine-art worlds and Main Street." Over time, such stereotypes, and image saturation, began to desensitize the public to such a degree that many marketers, TV news directors, screenwriters, fashion advertisers, and performers believed that the surest way to break through the morass was to use sex shock—the more inventive the better. More buck for more bang.

Porn was surging in the '90s not because of mobsters and creeps pushing product but because of an appetite across all demographics for the whole tasting menu. In a much-talked-about *New York Times Magazine* story on the growing national acceptance of adult entertainment, columnist Frank Rich found that Americans spent $10 to $14 billion a year on pornography—more, he calculated, than "professional football, basketball and baseball put together.[7]

---

6. In the '90s, photographers Jeff Burton, Ken Probst, and Larry Sultan—following Barbara Nitke's lead in the '80s—documented the on-camera frenzy and off-camera ennui of adult-film sets, gay and straight, creating bodies of work that sold well in galleries. Sultan created chilly tableaux showing porn actors, filmmakers, and crew members in their San Fernando Valley milieu: furnished upper-middle-class homes that were rented for the purpose, or sets that replicated suburban bedrooms. Sultan's stills, often depicting "breaks in the action," managed to place porn artifice inside a spooky American wholesomeness that was equal parts Helmut Newton, *Twin Peaks*, and *Pleasantville*. (Suzanne Stein, "Larry Sultan, 1946–2009,"SFMOMA.org, December 17, 2009; Jenna Garrett, "Photo du Jour: Boredom on an 80s Porn Set," FeatureShoot.com, June 17, 2014; William L. Hamilton, "The Mainstream Flirts with Pornography Chic," *New York Times*, March 21, 1999.)

7. Many publications would repeat these numbers, yet *Forbes* would eventually call them largely "baseless and wildly inflated." Citing stats from 1998 through 2001, Forbes.com asserted, "For the $10 billion figure to be accurate, you have to add in adult video networks and pay-per-view movies

"Size matters in the cultural marketplace," Rich would write. "At $10 billion, porn is no longer a sideshow to the mainstream like, say, the $600 million Broadway theater industry[8]—it is the mainstream." Indeed, it was hard to be more middle-of-the-road than General Motors, which owned the DirecTV satellite behemoth. Or more whitebread than AT&T, which charged customers by the minute for their phone-sex sessions. Or Time Warner, whose HBO, Warner Bros., and Warner Music divisions pushed sexual boundaries in their films and recordings. Or News Corp, which did the same on its Fox broadcast network. Or Marriott Hotels, which featured adult films on their TV menus. Porn no longer targeted the male and the frail. The audience included women *and* men *and* couples of all ages. And, gradually, female directors and producers began to take their share of the pie.

————

How, then, had porn been rebranded and reborn? The maiden culprit was the ascent of the videocassette in the '80s, which revolutionized porn (and vice versa). In prior ages, one could see filmed versions of sex acts only by going to a public place—a movie theater, a booth in a video store, or, in earlier times, a stag or bachelor party. In the '90s explicit tapes were conveniently stocked at Tower Records (remember Tower? remember *records?*), the corner video store, the adult paraphernalia parlor, *and* the online sex site. The films themselves had become more self-aware, bearing campier titles (*The Butt Sisters Do Baltimore*) or riffing on Hollywood features (*Foreskin Gump*) or porno *ad absurdum* (*President by Day, Hooker by Night*).

Plots and characters disintegrated as videos focused on themes or fetishes (*Anal Maniacs 3*). One popular genre was the "facial" compilation, which spliced together climax clips from other films, providing cascades of well-timed spunk as they frosted the upturned countenance of partner after partner. The penis itself, according to historian Debby Applegate (currently writing a biography of the legendary New York madam Polly Adler), emerged from porn's shadows for its perpetual close up. And breaking through all of

———

on cable and satellite, Web sites, in-room hotel movies, phone sex, sex toys and magazines—and still you can't get there....Skepticism is in order, though, because as David Klatell, associate dean of the Columbia Graduate School of Journalism notes, '[Pornography] is an industry where they exaggerate the size of everything.'" (Dan Ackman, "How Big Is Porn?," Forbes.com, May 25, 2001.)

8. By the 2010s, Broadway's annual ticket sales would soar to $1.37 billion. (Jesse Lawrence, "Broadway Just Had Its Highest-Grossing Year Ever," Forbes.com, July 10, 2015.)

the smut clutter was a new bumper crop: the amateur tape.[9] As camcorders became less costly, more totable, and equipped with more versatile lenses, there were fewer barriers to entry. The two-step process: go to Radio Shack; go home and draw the bedroom shades (tripod optional).

The appeal of these downmarket videos was their grunge-vérité: the more ooze and cooz, the noirier. In an industry dominated by airbrushed, well-toned, brand-name stars, filmed from multiple camera angles, there was a garden-fresh turn-on inherent in videos that were lone-lens, stripped-down, down-and-gooshy. In DIY porn, the sex act was human tartare: bring on the welts and hives and flushing. Indeed, the nameless bangers in these shameless tapes might even be into it not just for the paycheck or the infamy, but because they were *into* it.

Even so, the slicker flicks soldiered on. In the late 1990s, "thanks to Viagra," as writer R. V. Scheide has pointed out, "the flaccid penis [would] all but disappear...from porno films; the drug reportedly [would become] an industry mainstay." If anything, Viagra would help porn become bolder, colder, and, for many scenes, more interminable than ever. With their actors pharmacologically enhanced, directors could shoot more seamlessly and producers could schedule more films in a shorter span.[10]

Softcore and soft-focus were losing steam (though Cinemax—nicknamed "Skinemax"—pumped up its '90s lineup with light adult fare). Dramatic narrative had been supplanted by repurposed clips of orgies and tag teams. Establishing shots and tracking shots—and, oh, those oceans of shag carpeting—had gone the way of the buggy whip. But even if porn's cinematic conventions had been chucked out the basement window, no one seemed the

---

9. Nineties amateur tapes, which began as a "fringe fetish," according to journalist Ben Wallace, would become "one of pornography's most popular aesthetics—and, as such, one co-opted by the pros." (Benjamin Wallace, "The Geek-Kings of Smut," *New York*, February 7, 2011, 30.)

10. The new equation often proved a sore spot for the onscreen recipients. *Vanity Fair* columnist James Wolcott would call 1998 Year One of "Redi-Wood," stating that whatever benefits the drug brought to male staying power, "Viagra has resulted in a grueling strain on porn women, whose bodies are pounded by battering rams in scenes that can drag on near-forever. Couple this with anal sex's no longer being a specialty in a porn career...and the wear and tear on the body amounts to consensual rape." It was only a matter of time before many hardcore viewers began to believe that such roughhouse sessions were, in Wolcott's argot, "the marauding norm." (James Wolcott, "Debbie Does Barnes & Noble," *Vanity Fair*, September 2005.)

wiser. In 1997, according to the trade magazine *Adult Video News* (*AVN*), porn producers released some eight *thousand* titles.

Nineties news reports, tragically, included stories of porn stars lost to AIDS or suicide. Performers and friends flocked to memorials. HIV testing escalated. And yet the industry and the public perceived more rose than thorn. Business, in fact, was so brisk that the annual AVN Awards ceremony—the Golden Globes of hardcore—became more over-the-top and self-aggrandizing than ever. Each year, *AVN* would present honors in over *one hundred* categories, such as "Best Anal Themed Feature," as David Foster Wallace would observe in 1998 when covering the awards for *Premiere* magazine.[11]

As the videocassette trade gained traction, so did the cable and satellite side. From the 1980s through the early 2000s, premium TV, instead of cutting into video sales, at first did the opposite: winning over jittery viewers to content so raw that its skank factor was suddenly regarded as a plus. A business traveler, for instance, could check into any one of America's hotels or motels, and there on the set-top box would be a wad of adult features. (In some states or jurisdictions or hotel chains, the videos were sexually explicit; in others, they were spliced and diced to leave out graphic elements that a county judge might deem indecent.)

When business travelers got home, they could tune into the blue channels by dish or cable, order up pay-per-view movies, or surf the Web. They could dial into phone-sex lines, rifle through spank books, or visit local strip clubs or massage parlors or porn emporia. "People pay more money for pornography in America in a year than they do on movie tickets," Frank Rich would note. "As one [adult-film expert] put it, 'We realized that when there are 700 million porn rentals a year, it can't just be a million perverts renting 700 videos each.'" By decade's end, porn-video sales and rentals alone would reportedly account for more than $4 billion annually. (*Forbes*, however, would put that figure at "no higher than $1.8 billion.")

It was not uncommon for serious porn devotees to hail from red states,

---

11. Wallace would recount in his classic essay "Big Red Son" that when filmmaker Rob Black was bestowed with *AVN*'s 1998 Best Director/Video award for his porn feature *Miscreants*, he was lauded from the stage as "a guy who can take buttholes, midgets, and fried fish, and make a love story." The whole nine yards. (David Foster Wallace, "Big Red Son" [1998], in *Consider the Lobster and Other Essays* [New York: Little, Brown, 2006], 36.)

sometimes from counties with officials or judges known for outlawing erotic content if it failed to meet "community standards." (A 1973 Supreme Court ruling had established the smell test: content was obscene if thy neighbor— "[the] average person, applying contemporary community standards"— considered it so.) And yet the notion of a community standard was becoming altogether moot in the borderless online universe.

The major case in this regard was one involving Larry Peterman, from conservative Utah County, who managed a chain of video rental outlets.[12] (Peterman, along with his inventory of mainstream films, rented XXX videos to some four thousand people—"regular customers," according to court documents.) In 1996–97, Peterman and two codefendants were charged with peddling indecent films—in a predominantly red district in a heavily Mormon region. Peterman was threatened with jail time and his business went into a tailspin. But as his 1999 trial commenced, his attorney, Randy Spencer, was chagrined to find that the Provo Marriott—across the street from the courthouse—*also* rented pornos. In a given year, guests there had readily purchased some three thousand explicit in-room movies. According to the *New York Times*, the case was eventually thrown out because the "people in Utah County, a place that often boasts of being the most conservative area in the nation, were disproportionately large consumers of the very videos that prosecutors had labeled obscene and illegal." Moreover, their yearly satellite-TV consumption was "double the volume [of] most cities the size of Provo." By *this* "community standard," the county's argument against Peterman petered out.

Video's Blue Period was not just a function of supply-side bounty, pornographers' profit motive, or new distribution over the World Wide Web. Porn's prophylactic role also factored in. "The coincidence of AIDS—arriving at the same time as the development of technologies like VCRs and then the Internet, put us on two paths forever," says TV director Rob Klug, sitting in a CBS editing suite in Manhattan. "You could have intimacy—meaning you

---

12. Senator Orrin Hatch, the Utah Republican, has long been one of the nation's foremost antiporn crusaders. And the state, with its large Mormon population, has maintained so stiff an opposition to "obscene materials" that its lawmakers as recently as 2016 voted unanimously to designate porn as "a public-health crisis." ("Hatch Offers Anti-Porn Bill, Decries Judges," *Tulsa World*, June 5, 1996; interview with Robert Rosen; Belinda Luscombe, "Porn and the Threat to Virility," *Time*, April 11, 2016, 42.)

could die. *Or* you could have safe sex." Thus came a larger public appetite for porn, as the statistics attest. Says Klug, "We chose *not* to risk it. And we became less connected. We're all now texting, not talking. Clicking, not dicking."

In previous generations, sexual knowledge (sometimes highly misinformed) was imparted to preteens and younger teenagers by older siblings or "more experienced" friends. Junior high "health" seminars would get across the bare bones, literally. Parents, if they were the forthcoming kind, might convey more nuance. And come the mid-to-late '80s, the rise of AIDS forced sexual conversations out into the open. But the Internet made the discussion, whether roundabout or illicit, completely explicit. Kids learned not just the birds and the bees, but the whole buzzing hive.

Film producer Zak Tanjeloff was a twelve-year-old in Sarasota, Florida, in 1998. The erotic acceleration of the Internet, he now says, "coincided perfectly with my adolescent curiosity. For my friends and me, we didn't need sex-ed class when there were AOL, chat rooms, and Ask Jeeves to instantly answer any questions we had. Instead of rummaging through a parent's old collection of *Playboys*, we'd go to the house of the friend whose parents were less likely to barge in and we'd explore the [Web's] dark recesses with a casualness now common for people that age. Or we'd email each other links: Did you see *this*?

"Couple this incredible ease of access with the contemporaneous, incessant, and lurid details of the president's affairs being discussed and dissected everywhere, from CNN to talk-show monologues. To a curious twelve-year-old, it was serendipitous. The news served as a daily inspiration for late-night Web searches—'Hey Jeeves, what is a blowjob?' For my generation, this was the new normal."

––––––

How, then, to put the Internet porn genie back in the bottle? For a time, there were serious efforts by civic and church leaders, legislators and their constituents, many of them concerned parents. The decade saw a series of attempts—supported by both President Clinton (in a reelection year) and the Republican-controlled Congress—to curtail what many perceived to be a medium run rampant. First came the rudimentary V-chip and various forms of filtering software, which were meant to keep kids from being exposed to X-rated material on their electronic devices and TVs. Along with these stopgaps came the Communications Decency Act of 1996 (CDA), which sought to criminalize those who posted porn online without safeguarding it from the eyes of youngsters. (Under the law, websites and service providers were not necessarily liable if their users were the ones disseminating the allegedly offensive content.) The Supreme Court, however, would unanimously rule the CDA unconstitutional, calling it overly restrictive and a curb on free speech. Next came attempts to remedy the restrictiveness of the CDA: the Child Online Protection Act (COPA), the Child Internet Protection Act (CIPA), and the Child Pornography Prevention Act (CPPA). Though these bills were intended to penalize suppliers of content deemed to be "harmful to minors" and to outlaw porn that incorporated computer-generated images depicting kids (or adults who looked underage), various provisions of each act were also thrown out by the courts.[13]

The genie, however, was here to stay, tempting hundreds of millions of consumers, no matter their age. And by the turn of the millennium, the amateur ruled. Free nasty had sunk the business model of an entire industry. "If ten billion dollars [in annual porn profits] was accurate then," Frank Rich tells me today, "four billion dollars is accurate *now*. It's like Napster. The Internet decimated it."

---

13. Nancy Libin, an expert on digital privacy law and cyber security, a former counsel to Senator Joe Biden and later to the Center for Democracy and Technology, points out, "In *ACLU v. Reno*—the case that struck down the CDA—the [Supreme] Court distinguished the Internet from other kinds of broadcast media, like TV and radio. It found that the Internet was less intrusive because it requires users to take 'a series of affirmative steps more deliberate and directed than merely turning a dial.' Because it was not technically possible to screen Internet viewers by age or to block content harmful to kids without also blocking adults' access to constitutionally protected speech, the Court struck [down] the law on First Amendment grounds. COPA was an attempt to address the constitutional infirmities that the Court found in CDA....CPPA was struck down, [in turn,] because a majority on the Court found that virtual images [purporting to represent minors, either through computer-generated imagery or young-looking adults,] met neither the definition of 'obscene' or 'child porn' and the law therefore blocked lawful content." (Interview with Libin.)

CHAPTER 25

Chez Fleiss

"Lookit—my life," she says. "I've had tremendous highs. I spent one evening with Princess Diana. I've had dinner with Nancy Reagan. I also spent [part of] 1997 in solitary confinement in the penitentiary in Dublin, California."

I am at the desert hacienda of Heidi Fleiss. My host gained national notoriety after her high-profile arrest in 1993 on charges connected with running L.A.'s toniest prostitution ring. She would become widely known as "the Hollywood Madam." *People* magazine would refer to her as the "sex broker to the stars." Kid Rock would sing about her ("Start an escort service . . . find Heidi Fleiss."). Indeed, her operation had been such a sine qua non in the sin cycles of many of the world's power brokers that on any given night she would have "Heidi girls" on at least three continents and not infrequently aboard a private or corporate jet.

Chez Fleiss—surrounded by cacti, brush, and desolation—is located in a frontier town named Pahrump, Nevada. It consists of two trailers, which have been converted into a spacious ranch house. To get here, I have driven an hour along the parched perimeter of Death Valley without spying a human soul. And then, like some portent out of Castaneda, I see a vision. A titty bar. And its adjoining billboard announces her: "Ex–Hollywood Madam Heidi Fleiss book 'Pandering' autographed and sold at the Kingdom, All Nude Gentlemen's Club." Tempting, yes; but I decide to drive on to my destination.

Fleiss's property, on the barren outskirts of Pahrump, finally appears, up a winding dirt road. New signs await me: "Do Not Enter," "Keep Out." I park and Heidi Fleiss emerges with a macaw on her shoulder. "It's my Robinson Crusoe house," she says playfully as she greets me. She ushers me inside for

Perrier. I notice macaws and exotic birds of every color—I count twenty—on perches and ledges. I also spot splotches on the floor.

Fleiss shows little hint of her sleek former glory. She looks wan, her facial features sunken. She has recently gotten off crystal meth—"the white trash drug," she tells me. She has completed a stint on TV's *Celebrity Rehab with Dr. Drew.* (The public humiliation, she claims, was actually therapeutic.)

Indeed, she has reality TV in her blood. Mike Fleiss, a cousin, is one of the giants of the genre, having produced the breakout successes *Who Wants to Marry a Multi-Millionaire?*, *The Bachelor*, and *The Bachelorette.* Heidi, too, has appeared on a string of such programs (*Celebrity Big Brother*, *Sober House*, even Animal Planet's *Heidi Fleiss: Prostitutes to Parrots*). She is a woman straddling two cognitively dissonant lives: one tethered to the here and now, one pure façade; one steeped in addiction and criminality, one in sexual fantasy.

Then again, she is funny and whip-smart. Her opinions spew out in burbles. She is cocky and coquettish, though painfully self-conscious. She is also darkly transfixing, with an almost lupine spirit. "Charles Manson was captured a half hour from here," she says, as if to spook me.

Today, Heidi Fleiss is wearing gray Superbad sweatpants, house slippers lined in fluffy pink, and a blue sweatshirt speckled with macaw caca. Her two housekeepers, she explains, have "up and quit" two days before. She acknowledges her current state with a bright pop of self-deprecation: "I'm in my sweats cleaning up bird shit." But she is sanguine nonetheless. "My life [is] finally balanced out right now. Sure, it is a very unconventional and dysfunctional lifestyle I have, living with these birds. But, somehow, I make it work."

Initially, Fleiss had moved to Nevada (where prostitution is licensed and legal in certain counties) hoping to open an all-male brothel catering to women. But "Heidi's Stud Farm" went off the rails when she came up against local resistance, some legal issues, and, oddly, a new preoccupation. Fleiss, it turns out, had befriended Marianne Erikson, a neighbor who was elderly and bedridden. An ex-madam, Erikson used to run the exotic bird department at the Tropicana Hotel in Vegas, and upon retiring maintained a menagerie in her home trailer. "I would go and visit her," Fleiss recalls. "She had all her birds in cages with these big Frankenstein bolts, and the birds would be screaming and rattling the bolts."

In 2006, as Erikson lay dying, Fleiss called the paramedics. "Her last words were, 'You take care of my birds.' I told her, 'No.' But this is where I am. I fell in love with these birds and I lost interest in the sex business.[1] . . . I'll never turn my back on them." Most nights, she says, she is alone in this place on the edge of the desert. "In the evenings, they fly around here. I don't clip their wings. . . . I don't keep them in cages."

I am introduced to Paulina, Paul, Rodin, Freddie, and Simon. Golly used to work in a furniture store and likes to declare, "Half-off!" Suzy speaks Spanish; two others speak Mandarin. Reggie, Heidi insists, is gay. She describes his habit of pecking at another male, occasionally finding him in dirty-bird flagrante: "He turns him upside-down, sixty-nines him." Now and again, her feathered friends break into conversation, their calls suggesting a sort of cacophonous Greek chorus.[2]

———

Between 1991 and 1993, Heidi Fleiss ran a ring of high-end call girls, some five hundred at one time or another. They charged upwards of $1,500 a night. (Fleiss says she pocketed 40 percent.) Clients ranged from Fortune 500 execs to dissolute young heirs and royals, from rock icons to the free-spending studs at the studios. The typical Heidi "type," she explains, "look[ed] clean-cut and perfect. . . . I want[ed] a guy to know that she was born and raised in Beverly Hills, stepped off the cover of *Seventeen* magazine, but she's going to fuck like Jenna Jameson in the bedroom. She's going to be the nastiest girl on the planet. She's going to bring in other girls—do this, do that, do things you never even heard of. *That's* the girl."

Even so, Fleiss maintains, the sex itself was never hyper-kinky. "At the

———

1. Since then, Fleiss regained some interest in her old trade, working as a consultant to her longtime friend Dennis Hof, proprietor of seven Nevada brothels. "I advise him," she says. "Interior design. [Helping to] put together a museum on brothels." She monitors trends too. "There's a huge call for trannies now. A guy, if they're a little bit high, they are insane for trannies." But Fleiss's heart, she maintains, is with her more manageable flock. (Interview with Fleiss; John M. Glionna and Javier Panzar, "In Nevada, There Is Little Love Left for Brothels," *Los Angeles Times*, October 14, 2015.)

2. Before my visit, I had read up on multiple-pet owners. "Animal hoarding," according to a key research consortium that studies the practice, "is likely a final common pathway from a variety of traumatic experiences which result in dysfunctional attachment styles to people and lead to compulsive and addictive behavior." But Fleiss seems to have broken the mold and, per usual, defied convention. In her case, I feel I am in the company of someone determined to be a nurturer, caretaker, and provider for those she has taken under her wing. These are the very attributes, in fact, of the best madams. ("FAQs for Hoarding of Animals Research Consortium," Cummings School of Veterinary Medicine, Tufts University, vet.tufts.edu/hoarding/faqs-hoarding/.)

levels and money I'm dealing with," she says, "there is no time for anything like that—where people are going to [try] asphyxiation and die. There was nothing so abusive or so degrading that someone was going to, the next day, feel shameful or hurt.... If drugs and drinking [are] involved, there's, like, people you don't expect, all of a sudden, will want to suck a dick or whatever.... That kind of thing wasn't as weird as you thought. [Or] all of a sudden you want anal sex—a tennis racquet, but which end? Stuff like that... Okay, yeah, you'd never understand that *this* billionaire wants to wear lingerie. But so what?"

Her heyday, like the mayfly's, was brief. In her early twenties, she started turning tricks for the legendary Madam Alex. "I wish I was a better hooker," she laughs. "I couldn't compete with the other girls." She soon realized that her aptitude was not in servicing clients but in the service *business*. Before long she was running the show, then setting off on her own, and for two or three heady years, she had cornered L.A.'s top-tier sex trade.

Her original objective, she says, had been to make enough capital to switch careers (possibly to real estate), a dream of many a young entrepreneur. But she got hooked on the glamour, the octane, and the power. She fell in, she says, with "people who are 1 percent of the wealthiest in the world.... I remember when one client paid me $10,000 in $500 bills. A palette of silver bars showed up at the house [one day] that weighed like seven pounds each. I used to use them as doorstops.... I had one girl on the cover of *Seventeen* magazine, *Harper's Bazaar*—all working for me."

She recalls dispatching her troops to the Clinton inaugural in 1993; to Argentina, for polo season; to yachts in Acapulco and Monte Carlo. She had four phone lines at her house in Benedict Canyon; lovelies lounging by the pool; drugs aplenty. At her trial, a real estate grandee described shuttling Fleiss's damsels on his private plane. Even heads of state, she bragged, would phone her directly. "If I really came out and talked," she told Lynn Hirschberg in *Vanity Fair*, "I could have stopped NAFTA."

Today, Fleiss speaks with astonished wonderment. "It seems like another world ago. I was living in a world that was really not realistic. I mean, not too many twenty-five-year-olds go and buy a [multi]million-dollar house up in Beverly Hills like that and just live that lifestyle.... My neighbors were Bruce Springsteen, Bernie Brillstein, Jay Leno, and Jack Lemmon."

She shifts from past to present tense, as if reliving the rush. "It just keeps getting better and better, like the wave is never going to crash. I remember some days—I hate to put it [in] financial [terms]—I'd be, like, 'Okay, let's see if I can make $200,000 by the end of this week.' And I'd be, 'Oh my God, I made $300,000.'...Like you get in a *zone*....Everything was fun. I mean, girls are getting paid to fuck Charlie Sheen."

And the parties. "They didn't have sex for money at my house, but they would come hang out. It was social....You've got people like Jack Nicholson and Mick Jagger partying at your house"—not to imply that any of these guests partook of her stable's services. "I remember coming home and Prince was dancing in my living room."

Surely there had been flesh-peddlers who catered to the elite. But Fleiss was a new, '90s breed. She was in her twenties. She was hardly inconspicuous, driving around town in a '92 Corvette or a '67 Mustang. And she personified call-girl chic at a time when hookers were in sudden favor—in films like *Pretty Woman*, in fashion, in rap. Just months after making bail, she started a casual clothing line—Heidi Ware. She entertained offers for movies-of-the-week. She granted interviews. She posed in her Vette (in black boots and her signature shades) for Annie Leibovitz. She wore Norma Kamali and Dolce & Gabbana to the courthouse, and her state trial drew the likes of columnist Dominick Dunne and Sydney Biddle Barrows (the Mayflower Madam, dressed in Chanel).

She stood out in another way too. In her insular sisterhood, discretion had always been the watchword. But Fleiss was a slave to her addictions—and her ego. And she would eventually see it all implode because she was, at twenty-seven, a woman of her times: a chatterbox in an era of braggadocio.

In December 1992, she crowed to the *Los Angeles Times*, "Look, I know Madam Alex was great at what she did, but it's like this: What took her years to build, I built in one. The high end is the high end, and no one has a higher end than me....In this business, no one steals clients. There's just better service." Her gloating immediately put the LAPD on her tail. (She would eventually be jailed on federal charges of evading taxes and laundering money.)

"I sunk my ship—I did," she now allows, blaming no one but herself. "I was an idiot. And I have to take responsibility....We all knew what we were doing. The girls knew it was illegal. The guys knew it was illegal. I knew it was illegal. I didn't think I'd end up in...a federal prison. For *sex*? But [that's what happened]. They can say it was [for tax charges by] the IRS. There's nothing else to it but sex."

Fleiss went down fighting. She struck back when her black book was fought over by the law and the press. (The "black book," she tells me, consisted of a few red-bound Gucci day planners.) She lashed out when former lovers or members of her aviary tried to feather their nests by dangling secrets (interviews, audiotaped phone calls, incriminating videos) in front of the tabs and tabloid TV.

The main reason for her overnight celebrity? Her flock serviced celebrities. And if anyone personified flagrant sexual indulgence in the '90s it was her client Charlie Sheen. In video testimony at Fleiss's trial, the actor admitted that in a year's time he'd spent $53,000—two dozen occasions' worth—for Heidi-caliber companionship. (Though Sheen had ridden an '80s wave to stardom in movies like *Platoon* and *Wall Street*, he became a '90s caricature of self-destructive behavior.[3] Known, as he once put it, for "banging seven-gram rocks," Sheen told *Maxim* that by the year 2000 he'd bedded some five thousand partners. Fifteen years later, he would announce he was HIV-positive.) "He's the most well-known client [of mine]," Fleiss says, "because his traveler's checks were in my purse...when I was arrested. [Otherwise] there was no reason to give him up....I had people who spent a *lot-lot* more money with me."

Comparable offenders might have managed to get off lightly. But Heidi Fleiss had no such luck. She would serve three years, hard-core. And she survived it, she concedes, by adapting to her environment. Of prison, she reports, "It's lesbian hell. I had a girlfriend"—an airplane mechanic, she says,

---

3. Sheen dated and married models and actresses. He befriended porn stars. After procuring sexual services, he was known to leave a handsome tip over and above the steep fee. He battled substance abuse and got in trouble with the law repeatedly for incidents of violence against women. And in the perverse counter-karma that seemed to define tabloid personalities of the period, Sheen became, by the 2000s, the star of the sitcom *Two and a Half Men*—and, for a time, television's highest-paid actor. ("Charlie Sheen in Hospital for Drug, Alcohol Problems," CNN.com, May 22, 1998; Jim Rutenberg, "Charlie Sheen's Redemption Helps a Studio in Its Struggles," *New York Times*, February 4, 2002, C8; Karen Thomas, "So Bad, but Such Good Fun," *USA Today*, August 27, 2003, D3; Tracie Egan Morrissey, "Charlie Sheen's History of Violence Toward Women," Jezebel.com, March 2, 1001; "Charlie Sheen Breaks Silence, Tells Radar: 'I'm Fine...People Don't Seem to Get It,'" Radar .com, January 29, 2011; "Charlie Sheen's Porn Star Girlfriends," Radar.com, December 24, 2015; Mark Seal, "Charlie Sheen's War," *Vanity Fair*, June 2011, 173; Dorothy Pomerantz, "Hollywood's Highest-Paid TV Actors," *Forbes*, October 11, 2011.)

who was in on drug charges. "[Now] she has a huge company that's worth a few million dollars." Her second lover "looked like J-Lo. Men are my preference, but you're there, and you just do what you're going to do."

Her takeaway from the decade, she says—as a woman running her own business, as a sexual creature, and as a strong-willed individual—is that the era gave females new command over sex and power. "The world has changed with women and independence and money. [During] the '90s, I was living with Victoria Sellers[4] in my house in Beverly Hills and [we'd] say stuff like this: 'Do you want a blonde or a brunette tonight?' A blond or a brunet *guy*. I'd go, 'I don't care, as long as they don't call me back. I have work to do in the morning.' It just became a thing, I think, where women didn't feel so pressured that they have to marry the first guy that they have sex with. I don't know if [the attitude was more] casual—or realistic."

Men, she contends, cannot *not* sleep around. "Men will fuck mud," as she puts it. But in the '80s and '90s, she says, women became more pragmatic about the interpersonal hypocrisy that had previously been a largely male preserve. "Women [became more] confident. A woman felt, 'I can act on my impulse.'" She attributes much of this brave new sense of authority and self-possession to a single role model. "Madonna has a lot to do with everything. From 'Like a Virgin,' all her songs—I think Madonna is a catalyst, an incredible force of nature, [teaching] women, 'Be yourself' and 'Do what you want to do' and 'Express yourself.'"

Fleiss turns reflective. "I have very low self-esteem....I listen to everyone. But [in the end] I'm going to make my own decision, no matter what.... My image is: I'm associated with something bad—illegal, prison. So I have a different kind of stigma attached. I'm aware of it and it doesn't bother me. Look, I don't care what people think. If you care what people think or say—you're a prisoner. Your life is over."

Now that the dazzle and the crime and the punishment are behind her, I ask, what lasting mark did she make, in the end, on the decade and the culture?

She says she managed to relieve some pressure on the American conscience—on millions who were struggling with their angst and qualms surrounding infidelity. "Everyone has something," she figures, "a little bit of

---

4. The model and actress is the daughter of Peter Sellers and Britt Ekland.

scandal. Everyone really does. It's just whether you find out about it or not. It's human nature. You cannot help yourself. In the '90s, when people found out about what I was doing with my operation, it made everyone breathe a little bit easier: 'Phew, it's not only me.' They didn't feel they had a dirty little secret. All men will cheat. Women too."

Moreover, her own scandal, she believes, helped create and define a market for exposing the dirtiest secrets of public personalities—for better and for worse. "It was the time that *Hard Copy, Inside Edition,* and *A Current Affair* were exploding. They were *so* hardcore gossip. And so I was plastered on all of that. *Everyone* wants to be famous. So *anyone* could make an accusation about me. And many people did—and got paid for it. Some were true and some weren't true. I don't really care now—I can only laugh about it." But, looking back, she says, she sees herself as something of a tabloid trial balloon. "It was a weird celebrity time. My situation was on the cusp of that tabloid explosion. I went to prison from 1997 to the millennium. And that's when the Internet came. Paris Hilton. *The Bachelor*—which my cousin *owned....* A lot of this reality stuff is based on whatever went down with my arrest— and the tabloid culture of the era, which I'm not too proud of. I [helped] spawn this brain-dead television thing."

"Movie star," Gina, a scarlet macaw, cries out, as if listening in.

"I love Gina," Heidi says, shaking her head. "I just don't know how I wound up here. In Death Valley. With twenty macaws. I just don't know."[5]

---

5. When I phone her in 2015 to see how she's getting on, she tells me she has had a change of heart—and is on a new mission. "It took me a long time to understand the birds. Now I'm an [animal rights] activist. They do not belong as pets in my home or your home. There is no way to have a normal life and have a macaw. They *live a hundred years.* They are powerful fliers. They are not supposed to have their wings clipped and live in a cage. It's a huge, huge problem. I'm dedicating myself to two things," she promises. "There's not one sanctuary where they can live free. I need to create a place where [birds like these] can live. [This initiative] needs to be done, state by state. Secondly, I'm hoping to stop the breeding—to stop the pet trade. This is the rest of my life—to try and help them. That gives me hope." In the meantime, her loyal, radiant hens and cocks give her unconditional love, and company, in a world that has often betrayed or discarded her.

CHAPTER 26

Hard Currency

"In the '90s, with the exception of maybe Bangkok, Moscow was where you saw the most decadent behavior on the face of the earth," says my friend Brett Forrest, an American correspondent who spent years reporting from Moscow and Kiev. We are discussing how erotic commerce, after 1989, began to corrode certain sectors of society in Russia and the former Eastern Bloc as Communist governments disintegrated, one by one.

"The '90s," he insists, "were a particularly dark time for the Russian people, who have a dark history anyway, and who by then had had their instincts repressed since the 1917 revolution. In darker times, people are given over to vice. And vice came on with a vengeance. You're talking about the A-1 bad behaviors: murder, theft, violence, sexual violence. Total lawlessness. Important officials, as a matter of course, were being gunned down on the street. And when *that's* going on, sex ranks far down on the list of social ills. People thought they could get away with *any*thing: 'You're telling me I can't have sex with *three* fourteen-year-olds?'"

There were rumblings in the 1980s. That's when glasnost—the cultural and social "openness" campaign introduced by the reformist leader Mikhail Gorbachev—had, among other things, brought about a loosening of sexual mores, a public airing of sensually charged topics, and a glamorization of Western-style disinhibition in a land that for generations had suppressed such expression. Films became more risqué and socially provocative. Russians, especially Russian youth, became more sexually adventurous. And, as the business consultant and Slavic studies expert Katherine Avgerinos has described, it became acceptable, among certain peers, given the challenges of day-to-day survival, to accept alcohol or lodging or money for what in less dire times might have been considered "casual sex."

Soon all bets were off. The Berlin Wall was torn down in November 1989. The Iron Curtain opened. Regimes toppled. In December 1991, the Soviet government was officially dissolved and there was no dominant ideology to replace Communism. Into that vacuum swept a system of economic thuggery. Even as dwellings were privatized and people suddenly *owned* the apartments they lived in, the bulwarks of the economy (the state-owned industries, such as oil and metals) were sold at auction. "Very often the guys who ran the auctions *won* the auctions," explains Forrest, over drinks in Manhattan and then in phone interviews during his travels between Kiev and Istanbul. "It was a dark swindle: state-sponsored theft, all through the '90s." And a new class of spectacularly wealthy individuals—the oligarchs—became the central force in a Mafia-style racket with the Kremlin at its pinnacle. "It created a pervading mind-set," he adds. "'Okay, anything goes. If *these guys* are just stealing everything—and these guys are *the government*—I will too.' The decadence [that resulted] was fundamentally about exerting one's power.

"An aspirational attitude sprang up," Forrest remembers. "The United States is number one, and we want *that*—all these things that for years we were told were better and we couldn't have. When Russians finally got the chance to experience Western culture, they largely took the worst parts: conspicuous consumption, the emphasis on the individual, and boundless promiscuity, without recognizing the greater underpinnings of a stable, civil society. *All* behavior became permissible. You saw an upswing in drug use, partying, wild orgies. Out-and-out sexual excess was the order of the day, and largely still is. People were going after anything and everything, all in the greatest amounts. The ethos was, 'Push it further and harder, until I fall down.' And then, 'Get up from your stupor and do it all over again.'[1]

"In the '90s in Russia and Eastern Europe, things were hard on everybody,"

---

1. The scene was encapsulated in a '90s den of decadence called the Hungry Duck, a Moscow nightclub with female and male strippers and a history of violence, prostitution, underage debauchery—and what journalists Mark Ames and Matt Taibbi have called a "rape-camp" vibe. "The stories," wrote Andrew Roth, in an almost nostalgic recap in the *New York Times*, "were outlandish and often unverifiable: of barroom brawls where eyeballs were knocked out of their sockets, public sex in the booths and topless dancers falling off the bar." Not to mention two thousand lost passports—and eight wayward bullet holes lodged here and there. (Andrew Roth, "A Decadent Reminder of Russia Before Putin," *New York Times*, August 6, 2012, A7; Mark Ames and Matt Taibbi, *The Exile: Sex, Drugs, and Libel in the New Russia* [New York: Grove, 2000], 236; Katherine P. Avgerinos, "From Vixen to Victim: The Sensationalization and Normalization of Prostitution in

he says. "But at times like that, they're harder on women. Women, barred from professions of longevity, were reduced to relying on more base instincts for short-end money, propelling them into a spiral and perpetuating a system that ultimately worked against them." Slavic women by the thousands, often sold into sexual servitude under false pretenses, would be smuggled out by gangs in Kiev, Belarus, and Moscow, ending up in brothels from Germany to Turkey, Israel to Japan. By 1998, journalist Michael Specter would write in a *New York Times* exposé that "as many as 400,000 women under 30 [had left Ukraine] over a ten-year period," many having become ensnared in the sex trade.

The trafficking was the result of "a perfect confluence of circumstances," contends Forrest, who has written about the region's prostitution syndicates. "First, Slavic women are considered by many cultures as being, by and large, exceptionally beautiful. Secondly, in the first dozen post-Soviet years, women outside of the major population centers had zero professional, educational, or economic outlets. So they were readily available and easily preyed upon. Thirdly, there was a market for newly available [young women], which an extraordinarily ruthless syndicate could exploit. These gangsters had superior girls, at a cheaper rate, and they were more violent than the competition. It's pretty easy to see the profit margins. [To] a Russian guy in this business, a 'quality' girl from the Eastern Bloc would cost five times less than other prostitutes who might appeal to discriminating johns in the so-called First World. The business model? Bring these girls over to Belgium, put them up in a slave house, take care of the cops, rotate new girls in every month, and you have clients out the door."

Tragically, a similar formula was being applied around the globe by networks seeking to meet the needs of the local population—and to satisfy an ever more migratory executive class that, in the global economy, had come to expect five-star amenities.

———

The world was flush with new capital, new jobs, new economic opportunities[2]—and new ways to profit from sex.

Post-Soviet Russia," *Vestnik, The Journal of Russian and Asian Studies,* October 23, 2006, http://www.sras.org/normalization_of_prostitution_in_post-soviet_russia.)

2. Historian Douglas Brinkley recently told me that he sometimes considers the 1990s "the decade of the Two Bills: Bill Clinton and Bill Gates." Call it the Bill Epoch. (Interview with Brinkley.)

Excess capital, to be clear, had *always* been a stalking horse for the carnal. And as the world's financial health got rosier in the '90s, there was an expanding market for wanton commodities and services. In the upheaval that followed the collapse of regimes in Poland, Hungary, East Germany, Bulgaria, Czechoslovakia, Romania, and the U.S.S.R., democratic initiatives flourished, as did broad-brush capitalism. According to the *New York Times'* Thomas Friedman, "After the fall of the Berlin Wall, virtually every economy in the world moved to a capitalist system, which eventually made the world awash with money looking for investments." In China, despite the bloody crackdown on the student-led democracy movement (also in 1989), the nation had already begun its transition to a market economy. Indeed, a new term—"globalization"—came into wide use, denoting how the interdependence of world trade, markets, communications networks, and economic development had begun to exert profound cross-cultural, political, and social shifts across borders and oceans.

So where, in all of this, was *erotic commerce?* During this period of convulsive economic change, more new methods were devised to profit from illegal sexual practices than at any time in human history.

As mentioned, trafficking was on the rise. Women, often escaping economic hardship, fled overseas from Africa and Asia, from the Balkans and across Eastern Europe. Many would be promised legitimate jobs but then end up forced to become sex workers. The situation in the Pacific had its own dynamic. As a result of the 1980s recession in Japan, followed by the Asian financial crisis of 1997, so many regional women lost traditional means of employment—according to Siddharth Kara, the author of *Sex Trafficking*, and the Pulitzer Center's Deena Guzder—there was "a mass migration from the villages of rural Thailand, Burma, Laos and Cambodia into urban centers such as Bangkok and Chiang Mai... [where] destitute migrants were exploited in factories and brothels."

Ukraine, meanwhile, "replaced Thailand and the Philippines as the epicenter of global business in trafficking women," Michael Specter would report. "In Milan a week before Christmas, the police broke up a ring that was holding auctions in which women abducted from the countries of the former Soviet Union were put on blocks, partially naked, and sold at an average price of just under $1000."

It was not just "over there." U.S. law enforcement agencies, according to the *Times'* Nicholas Kristof—who would go on to become a standard-bearer for reporting on sex trafficking—saw an influx of sex workers from Russia, Eastern Europe, Latin America, Asia, and elsewhere. The worst spike of all, though, in Kristof's view, involved the American runaway: "Typically, she's a 13-year-old girl of color from a troubled home who is on bad terms with her mother. Then her mom's boyfriend hits on her, and she runs away to the bus station, where the only person on the lookout for girls like her is a pimp."

During the same period, the phenomenon of sex tourism took insidious root. Tour operators sold foreign "packages" that promised travelers a safe way to pay for sex or to watch sexually explicit performances that were often humiliating and sometimes vile. ("Reducing impoverished women's sexuality to a spectator sport is inherently degrading," writes Guzder.) Anthropologist Kathleen Nadeau would find that as American military bases in Asia were decommissioned or cut back, endangering nearby clubs and houses of prostitution, "sex tourism began to be promoted instead . . . [to the point where] loans offered by the World Bank and International Monetary Fund as a strategy for economic development [in Thailand and the Philippines]" were in effect supporting sex-holiday destinations. "Young women, gay men, and even children," Nadeau has noted, "[were] lured by often illicit recruiters to work in the teeming array of brothels, massage parlors, and sex bars that service mainly males from the United States, Europe, Australia, Japan, Korea, Malaysia, Singapore, and the Gulf states."[3]

Meanwhile, pornographers would push ever farther afield. Czech-born journalist Iva Roze Skoch, who divides her time between New York and Prague, has studied how the Eastern Bloc's breakup led to a surge in hardcore producers trying to enlist young models, performers, and cinematographers— people who would agree to work for lower wages than their stateside coun-

---

3. Closer to home, according to British journalist and social activist Julie Bindel, who helped found the organization Justice for Women, certain tourists in the '90s and 2000s (typically middle-aged women from North America and Europe) explored "the darker side" of fun-in-the-sun vacations, traveling to beachside destinations like Jamaica, Cuba, and the Dominican Republic with the intention of paying for sex with "beach boys" or guides. Bindel, writing about one such sex tourist— a forty-three-year-old Canadian woman who regularly traveled to Jamaica for trysts—pointed out, "The knowledge that many of her sexual partners are desperately poor does not seem to spoil her enjoyment." (Julie Bindel, "The Price of a Holiday Fling," *Guardian*, July 5, 2003.)

terparts. Czech culture enjoyed its libertine reputation,[4] and porn was not "specifically illegal" under Communist rule, says Skoch. "But the *production* of it was. Camcorders and good camera [gear] were banned because the government didn't want people using them on the street to document civil unrest. So after 1989 there was a flood of electronic equipment [from] Austria and Germany. It was just a matter of time before people realized that there would be a huge market for pornography.

"Talk about cultural imperialism," Skoch remarks. Local and foreign producers and directors set up shop in Eastern Europe "because it was easy to recruit men and because [many] American gay customers like seeing straight men in porn." Budapest (already a center for cinematic talent) and Prague, Skoch recalls, became hubs for the production of straight and gay porn. In an article she would publish on GlobalPost.com, Skoch wrote about one director who told her he liked to "recruit men who have typically never done porn or had sex with men before and market their inexperience as an asset.... He enjoys filming the first-timers, especially if they don't really like it. He zooms in on their faces clenched in pain."

––––––––

Eros and economics do not necessarily correlate. Recession or depression or political unrest can contribute to an environment ripe for sexual openness, abandon, or decadence. And yet supercharged economies—or societies going through periods of wide income disparity—can be similarly focused

––––––––

4. A Czech-born photographer I know, Hana Jakrlova, was in her twenties and living in Prague at the time. "Prior to the fall of the [Berlin] Wall, the control you had was over your mind, but you were always physically restricted. You couldn't move around. You could go to Yugoslavia once in five years, if you were lucky. But what you *could* control was your body. And so there was in Bohemia a history of libertine ways, more so than in Moscow and elsewhere. The freedom of sleeping around was a way to express yourself. In other areas of life you were not free. It wasn't about exploring; life generally sucked. But people found joy in sex and relationships.... Then, [after] the week of November 17, 1989—the week of the Velvet Revolution—*the next day* pornographic magazines appeared on the newsstands. They had never been allowed. Advertising became this aggressively childish [and] tasteless thing: 'Naked tits—and buy Skoda, a brand of Czech car.' Never before would you see a *billboard* under Communism. But now there was *a set of tits on a billboard*." Madonna Swanson, an American-born daughter of Czech émigrés, is a program manager who assists global companies after mergers and acquisitions. She too recalls the unapologetic attempt to profit off of women's bodies. "Day one, the Velvet Revolution," Swanson says. "Day two: in a heartbeat—boom—sex was everywhere from a marketing point of view. If you're selling a mobile phone, a sweater, below the bustline [models' clothing] was coming unraveled." (Interviews with Jakrlova, Swanson.)

on leisure interests that overvalue the erotic. And fin de siècle America was such a society.

For much of the '80s and '90s, the so-called New Economy was at a gallop, continuing, off and on, late into 2008. During Bill Clinton's time in office, "jobs were being created at an unprecedented pace," economist Joseph Stiglitz would point out in his book *The Roaring Nineties*. "By April 2000, [unemployment fell] below 4 percent for the first time in three decades.... For the first time in a quarter century, those at the bottom saw their incomes begin to grow, with the greatest ever reduction in welfare rolls (more than 50 percent in six years)." Bill Clinton had been at the controls for the country's broadest and most bounteous economic expansion in peacetime, and when he exited the Oval in the winter of 2001, America's ledgers were graced with an estimated budget surplus of $256 billion—projected to expand over the next decade to between $1 and $2 *trillion*. At the same time, small fortunes accumulated in the hands of a younger, tech-connected elite in ways that echoed the Gilded Age of a century before.

Yet these new riches allowed more people to devote more discretionary funds to leisure pursuits—often sexual (and *illegal*) pursuits. And such spending was often most visible among newly affluent men, many of whom believed that their wealth had earned them a rightful dominance (sometimes erotically charged dominance) over other human beings.

So-called massage parlors and men's spas—fronts for sexual favors—spread out from American cities to the suburbs. (They would become ubiquitous in the 2000s.) It was not uncommon for an upstanding fellow to plunk down a modest fee for a late-night, weekend, or after-work "happy ending"—a handjob administered perfunctorily to a prone patron after his full-body massage. "A rub-and-a-tug became an underground sexual phenomenon," says a friend of mine from the Midwest who sampled these establishments in the period between his two marriages. "There's a 'happy ending' place on every [other] corner in every [major] city. It became socially accepted."

But the most aboveboard expression of America's erotic economy was the rise of the strip club. Rebranded as "gentlemen's clubs," the establishments—between twenty-five hundred and five thousand of them, coast to coast—experienced exponential growth in the '80s and '90s. While the less savory strip joints still operated in smaller towns, metro areas opened spacious upscale clubs that offered nude or seminude dancers. In these nightspots a handful of performers could be found disrobing on a central dance floor; others would do the same on satellite stages; still others would circulate among the customers, dispensing intimate dances, sometimes with "friction" contact.

The women in slinky dresses, the mirrors, the flashing lights and throbbing music—interrupted every now and then by an emcee's directions ("Orchidea to the main stage")—gave the enterprise the feel of a forbidden theme park. Adding to the ambiance were clubs with dining areas, ATMs and fax machines, big-screen TVs tuned to sporting events, and bathrooms with attendants in black tie offering baskets of breath mints.

"What topless is doing is replacing disco," the writer D. Keith Mano told the *New York Times* in 1992 after the publication of his novel *Topless.*[5] The next year, novelist Carl Hiaasen came out with his own contribution to the genre: *Strip Tease*, a raucous tale about the lives and crimes inside the Florida strip-club scene. Its most notable passage described how clubgoers would pay top dollar to spar with a topless model in a wrestling tub piled high with creamed corn. To wit: "Erin remained baffled by the success of the nude wrestling exhibitions, which had become a red-hot fad in upscale strip joints. There was nothing erotic about grappling with a topless woman in a vat of cold vegetables, although the sodden realization came too late for most customers."

Stripper-themed films opened at the neighborhood multiplex. In 1995 came *Showgirls*, with Elizabeth Berkley, face glitter galore, and cartoonish maxims ("In America, everyone's a gynecologist"). It was followed by *Striptease*—based on Hiaasen's book—with Demi Moore (in lace-up boots and a rhinestone choker) taking it all off, and then taking down a corrupt congressman and his sugar baron chums.

Don Waitt, the publisher of *ED*, is one of the arbiters of the adult entertainment business. (The leading trade publication for the adult nightclub industry—*ED*, which launched in 1992, stands for *Exotic Dancer*, not "erectile dysfunction.") In Waitt's view, the '90s were a turning point. "It's a long way from the go-go lounges of the '60s, '70s, and '80s," he tells me. "The clubs evolved as the culture changed. They [began to] have steak restaurants and

5. True enough. As disco died a slow death, landlords and discotheque operators were left holding the bag. Many a pressured tenant decided to fill those empty spaces with adult entertainment.

valet parking and champagne. We reflect mainstream society more so than the porn industry and video and the Internet. We're really *not* porn. We're *real*. The Internet changed everything"—meaning that customers had come to expect their sexually charged performances in settings that were up-close, convenient, and quasi-private. And yet, Waitt says, the Web experience was *virtual*. Exotic dancers, in contrast, smiled and asked you your name. "The clubs have *thrived* in this period. You actually touch a girl and feel the sweat on her arms."

Strip clubs were touted as a relatively hygienic way to play out one's own safe-sex fantasy. But they were also about abundance. And no hassle. And creating the illusion that each and every customer, for that moment, was magically affluent, and actually *appealing* to the woman passing by. The kinder, gentler, gentrified clubs made the little guy feel at home next to the big spender. With their stages and hidden rooms and tempting choices, they had become topless Target stores: clean and consumer-friendly, stylish *and* garish. "The '90s," says Waitt, were a sort of new erotic dawn when "the asymmetry of supply" met the needs of "the lone, lustful, demanding man."

The critics, of course, were legion. Such establishments perpetuated sexual stereotypes. They exploited women, many of whom were economically and socially disadvantaged to begin with, and often the victims of abuse. They *closed* more career paths for dancers than they opened. They brought a criminal element to their neighborhoods. They eroded real estate values. They sent the wrong message within their communities.

But the recriminations did little to dissuade the crowds. At the higher-end clubs, movie, rock, and sports stars became regulars and their visits were chronicled in the local gossip pages, as promoters and owners sought to shine the celebrities' reflected luster onto a hitherto murky activity. Salesmen and clients, as well as employees who worked in team settings, white-collar or blue, would visit topless bars with colleagues on their lunch hours or at the end of a busy workweek, sometimes charging the tab to their employers.[6] Women were frequenting the clubs in greater numbers, often in groups, and sometimes at nightspots that offered nude male dancers. Many recording artists, encountering fewer traditional outlets for their music, were funneling their songs, especially hip-hop tracks, to DJs at gentlemen's clubs. Some

6. In these boom years, almost every male-bonding movie had an obligatory scene in which detectives, drug dealers, college buddies, or office grunts would meet for a pop at the local strip club.

strippers themselves were outspoken in the press (and in a number of memoirs) about how the economics of exotic dancing had handed *them* the levers of financial and sexual power in their transactions with their clientele.

––––––––

If there was a banner period when live adult entertainment had *arrived*, it was the fall of 1991, the season New York City became home to two new mega-clubs, both of which became legendary: the soon-infamous Scores and the more-than-a-mouthful Stringfellows Presents Pure Platinum. The latter was operated by a man named Michael J. Peter, who today calls it the era's most profitable American nightclub, by square foot. "Within three weeks," Peter recalls, "I'm making $250,000 a week. The money in New York versus every-place else [was astronomical], especially when you're catering to Wall Street, which is breaking your doors down. Every day, for every guy that's lost his ass in the market, there's somebody that made a killing—celebrating.... We had a waiting line every single night from Wall Street. You couldn't get in.

"Girls were dancing on a low table—like a cocktail table—and the chairs were around it. The customers would fight over 'em. I remember this one night, this guy saying, 'Com'ere and dance for me' to this hot girl. He's sitting there with his four buddies. He goes, 'Here's a hundred dollars.' The guy next to him goes, 'Here's *five* hundred dollars. Step six inches to the side. Focus on *me*.' The next guy goes, 'Here's a *thousand*.' The next guy goes, 'Here's *five* thousand.' The next guy goes, 'Here's the keys to my Corvette.' He gave her the car. 'You're with me. Screw them.' That's how it went."

It was Peter, in fact, whom many credit with conceiving, or at least shaping and formalizing, the idea of the high-end gentlemen's club in the United States. A compact former wrestling champ with a deep, oil-drum voice, he tells me the creation tale as we sit in his office in Oakland Park, Florida—a cross between a Burt Reynolds man cave and the gold-lacquered lair of a '70s record exec. (I spot signed photos of Don Ho—and Rob Lowe.)

In 1975, he says, he had a hotel-and-restaurant-management master's from Cornell, and was running his first disco, in Orlando. One day he was chastened to see that the parking lot of a local topless dive, the Booby Trap, was always jammed—at three in the afternoon. Curious, he paid a visit. Before entering the place (twin domes with nipples on the top, he recalls), he locked his wallet in his trunk, fearful of being rolled. Once inside, Peter shuddered at the scene, which he could barely make out through the darkness: dancers with tattoos (and one or two with missing teeth), dancers who appeared not to have showered, "table girls" who would sit down next to customers and then wheedle them into buying them drinks. "Every seat was full and it was businessmen, nicely dressed," he says, shaking his head. "And I said [to myself], 'These people are in this dump availing themselves of *this* kind of hustle?'" He wondered, as he took it all in: What if I created my own strip club where the lighting was inviting, the women were "10s," and the customers were *welcomed* and made to feel *inclined* to part with their money?

By the time he'd returned to his car, so he says today, a vision had crystalized. In *his* club, the dancers would wear evening gowns. The male staffers would sport tuxedos. Soon, he realized, there should be a runway and a stage. He would junk the standard jukebox for a female DJ.

He immediately shut down his disco and built a club from scratch. "I had a dressing room, a makeup artist, a woman who did your hair—and it was required. They couldn't cuss. They had to have manicures, pedicures. We gave them lessons in how to perform. We talked about eye contact and selling the fantasy. These guys had to believe that they could take you home to Mother." The format clicked, and he was soon in twenty cities.

Come the mid-'90s, he had opened clubs around the world, under three main banners: Thee DollHouse, Solid Gold, and Pure Platinum.[7] Against great opposition from an array of family-values groups, Michael J. Peter had helped perfect the swankier, Boomer-approved gentlemen's club. And he had managed, in the process, to commandeer a private jet, a yacht, several homes, and a fleet of luxury cars. "I had a $100 million company and ten thousand employees in the early '90s, at the height," he says, "before the government started going after me."[8] (Peter would be hounded by the Feds and did time for mail fraud. His conviction would be reversed and tossed out in 2002.)

But all that is champagne under the dam. I ask Peter if there was a single moment, looking back, that he cherishes most. He tells me about the time

---

7. Peter also started offshoots such as a gambling-and-nudie cruise-ship operation; *Platinum* magazine; and a film-and-video franchise. (Peter publicity materials; interview with Peter; Matt Schudel, "Michael J. Peter: The Solid Gold Touch," *[Broward and Palm Beach] Sun Sentinel,* October 3, 1993; Eric Conrad and Warren Richey, "Hedonism on High Seas: Nude Cruise Isn't NFL's Idea of Fun," *Sun Sentinel,* January 24, 1995.)

8. Press reports at the time verify his firm's valuation, estimating that his staff numbered five thousand strong. (Schudel, "Michael J. Peter.")

one of his dancers, in the late '70s, approached him with a request. "I met my fiancé here," she told him. "We've been engaged for two years. I want to get married *in* your club. You can [spread the word that dancers] are *real* people, that we fall in love." Peter came up with a plan. She would get married topless. The justice of the peace would be topless. The wedding party would drive in six topless cars—convertibles. Pure catnip for the local press.

The coup de grâce, he says, would come thirty years later. "I'm going up to my home in Orlando from the airport—in a yellow cab. I have a big set of gates, [with a sign] that says 'M. J. Peter Estate.' We pull up to the gates. She sees that sign and turns around. 'Michael, is that you?' She says, 'Do you remember me? You put on my wedding. I want you to know that I'm still married to that gentleman. My daughter has worked in one of your clubs for a number of years. And my *granddaughter* is getting ready to be old enough to audition. You're gonna have *three* generations.'"

Ah, the family that strips together.

Gentlemen's clubs advertised themselves as sites for adult entertainment, implying a passive audience. But many venues pushed the boundaries into active engagement. The lap dance, in which a partly or fully disrobed performer gyrates and then grinds into a seated customer's groin, had made headlines in 1994 after a Canadian judge declared that the activity was not illegal.[9]

Meanwhile, many clubs offered "VIP" or "champagne" rooms. These were dark, private sanctums, often separated by a divider or a curtain, in which customers paid large sums, ostensibly for a bottle of bubbly to be consumed in an agreed-upon time period. A fully clothed client—male or female—would sit or recline on a couch or chair. A preselected exotic dancer (or two) would strip, then commence to slither, caress, and body hump. In many such rooms, sex acts were hardly uncommon, though illegal if the client paid for them.[10] "From Sapporo to Zurich," says a friend who survived dozens of lap dances, "every VIP room in the '90s had a corner for a handjob and the promise of more. There was lots of 'wiggle room' [for sex play]—and lots of wiggle *rooms*."

---

9. The ruling was later overturned. ("Canadian Court Rules Lap Dancing Indecent," *Toledo Blade*, June 27, 1997.)

10. This ran counter to comedian Chris Rock's tongue-in-cheek axiom in his 1999 song parody, "No Sex": "No matter what a stripper tells you, there's no sex in the Champagne Room."

And after-hours hookups between performers and patrons, while nominally discouraged, were a convenient way for dancers to make extra cash.

As the Clinton economy continued heading nosebleed north, things got looniest in the big cities. A buddy of mine in finance explains. He takes out a piece of paper one night at the bar in New York's Algonquin Hotel and sketches out his theory about the impetus behind the boob-club boom in Manhattan and, by extension, the rest of the country. In his view, there was a small stratum at the top of a pyramid: "The Elite." Its subcategories were "The Private Equity Guys," "M&As[11] and Bankers," and "The Hedge Funds and the True Money Guys." At the bottom of the pyramid were regular working-class New Yorkers. But in the *middle* of the pyramid were the ones who made things tick: the *salesmen* who relentlessly pursued the wealthiest tier at the top.

My friend continues scribbling: "Bond salesmen, currency salesmen, buyers and traders, currency traders in 'the pits.'" The crazy money spent at adult entertainment clubs, he theorizes, was fueled by these "guys with tags" around their necks during the day—"the thousands of salesmen from Queens and Staten Island making two to three million dollars a year. The middle of the pyramid is where the bulk of this was happening: the numb-nuts. There were so many firms selling shit, what was the [only] way they get that banker to buy *their* shit? Coke 'em up and get 'em girls [and write it off as] client entertainment." As he sees it, "salesmen ordering marked-up bottles of vodka" were the ones who were driving everyone else in New York to go to pricey restaurants, dance clubs, and strip clubs.

Manhattan, of course, was not alone. Many cities vied for the title of the nation's strip-club mecca: Las Vegas, Houston, Dallas, Los Angeles, New Orleans, "Sin"-cinnati, and Central and South Florida, especially Tampa (where Joe Redner's Mons Venus club had given birth to the nude lap dance). But the '90s metropolis of men's clubs was Atlanta, a city, as Anne Berryman would report in *Time*, that was home to over forty strip joints. Conventioneers would flock there—some five and a half million a year—many of them not unaware of the fact that local ordinances allowed what Berryman would call a "rare combination of full nudity and alcohol, a mix of pleasure not offered in many other towns."

The center of Atlanta's scene, says a former sports executive who requests anonymity, was a venue called the Gold Club, considered by many con-

---

11. Mergers and Acquisitions.

noisseurs to have been lap-dance Valhalla. "The reason it was the über strip club of the time," he says, "is that Atlanta was the convention capital in the '90s, before Vegas turned from being family-centric to being its dirty old self." Every year, the Gold Club (and, to a lesser degree, the nearby Cheetah Lounge) hit max frenzy during the Super Show, run by what was then called the Sporting Goods Manufacturers Association. My executive source describes it this way: "The SGMA had companies like Nike, Reebok, and Adidas. It had all of the leagues' representatives. It had athletes. In essence, this was the annual meeting place for the sporting industry in the 1990s. But the *nightly* meeting place was the Gold Club. Could you imagine a confluence of male salesmen, buyers, jocks, and women [that was] a more combustible situation? There were so many guys raging with testosterone and money in their pockets that the clubs would fly girls in from around the country, just for the Super Show." (Many pro athletes steered clear, of course. But others came to expect such treatment when they breezed into town for away games, events, or corporate-sponsored functions. My contact remembers finding himself in a closed-off VIP area of a gentlemen's club in the Midwest. Next to him, he says, was a star quarterback of the day, "now a Pro Football Hall of Famer, and [I was] watching him with his hand, which had disappeared—*up to the wrist*—in the nether region of a dancer." He doesn't recall if it was the QB's throwing arm.)[12]

Art Harris, the reporter and TV producer, was based in Atlanta for the *Washington Post* and CNN during the 1990s. "The Gold Club," he recalls, "was considered the Taj Mahal. It was also the first time that a Yankee, Steve Kaplan"—who was indicted, though eventually cleared, on charges of paying protection fees to the Gambino family—"had come south and really made an impact in this field. It was brilliant marketing. The idea was to bring

---

12. "From the earliest days of business to the *Mad Men* era to the '90s to now, sex has gone with the territory when there's excessive money involved," says Scott Gutterson, a New York attorney and accountant. "The Wall Street guys—I have many clients who are brokers, bond guys in the many-millions-of-dollars-a-year range. They'd think nothing in the '90s about taking ten guys to the [redacted-name strip club] as a legitimate business expense—entertainment—where you could get a blowjob in the VIP room for a couple hundred dollars. The New York DollHouse was directly across from [one of the city's] IRS office[s]. I once went to an audit [at which my client had] $7,000 in receipts for a strip club. I did not do that infrequently. Because the law states, 'Entertainment is deductible if it is ordinary and necessary.' Some audits were successful, some weren't. In the '90s this was the mentality of those guys." (Interview with Gutterson.)

in and comp celebrities so the big spenders would follow [and take clients] to hang out at the same strip club and tip the same women who the stars were tipping.... Kaplan knew his demo: upper-crust frat boys, jock-sniffers, super-CEOs, the guys who love to hang out with each other and brag about who they had seen, whether it was Shaq or Mutombo or Rodman or players on other ball teams who came through town."

And then, in 1999, the jig was up. Kaplan and several cohorts were charged with prostitution, racketeering, fraud, and more. Witnesses spoke of a pattern of handouts given to strippers—at the direction of Gold Club bigwigs—as payment for pleasuring pro athletes right there in the back rooms. (NBA legend Patrick Ewing testified in court to having received a blowjob or two, gratis, while Kaplan allegedly watched.) VIP-room visitors, under oath, told of exorbitant charges that would materialize on their credit card statements. (One sorry customer testified that he'd been stiffed with a $28,000 tab—accumulated over a scant six hours.) Kaplan, while denying most of the accusations, accepted a plea bargain, paying $5 million in fines and spending more than a year in the slammer. The club itself was summarily shuttered.

––––––

There was one man who was not about to take all of this lap-dance madness lying down. His name was Rudy Giuliani, and he was the mayor of New York City.

Giuliani—already a successful U.S. attorney and a crimefighting mayor (not to mention a future presidential contender and adviser to Donald Trump)—continued with his plan to power wash the five boroughs. He was periodically up in arms about decadent art exhibits. He helped sanitize (some said "Disney-fy") Times Square. He cracked down on "quality of life" offenses such as squeegee-wielders who approached cars and forcibly cleaned drivers' windshields in exchange for pocket change. He sought to thin the ranks of the city's homeless. ("Streets do not exist in civilized societies," he proclaimed, "for the purpose of people sleeping there.") He quashed crime in Gotham, which hit a three-decade low.

Soon the man whom many considered a closet liberal (he was pro-choice, a supporter of domestic partnerships, and, as journalists liked to note, had roomed for a time with a gay couple),[13] was choosing to make an example of his

––––––

13. Giuliani was not averse to appearing in drag. At the 1997 Inner Circle show (an annual spoof revue for journalists covering City Hall), for example, the mayor played a convincing Marilyn, down

city's XXX establishments. Sex business, said Giuliani, "destroys the character of the city." The city council rewrote the zoning laws in an attempt to push out strip clubs, porn stores, and peep parlors by forbidding them to operate around schools, daycare centers, or places of worship, or in largely residential areas. When proprietors fought back in court, the city cooked up its "60/40" provision. Under the decree, businesses would be padlocked and shut down if 40 percent or more of their operations or inventory were explicitly sexual in nature.

It was a war of attrition. Randy Mastro, the deputy mayor for operations, appeared at a press conference armed with a baseball bat, announcing that his enforcers would fan out across the city to check on compliance: "This is the last dance for sex shops." In response, porn store clerks reshelved their inventory and strip club owners had their performers don bikinis. Next, Giuliani would encourage law-abiding citizens to take out their cameras and photograph patrons going into triple-X hangouts. Striking back, near-naked protestors marched; civil liberties lawyers filed countless motions; New York's VIP Club, to get around the new rules, converted some of its space to what was touted as "the world's first nude sushi restaurant." Back and forth they volleyed.

In other cities, local laws were comparably baroque. As of 1997, for example, it was forbidden to lap dance in Houston (a) while topless, (b) while closer than three feet to the said recipient's lap, or (c) under illumination greater than "one footcandle as measured at four feet above floor level." Many clubs and dancers found legal loopholes. New York City forced the closure of a spate of playpens. But for the most part the DJ played on.

Sunny Mindel, Giuliani's press secretary in the late '90s and into the next decade, agrees to have lunch with me at Aretsky's Patroon, in midtown. She explains some of the reasoning behind the crackdown. "Porn shops reduce real estate values," she suggests. "They are not a land-enhancement program. Even in neighborhoods where you might think they were welcome—the Village—people weren't 100 percent in love with having them around."

But it wasn't really about real estate values. It was about values. "He

---

to the pink dress, mascara, and beauty mark. Appearing that evening with the Broadway cast of *Victor/Victoria* (about a woman playing a man playing a woman), Giuliani joked, "I already play a Republican playing a Democrat playing a Republican." (David Firestone, "Jaws Drop as Giuliani Steals Show in Heels," *New York Times*, March 3, 1997; Sara Kugler, "Giuliani's Cross-Dressing Antics Debated," Associated Press via *Washington Post*, April 14, 2007; Nicole Levy, "The Inner Circle Opens Up," *Politico*/CapitalNewYork.com, March 14, 2014.)

worked on enforcement," Mindel says. "New York was cleaner and more livable. Most people would say that this was a *good* thing.... In Manhattan it was very easy to take a very narrow view. You had people like [columnist] Jimmy Breslin saying that [Giuliani] had ruined the cultural fabric of Times Square—*ruined* it.... Talk about 'defining deviancy down.'[14] At one point, back in the '90s, people had ceded their city to the point that they had put those 'No Radio' signs on their cars' [dashboards to dissuade people from breaking in]. It was a sense of a loss of the city, 'We are no longer in control.' And certainly Times Square became emblematic of that."

New York City, however, as Mindel points out, "is a lot more than Manhattan. It's a very narrow view to think that *any* of this [crackdown on porn] was a bad thing. Once a month for eight years [the mayor] held 'town hall' meetings. Ninety-six, all over the city. Wherever we went we heard the same issue: We'd like more police. They're selling drugs on my block. That porn shop—when is that going to go away? It's what New Yorkers *wanted*.... [The mayor] got to the point, I think, where he thought, 'This is crazy. How low can you set the bar? What are we talking about, *Divine Comedy*? "Abandon All Hope, Ye Who Enter Here?"'"[15]

Giuliani had his way for a time. But in the end, it was the owners of strip clubs and porn stores—and the civil libertarians—whose rights eventually outflanked those asserted by elected officials, civic leaders, and municipalities. Erotic commerce prevailed. And the banners of free speech and safe sex would fly, unmolested, above Lapland.

---

14. "Defining deviancy down" was a term coined by New York senator Daniel Patrick Moynihan in an influential 1993 essay. "Over the past generation," he argued, "the amount of deviant behavior in American society has increased beyond the levels the community can 'afford to recognize' and,... accordingly, we have been re-defining deviancy so as to exempt much conduct previously stigmatized, and also quietly raising the 'normal' level in categories where behavior is now abnormal by an earlier standard. This redefining has evoked fierce resistance from defenders of 'old' standards, and accounts for much of the present 'culture war' such as proclaimed by many at the 1992 Republican National Convention." (Daniel Patrick Moynihan, "Defining Deviancy Down," *American Scholar*, Winter 1993, 19.)

15. The rulings would soon lurch in the other direction. Giuliani's successor, Michael Bloomberg, would go on the *Late Show with David Letterman*, and when the host asked him about the role strip clubs played in drawing jobs and tourists to Gotham, Bloomberg cracked, "Adult bars are clearly part of it. That's what capitalism is all about." Indeed, as recently as 2017, the name "Trump" graced Atlantic City's Taj Mahal, once home to a Scores-branded strip club. (Elizabeth A. Harris, "Bloomberg Spars [Lightly] for 15 Minutes with Letterman," *New York Times*, September 30, 2010; Alexandra Villarreal, "As Atlantic City Struggles, a Strip Club is Helping Provide Jobs," *New York Observer*, September 12, 2014; "Reports: Trump's Name Taken Off...," *Philly Voice*, February 15, 2017.)

CHAPTER 27

The Lowest-Hanging Fruit

Patrick Carnes has a serious, clergyman's cast. The father of sex addiction therapy, he sits in his office in a lodge-style building, a place of dark wood and heavy silences. Carnes's sandy hair and soft-edged manner, along with the solemn setting, bring to mind the actor Red Buttons, as if rendered by Rembrandt.

At the time of my visit, the golfer Tiger Woods has recently come to Carnes's nearby Pine Grove campus, southwest of Hattiesburg, Mississippi. And on any given day as many as a half dozen celebrities are mixed in among those who wish to remain uncelebrated, participating in the center's programs for addiction and behavioral health care. It is an unseasonably mild October afternoon. Dr. Carnes, age sixty-seven, is wearing a heavy jacket of rust-colored corduroy.

Was there a turning point, I ask, when the general public began to take the concept of sex addiction seriously?

"Not until Bill Clinton," he says, without hesitation. "Nineteen ninety-eight." He is referring to the day the country was informed of the president's intimate and ongoing relationship with White House intern Monica Lewinsky. "I remember that afternoon the news broke. I was in my office [then in Wickenburg, Arizona,] and between one o'clock and three o'clock, two hours, we counted them up—we had 141 media contacts, just one right after the other. They all, of course, wanted a diagnosis of Bill Clinton on the phone. Was he a sex addict?"

Carnes speaks with a rasp, practically a whisper, as one might expect from someone who makes a living from talking to others in confidence. He affirms the bind that he faces as a therapist and as a spokesman for the field.

"As a clinician, I've never met Bill Clinton—how can I make a diagnosis?" he asks. "What reporters don't realize is that they needed to talk. They would say, 'I have watched this thing unfold and...I am convinced that there is sex [addiction].' They were making a diagnosis in their heads because there's someone who had so much to lose.

"If you look in writings of reporters at the time, like [*Newsweek*'s Michael] Isikoff on covering Clinton, or you look at [*Vanity Fair* contributor] Gail Sheehy, she did quite a job because she really asked the right questions. They used the language of therapy: the 'long reach' of trauma, anxiety reduction, denial. The whole culture started using a different set of language. If we were maybe thirty years behind alcoholism at that time, in understanding sex addiction, we probably made a leap of a decade or fifteen years within a six-week period. The dialogue about this issue among the reporting community: these people were talking to each other about this and were connecting the dots. And that was an extraordinary moment in history." (Carnes adds a caveat: "I wish the Clintons no ill, because I think they've suffered a lot and they both have persevered in their careers and I admire them both. I wouldn't want [it] ever to appear that I had felt any other way about them.")[1]

"Bill Clinton," he continues, "was not the first president who has been sexual in the White House under various different circumstances. Our history is *filled* with that.... [But] there are some things about power that we now understand that we didn't understand even then."[2]

---

1. Even so, Carnes did provide his expert opinion in the harassment case brought against Clinton by Paula Jones, stating that the governor's 1991 encounter with Jones and its aftermath had "caused Ms. Jones to suffer severe emotional distress" along with "consequent sexual aversion." The judge in the case, Susan Webber Wright, discounted aspects of Carnes's declaration, stating that they did "not suffice to overcome plaintiff's failure of proof on her claim of outrage.... [N]otwithstanding the offensive nature of the Governor's alleged conduct... [p]laintiff's actions and statements in this case do not portray someone who experienced emotional distress so severe in nature that no reasonable person could be expected to endure it." (Liza H. Gold, *Sexual Harassment: Psychiatric Assessment in Employment Litigation* [Arlington, VA: American Psychiatric Publishing, 2004], 3–5.)

2. Some contend that some of the attributes that draw people with type-A personalities to the thrills of high-level politics (the constant need for public attention, reward, or affirmation; the need to be empowered; the risk of public failure, humiliation, and punishment, and so on) can also draw them to other addictive behaviors. "Not everybody is comfortable with the idea that politics is a guilty addiction," the gonzo journalist Hunter S. Thompson declared in his book *Better Than Sex*. "But it *is*. They *are* addicts, and they *are* guilty and they *do* lie and cheat and steal—like all junkies. And when they get in a frenzy, they will sacrifice anything and anybody....That is addictive thinking.

Even if the nation and the addiction-and-recovery network had learned from that teaching moment, it is difficult to gauge whether the president's pattern of behavior actually constituted genuine addiction, compulsivity, or any other condition whatsoever. But that has not stopped others from trying. In a *Time* magazine account, Dolly Kyle Browning, for one—an attorney and former school chum of Clinton's, who has stated that the two of them kept up an affair over several years—described a supposed encounter in Texas in 1987 at which she said she opened up to Clinton about her struggles with sex addiction. Browning insisted that he became tearful, saying that he too confronted "temptation on every corner—How do you expect me to pass it up?...I can't even walk down the street without someone literally trying to pick me up." ("The President," according to *Time*, "now says he does not believe the conversation ever took place.")

Dr. Drew Pinsky, the rehab expert and love-life guru, offers his own take when I meet with him in Los Angeles: "Is Bill Clinton a sex addict? The piece that gets lost in the defining quality of sexual addiction is the loss of control. By the time somebody is so deeply engaged in sexual addiction that they feel like they've lost control—and suffer the consequences—they're really in. Go about seventy-five pages into his autobiography, *My Life*. There's alcoholism all over the place. His mom was an opiate addict. You're at risk. His relationship with Monica Lewinsky: was that sex addiction, out of control? It meets my criteria."[3]

Pinsky actually conducted a 2008 interview with Gennifer Flowers on his popular radio show, *Loveline*, in which she claimed that Clinton had contacted her two or three years before. "He wanted to come and see me," she said on air. "I clearly felt like he was in some sort of a program, where he needed to make [amends] to people.... He said... 'I'll wear a jogging outfit. I'll wear a hood.... Nobody will know it's me.' I said, 'No!...And please don't call me again.' " Flowers, who told Pinsky she was unnerved by the

---

That is politics—especially in presidential campaigns." (Hunter S. Thompson, *Better Than Sex: Confessions of a Political Junkie*, vol. 4. of *The Gonzo Papers* [New York: Ballantine, 1994].)

3. Ex–White House staffer Linda Tripp, when summoned to testify by the independent counsel investigating Clinton, declared that the president, as she understood it, took to using a datebook or calendar to tick off "all of the days he had been good [and] overcame the compulsion to be with someone sexually other than his wife." Note: Tripp's grand jury statements, whatever else they are, are also the testimony of a Clinton detractor. (Ken Gormley, *The Death of American Virtue: Clinton vs. Starr* [New York: Crown, 2010], 507.)

overture, insisted that the more she thought about it, the more "he seemed like...I have known people that have been in, for example, a twelve-step program...and how they have to, you know, go to these various people that they have wronged or that they have issues with and deal with it."

That said, this is *so* not about Bill Clinton. It is about a condition affecting men and women, their life partners and sex partners, their families and friends. Time to check under the proverbial hoodie.

——————

The concept of a person being *addicted* to sex, of course, didn't start in the '90s. But by that decade, researchers, health professionals, and marriage counselors were buying into the idea. Twelve-step programs for sexual dependency were drawing crowds. The wider treatment circuit was embracing intimacy disorders as a sort of last taboo. The first inpatient center to focus specifically on sex addiction—established in the 1980s, in Golden Valley, Minnesota— was gaining recognition. Judges were ordering perpetually straying spouses to seek help. Television talk shows were running segments ("Next hour: 'I'm a nympho'") that played up the high-drama sagas of shame, betrayal, and domestic devastation. Michael Ryan published his influential memoir *Secret Life* in 1995, about his own path to destructive seduction.[4]

On top of this, the new phenomena of online porn, chat lines, and connections for hookups risked turning impressionable Internet users into what the press often called sexaholics. (Early on, the disorder was referred to as "hypersexuality.") In the late 1990s, as the *New York Times*'s Jane E. Brody would report, Stanford's Al Cooper conducted in-depth analyses of obsessive erotic behavior online. He came to view cybersex as "the crack cocaine of sexual compulsivity," warning that "this is a hidden public health hazard exploding, in part, because very few are recognizing it as such or taking it seriously." Indeed, many people were still clinging to the notion that the player or the lech was a rather harmless type.

——————

4. As a teacher at Princeton, Ryan had been canned in the '80s for sleeping with students; he'd had unsafe sex with men and women during the early march of AIDS, and then slept, in turn, with other lovers, unprotected; he'd sought underage partners, having himself been molested as a young boy. Another particularly powerful study of sexual addiction is Susan Cheever's *Desire*, in which she states, "One primary characteristic of addiction is always a broken promise, whether it's a promise made to oneself or to another person." (Michael Ryan, *Secret Life: An Autobiography* [New York: Pantheon, 1995]; Susan Cheever, *Desire: Where Sex Meets Addiction* [New York: Simon & Schuster, 2008].)

Nineties headlines, meanwhile, were routinely announcing flameouts due to sexual obsession. "Hard to believe," says journalist Sam Kashner today, "but teacher-student sex became a 'beat' of mine at *GQ*." He cites the high-profile case of Mary Kay Letourneau, a married teacher with four children who had an ongoing sexual relationship with her thirteen-year-old pupil. (She went to jail for the crime in 1997, bore two of her ex-student's children, then married him and took his name.) In another case, a Berkeley professor, as Kashner recalls, "advocated [for] consensual relations between teachers and students as part of the Socratic method.

"Why was this kind of a '90s phenomenon?" he wonders. "The generations had gotten closer in age. Children were being more sexualized—in Britney Spears's first video she's dressed as a cheerleader. The shift came when the professors came to power in the academy and they had grown up sexually during the sexual revolution. For them, *Lolita*"—Nabokov's mid-'50s novel about a professor's obsession with the young object of his desire—"didn't register as it did to a previous generation. In the '80s and '90s, *Lolita* wasn't a paean to sexual longing and lost youth; it was just a guide to motels."

There was also a steady flow of news stories about men in power—members of the clergy, elected officials, athletes, performers, actors, and business figures—undone by destructive affairs or predatory behavior. Incidents involving pedophile priests regularly surfaced after years of silence, denial, and hush money. (The *Economist* estimated that from the late '80s onward, "thousands of claims for damages following sexual-abuse cases [cost the Catholic Church, on average, more than] $1 million per victim, according to lawyers involved.") Frequent, too, were accusations of sexual misconduct—or of behavior that might be perceived as unbecoming a public servant—against lawmakers and governors and political figures (Democrats *and* Republicans) throughout the '80s and '90s, including Jon Hinson, Robert Bauman, Thomas Evans, John Schmitz, Dan Crane, Gerry Studds, Brock Adams, John Tower, Buz Lukens, Bob Packwood, Dan Burton, Helen Chenoweth, Henry Hyde, and Mel Reynolds.

Specialists in the heartland, like their journalist colleagues in the capital, were also looking into the ways of the wayward heart. In May 1990, more than 250 psychologists, academics, and counselors gathered at a sex addiction summit in Minneapolis. *Time* magazine, which covered the event, described the polarized atmosphere. Many among them insisted on using the term "addiction" when treating patients with systematic and uncontrollable sexual dependency—a condition that had made patients' and clients' lives unmanage-able, often in truly destructive ways (a marriage dissolved; an arrest or a loss of one's livelihood; a downward, self-annihilating spiral). In contrast, many shrinks, therapists, and theorists insisted that these men and women suffered instead from what was mainly a psychological disorder, which manifested itself in compulsive behavior. By this interpretation, addiction amounted to a metaphor. Unlike heavy substance abusers, those who engaged in destruc-tive behavior patterns that involved activities like sex or gambling or overeat-ing did not go through observable symptoms of withdrawal when they halted their behavior. As such, their actions were merely compulsive, not true "habits" in the diagnostic sense. (The month of that conclave in Minneapolis, in fact, psychologist John Money of Johns Hopkins would tell *Time* that he viewed the "sex addiction" designation as something of a fad: "People trying to make money on it better hurry up. It'll probably dry up in five years." Go figure.)

Today, the sex addict tag is more widely accepted and is said to apply to between 3 and 6 percent of the adult population—a figure Carnes says may be far too low. Although the condition has not been officially classified in the prime psychiatric field guide, the *Diagnostic and Statistical Manual of Mental Disorders*, the categories of "process" or "behavioral" addictions (including sexual compulsivity) are now thought by many experts to have their own biochemical components. The brain of an individual ensnared in a cycle of hypersexual activity, for instance, produces its own feel-good spike of dopa-mine, not unlike the brain of the alcoholic.

A former colleague of mine—we'll call her Geraldine—is an accom-plished media publicist and mother, who is recently divorced. She has been in therapy for ten years. As she sees it, men and women tend to "ride out their compulsion in different ways." For many guys, she believes, it's all about the thrills associated with the sex—the encounter. In contrast, Geraldine and her peers, no matter their sexual orientation, often seem more preoccupied with the romance, with fantasizing about their partners and their feelings, sometimes all out of proportion to reality. "Women have a different way of acting out their demons," she tells me. "People I encounter at women's meet-ings often have 'relationship addiction'—that addiction of finding somebody and becoming obsessed with them to the extent that everything else goes away and you blank out. People say heroin is easier to give up than that high of being with another person, that intense, chemical rush.

"I had this compulsion to go outside of myself. I really liked the ritual of getting prepared for the sexual encounter, of anticipating it, the romance of the meeting. Sex, for me, was a way of connecting very intensely with these individuals [so as] to give my life meaning. But the actual experience was never that great. And afterwards, like most highs, the crash was incredible. So, so awful. It really is a hellish way of life."[5]

No matter how destructive such repetitive behavior can be to an individual's psyche, the general public, by and large, still regards sex addiction as a punch line—or a cinematic cliché. For those battling insatiable sexual urges, however, the condition is altogether real. Beginning in the 1970s, researchers began to notice behavior patterns that might suggest an underlying illness. Sex addicts often came from families with a history of addiction, sexual or otherwise. More than half exhibited multiple addictions. In many cases they had been sexually abused themselves early in their lives. And sexual compulsion, as with other addictive disorders, was typically chronic and progressive. Not for nothing, then, did treatment programs borrow heavily from AA's so-called *Big Book*.[6]

---

5. "For me, it was totally about sex, just sex—not that soft, romantic stuff," says another woman I know who has been in treatment for her own sex and alcohol addiction, and requests that she be referred to as Tiffany. "I think that's another face of addiction, closer to obsession and perhaps more female. But there are plenty of women who are sex addicts and don't give a fig for romance, cuddling, blah-blah—all the patronizing stuff that men think we long for."

6. Pat Carnes wrote his first paper on the concept of sex addiction in 1972. Later that decade, sexual-addiction programs, patterned on the twelve-step model, sprang up, taking real measures to counter some of the missteps of the '60s sexual revolution. New leaders emerged in the recovery movement, and a 1978 article in the *British Journal of Addictions*, by Jim Orford, was the first, Carnes says, to detail and identify "sexual dependency as a class of addiction in a peer-reviewed medical journal."

For Carnes personally, the most revelatory moment of all might have come in 1982. Right as his book *Out of the Shadows* was about to be published, a colleague asked him to join him at a conference at the University of Minnesota. The keynote speaker, Carnes recalls, was "a woman from an Ivy League university" who had a patient onstage with her: a pedophile, who was obese as a result of the high drug dosage he was taking to help curb his urges. "He was saying, 'I know that my weight has made me grotesque now, but I would do *anything* to get better, to stop my behavior.' And she would periodically make derisive comments about him as a person, and even used the [phrase], 'Hey, you pathetic fat slob,' and would get the audience to laugh at him.

"I walked out in tears," Carnes says. "What I saw was sexual prejudice. He was earnestly saying he wanted to get better. And I knew that people could. I went down, I sat next to the Mississippi River—the river flows right through the campus—and I just realized that there are these attitudes out there about people who do sexual things without any understanding or appreciation of it. My

Carnes had been known for his breakthrough book *Out of the Shadows* (1983), the classic in the field. Then in 1991, he published *Don't Call It Love*, which surveyed the lessons gleaned from a three-year study of a thousand individuals in various phases of recovery from sexual dependencies of all sorts. Carnes's work suggested that so-called sex addicts might have real reason for hope—and a path forward.

Many of Carnes's peers would cast doubt. They considered his beliefs "quackery," he says. "Sometimes in my career I feel the classic tied-to-the-mast-as-the-storm-comes-over-you, and I just endure it." Jill Vermeire, a respected sexual-addiction and marriage-and-family therapist in the L.A. and Phoenix areas, paints an overall picture. Pat Carnes was the "pioneer in dealing with these issues," she tells me, "the first person to speak out loud to the medical community and call this disorder 'sex addiction.'" Nonetheless, Vermeire says, Carnes was "very white-male, hetero-focused in the early years, very cognitive-behavioral. He changed his tune over time." In contrast, she says, "a lot of us work at the psychodynamics—going more into the childhood issues and the family of origin and the formative years. We do the trauma work *first*; Pat does that later. Pia Mellody, she's my mentor, ties in a lot of components and believes that love addiction or love avoidance is really the precursor to sex addiction.... Kelly McDaniel has written the best book, in my opinion, on female sex and love addiction [*Ready to Heal*]. She talks about something called 'mother hunger' and that craving and yearning for the mom who was the very first person that you have an intimate contact with, which women later find themselves seeking out through men or women."

———

Sexual addiction in the 1990s was occurring against a backdrop of other behaviors, even pathologies, that appeared to be on the rise. The most

———

friend came, and he sat down, put his arm around me, and he said, 'Pat, I just wanted you to see what you're going to be up against. When that book comes out, you're going to run into anger and laughter because the culture can't deal with the realities of what you're talking about.'"

Carnes forged ahead. By the 1990s he was heartened to see that there was a wider acceptance of addiction in general throughout American society. Phil Donahue, Oprah Winfrey, and others spoke the language of addiction and recovery. The self-help field became a movement. Megachurches, their pews overflowing, encouraged public disclosure, apology, and forgiveness. During the decade, as Carnes recalls, a national society emerged to address issues related to sex addiction; books on the subject began appearing regularly; and a sex-addiction medical journal was established. "In essence," he says, "if you were determined, you could find help." (Interview with Carnes.)

pernicious was the traffic in child porn. Some of this increase was due to the peer-to-peer sharing of imagery facilitated by the Web. Others would attribute the disturbing trend to how young people were being eroticized, seduced, and reduced by popular culture and consumer society, coincident with the arrested development of many young men, who were lingering longer in adolescent stages and habits. Carnes adds a further explanation: "I am seeing patients now who are in their late twenties [and early thirties] but in 1995 were ten or eleven on the Internet and they could go on a lot of different ways, but one, for example, is they started looking at child pornography because they were children. They were looking at kids the same age. They never dated, they never held the hand, they never kissed, because they're spending all the time on the Internet. They never socialized normally.... We are in an extraordinarily different space. That started in the mid-'90s and I hear that all the time."

A second phenomenon involved hardcore adult porn, which was increasingly sadistic and misogynistic. One of the first major studies to compare sexual violence across different media was conducted in the late 1990s by Martin Barron and Michael Kimmel. In their paper, published in the *Journal of Sex Research*, they looked at porn's migration from magazines (a pre-'80s medium) to videos (in the '80s) to the Internet newsgroup alt.sex.stories (in the '90s). They found "an increase in violent scenes from magazines to videos to the Usenet.... The more pornography is consumed at one level, the less arousing this material becomes [so that] this satiation leads the consumer to seek out newer, more explicit, and [sometimes] more violent forms of sexual material that will again arouse him/her." What Barron and Kimmel could not anticipate, however, was how porn videos by the next century would become platform agnostic, offering explicit and often violent scenarios that would be available on virtually any device.

Third, a generation's collective sexual unconscious began to process porn's tropes along with its two main mood states: exaggerated ecstasy or numb detachment. Indeed, writer Naomi Wolf had presaged this state of affairs in 1991, before the advent of the World Wide Web. "We must recognize young people born after 1960 as 'the pornographic generation,'" she ventured. "Children are growing up whose earliest sexual imprinting derives not from a living human being, or fantasies of their own: since the 1960 pornographic upsurge, the sexuality of children has begun to be shaped in response to cues that are no long human [but from] paper and celluloid phantoms.... Nothing comparable has ever happened in the history of our species; it dislodges Freud."

Freud had rightly noted that our earliest sexual cues come as infants. But if, as Wolf has suggested, an individual's initial exposure to erotic stimulation springs ever more frequently from inhuman, fetishized, self-centered representations of sex (the poor cousin of the intimate, passionate, mutually satisfying encounter), the more that particular individual, as a post-adolescent, risks becoming a thirdhand lover, a phony with pheromones.

———

Starting in the '90s, technology, in many ways, "isolated people from real human relationships," says Elisabeth Owen, an Austin, Texas, psychotherapist. Owen specializes in cofacilitating two-parent Boomer couples who are raising sons who have fallen between the cracks—many of them, in her description, college dropouts "holed up in their rooms with the door shut, playing video games or looking at pornography. [Online,] they have virtual relationships. Even sexuality has become an isolated, lonely, virtual experience. Real girls don't look like [the online] fantasy version. Nor do real guys."

This burrowing away into a form of electronic quarantine began as the Web gained prominence. "Girls are moving on," Owen says. "Girls are communicators and they are emotionally evolved in a way that boys of this generation are not, and they are eclipsing young men in education and in the job market, where communication skills are key. And the saddest thing to me is that in this age, the first and defining sexual experience for a boy is a virtual one on the Internet. This is what they've come to expect, sexually. They don't know how to relate to a woman. And women don't need them anymore in the same way—in terms of marriage and a financial anchor. I can't tell you how many of these boys have never even had a first kiss. They don't know what to do. And young women, they're pretty much inured to pornography—they're very aware of it and they're not shocked by it. Many girls think that boys who get into pornography on the Internet are losers and perverts. That's not attractive to girls. Girls like boys that talk to them—they want to talk about their feelings.

"It began in the '90s," she believes. "Many are in suspended adolescence until they're thirty years old. The boys that seem to do best are boys that are athletic and who have joined team sports. They learn to communicate as members of a team. Many of these boys who have finally found themselves have ended up joining the military because this gives them a structured rite of passage to become a male in our culture. This is one of the few vehicles that's concrete enough to grant them the recognition of being a man."

Such online activities have extracted a profound toll on marriages too. As noted by Pamela Paul in her book *Pornified*, Richard Barry, the head of the American Academy of Matrimonial Lawyers, remarked in 2003, "Eight years ago, [Internet] pornography played almost no role in divorces in this country. Today, there are a significant number of cases where it plays a definite part in marriages breaking up." Paul goes on to point out that "nearly two-thirds of the attorneys present [at an annual conference in 2003] had witnessed a sudden rise in divorces related to the Internet; 58 percent of those were the result of a spouse looking at excessive amounts of pornography online." (Around the same time, however, an Illinois State University study, focusing on the attitudes of women whose partners were habitual porn viewers, found that more than 50 percent of the respondents were either "neutral or even positively disposed to their lover's taste for smut," writes essayist Ross Douthat, while only a third of those surveyed considered Internet porn use "a form of betrayal and infidelity." The culture has certainly moved on, and not necessarily in a good way.)

Patrick Carnes, of course, looks at the dark clouds above the landscape of American sexuality and returns, naturally, to the subject of addiction. "The social costs are huge," he says. "The Internet has really ramped [it] up, because there are people who are now having trouble with sexual issues who are offenders that never would have gotten there if it hadn't been for the Internet.... You have fifty thousand new HIV cases every year, a portion of which comes out of [addictive behavior]. You're not showing up for work. You're putting yourself at risk legally. If you're spending thirty-five or forty hours doing cybersex, you're not doing much else."

When you factor in "abundance," Carnes contends, the risk of obsessive behavior can escalate. "Addiction is very related to availability," he says. "The more casinos we have, the more gambling problems. Sexual acting out—now a fifth-grader can do it.... The Internet was a game-changer because it was so easy to get access. Parents had no clue what their kids were doing because they didn't understand how to use a computer. As a result, what we have coming [on the horizon] is huge.

"The reason we have an obesity problem," he submits, by point of comparison, "is an abundance of food. And what food and sex have in common—different from all the other addictions—is they're wired for survival. They are wired right to the reward centers of the brain. A cocaine addict doesn't care how his cocaine is presented. But a food addict does. A sex addict would.... Other countries don't have the amount of food that we have. Other countries don't have the amount of sexual stimulation our kids get.

"I see a tsunami coming."

CHAPTER 28

Culture Wars, Part II

The Big Three culture-war clashes of the 1990s were over abortion, same-sex marriage,[1] and the concept of "traditional" marriage. And they were waged without letup. First and foremost, the nation was rocked by a major offensive regarding reproductive health, which drew all three branches of government to the front lines. That battle is being fought to this day.

———

On the eve of the 1992 Democratic National Convention, the Supreme Court hurled a grenade as it broke for summer recess. In a 5-to-4 decision in *Planned Parenthood v. Casey*, the justices narrowly upheld *Roe v. Wade*, the landmark 1973 case that affirmed a woman's "right to choose." Yet the ruling reverberated through the pro-choice movement. For the first time in two decades, the High Court—despite supporting *Roe* and barring states from placing an "undue burden" on those seeking an abortion—was putting restrictions on reproductive freedom. According to the majority opinion, a state (in this case, Pennsylvania) had the legal authority to insist on a twenty-four-hour waiting period before a patient would be allowed to terminate her pregnancy. Furthermore, the state could demand that a minor be required to secure the consent of one of her parents.

Shock waves followed. Many feared that the Court had opened the floodgates for new limits on a woman's ability to have an abortion. (And, lo, it had. In the years since, legislation and case law built around that Pennsylvania precedent have slowly chipped away at *Roe*.)

Bill Clinton made his move. He had yet to be named his party's

———

1. The term "marriage equality" was not yet in wide circulation.

presidential nominee. And it was not at all clear where he would stand on such restrictions. In the summer of '92, in fact, feminists were understandably wary, recalls his press secretary Dee Dee Myers. "It wasn't like he was their champion," she says, "[even though] he became that over eight years. Women's groups were suspicious because of his [extramarital behavior]. He was southern. He was a centrist; he was not a traditional liberal. He was pro-choice but he had supported some restrictions on abortion. And his language was different. It was 'abortion should be safe, legal, and *rare*.' So they didn't know what the 'rare' thing meant.... The one thing the country [believed]: people don't want to *hear* about abortion. They think there are too many abortions, but they don't want to get into telling women what to do—most people—[so as to] make it a big political issue.... Clinton got this instinctively. No one had to explain it to him or take a poll."

The day the decision came down, Clinton had set up a prearranged call with Kate Michelman, the head of NARAL Pro-Choice America. She phoned him after she left the courtroom, and Clinton was unequivocal. "It's awfully good news that *Roe* was upheld," he told her, adding, "I want you to know that you can count on me to continue to stand up for a woman's right to choose."

Clinton was good to his word. During his first week in the White House, he signed defiantly pro-choice directives, drawing his own line in the sand on matters of reproductive health, just as his predecessor, George Bush, had drawn his.

For a while, the pro-choice community had the political momentum. Its April 1992 gathering on the Washington Mall drew a half to three-quarters of a million. Voters across the country were electing candidates who forcefully defended a woman's freedom to choose. According to Gallup, supporters (53 to 56 percent of those surveyed) had now surpassed opponents, including those who would limit abortion to specific medical situations. On balance, those promoting choice were of a like mind: they were adamant that a woman's control over her own body was not the business of state or federal law, the workplace, or religious decree.

The '90s pro-choice legions were growing for various reasons. There was a new comfort level with a variety of contraceptive methods, thanks to improved education, marketing efforts, and the impetus in the late '90s to introduce the French pill RU-486 in the States. There was serious concern about teen pregnancy rates (even as those rates, and the overall number of abortions, *declined* during the decade). In black communities, *Time's* Kate Pickert recently recalled, "the term *reproductive justice* was coined... by black feminists who wanted to... speak to the needs of African-American women, whose abortion rate [was] 3½ times that of white women." Pro-choice defenders, moreover, were truly galvanized by the Supreme Court decision. "That case," says Kate Michelman, who remains active in the cause, "had come after twelve years of Republican presidents who'd been doing the bidding of antiabortion forces [whose power had been centered] in the nation's churches."

But most significant of all was a backlash against violent attacks by a cadre of pro-life activists, a backlash that shocked large segments of society and invigorated the pro-choice camp. "The '80s and the '90s saw a gathering of strength of the forces on the far right wing working to deny women the right to choose," Michelman insists. "Their extremism—demonstrated in their aggressive assaults on clinics and doctors—was [regarded] by the general public as desperate and unacceptable."

Despite all of this, however, it was the *anti*abortion movement that was gaining the upper hand in the longer-term culture war.

————

Most Americans who opposed abortion stood by their principles quietly, even stoically, and entirely out of public view. Many had arrived at their beliefs after having undergone the procedure themselves, or from firsthand experience with ultrasound imaging, neonatal surgery, or visits to the preemie units at their local hospitals. Many had been persuaded on religious grounds. But the most visible and vocal abortion opponents in the '80s and '90s were the most radical—and they were making serious political inroads.

At first, protestors had participated in so-called direct-action interventions, using methods ranging from blockades to vandalism to other tactics for forcing clinics to close. They set up "rescues": attempts to preempt planned patient consultations by protesting, occupying public spaces, or actually confronting pregnant women outside clinics and trying to persuade them to reconsider.[2] By the 1990s, "an estimated forty thousand individuals had

————

2. By the late 1980s, writes Carol J. C. Maxwell, these shifts were apparent in terminology "adopted by all pro-life direct action groups, new and old, Catholic and evangelical. Activists abandoned the

participated in sit-ins at abortion facilities and related locations in the United States," according to anthropologist Carol J. C. Maxwell in her book *Pro-Life Activists in America*. "Most had no previous experience with direct activism; this political involvement was a dramatic, portentous episode in their lives."[3] A large segment of this faction had become involved, in part, because they felt they were on the *losing* side of a vast cultural rift. "Many activists," Maxwell contends, "perceived themselves to be excluded from the mechanisms through which people control and change society. They spoke of their religious values as making them a targeted, disenfranchised minority vulnerable to the havoc wrought by a dominant, 'liberal,' 'humanist' majority."

But after hundreds of actions and thousands of arrests, many participants saw little result for their efforts. A splinter alliance perceived a need for drastic escalation. "When ten years of sit-ins had failed to recriminalize abortion," notes Maxwell today, "a call for violence surfaced—[from] an isolated minority. The injunction to murder came from the fringe. This was a like-minded group... decreasingly challenged in their own forums as dissenters abandoned them."

With increasing frequency, clinics and other facilities were set aflame or firebombed.[4] Protestors released acid into buildings, making them inoperative for weeks. And one by one the killings began. Between 1992 and 1996, two physicians, two clinic workers, and an assistant were slain. A half dozen more were wounded by gunfire.[5] Dr. George Tiller, of Wichita, was shot in

---

terms 'sit-in' and 'intervention,' with their rational, instrumental, and civil-liberties connotations, and adopted the term 'rescue,' based on a Biblical injunction, thus heightening the emotive character of their call to fulfill a duty to come to others' aid." (Carol J. C. Maxwell, *Pro-Life Activists in America: Meaning, Motivation, and Direct Action* [Cambridge: Cambridge University Press, 2002], 62–63.)

3. Maxwell cites statistics by Faye Ginsburg from "Saving America's Souls: Operation Rescue's Crusade Against Abortion." (*Fundamentalism and the State*, ed. Martin E. Marty and R. Scott Appleby [Chicago: University of Chicago Press, 1993], 557–88.)

4. The first "bombings and arsons," according to sociologist and minister Dallas A. Blanchard, started in 1977, peaked in 1984, and "picked up again in 1991." (Dallas A. Blanchard, *The Anti-Abortion Movement and the Rise of the Religious Right* [New York: Twayne, 1994], 54–59.)

5. According to Maxwell, "The trend toward violent acts suggests a shift on the part of a minority away from relatively passive attempts to 'save babies' toward more aggressive attempts to control others' behavior, tragically culminating in the ultimate measure of stopping providers by killing them." Such actions, while alienating many in the movement, also had the effect of terrorizing medical professionals and women who contemplated having an abortion. As Maxwell would write

both arms by an assailant. (Sixteen years later, Tiller—having been repeatedly called out by the conservative press for performing thousands of abortions—would be murdered in cold blood while dispensing leaflets at his church.)

Much of the country, including most abortion opponents, looked on with alarm in the 1990s. Attorney General Janet Reno, law enforcement agencies, and the courts mobilized. Congress passed and the president signed the Freedom of Access to Clinic Entrances Act. And yet the murderous violence was a goad to some extremists, who adopted new predatory tactics. Doctors and medical practitioners were targeted, their homes picketed, their families threatened. Physicians' names sprang up on antiabortion websites, their faces on "wanted" posters. Women seeking medical help were intimidated and shamed. "Patients were brazenly stalked and 'outed,'" Paul Solotaroff would recount in *Rolling Stone*, "their names emblazoned on picket signs, their front steps daubed with [red paint]."

Elsewhere, there was another kind of combat going on. In state legislatures, lawmakers had begun to follow Pennsylvania's lead. "Eighteen states now have legislation that mandates a waiting period," Tina Rosenberg would report in *Rolling Stone* in 1996. "Twenty-eight states require women under 18 to notify or get the consent of one or both parents. Thirty-three states deny Medicaid coverage to poor women even when abortion is necessary to preserve their health." Moreover, a ban on so-called partial-birth abortions—a late-term method to end pregnancy via "dilation and extraction"[6]—was passed by both houses of Congress, in 1995 *and* 1997. President Clinton vetoed it both times. (The ban, however, would go into effect with Bush II's signature, in 2003.)

The battlefront kept shifting. And by the close of the '90s, the right-to-life brigades had made concrete strategic gains. The laws they championed became the laws that prevailed. Their most radical acts proved to have been an effective deterrent. Clinics became scarce in many states. Health professionals left the practice in droves. Most young doctors-to-be opted out of training or specializing in reproductive health. "Abortion moved to the margins of medical

---

in 2002, assessing the right-to-life movement in the '90s, "The combined effect of a large, persistent pro-life movement and a limited number of acts of anti-abortion violence committed by a minority of abortion opponents may encourage fear and a concomitant reluctance to perform abortions despite support for legal abortion." (Maxwell, *Pro-Life Activists in America*, 79–80, 85.)

6. The procedure is used in instances of fetal abnormality or in cases involving a threat to the health of the would-be mother.

practice," according to journalist Emily Bazelon. "In 1995, the number of OB-GYN residencies offering abortion training fell to a low of 12 percent."

At the same time, the notions of conception, abortion, and viable life had been repositioned in the public mind. More women were exploring the medical, familial, moral, and religious consequences of terminating a pregnancy, asking, "When does human life actually commence?"

Through it all, those seeking reproductive health care and family planning services have arguably been made *less* safe as a result of the strategies adopted by antiabortion advocates in the '80s and '90s. Clinics have been shuttered. Restrictive laws are still on the books. Measures have emerged to curtail funding for legal abortion. More women have had to take out loans to pay for their care. Schools have done away with comprehensive sex-ed classes. And there has been a distressing rise in the number of women taking matters into their own hands and attempting self-induced abortions. These added burdens and perils, according to the National Organization for Women, have disproportionately impacted "low-income women...women of color, as well as immigrant women and young women."

"Women have to take days off work to get to clinics," says Kate Michelman. "I know of women who drive to neighboring states and sleep in their cars through waiting periods. It is taking us [back] to the days when women seeking an abortion were demeaned, humiliated, and made to feel like criminals." This has remained the barbarous reality across much of the nation, even though abortion remains *legal and protected* for every woman in the United States of America.

In 2016, the Supreme Court would deal a severe blow to the antiabortion cause by issuing its most impactful reproductive health opinion in a generation. The Court *reaffirmed* the pivotal 1992 ruling that forbade states (in this case, Texas) from putting an "undue burden" on any woman intending to terminate a pregnancy. The pro-choice camp had recouped its momentum—and the legal high ground—even if the Republican administration that took office in 2017 was avowedly pro-life, averse to funding Planned Parenthood, set on curtailing women's rights to abortion services, and determined to continue nominating justices who would ultimately roll back *Roe v. Wade*.

But let's return to the 1990s. As this confrontation got more heated, another was brewing on a second, decisive front: the struggle over domestic partnerships.

I am operating the video camera. Through the lens, my brother and his partner stand before a minister. They are encircled by dozens of friends and family in the courtyard arbor of Philadelphia's Rittenhouse Hotel. "This has to be an historical moment," says William Stayton, a pastor and psychotherapist. "If you can imagine: a Jewish man and an unreligious man being brought together by a Baptist minister. Eat your heart out, Jerry Falwell."

Stayton addresses my brother, Richard. "Will you be joined to Steven, to live together as friend, mate, and lover? Will you love and cherish him through all the changes of your lives?" Stayton then faces Richard's partner. "Steven, will you love him as a person, respect him as an equal, sharing joy as well as sorrow, triumph as well as defeat?" Each in turn asserts, "I will."

A friend, Ken George, steps forward. Heterosexual matrimony, he explains, typically holds the promise of affirmation. When a man and a woman are so joined, the couple's loved ones, through their presence, are decreeing that for years to come they will recognize and honor the newlyweds' relationship. This is not the case, George testifies, for same-sex partners. Instead, such couples, when ritually united, have historically tended to *lose* that support.

That day in Philadelphia, vows are exchanged, along with twin trinity rings of rose, white, and yellow gold. Then Stayton tells the assembled, "I present to you, Richard and Steven, partners in love." A kiss seals their bond. A pianist breaks into "Our Love Is Here to Stay."

The occasion is a commitment ceremony between Richard Friend and Steven Mauldin. The date is auspicious: June 24, 1994—the week that marks the twenty-fifth anniversary of the Stonewall riots, which forged what would become the modern LGBT movement in America.[7] In fact, the following morning, many guests head north to join tens of thousands at the closing ceremony of New York City's Gay Games and to attend events surrounding Stonewall 25.

Commitment ceremonies, while not uncommon at the time, were ahead of the curve. Straight and, to some degree, gay culture was largely resistant to the notion of same-sex *matrimony*.[8] True, a pioneering case in Hawaii in

---

7. LGBT or LGBTQ were designations that would become standard a generation later.

8. Attorney Evan Wolfson, a longtime advocate for marriage equality, founded the organization Freedom to Marry. Wolfson understood that for many lesbian and gay partners in the 1990s,

1991 had sought to force the state to officially recognize marriage equality. But Hawaii's citizens, like those in several other states, had other ideas, voting to deny legal recognition of same-sex partnerships. In the meantime, lesbian and gay couples by the thousands were formally announcing their love and commitment in public.[9] And through the work of lawyers such as Mary Bonauto, the first state supreme court in the union—Vermont's, in 1997—gave blanket protection and benefits to all, no matter their sexual orientation. In April 2000, both houses of the Vermont legislature went on to pass a bill, signed by the governor, letting town clerks grant licenses to same-sex couples. Their unions, according to the statute, would be recognized by the state as enjoying "the same benefits, protections, and responsibilities under the law... as are granted to spouses in a civil marriage."[10]

With two decades of hindsight, my brother—a diversity and leadership development expert with a PhD as a human sexuality educator—looks back fondly at the service. "There was a trend going on around commitment ceremonies," Richard says, "but with little of the marriage-equality component you see now. Had it been a legal marriage, I probably wouldn't have chosen it. In the '90s there was actually a politics around *not* calling it marriage because to do so was viewed as supporting a heterosexist ideology. Today, I fully support marriage equality. But at that stage it was all about creating a community ritual, about engaging those around us to stand up and make a commitment to us as a couple."

Steven, a textile expert, agrees. "It was partly political for Richard and

---

marriage was beside the point; to some, it was actually an expression of assimilation into straight culture. "Some thought marriage was 'patriarchal and exclusionary,'" he would later tell the *New York Times*, "while others said the gay rights movement 'was supposed to be about liberation,' not [about] joining heterosexuals." Steven Mauldin, my brother's partner, remembers the odd reaction the day of the ceremony: "The irony was that a lot of my gay friends took it less seriously than my straight friends. *Support* came mostly from heterosexual people. Literally, I had friends who thought it was a joke... hysterical." (Erica Johnston, "Meet Two Activists Who Brought Sweeping Change to the Gay Rights Movement," *Washington Post Magazine*, October 3, 2014; Sheryl Gay Stolberg, "In Fight for Marriage Rights, 'She's Our Thurgood Marshall,'" *New York Times*, March 28, 2013, A19; interview with Mauldin.)

9. Two of the '90s' most popular network shows, *Roseanne* and *Friends*, aired episodes featuring same-sex ceremonies. Later in the decade, the topic would become more standard fare on such programs as *Ellen* and *Will & Grace*.

10. In 2003, Massachusetts made history by issuing the country's first marriage licenses to gay and lesbian partners.

me to have the ceremony," he says, "to do it in an open way, to have it in a hotel—which would have turned us away just a few years before. And to do it on the anniversary of Stonewall was kind of like taking back the power and saying, 'I'm a human being. I have rights.' Having the ceremony was kind of like the ultimate coming-out."

"The beauty of such ceremonies at the time," Richard reflects, "was about formalizing a redefinition of what family is. It became our capacity to define our 'family of choice,' our 'family of friends,' on our own terms— above and beyond our 'family of origin.' Families *changed* in the '90s. We started to see and accept blended families, cohabitating couples, more and more grandparents raising kids, etcetera."

Another factor making their partnership particularly strong was the fact that Steven was HIV-positive, which no one in the family knew back then. "We never used language at the ceremony like 'forever' or 'in sickness and in health,'" Richard continues. "The whole HIV bubble that surrounded our lives and that period makes 'forever' an odd construct to commit to. He was diagnosed in March of '93. The diagnosis wasn't a reason for me to leave the relationship and it would have been patronizing to have [provided] more of a reason to stay. But we supported each other through it. The summer after the ceremony, he got really sick and almost died. And because he wasn't out about his status to his family or mine, that was hard and isolating."

Steven recalls, "You were seeing real change in the Clinton era with regard to progressive matters involving sex and gender rights. But it was almost like a reverse of that—in some ways—for gays. A lot of people had died. And [our commitment to each other] was just kind of, 'All right, what's the real meaning here? How do I exist in this?' In that period, it was a real political issue. And deeply personal. If I look back on it, I probably did want stability and a partner who cared for me and looked out for me, which was connected with my HIV status. When you think that you can die relatively easily, you look at things differently."

Though Steven and Richard decided to end their partnership in 1999, to this day they remain connected as "family of choice." Steven now admits, "I totally looked at the breakup as a failure in my life. We both saw it as a failure. We don't now. And I think it's good that we both are as close as we are still. I don't think a lot of straight people do that."

In the end, the civil-union and marriage-equality movements would stay the course and win the war. In the 2010s, leaders of both political parties would join forces in recognizing the constitutionality of domestic partnerships, even if many, especially on the right, had been forcefully resistant in the intervening years.[11] Finally, thanks to struggles waged in the '90s, the Supreme Court ruled in 2015 that marriage equality was indeed the law of the land. And so it shall remain for the near term, despite the current administration's rollback of transgender rights, its stated desire to have states (not the federal government) set the terms for domestic partnerships—and Vice President Mike Pence's history of opposing initiatives promoting LGBT equality.[12]

————

While the legal consensus was shifting in favor of marriage equality in the 1990s, domestic partnership laws faced one seemingly insurmountable roadblock: the Defense of Marriage Act. More than any other culture-war skirmish of the '90s, it was *this one* to which social conservatives claimed a resounding victory.

The 1996 Defense of Marriage Act—DOMA—was introduced by thrice-married congressman Bob Barr, the Georgia Republican; cosponsored in the Senate by the twice-married majority leader, Bob Dole; and backed by a bipartisan wave of legislators. DOMA had been devised for three reasons. First, it would create a federal law that would void any state statute that recognized same-sex marriage. Second, it would legally define marriage as being the exclusive right and privilege of heterosexual couples. Third, it would curry favor with "family-values voters" on the eve of the 1996 elections. "Lacking anything better to do," quipped the *Economist*, "America's Senate has been busying itself banning something that is not legal anyway.... What

————

11. "In the first half of 2016 alone," according to a *Washington Post* analysis, "87 bills that could limit LGBT rights have been introduced [in state legislatures], a steep increase from previous years." (E. Mason, A. Williams, and K. Elliott, "The Dramatic Rise in State Efforts to Limit LGBT Rights," *Washington Post*, June 10, 2016.)

12. The Trump administration, from the first, was dead set against reproductive choice. During his first two weeks in office, the president nominated a pro-life jurist to the High Court; he signed a directive denying aid to overseas nonprofits involved in matters of choice; he named a series of cabinet nominees, many of whom saw little daylight between church and state; and his vice president, Mike Pence, attended a large pro-life rally. "'Life' is winning," Pence told the crowd. "[We will] embrace a culture of life in America." (Elizabeth Landers, "Vice President Mike Pence Speech Right at Home at March for Life," CNN.com, January 27, 2017; Ben Kamisar, "Trump, Like Obama, Signs Flurry of First Week Executive Actions," TheHill.com, January 29, 2017.)

is marriage 'defended' from? Divorce? Illegitimacy? No. In Hawaii two men want to wed, and the state courts there may let them do so."

In truth, the institution of marriage was under pressure from every angle.[13] The rates for first marriages were declining. Couples were getting

---

13. Marriage was on the rocks for many reasons. First, even though faith is not a prerequisite to marital stability, many couples lacked a firm or common spiritual grounding to reinforce their commitment. While a greater number of Americans in the 1990s defined themselves as religious, they were increasingly less likely to adhere to a fixed set of values tied to a single organized religion. In many cases, their spiritual affiliation became a DIY matter. ("The Way" had become "Have It Your Way.") Between 30 and 40 percent of Americans were practicing a different faith than the one they'd been born with. Often the faithful were less connected to an established denomination or congregation with stable rules, roots, a hierarchy, and a system of belief that might reinforce conjugal fidelity or long-term commitment to a partner. Second, while marriage has been "extolled in the pulpits...since colonial times," writes sociologist Andrew Cherlin, "divorce has [also] been part of the individualistic side of American culture. Well before it was legal in Britain or France...divorce was legally available in America." Third, there were professional pressures building at the fin de siècle. Dual-career couples saw office demands cut into me time and we time. With one eye on the workplace, many young marrieds delayed or deferred having kids. And increased business travel or relocation, in a global economy, meant less family time and more opportunity for infidelity.

Popular culture played its part. The idea of an "affair" was consistently presented in fiction, movies, and television as stock, if stigmatized, behavior: less a moral lapse than a logical consequence of a character's personal flaws or a couple's struggles to communicate or express intimacy. ("It's not our partner we seek to leave with the affair," psychotherapist and sexologist Esther Perel advises, "it's ourselves.") The 1997 book *The Ethical Slut* would become a bestseller by advising readers how to navigate the moral dynamics of affairs and various forms of nontraditional companionship. In short, many who sought lovers beyond their committed partner or spouse were becoming more comfortable—despite all the pain inflicted or the risks and guilt and fallout—with what culture critic Sam Eichner calls "casual duplicity." Many others were maintaining numerous relationships (with or without their partner's knowledge) for reasons that were sexual, cultural, economic, social, or personal, with little duplicity involved whatsoever. This was how they chose to live and to love.

Meanwhile, extramarital relationships, as covered in news accounts, began to seem commonplace, if only because of the extensive media play given "sex scandals" befalling public figures. Political commentators worked themselves into a lather trying to explain the marriages of Bill and Hillary Clinton or Newt and Marianne Gingrich in much the same way they had focused on the marriage of Gary Hart and his wife, Lee, after the senator's affair with Donna Rice was made public. ("If it doesn't bother me," Lee told reporters in 1987, "I don't think it ought to bother anyone else.")

Forces on the right at times tried to shift the blame for the "marriage crisis" to the left, to minorities, to myriad "others," even if patterns of divorce, remarriage, and single parenthood were just as common in largely conservative, religious, or "red state" regions. As author Angela Stanley has noted, "Marriage as the norm in the United States has been on the decline for decades." An expert in African American social issues, Stanley has tried to dispel the myth that black women have played an outsize role in this overall "crisis." She asserts that part of the dynamic has been that "poor people of color, a disproportionate number of whom are black men, [were swept] into the criminal justice system....These men have significantly reduced employment and economic opportunities and are married later in life. Divorce rates, meanwhile, were slowing but still at near-record levels, affecting half of all marriages. (Nearly 30 percent of couples who wed at the start of the '90s were split up before the decade was out—even as more than two-thirds of '90s marriages *survived* fifteen years or more.) For many young single mothers, there was little or no stigma associated with bearing children early. Other partners or parents were forgoing matrimony altogether. Or they were choosing, whether married or unmarried, not to bear children. By the end of the 1990s, two statistics represented all-time lows: only one in four households had stay-at-home moms; only one in four consisted of two-parent families with kids.[14]

Another less obvious partnership pattern was emerging: *serial* monogamy. As Andrew J. Cherlin writes in his eye-opening book *The Marriage-Go-Round*, many Americans were on a partnership carousel, getting into relationships earlier and with more frequency—and then extracting themselves, instead of sticking it out if things weren't going right, only to recouple with new partners later on. A large demographic study comparing romantic relationships cross-culturally found that Americans between 1989 and 1997 "partner, unpartner, and repartner faster than do people in any other Western nation," as Cherlin put it. "They form cohabiting relationships easily, but they end them after a shorter time than people in other nations. They tend to marry at younger ages. After a divorce, they tend to find a new partner more quickly." The evidence pointed to a widespread personal desire—and cultural

---

sometimes viewed as less viable partners." At the same time, she points out, "significantly more black women than black men are earning college degrees." The result—along with many other factors—has meant that "black women marry later, but they do marry." (Interview with Gay Talese; Andrew J. Cherlin, *The Marriage-Go-Round: The State of Marriage and the Family in America Today* [New York: Knopf, 2009], 33, 166, 182, 186; Ryan Selzer, "Why You're Happily Married and Having an Affair," *Daily Beast*, November 2, 2014; Alex Williams, "Open Marriage's New 15 Minutes," *New York Times*, February 3, 2012; Sam Eichner, "Bill Simmons, Ben Affleck and Epic Man Caves," UrbanDaddy.com, June 23, 2016; Polly Vernon, "Is Anyone Faithful Anymore?," *Guardian*, March 6, 2010; Jonathan Rauch, "Cheatin' Hearts," *Chicago Tribune*, September 23, 1998; James V. Grimaldi, "Marianne Gingrich, Newt's Ex-Wife, Says He Wanted 'Open Marriage,'" *Washington Post*, January 19, 2012; Angela Stanley, "Black, Female and Single," *New York Times*, December 11, 2011, SR1, 6.)

14. In 2015 the Reverend William Hultberg, in his eighties, would tell me, "More than 50 percent of all marriages end in divorce. Fifty percent of all [American] births are out of wedlock or aborted. A *billion* dollars has been spent in the past twenty years fighting gay marriage. Give me a billion dollars and... how I could have helped heterosexual marriage." (Interview with Hultberg.)

sanction—for having a single, largely exclusive romantic partner at any one time. And if *that* one didn't work out, it was time for a do-over.[15]

Whatever the trends, social conservatives seemed poised to play the Defense of Marriage Act as a trump card in the 1996 presidential race. Bob Dole, who enthusiastically endorsed the legislation, was in line to become the Republican nominee for president. But before he got the nod, two remarkable twists would forever change the complexion of the decade.

First, Speaker Newt Gingrich, who'd been flying high the year before, took a nosedive.[16] In one of the most self-destructive political acts of the era, Gingrich and his fellow House Republicans overplayed their hand in a heated budget battle with Bill Clinton. Trying to pressure the president to cut a deal, the Speaker engineered not one but *two* shutdowns of the federal government. And the maneuver backfired in epic fashion. American voters, come election time, would place the blame squarely on the shoulders of the Grand Old Party. (As fate would have it, the November 1995 shutdown— resulting in fewer staffers traversing the halls of the West Wing—would *also* precipitate the first intimate encounters between the president and White House intern Monica Lewinsky.)

The second surprise: Clinton, conferring with adviser Dick Morris, had begun to tack center-right on his social agenda. The president, hoping to

---

15. Corollary 1: There appeared to be a need for stable partnerships, *period*, among a large segment of American adults—as if a fixed relationship were better than none at all; as if cohabitation brought a level of financial and emotional security; as if there were negative social or personal costs associated with being unattached or uncommitted. Corollary 2: The economic prosperity of the period had given "more Americans the time and money to develop their senses of self," writes Andrew Cherlin. "It suggests a view of intimate partnerships as continually changing as the partners' inner selves develop....It suggests that commitment to spouses and partners are personal choices [rather than lifelong vows] that can be, and perhaps should be, ended if they become unsatisfying." (Cherlin, *The Marriage-Go-Round*, 29–30.)

16. Well, *nearly* high-flying. In 1995 Gingrich was granted a ride on Air Force One and threw a hissy fit when the commander in chief, during twenty-four hours of flight time, chose not to exchange word one with him. And *then* Gingrich's host had had the chutzpah to allow the Speaker and the other passengers to deplane from the aircraft's tail exit. "Where," Newt fumed, "is their sense of manners?" The brat was out of the bag. The next edition of the *New York Daily News* bore an illustration of a whimpering Gingrich in a diappie, with the headline "CRY BABY—NEWT'S TANTRUM: He closed down the government because Clinton made him sit at back of plane." (Alexander Nazaryan, "Newt Gingrich, Crybaby: The Famous Daily News Cover Explained," New York *Daily News*, January 6, 2012.)

broaden his electoral appeal in the wake of Gingrich's 1994 midterm blitz-krieg, adopted what columnist Ross Douthat would later term "soft 'values' rhetoric on marriage and family." Clinton got on the school-uniform band-wagon. He endorsed the V-chip, which was intended to give parents more control over their kids' TV-viewing habits. He backed a sweeping welfare reform bill (as a way to incentivize people to work by forcing many off gov-ernment assistance, but leaving millions in the lurch),[17] prompting three high-profile assistant secretaries to quit. And in Clinton's most out-of-character move of all, he announced he would actually *sign* the Defense of Marriage Act, outlawing legal recognition of gay and lesbian couples.

Critics said that the president, mindful that a veto might cost him the popular vote, was pandering yet again, smokescreening but not inhaling. Maybe so. But in the end, Clinton was above all a survivor. The sanctity—and heterosexual purity—of the institution of marriage, instead of becoming a Republican cudgel, had been neutralized. (While same-sex marriage, mid-decade, appeared to be on the ropes, the tide would eventually turn. The majority of Americans would line up in support of marriage equality, with commentators such as columnist Frank Rich calling Clinton's support of DOMA "the most ignominious civil rights betrayal" of his presidency. But on this singular issue, for the remainder of the '90s, the right emerged victo-rious and the left was resigned to waging its battle in the courts.)

Clinton, again, had finessed a culture-war fracas. Gingrich, who'd worked with his nemesis and GOP moderates to cobble a historic bill to bal-ance the budget, swiftly saw his own approval numbers disintegrate, along with his power. He would be disciplined in 1997 by his fellow House mem-bers in a 395-to-28 vote—the first Speaker in history to receive such a rebuke for conduct unbecoming a congressman.

And what about Bob Dole? First, he would get trounced by Bill Clinton in the 1996 election, the incumbent having successfully "grabbed family val-ues for the Democrats," in the words of *Newsweek*'s Jonathan Alter.[18] Second,

---

17. The bill opened with this language: "1. Marriage is the foundation of a successful society. 2. Marriage is an essential institution of a successful society that promotes the interests of children." (Cherlin, *The Marriage-Go-Round*, 126.)

18. Many attribute Bill Clinton's 1996 victory to his new pet social causes, which drew the support of swing voters, not insignificantly the so-called soccer moms identified by the president's pollster and adviser Mark Penn.

in 1998 Dole would pull off what many considered a marketing masterstroke, and one that ingeniously blended politics, commerce, celebrity—and sexuality. The candidate, who'd lost to the national fall guy for sexual indiscretion, was hired by Pfizer—the makers of a new drug called Viagra—to help raise awareness about *erectile dysfunction*.

To be fair, Dole wasn't actually shilling for Big Pharma. He was putting a public face on a public health issue by lending his status as a statesman, war hero, and ED sufferer. (His condition, he said, was a consequence of his having undergone prostate surgery.) "It's a great drug," the senator would tell talk-show host Larry King, explaining how he'd been a volunteer in early Viagra trials. "My wife was a little startled."

Dole's communications director, Douglas MacKinnon, recalls the senator's decision to step forward, a red-state icon commending a little blue pill. "I'm not exaggerating," MacKinnon says, there were "hundreds and hundreds of jokes…at his expense. [But] it was huge in terms of someone with Bob Dole's profile being willing to put himself out there publicly on a pretty sensitive subject."

———

The timing was uncanny, not just in terms of the Clinton-Dole dynamic but the entire culture war dustup. In early 1998, revelations emerged that the president had been involved in another extramarital affair. News reports would include graphic descriptions of sexual matters and would provide Republicans with even more explosive family-values ammo. The scandal *plus* Pfizer's coincident rollout of Viagra *plus* Dole's TV spots ("erectile dysfunction, ED, often called 'impotence'") would gum up the political news cycle with the indelible stain of sex.

"It was the summer in America when the nausea returned, when the joking didn't stop," wrote Philip Roth in his novel *The Human Stain*. "It was the summer when a president's penis was on everyone's mind, and life, in all its shameless impurity, once again confounded America."

But first: the unlikely and largely untold story of Bob Dole's wonder drug.

CHAPTER 29

The Hardener's Tale

Viagra arrived in the spring of 1998. But it didn't truly seep into most American homes until the following winter—and not through the bedroom, but the living room. It happened on a series of successive Sundays. And before the year was out, an entire nation had collectively cringed.

By now, that deep male voice seems altogether innocuous. *In the rare event of an erection lasting more than four hours, seek immediate medical help.* But when those words were first uttered, they landed with the wallop of a blindside tackle. They caused many a parent (and countless children and yelping pets) to burrow into the sectional sofa.

Let's recount the shock wave.

Our families had gathered to watch football. We were digesting, quite possibly, a holiday meal. We were settling into the ebb and flow of a close game. Then all at once the Viagra ad commandeered the screen.

It is sunset. An elderly couple in jeans and cowboy boots is doing the box step. Cut to: a handsome, bronzed pair, just entering their twilight years. *They're dancing again*, comes the voice-over. *Glancing again. People holding, touching, and romancing again.* Next, a seated man in formal attire, possibly in a wheelchair, kisses his partner, who is perched on his lap. *Viagra works by improving a man's natural response. So with Viagra, a touch or a glance can again lead to something more.* The montage continues. Couples hug and sway on a dock, on a roof deck, in the kitchen after the dishes are done. The light is enchanting, the cinematography crisp. In three of the scenes, the women are so moved that—*bah-dum*—they kick up their heels.

At last, the possible downsides are announced: headaches, facial flushing, visual disturbances—along with the proviso that sexual activity can be physically demanding on the heart. In these first airings, the fearsome four-hour erection is never mentioned. But soon the warning is tacked onto the commercial, phrased so ingeniously as to trigger *greater* appetite for the drug.

Something new was going on in this inaugural ad.

Football is family time. The TV room is family space. So talk of uncontrollable erections elicited not groans but an icy hush. And in a flash, the retaining wall had collapsed between Poppy and the grandkids, between what preteens snickered about in school and what Mom and Dad did upstairs. Here was talk of sexual congress—out in the open, over chips and guac and wings. With nowhere to slink away to, each adult viewer was forced into a quiet complicity. Yes, they had to acknowledge: we actually copulated, at some stage, to bear the children sitting nearby.

TV audiences, true enough, were not unaccustomed to commercials about sexual health. In the '80s, as the AIDS crisis deepened, public service spots had been meant to shock so as to raise awareness and incite action. But those ads were less about sex than they were about death—and America's silence in the face of the disease. These new commercials were instead about the quality of consensual interaction among underserved couples. And so the whiplash of the transaction—football, fornication, football—jacked up the queasy.

Private, wholesome family time could no longer charade as being either private or wholly wholesome. More and more, in the days of more and more media, domestic space had become a cul-de-sac in the public square. And sexuality's grip on the public purse strings, through sponsored programming, ensured that such messages, even medically enlightened ones, could not be kept at bay, no matter one's age or upbringing, no matter one's religious belief or disbelief.

Here, then, during one of the most benign and G-rated rituals of the week—six years after Governor and Mrs. Clinton's Super Bowl date with *60 Minutes*—were the messy, miraculous, wacky facts of life, of modern science, and of commercial television.

Whence did the circuitous dance begin? How did Pfizer—the company that developed Viagra—go from creating that initial dose to that public do-si-do, giving rise to the fastest-selling prescription drug in the history of medicine?

The tale is a largely untold one. "One of the reasons you don't read a lot about the backroom stuff on Viagra," says David Brinkley, who headed up the team responsible for the drug's global marketing strategy, "is because we just don't talk about it. We have kind of—I won't say an understanding—we just don't talk."

But as luck would have it, enough time has passed since. And so Brinkley, along with some of the Viagra group's most senior scientists and consultants—all of whom have since left the company—feel comfortable opening up, for history's sake. At one point Brinkley admits, in comments echoed by his former colleagues, "This is actually the most in-depth discussion I've had with anybody [about Viagra] in ten years."

———————

The year: 1985. The cast: four chemists and five biologists working long hours in a backwater research lab in southeastern England. The setting: farms hidden amid marshes; narrow inland wharves; hedgerows and thatched cottages; sloping hillocks with clusters of hops and, everywhere, dewdrops of grazing sheep, plump and alabaster and immobile as porcelain.

The region: time-tousled Kent, in many ways an apt breeding ground for Pfizer's prized medicine. Up the road, the town of Canterbury, in fact, was practically the birthplace of the ribald tale. As Geoffrey Chaucer famously recounted, fourteenth-century Britons were known for trading bawdy stories on their annual pilgrimages through these parts. ("I beg you," Chaucer writes in *The Canterbury Tales*, "not to consider me vulgar [as I relay these pilgrims'] exact words...no matter how crude and low.")[1] Those journeys of penance were considered by puritans of the day to be little more than church-sanctioned debauchery—the medieval equivalent of sex tourism. And nearly a century and a half later, the much-married Henry VIII would make his own pilgrimages, to nearby Hever Castle, to woo and win Anne Boleyn. (Then, of course, there is the landscape itself: Kent's fields are veiled in layers of chalk that undergird the very ground, called the North Downs. These folds and ridges, notoriously white-flecked, imply an inherent fertility.)

Finally, there is the town proper: unassuming Sandwich, where, in the 1950s, Pfizer decided to establish one of its two prime research hubs. Three decades later, quite by accident, the company's scientists would devise a mol-

———————

1. In "The Merchant's Tale," for example, Chaucer describes the lechery that results when an elderly man takes what he believes to be aphrodisiacs.

ecule that would be central to a story of chemistry and kismet. Call it The Hardener's Tale.

That molecule: UK-92480.

––––––––

Among the men most responsible for that auspicious clump of atoms is a chemist named Simon Campbell, whom many consider the godfather of Viagra. Indeed, in 2014 the queen knighted him for "services to Chemistry" (and, by extension, to the general British blood flow).

Campbell's hair is gray now, brush-cut into a rebellious spike. His eyes are cobalt blue. His brow, knitted above a hawkish countenance, suggests intensity: Samuel Beckett by way of Ian McKellen. As he sits in his well-appointed flat in Kensington, the former president of the Royal Society of Chemistry, just entering his seventies, fixes a marksman's glare on his guest.

"Sandwich came close to being shut a few times," he says, revisiting Pfizer's dire pre-Viagra days. "We were living on a knife edge. The group hadn't been very productive in the late '70s and mid-'80s and we were under tremendous pressure—on a precipice." But part of the facility's turnaround, over the course of a generation, was due to Campbell and his knack for forging consensus, along with what he calls an unwavering commitment to "scientific excellence and rigor—and deep scientific understanding of what you need in a drug." Campbell managed and rallied the teams behind Pfizer's new drug candidates.[2] He minded the purse strings, the hiring, the construction of a massive research complex. He also played soccer in local leagues for most of those years, and became, says a close coworker, "renowned for his aggression."

On Campbell's watch, Sandwich rolled out the prostate drug Cardura, which brought in a billion dollars. ("I'm the sole inventor listed on the patent," says Campbell, not one disinclined to crow.) The same with Norvasc, for angina and high blood pressure. ("Over $5 billion sales—I'm one of three inventors on that patent.") The list winds on. By 1998, Pfizer had produced, coproduced, or acquired the rights to a portfolio of category-leading drugs such as Aricept, Celebrex, Lipitor, Trovan, and Zoloft.

But how to account for Campbell's team and its "discovery" of Viagra, a medicine that owes a goodly share of its existence to serendipity?

––––––––

2. Having joined the company in 1972, he retired in 1998 as the company's czar for worldwide drug discovery and medicinals, R&D Europe division.

Drug discovery, on the whole, is a laborious, hit-or-miss proposition. It is a process governed as much by Darwin (and the ruthless gleaning of natural selection) as by Machiavelli (the boardroom machinations, the industry hardball, the regulatory red tape). Indeed, in the pharmaceutical Ironman known as drug discovery, "only one of about seven million screened compounds," according to *Fortune* magazine, "has the right stuff to make it to market." To put it another way: it can take *twelve or more years* (on average)—and well north of $2 *billion*—to take a pill from thesis to molecule to pharmacy shelves. Given all of the biochemical, economic, and political roadblocks that await every major-market drug, it is a wonder any of them gets made, let alone one as initially miscast as Viagra.

———

During the mid-'80s, the question of how to erect a firm, determined penis was about the last thing on Simon Campbell's agenda, at least while he was making the rounds in Pfizer's labs. Instead, Campbell's attention, for a time, was focused on coronary arteries.

In the beginning, it was merely a hunch. Campbell (then director of discovery chemistry) and Dave Roberts (a medicinal chemist) had devised a compelling hypothesis. They wondered if one could curb high blood pressure by relaxing the smooth muscle in the body's blood vessels. Their proposed method was to introduce a compound into the bloodstream that would hike up levels of what scientists call cyclic GMP (cGMP), a natural substance in cells that, when elevated, is known to decrease tension in the heart's arteries.

The drug they had in mind would perform a sort of vascular blockade. It would take aim at an obscure enzyme that scientists—in the alphanumeric patois of med-speak—referred to as PDE5.[3] PDE5, which sounds more like the name of a cop show or a psoriasis shampoo, normally breaks down the cell substance cGMP. But the medicine that Campbell and Roberts were proposing would instead *block* PDE5, thereby pumping up levels of cGMP to relax smooth muscle, lower blood pressure, and increase blood flow. At the time, this was a new concept. "Little was known about the physiological role of cGMP," Campbell reflects—and even less about PDE5.

———

3. Enzymes are proteins that accelerate cellular reactions. The ones in saliva, for instance, break down the cracker you chew so that your body gets its nutrients, and the cracker tastes good because the enzymes release its sugars. (Interview with Dr. Michael Mendelsohn.)

Campbell and Roberts had uncovered evidence in research journals about a related compound called zaprinast that had actually lowered the blood pressure of anesthetized dogs. (Not that the dogs had been complaining of high blood pressure to begin with.) Intrigued, the scientists surmised that if they were to modify a zaprinast type of molecule, they might end up with a cardio drug that could zero in on spongy vascular muscle and dilate vessels in the body, including those in the heart.

They petitioned Pfizer to let one of its small units try to synthesize such a molecule. "We wrote that proposal in 1985, Dave and I," Campbell says. "We went through all the biology, all the chemistry, all the literature, and made a cogent [argument]." Pfizer would approve their modest proposal the following year. "It wasn't a big project. Four to six people in chemistry at the start. A dozen total. We [eventually] made two to three hundred compounds—not thousands."

That task in large part fell to Nick Terrett, who would spearhead the chemical strategy for constructing molecules that might fit the bill. Terrett—whose name would be one of the three registered on the patent for Viagra—is thorough, compulsively curious, and a self-described introvert.[4] In his lab-coated press pictures from those days (he was forty when the drug was finally launched) he has a cue-ball crown, salt-and-pepper beard, and dark-rimmed specs that bring to mind a young Sigmund Freud.[5]

Terrett and his colleagues were charged with constructing a single molecule, a Calderesque mobile of interlaced rings and clumps of atoms. That molecule's properties, in theory, would fit nicely into the PDE5 enzyme, like a lock into a key—blocking it, increasing cGMP levels, and relaxing the smooth muscle of the heart's arteries. Or at least that was the plan.

The obstacles were enormous. "The trick to inventing a drug," insists Terrett, is to make sure the compound hits its target without causing collateral damage. "It mustn't affect other biochemical mechanisms of the body. It must have properties that allow it to be ideally taken by mouth and get to the

---

4. The chemical patent lists Terrett, his boss David Brown, and senior chemist Andrew Bell. The names on the patent for the use of the compound to treat erectile dysfunction: Terrett and Peter Ellis.

5. Terrett left Pfizer in 2006. He is now the chief scientific officer at Ensemble Therapeutics, in Cambridge, Massachusetts.

appropriate cells *within* the tissues and the appropriate biochemical target *within* the cells, and then be excreted or metabolized."

To winnow down the permutations, as Terrett describes it, "there's a very slow, methodical, interesting process. You take these compounds and you modify their structures, atom by atom or group by group, fine-tuning their properties. You have to keep an eye on [whether] the drug [will] dissolve in the stomach before it can be absorbed through the gut into the bloodstream. You have to make sure it's going to be a nontoxic compound when it's put into animals and, ultimately, put into man. It's really a case of juggling twenty balls in the air at the same time."

For centuries, healers treating tribal cultures would often use mixtures of natural substances. But contemporary drugs are different. Unlike the practice in "native, traditional medicine," says Terrett, "[and among] shamans as well, that's quite often a combination of different elements. In Western medicine, what we're trying to do is find everything we need in *one* molecule."

To that end, beginning in 1986, Pfizer's chemists jiggered with a cocktail of atom bundles, swapping in various clusters. They then handed the compounds over to a cardiovascular biologist named Peter Ellis and a small squad who would test the proposed drugs on tissues—strips of aorta and other vessels from rabbits, rats, and dogs.

And for eighteen months nothing much happened. "To be absolutely fair," Terrett says, recoiling at the memory, "for the first year or so, we thought: exactly what were we *doing*? There was a sense of frustration and concern." Gill Samuels, another team member, would concur, telling the industry journal *Chemistry in Britain*, "There wasn't a great deal of confidence [within] the company that we could get a really potent and selective inhibitor."

Things looked bleak until a Pfizer biochemist named Frank Burslem joined them. Instead of dithering with vessels and tissues, Burslem went deeper. According to Jim Kling, reporting in the journal *Modern Drug Discovery*, Burslem used rat kidney and rabbit platelets to isolate one purified enzyme, allowing the pharmacologists to see how different drug samples would interact with it. Things quickly took a turn. The team discovered that one plucky enzyme in their experiments might be a better match for treating coronary artery disease. Suddenly, what had begun as a quest for treating high blood pressure had morphed into a medicine aimed at that condition's most deadly *consequences*: angina and heart attacks.

By 1989, one molecule seemed to have real promise. The scientists code-named it UK-92480, the single standout from among the sixteen hundred substances they'd tested. In short order, Peter Ellis was conscripted to make a pitch to Pfizer's top brass proposing that they try the drug on human beings. And—presto—the company consented, choosing the compound over twelve others (that were then being developed for various ailments by different Sandwich divisions).

To celebrate, a small party was thrown in a Pfizer conference room. "It was late afternoon," Terrett says. "It was low-key. It had alcohol—sparkling wine, nothing special. And some appetizers.... The critical point in a discovery program is when you say, 'This is the compound that we want to take the distance.'"

After congratulating the discovery team, Simon Campbell pulled Terrett aside. "Simon did his usual thing," Terrett says, laughing as he remembers his boss's sour expression. "He furrowed his brow and frowned at me, and he said, 'D'you know, it's a weak candidate. You're lucky to get it nominated.'"

Poor candidate or no, UK-92480—later christened with the generic name sildenafil—would move on to the next stage: clinical trials in healthy volunteers and then, with any luck, in patients with coronary thrombosis.

———

Pfizer's research facility in Sandwich is literally hidden in plain sight. One drives down Ramsgate Road through farmland and past cricket grounds. Along the lane rests an apple orchard, the Gazen Salts Nature Reserve, drowsy houseboats nestled along the river Stour. In the distance loom a half dozen silo-shaped structures along with large office buildings arranged in clusters. As Nick Terrett recalls the place in the zooming Viagra years, "We were in a very rural environment in a sleepy part of the country, which had stayed sleepy pretty much from the fifteenth century onwards." The Pfizer campus, however, was state of the art and perpetually abuzz.

Upon approaching the site, one encounters imposing fences and security gates. And today a visitor has come to call on Peter Ellis—the leader of the cardiovascular biology team that developed UK-92480—and to walk the halls where chemists first brewed that initial batch. The interloper states his name and intention into an intercom, enters the curved edifice ("Welcome to R&D HQ Europe"), and is escorted up an escalator and into an open-air atrium. It is all very Saarinenian: swooped railings, cascading glass, and amoeba-shaped swivel chairs.

One wall is etched with the names of Pfizer's progeny: Celebrex, Lipitor, Zoloft, Zyrtec among them. Farther along is a pedestal holding a bust of Sir Alexander Fleming, the father of penicillin. (Pfizer, which dates back to 1849, mass-produced the drug during World War II.) Pfizer's 390-acre site—upon this visit, at least—is a thriving hive. (It will be closed down, then sold off, then turned into a national "enterprise zone" in the mid-2010s.)

Peter Ellis approaches with a wide smile, friendly patter, and an armful of files. His goatee says: scholarly '70s—as in *1870s*. His grin is slightly conspiratorial, suggesting a cheeky Ricky Gervais. Ellis works as a Pfizer consultant, having left the firm the previous April. He is therefore free to divulge certain Viagra back stories that haven't been previously shared with outsiders.

Ellis, a Yorkshire-born biologist with a pharmacology PhD, used to be a competitive rower for Scotland. He ushers his guest into a small conference suite just down the hall from the lab where UK-92480 was first brewed. He shuts the door to the Naxcel Sterile Powder room. The walls are off-Pepto pink, roughly the color of Naxcel (used in animals to treat pneumonia and foot rot). Down the hall is the Benadryl room; next door, the Listerine room. Each is painted in its medicine's respective shade.

Ellis opens a file from his stack. In 1991, he says, Pfizer wanted to test the safety of what came to be known as sildenafil. To that end, a single modest dose was parsed out for several days to a handful of English volunteers—all of them male and seemingly free of heart disease. None had adverse reactions. Next, Ellis recalls, a second pool of healthy volunteers, this time in Wales, stayed in a medical facility for ten days and were administered the drug at various dose levels. The results—six years after Campbell and Roberts's first conjecture—were less than encouraging.

Not only did the drug have little effect on how well the heart pumped or the blood flowed or the vessels dilated, but it also caused mild side effects—backaches, throbbing in the temples, upset stomach. "The darkness for this compound," Ellis says, was that "the early, healthy volunteer trials showed it caused headaches and muscle aches and that when compared with nitrates"—nitroglycerin remains the drug of choice for treating angina—"[it] didn't obviously look any better."

Ellis, however, wasn't ready to cave. "You feel a real sense of ownership for the compound," he explains, "[due to] the investment in time and energy—and body and soul. . . . It's like a parent defending a child." He returned to the library, hunting down more research to support the original concept, and pressed on. "You have to have evidence. You can't just go back to senior management and *whinge*. In this dark phase, I was convinced that if we stayed with this drug long enough, we'd see long-term benefits. We had faith that this compound [could] deliver—for *angina*."

Then, out of nowhere, the needle moved.

The clinicians in Wales were intrigued after giving the drug to some of their volunteers. When the subjects were later asked about any side effects, Nick Terrett recollects, "They [would] say, 'Yeah, I've got a headache. I feel a bit dizzy.' What happened on this particular occasion was that many of the volunteers said, 'I've got erections.'"

Mike Allen, the supervisor of the study, was similarly surprised. While he was going over test results with one of the program administrators—explains science journalist Jim Kling—the investigator "mentioned that at 50 milligrams... [there were] some reports of penile erections." And the data suggested the arousals appeared to be delayed sometimes by a matter of days.

"None of us at Pfizer thought much of this side effect at the time," recalled Ian Osterloh, who was working with Allen, Terrett, and Ellis. "I remember thinking that even if it did work, who would want to take a drug on a Wednesday to get an erection on a Saturday? So we pushed on with the angina studies."

One person who wasn't surprised was Peter Ellis. He and Terrett had had a sneaking suspicion that the enzyme-blocking technique (for which Campbell and Brown were targeting the heart) *might* have another application: engorging the male member. They'd written a paper in 1988 saying as much—a document Ellis plucks from his file as proof. But his colleagues, in effect, were throwing cold water on the erections. "[Scientists] are always looking for problems and for reasons why things *wouldn't* work," Terrett recalls. "People said, 'If you are increasing blood flow through the body, why should it target the *penis* and not target every *other* tissue in the body? You won't get selectivity in the tissues." So the erection connection was put on the back burner. The team's mission remained: angina or bust.

Simon Campbell remembers that the prospects seemed grim during the Wales tests. "That was the final trial where we said, 'All right, if we don't see anything this time, that's the end of it.'" He admits he was skeptical. "My concerns at the [Sandwich] development stage"—as he'd warned Terrett at the launch party—"were [now being] reflected in the clinic: it didn't have robust cardiovascular activity, in my view. At the time, we had a dozen projects going on. We all supported it, but this one was a long shot."

Meanwhile, Ellis remained undeterred. He went so far as to recommend that his counterpart in urology, Per Andersson, inject a nip of sildenafil into an anesthetized monkey. "It was UK-92480 injected right into the penis," Ellis recalls. "It didn't work because the monkey was sound asleep. No sexual arousal. No drive."

Still, Pfizer agreed to move on to more extensive trials. And since the medicine had proven relatively tolerable, a new group of volunteers—eight in all, each with a history of angina—were sequestered in a British clinic in 1992. They were administered medium doses of sildenafil intravenously.

These results were similarly underwhelming. "Patients with coronary heart disease, who had [taken] UK-92480," says Terrett, "really showed no benefit at all—marginal benefit. The whole thing was really a disappointment." Campbell corroborates: "We were disappointed in the cardiovascular [results] and we didn't *know* what the erections *meant*. When we saw the erections, we didn't know the mechanism [behind them]."

Two years of pilot studies were turning out to be a wash, and the clock started winding down. It was time, many Pfizer insiders believed, to cut their losses and move on.

Ellis, Allen, Osterloh, and a handful of others, however, were like homicide detectives with a corpse and a mound of murky evidence but no motive. They kept poring over the facts of the case. Twenty-five milligrams: nada. Higher amounts of meds: modestly better blood flow, general achiness, and some swollen boners. They just couldn't make out the forest for the wood.

———

History may belong to the victors, distinguished by sword and deed and seed. But one needn't search too far to find a counter-tale—a literature of impotence.

In the Old Testament, King David, in old age, has trouble getting it up. In Egyptian tombs, there are occasional references to a man's fallen obelisk. Homer prescribes jimsonweed for the inoperative digit, and Shakespeare warns of alcohol's effects on "performance" problems. Goethe, on confronting the ravages of age, observes, "Now all my members are stiff, / All except one."

For centuries, different cultures had used a witch's cauldron of anti-dotes. According to Joseph Hooper in *Men's Journal*, the ancients believed sexual prowess was "best bolstered by ingesting foods that look[ed] like geni-tals, from phallic rhino horn to the labial oysters." India's Ayurvedic practi-tioners, some three thousand years ago, offered rare "rock salt from a mine in Sindh" for men seeking a lift. The ancient Greeks, notes Hooper, swore by "a plant called satyrion[6] [that] allows a man to perform 70 consecutive acts of intercourse" (though his partner was sometimes known to complain of headaches). Journalist R. V. Scheide provides a roster of historic remedies, including "centipedes, rotten fish, [and] bear bile." And David M. Friedman, in his seminal book on the cultural history of the penis, *A Mind of Its Own*, chronicles how different societies over the millennia have recommended the restorative powers that came from consuming ground-up animal testes.

For much of the last century, scientists and charlatans dipped into their kit bags to treat the unascendant appendage. Erections were held aloft—or at least promised to be—by creams, gels, lotions, under-the-tongue tablets, and liquid supplements such as ye olde Spanish fly (actually beetle extract). There were acrylic splints and implants made of animal bone or cartilage. There were hand pumps and vacuum versions and electrode-wired strap-ons. There was a type of surgery called revascularization, which could reroute the groin's arter-ies in a manner akin to a coronary bypass. For one popular treatment—meant to deliver pellets to the urethra, according to Gina Kolata in the *New York Times*—"the patient [would] himself insert suppositories into the end of the penis with a tiny plunger." Just so.

Then came an event, in 1983, that would set the stage for everything that followed. It happened in, of all places, Las Vegas, at a gathering of several hundred doctors at that year's meeting of the American Urological Association.

British physiologist Giles Brindley, a fifty-seven-year-old renegade, stood onstage and addressed the assembled. Several attendees later recalled that they found it odd that Brindley was wearing sweatpants. "I have lots of slides to show, and I'm the subject in all these slides," he began. "I've injected… phentolamine…into my corpus cavernosum today, and the erection that's pushed aside by my trousers at the moment is in fact now virtually full." After

---

6. In Greek mythology, satyrs were followers of Dionysus and were sometimes depicted with erections.

the loud chuckles and clapping subsided, Brindley discussed how he had previously injected fifteen impotent patients, eight of whom had achieved erections. "Seven of them had sexual intercourse while under cavernosal alpha blockade...most of them for the first time for years."

Emerging from behind the speaker's rostrum, Brindley promptly dropped trou and exposed a healthy erection. The crowd was momentarily speechless. His associates, almost exclusively male, craned their necks to see the goods. The doctor was *out*. And he proceeded to parade around the lecture hall, his specimen swaying slightly. So as to prove he wasn't playing a parlor trick, as one urologist would later testify, "He walked down the aisle and let us touch it. People couldn't believe it wasn't an implant."

Brindley, on that memorable Vegas stage, had instantly caught the attention of his peers in the penile colony. In short order, scientists began experimenting. Doctors began offering office booster shots. "I had patients on injection that very next week in Boston," says Dr. Irwin Goldstein, who had sat agog that day. Soon there were anecdotal accounts of Brindley blasts being given to actors in adult films (to help them better master their parts) and to elderly L.A. moguls willing to pay top dollar (for that extra margin while squiring dewy ingénues).

Brindley had laid down a gauntlet. Was it now possible, experts wondered, that any guy at any age at any time could simply buy himself a swig of added manhood? The implication was that medical science might be on the road to establishing "a new masculine ideal," in the words of author Meika Loe in her book *The Rise of Viagra*.

And yet doctors in the late '80s and early '90s were more concerned with examination-room reality. That's because impotence—partly due to the graying of the population—was becoming a hot topic in medical and media circles. In response, a panel convened by the National Institutes of Health formally proposed rebranding the term "impotence," instead calling it "erectile dysfunction." "Impotence," says urologist Goldstein, "was felt to be pejorative and discriminatory, an irrelevant term [like] another sort of nonscientific word—'frigid.'"

Goldstein had his own role to play in the impotence tale. "The baron of boners," in the words of a fellow Boston-trained physician, Goldstein is a colorful, charismatic doctor, who at the time was the press's go-to guy for

ED. (He is currently the director of sexual medicine at Alvarado Hospital, in San Diego.) For him, the landscape shifted one day in 1989 when a colleague, John McKinlay, walked into his Boston office one afternoon carrying a batch of books. Goldstein had been one of the coauthors of a recent article on impotence published by the *New England Journal of Medicine*. In it, Goldstein now says, he had bemoaned the fact that "there were no epidemiologic studies of impotence that were current and modern, and that we were really relying on [Alfred] Kinsey's data [from] back in the 1950s." McKinlay, however, had been engaged in studies that drew a correlation between hormonal changes and the aging process—and had the detailed statistics to show significant falloff in sexual function. "In his hands," says Goldstein, "were three large books—on each side of his body. And he put the six books on the chair, and said, '*Here* is the epidemiology of sexual dysfunction, right on this chair.'"

That data became the basis of Goldstein's monumental work in the field—the Massachusetts Male Aging Study (MMAS). Initially, it was an attempt to understand how testosterone and other hormones impacted aging. Soon, however, it amassed interviews with 1,290 subjects and would become a clarion call about how pervasive ED was among men of advancing years. By 1994, the National Institutes of Health would use the study's results to boldly assert that as many as thirty million Americans over the age of forty actually experienced some degree of erectile dysfunction—roughly half of all middle-aged males.

That figure was "triple the number previously regarded as impotent," so David Stipp and Robert Whitaker would state in *Fortune*. "To hear the experts tell it, E.D. was now an epidemic. A majority of men over 40 were now seen as suffering from erectile dysfunction—yet fewer than 5% were seeking treatment." Goldstein's findings, when later published in the *Journal of Urology*, literally rewrote the entire library on impotence.

Critics predictably balked. Thirty *million* sufferers sounded way out of line. What man over forty, at some point in his coital travails, *hadn't* had a bit of funk in his wagnall? Certain foes of Big Pharma aired their own suspicions. It seemed that there might be a movement afoot to let drug companies, physicians, and health care providers have their way with the phallus, just as so many other corners of the brain and body had been overmedicated in the last two decades, largely at the behest of Baby Boomers looking for another quick fix for their afflictions. ED, never before a household term, would soon become a catchphrase—and a catchall. A man could be said to be mildly or moderately impaired, according to the NIH and Goldstein's study (begun in 1987 and published in full in 1994), if he was not able to achieve sustained firmness that was consummate with "satisfactory sexual performance." To many, the definition seemed to cut a pretty broad swath.[7]

With ED treatments on the uptick—not to mention Brindley's show-and-tell—drug makers were beginning to take notice. Even so, Pfizer appeared to be moving toward halting the UK-92480 trials. And then, as a quiet corollary, an intriguing new thesis emerged. And it would turn all previous thinking about erections on its figurative head.

———

"At this same time," Nick Terrett reflects, "there were people like Lou Ignarro and Ferid [Murad], who were looking into erectile dysfunction and beginning to realize that it was driven by a mechanism that was totally consistent with the mechanism of sildenafil. Some people were working with animals, some with isolated penile tissue, some on human volunteers, and this picture was coming together. There were a number of [articles in scientific] publications in the early '90s, which started to gel into a theory.

"And for the first time, people began to understand how it was that sexual stimulation resulted in nervous signals to the penile tissue which then resulted in the production of cyclic GMP which we were then amplifying

———

7. "The general increase in the medicalization of impotence," writes Meika Loe, "coincided with technological innovation [such as] the surgical implantation of a penile prosthesis, performed by urologists. Thus, the problem of impotence transferred from psychologists to surgeons or, more specifically, urologists." Loe goes on to quote Lynne Luciano, the author of *Looking Good: Male Body Image in Modern America*: "As the urology profession tried to bring more treatment areas under its control, male sexual dysfunction would be declared a disease rather than a psychological disorder. Virtually overnight psychogenic conditions were downgraded to contributing factors." This shift, in turn, set off what journalist John Leland has described as "a turf war between shrinks and urologists" as scientists, creating drugs like Viagra, and the pill before it, "reduce[d] complex human endeavors to biology, then monkey[ed] with the biology." (Meika Loe, *The Rise of Viagra: How the Little Blue Pill Changed Sex in America* [New York: New York University Press, 2004], 39; Lynne Luciano, *Looking Good: Male Body Image in Modern America* [New York: Hill & Wang, 2001]; John Leland, "A Pill for Impotence?," *Newsweek*, November 17, 1997; Jay Baglia, *The Viagra Ad Venture: Masculinity, Media, and the Performance of Sexual Health* [New York: Peter Lang, 2005], 25; David M. Friedman, *A Mind of Its Own: A Cultural History of the Penis* [New York: Penguin, 2001], 294–97.)

with our drug. And"—he hesitates as he says the phrase—"it all started to hang together."

A Unified Erection Theory?

"Yes." He laughs. "UET."

Actually, it was the thesis of Dr. NO, as in nitric oxide. NO turned out to be a molecule that lines all types of blood vessels. In theory, NO, as applied to erectile function, went something like this: An erection results when the interior nerves of the penis relax enough to allow blood to course through the shaft's two main chambers. Nitric oxide, so medical sleuths found, is a signaling substance that acts as a medium through which cells communicate, like the current in a telephone wire. In men who are unencumbered in their performance, sexual cues prompt the nerve cells of the penis to generate NO. NO, in turn, prompts enzymes to generate cGMP, letting penile vessels open up so that blood floods in. If a man remains aroused by those cues, his penis remains blood-filled. But soon after that first wave of cGMP, a second enzyme—a PDE, acting as a constrictor—starts to degrade and reduce the cGMP, "dousing" the erection.

The behavior of the newly detected nitric oxide was a revelation. *Science* magazine went so far as to name NO the 1992 "Molecule of the Year." The case for NO began to build. (Indeed, before the decade was out, Robert Furchgott, Louis Ignarro, and Ferid Murad would snag a Nobel for discovering NO and its effects.) And the Pfizer team no longer seemed to be grasping at straws. They started to see how NO might be the root cause of those incidental erections in the clinic. What sildenafil might have been doing was blocking the PDE enzyme, thereby helping keep the patients otherwise engorged.

"The Eureka moment for me," Simon Campbell affirms, came when the journal articles he was reading about NO jibed with the Wales results, which jibed with early conjectures at Pfizer by Ellis, Terrett, and Mike Allen, who'd forecast that the drug might work for impotence. "There were papers linking nitric oxide and cyclic GMP with erections. And *we're* seeing erections."

Skepticism within the Pfizer hierarchy, however, echoed a resistance in society at large. People tended to believe that the force behind a hard-on existed between the ears. "When you consider the doctors' perspective of impotence back in the early '90s," Terrett reflects, "they said, 'Well, if it's not a patient with spinal injury or a prostatectomy due to diabetes or multiple sclerosis, it's psychosomatic.' And so there was a concern that if it's a psychological problem, why would a drug actually help? It was a cultural perception." In addition, large pharmaceutical firms at the time were dealing with the AIDS crisis by introducing antiretroviral drugs, says Terrett, and a pill designed to *promote* sexual activity had its share of detractors.

With UK-92480's chances dwindling as an angina medicine, Pfizer faced new decisions—and hurdles. If the team actually changed course to test the drug as a way to treat ED, how would researchers set up a protocol for measuring their subjects' levels of arousal? How could the clinical crew persuade their managers at decidedly conservative Pfizer that there was a market for an oral penis pill? And did men in general have the stomach—or the cojones—for a product that let their physicians, lovers, and insurance providers in on the secret that they needed *a drug* to perform one of the most natural and human of activities? "In the early 1990s," Campbell says, "we were never sure impotence was a problem, that it caused a lot of tensions in families and breakdowns in relationships. People didn't talk about it."

Ellis and the team, cognizant of all the persuasive nitric oxide cases, made a plea to Pfizer execs to shift gears from the coronary to the urinary. "We had to present a case before the governance [board]," Ellis recalls, "to say we should take this candidate before a patient with erectile dysfunction. The senior governance body said, 'Not looking good, guys. Why should it work in people with erectile *dys*function? It has only been shown to produce erections in *healthy* males.' The jury was split."

But after weeks of internal debate—a full year after that group of volunteers' first stirrings—senior management came around. In late 1993, clinical trials would commence in Bristol, England, on sixteen men with ED. And overseeing the patients would not be a chemist or a biologist or a cardiologist, but a genial urologist named Clive Gingell.

———

It is a clear blue Friday in June, "open day" at the University of Bristol. The college green teems with parents and prospective students who enjoy picnic lunches as a band plays folk rock. Considered by many Britons to be "the birthplace of America" (because explorer John Cabot first shoved off from its banks), Bristol played a central role as the cradle for the hatchling Viagra.

In a sentimental mood, Clive Gingell (pronounced *gin-gel*, with two soft Gs) recounts his boyhood Fridays—born in Wales, growing up in Kettering, Northamptonshire—before his family moved to the Welsh coal-mining valley of Rhondda. "[There] was an open cattle market on a Friday," he says, sitting in his office at the Litfield House Medical Centre, "and [as a boy] I did walks with my little dog."

That boy, an architect's son, is now a retired physician with a Spencer Tracy wedge of a face—expressive and handsome and topped off by a mane as white as chalk. A past president of the urology division of the Royal Society of Medicine, he is the recipient of the St. Peter's Medal (for "notable contribution to the advancement of Urology").

Gingell is genuinely esteemed. Whenever a peer speaks of him, it is with a warmth that has no doubt been reciprocated in kind, over years. Equally evident has been the gratitude from those in his care. "I had a very large number of patients with erectile dysfunction," Gingell says, "[and ran] a weekly outpatient clinic. It was a topic most urologists didn't want to get involved in. It is a *very* common problem. The only treatment in the early '80s was intrapenile injections. And you had to commit yourself to teaching [men how to inject themselves].

"The problem was it worked *too well* in some patients, who developed prolonged and sometimes painful erections. If they didn't have poor blood flow and it was more psychogenic, [the dose could be] *too* effective and they would go into a priapism.[8] We had to be called in every so often to treat a four-hour erection. And you'd have to stick a rather long needle in to get the stale deoxygenated blood out, like a cramp in a muscle. You'd have to detumesce it. You had to be jolly careful."

Gingell's role in the Viagra saga began in 1993 when two doctors from Pfizer's clinical research came calling. Mike Allen and Mitra Boolell—both of whom had been acquainted with the urologist's work from their days as med students at Bristol—traveled from Sandwich to see if he'd agree to coordinate the trials for Pfizer's new drug. Allen and Boolell, recalls Gingell, began by describing the unaccountable erections they had seen in Wales. "Mitra said, 'We want to start by treating people who have no obvious cause

---

8. Priapus is a Greek fertility god typically depicted with a lance-length phallus. In a first-century AD mural that survived the devastation of Pompeii, Priapus can be seen opening his toga, the better to settle—and weigh—his hammerheaded feller on a set of scales. (Maggie Paley, *The Book of the Penis* [New York: Grove, 1999], 22.)

for their problem—people with nonorganic ED. Meaning: largely psychologically based." The candidates would need to be relatively young and fit.

And how would they go about taking the measure of these men in full? They would need a RigiScan. The device, perfected in the mid-'80s, was the size of an electric razor and resembled a large computer mouse coupled with a tricked-out calculator. A tiny triumph of sex-research engineering, the RigiScan—available in mah-jongg tile ivory—was meant to mechanically quantify an erotic process that hitherto had been understood by its qualitative facets. Here was a contraption that could actually measure an erection's firmness, circumference, and duration; in short, a peter meter.

Two white loops, like small lassos, extended from the RigiScan console. They would be slid in ring-toss fashion down the length of the penis—one around the base of the shaft, the other around the tip. As arousal commenced and fresh blood flowed into the pubic area, a mini-motor inside the control unit would subtly tighten the wires around the patient's own unit until there was a degree of resistance. "The device was set to measure the circumference (tumescence) and rigidity (hardness) continually throughout the experimental period," Ellis explains. "The data was then expressed primarily as duration of rigidity greater than 60 percent, representing the minimum for penetrative intercourse, and 80 percent to represent a full erection."[9]

The Bristol volunteers would be wired up and then shown to their rooms for some private time. "At Pfizer, we thought you needed arousal [to activate the drug]," Ellis says. "And they came up with RigiScan-plus-pornography as the answer—the enabling methodology."

Yes, porn. The scientists had determined that to get any observable results, tolerable doses of triple-X fare had to be administered along with the drug. But who had a viable stash (at a time when hardcore hadn't gone main-

---

9. Irwin Goldstein, in an interview with Jack Hitt for the *New York Times Magazine*, would go on to describe the pertinence of such percentages. "At a certain point all sex is mechanical," he ruminated, apropos of heterosexual union. "The man needs a sufficient axial rigidity so his penis can penetrate through labia, and he has to sustain that....I am an engineer...and I can apply the principles of hydraulics to these problems." To wit: the " 'typical resistance' posed by the average vagina," writes Hitt, "is a measurable two pounds. The key is to create an erection that doesn't 'deform' or collapse when engaging that resistance." (Jack Hitt, "The Second Sexual Revolution," *New York Times Magazine*, February 20, 2000.)

stream)? "U.K. law," says Ellis, "specifically excluded use of erotic material of a strong sexual nature. Thou shalt not show an erection or a couple engaged in coitus."

Clive Gingell's grin widens as he remembers. "Mitra and Mike Allen [asked and] I said, 'Yes, we've got a RigiScan. Yes, we've got [hardcore] videos.'" Gingell stops and laughs. "You want to ask me where we got them? Amsterdam and Hamburg. They were brought in"—he reaches over and picks up a briefcase, to illustrate—"by hand luggage. And we had some top-flight magazines as well. They [were leftovers that] had been used for other cases such as patients with prostate cancer. . . . So we had to have a *choice* of offerings—all types, a variety of what's going on between people. Some [sexual activities] that some would find arousing, others wouldn't. We'd come back from conferences in Europe—and *have* them."

Gingell had the patient pool, the expertise, the staff, and the compassion required for treating men with ED. He also had the RigiScans and a lending library of porn tapes and stroke books. He readily agreed to wrangle the patients and administer Pfizer's studies. And in late 1993, Gingell reconfigured a ward in the style of a sleep lab, working with research registrar Ken Desai and an exactingly precise doctor named Sam Gepi-Attee. "I had to do this in a private setting on evenings and weekends," Gingell remembers, discussing the need for patient confidentiality and the sensitivity of bringing lewd movies and magazines onto public hospital grounds.

Three times a day, for seven days, sixteen ED outpatients would go about their daily business, ingesting a pill containing either a placebo or a small 25-milligram dose of sildenafil. They would be asked to maintain a journal, dutifully marking down the number of erections they maintained, how hard each hard-on seemed, and the probable cause. At the end of the week, they would be admitted to the ward, rigged up with RigiScans, and sequestered in their rooms. Then they would settle in with fresh batches of porn and for two hours research aides would monitor the subjects' firmness, width, frequency, and duration—either reviewing the results later (as downloaded data) or in real time in an adjoining room (as graphs on printout paper).

Since 25 milligrams was a minimal dose, Gingell and his partners back in Sandwich were keeping their power dry. Pills of much higher potency had been required to get an appreciable rise in Wales. But, lo and behold, the men's journals and their printouts proved promising: those taking the placebo reported little change; those taking sildenafil occasionally reported a new spunk in their junk.

Underwhelmed but not discouraged, Pfizer recommended that Gingell run another pilot study, this time with a dozen men taking tablets of differing strengths, from 10 to 25 to 50 milligrams—but only a single dose a day. By day three or four, some of the subjects at the higher levels actually remarked that they were getting "spontaneous erections"—this among some men who had been troubled by impotence for years.

Then, at the tail end of that second study, in 1994, the chief aide on the Bristol trial called Pfizer's Ian Osterloh in Sandwich. He had, he said, some stunning news.

CHAPTER 30

Homo Erectus

Dr. Ian Osterloh has asked to meet in Canterbury at the Old Gate Inn. The pub, dating from 1728, sits along a main thoroughfare on the path of the Pilgrims' Way, heralded by Chaucer. As Osterloh sits in the back garden, sparrows dart and flit from the inn's roof to the nearby geraniums. Just on the horizon looms Canterbury Cathedral, for years a home to honeybees—raised by Benedictine monks to generate income from the insects' golden bounty. In a way, Osterloh is here to talk about the birds and the bees.

Osterloh, a physician-scientist with a mantislike presence, has been dubbed Dr. Viagra for his early role as the drug's chief medical spokesman. His dark eyebrows are upturned in the manner of *Flash Gordon*'s Ming the Merciless. They offset a white shock of hair that sweeps across his balding crown. Now an independent medical consultant, Osterloh has an engaging air, a dimple, and a soft-spoken, almost courtly manner.

Today he is recalling his reservations about whether UK-92480 would have any effect at all on Clive Gingell's band of volunteers. "We were cautious," he says. "As researchers you can have a lot of false dawns."

That is, until he got a call from the Bristol team. "Sam Gepi-Attee, the senior research registrar—who did the actual nuts and bolts of the study— phoned up and said, 'You don't need a statistician. This drug is working. You have to see these [RigiScan] tracings!' He was excited. When the data came out, everybody got *really* excited because it was only a single dose and the drug was clearly working. Ten milligrams had some effect. But 25 was better. And 50 was better still. And the placebo had very little effect." According to Larry Katzenstein, in Viagra's so-called "blue book" (a concise official history of the drug's discovery and launch), the registrar was even more animated when he informed Pfizer's Mitra Boolell, telling him, " 'These patients are phoning me that they want more tablets and saying this has changed their lives.' In fact, the patients' partners were calling too."

That spring, a small Pfizer team flew to a urological convention in San Francisco to present the company's findings in a private conference room. And there was already some buzz. "[It was] at some ridiculous time in the morning," Osterloh says, "at 5 a.m. or 6 a.m., at two breakfast meetings. We did it twice because these meetings are always overscheduled and packed.... Irwin Goldstein came up to me beforehand because he'd heard [rumors], and said, 'Tell me, Ian. What is this drug? You can tell me! Tell me the mechanism action.' I said, 'I can't. Wait till the meeting next morning.' He said, 'You can tell *me*.' I said, 'It's *vasodilation*.' "

Goldstein has no recollection of that exchange, but the events of the morning remain clear as crystal to him. "I remember the day as I remember the day that I heard that President Kennedy was assassinated—and 9/11," he offers in a phone conversation. "I can tell you every second of it. I remember walking up the hills of San Francisco to find this hotel. It was dusky. I remember registering. I remember sitting, listening to some British individuals, heavy accents, report that there was this agent that [prompted erections]. I recall specifically standing up, saying, 'It's not likely and not possible.' I was very vocal. I said, 'You have a certain amount of blood flowing around your body—around five liters a minute, every minute. But only about 10 milliliters [goes into] the genital tissues. It seemed impossible to get a drug that you took in the mouth that could end up in the penis affecting its functions when only around .1 percent of the blood was ever going to the penis.' "

"I remember the opposite," Osterloh counters. As he tells it, Goldstein "broke into applause [when we finished] and said, 'That's the most interesting thing I've ever heard.' That is my very clear recollection. Irwin was *not* playing the devil's advocate. He'd been an enthusiast from the get-go." (Goldstein begs to differ, insisting that not long ago he listened to a tape recording of the session.)

Whatever the case, most attendees were galvanized. "The enthusiastic response on the part of the [urology] community there validated that this was positive," Osterloh says. "This was ammunition we could use [with Pfizer management] to further justify the next and very expensive stage of research. We had a few drinks that night—but not huge numbers [because we'd awakened] so bloody early in the morning. We went to have *breakfast* to celebrate." Nick Terrett concurs: "The people who heard [the San Francisco presentation] just thought it was unbelievably incredible. My manager, David Brown—I remember him saying to me one day around this time, 'You know, this could be the biggest drug that Pfizer will have in the future. If this goes the distance, this could be absolutely huge.'"

But they had to proceed gingerly. At this point they had only a couple dozen erections in hand.

The first Phase II study commenced, expanding the pool to 350 men in Scandinavia, France, and elsewhere in the U.K., with Bristol hosting additional tests. Many volunteers were resistant to the idea of placing guy wires on their willies. So Osterloh took on the task of creating a home monitoring system that was more user-friendly. He introduced a fifteen-item questionnaire—updating a template he'd seen at a conference—that ranged from the less tangible ("How would you rate your level of sexual desire?") to the purely mechanical (In the past four weeks "how often were you able to penetrate your partner?")[1]

The tests continued through 1995. At one point a clinician phoned to say that one of the subjects, accustomed to his nightly fix, had panicked when he'd been given a placebo. "The tablet has stopped working!" he insisted. "Another patient," Osterloh would recount in *Viagra*, the Pfizer-commissioned chronicle of those early days, "reported that his wife got so angry when the tablets stopped working that she threw them into the fireplace." In time, subjects would sneak pills for their friends or hoard them, claiming to have flushed their extra tablets down the john.

Finally, the results were presented at a pivotal meeting back at Pfizer research headquarters. Osterloh remained apprehensive. "I was beginning to feel a bit nervous," he says. "I'd made the case for this compound for a while.

---

1. That fall a panel of about fifteen experts had gathered in Orlando to perfect and endorse the questionnaire for wider use among urologists and to hear further results of Pfizer's newest volunteers. "I was invited by [Pfizer's] Dr. David Cox—which is a sort of interesting name," says Goldstein. "At the meeting emerged the International Index of Erectile Function"—which remains a respected method for determining impotence and for helping judge the efficacy of a given ED regimen. "It was the sentinel event, really," Goldstein asserts. "At that very moment the field shifted." No longer were invasive penile devices required; all a patient needed was a pencil. (Interview with Goldstein.)

I designed the study and we'd used a lot of instruments that hadn't been used before. So all sorts of things could have gone wrong. The patients were older. They had more background medical conditions.

"We all gathered in one fairly small meeting room in Sandwich," Osterloh continues. "I remember the *buildup*—the statistician, John Kirkpatrick, keeping us all in the dark. I remember the tension. And even when we all got there, John went through a lot of preambles. Eventually someone said, 'C'mon, John, cut all this out. Give us the results.'"

Kirkpatrick's results, Osterloh says, "were absolutely fantastic. We had a *90* percent response to the 50-milligram dose. Almost as high at 25. And almost as high for [a question posed to every respondent]: 'If this treatment is available after the end of the study, would you want to continue taking it—Yes or No?' Everything supported it: the diaries, the sexual function questionnaire [asking about] erection, ejaculation or orgasm, satisfaction, relationship-with-partner. They all went *up*."

"Oh boy, oh boy, yes," Peter Ellis now says, pulling another page from his file. "That study was [number] 353. People with psychogenic problems, no known cause, who take the tablets home doing normal things—we hope!" he chortles—"with their wives and partners. Typically, [a result] makes a few millimeters of mercury difference: you're looking for a small effect in a moderate number of patients. *These* results were absolutely incredible!"

But it wasn't time to celebrate just yet. "We're a boring lot, us scientists," Ellis clarifies. "There's absolute delight and joy but not quite going-out-for-a-steak-dinner. This piece of data raced the mind ahead to the next hurdle. Whoopee!—fantastic!—*next* question. Will it work in patients with...diabetes, multiple sclerosis, hypertension, spinal cord injury?"

––––––––

Over the next two years, the ranks of UK-92480 recipients would swell to some five thousand men in twenty-one studies in thirteen countries. And through it all, the data continued to be extraordinary: erections for three-quarters of all participants, including those with erectile dysfunction due to injury or a prevailing ailment. Most of the side effects were mild: nausea, headaches, flushing, clogged nasal passages. Some of the subjects spoke about an odd bluish tinting in their fields of vision. (Thus would the drug develop one of its many nicknames: the Blue Haze. Other tags: the V-Train, Vitamin V, "poke," and the Pfizer riser.)

Though things seemed promising, the drug's practical impact was lost on some members of the discovery team. Most of the UK-92480 scientists were in their forties or younger and had less of a real-world connection to a product intended for a more elderly demographic. But no matter. Pfizer's CEO, Bill Steere, "was a bit older than us," Simon Campbell says. "His friends told him there *was* a problem [with ED in their peer group]"; the senior set seemed ready, willing, and saleable. (Nine months after the drug's launch, Steere would tell *Newsweek* that "no fewer than 20 of his colleagues running Fortune 500 companies are enthusiastic [Viagra] users.")

Still and all, men with ED were an elusive group. The vast majority had never sought treatment. To meet the challenge, Pfizer, with Steere in the lead, went about the business of figuring out how to market a medicine with a largely unknown user base—and a potentially incalculable upside.

The drug, at this critical juncture, would now need a brand name. But how did the christening gods ever arrive at ... Viagra?

Executives, so the story went, had settled on a word that rhymed with "Niagara" (think gushing waterfalls and blushing newlyweds) and one that began with a hard V (implying virility and vitality). "The press," says Ellis, would eventually decode the name as having been derived from "the power of Niagara Falls, [and for] *via*, the Roman word for road." One could make the case that *viag* implied vigor; *ag* and *vie*, aggressiveness; *agra*, fertility. There was also the view that the word evoked *vagina*, the male organ's ideal hetero destination.[2]

What's more, V turns out to be a potent letter in the pharmaceutical quiver. Lexicon-branding.com, in comparing Viagra to a subsequent competitor, Cialis, favors Viagra's "prominent initial V as one of the fastest, biggest, and most energetic sounds [in the branding firm's] sound symbolism research. As such, it sets the tone for the name, and hence the drug, to be also fast, energetic, and, in context, big."

All of this, in the end, was poppycock.

For the real story, I contact David Brinkley, who would eventually steer

---

2. A Latin American knockoff would be named Eviva—as in "revive"—perhaps a linguistic nod to apple-plucking Eve. And in the Middle East one homespun version would be called, simply, Erecto 100.

the marketing plan for the drug. He confides that Pfizer, like many large companies, maintains a "name bank." And during the interval when UK-92480 was being considered, there were two designations not yet assigned to products. One was Viagra. The other was Alond—like Almond, minus the M.

Viagra, as it happens, had previously been cleared as the name of a tablet intended to treat men with enlarged prostates, an alpha-blocker not dissimilar to a popular antihypertension drug called Cardura. The marketing team settled on Viagra as the name of the Cardura spin-off, says Brinkley, "partly because it sounded a little bit like Niagara—unstoppable flow of water. And it connoted, sort of, 'big urination.'" But urologists and primary care physicians were already big fans of Cardura and they balked at prescribing a comparable drug with a different name. So Viagra was discarded and thrown back into the Pfizer hopper, along with Alond.

Both names had been vetted for copyright and trademark infringement. Both, insists Brinkley, had undergone "linguistic validation to make sure it doesn't mean something weird in different languages around the world, or there's no unintended meaning." But which of the two was more appropriate to grace sildenafil, a tonic for erectile dysfunction?

The two names were proposed to Pfizer's marketers and executives. "The opinion was fairly evenly divided," Brinkley says. "Some people liked [Alond] because they thought it sounded like 'elong,' a little bit like 'elongate.' That sounded too weak for me. I just thought it sounded very soft, feminine, and—this will reveal the depth of my ridiculousness—it sounded like a French drug for women. *Al-londe.* Like *Allons-y*—[French for] 'Let's go.' In the end, I kind of went with my gut, which is that Viagra was harder. Vs are very hard and masculine, and the G-R, the *gruh*, when you pronounce it, it comes out much more forcefully and much more hard-edged—and I thought that was a better brand image than Alond." Niagara Falls and honeymoons, he claims, had nothing to do with the choice. "All of that stuff I used to read with great amusement. How we did it was: We went to the name bank. There were two names. There was a sort of eenie-meenie-miney-moe, and we settled on one that sounded more masculine."

At first glance there is little in Brinkley's background that would indicate that the father of two might be the ideal candidate to man Viagra's marketing push. He had trained for a job in finance. He had earned a graduate degree from Johns Hopkins—in international studies. He had worked for the World Bank. Indeed, he *looked* like a banker (or, for that matter, a teller): lean, clean-cut, and boyish. At one point, he says, he even interviewed with the CIA.

When asked why he backed off from pursuing a job in espionage, he answers candidly: "Well, eventually I came out as gay. And back then you couldn't get a security clearance if you were gay. In fact, that only changed with [practices under Bill] Clinton. I came out in '91. I was 'out' when I was heading up the Viagra team."

Brinkley explains that to his superiors his sexual orientation was a moot point. "Within Pfizer, which has a fair amount of Big Corporate America built into it," he says, "we were a really eclectic team, really diverse ethnically, age-wise, demographically—with a number of rebels to take what was essentially an explosive topic and push some boundaries. That was one of the coolest things about it, actually. The woman who was head of market research is a PhD, vegan, third-degree brown-belt taekwondo Trekkie, who, like, goes off to Montana and Wyoming in the winter to stalk *big* cats."

Even though the company, as Brinkley describes it, was "conservative and old-fashioned, they weren't retrograde. Probably half of all the management were women, which in the late '90s was still remarkable. My boss was a woman. The head of U.S. pharmaceuticals was a woman, Karen Katen.... It was very progressive with respect to religion—literally a United Nations of ethnicity and religion—only two or three blocks from the U.N. at 42nd and Second Avenue, with a large number of LGBT folks."

In Brinkley's view, and the company's, he fit in just fine. "I had a picture of my husband—or my partner—and my children on my desk," he says. "I took my partner to all corporate functions. We danced. We held hands. So it wasn't a big deal. Did the chairman know that I was gay? Probably not. It probably never would have occurred to him.... But in the Pfizer culture I wasn't wearing rainbow ties every day to work [or saying], 'I'm here, I'm queer, get used to it.' It was a very professional culture. We were still required to wear suits at the time—suits and ties, I don't mean jackets and slacks."

If anything, he says, his orientation might have been considered a plus. "I bring a lot of different [perspectives]," he says. "When it comes to sexuality, I think one of the good things is that I was married to a woman for quite a while and I have two kids and all. So I've been lucky enough to experience both sides of the sexuality coin."

As the trials were due to be phased out, volunteers began clamoring to continue getting access to tablets. According to Pfizer's own thumbnail history, *Viagra*, the company "received a deluge of letters," recalled Richard Siegel, the firm's then-senior medical director of sexual health. "A man had gotten engaged to be married while he was in the study, and he wrote that his fiancée was threatening to break it off if he stopped taking the medication." Faced with many requests like this one, Pfizer made a decision early on to allow any test subject to receive the drug gratis as part of what is called an open-label extension.

"[The] patients in our trial used to send us letters," says Brinkley. "We used to sit around in team meetings—the marketing group or the medical group—and take turns reading them. At the end of about five minutes' worth of these letters, everybody on the team is sobbing. These were the most beautiful, heartfelt, heartwrenching letters I'd ever read. We talked with people who suffered from erectile dysfunction and we talked to their spouses. They rarely ever talked about [erections]. That's not their language. That's not their feeling. Almost invariably, and very quickly, they would take [the conversation] away from the physical act and describe what it was that was missing since they hadn't had sex. 'I miss talking. I miss cuddling. I miss intimacy. I miss making love to my wife. I miss being *made love to*'—or whatever it was. But it was rarely ever about having a hard penis."

Indeed, one of Gingell's volunteers from January 1995—a rare participant from the period of the Wales-Bristol trials who agrees to go on the record—speaks of Viagra as helping him in a deeper, spiritual way. Pravin Agravat is a single man from Leicester, England. In 1989, as a hospital catering assistant, he was pulling a portable food cart when it hit a slick of detergent on the floor and skidded out of control—and into his groin. Rendered impotent by the incident, which stanched his genital blood flow, he consulted specialists for years. Most, he says, told him, "You're a young lad; don't worry, we'll get you back on track"—all to no avail.

Even so, Agravat recalls, one of his urologists told him, "Every time I've seen you, you're smiling. Other men who come in here, they look really depressed." With his beaming demeanor and Indian-inflected English, Agravat insists that he relied on his faith. "We have the *Bhagavad Gita*. The book says, 'You are getting fruits from your actions. You get what's *destined*.' [In] my religion, how you see people, how you treat people, colors your attitude. So I had confidence that despite the injury and because I'm young, it would be okay."

Sympathetic to Agravat's condition, Clive Gingell agreed to take him on as an extra participant in the RigiScan studies. During the trial, Agravat had only minimal response to the drug. But once Viagra became available, his GP procured him some tablets. "Straightaway, I had a different reaction," he says. "Within forty to fifty minutes, the blood started pumping, rapid, and for the first time in ten years I had normal penile responses. I looked down, and 'Bing!' "—he pounds a fist into an open palm.

"Then, just the thought of the *packet*—there were four in a packet—got me excited. Within a couple of months, I [tried it] with a longtime friend... someone who understands me for three or four years. And she was *more than* happy to do it." The results, he says, were spot-on. "The drug made me more fulfilled as a human being," he attests. "And yet if Viagra had never come along, I would still have no regrets, even if I had never been able to have sex again. That's because Viagra replaced only the avenue of sexual intimacy and did not alter my spiritual life, which was already rewarding and full, openhearted and simple and calm."

Of his role in the Bristol studies, Agravat says, "I think I was destined to be in the study. We were pioneers in a way. Imagine if someone were taking nitrates and had a heart attack. No one asked me before the trials about a heart condition. We were risk-takers. There were all sorts of side effects. If it wasn't for the people participating in the trials, there would be no Viagra."

––––––––

There was still major spadework required before a rollout. Launch teams were formed to do extensive research among physicians, consumers, and middlemen-providers.[3] But how to anticipate the cultural and social reverberations of a pharmaceutical *for erections*? To that end, Pfizer set up the Viagra Issues Management (VIM) team, a core group of consultants. "The meetings were in New York," Osterloh says. "On the panel was somebody specializing in psychiatry and psychology [with regard to] erectile dysfunction, a medical ethicist, a cardiologist, an ophthalmologist, [a specialist] in female sexual

––––––––

3. Pierre Wicker, the man at Pfizer with overall responsibility for the clinical trials, kept the tests on track (along with the channels to the FDA) and helped line up key experts for their advice, including Goldstein, Ray Rosen, Harin Padma-Nathan, and urologist Tom Lue. (Various interviews.)

problems." In addition, Pfizer canvassed experts versed in sociology, religion, sexual health, education, and the law. The company enlisted "University of Pennsylvania bioethicist Arthur Caplan to pepper them with hypotheticals," as *Newsweek's* Daniel McGinn and Anjali Arora would report. The range of topics considered: "What if nursing homes complain about requiring more private rooms to facilitate patient romance? Should Alzheimer's patients receive the drug?"

Pfizer elicited early feedback from women's organizations. "It's a very delicate subject—male sexual function and penises and enabling sex and all," Brinkley contends. "So [in] reaching out to women's groups, [we stressed,] 'We're trying to restore something and actually create intimacy between couples—and that's a laudable goal. What we're not trying to do is make men, you know, super-potent heroes, where they're out banging everything that moves.'"

What Brinkley and his colleagues *didn't* foresee was the depth of the antagonism from those who viewed the drug in terms of sexual politics: as an offshoot of the men-centered worlds of Big Pharma and mainstream medicine. Many viewed Viagra as a restorative advancement designed not for the couple, as Pfizer was inferring, but for the man intent on having his way—no matter whether or not a companion clitoris came into play. In a chorus that would grow louder once the drug was introduced, these voices demanded to know why pharmacologists had not yet managed to perfect a so-called pink pill—the long-sought medicinal breakthrough that could facilitate or enhance *female* orgasm?[4]

The idea that Viagra was a he-man's drug concocted *by* men *for* men—as an outgrowth of a male-dominated industry—is "pretty ridiculous," Goldstein protests, an overlay of sexual politics on a medicine that sprang up organically from compelling physiological observations. "I think people who describe it in [these] terms are not part of the reality of history. . . . The drug Viagra and the term 'erectile dysfunction' emerged from individuals, including those in our own laboratories, that studied basic science."

Meanwhile, Pfizer officials had to appease the group *least* likely to embrace the drug: the Vatican. On a trip to Rome, according to Ellis and Osterloh, a small Pfizer delegation made the case that Viagra would not pro-

---

4. Viable drug candidates for women would not emerge until the mid-2010s.

mote values antithetical to those espoused by the church. "You can imagine, with the Catholic Church's position on contraception," says Ellis, "how they [might] view a drug that intervened in the normal reproductive process. Of course, Viagra would, in theory, facilitate procreation. Back at that time, Pfizer was aware that we were walking a tightrope between a drug for a serious condition, which could substantially enhance and enrich family life, versus the potential for drug abuse. So we were really focused on: this is a serious product...with real *relationship* benefits, [meant] for treating the couple and the family. The outcome was: it was *endorsed* by the Vatican." (Pfizer executives, contrary to press accounts, did not have an audience with the pope, nor did the pontiff "bless" the pill.)

———

Liberation through medication had become the American way. A reliable erection, in effect, would soon become tantamount to an entitlement, one that medical science had beneficently conferred on all males of *shvantz*-bearing age—and one that should damn well be covered by an HMO. Men, and the women (or the men) who loved them, were due their Hummers, their surround-sound entertainment centers, and their sustained extremities. And this message beat in time with the pulse of an already overmedicated nation. (Over the course of the decade, prescriptions jumped 50 percent—an astounding increase.)

Many Boomers in the '90s, meanwhile, still measured themselves by the yardsticks of their youth. Though they had aged in calendar years, many believed they could use newfound compounds to eke some extra mileage out of their battered physiques and psyches. Thus they became assuaged, and in some cases ravaged, by Ambien and Xanax, Lipitor and Crestor, Prozac and Vioxx and OxyContin, while their children scarfed down their own pharmacopeia of Accutane and Adderall and Ritalin.

In the meantime, the FDA, aided by deregulation in the drug sector, began to greenlight more pharmaceuticals more quickly, allowing firms to recoup their hefty development outlays. The Web made it easier, for good or ill, to purchase pills online. Drug companies would tout new tablets and their side effects in magazine ads, appealing directly to patients and taking the family doctor out of the equation. Consumers, according to Jack Hitt in the *New York Times Magazine*, were being told "to take charge of their own health care; politicians [were] debat[ing] a 'patient's bill of rights.'

H.M.O.'s themselves [were] built on the idea that individuals will decide the general direction of their care." And after years of popping vitamins, supplements, and herbal remedies, health-conscious individuals were increasingly open to alternative therapies.

Taken together, these trends propelled American drug expediency and, to a large degree, compounded the prevalence of drug dependency. Many consumers became predisposed to devaluing behavior modification in favor of treating almost any physical or mental impediment with a tablet. The impulse dovetailed neatly with the sin-again/saved-again paradigm that was trickling down from the pulpit and the presidency.

Viagra, to many, was certainly the sin-again drug. But it was also emblematic, to many observers, of how male power was on the rebound. "Medical professionals and patients," writes Meika Loe in her book *The Rise of Viagra*, had begun to view their manhood "in the language of 'trouble' and 'repair' as they grapple[d] with 'deficient' body parts.... They imagine their bodies as machines, and they use Viagra as a tool for fixing their broken masculinity." Indeed, Viagra coincided with the boy-toy extension boom, a phase in which computer science, athletics, medicine, military R&D, and biotechnology had enhanced the body's capabilities through ever more inventive anatomical add-ons. Come the 1990s, we had evolved into what naturalist-photographer James Balog at the time termed "Techno Sapiens." We had joysticks for our computer games, headsets for our telephonic conversations, and ever more sophisticated prosthetics. We had night-vision scopes for the battlefield and law enforcement. We had what came to be known as "wearable technology": our adventure gear allowed us to trundle up cliffs and down into ice caves; our hazmat suits let us navigate despoiled worlds after we'd made a royal mess of them. In this context, Viagra was just the top-line accessory.

This was not merely about profit or prowess or even sexual health. In the course of a year or two, cultural perceptions about the mechanics of what made a man virile would change irrevocably. A man, made hard *virtually*, could now perform *actually*—the word "perform" reflecting both the sex act and the new play-acting that was enveloping much of the culture.

———

Simon Campbell recalls the party vividly. It remains, he insists, one of "the Eureka events" on his personal Viagra highlight reel.

"It was, to my memory, late afternoon," Campbell says. The company in September 1997 had just filed Viagra's application documents to U.S. and European authorities, seeking official approval for consumer use. That week a thousand staffers from Pfizer Central Research listened as Campbell stood at a lectern and called Viagra "a feather in everyone's cap." Then a live band took over, flanked by bouquets of helium balloons. Clowns weaved about on unicycles and stilts. Jugglers in bowler hats tossed clubs in front of a poster declaring, "Erectile dysfunction impairs sexual performance." A balloon sculptor handed out suggestive swords. Pfizer had even hired two impersonators dressed up as the ditzy, druggy Eddy and Patsy from the British sitcom *Absolutely Fabulous*, then at its apex. "They went through the crowd startling people," Campbell recalls, "[offering] a string of Viagra jokes [with] double meanings."

Campbell's colleagues, though, would quickly dispense with the balloons and the bubbly. This was serious business—a *business* above all else.

Pfizer Command, in a matter of days, began its surefooted march toward consumers' medicine cabinets. A price point was set for each pill: ten bucks a bump. A dose scale was devised: 25, 50, and 100 milligrams. A shape was selected: a soft-edged diamond. A color was chosen: Viagra blue, Pantone No. 284U—a deep sky blue in the family of the Pfizer logo's PMS285. (The powder blue color was meant to denote masculinity.) A manufacturing facility was established: in Ringaskiddy, Ireland, where, over the course of three weeks, batches of pure V (sildenafil citrate) would metamorphose into a white powder. These lots would then be shipped to France, America, and Puerto Rico, where they would be cut with other substances and given their distinctive blue cast.

Meanwhile, the insurance companies were courted. From the start, most agreed to cover their patients' intake, though many would authorize only six tablets a month. Critics would take umbrage that the male-governed medical and insurance establishments had predictably decided to assume the cost of the little blue pill—but not the birth control pill. Such favoritism, they said, once again revealed the sexist priorities that placed the health concerns of men over those of women.[5] Opposition was amplified among certain "family

---

5. No surprise, this. According to Dee Dee Myers, "As crazy as it seems, it wasn't until the early 1990s that clinical health studies routinely included women....In the 1980s, for instance, a study examining risk factors associated with heart disease studied 15,000 men—and no women." The change was largely spurred on by Dr. Bernadine Healy, President George H. W. Bush's appointee to head the National Institutes of Health in 1991. "Within months," according to Myers, Healy "made

values" constituencies for whom *both* pills—one encouraging conception, the other contraception—were deemed unsuitable for HMO or insurance coverage. (And never the twain shall be reimbursed.)

Wall Street, for its part, was duly seduced. For two years, results of the ongoing trials had been touted in the science and business press. In 1997, *Fortune* genuflected, naming Pfizer that year's most admired pharmaceutical company. The *Journal of the American Medical Association* sang the drug's praises, pre-launch. That June, Irwin Goldstein told the less scientific but equally physiocentric journal *Playboy*, "We're in the midst of an exciting revolution, a new area of sexual medicine called sexual pharmacology."[6] Talk of a Pfizer wonder drug swept from doctors' waiting rooms to the trading desks at investment firms, where brokers watched the bulge in the company's stock price.

Viagra would be introduced first in America. But its success was no sure thing. A dormant side effect might emerge to scuttle it. American consumers, out of shame or any number of aversions, might choose to avoid it in droves. Most critically, the FDA might delay its authorization or insist on more trials for what was being presented as a new class of drug.

———

It was this very angst—about Washington's imminent approval—that hovered like a snow squall over midtown Manhattan as Team Viagra convened in the spring of 1998. They had come for a press conference at Pfizer headquarters to announce that the company, at last, was launching its long-awaited tablet. But the timing was anyone's guess. "We were hanging on the FDA," Campbell says. "I spent five days in New York waiting for the FDA to come through with its decision. I don't recall any sightseeing. We were practicing [our presentation for the media], doing science. People were pretty tense.... You've invested so much in it, you feel, 'Is something going to go *wrong*?!

it clear that women could no longer be excluded from the agency's clinical trials.... It wouldn't have happened without Healy—and the [growing number of] women in Congress [in the 1990s]." (Dee Dee Myers, *Why Women Should Rule the World* [New York: HarperCollins, 2008], 55–56.)

6. Michael Mendelsohn, the former head of cardiovascular research at Merck, has a different perspective. "How many drugs do you know that created their own disease? In reality—no matter who coined the term, and when—erectile dysfunction didn't really exist before Viagra. Men who never really knew they *had* erectile dysfunction now had a way to name it and a way to treat it." (Interview with Mendelsohn.)

Is someone at a high level at the FDA going to shut it down?'" The medical community—and ED-afflicted couples, quietly shouldering their own burden—looked on at an anxious remove.

On Friday, March 27, 1998, at 10:57 a.m., a fax quietly unfurled at a command center that David Brinkley had set up at Pfizer's offices. It was the FDA, in D.C., giving Pfizer, in New York, its thumbs-up.

"It happened on my birthday—I was fifty-seven," remembers Campbell, who that afternoon stared down a phalanx of reporters and presented the drug discovery story. Osterloh, who would soon become the televised face of Viagra, spoke about the nuances of PDE5. He spoke about cyclic GMP. He spoke about the best way to take the pill: an hour before intercourse, supplemented by sexual stimulation to allow the drug to kick in. Concurrently, the FDA was fielding its own press questions, and trotted out its chief of drug evaluation and research, Dr. Janet Woodcock—no misprint, that. "Nothing works for everyone," she said, "but this will be another choice [for patients], a medication that can be taken conveniently."

No one, however, was prepared for the deluge.

The next morning, the *New York Times'* headline read: "Huge Market Seen [for] Impotence Pill." The *Wall Street Journal* heralded "a new medical era." *Time* ran a cover story in which writer Bruce Handy wondered, "Could there be a product more tailored to the easy-solution-loving, sexually insecure American psyche than this one?...What else can one say but Vrooom! Cheap gas, strong economy, erection pills—what a country!" (One psychiatrist fretted about all the hype, telling *Time*, "[Patients] think Viagra is magic, just like they thought the G spot worked like a garage-door opener.")

In a matter of days, the national hankering for Viagra crossed the threshold into frenzy. Word surfaced that in California, thieves pilfered a stash from a medical office. Patients began demanding to be moved to the head of their urologists' queues—some out of medical desperation, some merely jonesing for the next, best kink. Certain physicians began to shelve their tee times and schedule Wednesday and Saturday hours to accommodate the overflow. Dr. Stanley Bloom, a New Jersey urologist, told the *New York Times* that he'd developed writing cramps from filling out scrips. Some doctors began shipping out pills by FedEx or setting up online dispensaries. All told, medical practices wrote two million prescriptions during the drug's first two months on the market. Websites sprouted up, pushing pills—and starting a racket that became so lucrative that "unsolicited Viagra pitches," according to California writer R. V. Scheide, would soon comprise one fourth of all email spam.

Press attention very nearly overwhelmed the marketing team. "The phone calls were continuous for at least four months," according to Mariann Caprino, of Pfizer's corporate communications office. Brinkley says he hired a clipping service to "scan five thousand periodicals around the world—and websites, [which] were still nascent at the time." The day after launch, they got fifty clippings. "Three weeks later, we were going through mountains."

Comedians went on a Viagra jag. *How is Viagra like Disneyland?* It's a one-hour wait for a three-minute ride. *Heard the one about the Viagra computer virus?* It turns your floppy disc into a hard drive. And, perhaps most enduringly, a mock news alert became the stuff of Viagra lore: *A truckload of Viagra was stolen today. Police are looking for a gang of hardened criminals.*

"It would have been hard to predict how quickly Viagra got into the public discourse," Brinkley says. "Before approval, we used to wonder, 'Gee, I wonder if Jay Leno will ever make a joke.' And then, of course, he ended up telling a Viagra joke every night for weeks." (Over the next five years, the *Wall Street Journal* noted, Leno would log 944 V-gags.) One Leno punch line imagined a rejected Viagra slogan: "Church won't be the only place that Granny shouts, 'Bingo!'" *Newsweek* described a "shell-shocked" Pfizer chairman Bill Steere, who contended he would "fall asleep to Leno's Viagra jokes, wake up to [Don] Imus's and come home to his wife's latest.... 'Nobody used to talk about impotence,' says Steere. 'Now [men] come up to me and tell me about their Viagra moments. I can't believe the things people say.'"

All the while, Osterloh would press on at press conferences, trying to treat the subject with the gravity it deserved. He was probed by questioners such as journalist David Friedman, who asked him if he'd ever tried old blue himself. "Certainly not," the doctor sniffed. The reserved, bookish Osterloh remembers one mortifying appearance in a London television studio. "They break for news," he says, "and then suddenly some other guests come in and they start talking about some general TV soaps and the sexual lives of these actors and actresses...and they're asking me my opinion. And I can't say anything for a second. And they all looked at me, waiting for my answer to the question, as if I'm from another planet." (Osterloh today relays a favorite from that first year, courtesy of the British comedian and entertainer Bob Monkhouse: "Quite a good one, actually. He said, 'It says on the packaging,

"Take it about an hour before commencing intercourse." Good idea. It gives you time to find someone.' ")

––––––––

By this point the marketing team had settled on two possible approaches for introducing the drug to consumers: advertising that stressed either the performance angle (appealing to men hoping to restore their sexual capacity) or the intimacy angle (appealing to partners hoping to revitalize their relationship). Focus groups were asked to choose between various scripted scenarios: two men in a boat (discussing their exploits of the previous evening) versus, say, a dog waiting outside a closed bedroom door (with a tagline: "Man's New Best Friend.") The winning concept, of course, turned out to be the Dancing Couples.

After a time came the performance play. Photographer Michael O'Brien—a portraitist known for this use of warm, suffused lighting and his Norman Rockwell knack for making everyday people look heroic—was signed up to do a series of print ads. O'Brien is a laconic, aw-shucks Memphis native. He remembers the assignment as "celebrations of accomplished and cool males—sort of male clichés, like a man working on a sports car, or a man having an artist's studio in his backyard—so here's a very virile, artistic, creative [type]. They'd done tons of market research, so they had it exactly: he's, like, forty-six-and-a-half to fifty-four-and-two-thirds, and had this much income.

"Being the photographer involved, it's our job to hire a casting agent," he remembers. He tried to fill the bill of the creative director of Cline Davis & Mann, Pfizer's ad agency for the Viagra account. "We looked at hundreds of guys," he says, looking for "the alpha male. The alpha male is a man who knows who he is. He has an inner security and self-confidence and carries himself that way. He's not the wimp or 'the indecisive.' He's the male that's *sure*. He just has this one little problem. 'ED,' they say."

The ideal model, O'Brien says, "might have a beard and look very powerful. Very *present*. It was not television—so it didn't matter how [he] talked. If he looked too fey he wouldn't be cast. He had to be strong, masculine, not effeminate. Not Alan Alda. More Robert De Niro or Robert Mitchum. But not so much that it's a caricature."[7]

––––––––

7. The five-day shoot, in Santa Barbara, required a posse. On hand, by O'Brien's tally, were the models cum actors, two or three photo assistants, a stylist, an assistant stylist, a producer, the ad

Soon came the endorsement commercials from athletes like Pelé, and baseball's Rafael Palmeiro ("I take fielding practice, I take batting practice, I take Viagra"), and NASCAR drivers, who would emblazon their cars in Viagra blue.[8] Indeed, sports and Viagra would become a man crush made in marketing heaven. Both, to put it plainly, focused on men and their balls. And the big game, Pfizer recognized, was precisely where an advertiser went to attract a mass male audience. The Y-chromosome bonanza associated with professional sports gave the erectile-impaired a cover: I may not be hitting them out of the park, but I'm still on the field.

Subsequent commercials, writes communications professor Jay Baglia in his book *The Viagra Ad Venture*, were laden with "male signifiers [such as] tools, buildings, flag poles, masts, columns," along with heavy visual references to "the powder blue color of Viagra." (By 2004 Pfizer would get much bolder, winking at its own use of euphemism. According to Baglia, in one spot, "featur[ing] the rock anthem 'We Are the Champions' by Queen, men burst from their homes on a suburban street...dancing and high-fiving each other [in a neighborhood of] penis-shaped white picket fences.")

———

As with any drug, success was tied to the mojo of the sales team. And Pfizer's might as well have been recruited from Straight-Arrow Central Casting. "Our trainers joked that the sales force was comprised of the 'Three Ms,'" former Viagra salesman Jamie Reidy would put it, "Military, Minorities, and Mormons." Reidy would characterize Pfizer's pharma reps as men and women who were physically attractive, clean-cut or well-coiffed, and "used to tak-

———

agency's art director, an assistant art director, and two or three account representatives from Pfizer. In addition to creating five portraits of five males in various natural environments, the agency asked for one more situation. "We had to do a set of pictures of this couple walking over a hill and being lovey-dovey," O'Brien says. "They had to kiss each other and all this stuff. It gave me the heebie-jeebies. I just felt awkward that two strangers, who hadn't known [each other], being [affectionate. I had] them on these hills above the clouds, and holding hands, and bumping into each other. Sunrise and sunset...romantic. They did it again and again." As O'Brien remembers it, one of the agency or client reps repeatedly encouraged more touching rather than less. "They were saying they really have to get ooey-gooey. I mean, gooey, but not ooey. [I was hired] because they thought I could do ooey-gooey good." (Interview with O'Brien.)

8. Pfizer would actually go on to erect stations at NASCAR tracks where fans could go and get diabetes screenings and high blood pressure tests at no charge—a commendable initiative since both conditions, like ED, can presage serious heart issues. (Only in America could car races be conceived as plausible, unironic, even laudable venues for erectile-dysfunction education. *Gentlemen, start your engines.*)

ing orders." They were competitive types with a generally "elevated intensity," who, once they'd been indoctrinated by their trainers, all "bled Pfizer blue."

"Pfizer was recruiting extensively among ex-military," David Brinkley remembers, "because they're great team players, very disciplined. They're self-starting." The hitch was that once they were confronted with the subject of Viagra, many were at a loss. "You've got this group of really go-get-'em, very testosterone-ized people in a room, but [impotence was] outside their realm of experience. So we have to give them a lot of context so they can handle the inevitable—hmmm—childishness that comes with talking about sex and sexual function."

Eleven days after the FDA's go-ahead, more than a hundred company reps from the urology division hunkered down at Miami's Doral Golf Resort and Spa "for a thirty-six-hour crash course on Viagra," Reidy would recount in his book *Hard Sell: The Evolution of a Viagra Salesman.* Before arriving, they'd been sent reams of reading material covering human sexuality, sexual dysfunction, sociology, prospective competitors, side effects. They made a point of studying the fine print on the so-called package inserts—those thin scrolls that accompany pill boxes and outline various precautions, interactions with other drugs, and when to drop the K-Y Jelly and head for the ER. "We memoriz[ed] success rates and side-effect percentages," Reidy writes. "We rehearsed sales pitches until we knew them cold. We were ready for war."

A month later, the company hosted the product's official launch. Several thousand employees descended on Orlando, including reps from all five of Pfizer's divisions, each of whom on their sales calls would be required to know the ins and outs of Viagra. They viewed PowerPoints, attended breakout sessions where they practiced real-life sales scenarios, watched training films in which actors would stage embarrassing or tense encounters in the field. "We had to give them training on how to deal with sensitivity, with the topic of sexual function," says Brinkley, "how to talk naturally in a business setting about penises and vaginas and ejaculatory dysfunction, how to recognize when an inappropriate situation is developing. . . . We actually had training on potential sexual harassment situations for our reps because a good number were female, and we had a responsibility as an employer to create a working environment for them that isn't hostile."

The reps gorged on a buffet meal at the Universal theme park. Viagra goody bags were dispensed. The capstone of the retreat was a presentation that turned into a pep rally. "When we got [to] the auditorium," Simon Campbell remembers, "there were no seats for us. So Pete Ellis or Ian went down and removed all the 'reserved' signs on the seats [and we sat down]. When the people who belonged to those 'reserved' signs came and saw us, they said, 'What are you doing in our seats?' We said, 'We discovered Viagra.' And they said, '*Have*'em.'"

Ian Osterloh, in his usual role as Viagra's understated hombre, energized the troops and garnered a standing-O. Then CEO Bill Steere whipped them into a fervor. "The hype at the meeting was incredible and almost evangelic," Peter Ellis says. "Everything was big and bolder than life. There was a great light show. I remember being somewhat bowled over by the very exuberant American approach as compared to the reserved British, stiff-upper-lip caricature.

"I think the reps got commissions and if they met sales targets they'd get a form of reward such as 'Go on holiday with the family.' One guy got onstage and said, 'Here is the current advance sales—and here is the target.' And already the sales had *exceeded* the target. At that, everyone in the room stood on their seats cheering—because they knew that they'd made their sales targets and would be getting their bonuses without having yet left their initial launch meeting! This was hilarious for us. The whole room was erupting around us and we're feeling very bemused by it all: 'Good *God*.'"

But just on the horizon, the thunderheads formed.

————

"There was an eminent ophthalmologist, Dr. Michael Marmor, going on the radio the next day," Ellis recalls, "to say that Viagra had the potential to make people go blind. He was the secretary of one of the large ophthalmology societies and there had been a misprint in the approval on the FDA website...which led to this misunderstanding. There was a core group of us who were up most of that night troubleshooting the issue and we missed much of the evening festivities—the whole of the Universal theme park—because we were compiling the real data for this ophthalmologist to reassure him that what he'd seen was wrong."

And then people started to die. Less than two months after launch, both Pfizer and the FDA revealed the sudden deaths of six men who had recently taken the drug. Since the announcement lacked specifics, it was unknown if any of the patients had also been on nitroglycerin for heart conditions—or if any were elderly (three-quarters of the million-plus prescriptions were made out to older men, some of them cardio patients, who are not unknown to have suffered heart attacks after strenuous exertion). Pfizer began getting hit with wrongful-death litigation; by fourteen months out, more than five hundred had died.

While independent monitors determined that none of the volunteers in Pfizer's clinical trials had ever died due to "a heart attack, stroke, or life-threatening arrhythmia within six months of taking the drug," these new fatalities were cause for alarm. First, blindness; now myocardial infarction. And even though the Viagra-induced ER visit would in time become a comedic staple (Jack Nicholson's gallivanting character in the 2003 film *Something's Gotta Give*, for instance, would twice be rushed to the hospital after riding the V-Train), in those first few months there was considerable concern among physicians and patients and their partners.

Not that this deterred Joe Rep. Pfizer's sales force kept meeting and exceeding its targets. "Nobody took Viagra and then, boom, had a heart attack," Reidy would write. "Rather, they took Viagra, *had sex*, and then had a heart attack. The activity killed them, not the drug.... '*Of course* they're having heart attacks and dying,' an exasperated urologist barked at me.... 'If you wouldn't let a guy carry a suitcase up a flight of stairs, then he shouldn't be fucking!'" Pfizer, of course, reiterated its warnings. The company told health care providers, ER teams, and paramedics that the blue meanie shouldn't be doled out to the out-of-shape—and that a nitrate-Viagra combo was verboten.

In the face of all these stories, *recreational use* proliferated. *Time* was reporting on retirees planning Viagra bashes in the Poconos. *Penthouse* wrote about the comings and goings of the man who ran Nevada's Moonlite Bunny Ranch—on a junket to Amsterdam and armed with some baby blue. ("I ended up partying with six different girls that night," he decreed.) Club kids began popping pills casually, David Friedman would note, "often [taking them] in conjunction with Ecstasy, a party drug that enhances sexual desire but can inhibit sexual performance." (The resulting cocktail was dubbed Sextasy.) A popular Viagra-plus-methamphetamine mix would facilitate sex marathons that became notoriously debauched, according to the *Boston Globe*'s Diedtra Henderson. She quoted a source who insisted, "We're talking days. Days, not hours... no eating, no sleeping." Discussing the public-health consequences of such activities, Meika Loe would write, "Gay publications such as the *Advocate* [warned] about the potentially lethal combination of Viagra with crystal meth, poppers, and Ecstasy, as well as the potential for 'risky sex' and HIV transmission with such drugs."

It would take several years before a credible statistical correlation would be drawn between STD transmission and recreational Viagra use. And there would also be a pattern of "senior scare" stories on local and entertainment-news programs. These described wives who were exhausted by husbands with new skin in the game; by "Viagra studs" who had fled their longtime partners to strike out on their own; by voracious Viagra addicts—male and female alike—who went on binges; by elderly husbands who had infected spouses with STDs after having used the drug while visiting prostitutes; and by predictions of a bumper crop of babies sired by aging "Viagra dads." (This turned out to be a demographic dud. The National Center for Health Statistics would show, ten years later, that "fatherhood rates among older men," according to Hilary Stout in the *New York Times*, "[had] not risen since Viagra came on the market, [remaining] exactly where they were in the early '80s.")

Almost from the start there was a conservative backlash. Pfizer, no matter how careful it had been in trying to divine the public's reaction to the drug, could not have foreseen the political throw-weight it possessed as a totem of the culture war. With reports of an illicit White House affair dominating the Web and the late-'90s newswires—concurrent with ED bulletins commanding the science, business, and lifestyle headlines—certain elements began to attack Viagra as a lax-values drug. Viewed through this lens, Viagra was a pharmacological outlier with antecedents in the '60s (the pill, which had propelled contraception) and the '70s and '80s (the age of party drugs, which had further diluted the nation's moral fiber). Soon the whispers crescendoed: the drug was being downed by porn stars like hors d'oeuvres. The drug was being sold for recreation, not procreation.

"When it became like a national punch line," Brinkley recollects, "a lot of conservative groups would say, 'This is trivializing sexual relations. This is typical of American culture where sex is everywhere.'" And when media pieces appeared offering conjectures that gay men were disproportionate users of Viagra, Brinkley took offense. "[Why] gay men got singled out as a demographic other than their titillating value for the mainstream press, I don't know—but there were a series of articles that ran. Then there was even some speculation kind of on the fringe, from conservatives, that Viagra was going to increase AIDS in America—that giving gay men erections and then enabling them to have unsafe sex, that somehow there was going to be an explosion in HIV.

"When I'd read these articles—those became some of the most upsetting to me," he confides—"I, maybe in the back of my mind, wondered, 'Well, if somebody found out I was gay and they tried to connect the dots, that they would think it's again part of [some] Velvet Mafia.'" But it would be preposterous, he insists, to draw any conclusions about such an agenda—whether in pharmaceuticals, advertising, or Hollywood. "Really? Have you ever seen five gay men try to figure out where to go to dinner? And you think we're trying to take over the country? I mean, come on."

The rumors of blindness. The death knell. The recreational use and abuse. The cultural and religious resistance. None of it seemed to make much of a dent. Two years on, Viagra was being prescribed at a pace of seven pills *a second*—with a supply being dispensed, as it happens, to one out of every twenty-five adults in Palm Beach County, Florida. In that same time frame, 93 percent of Americans would become familiar with the Viagra moniker (and its purpose)—a brand-name recognition that rivaled that of Coca-Cola, which had been around since 1886.

Meanwhile, women were experimenting too. Research indicated that genital blood flow was enhanced when a member of *either* sex partook. For Salon.com, Susie Bright popped some blue and wrote about her multiple climaxes, including one that came on "like the most delicate, melting chocolate cream egg cracking inside." On *Sex and the City*, Samantha—Kim Cattrall's character—did the same. (She would later admit to taking some in real life, as reported in the British press: "All that business about multiple orgasms? It's true. I'm not just having two or three. It's four or five.")

From the boudoir to the boardroom, the storm surge lifted all boats, including Pfizer stock. Company shares on the day prior to the New York press conference had stood at an already lofty $95 each. By the end of a year, the stock had risen nearly 40 percent, then split—with Viagra's gross revenues eclipsing a billion dollars. By the end of the decade, according to Simon Campbell, "more than 150 million tablets [had] been dispensed worldwide [in] over 100 countries."

I am on a flight to New Orleans. I am seated next to a man who tells me he's on the rebound from hip replacement surgery. An athletic African American, he turns out to be fifty-one, married for twenty years, and the father of a teenage daughter. All at once, I experience something I never would have encountered in the 1990s—a time when men typically didn't talk openly to strangers about their setbacks in the sack.

After exchanging pleasantries, the passenger introduces himself as D. (name withheld), from Dayton, Ohio. He mentions his job in the pharmaceutical industry and I discuss my visit to Pfizer in search of the story of Viagra. And in a sudden, unsolicited outpouring, he cannot stop gushing about the wonders of the drug.

Six years before, D. says, he began taking high blood pressure medication for what he describes as "a condition affecting African Americans that is also caused by diet and other factors. It had an immediate effect on 'quality of performance.' You could get the job done, but it was a *job*." Despite this impediment, he says, he continued with his medication. "If I didn't take it, I was going to die."

As for the unfortunate side effect, he reasoned, "Maybe this was karma. I thought I had the game nailed in my twenties because I had total control of the outcomes of my physical pursuits. The only thing that made [my new reality] cool was: when I was younger I had had my share. And when it came to a screeching halt, I thought, 'Everybody gets theirs and if you overdo it, you pay the price later on.'"

Karma—with a caveat. On one of his monthly visits to his psychiatrist, D. says, he mentioned his diminished erectile function, and without hesitation she wrote out a prescription. "I [had] thought that having a regular sex life was out the window," he claims, "and I'd pretty much come to peace with it. But [the drug] was like a *gift*. With the Viagra I had such a strong erection that it almost scared me.... This Viagra thing has added *joy* to my day-to-day."

Two of his friends—both of whom have survived prostate cancer surgery—are also users. "They were highly stressed with this bad boy," he says, but now "it made them men. It had restored a sense of self-esteem." He then takes the long view. "These guys [at Pfizer] that pulled this together—I don't think they knew the impact it would have on people's mind-set. This is a game-changer."

The game would never be the same. After all the lab-tested molecules; the internal memos; the rooms with men hooked up to RigiScans; the Nobel Prize in Medicine (for the men who deduced the secret of nitric oxide), Pfizer's scientists had understood the significance of the unambiguous attraction of human bodies and, in turn, of minds and spirits. They had set their sights on connecting couples, literally, through chemistry. And they had succeeded beyond their most implausible fancies.

What got lost sometimes in the consumer's mind and in the culture's miasma was the deeper purpose of the drug. All the wood in the world wouldn't make up for the inner passion and emotional capacity required of the user and his partner.

In the end, Viagra, as a medical watershed, was profound and far-reaching. In the early 1990s, among a few men in Wales and Bristol, a nameless compound's minor side effect had been identified. That compound was then tapped, harnessed, and dispensed across the globe. Within a few short years, it would help millions interact, and deeply, again and again. And all because of the unique properties of a peculiar molecule.

That molecule's story came down, as so many tales do, to the wisdom of promoting human relationships. It came down, finally, to recognizing those persistent, primal connections that have forever ruled creation.

CHAPTER 31

The Internet and the Intern

The punctures, one after the other, finally pierced the veil. Between the private and the public. Between the real and the virtual. Between politics and sexual politics. And by the late 1990s it appeared as if all of the scandals and clandestine tapes and careening squad cars—along with the entire culture war itself—had been meant as a preamble to a single, preposterous morality play.

Today, of course, the details are familiar; the saga itself, brutal, futile, and contemptible.

A *Newsweek* reporter named Michael Isikoff, in reporting on Paula Jones's sexual harassment case against Bill Clinton, would come to learn about an intimate consensual relationship between the president and a White House intern named Monica S. Lewinsky. (Internet wag Matt Drudge would actually be the one to publicly expose the intern's name.) Isikoff would discover that Lewinsky—twenty-two years old when the relationship began—had been confiding in a coworker, Linda Tripp, about the romance. And Tripp in turn had begun secretly audiotaping Lewinsky, amassing over twenty hours' worth of recordings of their private conversations, some of them related to the affair.[1] On a parallel path, prosecutor Kenneth Starr, while investigating the president on several fronts, would become aware of Clinton and Lewinsky's interactions—and of Tripp's tapes—prompting him to widen the focus of his probe.

---

1. Tripp's taping, many believed, stemmed from her animus toward Clinton and/or her plans to write a book. She would deny this, telling CNN's Larry King that she had taped Lewinsky so as to "prove" that Lewinsky had had an affair, thus ensuring that Tripp herself could not be "set up for perjury." ("Tripp Had 'No Choice' but to Make the Tapes," CNN.com, February 16, 1999.)

Then things got *really* rancid. Starr, partly pressured by the timing of upcoming depositions and the pending publication of *Newsweek*'s article about the relationship, decided to go for broke. He sent his minions after Lewinsky to get her to open up before the news story broke open.

On January 16, 1998, a small group of U.S. attorneys and FBI agents cornered Lewinsky in a Pentagon City mall. They brought her to a nearby hotel room, where she was met by prosecutors from Starr's office. And then, according to her account, they threatened her with as many as twenty-seven years in prison for having signed a false affidavit about her relationship with the president. They discouraged her from calling a lawyer. They started inter-rogating her. They asked her to wear a recording device to secretly audio-tape Clinton's aides and, if need be, the president—which she refused to do. At wit's end, Lewinsky requested to be allowed to telephone her mother for advice. Permission granted, she implored her to hurry down from New York and join her. When her mother arrived, both she and her daughter were subpoenaed.

After the shakedown came the takedown. Investigators would rifle through Lewinsky's bookstore purchases. They would canvass her friends and colleagues about her habits and history. They would take possession of her personal property, from items as innocuous as printouts of her GRE scores, to gifts from the president, to a telltale blue dress bearing traces of the president's DNA (which Tripp, according to Lewinsky, had encouraged her to hold on to for safekeeping). They went into Lewinsky's computer and fished out drafts of unsent love letters that had been stored in her personal email account. (The drafts, which were equivalent to her private musings, were later published worldwide.) Above all, the independent prosecutor, in exchange for granting her immunity, would require Lewinsky—under threat of perjury for having signed the affidavit—to appear three times to give grand jury testimony and graphically describe personal encounters she had had with the president.

Lewinsky, as a consequence of her legal and media exposure, would be publicly shamed and derided by the White House and its surrogates, by media commentators, by fellow feminists who supported Clinton's policies—and by former acquaintances who saw an opportunity to shine in the sulfurous limelight. For months she would remain traumatized by the initial ordeal with the authorities, shaken by the legal and press onslaught, and humiliated by the public dissemination of details about her personal life. Her family, alarmed, began to worry if she might choose to end her life.

The president, for his part, endured his own takedown. During his video-taped deposition in the Jones case, he would be pushed to discuss alleged sexual activities involving various women. He would deny, falsely, that his relation-ship with the former intern had been sexual in nature, and would insist to the American public, while standing at a podium and waggling his forefinger, "I did not have sexual relations with that woman, Monica Lewinsky."[2] For months, he would witness the anguish of his wife and daughter as well as the feelings of betrayal and distress expressed by members of his cabinet, his administration, and America at large. For spiritual counsel, he would turn to the Reverends Tony Campolo, Jesse Jackson, Gordon MacDonald, and J. Philip Wogaman. His presidency would stagger to the edge of a precipice. His legacy and reputa-tion would be tarnished for a lifetime. "The yurts of Mongolia," ex–Clinton aide Paul Begala would remark in 2016, "know that Bill Clinton was accused, and in fact was, unfaithful to his wife."

––––––––

In 1998, the country was convulsed and in many ways repulsed. From the moment the rumors of the Clinton-Lewinsky relationship surfaced, the immediate message that the president conveyed to the nation, in the view of Republican political strategist Mike Murphy, damaged both the presi-dent and the office. "There used to be an elevation [to the presidency]," he remarks today. "I think Clinton brought 'the president' down to just another... politician. When he stood in front of the [presidential] seal and said he didn't have sexual relations with Monica Lewinsky, and kind of invoked the power of the presidency and that moral authority to cover a lie about his personal life, I thought that was kind of a crossing point [in the] culture at large. It was no surprise that the biggest applause line [of his successor] George W. Bush's campaign was when he would say he would bring honor and respect back to the Oval Office. . . . I mean, Nixon gets a lot of blame—it kind of started with Watergate. [But] Clinton did his part to cement that image."

For the next eight months, the carnival stayed open 24/7. Starr's team com-

––––––––

2. My daughter, Molly, a schoolteacher, told me that in one of her education seminars in college, she and her classmates watched the video as part of a lesson plan that covered how to recognize the body language and facial expressions of people who are lying.

piled its case. Leaks circulated like a contagion. The media and the public would latch on to every salacious shred, as if the artifacts of the O. J. Simpson case (the knife, the Bruno Maglis, and the bloody glove) had been magically supplanted by new totems (the Tripp tapes, a beret, and a blue dress). Finally, in late summer, rafts of material compiled by the independent counsel's office were packed into file boxes. Among the items: videos of Clinton's and Lewinsky's testimony, transcripts of personal conversations, logs of Oval Office comings and goings, numbingly clinical descriptions of sex acts, and page after page of sheer hearsay. The lot of it had been collated, scrutinized, and interpreted, and the results were crammed into a multivolume, 7,793-page data dump. The price tag for the entire Starr investigation: more than $70 million in taxpayer dollars.

And then the melodrama turned utterly Kafkaesque.

The Starr commission's findings were handed over to Speaker Newt Gingrich and the Republican-run House of Representatives. And the lawmakers, in their zeal, decided to release them. Grand jury testimony, often kept sealed, was effectively unsealed. Nuggety portions of Tripp's tapes were posted online for all to hear. The centerpiece of the committee's work, the 445-page Starr Report, became a night-table curio, rocketing to the top of the bestseller lists. It would prove, in time, to be the ur-text of 1990s Washington.

JFK adviser Arthur Schlesinger Jr., writing in his personal journal, would call the report "the most salacious public document in the history of the republic." Journalist Renata Adler, in a scathing exegesis in *Vanity Fair*, would refer to Starr's dissertation as "a voluminous work of demented pornography [that amounted to] an attempt, through its own limitless preoccupation with sexual material, to set aside, even obliterate, the relatively dull requirements of real evidence and constitutional procedure." The *Washington Post*'s Peter Baker and Susan Schmidt would assert that the decision to publish the report's findings "follow[ed] an emotional debate on the House floor about the propriety of releasing a document that none of its members, let alone Clinton or his lawyers"—not to mention Lewinsky or *her* lawyers—"had even read. Within minutes after it was posted on the Internet, millions of Americans jammed Web sites... [and] found themselves stunned by the breathtaking amount of detail included about Clinton's sexual adventures with Lewinsky."[3]

---

3. Every media outlet—from Drudge to *Entertainment Tonight* to *Fortune* to the *Star*—would cover it ad nauseam. "The story that caromed off the keyboard of an Internet tipster," wrote the *New*

In short order, the House of Representatives, spearheaded by Gingrich, along with Bob Livingston, Dennis Hastert, and cohorts, compiled their case against the president. No matter that Gingrich was involved in his own affair at the time.[4] Or that Livingston, Gingrich's designated successor, would withdraw his name from nomination in 1999 amid rumors of his *own* extra-marital activities. Or that *his* replacement, Dennis Hastert, would eventually be branded a "serial child molester" and sent to jail. The legislators and their colleagues pressed ahead in earnest, charging Clinton with engaging in impeachable offenses that included abusing his power, maintaining a relationship with a subordinate, and perjuring himself about it.

Ten days after the data's release, a video of Clinton's testimony would be made public by the House Judiciary Committee. It showed the president sitting in the White House and being grilled by anonymous prosecutors whose disembodied voices were piped in teleconference-style through video and audio hookups. (Q: "Did Kathleen Willey ever give you permission to take her hand and place it on your genitals?" A: "No, she didn't.") In a matter of days, two images would fuse in America's mind: that of a president's frosty

---

York Times' Janny Scott ten days into *le scandale*, "appears to many in journalism to have blurred the boundaries between mainstream and tabloid news.... Editors have found themselves debating whether to use words like 'semen' on the nightly news." (Janny Scott, "A Media Race Enters Waters Still Uncharted," *New York Times*, February 1, 1998, A1.)

4. To give House Speaker Newt Gingrich his due, he maintained that he pushed for Clinton's impeachment on the grounds that the president had been untruthful at his deposition. Looking back on the period, Gingrich would tell *Newsweek* that he had had a private conversation with Clinton chief of staff Erskine Bowles in which Gingrich recalls Bowles saying, " 'Look, virtually every guy I know has had an affair.' . . . I said, 'This isn't about Bill Clinton groping some girl. This is about the president of the United States, who is a lawyer, sitting in front of a federal judge, lying under oath, in a case in which it is a felony.' "

That said, the march toward impeachment was part of a holier-than-thou crusade that the Republicans in the '80s and '90s had refined to an art. The ethical buzzsaw would claim Gingrich himself when he was forced to resign as Speaker in 1998 after an internal House probe. (The IRS would later clear him of violating any tax provisions.) Historian Steven Gillon would eventually make the case that Gingrich, ironically, "never acknowledged or accepted his role in creating the culture of ethical inquisition that would eventually destroy him." Destruction, of course, would eventually give way to resuscitation. Gingrich would reemerge in the 2010s as a presidential candidate and later a loyalist in the Trump camp's culture-war campaigns. (Jake Tapper, "Gingrich Admits to Affair During Clinton Impeachment," ABCNews.go.com, March 9, 2007; Peter J. Boyer, "Newt Wants You!" *Newsweek*, December 19, 2011, 34; "Scars Remain From Gingrich Ethics Case," AP via *USA Today*, December 25, 2011; 1997 Steven M. Gillon, *The Pact: Bill Clinton, Newt Gingrich, and the Rivalry That Defined a Generation* [Oxford: Oxford University Press, 2008], 105.)

denial at a lectern—and that of a president, in excruciating verbal gymnastics, trying to amend and parse that denial. (Quoth President Clinton, "It depends on what the meaning of the word 'is' is.")

But just as his *60 Minutes* appearance in 1992 had proved to be a potent character tonic, here was another filmed interrogation that, counterintuitively, engendered a degree of public sympathy. "It was the turning point for him to get out [of the thicket]," says Dee Dee Myers, his former press secretary. When the footage was released she was in Los Angeles and miked up to comment about it on NBC. "It was going to be [aired] after the *Today* show or [on MSNBC]," she recalls. "We did the seven-to-eight [o'clock] segment....And I started watching this thing. And they actually broadcast the tapes. *The whole thing*...As I watched, I thought, first of all, these questions are absurd. They're trying to get him to talk about how many angels are dancing on the head of a pin...They're asking him completely inappropriate questions. And it ended up being the turning point—and there's some pretty embarrassing stuff—but [viewers were wondering], Why are we *seeing* this? Why did they ask these questions? Why did they release the tape? Why are we going through this as a country?"

Clinton's former communications director and close adviser George Stephanopoulos would have an even more visceral reaction that day. According to his memoir *All Too Human*, he watched while sitting in a room at ABC News. And the video's harsh lighting, single-camera perspective, and the jarring crosstalk by unseen speakers gave the deposition "the quality of an amateur porn flick," making Stephanopoulos "feel as if I were eavesdropping on a private encounter." Once the dialogue moved on to sexual topics, he writes, "I felt a tug inside....The whole scene was heartbreaking....He was a man alone with his failings before the whole world, a man forced to confess sins that had devastated his family and undone the hopes of his life, a man ashamed....Off camera, I quietly started to cry."

Much of the nation, watching on television or online, was distraught as well—distraught for itself and its flawed leaders, its wanton voyeurism, its scorched-earth politics, and its children, who were now forced to witness such sorry spectacle. "At the end of the day, the Republicans were hurt more," in the estimation of Mark Corallo, who had served as an aide to the GOP's Livingston. "We became the party of the moral jihad. I'm as guilty as anyone. We all got wrapped up in it."

The late Jonathan Schell, the writer and arms-control advocate, had a unique take. While discussing Clinton's impeachment in an article for *The Nation* in 1998, Schell proposed that the O. J. Simpson drama in fact had been the beta test for the congressional proceedings. That decade, America had created what Schell called a "new media machine" that chose to elevate "the trifling (sex and lies about sex) to the earth-shaking (impeachment of a president and damage to the constitutional system)... [and] may have fatally tipped a newly endangered balance of power: the balance between fantasy and reality."

Schell surmised that if "a history of this secondary reality is ever written, a pivotal chapter, I believe, will concern the trial of O. J. Simpson, in which the media, making use of materials offered by the real world, managed to construct a drama indistinguishable from a soap opera." The Bronco ride, in Schell's telling, was the centerpiece—the archetypal movie chase, broadcast live before a national audience. "At that moment," he contended, "virtual reality and plain old-fashioned reality were inextricably fused in some new way." He went on to suggest that the Simpson and Clinton trials were working off the same media script in which "highly diverting ascertainable facts mingling sex and crime were presented as, among other things, entertainment."

And yet in Schell's mind the two cases had vastly different ramifications. "The O.J. trial marked the apotheosis of infotainment—the use of factual material to amuse," he wrote. By contrast, "the Monica and Bill story started that way too.... Only a minority, for instance, has ever thought that Clinton should—or would—actually be impeached. But then the story was given a fateful turn. The soap opera suddenly became serious and real. Against the public's wishes and its expectations, Clinton actually was impeached.... The whole country found itself trapped inside a television program."

The Boomers had cut their teeth on shared televised or mediated stories. Their sense of the wider world had often been shaped by its transmission in virtual space: from assassinations to moonshots; from a war in Southeast Asia to a war in the Persian Gulf.[5] Boomers, settling down in the '80s and '90s

---

5. Along the way, fact and fiction got tangled up. In the 1980s, ex-actor Ronald Reagan, while threatening to veto a bill that would raise taxes, dared Congress to "Go ahead, make my day," invoking the words of actor Clint Eastwood (playing Dirty Harry in the film *Sudden Impact*). In the '90s, U.S. bomber pilots in the Gulf War, having grown up playing video games, monitored their targets on airborne displays fashioned after... *video games*. In the new century a vice presidential candidate

and raising families, spent more and more time *watching*. Their desire, at the end of their workdays, was for escape, thrills, and the whole variety show. At first the audience tuned in because it was good dirty fun—no harm in that. But the harm came when the lure turned out to be the heat and the slime, not the substance of the high crimes and misdemeanors.

If JFK had been the first president to triumph because of TV, and Nixon the first to be done in by audiotapes, then Clinton was the first to be done in by audio- *and* videotapes. Trump, by extension, was the first president to triumph through *reality* TV. And he triumphed *regardless* of the fact that an audio track for a celebrity news program, *Access Hollywood*, had recorded some off-camera banter in which he'd boasted about how his star power enabled him to kiss women or grope for their genitals with little risk of reprisal. In an earlier America, such footage would have sunk any would-be president. But in the age of reality shows, WikiLeaks, and naked selfies, the body politic merely rolled a jaundiced eye.

———

Dr. Drew Pinsky, the physician, internist, author, and psychiatry professor, has made a career out of counseling Gen-Xers and millennials about sex—and by helping patients (celebrities, most notably) cope with addictive disorders. Over a coffee in L.A., then at his radio studio, he talks about how the culture became preoccupied in the '90s with delving into the personal lives and behavior patterns of strangers and public personalities.

First, he says, individuals were leaving an ever-larger data "footprint"—audiotapes, videotapes, receipts, photos, surveillance footage, and so on—that allowed outsiders to document shameful actions. Second came "the

---

(Governor Sarah Palin) would land her own reality show, a presidential candidate (Governor Rick Perry) would perform on ABC's *Dancing with the Stars*, and an NBC reality TV personality (Donald Trump) would become president of the United States. The real and virtual worlds—as anticipated by sci-fi sages such as Philip K. Dick and William Gibson—had merged.

To some degree, America's ever more surreal national politics had fallen into the mediated world's hobbit hole. And Trump became its apotheosis: a creature of media as much as Reagan had been a creature of the Hollywood studio system. In equal measure, much of geopolitical behavior—even global conflict—became indistinguishable from propaganda, presented *for* media consumption. (Even terrorist organizations formed media units to recruit volunteers or dispense atrocity videos across the Internet.) As Shakespeare had advised, "All the world's a stage"—and we watched, sometimes mesmerized, often incensed, on our plasma screens, our laptops, our iPhones. (William Shakespeare, *As You Like It*, act 2, scene 7, [First Folio, 1623], www.folger.edu/as-you-like-it.)

normalization of humiliation," a phenomenon he traces to the 1980s talk-and-trash TV programs such as *The Jerry Springer Show*. Third, he insists, both the cheap thrills of pop culture and the deep traumas that result from domestic disarray, neglect, and abuse (often the result of intense economic challenges) combined to make people predisposed to "the vice of envy, the most deadly sin, the most destructive of human emotions. Envy is not jealousy, which is a craving for another's possession or trait or partner. Instead, envy requires action, which is knocking the person down to my size. They make me feel bad, they diminish me, so I have to bring *them* down. I have to make myself feel empowered over them. Envy is a highly narcissistic impulse. Envy is a product of trauma. And envy is what we are steeped in right now."

Fourth and foremost, Pinsky says, is a narcissism that has been baked into the American mind-set. "If you go back to Christopher Lasch's [1979] book *The Culture of Narcissism*, he predicted it [correctly], although even he didn't predict the profundity of what would happen. Narcissism—which Freud debated even existed—is now rampant. You go down to the psych hospital and [countless] admission page[s have] what's called a Cluster B diagnosis, which is a narcissistic disorder. Everybody. We've all got it. It's in our system. It's in our psyches."[6]

Pinsky telescopes back in time to compare our era to an extreme paradigm: the Aztecs. "Where you see narcissism emerge as a personality style in a culture, you see a high incidence of childhood trauma and disrupted families, as we have in our society today. We're *not* the Aztecs. [Their] codex of how to raise children would call for rules about how you hold them over fires, you bite them, you do horrible things to them, ostensibly to make them great warriors. We're not quite [as bad as] that. When we focus our violence

---

6. Pinsky examines the connection between violence and narcissism. "René Girard is a social scientist and philosopher who basically theorizes that society is organized around the focus of violence: a common enemy or scapegoat. That special enemy galvanizes us and we unify or we metabolize our violence by focusing it together on one [object]. He would argue that human sacrifice was always part of religion, and that's how we organize violent societies. When you look at *really* violent, narcissistic societies, where there's lots of childhood trauma, you start to see the sacrificial impulse coming out. And I believe that all of what we do to celebrities is out of a sacrificial impulse. We make [or] elevate a god and then destroy it."

on someone else, we feel guilty, we feel ashamed. And to relieve us of that, we like redemption and resurrection, which lets us do the sacrifice, then cleanses us of our guilt for having done so. When we gather together and destroy somebody, we feel bad for that person and [for having] taken them down. And when they redeem themselves, it makes us feel good. So now we've completed our power cycle."

Where, then, did this power cycle begin? "This started with O.J.," he declares. "That's really the moment." Not only were we sanctioning celebricide, but we were watching it as a daily ritual. "That's when reality programming began, and the news media gave up on trying to be journalistic. It is summed up well in the [2016 ESPN] *30 for 30* documentary *O.J.: Made in America*, in which journalists and producers are expressing that after a while they threw up their hands, [saying, in effect,] 'If that's what they want, that's what they get.' It became more about the consumerism than about the journalism."

Three years after the Simpson trial, the zenith of the media-age sacrifice was Monica Lewinsky's, made all the more riveting because it involved sexual relations *and* the American presidency *and* "the politics of personal destruction"—a phrase popularized by (*drum roll*) Hillary Clinton. Pinsky hazards an assessment of that curious process. "The takedown mentality, at the beginning, is really directed at Bill," he says. "But it is sort of led by Hillary, in a way, *toward* Monica and away from her husband. Many times women will make the mistake of [seeking retribution against] the woman involved in the affair rather than the man choosing the affair. So I think a lot of that energy *started* this." By the same measure, he adds, "We didn't have a social media yet to act it out. So it was a press frenzy, first, around Bill. But once that sort of settled, the need for the 'sacrifice' began to focus on Monica. And the new domain of the Internet really began to flex its muscle. She became literally a punch line.

"In a weird way we were satisfied with Bill Clinton's administrative skills and his record, and wanted him to stay [in office], but we still needed some blood. That's Monica. It's the first case of somebody being dehumanized through this mass, mob action. There was never any concern as to whether these attacks were hurtful to this individual. Monica was really Case One for the online mob. The narcissistic shift was larger now. And the city square where the mob gathered was the biggest in history: the Internet."

Ultimately, nothing on the mass media continuum "creates more of a response than sex and violence," Pinsky says, citing the Simpson trial, the sex tapes of the era, and the White House scandal. "There were no longer taboos against either. Shroud them with a little bit of euphemism [perhaps], but sex and violence had become part of what we saw every day—just another feature of the sexual revolution, the tabloid era, the violence in our culture [coming to] our many screens. We craved it."

The deeper lesson of the '90s, says Pinsky, is that two successive generations had become the unwitting victims of the '60s sexual revolution. The American libido, aided by the pill and abetted by the free-love Age of Aquarius, never got put back in the lockbox. "Sex is deeply embedded in the human experience and ultimately it's one of the deepest expressions of human intimacy. That's why Freud talked about it so much. For twenty years, we pretended that wasn't the case, and it came back to hit us. During the Swinging '60s and '70s it was never really contemplated that *nonadults* would begin engaging in recreational sex...using one another as objects of recreational satisfaction. [But as we have witnessed] throughout history, we are human beings. And, lo and behold, it turns out that sexuality has physical, emotional, and spiritual consequences, and we were completely unwilling to acknowledge it. So as people were getting harmed, first physically and then emotionally, it became obvious that the people who continued to use humans as objects, regardless of the effects they were having on them, were unable to control it. That's a problem. That's sex addiction."

If there is a silver lining in all of this, Drew Pinsky notes, it is the return to the recognition of the importance of one's closest acquaintances and family members—and the inherent value placed on sustainable intimacy. Today's youth, according to several studies, are having *less* sex, not more, and less sex that is purely physical. "There's been a refocus on children and families," he proposes, "an increasing stability in relationships in the new millennium. My kids understand, strangely enough, that sexuality is part of a deep interpersonal experience with tons of implications."

––––––

In the end, a politicized legal case, a constitutional crisis, and a muck-drunk media ran roughshod over an intern's private life. For Paula Jones to effectively press her case against Bill Clinton...for Kenneth Starr to press *his* case against Bill Clinton...for the Republican Congress to press *its* impeachment case against Democrat Bill Clinton...(and for the press to cover it 24/7), Monica Lewinsky had to be placed on the altar.

For the last word, it seems appropriate to hear from her—the Internet age's inaugural citizen-victim of sexual shaming.

"I was the first to have my identity and reputation savaged by the virality of the Web," says Lewinsky in a series of conversations in New York and Los Angeles. "Today, unfortunately, people are routinely cyberbullied with impunity.[7] But back in 1998, I happened to be the first one to walk into that barrage. And overnight I was branded a tramp, a floozy, an unstable stalker"—the latter characterization coming courtesy of Team Clinton. "I was outed by Drudge, used as a political pawn by the Republicans, and scapegoated by the White House. My reputation was shot so that the president could hold on to power. In the process, my identity was distorted and I was left voiceless [and unable to correct the record] because I was in the middle of a judicial process and had to remain silent. My human rights and civil rights were thrown out the window."

Now forty-four, with a master's in social psychology from the London School of Economics, Lewinsky is an antibullying advocate, a public speaker, and a contributing editor at *Vanity Fair* (where I have served as her editor at the magazine). She says she has learned firsthand that public personalities as well as unknown individuals who are suddenly thrust into the public eye "have two identities," as she puts it. "One is the true self—a human being with an inner spirit, a rich character, and a definable personality. They're known to others by their behavior and character, their strengths and faults. The second self is a caricature made up by the media, PR people, gossip, enemies, or outsiders. It often has no resemblance to the real person. And when this false identity hijacks the person's reputation, it's almost impossible to shake it."

Producer and screenwriter Aaron Sorkin once remarked that "everyone

---

7. The phrase itself is a rather new construct, as Jessica Bennett has noted, in *Time*. "'It was a different time back then. There was no consciousness raised about slut-shaming. *Bullying* wasn't even in the vernacular,' says Leora Tanenbaum, the author of *Slut!*, which first established the term *slut-bashing* (a precursor to *slut-shaming*) when it came out in 1999. 'People who were decision-makers and influential writers were making comments about [Lewinsky's] hair and body. It was a textbook case of the sexual double standard.'" (Jessica Bennett, "The Shaming of Monica: Why We Owe Her an Apology," *Time*, May 9, 2014.)

who works in Hollywood has two personalities: their real one and the one assigned to them by rumor." In a similar way, Lewinsky had her "rumored self" chiseled in stone by others. "There is a social representation of Monica Lewinsky out there," she attests, "who is supposedly rich, spoiled, a conniver. She's bitchy and a bit of a ditz—*none* of the things that line up with my true identity or personality. I really was a social canvas and I had no part in painting [the picture], in being able to say, 'This is actually who I am.' That Other Monica existed—still exists—in a parallel universe, in a narrative I couldn't take back.

"Sociologist Erving Goffman has explored the notion of 'frontstage/backstage': what we choose to share with the public and what we choose to keep private. Private doesn't necessarily mean just within ourselves. Private means: within our circle of people, a boundary which we create. That boundary collapsed for me. My private self became a public commodity. I lost my sense of social identity *and* self-identity. My private conversations were there to be read. A copy of my brother's SAT scores was taken *as evidence.* I became a test case for something that is still unresolved in a post–Edward Snowden world: How do we guard against a government intent on prying into our most private information? How do we guard against being taken out of context if we're public people—or being ridiculed on social media [if we're] private individuals?"

Lewinsky speaks at length about Jeffrey Rosen's book, published in 2000, *The Unwanted Gaze: The Destruction of Privacy in America.* She draws my attention to pertinent passages. "During the impeachment drama," writes Rosen, "privacy law failed to keep Kenneth Starr out of the bedroom of Monica Lewinsky, whose experience was a dramatic rebuke to the claim that women have no privacy to lose.... The Lewinsky affair has challenged us to refine the legal definition of sexual harassment so that the privacy and autonomy of individual women and men are preserved rather than invaded."

Rosen, a George Washington University Law School professor who serves as the president and CEO of the National Constitution Center, argues in his book that the creation of the independent counsel act,[8] along with various

---

8. The law validating the authority of special prosecutors—set up after the Watergate scandal in the 1970s—lapsed in 1999 after the Clinton impeachment debacle. (Carol Elder Bruce, "An Independent Counsel Law Needs to Be Restored," *New York Times,* June 13, 2012.)

rulings by the High Court from the 1970s through the '90s (such as the right to subpoena private diaries and an overhaul of sexual harassment laws), have served to undercut personal-privacy protection. The Supreme Court, Rosen notes, has failed to adequately address "our ability to control the conditions under which we make different aspects of ourselves accessible to others."

Indeed, for many, the pervasiveness of social media since the 1990s has made the very concept of privacy, in the words of Facebook founder Mark Zuckerberg, an evolving "social norm." Online, privacy has become a fluid concept. "If those creepy targeted ads on Google hadn't tipped you off," writes journalist Kate Murphy, "then surely Edward J. Snowden's revelations, or... [actress] Jennifer Lawrence's nude selfies, made your vulnerability to cybersnooping abundantly clear." Murphy goes on to quote sociologist Christena Nippert-Eng, the author of *Islands of Privacy*: "When people want privacy there's often this idea that, 'Oh, they are hiding something dirty,' but they are really just trying to hold onto themselves."

"The action brought against me," Lewinsky says, "was called *United States versus Monica Lewinsky*. My country was prosecuting me, essentially, for trying to keep private the fact that I had fallen in love with my married boss." She argues that in order to make their respective cases against the president, Paula Jones, Kenneth Starr, and the Congress "first had to make their case against me by exposing my private life and subjecting me to this inquisition. It was litigation as harassment. There was a closed-door, detail-by-detail grand jury deposition, which was ultimately released and made public. It was an assault. I was violated. And I was traumatized by having been violated. Violation of privacy is really just an abstract concept until it happens to you."

What does Lewinsky believe happened in the '90s to make individuals' private lives so susceptible to unwarranted intrusion and exposure? She sees five contributing causes. First came the increased "tabloidization of celebrity in tandem with the surface treatment of politics."[9] Next came the news-channel wars. "It wasn't until '96, with the birth of Fox News and

---

9. "Election cycles," Lewinsky notes, "started to take on more of an entertainment value and a Hollywood luster. *People* magazine superseded *Time* magazine. Reagan, surely, had changed some things, but the Clintonian style shifted it further. There was a silent campaign going on to make the voter ask: who is the candidate I most want to have a beer with? The family of the candidate was suddenly significant. Does the candidate have charisma? All of these attributes, which we came to

MSNBC, in opposition to CNN," Lewinsky says, "that you started to see the shift. That fierce and often partisan contest in a twenty-four-hour news cycle made news a *business* first, and [viewers] went from being interested in significant events—'Is this newsworthy?'—to being consumers of information and entertainment that 'sells': 'Does this bring the network value?' Again, this created an inducement for more tabloidization and more defaming and shaming. It became this 'gotcha culture.' "[10]

Third, of course, was the Internet. The World Wide Web, she says, "amplified the competition for new smears that could provide some prurience. Now you were getting rumors twenty-four hours a day—you didn't have to wait for the next cycle.... In my instance the intensity surrounding the 'sting' in the hotel room had a lot to do with Drudge saying that *Newsweek* was holding back on a story [about my time in the White House]. I think it was the first time that a 'nonlegitimate' news source, as it was called then, was the catalyst for one of the biggest news stories."

These all coincided, she believes, with a fourth factor: a change in "sexual mores in the '80s and '90s.[11] We became more permissive as a society even if the culture's puritanical [roots] still made us feel shame about our voyeurism and our behavior. We were grappling with issues of morality in a way that we hadn't before. The Boomer generation and the Me generation and all the therapy—with people wanting a more self-focused life—were processing a very wide spectrum of behavior that some people considered moral and others considered immoral.[12]

---

ascribe to the kind of leader we wanted, are really useless when it comes to *leading*. So the private life and the surface personality overtook the public role of the public servant."

10. Quoth Clinton himself on *60 Minutes*, back in 1992: "What the press has to decide is: Are we going to engage in a game of 'gotcha'?" ("Clinton Conceded Marital 'Wrongdoing,'" *Washington Post*, January 26, 1992.)

11. "Mores were also a matter of economics," Lewinsky adds. "Look at [the 2013 film] *The Wolf of Wall Street*—the story line took place late '80s, early '90s. Did this great influx of wealth end up becoming an opportunity for us to move forward in a way that [promoted] higher consciousness? No. Many people used that new money to open their sexual appetites. They had more resources, more time, which led to inhibitions being expunged. So people were giving into some darker sides of themselves—drinking more, doing more drugs—which led to more sexual liberation as an aftershock to the '60s sexual revolution."

12. Lewinsky acknowledges that popular culture also played a major role in affecting sexual mores. Indeed, the neighborhood where Lewinsky grew up is a short drive from the communities depicted

"All of these things slowly chipped away at the division between private and public. So once we started to chip away at the privacy of a *public* person, that slowly trickled down into the privacy of a *private* person.

"What happened between Bill and myself," she continues, "was not new for him. It was not new for other presidents.... Older men and younger women in inappropriate relationships have been around for a long time. Since the beginning of time, girls have been talking to their girlfriends about their relationships, and people have been denying sexual things [to keep them from being made public]. What had changed was the culture: the landscape of the media, the treatment of politicians as 'power personalities,' plus people's mores, plus more tabloids and tabloid TV, which had no ethics, no standards."

Monica Lewinsky, like Schell and Pinsky, also finds the O. J. Simpson case, coming three years before hers, to have been a force multiplier. "There was a seismic media shift in which people were being inundated by scandal. This was the beginning of the change of our attention span for certain stories which further eroded privacy as the press made that erosion more acceptable. O.J. literally happened in my backyard. My dad lives about two blocks from where Nicole Simpson and Ronald Goldman were murdered. At the time, 1994, I was in college—I was living in Oregon—so I didn't pay a lot of attention to it. I was at a Grateful Dead concert in Eugene the day of the Bronco chase. But examining it in hindsight, I see that it spawned the whole talking-heads culture, which became a very, very big part of what happened in '98—the whole glamorizing of pundits along with the lawyers and the judges. Some of the same talking heads covering the Simpson trial morphed into those from 1998.[13] But in my case, it was even more magnified: the direction of the country was on the line.

---

in some of the most provocative television shows of the '90s: *Melrose Place, Baywatch,* and *Beverly Hills 90210.*

13. Writing in the *Columbia Journalism Review* in the summer of 1998, Lawrence K. Grossman, formerly the president of NBC News and PBS, would observe, "Like a recurring nightmare, an improbable connection was made between [Monica Lewinsky's] dress and the O. J. Simpson murder case. Former Los Angeles police detective Mark Fuhrman, [the LAPD detective who happened to be] a key witness in the Simpson trial, appeared on MSNBC, the cable news channel that gained the dubious reputation of programming 'All Monica, All the Time.' Fuhrman revealed that he had been contacted the previous October by his one-time book agent [Lucianne] Goldberg, who asked him how DNA could be extracted from a dress." (Lawrence K. Grossman, "The Press and the Dress," *Columbia Journalism Review,* June 1998.)

"The added 'X factor,'" Lewinsky surmises, was the politics of the culture war in all of its shadings. "You had this religious thread. The religious right's influence on the extreme right wing in that decade fomented the attitude that *this is wrong*. This fit in with the whole notion of private or interpersonal decisions and practices being judged: choice versus pro-life, sexual orientation, and a lot of other issues that allowed those on the religious right to judge others [as being immoral].

"The irony was the hypocrisy. The Republicans and the leaders of the religious right were hardly bastions of virtue. And the media put on a puritanical front, even though some of them were hardly averse to doing what they had to do to get to their positions in front of the camera. For preachers and congressmen and commentators to talk so disdainfully about 'tawdry' behavior was a bit disingenuous."

Vanessa Grigoriadis, in *New York* magazine, would make the point that Monica Lewinsky had become "many...things, a global icon, a cautionary tale, the individual on whom America projected its feelings about sex and power and politics." But Lewinsky had never remotely expected to become a role model in the arena of human sexuality. Even so, she now finds that strangers come up to her in social or public settings to thank her or to ask her if they can hug her. (I have witnessed such encounters.) "There are pockets of communities in our world," she explains, "that have been persecuted for their sexuality, and I think that [among certain] people, there is a sense of understanding and empathy [because they] know what it's like to be judged specifically on one's sexual choices. They see some aspect of themselves in my own experiences. They express, to me, compassion, for which I am grateful."[14]

---

14. Lewinsky's persona, she says, was defined in part by her upbringing and her role models. "Pop icons of my generation," she reveals, "were Molly Ringwald in those John Hughes films. Her characters were probably a really good example of what I was trying to be: more open and [more comfortable with] exploring the boundaries than in previous generations where you were shut down about your sexuality and your acceptance of others' behavior and orientation." That said, Lewinsky was not ready for either the scorn or the praise that came her way simply for being a modern young woman. Sex-positive feminist Susie Bright, for one, actually swooned over her in an article for *Ms.*, labeling Lewinsky "our living Helen of Troy" and "a sexual superstar," reminding readers that "the day after Monica's interview [with TV host Barbara Walters], the lipstick she was wearing— Club Monaco brand, in the color 'Glaze'—sold out at cosmetics counters." Bright would go on, "I understood Monica's universal erotic appeal. But it's through her *words* that I have discovered Monica's big secret: she has a big IQ....She may be naïve about love, but she is good with the law. Monica Lewinsky wanted to *be* president when she was in the second grade....In [school she]

What's more, Lewinsky became a symbol of how gender politics apply in what many would consider a hostile work environment. "I lost my job at the White House because of this," she says. "I was transferred to a job [at the Pentagon] where I was actually making more money, but that was not by my choice. There were real-world negative consequences for me. And so, in looking back at my predicament, new ethical and legal precedents in sexual harassment laws were tested out: where does a consensual sexual relationship overlap with others' view that that relationship constituted workplace harassment and sexual coercion?"[15]

In the summer of 1998, the case for impeachment crescendoed. For a brief moment, though, one man in particular, and in particularly disarming fashion, tried to throw up a roadblock.

Connecticut senator Joseph Lieberman had been one of Bill Clinton's early, ardent supporters. The senator had taken the president at his word when he'd denied having had an affair. Yet over the months, the truth tumbled out, and Lieberman bridled. Clinton, in his view, had betrayed the public trust. Moreover, in the words of Lieberman's chief speechwriter at the time, Daniel Gerstein, the senator believed the president "wasn't owning up to the severity of his misconduct" nor acknowledging that his actions "eroded the office he held."

---

excelled [and became one of many] thwarted [and] gifted young women. . . . This big girl should have been mentored to run the world, not run little games around the little men inside it." (Interview with Lewinsky; Susie Bright, "The Beauty & the Brains," *Ms.*, June 1999.)

15. For all the talk of progress in this arena, Anita Hill tells me, society often avoids the root of the matter. "My issue isn't with [the culture's] permissiveness," she says. "The problem is the overexposure and the sense of entitlement that people have toward others; that culture tells you they're able to participate with you sexually in any way they want. For young women there is this false sense that they are in control of their sexual expression. They feel it's okay to be sexually explicit because 'I'm making that choice.'" Hill illustrates her point with an incident she recalls at Brandeis, where she teaches. "The other day a [female undergraduate] student told me a group of friends got together, male and female, and they routinely did it and called it Porn and Doughnuts. They got together and watched porn. Part of the thinking, she said, [was] 'We're agreeing to do it, so the pornography's not problematic. We're all in an equal place.' She also said that during one of the scenes, a woman said, 'Oh, that looks like that would hurt,' but there was no response from the men, [who] didn't object. They just sat there and just ate the doughnuts. In [these women's] minds, their having chosen to participate made it okay, so whatever happened after that was okay. It gets to the issue of agency: your ability to control your sexuality, *own* your body, and use it as you want to and not be exploited." (Interview with Hill.)

The senator—as a Democrat, an observant Orthodox Jew respected for his principles, and a Washington divining rod on issues of ethics—felt he had the moral clout to reprimand the president but also to *dissuade* his fellow lawmakers from forging ahead with a trial so rare that it had but a single precedent: the impeachment of Andrew Johnson in 1868. Lieberman decided to go to the Senate floor, just before legislators broke for the Labor Day weekend, to deliver what many would come to see as the most impactful speech of his career.

"It was really an extraordinary moment of political theater," Gerstein reflects.[16] No one in the Congress knew where the senator really stood on the matter. Few realized he was even scheduled to speak. "Most everything in Congress is very scripted and rather predictable—it's kabuki. This was one of those rare moments where you don't know *what* was going to happen."

Gerstein remembers heading to the Hill with Lieberman, speech in hand, by underground subway. They conversed very little, Gerstein says, because "the significance of the moment was kind of heavy." Upon their arrival, the setting they encountered was eerie. The Senate was in pro forma session and so the chamber turned out to be virtually unoccupied. Only two other members were present, both Republicans: one presiding (the Senate, like the House, was in the hands of the GOP) and one addressing the empty room.

Lieberman, Gerstein recalls, "[takes his seat, then] rises to ask for recognition and starts into his speech. And word starts filtering out [via] C-SPAN and the [Senate] cloakrooms. Republican members start streaming in because they recognize the significance of it." The lawmakers took their places, one after another, as if in a scene from a movie. But no Democrats were among them. "I would say the majority of the Republican caucus [had gathered. Meanwhile, Democrats] Bob Kerrey and Dan Moynihan, watching [on TV monitors from their offices], understood what the optics looked like and what message that would send if it was a bunch of Republicans there. And they both, independently, dropped what they were doing and rushed to the Senate floor."

Lieberman had recently stood at that same spot and excoriated entertain-

---

16. Gerstein, who helped draft Lieberman's public remarks, was also in charge of his "values" portfolio, covering legislative matters related to subjects like teen pregnancy, fatherhood, and sex and violence in the entertainment industry. Today he runs a strategic communications firm.

ment moguls for "weaken[ing] our common values." Now he was doing the same to Bill Clinton, whom he described as having even *more* sway "on our culture, on our character, and on our children":

> I must respectfully disagree with the president's contention that his relationship with Monica Lewinsky and the way in which he misled us about it is nobody's business but his family's and that "even presidents have private lives," as [the president] said. Whether he or we think it fair or not, the reality is, in 1998, that a president's private life is public. Contemporary news media standards will have it no other way. And surely this president was given fair notice of that by the amount of time the news media has dedicated to investigating his personal life during the 1992 campaign and in the years since.
>
> But there is more to this than modern media intrusiveness. The president is not just the elected leader of our country....The president is a role model. And because of his prominence the moral authority that emanates from his office sets standards of behavior for the people he serves....No matter how much the president or others may wish to compartmentalize the different spheres of his life, the inescapable truth is that the president's private conduct can and often does have profound public consequences....I fear that the president has undercut the efforts of millions of American parents who are naturally trying to instill in our children the value of honesty....I am afraid that the misconduct the president has admitted may be reinforcing one of the worst messages being delivered by our popular culture, which is that values are fungible.

Lieberman's remarks were lacerating. But implicit in his comments was an underlying message: despite Clinton's misdeeds, impeachment was too grave a penalty. "Let us be guided," he advised, "by the conscience of the Constitution, which calls on us to place the common good above any partisan or personal interest." Lieberman's overall intention had been to mute "the hysteria," says Gerstein. "He felt strongly that there was a need to separate the moral implications from the legal implications. By condemning the president's behavior on moral grounds, it became easier to then pivot and sort of say, 'But these aren't impeachable offenses and there are other ways to hold the president accountable, short of a constitutional crisis.'" (Lieberman would argue instead for a formal censure.)

Over time, the senator's intercession was considered a boon to the president. While chastened, Clinton was reportedly "gratified" by Lieberman's words of caution, delivered at such a crucial juncture. The next morning, in fact, Clinton was contrite, contending, "I agree with what he said." And in his autobiography Clinton would insist, "I knew he was a devoutly religious man who was angry about what I had done, and he had carefully avoided saying that I should be impeached."

The Impeachment Express, nonetheless, had already left Union Station. In October, the House of Representatives agreed to hold an inquiry. In December, its members cast votes along party lines and impeached William Jefferson Clinton for perjury and obstruction of justice. In January and February 1999, the Senate, after public hearings, held a trial that would determine whether the legislative branch would remove the nation's chief executive.

Like other televised, make-or-break spectacles that decade, the Senate proceedings and the historic roll-call vote, kept the nation in thrall. Arguing for the defense was retired senator Dale Bumpers, a longtime Arkansas friend and colleague of Clinton's. He proved to be the president's most valiant and effective advocate. Standing in front of a packed Senate chamber, Bumpers recalled that the founding fathers had spent months debating the method and meaning of impeachment, and that the procedure's "greatest danger," in the prescient words of Alexander Hamilton, "[was] that the decision will be regulated more by the comparative strength of [the political] parties rather than by the real demonstrations of innocence or guilt."

Bumpers, in his folksy, measured manner, went on to ask, "How did we come to here? We are here because of a five-year, relentless, unending investigation of the president. Fifty [m]illion dollars, hundreds of FBI agents fanning across the nation examining in detail the microscopic lives of people. Maybe the most intense investigation not only of a president but of anybody ever.... I doubt that there are few people, maybe nobody in this body, who could withstand such scrutiny." In his most memorable passage, Bumpers reduced the impeachment case to three words: "H. L. Mencken said one time, 'When you hear somebody say, "This is not about money," it's about money.'" Bumpers paused and then went on. "And when you hear somebody say, 'This is not about sex,' it's about sex."

He'd laid down a clear-eyed case for the defense, and appealed, many believed, to the legislators' collective conscience. Finally, after the independent counsel's five-year investigation, after Paula Jones's four-year lawsuit, and after the second-ever impeachment in the history of the House of Representatives, the Senate voted to acquit the president on both charges. Clinton would remain in office and complete his second term.

––––––––

In many ways the impeachment proceedings, coming after the itemized inanities of the Starr investigation, had exposed not the indecency of intimate acts between consenting adults but the indecent divisiveness of partisan Washington. One might argue that a majority of Americans—as evidenced by Bill Clinton's rising favorability ratings during his last years in office—believed that things had gone awry and that a dark politics of revenge and character assassination were in perpetual play. (After he was impeached, Clinton's approval numbers soared to 73 percent.)[17] Indeed, the consensus among the citizenry appeared to be that private romantic or sexual matters, whether a president's or their own, should be left private.[18]

Still and all, Bill Clinton *had been impeached.* And while much of America

––––––––

17. Bill Clinton, upon departing the presidency, posted a favorability index of 68 percent, essentially tying him with Ronald Reagan at the same stage. Hillary Clinton, for that matter, was similarly well liked at the height of her husband's troubles. "She was often more popular when she was suffering a traditionally feminine humiliation," posits the *New Yorker*'s Margaret Talbot. "As First Lady, her approval ratings rose after the Monica Lewinsky revelations and during Kenneth Starr's investigation.... Like the female protagonist of a quest narrative—or, perhaps, of a dystopian fantasy—Clinton has made it through all her challenges to face [Donald Trump], the bull-headed Minotaur of sexism at the end of the maze."

As recently as 2014, a poll by the *Wall Street Journal*, in conjunction with NBC News and the Annenberg Survey, revealed Clinton to be the "most admired" president of the previous twenty-five years. ("Clinton's Approval Rating Up in Wake of Impeachment," CNN.com, December 20, 1998; Megan Thee-Brenan, "Poll Finds Disapproval of Bush Unwavering," *New York Times*, January 17, 2009; Margaret Talbot, "That's What He Said," *New Yorker*, October 24, 2016, 20; Janet Hook, "Poll: Clinton Most Admired President of Past 25 Years," *Wall Street Journal*, June 15, 2014.)

18. Jeffrey Rosen, citing sociologist Émile Durkheim, writes of the lasting impact of public trials as collective rituals: "The process of identifying and punishing exemplary violations of moral and social rules is the process by which we identify what, precisely, those rules are. By insisting that Clinton be acquitted and [Justice Clarence] Thomas confirmed, perhaps the public established clear limits on what kinds of violations of privacy it would tolerate, and, in the process, it reasserted the boundaries between the public and private sphere." (Jeffrey Rosen, *The Unwanted Gaze: The Destruction of Privacy in America* [New York: Random House, 2000,] 157.)

expressed resentment about the motivations that had led to his trial, the national fatigue with his ethical elasticity became a millstone for the Democratic Party, determining how the *next* decade played out.

Mark McKinnon was a longtime strategist for George W. Bush. He tells me that the reason the Texas governor defeated Vice President Al Gore in the 2000 election had little to do with Bush's proposed policies or the state of the economy or the ballot confusion in Florida. "In any presidential election, the conventional wisdom is that it's either going to be a 'status quo' or a 'change' election," McKinnon offers. "The first question [in any poll] is, 'Is this country, city, or state headed in the right direction or off on the wrong track?' If the 'right track' number is over 50 percent, then we call it a status quo election [and] people are generally satisfied with the incumbent candidate or party." In 1999 and 2000, he recalls, the Clinton-Gore numbers were all positive. The nation and the economy, most voters believed, were on the right track. "By all conventional metrics, it looked like a home run for Gore.... Strategically, it looked like an impossible hill [for Bush] to climb.

"But from the very beginning," says McKinnon, "Bush had been talking about the importance of restoring integrity to the office of the presidency and talking about a cultural change—[insisting that] we needed to take more responsibility, accountability. This was all 'coded speak' for Clinton and all the Clinton problems.... So underneath that election and that time in our history, people felt that we'd kind of rolled off our moral axis and wanted to restore some order, and George Bush became the vessel for that. We looked at the [polling] numbers and there was no other way to explain it with the economy being so good. It turned out they voted on a constellation of attributes, the most important of which was strong leadership, and then character, and then values.

"The conventional metrics changed...to moral metrics. The line that got roars [on the campaign trail] was when he said, 'When I put my hand on the Bible, I'll restore the honor and integrity to the office of the presidency.'"

McKinnon, despite all of this, says that he does not believe Clinton should have been impeached. And Lewinsky, to this day, is of two minds about the verdict. "There were even plenty of Republicans," she says, "who felt, 'Okay, enough already—let's just move on.'" But she remains firm in her contention that Clinton had much of it coming. "I can see both sides of everything," she insists. "By no stretch of the imagination do I think that anything Ken Starr did was right, any step of the way. But I can see where somebody who is continuing to lie and evade the truth—even though he shouldn't have had to be telling the truth about certain things—[needed to be] held accountable. What is the recourse when someone starts to thumb his nose in the face of the law that way? There's no question that I did that too, but *he* was the president. For the head of the nation's law enforcement to not be following the rules is a bit of a challenge. . . . I don't know what the deciding factor for impeachment should be [but] we had a president, under oath, lying."

At the heart of the matter—despite the many handmaidens of Clinton's undoing, including Starr, Gingrich, and that vast right-wing conspiracy—the president's precipitous fall was self-induced. As any student of Greek tragedy can attest, a hero's demise, even when orchestrated by his enemies, is intrinsically the result of the protagonist's own hubris.

Afterword:
The Trumpen Show

The curtain closed on the 1990s. But the culture-war drama played on.

And after a prolonged period of division and collision, the stage was set for the 2016 campaign cycle. The stars were Hillary Clinton and Donald Trump. The genre was black comedy. And the last act, as it turned out, was a madcap sequel to the Reagan and Gingrich revolutions.

When the house lights came up, on November 9, 2016, the audience sat stunned. America, in a culture-war reversion to the 1980s, had managed to elect another tanned and privileged media creature, another septuagenarian disrupter. Trump in some ways was Ronald Reagan Remade—as a Sith Lord with French cuffs. But while Trump, like Reagan, purported to speak for the American Everyman, he and his minions were essentially forging an offensive against the underclass he professed to champion—and against the advances of women, people of color, LGBT individuals, immigrants, and others who had been marginalized by society. Trump's was a movement that would test the boundaries of racial tolerance, gender inclusion, religious acceptance, and voting rights; a movement intent on rolling back liberalism, feminism, globalization, *Roe v. Wade*, and everything that the Clintons had represented.

A recap is in order. Eight years of Bill Clinton had led, inevitably, to eight years of George W. Bush, who had vowed to bring dignity back to the West Wing. (In a totemic repudiation of Clinton, Bush would store Saddam Hussein's pistol, captured during the Iraq War, in the same study adjacent to the Oval Office where some of Clinton's after-hours encounters had occurred.)

But Bush's presidency was a fraught one. During his tenure, Al Qaeda terrorists launched the deadliest foreign assault on America since the 1940s. Bush began a foolhardy, unwinnable war in Iraq, which in time would further inflame the region. He bungled the emergency response to Hurricane

Katrina, deepening a deadly humanitarian crisis. He was at the controls when the economy, as part of a global recession, went into a tailspin.

The cumulative effect? "George W. Bush's failures pushed the Democratic Party to the left," Peter Beinart would contend in the *Atlantic*. And Bush's successor, Barack Obama, would become, in Beinart's judgment, "the most tangible result" of the Bush fiascos, making many "Democrats unapologetically liberal." (Voters, to be sure, continued to swing right at the local level and in their selection of governors and congressmen.)

But Obama, for all his successes in health-care, counterterrorism, and rejuvenating the hobbled economy, racked up his *own* series of disappointments. And so the Obama era—hampered by Washington gridlock (in large measure the fault of a deliberately intransigent Republican Congress)—gave impetus to restive forces across the political spectrum. Soon arose the Occupy movement; the Tea Party movement; the Black Lives Matter movement; and the candidacies of a self-proclaimed socialist, Bernie Sanders, and a self-styled populist, Donald Trump.

As this book has sought to establish, America from the '90s onward had actually moved *left*. Citizens in red states and blue consistently expressed a desire—as Mitt Romney's 2012 campaign strategist Stuart Stevens described it during Trump's 2016 presidential run—to have "a growing benevolent government, as long as they [didn't] have to admit they need[ed] it."[1] The nation's progressive drift was at its most pronounced in the tug-of-war over "values." In their sexual attitudes, Americans had adopted more liberated views. In popular culture, expressions of erotic desire became commonplace. In relationships, new templates were established for human intimacy and the structure and definition of family. In the workplace and elsewhere, sexual harassment and gender equity were codified in law and in practice. In these regards, the values and norms of the left had won decisively. The future had triumphed over the past.

And yet on many of these fronts the culture was still on a war footing. Battles continued to rage over abortion, marriage equality, legal and social

---

1. If Democrats had tacked left in their attitudes, so too had GOP voters, especially millennials. Wrote columnist David Brooks, during the 2016 campaign, "According to the Pew Research Center, young Republicans are much more moderate than older Republicans. Among millennials who lean Republican, only 31 percent have consistently conservative views." (David Brooks, "The Self-Reliant Generation," *New York Times*, January 8, 2016, A23.)

safeguards for LGBT rights, and a host of other issues involving civil and voting rights, affirmative action, criminal-justice reform, income disparity, political correctness, identity politics, and Americans' lack of moral fixity. In *these* struggles, the far right was gaining traction. What's more, after twenty-four years of Clinton, then Bush, then Obama, tens of millions of Americans recoiled at the notion of entrusting their future, once again, to the Washington establishment.

In 2016, two consummate Boomers, HRC and DJT, entered the ring and fought the culture war's ultimate elimination round. The stakes were higher than ever. The invective was louder. The candidates, scraped and bloodied, hugged the ropes from time to time.

At the final bell, the refs—America's voters—could well have said, *Enough*: enough with our nagging '90s hangover; enough with the tabloid drift, the reality programming, the digital sabotage, the media-contrived confrontation, the race-baiting, the mansplaining, the egomania and xenophobia and homophobia and misogyny and sexual shaming and crude public references to human anatomy.

But, *nahhh*...

They chose, instead, the hair of the dog—comb-over and all.

And even though the ex–First Lady/senator/secretary of state had landed a larger share of the popular vote, America's electoral loyalties in the end went to a real-estate mogul turned reality-TV star.

———

Every TV pundit worth his mousse had a theory about why Donald Trump won, why Hillary Clinton lost, and why the outcome had been preordained. The culprits were disgruntled white men; women "complicit...in their own oppression" (as columnist Suzanne Moore put it); Russian hackers; eleventh-hour meddling by the FBI director; the Trump team's superior data analytics; and "conspiracy theories...a generation in the making," as former *New York Times* executive editor Jill Abramson surmised. "As in any good Agatha Christie mystery, there are so many suspects that it's hard to find the real killer." Trump won, they said, because he'd projected nationalist pride and isolationist resolve, sentiments that were also resonating across Europe. Trump won because he was considered a businessman who could fix things; because he was the most tenacious and engaged candidate. Trump won because he was Rocky Balboa, an underdog who'd kiboshed *sixteen* other

Republicans in the primaries—and who'd gained voter sympathy after being relentlessly pummeled by the press and the leaders of both parties. Trump won because he'd pledged to address one or more of a given voter's overriding fears: unchecked immigration, escalating terrorism, legalized abortion, expanding government, declining job prospects, and everything from globalization ("a broken system") to Obamacare ("a disaster").

Time and again, observers pointed to the gender equation. They argued that Trump was an alpha-male protector in a time of crisis. Or that many men had viewed him as a revivalist figure—a leader who would bring back a brawny, Old Spice–scented America where every guy could keep his gun, his gal, and his job. And yet Trump was swept into office on a tide of female voters too. While a majority of women had supported Hillary Clinton—by a factor of 54 to 42 percent—Trump had secured the backing of 53 percent of white women voters (62 percent of his female voters did not have college degrees). What would have possessed them to cast ballots for a candidate who had disparaged women as "pigs" and "dogs" and had bragged about groping women's privates without their consent?

Possible motivations were all over the lot. Some pro-Trump women evidently disregarded his flashes of chauvinism and could justify such statements, having heard them frequently at home, at work, or on the street. Some were willing to cut him some slack because they trusted he'd deliver a brighter tomorrow. Many took cues from their partners or peers, contends journalist Emily Jane Fox, my *Vanity Fair* colleague: "People [often] underestimate how sexist women are. When you yourself have never been treated equally as a woman—paid fairly, promoted commensurately, treated with respect—you don't, then, treat other women as equals. If you in your life are harassed, assaulted, put down, left behind, and you've accepted that behavior as either the norm or an unfortunate, undeniable reality, then seeing a man treating women that way doesn't strike you as out of the ordinary."

Historian and journalist Susan Faludi had seen it all coming. Back in 1991, in her book *Backlash*, she'd explained how women's legal, social, and economic advances were running smack into a wall—a "backlash" from threatened men and a patriarchal ruling class. Though women's rights would expand even further during Bill Clinton's time in office, society's male bias had remained intact. And so, twenty-five years later, the triumph of Trump was a culture-war reversion. "As the culture moves further away from the conservative ideal," Faludi would posit on the eve of the 2016 vote, "as women gain freedoms, minorities assert rights, same-sex marriage proves commonplace—the monster howls grow louder. But the howls say nothing new. This election is the decisive battle in a Thirty Years' War."[2]

A Thirty Years' War. In this ongoing culture clash, the left may have won the majority of the nation's hearts and minds. But the right, to be sure, was winning the ground war.

————

For all this, it was hard to miss the 1990s underpinnings of the 2016 campaign cycle.

First off, many Trump voters had fallen for him in precisely the same way they'd fallen for Bill Clinton. They had warmed to his neediness, his naughtiness, his Boomer narcissism, and his come-ons. ("I love the poorly educated," he crowed after winning the Nevada caucuses. "I love Hispanics!" he tweeted. "The best taco bowls are made in Trump Tower Grill.") During the 2016 primaries, columnist John Saward had visited the county with the nation's highest percentage of Trump supporters—in economically strapped West Virginia. Saward's takeaway could have just as easily applied to '92-vintage Clinton: "Trump is politician as pickup artist, as infomercial salesman; someone who will in a single breath pulverize your self-esteem and then convince you that he is the only one who can put you back together again.... He's going to take you home tonight, you have such beautiful eyes, baby, what are you doing here all alone? *I can make you great again.*"

Second, many Trump voters had finally OD'd on the *actual* Clintons. They had had enough of Hillary's *inevitability,* her chattering emails, Bill's rattling closet, the Clinton brand, the Clinton Foundation,[3] the Clinton mumbo-jumbo. Some voters dreaded the mere *idea* that with each new American morning, Hillary *and Bill* would be back in the People's House.

Third, many regarded Trump as a fearless, independent "outsider." He was a counterforce to the Clintons' America: a country many believed to be hamstrung by big government, a liberal agenda, a welfare-state mentality,

————

2. Much of the animus, asserts Faludi, can be traced to "1992, when [Clinton's] husband destroyed the myth of Republican invincibility and Hillary Clinton was anointed the feminine face of evil." (Susan Faludi, "How Hillary Clinton Met Satan," *New York Times,* October 29, 2016.)

3. The foundation presented an eerie conflict-of-interest template for the Trump Organization.

a diminished military, and a rise in what came to be denigrated as political correctness at the office, on campus, and in the drip-drip-drip of rules and quotas and laws protecting the less privileged.[4]

Indeed, the '80s and '90s had helped make voters *accustomed* to Trump himself. Trump was a *celebrity*. He was a real estate "tycoon." He was a *brand*.

Trump was also a horndog, a braggart, and a social-media-holic—*just like voters were*. Trump, unlike the typical public servant, was *selfish* (and committed to self-preservation)—*just like voters*, who were bone tired of giving and forgiving.[5] Trump projected *power*: his bravado, not to mention his thin skin, might actually spook America's enemies. (Hadn't Reagan and Bush, after all, been feared as "cowboys"?) Trump was a press basher who was, paradoxically, a media queen. (Who but a press lush would have phoned up members of the media back in the day and, pretending to be a publicist, represent *himself* as a client?)

Most important of all, he was a *reality-TV star*. This was Trump's trump card, especially when courting a public with a compromised rumor-immune system. Not to belabor the obvious, but Donald Trump knew how to treat politics *as a reality show*.

At first, skeptics had viewed Trump's candidacy as his way of burnishing his brand.[6] But once he'd gotten a debate or two under his belt, he found his politi-

---

4. Political correctness, writes Moira Weigel, the culture critic and literary scholar, was the perfect straw man on which to hang Trump's ideology. PC, by this theory, was devised in part to galvanize voters against "powerful, unnamed" forces working against establishment interests; in reality, the new guardians of public conscience and behavior were actually trying to create social and legal sanctions against sexism, racism, prejudice, and hostility against those who were traditionally denigrated as "others." As Weigel points out, "Most Americans had never heard the phrase 'politically correct' before 1990, when a wave of stories"—in particular a Richard Bernstein article for the *New York Times*—"began to appear in newspapers and magazines... [lamenting how] the country's universities were threatened by a 'growing intolerance, a closing of debate, a pressure to conform.'... PC was a useful invention for the Republican right because it helped the movement to drive a wedge between working-class people and the Democrats who claimed to speak for them.... [The act of opposing] political correctness also became a way to rebrand racism in ways that were politically acceptable in the post-civil-rights era." (Moira Weigel, "Political Correctness: How the Right Invented a Phantom Enemy," *Guardian*, November 30, 2016; Richard Bernstein, "The Rising Hegemony of the Politically Correct," *New York Times*, October 28, 1990.)

5. Many voters identified with aspects of what appeared to be his isolation: they, too, were averse to self-analysis, remote, impulsive, indiscriminately discontent, and, at times, lonely.

6. After all, Trump had hinted he might run for president in 2000, suggesting Oprah Winfrey as his running mate. Then he cried "wolf," as in Blitzer, every four years thereafter. In 2015, while considering throwing his hat in the ring once more, Trump reportedly made "calls from a

cal métier. And the news divisions at the network and cable outlets began to cast him in the lead. Soon they were marketing the presidential race like a prime-time series. On *two dozen* evenings, TV provided live coverage of the primary and caucus results. Over the course of fifteen months, there were *thirty-one* debates, town halls, and forums. In addition, Trump's campaign rallies and primary-night speeches were sometimes broadcast or streamed live. (Jeff Zucker, the head of CNN, was going all-in on Trump. No wonder: he'd been the executive at NBC who'd help steer the success of Trump's own reality show, *The Apprentice*.) This saturation coverage got viewers hooked on *The Great Race*. The networks, in effect, were simulcasting an episodic TV series. The program merged three formats, all of which had been perfected during the 1990s: the reality show, the talk show, and the monthslong TV-news saga (e.g., Conflict in the Gulf '90–'91, the O.J. Trial '94–'95, and the March to Impeachment '98–'99, not to mention Bush v. Gore '00–'01).

The reality genre turned out to be tailor-made for Trump: the serialized nature of the race, the faux suspense, the obsession with *process*. So too was the fixation on the week's winners ("We are going to win big-league, believe me") and losers ("I like people who *weren't* captured"). This was a format Trump knew intimately. And he solidified his hold on voters early on, through the debates, which suited his showman's flashiness and his insult-comic style.

As the Republican candidates lined up on the debate stage, Trump would be positioned at the center lectern. He would field more questions than his competitors. The setting had hints of *Survivor* and *The Apprentice*. At times, the moderators focused less on the candidates' policies than on their views about one another: "Senator Cruz, you suggested Mr. Trump 'embodies New York values.' Could you explain what you mean by that?" This line of questioning encouraged conflict and played to Trump's strengths, amplifying his tendency to razz his rivals.

Meanwhile, the postmortems by experts and the candidates' surrogates would reverberate for days across websites, social media, the print press, and the news and opinion programs, prolonging the agony and the exegesis.

---

summertime vacation in Scotland to buddies back in New York," according to Politico, and "answer[ed] his own question with a reference to his eleventh-hour decision to skip the 2012 presidential race: 'If I pull out again, nobody is ever going to believe me again.'" (Gwen Ifill, "Before 2016, Donald Trump Had a History of Toying with a Presidential Run," PBS.org, July 20, 2016; Glenn Thrush, "10 Crucial Decisions That Reshaped America," Politico.com, December 9, 2016.)

All along, Trump was playing by reality-TV rules. He didn't "prepare." He played his malaprops and bluster as *authenticity.* He "spun" his performance in pre-interviews and post-interviews. He inserted his family into the process, which helped bolster his appeal and fill out his back story. He spread hearsay ("I'm hearing…"; "Everybody is saying…"). When things weren't going his way, he blamed his mic or his earpiece. He cast doubt on the moderators. He whined and he sulked and he scowled.

Trump seemed to have the facility to say whatever sounded sensible or outrageous in the moment. He would build a "beautiful wall" along the Mexican border—which Mexico would pay for. He would announce, in one of his debates with Clinton, that she should be put in jail. He would alter his positions, debunk candidates he'd previously praised, deny saying things he'd said. While the other presidential hopefuls, by and large, gave fact-based responses, Trump understood that on reality programs the cleverest half-truth can mortally wound an opponent and the craftiest player often wins—and *wins over* the audience. By building on the foundation set by Bill Clinton and George W. Bush, Trump was elevating the long lie into performance art.

Before honing the reality craft on *The Apprentice*, in fact, Trump had learned from the clown princes of the trade: pro wrestlers. In 1988, he'd first wooed World Wrestling Entertainment (then called WWF) matches to his Trump Plaza arena in Atlantic City. It was the golden age of conservative populism, as Stephen L. Miller has described it in the *National Review,* and "pro wrestling's biggest stage was where Donald Trump the populist was born." In the late '80s and into the '90s, Trump came to respect the stars of the sport, along with their kayfabe, their theatrical antics, and their targeting of "evil" enemies who would be summarily vanquished. "He became a master at trash talk, smack downs, and sheer television entertainment," according to CNN political analyst David Gergen, and it would culminate in Trump's 2007 appearance *in the ring*, where, having emerged victorious (when his designated wrestler stand-in beat WWE honcho Vince McMahon's), Trump got to shave McMahon's head—as the fans went wild. "Trump's blue-collar base," writes Miller, "believes he's one of them. He loves the pageantry of it all as much as they do, and he's spent years upon years cultivating them. These people are fans of Trump more than they are fans of conservatism. They believe he can do to ISIS what he did to Vince McMahon's dome."

"Pro wrestling fans understand they are watching a contest that is usually fixed," adds Gergen. "More than anything, they want to be entertained." This gut instinct about his audience put Trump in great stead in the GOP debates where, in the estimation of Judd Legum, the editor-in-chief of Think-Progress.org, the entire slate of candidates proved to be no match for him: "Trump is behaving like a professional wrestler while Trump's opponents are conducting the race like a boxing match. As the rest of the field measures up their next jab, Trump decks them over the head with a metal chair."

———

The debates would lay the reality-TV groundwork for all that followed. The snippy contestants, the unpredictable star, the shifting alliances, the offstage histrionics became addictive, not only to the audience but also to the news establishment. The networks began to bank on the ad revenue that came from these unscripted, low-cost, highly anticipated programs, which proved a ratings bonanza. More debates were scheduled. The series snowballed. The star was given more and more airtime. The trivia of the race became magnified in the news cycle and in the culture.

When the Republican National Convention rolled around, Trump broke with tradition and decided to put in an appearance *all four nights*. And come the general election, he had a distinct advantage. While Hillary Clinton at her rallies would enlist the likes of Barbra and Bruce and Beyoncé, Trump, thanks to his fan base and his months of debate exposure, could draw on a wider audience that considered him on par with his fellow reality peeps and tweeters. He had the Kardashians *and* Kanye *and* the Hiltons. He had the Duck Dynasty crew *and* World Wrestling Entertainment, Inc. *Yentl* compared with Kimye? No contest. (As pure entertainment, Trump had already won. His show was *The Bachelorette*; Clinton's was a public-TV fund drive.)

Reality television and pro wrestling, however, were just the baseline. Trump's success came from his mastery across the mediasphere. He was the sultan of the piquant tweet.[7] He was the phantom of the radio-show phone-in

———

7. The *Washington Post*'s Jenna Johnson would note, as Trump was about to take office, "With one tweet last week, Trump inflamed a conflict with China. With another tweet on Tuesday, Trump caused Boeing stock to plummet. With a third on Wednesday night, Trump prompted a series of threatening calls to the home of a union leader who had called him a liar." (Jenna Johnson, "Donald Trump Attacks a Private Citizen on Twitter," *Washington Post*, December 8, 2016.)

(Alex Jones)[8] and the TV schmooze (*Morning Joe*, *Hannity*, and, one notable Sunday morning, CBS *and* NBC *and* Fox *and* CNN). Fox News founder Roger Ailes for a time was an unofficial Trump adviser.

Upon taking office, Trump—with his own star on the Hollywood Walk of Fame—would call in the media moguls. His treasury secretary Steven Mnuchin had invested in media companies and films (*Mad Max: Fury Road*; *The LEGO Movie*). Trump's chief White House strategist, Steve Bannon, had been a film-maker, Breitbart News executive, and shareholder in the *Seinfeld* franchise. Close Trump advisers included people as varied as Peter Thiel (the social-media and data-mining kingpin), Veterans Affairs point man Ike Perlmutter (who made a fortune off of action heroes at Marvel Entertainment), and Trump's son-in-law Jared Kushner (former publisher of the *New York Observer*). Trump's pick to head up the White House Strategic Development Group? Hollywood talent-agency CFO Chris Liddell. Trump's choice to lead the Small Business Administration? Linda McMahon, who'd helped start WWE, the pro-wrestling juggernaut.

More importantly, though, media and show biz were the oxygen that animated—indeed, validated—Trump's public persona. Here was a man whose Trump Tower office was plastered with magazine covers of himself. He'd played himself in movie cameos. He'd hosted *Saturday Night Live*. (When *SNL* made fun of his tweeting, however, Trump would take to Twitter to slam the show as "totally biased, not funny…just can't get any worse….Sad.")

While President Bush had not been a heavy news consumer (claiming he relied on "people on my staff who tell me what's happening in the world") and Obama had professed an aversion to cable punditry, Trump was an inveterate channel surfer. "He's the Hate-Watcher in Chief," in the words of *Times* columnist James Poniewozik. "Trump sees something in the news; he gets mad; he tweets; that becomes the news; repeat." None other than William Kristol, the neoconservative standard-bearer, would admit that the man he'd so devoutly bashed throughout the campaign "understands today's media better than the media understands themselves."[9]

---

8. Trump was known to call into Howard Stern's show. The low points: discussions of boob jobs, anal sex, and his wife's tidy bowel-related behavior. (Andrew Kaczynski, "Trump Isn't Into Anal, Melania Never Poops, and Other Things He Told Howard Stern," Buzzfeed.com, February 16, 2016; David Remnick, "American Demagogue," *New Yorker*, March 14, 2016.)

9. Adds millennial Tim Zahner, an online marketer, "In the age of 24/7 content and social media, we've reached 'clutter of voice.' And Trump knew that to break through that clutter he had to move to the

Trump World would become *The Truman Show, 2017.* The President-Protagonist, unlike Jim Carrey's character in the 1998 film, was not an unsuspecting patsy being "cammed" as part of a theme-park-style reality show. Instead, *The Trumpen Show* was a genre all its own. Its creators had taken control of the political backdrop of the nation, along with the theater curtain called the news media, and retrofitted it. And day and night, a riveted audience was presented with diatribes and pantomimes and magic acts while way, way up there, perched in the rafters, sat the marionettist. He was the President as the Wizard-Behind-the-Curtain. He was the Bannon & Bailey ringmaster. He was the Trumpen Prole puppeteer, watching and tweaking and tweeting and presiding. He was *The Trumpen Show*'s star *and* producer, a man tormented by negative reviews—and consumed with his box office numbers. He was *Donald ex machina.*

It sounds like hyperbole. But a good case can be made that a Trump presidency would never have been possible had the 1990s not normalized and formalized personal branding, reality programming, 24/7 news, tabloid scandal coverage, and online self-expression. Trump *was* his media echo. What's more, Trump seemed to understand that harnessing the twin-engine force of traditional media *and* social media was the new mode for asserting power, for manipulating public opinion (so as to acquire power), for humiliating or undermining others (who were *displaying too much* power), and for perpetually deflecting or diverting the influence of those in *other* power centers (so as to *maintain* power). Kim Kardashian knew it, ISIS knew it, Vladimir Putin knew it, Trump knew it.

Trump was *the* candidate for the press-processed age. Since the 1990s, voters had become more media-dependent than ever. More Americans had more digital screens in their lives and more time on their hands—including the housebound, the retired, the out-of-work. And they were absorbing and sharing more unvarnished opinion—from Rush (syndicated nationally since 1988), to Drudge (b. 1995), to Fox News (b. 1996), and their progeny—than in previous election cycles. Now, the televised, pundit-spun presidential race had *become* the race itself. And the Internet's inversion of the opinion bell curve had brought more extreme voices to the fore. The hard line—and attendant

extreme. We've seen this across society, pop culture, the Middle East. Trump knew that a loud and angry voice was more important than any policy he put forth." (Interview with Zahner.)

bile—was *intended* to push viewers', listeners', and readers' buttons. At the same time, many disaffected Americans were taking ideological refuge in the new boom of extremist online outlets, conspiracy newsletters, hate-mongering blogs, and synthetic news sites that were profiting off false and often scurrilous stories. Some sites were disavowed by the Trump camp; others, not so much. This was governing by the long lie—in an era when fabrication was made valid through ceaseless reiteration.

Nearly seventy years ago, there had been inklings. The German social theorist Theodor W. Adorno, of the influential Frankfurt School, had suffered firsthand under fascism's vise. And in 1949 he had prophesized the meshing of the virtual and the real, the lie and the truth, as well as the perpetual media manipulation in America—manipulation that would come to characterize the 1990s and the years ever after. Alex Ross, in the *New Yorker*, recently summarized Adorno's prescience vis-à-vis the current age: "As early as the forties, Adorno saw American life as a kind of reality show: 'Men are reduced to walk-on parts in a monster documentary film which has no spectators, since the least of them has his bit to do on the screen.' Now a businessman turned reality-show star has been elected President. Like it or not, Trump is as much a pop-culture phenomenon as he is a political one."

———

The election results augured a new and chilling American chapter. The alarming spike in post-election hate crimes and incidents of violence and harassment were clear evidence: certain voters felt that Trump's conquest had vindicated their views. And through it all, there was an unmistakably '90s tenor. The nation's politics were so polarized—and the culture-war battles had been fought for so long—that there was no avoiding it. In the 2016 campaign cycle, synthetic reality had been made flesh. Here, too, had come the Hillary backlash. The Bill flashbacks. The social-media addiction. The kinky dossiers. The tabloidism and venom and gutter talk. (In 1998, for the first time, the *New York Times* had run the word "fuck," and quite prominently—in reference to Clinton. In 2016, the *Times*'s front page quoted Trump *himself* using the words "fuck" and "pussy.")

The gutter, indeed. In some ways, the victory of Donald J. Trump would never have been conceivable had America not withstood, survived, and then assimilated the coarseness of the Naughty Nineties. How else would the electorate have been comfortable with a thrice-married president who had a fondness for fashion models, a history of hosting beauty contests, and a string of accusers describing harassment, unwanted advances, or assaults (all of whose claims he denied)? How else would Americans have voted for a candidate who would announce, "We're gonna knock the shit out of ISIS," and "You can tell [U.S. companies who return from overseas] to go"—mouthing the verb—"themselves"? How else to justify supporting a man who'd described his years of successfully avoiding STDs as "my personal Vietnam," or who'd once remarked, "I'm automatically attracted to beautiful [women]. I just start kissing them.... When you're a star they let you do it. You can do anything.... Grab 'em by the pussy"?

In very real ways, in Trump Times, the '90s were collapsing back into themselves. "Many of the same players have returned to the political stage," says my friend Henry Schuster, a TV news producer, "but they are fighting with bazookas now. On one side of the culture war you had the resurrected Clintons. You had Biden. You had Carville and Stephanopoulos, this time as commentators or news anchors. You even had a reborn David Brock—Saul, the Pharisee, had become Paul, the Apostle. On the other side there was Trump. There was Giuliani. And Newt and Callista Gingrich. And Ann Coulter, with a best-selling Trump book. And Kellyanne Conway, whose husband, George Conway III, had worked pro bono for Paula Jones's legal defense. And don't forget that Trump, before one of the Hillary debates, even resurrected three Clinton accusers—including Paula Jones."

Here, too, was Rupert Murdoch in the catbird seat. And Fox News, as state TV, airing Hannity and O'Reilly (until his 2017 ouster) in prime time. And sometime-Trump-ally Roger Stone, offstage right (the same political operative who had resigned from Bob Dole's campaign in 1996 after photos emerged from a supposed Stone "swinger" ad). And no less than *Pamela Anderson* hanging out with WikiLeaks founder Julian Assange after he'd disseminated the hacked emails of Hillary Clinton's team. It was a virtual Nineties reunion—for the kids in the naughty class.

"Let's face it," adds Schuster. "The Internet back then is where social media is now. In the '90s, the Drudge Report scooped *Newsweek*'s scoop on the Lewinsky scandal. And *The Starr Report* brought about the real explosion of the Web, the moment everyone went online to read a combination of politics and porn and soap opera. *Now* you have a candidate who becomes the president and *he's* the one playing the role of Matt Drudge. In Leninist terms, he's seized the means of production. He's tweeting. He's elevating hard-right news. He's trying to emasculate the mainstream press. And through social media he makes all facts and rules negotiable, all flaws seem like virtues.

"In the '90s we had a daily diet of news about a president's private affair, which embarrassed the nation—and most especially the First Lady, 'the wronged woman.' Now, we're so used to all the dirty politics and sex and scandal that it doesn't raise an eyebrow when the *New York Post* runs some old pictures of the First-Lady-to-be romping around nude, with another woman, for a photo shoot in a European magazine. This is how far we'd come. Many conservatives and evangelicals, who might otherwise look askance at a guy who'd marry a woman [depicted in] a sexy photo shoot, decided they'd rather attack *Hillary*. Their ends—getting pro-life judges on the Supreme Court— justified the means."

As if by some universal law of media physics, then, the Naughty Nineties had inevitably imploded to become the Tawdry Teens. All truth had become malleable, all secrets exposed. What's more, the same people who were repulsed by this new reality were also secretly fascinated. They watched *compulsively*, which is how we watch reality TV. "What if Donald Trump understood the Naughty Nineties better than any of us?" asks Schuster. "He's the one, after all, who managed to flip everything on its head."

Somehow there was a cold Karma to it all. The week of Trumph's victory, *Newsweek*'s Nina Burleigh would summarize it this way: "Amid Trump confirming the size of his manhood on national TV, the return of Bill Clinton's sexual-assault accusers and a nearly campaign-capsizing FBI announcement regarding Anthony Weiner's sexting, election 2016 was punctuated by penises—which is apt, since this often vitriolic campaign was a national referendum on women and power." And men and power. And race and power. And the substitution, in American politics, of rage for reason, entertainment for information, and nerve for experience.

True, Hillary Clinton had won the popular vote. But America got what an overwhelming share of the commonwealth had been asking for since the 1990s. In the electoral reckoning, civility had been trumped by hostility, respect by chauvinism, tolerance by bigotry, truth by fabrication and deceit, privacy by exposure, modesty by exhibitionism, achievement by fame, shame by shamelessness, and bridges by walls.

For this round, anyway.

Acknowledgments

This book would not have been possible without the support, encouragement, and infinite patience of Nancy and Sam.

I am also grateful beyond words to my parents and my brother, Richard, along with the entire Paulsen-Rooney-Nalle clan—and all of the Bermans. I have been guided throughout by the spirit of Molly. And Marc. And Janet. As well as Brad, Kevin, Ann, and Joe.

Hats off to Sean Desmond for staying the course and shaping the manuscript, and for mobilizing the entire Twelve Books cadre, including Libby Burton, Rachel Kambury, Carolyn Kurek, Brian McLendon, Paul Samuelson, Cheryl Smith, Michelle Figueroa, and Eric Rayman. Much bowing and scraping, too, to Jonathan Karp, Cary Goldstein, and Jamie Raab for signing up the book in the dark days of the recession. (Thanks to Deb Futter and Susan Lehman as well.)

I am beholden to Joy Harris for *everything*. She has been an anchor, a buoy, and a life preserver. *The Naughty Nineties*, furthermore, would not exist without the Research A-Team, led by the utterly indefatigable and kindhearted Julianne Pepitone Caughel. Hats off, as well, to the incomparable Cynthia Cotts, and to Matt Kapp and Ted Panken, resilient both.

I owe a deep debt to the generosity and goodwill of my longtime editor and friend Graydon Carter, who gave me the flexibility and confidence to pursue this project. I am also thankful for my steadfast confidants Chris Garrett, Aimée Bell, and Cullen Murphy, along with the entire *Vanity Fair* family. Harry and Gigi Benson were always in my corner. And the late Christopher Hitchens, an early supporter, urged me to throw in my lot with Twelve.

The idea for *The Naughty Nineties* came out of a dinner conversation with cardiologist Michael Mendelsohn, who related a tale about the discovery of the medicine that would eventually become Viagra—initially a heart drug that had one curious side effect. Mike will forever have my gratitude for his advice and unwavering friendship (Viv's, too), along with that of Howie and Marc, Kot and Karrie, and Lester and Peggy. Pam and Stuart were my sage supporters and advisers.

Huge thanks to my hosts Chez Rooney (in New Rochelle, New York, and Dorset, Vermont) and Chez Nalle (Newport, Rhode Island), and to Aidan Sullivan (for the Barbican digs) and the Riders (for their Fire Island "writer's colony"). My appreciation, as well, goes to the Adasheks, James Balog, Jon and Philippa Bender, Jessica Diner, John Frook, Anne and Sandy Halstead, Jeff and Michelene Hogan, Monica Lewinsky, David Moore, James Nachtwey, the entire Naudet family, Mary Beth O'Neill, Steven Reisner, Tracey Ryans and Cecile Barendsma, Liz and Bob Sauer, Aaron Schindler, Mark Seliger, the Silvermans, Tara and Bill Simko, Rachel Smith, Shelley Waln, Chris Whipple, and Bruce Wolf. Much love to Jackie and Juliet, Drew and Rita, David and Paulette, Betsy and Don, Cheryl and Abe, and Chet and Dori.

At my side, along the way: Sarah Bracy Penn, not to mention Isabel Ashton, Cat Buckley, Jack Deligter, Lenora Jane Estes, Jessica Flint, Mary Alice Miller, Lily Rothman, Becca Sobel, and Feifei Sun.

Cullen Murphy indulged me with his charitable offer to read the manuscript. He provided invaluable insight, as did a host of readers, who took on specific chapters, including Lucia Brawley, Susan Cheever, Stephen Claypole, Bronwyn Cosgrave, Jack Delighter, David Ewing Duncan, Steve Fine, Brett Forrest, Richard Friend, Ken George, Michael Kimmel, David Kirkpatrick, Marc Kravitz, Donald Liebenson, Carol J. C. Maxwell, Michael Mendelsohn, Amy Paulsen, Nancy Paulsen, Robert Rosen, Mark Rozzo, Luc Sante, Henry Schuster, Harriet Seitler, Aidan Sullivan, Kirsten Swinth, Sam Tanenhaus, Jim Warren, and Susan Zirinsky.

Some 260 people were kind enough to allow me to interview them, including Pravin Agravat, Woody Allen, Debby Applegate, Ken Aretsky, Judy Bachrach, James Balog, Tommy Baratta, Lisa Baron, Harry Benson, John Wayne Bobbitt, Lorena Bobbitt, Lucia Brawley, Susie Bright, David Brinkley, Douglas Brinkley, Simon Campbell, Patrick Carnes, James Carville, Michael Ciaravino, Stefanie Cohen, Ryan Cook, Bronwyn Cosgrave, Alan Cumming, "D.," Nicole Daedone, "Dani," Lanny Davis, Joey DelVecchio, Tony DiSanto, Michael Douglas, David Ewing Duncan, Sian Edwards-Beal, Abby Ellin, Peter Ellis, Emel, Bruce Feirstein, Donna Ferrato, Helen Fisher, Heidi Fleiss, Brett Forrest, Emily Jane Fox, Molly Friend, Richard Friend, Sam Friend, "Geraldine," Daniel Gerstein, Clive Gingell, Gary Ginsberg, Irwin

Goldstein, Scott Gutterson, Anthony Haden-Guest, George Hamilton, Bruce Handy, Dian Hanson, Harley, Art Harris, Jonathan Harris, Jack Hayford, Anita Hill, Christopher Hitchens, William Hultberg, Samir Husni, Jesse Jackson, Hana Jarklova, Abigail Jones, Paula Corbin Jones, Reese Jones, Sam Kashner, Jim Kennedy, Anne Kent, Michael Kimmel, David Kirkpatrick, Rob Klug, Steven Kotler, Steve Kroft, Monica Lewinsky, Nancy Libin, Donald Liebenson, Robert Longo, Douglas MacKinnon, Sari Markowitz, John Marquis, Katherine Martin, Mary Matalin, Steven Mauldin, Carol J. C. Maxwell, Stephen Mayes, Bill McCartney, Mark McKinnon, Michael Mendelsohn, Jane Metcalfe, Jessica Stern Meyer, Kate Michelman, Sunny Mindel, Mike Murphy, Dee Dee Myers, Rosie Nalle, Chris Napolitano, Jean-Jacques Naudet, Michael O'Brien, Ian Osterloh, Elisabeth Owen, Janea Padilha, Jonice Padilha, Joyce Padilha, J. P. Pappis, Joel Paul, Amy Paulsen, Nancy Paulsen, Dan Payne, Julianne Pepitone, Michael J. Peter, Drew Pinsky, Racheli, Jonathan Rauch, Howard Read, Judith Regan, Frank Rich, Jennifer Rider, Joan Rivers, Michael Rooney, Cindi Harwood Rose, Franklin Rose, Robert Rosen, Julian Sancton, Henry Schuster, Ella Schwalb, Lester Schwalb, Ingrid Sischy, Iva Roze Skoch, Sharon St. Romain-Frank, William Stayton, Patricia Steele, Aidan Sullivan, Madonna Swanson, Kirsten Swinth, Sam Tanenhaus, Zak Tanjeloff, Terry Teachout, Nick Terrett, "Tiffany," Stacy Tompkins, Anna Maria Tornaghi, Bruce Tulgan, Scott Turow, Jill Vermeire, Don Waitt, James Warren, Jamieson Webster, Joan Williams, Jim Windolf, Rachel Winter, Michael Wolff, and Tim Zahner.

I apologize to the many others who were gracious in granting me an interview but who, because of space, ended up on the cutting room floor, among them: Julia Allison, Samantha Appleton, (the woman formerly known as) Danni Ashe, Heike Bachmann, J. Ross Baughman, Patrick Baz, Brian Bedol, Leslie Bennetts, Lauren Bishop, Harold Bloom, Stephanie Bornstein, Jimmie Briggs, Jerry Burke, David Burnett, Stephen Claypole, David Cogan, Michael Davidson, Tracy Tucker Davis, Phil de Picciotto, Jamilla Deville, Billie Dixon, Ayperi Ecer, Maureen Egen, Robert Farrell, Colin Finlay, Elena Ochoa Foster, Carolina Garcia, Philip Gefter, Cary Goldstein, Andrew Hearst, Kathy Hilton, Jim Kelly, Larry Kirshbaum, J. L., Richard Land, Stuart Lefstein, "Lynn," Cindy Margolis, Jim McHugh, Charles Melcher, Doug Menuez, Christian Miranda, Edie Mirman, Alice Mohr, Fawnia Mondey, Tina Naiga, Nora Nalle, Nansci Neiman, Cheryl Norton, Kerry O'Day,

Beth Ouellette, Howard Owen, Terence Pepper, Joe Peyronnin, Eli Reed, Reza, David Rhodes, Leigh Ann Rooney, Erica Rose, Tracey Ryans, George Schlatter, William Seabloom, Mark Seliger, "Sherry and Scott," Ben Silverman, Gay Talese, Susan Trento, Linda Troeller, Madison Vain, Greg Van Alstyne, Neil Wexler, and Aly Zafonte.

I also want to recognize Cara Tripodi and those in recovery at STAR Sexual Trauma & Recovery in Wynnewood, Pennsylvania.

Key writing and research was done with the help of Soho House New York, the Larchmont and New Rochelle (New York) public libraries, the New York Public Library, and the William J. Clinton Presidential Library, in Little Rock, Arkansas. Big shout-outs to everyone on Kingsbury Road and to all my friends at the International Center of Photography, the W. Eugene Smith Memorial Fund, and the *Vanity Fair* photo department.

Additional thanks to Emin Acar, Ken Alexander, Barbara Alper, Melinda Anderson and John Moore, Sam Anson, Periel Aschenbrand, Derrick Ashong, Barry Avrich, Anna Badoian, John Banka, Tony Bannon, John Banta, the Barbashes, Bob Barnett, the Barrs, Christy Barry, Anne Beagan, Jonathan Becker, Ari Bergen, Sue and Chadd Berkun, Melanie Berliet, Chuck Berman, Nina Berman, Rich Bernstein, Justin Bishop, Carol Blue, Pete Bonventre, Adam Bookbinder, Patti Bosworth, Marie Brenner, Todd Brewster, the Brockways, Dana Brown, Dan Buck, Chuck Burack, Bobbi and Russell Burrows, Billy Bush, Andrew Bushell, Veronica Cagliero, Michael Callahan, Dan Callaro, Cindy Cathcart, Neil Cerutti, Deepak Chopra, Adam Ciralsky, Rich Clarkson, Stephen Claypole, Gwen and Alvin Clayton, Stefanie Cohen, Cindy and John Conroy, Barbara Corcoran, Charlotte Cotton, Stephan Crasnaenscki, Pat Craven, Kenneth Cummings, Gwen Davis, Wendy and Chuck Dickson, Chris Dixon, Adam Dolgins, Roberta Doyle, Keith Duval, Paul Elie, the Emmanuels, David Fahey, Michael Feinstein and Terrence Flannery, Mary Fiance, Ralph Fiennes, Colin Finlay, Hilary Fitzgibbons, Cynthia Fox, the Frames, Will Friedwald, Jim Gaines, Tim Geary, Jessica Glick, Risa Goldberg, Marti Golon, Suzzette Gomes, Linda Gomez, Mark Gompertz, Ben Greenman, Michelle Grey, Theresa Grill, Barbara Grossman and Michael Gross, Chris Guglielmo, Scott Gummer, Laura Haim, Nabil Hajaji, David Hajdu, Mary Ann Halford, Naomi Harris, Glen Hartley, Shelby Hartman, Marvin Heiferman, Tim Hetherington, Dan and Tom Higgins, Eric Himmel, David Hirshey, Jason Hodes, Mike Hogan,

Bill Hooper, Ann Hughes, Al Hunt, Bill Hunt, Punch Hutton, Alison Jackson, Laura Jacobs, Don and MaryEllen Johnston, Sebastian Junger, David Kamp, Shwan and Kim Karim, Michael Katsobashvili, Katherine Keating, Mara Keisling, Jon Kelly, David Hume Kennerly, George Kindel, Oren Kirnsky, Emma and Jonah Kravitz, Beth Kseniak, Eliane and J. P. Laffont, Leah Laiman, Brian and Linda Lanker, Beth Laski, John Leo, Regis Lesommier, Michael Levine, Amelia Levitan, John Levy, Ruth Levy, Anjali Lewis, the Loebs, John Loengard, Leslie Long and Larry Wall, Jay Lovinger, Matt Lynch, Nathalie Majlis, Kia Makarechi, the Manzaris, Sara Marks, Guy Martin, Pam McCarthy, the Meaneys, Stephanie Mehta, Susan Meiselas, Daniele Menache, Peter Meyer, John Middleton, Alison Morley, Chris Murray and Govinda Gallery, Sara Nelson, Dan Okrent, Alexander Olch, Maureen Orth, Howard Owen, Jamie Pallot, the Pcinados, Frank Pelligrino Jr., Jake Perlin, Nathaniel Philbrick, Robert Pledge, Henry Porter, Jeffrey Posternak, Todd Purdum, Jerry Rafshoon, J. Ralph, Tom Ramey, Janet Reeves, Ken Regan, Shiya Ribowsky, Michael Riedel, Fred Ritchin, Lisa Robinson, Barbara Romer, Jane Root, Clifford Ross, Shelley Ross, George Rush, Juliet Rylance, Marta Salas-Porras, Nancy Jo Sales, Peggy Samuels, Roger Sandler, Ira Sapir, Janice Saragoni, Jane Sarkin, Charlie Scheips, Mark Seal, Mohammed Sekhani, Mark Sennet, Henry Shaw, Samantha Shefts, Tala Skari, Rachel Sklar, Celeste Sloman, John Sloss, Marya Spence, Betsy Cannon Smith, Jeffrey Smith, Krista Smith, Sara Solfanelli, the Sommers, Robert Soros and Jamie Singer, Susan Squire, Dick Stolley, Doug Stumpf, Kevin Tedesco, Sabina and Richard Tompkins, Ralph Toporoff, Bryant Toth, Charles Traub, Joseph and Susan Trento, Mike Tucker and Petra Epperlein, Jean Ufer, Matt Ullian, the Vandenbelts, Helene Veret, the Vogelmans, Shawn Waldron, Tom Walker, Basil Walter, Robert Walsh, Dick Waterman, Susan Watts, the Welbers, Sheila Weller, Richard Weschler, Katic Whelan, Susan White, Isaiah Wilner, Alex Witchel, James Wolcott, Libby Wotipka, Gayle Wycoff, Andrew Wylie, and all the Zahners.

Finally, here's to SamFriendMusic.com and the New Orleans Swamp Donkeys. And much love to Molly's charmed circle: Greer, Nora, Rosie, Leigh Ann and Vanessa, Alex, Dwyer and Patrick, Hank and Rebecca, Eliot, Jake, Lauren, Raphaelle, Sandra, Lisa, Leslie, Katerina, Serena, and the whole gang, too numerous to name.

Sources

CHAPTER 1: A Wednesday in November

Interviews: Lucia Brawley, David Ewing Duncan, Michael Mendelsohn, Cullen Murphy.

American Psychological Association, "Study Shows a Significant Increase in Sexual Content on TV," apa.org, May 2001.

Nicholas Bakalar, "Triplet and Higher-Order Births in U.S. Down 41%," *New York Times*, May 30, 2016.

Jonathan Bernstein, "Surviving the Fall," *Spin*, October 1995, 126.

Andrew J. Cherlin, *The Marriage-Go-Round: The State of Marriage and the Family in America Today* (New York: Knopf, 2009), 15.

William J. Clinton, "Inaugural Address," January 20, 1993, American Presidency Project, University of California, Santa Barbara, www.presidency.ucsb.edu/ws/?pid=46366.

"Clinton Accused: Time Line," *Washington Post*, September 13, 1998, A32.

Adam Cohen, "The Speaker Who Never Was," *Time*, December 21, 1998.

Steve Conner, "Nobel Prize for Work That Led to Viagra Discovery," *Independent*, October 12, 1998.

Mary H. J. Farrell, "The Trumps Head for Divorce Court," *People*, February 26, 1990.

Sigmund Freud, *Civilization and Its Discontents* [1930] (New York: Norton, 1961), 44.

Steven M. Gillon, *The Pact: Bill Clinton, Newt Gingrich, and the Rivalry That Defined a Generation* (New York: Oxford University Press, 2008), 162.

Dan Gilgoff, *The Jesus Machine: How James Dobson, Focus on the Family, and Evangelical America Are Winning the Culture War* (New York: St. Martin's, 2008), 104.

Bill Glauber, "Diana to Spill the Royal Beans…," *Baltimore Sun*, November 15, 1995.

Carey Goldberg, "Redefining a Marriage Made New in Vermont," *New York Times*, December 26, 1999.

Hawes Publications, "The New York Times Best Seller List," Hawes.com, www.hawes.com/1995/1995-11-26.pdf. (Note: According to a *Times* spokesperson, the list is routinely announced on the preceding Wednesday.)

Marcia E. Herman-Giddens et al., "Secondary Sexual Characteristics and Menses in Young Girls Seen in Office Practice: A Study from the Pediatric Research in Office Settings Network," *Pediatrics* 99, no. 4 (April 1997).

Sean Holton, "It's History or Was It Just a Day at Hooters?," *Orlando Sentinel*, November 16, 1995.

"Inquiry into Calvin Klein Ads Dropped," Associated Press via *New York Times*, November 16, 1995.

Ryan Jaslow, "Aging Dads More Likely to Have Kids with Autism, ADHD, Schizophrenia and More," CBSNews.com, February 26, 2014.

"Justice Department Plans No Charges over Calvin Klein Ads," Associated Press via *Los Angeles Times*, November 16, 1995.

Gina Kolata, "U.S. Approves Sale of Impotence Pill; Huge Market Seen," *New York Times*, March 28, 1998.

Howard Kurtz, *Spin Cycle: Inside the Clinton Propaganda Machine* (New York: Free Press, 1998), 150.

Jennifer Latson, "The Princess Diana TV Interview That Made History," Time.com, November 20, 2014.

Mark Leibovich, "Being Hillary," *New York Times Magazine*, July 19, 2015, 52.

Michael D. Lemonick, "Teens Before Their Time," *Time*, October 22, 2000.

Robert Lenzner, "The Bernanke Bull Market Is the Third Strongest in Modern Stock Market History," *Forbes*, July 22, 2013.

David Leonhardt and Geraldine Fabrikant, "After 30-Year Run, Rise of the Super-Rich Hits a Sobering Wall," *New York Times*, August 21, 2009, A1, 16.

Herbert Marcuse, *Eros and Civilization: A Philosophical Inquiry into Freud* [1955] (New York: Vintage, 1962), vii–x, 3, 183–85, 193–97.

Claire Cain Miller, "The Divorce Surge Is Over, but the Myth Lives On," *New York Times*, December 2, 2014.

Brian Naylor, "Not-So-Fond Memories from the Last Government Shutdowns," NPR.org, September 20, 2013.

"Netscape Announces Plan to Split Stock 2-for-1," Bloomberg Business News via *New York Times*, November 15, 1995.

Frank Newport, "Presidential Job Approval: Bill Clinton's High Ratings in the Midst of Crisis, 1998," Gallup.com, June 4, 1999.

"The Nobel Prize in Physiology or Medicine 1998" (press release), NobelPrize.org, October 12, 1998, www.nobelprize.org/nobel_prizes/medicine/laureates/1998/press.html.

Ashley Reich, "Newt Gingrich: Marriages, Divorces, Affairs Timeline," *Huffington Post*, May 11, 2011.

Joshua Rich, "Countdown! The 10 Best Bond Girls," *Entertainment Weekly*, March 30, 2007.

Lydia Saad, "Americans Choose 'Pro-Choice' for First Time in Seven Years," Gallup.com, May 29, 2015.

David Sanger, "Government Shutdown Cost Is Estimated at $700 Million," *New York Times*, November 23, 1995.

Janny Scott, "A Media Race Enters Waters Still Uncharted," *New York Times*, February 1, 1998, A1, 19.

David Segal, "Hooters Vows to Decide Where the Boys Aren't," *Washington Post*, November 16, 1995.

———, "Naming the '00s," *New York Times*, November 15, 2001.

Leonard Sloane, "Broad-Based Stock Rally Is Continuing," *New York Times*, November 17, 1995.

Donald J. Trump, "The Inaugural Address," January 20, 2017, www.whitehouse.gov/inaugural-address.

Louis Uchitelle, "The Richest of the Rich, Proud of a New Gilded Age," *New York Times*, July 15, 2007.

Josh Voorhees, "The *New York Times* Drops an F-Bomb, but Was It the Grey Lady's First?," *Slate*, August 26, 2013.

Washington Post, eds., *The Starr Report: The Findings of Independent Counsel Kenneth W. Starr on President Clinton and the Lewinsky Affair* (New York: PublicAffairs, 1998), xiii, 50–52.

Elizabeth Weil, "The Incredible Shrinking Childhood: How Early Is Too Early for Puberty?," *New York Times Magazine*, April 1, 2012, 32–33.

Paul Weyrich, "Letter to Conservatives," February 16, 1999, www.nationalcenter.org/Weyrich299.html.

CHAPTER 2: Down the Rabbit Hole

Interviews: Michael Davidson, Helen Fisher, Richard Friend, Peggy Samuels, Harriet Seitler, Jamieson Webster.

Daniel J. Boorstin, *The Image: A Guide to Pseudo-Events in America* [1962] (New York: Vintage, 1992).

David Brooks, *Bobos in Paradise: The New Upper Class and How They Got There* (New York: Simon & Schuster, 2000), 10–11.

Candace Bushnell, *Sex and the City* (New York: Grand Central, 1996), vii–viii, 54, 61.

———, "Sex and the City: New York's Last Seduction—Loving Mr. Big," *New York Observer*, April 24, 1995.

Tamal M. Edwards, "Who Needs a Husband?: Single by Choice," *Time*, August 28, 2000.

Helen Fisher, *Anatomy of Love: A Natural History of Mating, Marriage, and Why We Stray* (New York: Ballantine, 1994), 72, 154, 164.

———, "Why We Love, Why We Cheat," TED Talk, September 2006, www.ted.com/speakers/helen_fisher.html.

Michel Foucault, *The History of Sexuality*, vol. 1, *An Introduction* [1976] (New York: Vintage, 1990), 3–5, 32–33, 47–48, 156.

Margaret Mead, *Coming of Age in Samoa: A Psychological Study of Primitive Youth for Western Civilization* [1928] (New York: HarperCollins, 2001).

Desmond Morris, *The Naked Ape: A Zoologist's Study of the Human Animal* (New York: McGraw-Hill, 1967).

"Most Memorable Quotes from 'Sex and the City,'" *New York Daily News*, May 16, 2008.

Douglas Palmer, *Seven Million Years: The Story of Human Evolution* (London: Phoenix, 2006).

Amy Sohn, *Sex and the City: Kiss and Tell* (New York: Pocket, 2004).

Margaret Talbot, "Girls Will Be Girls," *New Yorker*, April 16, 2012, 39.

Timothy Taylor, *The Prehistory of Sex: Four Million Years of Human Sexual Culture* (New York: Bantam, 1997).

Nicholas Wade, *Before the Dawn: Recovering the Lost History of Our Ancestors* (New York: Penguin, 2006).

Heather Wagner, "How Sex Changed the City," VanityFair.com, May 27, 2010.

CHAPTER 3: The Night We Met the Clintons

Interviews: James Carville, Gary Ginsberg, Jim Kennedy, Steve Kroft, Mary Matalin, Mark McKinnon, Mike Murphy, Dee Dee Myers.

Peter Baker and Lorraine Adams, "Clinton Team Picks Apart Jones's Life," *Washington Post*, February 23, 1998.

Dan Balz, "Clinton Concedes Marital 'Wrongdoing,'" *Washington Post*, January 27, 1992, A1.

Richard L. Berke, "Democrats Hope to Persuade Voters to Tune In to Tradition," *New York Times*, July 6, 1992.

Sidney Blumenthal, "The Secret War for the White House," *Vanity Fair*, June 1992, 60–64.

David Brock, "Living with the Clintons," *American Spectator*, January 1994.

John Carmody, "The TV Column," *Washington Post*, January 28, 1992.

George J. Church, "Is Bill Clinton for Real?," *Time*, January 27, 1992.

Francis X. Clines, "At Breakfast with Godfrey (Budge) Sperling, Jr.; Politicians and the Press, Once Over," *New York Times*, January 10, 1996.

Bill Clinton, "Dukakis Nomination as Presidential Candidate," C-SPAN Video Library, July 20, 1988.

————, *My Life* (New York: Vintage, 2005) 385–86.

Hillary Rodham Clinton, *Living History* (New York: Scribner, 2003), 107.

E. J. Dionne Jr., "Clinton Traces Decision Not to Run for President to Family Obligations," *New York Times*, August 16, 1987.

Maureen Dowd, "The Comeback Vegan," *New York Times*, September 5, 2012, A27.

"Excerpts from Depositions Taken by Clinton's Lawyer, Gennifer Flowers," *New York Daily News*, March 21, 1998.

"Gennifer Flowers," CNN.com, 1996, http://cgi.cnn.com/ALLPOLITICS/1996/candidates/democrat/clinton/skeletons/flowers.shtml.

Gennifer Flowers with Jacquelyn Dapper, *Passion and Betrayal* (Del Mar, CA: Emery Dalton, 1995), 1–6, 54, 86–91, 95, 103, 157–58.

Ken Gormley, *The Death of American Virtue: Clinton vs. Starr* (New York: Broadway, 2010), 177–78.

Chris Hegedus and D. A. Pennebaker, directors, *The War Room*, 1993, produced by R. J. Cutler, Wendy Ettinger, and Frazer Pennebaker.

Don Hewitt, *Tell Me a Story* (New York: PublicAffairs, 2002), 183.

"In 1992, Clinton Conceded Marital 'Wrongdoing,'" *Washington Post*, January 26, 1992.

Joe Klein, "Bill Clinton: Who Is This Guy?," *New York*, January 20, 1992.

Steve Kornacki, "When Bill Clinton Died Onstage," *Salon*, July 30, 2012.

Steve Kroft, "Governor & Mrs. Clinton," *60 Minutes*, CBS News, January 26, 1992, produced by L. Franklin Devine, available at www.youtube.com/watch?v=lwXE52e9JFg.

Howard Kurtz, *Spin Cycle: Inside the Clinton Propaganda Machine* (New York: Free Press, 1998), 150.

Gene Lyons, "The Roots of the Clinton Smear," *Salon*, February 5, 1998.

Norman Mailer, "Tough Guys Don't Dance" (book excerpt), *Vanity Fair*, August 2002, 79.

David Maraniss, *First in His Class: A Biography of Bill Clinton* (New York: Touchstone, 1995), 438–41.

Mary Matalin and James Carville with Peter Knobler, *All's Fair: Love, War, and Running for President* (New York: Touchstone, 1995), 6–7, 103–11.

Dick Morris, *Behind the Oval Office: Getting Reelected Against All Odds* (New York: St. Martin's, 1999), xxx.

"My 12-Year Affair Bill Clinton," *Star*, February 6, 1992.

"Political Rivals to Marital Partners," *New York Times*, November 26, 1993.

Thomas B. Rosenstiel, "Clinton Allegation Raises Questions on Media's Role," *Los Angeles Times*, January 29, 1992.

Gail Sheehy, "Hillary's Choice," *Vanity Fair*, February 1999.

Hedrick Smith, *The People and the Power Game*, PBS, 1996, Hedrick Smith Productions in association with South Carolina Educational Television, produced by Pat Roddy and Barak Goodman.

George Stephanopoulos, *All Too Human: A Political Education* (Boston: Little, Brown, 1999), 31, 54, 56–62, 64–67.

David Stout, "Testing of a President: The Other Woman; Flowers Acknowledges Earning $500,000 from Scandal," *New York Times*, March 21, 1998.

Pat Summerall and Jon Madden, "Super Bowl XXVI," video courtesy CBS Sports via CBS News, January 26, 1992.

Michael Takiff, *A Complicated Man: The Life of Bill Clinton as Told by Those Who Know Him* (New Haven, CT: Yale University Press, 2010), 113.

Clive Thompson, "The Blog Establishment: The Early Years," NYMag.com, http://nymag.com/news/media/15971/.

CHAPTER 4: The Bubba Boomer

Interviews: Harry Benson, Douglas Brinkley, Dee Dee Myers, J. P. Pappis, Nancy Paulsen, Jamieson Webster.

R. W. Apple Jr., "Edward S. Muskie" (obituary), *New York Times*, March 27, 1996.

Karen Ball, "It's in the Cards," *New Yorker*, March 31, 1997, 35.

Paul Begala, "The Worst Generation," *Esquire*, April 2000.

William J. Bennett, *The Death of Outrage: Bill Clinton and the Assault on American Ideals* (New York: Touchstone, 1999), 24.

Harry Benson, *First Families: An Intimate Portrait from the Kennedys to the Clintons*, edited by Gigi Benson and David Friend (Boston: Bulfinch, 1997), 122–23.

Donald Bernhardt and Marshall Eckblad, "Black Monday: The Stock Market Crash of 1987," FederalReserve History.org.

"Bill Loves Bill," *New York Post*, "Page Six," September 30, 2000.

Karen Breslau, "Hillary Clinton's Emotional Moment," *Newsweek*, January 6, 2008.

William F. Buckley Jr. and Harry Benson, "The Way They Are," *Vanity Fair*, June 1985.

David G. Cannon, *Hey, Bubba!: A Metaphysical Guide to the Good Ol' Boy* (Atlanta: Peachtree, 1990), vii, 3–9, 28, 73.

Graydon Carter and David Friend, eds., *Vanity Fair's Hollywood* (New York: Viking Studio, 2000), 10–11.

Eleanor Clift, "Shooting Down Birds—And Rumors," *Newsweek*, January 9, 1994.

Bill Clinton, *My Life* (New York: Random House/Vintage, 2004), 4, 8–15, 19–26, 30–31, 39–40, 48–52, 55–63, 67, 246, 315, 365–66.

———, "Interview on MTV's 'Enough Is Enough' Forum," April 19, 1994, American Presidency Project, University of California, Santa Barbara, www.presidency.ucsb.edu/ws/?pid=49995.

———, "Remarks at the DNC," delivered September 5, 2012, Charlotte, NC, via CBSNews.com, www.cbsnews.com/news/transcript-bill-clintons-remarks-at-the-dnc/.

Robert Dallek, *Flawed Giant: Lyndon B. Johnson and His Times, 1961–1975* (New York: Oxford University Press, 1998), 491.

Ann Devroy, "A Bonding Experience at Camp David," *Washington Post*, February 5, 1993.

———, "Camp David Sessions Set Distinct Tone—Clinton Aides and Cabinet Join in Teamwork Exercises," *Washington Post*, February 7, 1993.

"'Doonesbury' at 35: Still Spry or Showing Its Age?," *Editor & Publisher*, November 12, 2005.

Maureen Dowd, "Fighting the Wimp Factor," *New York Times*, February 16, 2000.

Michael Duffy and Dan Goodgame, "Warrior for the Status Quo" [Box: "Atwater on Defeating Bush"], *Time*, August 24, 1992, 35.

Laura Fitzpatrick, "Top 10 MTV Moments," Time.com, February 10, 2010.

Gennifer Flowers with Jacquelyn Dapper, *Passion and Betrayal* (Del Mar, CA: Emery Dalton, 1995), 77.

David Friend, "Nobody Loved It Better," *Vanity Fair*, December 2000.

———, *Watching the World Change: The Stories Behind the Images of 9/11* (New York: Farrar, Straus & Giroux, 2006), 61.

"The Choice '96," interview with Paul Greenberg, *Frontline*, PBS, www.pbs.org/wgbh/pages/frontline/shows/choice/bill/greenberg.html.

Steve Gillon, *Boomer Nation: The Largest and Richest Generation Ever and How It Changed America* (New York: Free Press, 2004), 2–4, 8, 13.

Elisabeth Goodridge, "Front-Runner Ed Muskie's Tears (or Melted Snow?) Hurt His Presidential Bid," *U.S. News & World Report*, January 17, 2008.

Paul Greenberg, "Why Yes, I Did Dub Bill Clinton 'Slick Willie,'" *Free Lance–Star* (Fredericksburg, VA), June 28, 2004.

Jack Healy, "Dow, First Time in a Year, Breaks Through 10,000," *New York Times*, October 14, 2009.

Chris Hegedus and D. A. Pennebaker, directors, *The War Room*, 1993, produced by R. J. Cutler, Wendy Ettinger, and Frazer Pennebaker.

David Itzkoff, "Comedy Ahead of Its Time (If That Time Ever Comes)," *New York Times*, May 7, 2009.

Douglas Jehl, "Bill, Hillary and Other Plain Folks Are All Set for One Heady Weekend," *New York Times*, December 31, 1993.

———, "A Mustang and a Boy Named Bill," *New York Times*, April 18, 1994.

Virginia Kelley with James Morgan, *Leading with My Heart* (New York: Simon & Schuster, 1994), 296.

Michael Kinsley, "The Least We Can Do," *Atlantic*, October 2010, 62–72.

Joe Klein, *The Natural: The Misunderstood Presidency of Bill Clinton* (New York: Doubleday, 2002), 59.

Michael Kruse, "The Woman Who Made Hillary Cry," Politico.com, April 21, 2015.

Howard Kurtz, *Spin Cycle: Inside the Clinton Propaganda Machine* (New York: Free Press, 1998), 71–73.

Wendy Leigh, "Marilyn and Jackie's 11-Year Itch," *Guardian*, June 22, 2003.

David Maraniss, *First in His Class: A Biography of Bill Clinton* (New York: Touchstone, 1995), 21–31, 39–41.

Mary Matalin and James Carville with Peter Knobler, *All's Fair: Love, War, and Running for President* (New York: Touchstone, 1995), 85, 129–31.

Bill Maxwell, "Clinton's Earthy, Southern Personality Allows the Bashers to Get Personal," *Gainesville (FL) Sun*, June 3, 1994.

———, "Who Is 'Bubba' Anyway and What Is 'the Bubba Factor'?," *Gainesville (FL) Sun*, March 20, 1992.

Kevin Merida, "It's Come to This: A Nickname That's Proven Hard to Slip," *Washington Post*, December 20, 1998.

Dick Morris, *Behind the Oval Office: Getting Reelected Against All Odds* (New York: St. Martin's, 1999), xiv, xviii, xxvi–vii, xxxii, 31, 84.

Joyce Carol Oates, "The Woman Before Hillary" (review of Virginia Kelley's *Leading with My Heart*), *New York Times Book Review*, May 8, 1994.

"Oil Prices Up 87 Cents at Year-End," Associated Press via *New York Times*, January 1, 1991.

"Petroleum Chronology of Events 1970–2000," U.S. Energy Information Administration, www.eia.gov.

John Powers, "The Kennedy Mystique Explained in Ten Words," Vogue.com, November 11, 2013.

Todd S. Purdum, "In Brief Visit, Clinton Shmoozes at Renaissance Meeting," *New York Times*, January 1, 1995.

———, "At Home with Virginia Kelley; Bets Dark Horses. Raised One, Too," *New York Times*, August 13, 1992.

Andrew Rosenthal, "Bush Encounters the Supermarket, Amazed," *New York Times*, February 5, 1992.

Shelley Ross, *Fall from Grace: Sex, Scandal, and Corruption in American Politics from 1702 to the Present* (New York: Ballantine, 1988), xiii–xv.

William Safire, "Bubba, Can You Paradigm?," *New York Times*, October 21, 1990.

———, *Safire's Political Dictionary* (Oxford: Oxford University Press, 2008, based on Random House Reference, 1993), 85.

Gail Sheehy, "Hillary's Choice," *Vanity Fair*, February 1999.

Philip Sherwell, "Bill Clinton's Temper May Be a Liability for Hillary," *Telegraph*, January 19, 2008.

John Solomon, "A Wimp He Wasn't," *Newsweek*, March 20, 2011.

Steven D. Stark, "Practicing Inclusion, Consensus: Clinton's Feminization of Politics," *Los Angeles Times*, March 14, 1993.

Jennifer Steinhauer, "John Boehner and the Politics of Crying," *New York Times*, November 7, 2010, WK4.

George Stephanopoulos, *All Too Human: A Political Education* (Boston: Little, Brown, 1999), 135–36.

Sara Stewart, "All the President's Women," *New York Post*, November 10, 2013.

Ben Train, "Air Elvis," *Vanity Fair*, October 1992, 84.

G. B. Trudeau, "G. B. Trudeau's Doonesbury" (syndicated cartoon strip, *Washington Post*), November 3, 1984, doonesbury.washingtonpost.com/strip/archive/timeline/1980.

R. Emmett Tyrrell Jr., "Adding Up the Election's Most Telling Results," *Washington Times*, November 8, 1992.

Celia Walden, "As Francois Hollande Visits America, Will Women Swoon over This Gallic Lothario?," *Telegraph*, February 10, 2014.

Margaret Garrard Warner, "Bush Battles the 'Wimp Factor,'" *Newsweek*, October 19, 1987.

Jennifer Warren, "For Clinton Press Aide, Climb Was Steep, Rapid," *Los Angeles Times*, October 14, 1992.

Marjorie Williams, "Day of the Jackals," *Vanity Fair*, November 1996, 88.

———, "Love on the Run," *Vanity Fair*, July 1994, 78.

Michael Wolff, "The Kennedys: Is Sex Part of History?," Newser.com, February 18, 2010.

Bob Woodward, *The Agenda: Inside the Clinton White House* (New York: Simon & Schuster, 1994), 28, 255, 278–80, 324.

CHAPTER 5: On the Third Wave

Interviews: Susie Bright, Alan Cumming, Julianne Pepitone, Kirsten Swinth, Jill Vermeire.

Jennifer Baumgardner and Amy Richards, *Manifesta: Young Women, Feminism, and the Future* [2000] (New York: Farrar, Straus & Giroux, 2010), xii, 14–15, 21, 79, 91–92, 130–37, 242–43, 255, 276, 290–91.

Sarah Boxer, "One Casualty of the Women's Movement," *New York Times*, December 14, 1997.

Sarah Crichton with Debra Rosenberg, "Sexual Correctness: Has It Gone Too Far?," *Newsweek*, October 25, 1993.

Lizzie Crocker, "Stop Moaning About Women's Soccer Pay," *Daily Beast*, July 10, 2015.

Charles R. Cross, *Heavier Than Heaven: A Biography of Kurt Cobain* (New York: Hyperion, 2001), 167–69.

Barbara Crossette, "An Old Scourge of War Becomes Its Latest Crime," *New York Times*, June 14, 1998.

David Davis, "How the Most Iconic Photo in Women's Soccer Was Almost Never Taken," Deadspin.com, June 8, 2015.

Clarissa Pinkola Estés, *Women Who Run with the Wolves: Myths and Stories of the Wild Woman Archetype* [1992] (New York: Ballantine, 1997), 498.

Susan Faludi, *Backlash: The Undeclared War Against American Women* [1991] (New York: Three Rivers, 2006), xi–xii, 10–11, 243, 461, 466.

Ann Friedman, "Stop Pitting Women Against Each Other over Hillary Clinton," The Cut, NYMag.com, February 9, 2016.

Tad Friend, "Yes" (or "The Rise of 'Do Me' Feminism"), *Esquire*, February 1994, 47–56.

John Gallagher, "Attack of the 50-Foot Lesbian," *Advocate*, October 1994.

Steve Gillon, *Boomer Nation: The Largest and Richest Generation Ever and How It Changed America* (New York: Free Press, 2004), 202.

Sander L. Gilman, *Making the Body Beautiful: A Cultural History of Aesthetic Surgery* (Princeton, NJ: Princeton University Press, 1999), 244–45.

Melinda Henneberger, "Naomi Wolf, Feminist Consultant to Gore, Clarifies Her Campaign Role," *New York Times*, November 5, 1999.

Kim Hubbard, "The Tyranny of Beauty," *People*, June 24, 1991.

Kay S. Hymowitz, *Manning Up: How the Rise of Women Has Turned Men into Boys* (New York: Basic Books, 2011), 58, 67–71.

Caryn James, "Critic's Notebook: Feminine Beauty as a Masculine Plot," *New York Times*, May 7, 1991.

Michael Kimmel and Gloria Steinem, "'Yes' Is Better Than 'No,'" *New York Times*, September 5, 2014, A27.

Rick Koster, "Lilith Fair-ness," *Houston Press*, July 31, 1997.

Claire Landsbaum, "How the Success of Marvel's Female Superheroes Heralds a More Inclusive Age of Comics," Vulture.com, May 21, 2015.

Neil A. Lewis, "In Selecting Federal Judges, Clinton Has Not Tried to Reverse Republicans," *New York Times*, August 1, 1996.

M. G. Lord, "This Pinup Drives Eggheads Wild," *Newsday*, October 6, 1991.

Charles McGrath, "Why a Fallen Angel Is a Centerfold," *New York Times*, November 6, 2011, SR5.

Terry McMillan, *Waiting to Exhale* [1992] (New York: NAL, 2006), 101, 213, 346–48, 398.

Sara Marcus, *Girls to the Front: The True Story of the Riot Grrrl Revolution* (New York: Harper Perennial, 2010), 16, 19, 25–27, 38, 42, 76–81, 89.

Michele Moses, "Erasing Feminism from Take Our Daughters to Work Day," *New Yorker*, May 13, 2015.

Rebecca Munford, "Wake Up and Smell the Lipgloss: Gender, Generation and the (A)politics of Girl Power," in *Third Wave Feminism: A Critical Exploration*, edited by Stacy Gillis, Gillian Howie, and Rebecca Munford (Basingstoke, Hampshire: Palgrave Macmillan, 2004), 266–274.

Dee Dee Myers, *Why Women Should Rule the World* (New York: HarperCollins, 2008), 88–89.

Clarence Page, " 'Thelma & Louise': A Reel-Life Tale of Women and Power," *Chicago Tribune*, June 12, 1991.

Camille Paglia, "Perspective Needed—Feminism's Life: Denying Reality About Sexual Power and Rape," *Newsday* via *Seattle Times*, February 17, 1991.

———, *Sex, Art, and American Culture: Essays* (New York: Vintage, 1992), xi, 24, 37, 49–54, 68, 101–24, 242, 264–65, 269, 303–5, 319.

———, *Sexual Personae: Art and Decadence from Nefertiti to Emily Dickinson* (New York: Vintage, 1991), 5–12, 17–20, 23, 27–31.

Lisa Palac, *The Edge of the Bed: How Dirty Pictures Changed My Life* (Boston: Little, Brown, 1997), 160.

Ashley Parker, "Road Trip Helps Romney Brush Up on Banter," *New York Times*, June 18, 2012.

Marc Peyser and Johnnie L. Roberts, "The Katie Factor," *Newsweek*, April 17, 2006.

Mary Pipher, *Reviving Ophelia: Saving the Selves of Adolescent Girls* (New York: Ballantine, 1994), 12–13, 23, 27–28, 53, 70, 218–19.

Carla Power, "Sex Objects, Sex Subjects," *Newsweek*, January 5, 1998.

"Progressive Era to New Era, 1900–1929: Women's Suffrage in the Progressive Era," Library of Congress, loc.gov/teachers.

Katie Roiphe, "Date Rape Hysteria," *New York Times*, November 20, 1991.

Melena Ryzik, "A Feminist Riot That Still Inspires," *New York Times*, June 5, 2011, AR20.

David Sheff, "Playboy Interview: Camille Paglia," *Playboy*, May 1995.

Francesca Stanfill, "Woman Warrior," *New York*, March 4, 1991.

Alessandra Stanley, "Semantics Stalls Pact Labeling Rape as a War Crime," *New York Times*, July 9, 1998, A3.

Betsey Stevenson, "Title IX and the Evolution of High School Sports," *Contemporary Economic Policy* 25 (2007): 486–505.

Katie Thomas, "Sexual Violence: Weapon of War," *Forced Migration Review*, January 2007, 16.

Karen Tumulty, "Twenty Years On, 'The Year of the Woman' Fades," *Washington Post*, March 24, 2012.

Brad Tuttle, "Women's Soccer Gets a Parade and Huge TV Ratings, but Not Equal Pay," *Money*, July 10, 2015.

Sheila Weller, "The Ride of a Lifetime: The Making of Thelma & Louise," *Vanity Fair*, March 2011.

Naomi Wolf, *The Beauty Myth: How Images of Beauty Are Used Against Women* [1991] (New York: Harper Perennial, 2002), 10–13, 16, 171, 208, 281.

CHAPTER 6: Empowerment Icons

Interviews: Bruce Handy, Anita Hill, Jim Kelly, Joel Paul, Terence Pepper, Howard Read, Ingrid Sischy, Joan Williams.

Jill Abramson, "Women on the Verge of the Law: From Anita Hill to Sonia Sotomayor," *New York Times*, July 18, 2009, WK1, 3.

"ASME's Top 40 Magazine Covers of the Last 40 Years," American Society of Magazine Editors, Magazine.org, October 17, 2005.

Peter Baker and Amy Chozik, "Hillary Clinton's History as First Lady: Powerful, but Not Always Deft," *New York Times*, December 5, 2014, A1, 13.

"Biden Runs Better Than Clinton Against Top Republicans" (press release), Quinnipiac University, August 27, 2015.

David Brock, *Blinded by the Right: Confessions of an Ex-Conservative* (New York: Three Rivers, 2002), 95, 100–102, 107, 121–24, 259, 270, 346–48.

———, *The Real Anita Hill: The Untold Story* (New York: Free Press, 1993).

David Brooks, "Hillary Clinton's Big Test," *New York Times*, March 13, 2015, A29.

Libby Brooks, "Gay for Today," *Guardian*, November 2, 1999.

Roger Catlin, "You Can Tell This Book by Its Cover," *Hartford Courant*, October 21, 1992.

"Chicago Gay & Lesbian International Film Festival: *The Real Ellen Story*," *Chicago Reader*, November 12, 1998.

Amy Chozik, "Clinton Faces Test of Record Aiding Women," *New York Times*, March 9, 2015, A1, 11.

Hillary Rodham Clinton, *Living History* (New York: Scribner, 2003), 119.

———, "Remarks to the U.N. 4th World Conference on Women, Plenary Session," Beijing, September 5, 1995, www.americanrhetoric.com/speeches/hillaryclintonbeijingspeech.htm.

Adam Clymer, "Strom Thurmond, Foe of Integration, Dies at 100," *New York Times*, June 27, 2003.

Andrew Cohen, "The Sad Legacy of Robert Bork," *Atlantic*, December 2012.

Nancy Collins and Annie Leibovitz, "Demi's Big Moment," *Vanity Fair*, August 1991, 8, 96–101.

Jennet Conant and Annie Leibovitz, "Demi's Body Language," *Vanity Fair*, August 1992, 118.

Michael Crowley, "Sen. Orrin Hatch," *Slate*, February 20, 2004.

Elizabeth Diaz, "Hillary Clinton: Anchored by Faith," *Time* (special issue), *Hillary: An American Life*, June 27, 2014.

Maureen Dowd, "Supremely Bad Judgment," *New York Times*, October 24, 2010.

———, "When Hillary Killed Feminism," *New York Times*, February 14, 2016, SR9.

Alan Duke, "Strom Thurmond's Secret Biracial Daughter Dies at 87," CNN.com, February 6, 2013.

"Ellen to Dine with President," Reuters via ABCNews.com, November 6, 1997.

Priya Elan, "Looking Back at Madonna and *Sex*," *Guardian*, April 25, 2012.

Em & Lo, "Of MILF and Men," *New York Times Magazine*, April 22, 2007.

Emma Green, "A Lot Has Changed in Congress Since 1992, the 'Year of the Woman,'" *Atlantic*, September 2013.

Jim Farber, "Dancers in Madonna's 'Truth or Dare' Had Truths of Their Own," *New York Times*, April 13, 2016, C1, 6.

Thomas Friedman, "Moore's Law Turns 50," *New York Times*, May 13, 2015, A27.

David Friend, in *Vanity Fair 100 Years: From the Jazz Age to Our Age*, edited by Graydon Carter with David Friend (New York: Abrams, 2013), 292–93.

———, "Vanity Fair, 1983–Now: A New Magazine for a New Age," in *Vanity Fair: The Portraits: A Century of Iconic Images*, edited by Graydon Carter with David Friend (New York: Abrams, 2008), 23.

Vicki Goldberg, "Madonna's Book: Sex, and Not Like a Virgin," *New York Times*, October 25, 1992.

Andrew Goldman, "Anita Hill's Long Memory," *New York Times*, September 30, 2011.

Marcia D. Greenberger, "What Anita Hill Did for America," CNN.com, Oct. 22, 2010.

Linda Greenhouse, "Bork's Nomination is Rejected, 58–42; Reagan 'Saddened,'" *New York Times*, October 24, 1987.

———, "Supreme Court Rejects Clinton's Request for Delay in Paula Jones Suit," *New York Times*, May 28, 1997.

Bruce Handy, "Roll Over, Ward Cleaver," *Time*, April 14, 1997.

Patrick Healy, "Early in 2016 Race, Clinton's Toughest Foe Appears to Be the News Media," *New York Times*, March 12, 2015, A18.

Bill Hewitt, "She Could Not Keep Silent," *People*, October 28, 1991.

Anita Hill, "The Smear This Time," *New York Times*, October 2, 2007.

Christopher Hitchens, "What's Love Got to Do with It?," *Vanity Fair*, September 1993, 74–80.

Stephen Holden, "Madonna Makes a $600 Million Deal," *New York Times*, April 20, 1992.

———, "Madonna Video Goes Too Far for MTV," *New York Times*, November 28, 1990.

Caryn James, "Beneath All That Black Lace Beats the Heart of a Bimbo...," *New York Times*, December 16, 1990.

Jackie Judd and Ted Koppel, "Making Hillary Clinton an Issue," *Nightline*, ABC News, March 26, 1992.

Michiko Kakutani, "Madonna Writes; Academics Explore Her Erotic Semiotics," *New York Times*, October 21, 1992.

Tamara Keith, "Hillary Clinton's Privacy Problem," *All Things Considered*, NPR, March 12, 2015.

Michael Kelly, "Saint Hillary," *New York Times Magazine*, May 23, 1993.

Alex Keshishian, director, *Madonna: Truth or Dare*, Boy Toy, Inc., Propaganda Films, Miramax, 1991, produced by Madonna et al.

Laura Kipnis, "Medusa for President," in *Thirty Ways of Looking at Hillary: Reflections by Women Writers*, edited by Susan Morrison (New York: Harper, 2008), 152–53, 157.

Elizabeth Kolbert, "Most in National Survey Say Judge Is More Believable," *New York Times*, October 15, 1991.

Nicholas Kristof, "Debunking the 'Crooked Hillary' Myth," *New York Times*, April 24, 2016, SR11.

Howard Kurtz, *Spin Cycle: Inside the Clinton Propaganda Machine* (New York: Free Press, 1998), 78, 83–84.

Clifford Krauss, "The Old Order Changes In Congress—A Little," *New York Times*, November 8, 1992.

Steve Labaton, "Elusive Papers of Law Firm Are Found at White House," *New York Times*, January 6, 1996, A1, 7.

Robert La Franco, "Madonna's Hedge," *Forbes*, September 23, 1996.

Sam Lansky, "Staying in Vogue," *Time*, March 9, 2015, 46–47.

Annie Leibovitz, "Annie Gets Her Shot," *Vanity Fair*, October 2008.

———, *Annie Leibovitz at Work* (New York: Random House, 2008).

"Letters (to the Editor): The Naked Truth," *Vanity Fair*, October 1991, 36–40.

Ariel Levy, "Cheating," in Morrison, *Thirty Ways of Looking at Hillary Clinton*, 91.

Ryan Lizza, "How to Beat Hillary Clinton," *New Yorker*, October 13, 2015.

Madonna, *Sex* (New York: Warner, 1992).

Norman Mailer, "Women We Love: Norman Mailer on Madonna," *Esquire*, August 1994.

Sara Marcus, *Girls to the Front: The True Story of the Riot Grrrl Revolution* (New York: Harper Perennial, 2010), 24.

Jane Mayer and Jill Abramson, *Strange Justice: The Selling of Clarence Thomas* (New York: Plume, 1995), 55–57, 105–11, 115, 130–39, 215, 221–37, 241–42, 248–51, 330–31.

Lorrie Moore, "Boys and Girls," in Morrison, *Thirty Ways of Looking at Hillary Clinton*, 33.

"Most Admired Man and Woman," Gallup.com, December 27, 2016.

Emily Nussbaum, "Justify My Love," *New York*, August 3, 2009, 49–52.

Maureen Orth, "Madonna in Wonderland," *Vanity Fair*, October 1992, 206, 212, 298.

Camille Paglia, "Madonna II: Venus of the Radio Waves," in Paglia, *Sex, Art, and American Culture: Essays* (New York: Vintage, 1992), 6–13.

Chuck Philips, "Anger over Madonna Single," *Los Angeles Times*, January 4, 1991.

Katha Pollitt, "Hillary Rotten," in Morrison, *Thirty Ways of Looking at Hillary Clinton*, 18.

Todd S. Purdum, "Hard Choice for White House on Hillary Clinton and China," *New York Times*, August 17, 1995.

Anna Quindlen, "The End of Swagger," *Newsweek*, February 3, 2009, 64.

Jonathan Rauch, "Why Hillary Clinton Needs to Be Two-Faced," *New York Times*, October 23, 2016, SR3.

Hillary D. Rodham, "1969 Student Commencement Speech," Wellesley College, Wellesley.edu.

Patrick Rogers, "Girls Night Out," *People*, May 12, 1997.

Katie Roiphe, "In Favor of Dirty Jokes and Risqué Remarks," *New York Times*, November 13, 2011, SR4.

Alyssa Rosenberg, "How Coming Out Became Cool for Celebrities," *Atlantic*, January 2012.

Austin Scaggs, "Madonna Looks Back: The Rolling Stone Interview," *Rolling Stone*, October 29, 2009, 51.

Matthew Schifrin and Peter Newcomb, "A Brain for Sin and a Bod for Business," *Forbes*, October 1, 1990, 162–66.

Alex Seitz-Wald, "Clinton's 'Right-Wing Conspiracy' Comes Full Circle with Trump Shake Up," NBCNews.com, August 18, 2016.

Larry J. Sabato, "Media Frenzies in Our Time: Senator Robert Packwood's History of Sexual Harassment—1992," WashingtonPost.com, March 27, 1998.

"Senators For: Resolving Uncertainties in Favor of Nominee," *Washington Post*, October 16, 1991.

Gail Sheehy, "Hillary's Choice," *Vanity Fair*, February 1999, 139.

Martha Sherrill, "Hillary Clinton's Inner Politics," *Washington Post*, May 6, 1993, D1.

Ingrid Sischy, "Madonna and Child," *Vanity Fair*, March 1998, 212.

Jill Smolowe, "She Said, He Said," *Time*, October 21, 1991.

Alessandra Stanley, "Ellen, 'Idol' and the Power of Niceness," *New York Times*, April 4, 2010, AR1, 19.

Sheryl Gay Stolberg, "Standing by Her Story," *New York Times*, March 16, 2014, AR1, 16.

Kara Swisher, "We Love Lesbians! Or Do We?' Hot Subculture—Or Just New Hurtful Stereotypes?," *Washington Post*, July 18, 1993.

Brian Tau, "Hillary Clinton Hits Low on Favorability, Trustworthiness in Poll," blogs.WSJ.org, August 27, 2015.

Virginia Lamp Thomas, "Breaking Silence," *People*, November 11, 1991.

"The Thomas Nomination: Excerpts from Senate's Hearings…," *New York Times*, October 12, 1991.

———: "Excerpts from Senate's Hearings…," *New York Times*, October 13, 1991.

———: "Hearing Captures Big TV Audience," *New York Times*, October 13, 1991.

———: "Statements to Senators from Witnesses for Anita Hill," *New York Times*, October 14, 1991.

Jeffrey Toobin, "Partners," *New Yorker*, August 29, 2011, 41, 45–46.

Nina Totenberg, ed., *Complete Transcripts of the Clarence Thomas–Anita Hill Hearings: October 11, 12, 13, 1991* (Chicago: Chicago Review Press, 2005).

Karen Tumulty, "Clintons and Controversy: The Circus Is Back in Town," *Washington Post*, March 10, 2015.

Patrick E. Tyler, "Hillary Clinton, in China, Details Abuse of Women," *New York Times*, September 6, 1995.

Wendy Wasserstein, "Hillary Clinton's Muddled Legacy," *New York Times*, August 25, 1998.

Jacob Weisberg, "Desperately Leaking Susan," *Vanity Fair*, June 1996, 177.

James Wolcott, "Lover Girls," *Vanity Fair*, June 1997, 67.

Ned Zeman, "A Stomach for Controversy," *Newsweek*, July 22, 1991, 51.

CHAPTER 7: The Crying Game

Interviews: James Carville, Lanny Davis, Art Harris, Steve Kroft, Mark McKinnon, Dee Dee Myers, Dan Payne, Patricia Steele.

"Allegations of Clinton Marital Infidelity," C-SPAN Video Library, Press Conference at Waldorf-Astoria, New York, NY, January 27, 1992, Dick Kaplan, Blake Hendricks, and Gennifer Flowers, www.c-spanvideo.org/program/23995-1.

Matt Bai, "Legend of the Fall," *New York Times Magazine*, September 21, 2014, 39, 60.

Jim Bakker, "Transcript of…Personal Statement," *Charlotte Observer*, March 20, 1987.

Randall Balmer, "Still Wrestling with the Devil: A Visit with Jimmy Swaggart Ten Years After His Fall," *Christianity Today*, March 2, 1998.

Bart Barnes, "Marion Barry Dies at 78," *Washington Post*, November 23, 2014.

Susan Wise Bauer, *The Art of the Public Grovel: Sexual Sin and Public Confession in America* (Princeton, NJ: Princeton University Press, 2008), 3–5, 115–17, 143–51, 159–61, 174.

Emily Bazelon, "Mr. Home-Wrecker Goes to Washington," *Slate*, May 8, 2007.

Richard L. Berke, "Formal Reprimand of Rep. Frank Is Urged by House Ethics Panel," *New York Times*, July 20, 1990.

———, "Panel Focused on Frank's Use of Office," *New York Times*, July 21, 1990.

Margaret Carlson, "A Skeleton in Barney's Closet," *Time*, September 25, 1989.

Janet Cawley, "Baby Boomers Ready to Accept the Torch," *Chicago Tribune*, September 20, 1992.

"The Clinton Years," ABC News *Nightline* and PBS *Frontline*, in association with WGBH Boston, January 15, 2001.

Bill Clinton, "Letter to Colonel Eugene Holmes" (Reserve Officer Training Corps), December 3, 1969, via *Nightline*, February 1992.

———, *My Life* (New York: Random House/Vintage, 2004), 388–89, 392, 404.

Hillary Rodham Clinton, *Living History* (New York: Scribner, 2003), 106.

Laura Collins, "Two Decades After Her Affair with Bill Clinton, Gennifer Flowers Reveals...," *Daily Mail*, September 18, 2013.

Jennet Conant, "The Ghost and Mr. Giuliani," *Vanity Fair*, September 1997, 154–72.

Frank Davies, "A Good Story, Even Without Famous Son," *Baltimore Sun*, May 9, 1994.

E. J. Dionne Jr., "Courting Danger: The Fall of Gary Hart," *New York Times*, May 9, 1987.

———, "Gary Hart, The Elusive Front-Runner," *New York Times*, May 3, 1987.

———, "Paper and Hart in Dispute over Article," *New York Times*, May 4, 1987.

Gennifer Flowers with Jacquelyn Dapper, *Passion and Betrayal* (Del Mar, CA: Emery Dalton, 1995), 71–75, 110–14.

Barney Frank, *Frank: A Life in Politics from the Great Society to Same-Sex Marriage* (New York: Farrar, Straus & Giroux, 2015), 142–43.

Steven M. Gillon, *The Pact: Bill Clinton, Newt Gingrich, and the Rivalry That Defined a Generation* (New York: Oxford University Press, 2008), 101.

Allan R. Gold, "Rep. Frank Acknowledges Hiring Male Prostitute as Personal Aide," *New York Times*, August 26, 1989.

Barak Goodman, director, *American Experience*, "Clinton," interview with Dee Dee Myers, PBS, www.pbs.org/wgbh/americanexperience/features/interview/clinton-myers/.

Art Harris, Earl Miller, and Bob Guccione, "Gennifer Flowers," *Penthouse*, December 1992, 66–76, 153–60.

Gary Hart, "Transcript of Hart Statement Withdrawing His Candidacy," *New York Times*, May 9, 1987.

Patrick Healy, "Bill Clinton's 1992 Make-or-Break Stand in New Hampshire," *New York Times*, February 9, 2016.

Chris Hegedus and D. A. Pennebaker, directors, *The War Room*, 1993, produced by R. J. Cutler, Wendy Ettinger, and Frazer Pennebaker.

Gwen Ifill, "Clinton Thanked Colonel in '69 for 'Saving Me from the Draft,'" *New York Times*, February 13, 1992.

Joan Kaufman, "The Fall of Jimmy Swaggart," *People*, March 7, 1988.

Joe Klein, *The Natural: The Misunderstood Presidency of Bill Clinton* (New York: Doubleday, 2002), 24–25, 40–41.

Howard Kurtz, *Spin Cycle: Inside the Clinton Propaganda Machine* (New York: Free Press, 1998), 99.

Matt Labash, "A Rake's Progress: Marion Barry Bares (Almost) All," *Weekly Standard*, September 7, 2009.

Jim McGee, Tom Fiedler, and James Savage, "The Gary Hart Story: How It Happened," *Miami Herald*, May 10, 1987.

Kira Marchenese and Sascha Segan, "Marion Barry: Making of a Mayor," WashingtonPost.com, May 21, 1998.

David Maraniss, *First in His Class: A Biography of Bill Clinton* (New York: Touchstone, 1995), 439–43.

James Martinez, "Donna Rice Denies Spending Night with Gary Hart," Associated Press, May 5, 1987.

Mary Matalin and James Carville with Peter Knobler, *All's Fair: Love, War, and Running for President* (New York: Touchstone, 1995), 112–13, 141–42, 167–68, 270.

Kate O'Beirne, "Bread and Circuses: Senator Bob Packwood's Public and Private Stance on Women," *National Review*, October 9, 1995.

Anne-Marie O'Neill, "Three's a Crowd," *People*, May 28, 2001.

Michael Oreskes, "Rep. Frank Asks for Full Inquiry by Ethics Panel," *New York Times*, August 29, 1989.

Frank Phillips, "Frank Tells of His Despair During '89 Sex Scandal," *Boston Globe*, August 14, 2004.

Dick Polman, "Those Aren't Rumors," *Smithsonian*, April 2008.

Frank Rich, "She Gets Mail," *New York Times*, April 8, 1998.

Alan Richman, "Donna Rice: 'The Woman in Question,'" *People*, May 18, 1987.

Campbell Robertson, "Politicians Are Slowed by Scandal, but Many Still Win the Race," *New York Times*, July 17, 2013.

Jack Rosenthal, "Echoes of the New Frontier," *New York Times*, January 17, 2009.

Walter Shapiro, "Fall from Grace," *Time*, May 18, 1987.

George Stephanopoulos, *All Too Human: A Political Education* (Boston: Little, Brown, 1999), 68–69, 74–75, 79, 86.

Michael Takiff, *A Complicated Man: The Life of Bill Clinton as Told by Those Who Know Him* (New Haven, CT: Yale University Press, 2010), 113–15, 119, 121.

Steve Talbot, "Why the Public Hates the Press" (interview with Paul Taylor), *Frontline*, PBS, May 1996.

Robin Toner, "Hart Drops Race for White House in a Defiant Mood," *New York Times*, May 9, 1987.

Thomas Vinciguerra, "My Bad: A Political Medley," *New York Times*, June 9, 2011, A27.

Michael Wolff, "It's the Adultery, Stupid," *Vanity Fair*, June 2008, 94–98.

"Woman Riding in Swaggart Car Says She's a Prostitute," Associated Press via *Los Angeles Times*, October 12, 1991.

"The Women in Giuliani's Life," CBSNews.com, May 11, 2000.

Bob Woodward, *The Agenda: Inside the Clinton White House* (New York: Simon & Schuster, 1994), 32–33.

CHAPTER 8: A Vagina Travelogue

Interviews: Tommy Barrata, Jimmie Briggs, Nicole Daedone, Joey DelVecchio, Emel, Heidi Fleiss, Danielle G., George Hamilton, Sari Markowitz, John Marquis, Katherine Martin, Chris Napolitano, Kerry O'Day, Janea Padilha, Jonice Padilha, Joyce Padilha, Anna Maria Tornaghi.

Gary J. Alter, "Clitoropexy/Clitoral Hood Reduction," www.altermd.com/clitoropexy_clitoral_hood_reduction.htm.

Patricia Bosworth, *Jane Fonda: The Private Life of a Public Woman* (New York: Houghton Mifflin, 2011), 1.

Susannah Breslin, "Designer Vaginas," *Harper's Bazaar*, November 1998.

Paddy Calistro, "Guide to Los Angeles Area Beauty Spas," *Los Angeles*, April 1995.

Stephanie Clifford, "Philosophical Waxing Eases the Ouch," *New York Times*, April 17, 2010.

Robert Coover et al., *Playboy: The Complete Centerfolds* (San Francisco: Chronicle Books), 2007.

Rebecca DiLiberto, "Bikini Waxing," *In Style*, May 2003.

"Directory/Waxing," *Allure*, July 2007, 126.

Betty Dodson with Carlin Ross, "Betty's Response to *The Vagina Monologues*," DodsonandRoss.com, March 15, 2001.

Simon Doonan, "The Last Wax of Summer; Kate's Cut Is a Triumph," *New York Observer*, August 28, 2000.

Jancee Dunn, "The Man Who Loved Hair," *Allure*, August 2003, 154–56.

Eve Ensler, *The Vagina Monologues* [1998] (New York: Villard, 2008), xxxix–xli, xliii, 6, 9, 19–21, 67–70, 105–11, 170–73, 198.

———, "V to the Tenth," Feminist.com, February 2008, www.feminist.com/violence/vday1.html.

Ashley Fetters, "The New Full-Frontal: Has Pubic Hair in America Gone Extinct?," *Atlantic*, December 2011.

Krista Foss, "New Hot Cosmetic Surgery for Women," *Toronto Globe and Mail*, November 10, 1998.

Yvonne K. Fulbright, "Should You Nip/Tuck Your Private Parts?," FoxNews.com, May 20, 2008.

Fiona J. Green, "From Clitoridectomies to 'Designer Vaginas': The Medical Construction of Heteronormative Female Bodies and Sexuality Through Female Genital Cutting," *Sexualities, Evolution and Gender* 7, no. 2 (August 2005): 153–87.

Germaine Greer, "This V-Word Is No Victory for Women," *Telegraph*, March 1, 2002.

George Gurley, "What's New, Pussycat? 90's Women Adopt Sleek New Look Down Below," *New York Observer*, November 23, 1998.

Carrie Havranek, "The New Sex Surgeries," *Cosmopolitan*, November 1998.

Valli Herman-Cohen, "Gene Shacove, 72; Stars' Hairstylist" (obituary), *Los Angeles Times*, September 8, 2001.

Christopher Hitchens, "On the Limits of Self-Improvement, Part II," *Vanity Fair*, December 2007.

Christina Hoff Sommers, "Sex, Lies, and *The Vagina Monologues*" (lecture), Young America's Foundation 26th Annual National Conservative Student Conference, Washington DC, August 25, 2004, www.aei.org.

Jan Hoffman, "Doctors Worry About Women's Preference for the Cleanshaven 'Barbie Doll Look,'" *New York Times*, June 30, 2016, A16.

I Love Vagina, LLC, "About Us," www.ilovevagina.net/aboutus.asp.

Rachel Johnson, "Bush Whacked," *Spectator*, May 18, 2002.

Doree Lewak, "Gwyneth Paltrow's Favorite Brazilian Waxers Are Broke," *New York Post*, July 3, 2016.

Meika Loe, *The Rise of Viagra: How the Little Blue Pill Changed Sex in America* (New York: New York University Press, 2004), 127.

Jill Mahoney, "Designer Vaginas: The Latest in Sex and Plastic Surgery," *Toronto Globe and Mail*, August 13, 2005.

Douglas Martin, "Larry Mathews, a 24-Hour Hairdresser, Dies at 86," *New York Times*, August 5, 2007.

Kaya Morgan, "Angus Mitchell: First Family of Hair," *Island Connections*, www.islandconnections.com/edit/mitchell.htm.

Desmond Morris, *The Naked Woman: A Study of the Female Body* (New York: St. Martin's, 2004), 198–200, 218.

Dominique Mosbergen, "G-Shot for Your G-Spot: Vagina Injection Said to Advance Sexual Pleasure Gains Popularity," *Huffington Post*, October 23, 2012.

The Official I Love Vagina Blog, https://ilovevagina.wordpress.com/ilv-charity/.

Janea Padilha and Martha Frankel, *Brazilian Sexy: Secrets to Living a Gorgeous and Confident Life* (New York: Perigee, 2011), 12–13, 17, 30, 67, 74–75.

Camille Paglia, *Sexual Personae: Art and Decadence from Nefertiti to Emily Dickinson* (New York: Vintage, 1991), 13–14.

Tony Pendleton, "Bikini Kill," *Notorious*, September/October 1999, 56.

Katha Pollitt, *Virginity or Death!: And Other Social and Political Issues of Our Times* (New York: Random House, 2006), 10.

Lisa Rapaport, "Designer Vagina Surgery Is a $5,500 Risk, Doctors Say," Bloomberg.com, August 31, 2007.

Stephanie Rosenbloom, "What Did You Call It?," *New York Times*, October 28, 2007.

"Sexy Brazilian, Secrets Included at J Sisters Salon," Paris by Appointment Only, August 20, 2009, www.parisbao.com/international/sexy-brazilian-secrets-included-at-j-sisters-salon/.

Christine Shea, "Stop the Hair-Removal Insanity!," *Glamour*, August 2004, 60–62.

Natasha Singer, "The Revised Birthday Suit," *New York Times*, September 1, 2005.

Jill Smolowe, "Gone Too Soon," *People*, November 5, 2001.

Amy Sohn, *Sex and the City: Kiss and Tell* (New York: Pocket, 2004), 96.

Joyce Wadler with Melena Z. Ryzik, "Boldface Names," *New York Times*, March 10, 2004.

"Wax Job," *People*, August 14, 2000.

"Vaginal Cosmetic Surgery: Labiaplasty, Vaginoplasty, and Clitoral Unhooding—Feminine Cosmetic Genital Surgery (FCGS)," LabiaplastySurgeon.com.

Christina Valhouli, "Faster Pussycat, Wax! Wax!," *Salon*, March 9, 1999.

CHAPTER 9: The Glory of O

Interviews: Susie Bright, Patrick Carnes, Nicole Daedone, Colin Finlay, Harley, Reese Jones, Steven Kotler, Michael Mendelsohn, Nancy Paulsen, Racheli, Marta Salas-Porras, Linda Troeller.

Diane Ackerman, "Fruit Flies and Love," *New York Times*, January 14, 2012, SR5.

Decca Aitkenhead, "The Buzz: How the Vibrator Came to Be," *Guardian*, September 7, 2012.

Vanessa Allen, "That 'Five Hours of Tantric Sex' Was a Drunken Boast Says Trudie," *Daily Mail*, December 29, 2011.

Daniel Bergner, "Women Who Want to Want," *New York Times Magazine*, November 24, 2009.

Sarah Boxer, "Batteries Not Included," *New York Times*, March 21, 1999.

William J. Broad, "I'll Have What She's Thinking," *New York Times*, September 28, 2013.

Jane E. Brody, "Personal Health," *New York Times*, April 17, 1985.

Patricia Leigh Brown and Carol Pogash, "The Pleasure Principle," *New York Times*, March 13, 2009, ST1, 8–9.

Natasha Burton, "A Brief History of the Rabbit," Cosmopolitan.com, February 9, 2015.

Michael Castleman, "Desire in Women: Does It Lead to Sex? Or Result from It?," *Psychology Today*, July 15, 2009.

Haakon L. Chevalier, "The History of the Chevalier Estate," 2009.

Tracy Clark-Flory, "Ready, Set, Masturbate!: The Mastermind Behind 'International Masturbation Month,'" *Salon*, May 18, 2014.

Nicole Daedone, *Slow Sex: The Art and Craft of Female Orgasm* (New York: Grand Central, 2001).

Carol Anderson Darling and J. K. Davidson, "Enhancing Relationships: Understanding the Feminine Mystique of Pretending Orgasm," *Journal of Sex and Marital Therapy* 12, no. 3 (February 1986).

Adrian Deevoy, *Cosmopolitan*, April 1996, via Sting.com, www.sting.com/news/article/4182.

Sharon Doyle Driedger, "Mystical Passion," *Maclean's*, September 16, 1996, 44–45.

Maya Dusenbery, "Timeline: Female Hysteria and the Sex Toys Used to Treat It," MotherJones.com, June 1, 2012.

Florence Fabricant, "After 'L.A. Law,' a Pursuit of Passions for Food and Life," *New York Times*, May 22, 1996.

Bryony Gordon, "Trudie Styler: 'Tantric Sex? All Day Long? With Sting? If Only…,'" Telegraph.co.uk, December 29, 2011.

Lori Gottlieb, "The Egalitarian-Marriage Conundrum," *New York Times Magazine*, February 9, 2014, 32.

Anne Harding, "Rosemary Basson: Working to Normalise Women's Sexual Reality," *Lancet*, February 3, 2007.

"The History of Female Sex Toys," *Huffington Post* (U.K.), February 10, 2014.

Hilary Howard, "Vibrators Carry the Conversation," *New York Times*, April 20, 2011, E1, 9.

Douglas Jehl, "Surgeon General Forced to Resign by White House," *New York Times*, December 10, 1994.

N. R. Kleinfeld, "How Cuisinart Lost Its Edge," *New York Times*, April 15, 1990.

Carol Krucoff, "No Longer a Stretch: Yoga as Healing Tool," *Los Angeles Times*, August 14, 2000.

Ruth La Ferla, "Good Vibrations, Upscale Division," *New York Times*, October 3, 2004.

———, "Toy Story, the Adult Version," *New York Times*, January 8, 2009, E8.

Edward O. Laumann, Anthony Paik, and Raymond C. Rosen, "Sexual Dysfunction in the United States: Prevalence and Predictors," *Journal of the American Medical Association* 281, no, 6 (February 10, 1999).

Ariel Levy, "Novelty Acts," *New Yorker*, September 19, 2011, 84–87.

Rachel R. Maines, *The Technology of Orgasm: "Hysteria," the Vibrator, and Women's Sexual Satisfaction* (Baltimore: Johns Hopkins University Press, 1999).

Lynn Margulis and Dorion Sagan, *Mystery Dance: On the Evolution of Human Sexuality* (New York: Summit, 1991).

Chris Mundy, "Sting: Mr. Natural," *Rolling Stone*, May 27, 1993.

Tara Parker-Pope, "Estrogen Lowers Breast Cancer and Heart Attack Risk in Some," NewYorkTimes.com, April 5, 2011.

Carol Queen, "Really Safe Sex: Relaxing, Healthy, Feels Good and It's Free: Let's Give a Hand for National Masturbation Month," SFGate.com, May 26, 2002.

Frank Rich, "The Last Taboo," *New York Times*, December 18, 1994.

Carlin Ross, "Betty Reintroducing the Electric Vibrator as a Pleasure Device," DodsonandRoss.com, February 26, 2013.

Steve Rubenstein, "San Francisco 'Feel-Good' Fundraiser," *San Francisco Chronicle*, April 29, 2009.

Melena Ryzik, "Company Finds 'Grey' and Pink Yield Pure Green," *New York Times*, August 4, 2012, A8.

"'Seven Hours Includes Movie and Dinner!': Sting Clarifies Those Infamous Comments About Tantric Sex with Trudie Styler—Twenty-Four Years On," *Daily Mail*, October 24, 2014.

Natasha Singer and Duff Wilson, "Menopause, as Brought to You by Big Pharma," *New York Times*, December 13, 2009.

Mary Spicuzza, "Sex and Sensuality," *SF Weekly*, April 4, 2007.

James Tapper, "Dad's Tantric Sex? That Was Made Up by Bob Geldof, Says Sting's Daughter Coco Sumner," *Daily Mail*, August 17, 2009.

Christopher Trout, "The 46-year-old Sex Toy Hitachi Won't Talk About," Engadget.com, August 27, 2014.

"The Walk-Through: Stinson Beach Estate," SFGate.com, August 5, 2009.

Kelsey Wallace, "May: The Merry, Merry Month of Masturbation!," BitchMedia.com, May 18, 2009.

"WHI Study Data Confirm Short-Term Heart Disease Risks of Combination Hormone Therapy for Postmenopausal Women" (press release), National Institutes of Health, February 15, 2010.

Naomi Wolf, *The Beauty Myth: How Images of Beauty Are Used Against Women* [1991] (New York: Harper Perennial, 2002), 131–32.

"Writer Haakon Chevalier Dies at 83," Associated Press via *Los Angeles Times*, July 18, 1985.

CHAPTER 10: Culture Warriors, Man Your Battle Stations

Interviews: Frank Rich, George Rider, Jennifer Rider, Susan Trento.

Gregory Acs et al., *The Moynihan Report Revisited*, via Urban Institute, Open Society Foundations, Fathers Incorporated, June 2013.

Laurence Barrett, "Pulpit Politics," *Time*, August 31, 1992, 34.

David Bauder, "Odd Couple: Rachel Maddow and Pat Buchanan," Associated Press via *USA Today*, June 10, 2008.

Max Blumenthal, *Republican Gomorrah: Inside the Movement That Shattered the Party*, (New York: Nation Books, 2009), 24–25.

Sidney Blumenthal, "Christian Soldiers," *New Yorker*, July 18, 1994.

David Brock, *Blinded by the Right: Confessions of an Ex-Conservative* (New York: Three Rivers, 2002), 132–37.

Patrick J. Buchanan, Address, Republican National Convention, Houston, August 17, 1992, Buchanan.org.

George Bush, "Remarks Accepting the Presidential Nomination at the Republican National Convention in Houston," August 20, 1992, American Presidency Project, University of California, Santa Barbara, www.presidency.ucsb.edu/ws/?pid=21352.

Bill Carter, "CBS Is Silent, but Then There's the Next Season," *New York Times*, May 21, 1992.

Census and You, U.S. Census Bureau, vol. 27, issue 1.

Adam Chandler, "The Sad Fate (but Historic Legacy) of the Houston Astrodome," *Atlantic*, November 2013.

Bill Clinton, Acceptance Speech, Democratic National Convention, New York City, July 16, 1992, *New York Times*.

———, *My Life* (New York: Vintage, 2004), 419–20, 425.

"Bill Clinton's Vietnam Test" (editorial), *New York Times*, February 14, 1992.

Hillary Rodham Clinton, *Living History* (New York: Scribner, 2003), 84–85.

Adam Clymer, "Bush's Gains from Convention Nearly Evaporate in Latest Poll," *New York Times*, August 26, 1992.

Fred R. Conrad, "AIDS Activist Mary Fisher Is Defined by Words, Not Disease," *New York Times*, August 23, 2012.

Cathleen Decker, "Clinton Makes Appeal to Conservatives in California," *Los Angeles Times*, July 27, 1992.

Andrew Delbanco, "In the Kingdom of This World," *Washington Post Book World*, July 7, 1996.

Maureen Dowd, "Been There, Done That," *New York Times*, April 18, 1996.

Diane English, "Speaking of Dan Quayle and 'Murphy Brown,'" *Los Angeles Times*, March 27, 2013.

"Family Matters," *Newsweek*, August 31, 1992, 6.

Howard Fineman, "Playing the 'V Word,'" *Newsweek*, June 8, 1992, 23.

———— and Ann McDaniel, "Bush: What Bounce?," *Newsweek*, August 30, 1992.

Margalit Fox, "Erich Segal, Classicist Who Wrote Populist Blockbuster 'Love Story,' Dies at 72," *New York Times*, January 20, 2010, A15.

David Frum, *Dead Right* (New York: Basic Books, 1994), 16–17, 21.

"George H. W. Bush: Impact and Legacy," George H. W. Bush Home Page, Miller Center, MillerCenter.org.

"John Frohnmayer's Noisy Exit" (editorial), *New York Times*, March 25, 1992.

Dan Gilgoff, *The Jesus Machine: How James Dobson, Focus on the Family, and Evangelical America Are Winning the Culture War* (New York: St. Martin's, 2008), 96–99.

Elizabeth Glaser, "1992 Democratic National Convention Address," New York, NY, July 14, 1992, www.american rhetoric.com/speeches/elizabethglaser1992dnc.htm.

Tom Gliatto, "Nobody's Pussycat," *People*, November 9, 1992.

Jonah Goldberg, "The Wisdom of Dan Quayle," *Los Angeles Times*, March 26, 2013.

Laurie Goodstein and Pierre Thomas, "Clinic Killings Follow Years of Antiabortion Violence," *Washington Post*, January 17, 1995, A1.

Bob Goodwin, "Bush's New Hampshire Problem," TheHill.com, October 30, 2015.

Lloyd Grove, "Media to the Left! Media to the Right! The GOP, Shooting the Messengers," *Washington Post*, August 20, 1992.

Jane Hall and Judith Michaelson, "Murphy to Give Birth Again on Labor Day Rerun," *Los Angeles Times*, May 22, 1992.

Emily Heil and Helena Andrews, "The Chelsea Clinton Cheat Sheet," WashingtonPost.com, April 18, 2014.

Melinda Henneberger, "Author of 'Love Story' Disputes a Gore Story," *New York Times*, December 14, 1997.

Christopher Hitchens, *Hitch-22: A Memoir* (New York: Twelve, 2010), 106.

Jan Hoffman, "TV Shouts 'Baby' (and Barely Whispers 'Abortion')," *New York Times*, May 31, 1992.

Stephen A. Holmes, "Perot Says Democratic Surge Reduced Prospect of Victory," *New York Times*, July 17, 1992.

William H. Honan, "Head of Endowment for the Arts Is Forced from His Post by Bush," *New York Times*, February 22, 1992.

Jason Horowitz, "Inside Clinton's Outrage Machine, Her Allies Push the Buttons," *New York Times*, September 23, 2016, A21.

Gwen Ifill, "Clinton Team Challenges G.O.P. in Effort to 'Set Record Straight,'" *New York Times*, August 18, 1992.

————, "Clinton Selects Senator Gore of Tennessee as Running Mate," *New York Times*, July 10, 1992.

Molly Ivins, *You Got to Dance with Them What Brung You: Politics in the Clinton Years* (New York: Random House, 1998), xvi–xix.

Barbara Jordan, "Change: From What to What," Keynote Address, Democratic National Convention, New York, NY, July 13, 1992, Gifts of Speech, Sweet Briar College, http://gos.sbc.edu/j/jordan2.html.

Andrew Kaczynski and Ilan Ben-Meir, "When 17-Year-Old Rachel Maddow Came Out Publicly in Her College Newspaper," BuzzFeed.com, January 8, 2015.

Michael Kelly, "Clinton and Bush Compete to Be Champion of Change," *New York Times*, October 31, 1992.

"King Herod," BBC Religions, September 18, 2009, www.bbc.co.uk/religion/religions/christianity/history/herod/ shtml.

David D. Kirkpatrick, "Firing Up the Faithful with Echoes of Culture War Rhetoric," *New York Times*, September 5, 2008.

Joe Klein, *The Natural: The Misunderstood Presidency of Bill Clinton* (New York: Doubleday, 2002), 11.

————, "Whose Values?," *Newsweek*, June 7, 1992, 19–22.

Nicholas Kristof, "When Liberals Blew It," *New York Times*, March 11, 2015.

Daniel Larison, "Did Buchanan's Convention Speech in 1992 Damage Bush?," *American Conservative*, January 13, 2012.

"Letterman on Dan Quayle and Murphy Brown . . . ," Associated Press, May 21, 1992.

"Los Angeles Riots: Remember the 63 People Who Died," LATimes.com, April 26, 2012.

Norman Mailer, "By Heaven Inspired," *New Republic*, October 12, 1992.

Mary Matalin and James Carville with Peter Knobler, *All's Fair: Love, War, and Running for President* (New York: Touchstone, 1995), 233, 309.

Tanya Melich, *The Republican War Against Women: An Insider's Report from Behind the Lines* (New York: Bantam, 1996), x–xi, 256–59, 266, 271.

"Modest Bush Approval Rating Boost at War's End," Pew Research Center, April 18, 2003, www.people-press .org/2003/04/18/modest-bush-approval-rating-boost-at-wars-end/.

Lance Morrow, "Family Values," *Time*, August 31, 1992, 22–27.

"MSNBC's Cultural Odd Couple," *Washington Times*, October 8, 2008.

Adam Nagourney, "'Cultural War' of 1992 Moves in from the Fringe," *New York Times*, August 29, 2012.

Timothy Noah, "Why Don't War Heroes Win?," *Slate*, November 3, 2008.

Robert Orsi, "The Christian Right Reaches For Power, Not Influence...," *Baltimore Sun*, July 14, 1996.

Robert Pear, "Platform: In a Final Draft, Democrats Reject a Part of Their Past," *New York Times*, June 26, 1992.

Degen Pener, "On the Front of Newsweek, a Conflict of Values," *New York Times*, June 7, 1992.

Jonathan Peterson, "One-Liners Fly Fast and Furious as Both Sides Aim to Get In Last Zinger," *Los Angeles Times*, August 21, 1992.

Dan Quayle, "Address to the Commonwealth Club of California," May 19, 1992, www.vicepresidentdanquayle.com/speeches_StandingFirm_CCC_1.html.

Ronald Reagan, "Address at Republican National Convention," Houston, August 17, 1992, www.cnn.com/SPECIALS/2004/reagan/stories/speech.archive/rnc.speech.html.

Phil Reeves, "TV Soap Drops Hot Potato on Quayle," *Independent*, September 22, 1992.

"Republican Party Platform of 1992," August 17, 1992, American Presidency Project, University of California, Santa Barbara, www.presidency.ucsb.edu/ws/?pid=25847.

Frank Rich, "Stag Party," *New York*, March 25, 2012, 19–26.

Larry Rohter, "Candidate's Wife; Unrepentant, Marilyn Quayle Fights for Family and Values," *New York Times*, October 28, 1992.

David Rosenbaum, "Republican Platform; G.O.P. Drafting Stand for Total Ban on Abortion," *New York Times*, August 11, 1992.

Andrew Rosenthal, "Sununu Resigns Under Fire as Chief Aide to President," *New York Times*, December 4, 1991.

William Safire, "The Me-Too Democrats," *New York Times*, July 16, 1991.

Isabel Sawhill, "20 Years Later, It Turns Out Dan Quayle Was Right About Murphy Brown and Unmarried Moms," *Washington Post*, May 25, 2012.

Katharine Q. Seelye, "Molly Ivins, Columnist, Dies at 62," *New York Times*, February 7, 1, 2007.

"Senator John McCain's Convention Speeches," *New York Times*, September 4, 2008.

Tim Stanley, "A New Culture War? Nah," CNN.com, February 16, 2012.

Roberto Suro, "The Religious Right; Bush Gets Full Support at Religious Gathering," *New York Times*, August 23, 1992.

Mimi Swartz, "Being Dan Quayle," *Life*, September 1992, 28.

Richard Todd, *The Thing Itself: On the Search for Authenticity* (New York: Riverhead, 2008), 162.

Robin Toner, "Bush Jarred in First Primary; Tsongas Wins Democratic Vote," *New York Times*, February 19, 1992.

———, "Bush Vows a Tough Campaign as G.O.P. Opens Its Convention," *New York Times*, August 18, 1992.

———, "Perot Re-enters the Campaign, Saying Bush and Clinton Fail to Address Government 'Mess,'" *New York Times*, October 2, 1992.

Ken Tucker, "Dan Quayle Complains About 'Murphy Brown,'" *Entertainment Weekly*, June 5, 1992.

Ryan Walters, "The Republican Establishment's 20-Year War on Conservatives," *Mississippi Conservative Daily* via Buchanan.org, August 19, 2014.

Paul West, "Clinton Issues Fiery Call to Democrats, Perot Backers," *Baltimore Sun*, July 17, 1992.

Barbara Dafoe Whitehead, "Dan Quayle Was Right," *Atlantic*, April 1993.

Michael Wines, "Views on Single Motherhood Are Multiple at White House," *New York Times*, May 21, 1992.

Bob Woodward, *The Agenda: Inside the Clinton White House* (New York: Simon & Schuster, 1994), 332.

CHAPTER 11: Wanderlust

Interviews: Anonymous AOL source, Tony DiSanto, David Ewing Duncan, Donna Ferrato, Ben Greenman, Jonathan Harris, Andrew Hearst, Reese Jones, David Kirkpatrick, Jane Metcalfe, Aidan Sullivan, Michael Wolff.

Patchen Barss, *The Erotic Engine: How Pornography Has Powered Mass Communication from Gutenberg to Google* (Toronto: Anchor Canada, 2011), 64–65.

Jamie Beckett, "The Inventor's Mouse Revolution," *San Francisco Chronicle*, December 10, 1998.

Stewart Brand, "Scream of Consciousness" (interview with Camille Paglia), *Wired*, January 1993.

———, "Spacewar," *Rolling Stone*, December 7, 1972.

———, "We Owe It All to the Hippies," *Time* (special issue), Spring 1995.

Louis M. Brill, "1986–1991 Event Archive: The First Year in the Desert," Burning Man, http://burningman.org/culture/history/brc-history/event-archives/1986-1991/firstyears/.

Dina Cheney, "Louis Rossetto '71 Goes from *Wired* to Chocolate," *Columbia College Today*, Summer 2013, college.columbia.edu.

Alan Deutschman, "The Gods of Tech," *Vanity Fair*, July 2000.

Stacy Finz, "Couple's TCHO Ventures Sets the Bar for Chocolate," SFGate.com, October 5, 2013.

Nick Gillespie, "We're Creating Our Own Evolutionary Next Step," Reason.com, February 27, 2014.

Brooke Gladstone, "Sex and Technology," *On the Media*, NPR.org, November 29, 2002.

Katie Hafner, "Old Newsgroups in New Packages," *New York Times*, June 24, 1999, G1, 10.

Samir Husni, "Battle of the E-Mags," *Forbes ASAP*, August 21, 2000.

Walter Isaacson, "The Great Connectors," *Vanity Fair*, October 2014, 188–90.

Jennifer A. Kingson, "Happy Birthday, WWW," *New York Times*, May 7, 2013.

Michael Lewis, "The Search Engine," *New York Times*, October 10, 1999.

A. J. Liebling, "The Wayward Press: Do You Belong in Journalism?," *New Yorker*, May 14, 1960.

David Lumb, "A Brief History of AOL," FastCompany.com, May 12, 2015.

Harry McCracken, "20 Years of AOL Annoyances and Foul-Ups," *PCWorld*, April 28, 2009.

Declan McCullagh, "Blogs Turn 10—Who's the Father?," CNET News, March 20, 2007.

Brian McCullough, "Those Free AOL CDs Were a Campaign for Web Domination. It Worked," Mashable.com, August 21, 2014.

John Markoff, "A Free and Simple Computer Link," *New York Times*, December 8, 1993.

———, *What the Dormouse Said: How the Sixties Counterculture Shaped the Personal Computer Industry* (New York: Penguin, 2006), xii–xiii, xviii–xxi, 110–13, 127–28, 174–75.

Otis Port, "How the Net Was Born—And Where It's Headed," *BusinessWeek*, November 1, 1999.

Hugh Schofield, "Minitel: The Rise and Fall of the France-wide Web," *BBC News Magazine*, June 27, 2012.

David Shedden, "Today in Media History: The First Internet Search Engine Is Released in 1990," Poynter.org, September 10, 2014.

Clay Shirky, "Newspapers and Thinking the Unthinkable," Shirky.com, March 13, 2009.

Danny Sullivan, "A Eulogy for AltaVista, the Google of Its Time," SearchEngineLand.com, June 28, 2013.

Gerard Van der Leun, "This Is a Naked Lady," *Wired*, January 1993.

Kyle VanHemert, "How a Band of Rebels and Pioneers Launched *Wired*'s First Website 20 Years Ago Today," Wired.com, October 27, 2014.

Michael Wolff, *Burn Rate: How I Survived the Gold Rush Years on the Internet* (New York: Touchstone, 1999).

———, "You've Got Sex," *New York*, December 23, 2002.

———, "Why Your Kids Know More About the Future Than You Do," *New York*, http://nymag.com/nymetro/urban/family/features/679/index3.html.

CHAPTER 12: The Wild Blue Web

Interviews: Susie Bright, Sian Edwards-Beal, Abby Ellin, David Kirkpatrick, Stephen Mayes, Doug Menuez, Luc Sante, Greg Van Alstyne, Rachel Winter.

Dan Ackman, "How Big Is Porn?," *Forbes*, May 25, 2001.

Aimee Lee Ball, "Are 5001 Friends One Too Many?," *New York Times*, May 30, 2010, ST1, 11.

John Battelle, "The Birth of Google," *Wired*, August 2013.

Meredith Bennett-Smith, "Why Do Virginia, 13 Other States Want to Keep Their Anti-Sodomy Laws a Decade After SCOTUS Ban?," *Huffington Post*, April 9, 2013.

Charlie Brooker, "The Dark Side of Our Gadget Addiction," *Guardian*, December 1, 2011.

David Brooks, "The Crowd Pleaser," *New York Times*, February 10, 2012, A27.

Donn Cooper, "Doris Duke: Vanishing Soul," *Oxford American*, Winter 2008, 73.

David Cotriss, "Where Are They Now: The Globe.com," *Industry Standard*, May 29, 2008.

Maureen Dowd, "Stars and Sewers," *New York Times*, February 20, 2011, WK11.

Philip Elmer-DeWitt, "Battle for the Soul of the Internet," *Time*, June 24, 2001.

Vanessa Grigoriadis, "The New Position on Casual Sex," *New York*, January 6, 2003.

Rufus Griscom, "Ten Years of Nerve: A Retrospective," Nerve.com, June 26, 2007.

J. C. Herz, *Surfing on the Internet: A Nethead's Adventures On-Line* (Boston: Little, Brown, 1995), 164.

Amanda Hess, "Why Women Aren't Welcome on the Internet," *Pacific Standard*, January 2014.

Michael Hirschorn, "The PC Porn Queen's Virtual Realities," *Esquire*, June 1993, 57–60.

William C. Hughes, *James Agee, Omnibus, and Mr. Lincoln: The Culture of Liberalism and the Challenge of Television, 1952–1953* (Lanham, MD: Scarecrow, 2004), 25.

"Illinois C. to Sue Craigslist as Prostitution Hub," WCBSTV.com, March 5, 2009.

Robin Kawakami, "Todd Krizelman and Stephan Paternot," BusinessInsider.com, September 18, 2008.

Janet Kornblum, "eHarmony: Heart and Soul," *USA Today*, May 18, 2005.

Irene Lacher, "Sex in the Future? Can You Say 'Communication'?," *Los Angeles Times*, June 7, 1998.

Jaron Lanier, *You Are Not a Gadget* (New York: Vintage, 2011), 14–19, 60–63.

Mark Leibovich, "The Man the White House Wakes Up To," *New York Times Magazine*, April 25, 2010, 38.

Rudy Nadio, "Buying Into Bytes," *Brandweek*, December 8, 1997.

Andrew Adam Newman, "Dating Website Emphasizes Like, Rather Than Love," *New York Times*, November 5, 2014.

Lisa Palac, *The Edge of the Bed: How Dirty Pictures Changed My Life* (Boston: Little, Brown, 1998), 72–73, 89–93, 99–101, 103–17.

Sam Parker, "How Many Friends Can One Man Have?" (interview with Robin Dunbar), *Esquire* (U.K.), July 2014.

Pamela Paul, *Pornified: How Pornography Is Damaging Our Lives, Our Relationships, and Our Families* (New York: Henry Holt, 2005), 59, 268–69.

Nick Paumgarten, "Looking for Someone," *New Yorker*, July 4, 2011, 39–41, 46.

Douglas Quenqua, "Recklessly Seeking Sex on Craigslist," *New York Times*, April 19, 2009, ST1, 8.

Frank Rich, "Naked Capitalists," *New York Times Magazine*, May 20, 2001.

Sarah E. Richards, "You Don't Have to Be Jewish to Love JDate," *New York Times*, December 5, 2004.

David Riesman with Nathan Glazer and Reuel Denney, *The Lonely Crowd: A Study of the Changing American Character* [1950] (New Haven, CT: Yale University Press, 1961), xx–xxi.

Peter Rubin, "Pornocopia: The Immersive Future of Virtual Reality Sex," *Wired*, March 2015.

Evelyn M. Rusli, "How Reid Hoffman of LinkedIn Became Tech's Go-To Guy," *New York Times*, November 6, 2011, BU1, 5.

"Salon.com & Nerve.com Launch Online Personals Service," *Salon*, December 4, 2000.

Greg Sandoval, "The End of Kindness: Weev and the Cult of the Angry Young Man," TheVerge.com, September 12, 2013.

Betsy Schiffman, "FTC, Credit-Card Cos. Bump, Grind Web Porn," *Forbes*, August 25, 2000.

Brad Stone, "Craigslist to Remove 'Erotic' Ads," *New York Times*, May 14, 2009, B1, 6.

———, "Sex Ads on Craigslist Attract More Revenue, and More Scrutiny," *New York Times*, April 26, 2010, B1.

Sherry Turkle, *Life on the Screen: Identity in the Age of the Internet* (New York: Simon & Schuster, 1995), 20–21, 186, 223–24.

Greg Van Alstyne, "Cyberspace and the Lonely Crowd," Nothingness.org, 1994.

Michael Wolff, "You've Got Sex," *New York*, December 23, 2002.

CHAPTER 13: Don't Ask, Don't Tell

Interviews: Stephanie Bornstein, Richard Friend, Dee Dee Myers, Ingrid Sischy, Joan Williams.

"1988 Presidential General Election Results," U.S. Election Atlas, http://uselectionatlas.org/RESULTS/national.php?year=1988.

"1992 Presidential General Election Results," U.S. Election Atlas, http://uselectionatlas.org/RESULTS/national.php?year=1992.

"About Vice President Biden's Efforts to End Violence Against Women," WhiteHouse.gov, www.whitehouse.gov/1is2many/about.

Brett Atwood, "MTV Renews 'Choose or Lose,'" *Billboard*, February 3, 1996.

Brian Bender, "Pentagon Airs Criticism of 'Don't Ask,'" *Boston Globe*, September 30, 2009.

Richard L. Berke, "Clinton in Crossfire," *New York Times*, July 20, 1993.

———, "The Gay Troops Debate: Clinton Is Back in the Storm's Eye," *New York Times*, March 28, 1993.

Dallas A. Blanchard, *The Anti-Abortion Movement and the Rise of the Religious Right: From Polite to Fiery Protest* (New York: Twayne, 1994), 118.

Bettina Boxall and Edwin Chen, "Nunn, Dole See Perils in Lifting Military Gay Ban," *Los Angeles Times*, November 16, 1992.

Taylor Branch, *The Clinton Tapes: Wrestling History with the President* (New York: Simon & Schuster, 2009), 5–6.

Elisabeth Bumiller, "Obama Ends 'Don't Ask, Don't Tell' Policy," *New York Times*, July 22, 2011.

Robert Catlin, "Politicizing of MTV Culminates In Rock 'N' Roll Inaugural," *Hartford Courant*, January 20, 1993.

Bill Clinton, "How We Ended Welfare, Together," *New York Times*, August 22, 2006.

———, *My Life* (New York: Random House/Vintage, 2004), 318, 372, 471, 474, 477, 480–86, 706.

Bill Clinton, "We Force the Spring," Inaugural Address, Washington, DC, January 20, 1993, *New York Times*, January 21, 1993.

"Clinton Backs Bill to Bar Job Bias Against Gays," *Chicago Tribune*, October 21, 1995.

"The Clinton Presidency: Timeline of Major Actions," WhiteHouse.gov, https://clinton5.nara.gov/WH/Accomplishments/eightyears-02.html.

Amy Chozick, "Hillary Clinton's Gay Rights Evolution," *New York Times*, August 29, 2014

Adam Clymer, "Lawmakers Revolt on Lifting Gay Ban in Military Service," *New York Times*, January 27, 1993.

Yoji Cole, "'Don't Pursue, Don't Harass': The Other Half of 'Don't Ask, Don't Tell,'" DiversityInc.com, June 15, 2004.

Helen Dewar, "Congress Passes Family Leave," *Washington Post*, February 5, 1993.

Maureen Dowd, "Defending the Long Gay Line," *New York Times*, February 2, 2010.

"Empowering Women in Sports," Feminist Majority Foundation, www.feminist.org/research/sports/sports12.html.

"Family and Medical Leave Act: Overview," U.S. Department of Labor: Wage and Hour Division, dol.gov/whd/fmla.

Alyssa Fetini, "Top 10 Oprah Moments: 8. Putting Democracy to Work," Time.com, May 25, 2011.

Barney Frank, *Frank: A Life in Politics from the Great Society to Same-Sex Marriage* (New York: Farrar, Straus & Giroux, 2015), 161.

Nathaniel Frank, *Unfriendly Fire: How the Gay Ban Undermines the Military and Weakens America* (New York: Thomas Dunne, 2009), xxi–xxiii, 33, 38–39, 48–56, 70–72, 95–97.

Barry M. Goldwater, "The Gay Ban: Just Plain Un-American," *Washington Post*, June 10, 1993, A23.

"Guidelines for Employers on Sexual Harassment," 'Lectric Law Library, www.lectlaw.com/files/emp32.htm.

Hendrik Hertzberg, "Stonewall Plus Forty," *New Yorker*, July 6, 2009, 23–24.

Fred Hochberg, "In Government and, Incidentally, Gay," *New York Times*, February 10, 2001, A15.

"HRC Condemns Wyoming Hate Crime and Says Religious Right's Anti-gay Rhetoric Creates Climate Conducive to Violence" (press release), Human Rights Campaign, October 10, 1998.

Carl Hulse, "Senate Ends Military Ban on Gays Serving Openly," *New York Times*, December 9, 2010, A1, 34.

"Inaugural Events Sing a Song of Diversity," *Los Angeles Times*, January 13, 1993.

"Jan. 17–23: Roe's Momentous Anniversary; Undoing Republican Rulings, Clinton Lifts Bans Meant to Curb Abortions," *New York Times*, January 24, 1993.

Edward M. Kennedy, *True Compass: A Memoir* (New York: Twelve, 2009), 451–52.

Joe Klein, *The Natural: The Misunderstood Presidency of Bill Clinton* (New York: Doubleday, 2002), 44–45.

Lawrence J. Korb, "The Costs of Don't Ask, Don't Tell," Center for American Progress, AmericanProgress.org, March 2, 2009.

Adam Liptak, "Looking for Time Bombs and Tea Leaves on Gay Marriage," *New York Times*, July 20, 2010, A11.

"The March for Life, 1993: The View from the Ellipse," *Crisis*, www.crisismagazine.com/1993/the-march-for-life-1993.

Dick Morris, *Behind the Oval Office: Getting Reelected Against All Odds* (New York: St. Martin's, 1999), xvii, 270, 288, 307–8.

Lance Morrow, "The Torch Is Passed," *Time* (Man of the Year), January 4, 1993, 22–25.

Peggy Noonan, "Bush's Defeat: Insider's Analysis," *New York Times*, November 5, 1992.

Jon Pareles, "As Rock Beat Fades, Clinton's Presidency Opens on a Soft Note," *New York Times*, January 21, 1993.

"Policy Concerning Homosexuality in the Armed Forces," U.S. Code, Title 10, Subtitle G, Section 654, January 24, 1994, mit.edu/committees/rotc/code.html.

"President Clinton Signs the National Child Protection Act," Associated Press via *New York Times*, December 21, 1993.

Roger Rosenblatt, "Teaching Johnny to Be Good," *New York Times Magazine*, April 30, 1995.

Julie Rovner, " 'Partial-Birth Abortion': Separating Fact from Spin," NPR.org, February 21, 2006.

Eric Schmitt, "Military Cites Wide Range of Reasons for Its Gay Ban," *New York Times*, January 27, 1993.

———, "President's Policy on Gay Troops Is Backed in Vote of Senate Panel," *New York Times*, July 24, 1993.

"Scuttle 'Don't Ask, Don't Tell' " (editorial), *New York Times*, May 23, 2010.

Larry Shaughnessy, "U.S. Allies Say Integrating Gays in Military Was Nonissue," CNN.com, May 19, 2010.

Jube Shiver Jr., "The Hip-Hot Bash: MTV Ball Becomes the 'Hottest Ticket in Town,'" *Los Angeles Times*, January 13, 1993.

George Stephanopoulos, *All Too Human: A Political Education* (Boston: Little, Brown, 1999), 122–28, 133.

Michael Takiff, *A Complicated Man: The Life of Bill Clinton as Told by Those Who Know Him* (New Haven, CT: Yale University Press, 2011), 151–55.

Sharon Terman, "The Practical and Conceptual Problems with Regulating Harassment in a Discriminatory Institution," Center for the Study of Sexual Minorities in the Military (Palm Center), University of California, Santa Barbara, May 2004, http://archive.palmcenter.org/files/active/0/200405_Terman.pdf.

Robin Toner, "Anti-Abortion Movement Prepares to Battle Clinton," *New York Times*, January 22, 1993.

Tom Vanden Berg, "Military Transgender Ban Set to End Next May," *USA Today*, August 25, 2015.

Myrna Watanabe, "With Five-Year Ban on Fetal Tissue Studies Lifted, Scientists Are Striving to Make Up for Lost Time," *Scientist*, October 4, 1993.

Rick Weaver, "Sexual Harassment 'Affirmative Defense' Defined by Supreme Court," Orange-County-Attorney.blogspot.com, May 27, 2009.

"Will Powell Quit over Gay Issue?," *Philadelphia Daily News*, January 25, 1993.

CHAPTER 14: The Age of the Long Lie

Interviews: Steve Kroft, Dee Dee Myers, Jonathan Rauch, Frank Rich, Gay Talese.

William J. Bennett, *The Death of Outrage: Bill Clinton and the Assault on American Ideals* (New York: Touchstone, 1999), 16–21, 29–30.

Carl Bernstein, "Watergate's Last Chapter," *Vanity Fair*, October 2005, 340–41.

Graydon Carter, "Donald Trump: The Ugly American," *Vanity Fair*, October 2016.

Bill Clinton, *My Life* (New York: Random House/Vintage, 2004), 387, 445.

"The Choice '96," interview with Paul Greenberg, *Frontline*, PBS, www.pbs.org/wgbh/pages/frontline/shows/choice/bill/greenberg.html.

Kathleen Hall Jamieson, "What Those Polls Are Telling Us," *Washington Post*, March 22, 1998.

Joe Klein, "The Politics of Promiscuity," *Newsweek*, May 9, 1994.

Nicholas Kristof, "When a Crackpot Runs for President," *New York Times*, September 15, 2016.

Howard Kurtz, *Spin Cycle: Inside the Clinton Propaganda Machine* (New York: Free Press, 1998), 294.

Mary Matalin and James Carville with Peter Knobler, *All's Fair: Love, War, and Running for President* (New York: Touchstone, 1995), 400–402.

Frank Newport, "Presidential Job Approval: Bill Clinton's High Ratings in the Midst of Crisis, 1998," Gallup.com, June 4, 1999.

Robert Pear, "The Buck Stops Here," *New York Times*, July 19, 1987.

"Presidential Approval Ratings—Bill Clinton," Gallup.com.

Jonathan Rauch, "Cheatin' Hearts: Living with Adultery, or, It's Better to Pretend Not to Know," *Chicago Tribune*, September 23, 1998, N19.

———, "High Lying," *New Republic*, April 20, 1998, 42.

———, "Law and Disorder," *New Republic*, April 30, 2001.

———, "Live and Let Lie," *New Republic*, September 2, 1997, 24–28.

Frank Rich, "Fantasyland: Denial Has Poisoned the GOP and Threatens the Rest of the Country Too," *New York*, November 19, 2012, 18–20.

———, *The Greatest Story Ever Sold: The Decline and Fall of Truth, from 9/11 to Katrina* (New York: Penguin, 2006), 2–3, 87, 125, 163, 181.

Steven V. Roberts, "Reagan Says Aides Had Duty to Tell of Fund," *New York Times*, August 13, 1987.

Jeffrey Rosen, *The Unwanted Gaze: The Destruction of Privacy in America* (New York: Vintage, 2001), 144.

William Safire, "Blizzard of Lies," *New York Times*, January 8, 1996.

Lisa Taddeo, "Why We Cheat," *Esquire*, April 2012.

Michael Tomasky, "It's Time for the Media to Step Up and Call Out Donald Trump's Many Lies," *Daily Beast*, September 8, 2016.

CHAPTER 15: The Oversexed, Underexamined, Media-Soaked *Yadda Yadda* of Everyday Life

Interviews: Debby Applegate, Heike Bachmann, Patrick Baz, Brian Bedol, Stefanie Cohen, Ryan Cook, Alan Cumming, Father Robert Farrell, Donna Ferrato, Helen Fisher, Elena Ochoa Foster, Anthony Haden-Guest, Abigail Jones, Robert Longo, Jim McHugh, Sunny Mindel, Beth Ouellette, Howard Owen, Amy Paulsen, Julianne Pepitone, Drew Pinsky, Judith Regan, Reza, Julian Sancton, Ingrid Sischy, Linda Troeller, Bruce Tulgan.

Ron Athey, "Polemic of Blood: Ron Athey on the 'Post-AIDS' Body," *Walker* magazine, March 19, 2015, Walker Art Center, www.walkerart.org/magazine/2015/ron-athey-blood-polemic-post-aids-body/.

Richard Avedon, "Swinton's Time," *New Yorker*, March 8, 1993.

David Barstow, "Art, Money and Control: A Portrait of 'Sensation,'" *New York Times*, December 6, 1999.

———, "'Sensation' Exhibition Closes as It Opened, to Applause and Condemnation," *New York Times*, January 10, 2000.

Emily Bazelton, "Trolls, the Bell Tolls for Thee," *New York Times Magazine*, April 24, 2011, 9–10.

Jack Beatty, "Sex and the Social Critic: In Reviews of Stanley Kubrick's Last Film, the Critics' Eyes Were Shut to Its Wider Implications About Modern Society," *Atlantic*, August 25, 1999.

"Behind the Cover: Britney Spears, Photographed by David LaChapelle," RollingStone.com, September 30, 2004.

Jacob Bernstein, "She's Back. Watch Out," *New York Times*, February 8, 2015, ST1, 10.

Charles M. Blow, "The Demise of Dating," *New York Times*, December 13, 2008, A21.

Kathleen A. Bogel, *Hooking Up: Sex, Dating, and Relationships on Campus* (New York: NYU, 2008), 2–8, 20, 25, 39–41, 85, 184.

Robert H. Bork, *Slouching Towards Gomorrah: Modern Liberalism and American Decline* [1996] (New York: Regan-Books, 2003), 131–33.

L. Brent Bozell III, "TV's Morality, Standards: Loose Across the Board," Creators Syndicate, April 29, 1997.

David Brooks, "The Flock Comedies," *New York Times*, October 22, 2010, A35.

Barbara Brotman, "Howard Stern's Breakup Raises Universal Issues," *Chicago Tribune*, October 27, 1999.

Joan Juliet Buck, "Carrie Retakes Hollywood," *Vanity Fair*, August 1990, 130–32.

Joy Duckett Cain, "The Growing Pains of Salt 'N' Pepa," *Essence*, October 1994.

Ken Camp, "Study Finds TV Sex More Pervasive," Texas Baptist Communications, February 19, 2001.

Dan Carnevale, "With the Latest Technology, Students Find That Creating Fake ID's Is Easy," *Chronicle of Higher Education*, April 19, 2002.

Bill Carter, "This Year's Hot TV Trend Is Anatomically Correct," *New York Times*, September 22, 2011, C1, 7.

Susan Cheever, "Innocence Betrayed" (review of Kathryn Harrison's *The Kiss*), *New York Times*, March 30, 1997.

Steven Church and Sophia Pearson, "'Girls Gone Wild' Files Bankruptcy to Fight Vegas Debt," Bloomberg.com, February 28, 2013.

Roger Cohen, "Bret Easton Ellis Answers Critics of 'American Psycho,'" *New York Times*, March 6, 1991.

Holland Cotter, "Poised for a Final Close-Up and Moving On: Cindy Sherman, Metro Pictures," *New York Times*, May 27, 2016, C22.

Sarah Crompton, "Sarah Lucas…," *Guardian*, May 10, 2015.

Theodore Dalrymple, "Trash, Violence, and Versace: But Is It Art?," *City Journal*, Winter 1998.

Christopher B. Daly, "Not Banned in Boston: Mapplethorpe Exhibit Opens," *Washington Post*, August 2, 1990.

Steven Daly and David LaChapelle, "Britney Spears: Inside the Heart and Mind (and Bedroom) of America's New Teen Queen," *Rolling Stone*, April 15, 1999, 61–65.

Brad Darrach with Judy Ellis, "Jerry Seinfeld Lets It All Hang Out," *Life*, October 1993, 78–86.

Mike D'Avria, "The Sexual Proclivities of *Friends*," Splitsider.com, July 2011.

A. DeCurtis, "Naughty by Nature's Surprise Success," *Rolling Stone*, October 17, 1991.

Benoit Denizet-Lewis, "Friends, Friends with Benefits and the Benefits of the Local Mall," *New York Times Magazine*, May 30, 2004.

Joseph Dionisio, "'90s Mouseketeers Turned Big Cheeses," *Newsday* via *Seattle Times*, November 9, 2007.

Mia Fineman, "The Image Is Familiar; The Pitch Isn't," *New York Times*, July 13, 2008, AR22.

Joe Flint, "'Dawson's Creek' Is Named the Filthiest TV Series," *Entertainment Weekly*, August 6, 1998.

David Fricke, "The Naked Truth: Despite Their Appearance, the Chili Peppers Play Music That Comes from Their Hearts," *Rolling Stone*, June 25, 1992.

Tad Friend, "First Banana: Steve Carell and the Meticulous Art of Spontaneity," *New Yorker*, July 5, 2010.

"Friends," *Entertainment Weekly*, September 15, 2001.

Mary Gaitskill, "On Not Being a Victim," *Harper's*, March 1994.

Matthew Gilbert, "'Melrose Place' Basks in Bad: Its Villainy Makes It a 'Dynasty' for the '90s," *Boston Globe*, May 18, 1994, 69.

Sander L. Gilman, *Making the Body Beautiful: A Cultural History of Aesthetic Surgery* (Princeton, NJ: Princeton University Press, 1999), xix, 4–6, 32–33, 214–15.

Merle Ginsberg, "Nicole Kidman on Life with Tom Cruise Through Stanley Kubrick's Lens," *Hollywood Reporter*, October 24, 2012.

Anthony M. Giovacchini, "The Negative Influence of Gangster Rap and What Can Be Done About It," *Poverty & Prejudice: Media and Race*, Stanford.edu, June 4, 1999.

Andrew Goldman, "Blood Sugar Sex Fatherhood," *New York Times Magazine*, March 4, 2012, 12.

Walter Goodman, "HBO Offers Another View of 'Real Sex,'" *New York Times*, August 14, 1992.

Renee Graham, "MTV's 'Real World' Turns into 'The Carnal Camera Show,'" *Boston Globe* via *San Diego Union-Tribune*, September 26, 2004.

Elon Green, "The Dirty Talk of the Town: Profanity at 'The New Yorker,'" TheAwl.com, May 31, 2011.

Mel Gussow, "Artists See No Decency in Ruling on Grants," *New York Times*, July 2, 1998.

Anthony Haden-Guest, "Art or Commerce?," *Vanity Fair*, November 1991, 200–204.

Joe Hagan, "Bjork Icon," *Newsweek*, June 19, 2003.

Judith Halberstam, *In a Queer Time and Place: Transgender Bodies, Subcultural Lives* (New York: New York University Press, 2005), 137–41.

Jason D. Hans, Martie Gillen, and Katrina Akande, "Sex Redefined: The Reclassification of Oral-Genital Contact," *Perspectives on Sexual and Reproductive Health* 42, no. 2 (June 2010).

Suzy Hansen, "Vagina Mama-Log," *New York Observer*, February 26, 2006.

Thomas Hayden, "Barenaked Ladies Exposed," Newsweek.com, October 5, 2000.

John Heilpern, "Angels in America: Indeed, the Millennium Approaches," *New York Observer*, May 20, 1993.

Michael Hiltzik, "'Deep Throat' Numbers Just Don't Add Up," *Los Angeles Times*, January 24, 2005.

Christopher Hitchens, "As American as Apple Pie," *Vanity Fair*, July 2006.

David Hochman, "Playboy Interview: Dr. Drew Pinsky," *Playboy*, July 2008.

Matthew Jacobs, "13 Facts You May Not Know About Stanley Kubrick's 'Eyes Wide Shut,'" *Huffington Post*, July 18, 2014.

Michiko Kakutani, "Comic Novellas on Metamorphoses" (review of Will Self's *Cock & Bull*), *New York Times*, May 31, 1993.

"Kate Winslet: Bio, Pics, Clips," MrSkin.com.

Natalie Kitroeff, "In Hookups, Inequality Still Reigns," NYTimes.com, November 11, 2013.

Gina Kolata, "Editor of A.M.A. Journal Is Dismissed over Sex Paper," *New York Times*, January 16, 1999.

Howard Kurtz, "Tina Brown Quits the New Yorker," *Washington Post*, July 9, 1998.

Roger N. Lancaster, "Sex Offenders: The Last Pariahs," *New York Times*, August 21, 2011, SR6–7.

Molly Langmuir, "Masturbation, Nudists, and Street Interviews: An Oral History of HBO's *Real Sex*," Vulure.com, July 30, 2013.

John Leland, "Bisexuality," *Newsweek*, July 17, 1995.

———, "The Selling of Sex," *Newsweek*, November 2, 1992.

John Leo, "Raging Hormones on TV," *U.S. News*, January 25, 1998.

Jo Ann Lewis, "Corcoran in Red After Art Debacle," *Washington Post*, October 26, 1990.

David Lipsky, "To Be Young & Gay," *Rolling Stone*, August 6, 1998.

Daniella Luxembourg and Amalia Dayan, with Alison M. Gingeras, *Jeff Koons: Made in Heaven Paintings* [1990–91] (New York: Luxembourg & Dayan, 2010).

Sarah Lyall, "Art That Tweaks British Propriety," *New York Times*, September 20, 1997.

Jenny McCarthy, *Jen-X: Jenny McCarthy's Open Book* (New York: HarperCollins, 1997).

Norman Mailer, "Women We Love: Norman Mailer on Madonna," *Esquire*, August 1994.

Janet Maslin, "Jobless? Broke? Men, You Can Always Strip," *New York Times*, August 13, 1997.

———, "When a Not-So-Bad Girl Turns Very, Very Bad," *New York Times*, March 31, 1989.

"Mayor Giuliani Announces Appointment of Sunny Mindel as Press Secretary" (press release), Archives of the Mayor's Press Office, June 7, 1999, www.nyc.gov/html/om/html/99a/pr214-99.html.

Daniel Mendelsohn, "But Enough About Me," *New Yorker*, January 25, 2010, 68–74.

Daphne Merkin, "Unlikely Obsession," *New Yorker*, 98–99.

Denene Millner, " 'Booty Call' Man Hot Comic Bill Bellamy Is Out to Prove He's More Than a One-Joke Hunk," *New York Daily News*, July 30, 1997.

Judith Newman, "The Devil and Miss Regan," *Vanity Fair*, January 2005, 52–68.

Chris Norris, "Hitting Bottom: Dr. Drew Pinsky…Is This Therapy or Tabloid Voyeurism?," *New York Times Magazine*, January 3, 2010.

Emily Nussbaum, "Mary, Mary, Less Contrary," *New York*, November 6, 2005.

"O.J.'s Fake Tell-All Goes Bust!," *Entertainment Weekly*, August 31, 2007.

John Ortved, "Simpson Family Values," *Vanity Fair*, August 2007, 94.

Pamela Paul, "So, Hook-Ups Do Mean More Sex?," *New York Times*, May 9, 2010, ST6.

Peter Plagens, "The Young and the Tasteless," *Newsweek*, November 18, 1991.

Robin Pogrebin, "The Determined Troupe You Don't See: The Creators of 'The Full Monty,' Like Its Heroes, Had Something to Prove," *New York Times*, October 31, 2000.

Katha Pollitt, "With Love and Squalor" (review of Joyce Maynard's *At Home in the World*), *New York Times*, September 13, 1998.

J. D. Reed, "A Life on the Edge: Shannen Doherty's Wild Ways May Be Hazardous to Her—And Her Career," *People*, June 14, 1993.

Frank Rich, "The Greatest Dirty Joke Ever Told," *New York Times*, March 13, 2005.

Katie Roiphe, "The Naked and the Conflicted," *New York Times Book Review*, December 31, 2009, 1, 8–9.

Jim Rutenberg, "Unbleeped Bleep Words Spread on Network TV," *New York Times*, January 25, 2003.

Stephanie A. Sanders and June Machover Reinisch, "Would You Say You 'Had Sex' If…?," *Journal of the American Medical Association* 281, no. 3 (January 20, 1999): 275–77.

Kelefa Sanneh, "The Reality Principle," *New Yorker*, May 9, 2011, 72–77.

"Sarah Lucas: Self Portrait with Fried Eggs, 1996," Tate.org.uk.

Peter Schjeldahl, "The Elegant Scavenger: John Currin's Low Comedy of High Style," *New Yorker*, February 22, 1999.

Karen S. Schneider, "The Game of Love," *People*, March 28, 1994.

Jennifer Schuessler, "Shock Me If You Can," *New York Times*, September 16, 2012, AR1, 10.

———, "Shock Me, Please: Does Art Still Have the Energy?" (roundtable with Roberta Smith, Ben Brantley, A. O. Scott, and Alastair Macaulay), NYTimes.com, September 27, 2012.

Janny Scott and Geraldine Fabrikant, "Change at the New Yorker: The Editor," *New York Times*, July 9, 1998.

"Sensational Hit for Royal Academy," BBC News, December 30, 1997.

Abhishek Seth, "How Baywatch Unknowingly Changed the World: The Untapped Power of TV Shows," *Huffington Post*, September 25, 2013.

"Sex on TV: Content and Context" (press release), Kaiser Family Foundation, February 9, 1999.

Susan Shapiro, "Going for the Lion's Share: Judith Regan," *New York Times Magazine*, July 7, 1994.

William Shawcross, "Murdoch's New Life," *Vanity Fair*, October 1999, 320.

Michael Shnayerson, "Women Behaving Badly," *Vanity Fair*, February 1997, 54–60.

"Shoshanna Lonstein Gruss," CrainsNewYork.com, 2008, mycrains.crainsnewyork.com/40under40/profiles/2008/10096.

"The Small Screen Gets Smaller," Nielsen Media Research via *Time*, March 26, 2009, 62.

Roberta Smith, "That Was No Lady, That Was My Wife," *New York Times*, October 13, 2010.

Dan Snierson, "Bring on 'The Man Show,' " *Entertainment Weekly*, July 16, 1999.

Amy Sohn, "The Final Episode," *New York Press*, August 25, 1999.

Susan Sontag, *On Photography* [1977] (New York: Picador, 2001), 19–21.

Howard Stern, *Private Parts* [1993] (New York: Pocket, 1996), 8, 28, 77, 87, 265, 348–49, 436, 560–73.

Neil Strauss, "The Happiest Man Alive: The Long Struggle and Neurotic Triumph of Howard Stern," *Rolling Stone*, March 31, 2011, 40–47, 76.

———, "Marilyn Manson: Sympathy for the Devil," *Rolling Stone*, January 23, 1997.

Charles Strum, "Taste Schmaste! This Is Just About Laughs," *New York Times*, June 13, 1999.

Janice Hopkins Tanne, "JAMA Editor Fired over Sex Article," *BMJ*, January 23, 1999, www.ncbi.nlm.nih.gov/pmc/articles/PMC1114712/.

Kate Taylor, "Sex on Campus: She Can Play That Game, Too," *New York Times*, July 14, 2013.

Calvin Tomkins, "Lifting the Veil: Old Masters, Pornography, and the Work of John Currin," *New Yorker*, January 28, 2008.

Neal Travis, "...Seinfeld to Marry...," *New York Post*, November 9, 1999.

Linda Troeller, *The Erotic Lives of Women* (London: Scalo, 1998).

Bruce Tulgan, "Meet Generation Z: The Second Generation Within the Giant 'Millennial' Cohort," Rainmaker-Thinking.com, 2013.

Sarah Van Boven, "The Doctor Is Always On," *Newsweek*, June 15, 1998.

Dini von Mueffling, "Bloomingdale's or Bust! The Rise of Shoshanna Lonstein (Jerry's Ex)," *New York Observer*, January 17, 1999.

Sarah Vowell, "La Vie En 'Melrose,'" *Salon*, May 24, 1999.

Daniel J. Wakin, "Schuyler Chapin, Champion of Arts in New York, Dies at 86," *New York Times*, March 8, 2009.

David Foster Wallace, "John Updike, Champion Literary Phallocrat, Drops One; Is This Finally the End for Magnificent Narcissists?," *New York Observer*, October 12, 1997.

Sharon Waxman, "Sex on TV: Study Finds More, Sooner but Safer," *Washington Post*, February 7, 2001, C1, 8.

Elizabeth Weil, "The Incredible Shrinking Childhood: How Early Is Too Early for Puberty?," *New York Times Magazine*, April 1, 2012, 32–33.

Bernard Weinraub, "Getting Real Before Anyone Else: MTV's 'World' Rolls On with Voyeurs on Its Coattails," *New York Times*, February 21, 2001, E1.

Joanne Weintraub, "Tina Brown's New Yorker," *AJR*, April 1995.

Isabel Wilkerson, "Test Case for Obscenity Standards Begins Today in an Ohio Courtroom," *New York Times*, September 24, 1990.

Mary Elizabeth Williams, "Woof! There It Is! Snoop Dogg Asks Not What Porn Can Do for Him, but What He Can Do for Pornography," *Salon*, March 15, 2001.

James Wolcott, "Act I, Obscene Too," *Vanity Fair*, March 1999.

———, "'Roid Rage Threatens the American Soil," VanityFair.com, June 6, 2008.

———, "The Young and the Feckless," *Vanity Fair*, September 1999.

Tom Wolfe, "The 'Me' Decade and the Third Great Awakening," *New York*, August 23, 1976.

Rachel Wolff, "A Townhouse Full of High-Art Smut: Naked Koons Returns," *New York*, October 1, 2010.

"Word Nannies: The Supreme Court Endorses FCC Overkill" (editorial), *Chicago Tribune*, May 2, 2009, A14.

Wesley Yang, "The Sex Diaries," *New York*, November 2, 2009, 36.

CHAPTER 16: Botox, Booties, and Bods

Interviews: Bronwyn Cosgrave, Molly Friend, Anne Kent, Julianne Pepitone, Joan Rivers, George Schlatter, Jim Windolf, Aly Zafonte.

Erin J. Aubry, "Back Is Beautiful," *Salon*, July 15, 1998.

———, *Black Talk, Blue Thoughts, and Walking the Color Line: Dispatches from a Black Journalista* (Lebanon, NH: UPNE/Northeastern Library of Black Literature, 2011).

Peter Baker, "Clinton Blasts 'Glorification of Heroin' in Magazine Fashion Photo Spreads," *Washington Post*, May 22, 1997.

Sandra Ballentine, "Blowin' in the Wind," *W*, October 3, 2013.

Ingrid Banks, "Hair Still Matters," in *Feminist Frontiers*, 6th ed., edited by Laurel Richardson, Verta Taylor, and Nancy Whittier (New York: McGraw-Hill, 2004), 110–11.

"Barbie: History, 1990s," www.barbiemedia.com/about-barbie/history/1990s.html.

Alexei Barrionuevo, "Off Runway, Brazilian Beauty Goes Beyond Blond and Blue-Eyed," *New York Times*, June 8, 2010, A1, 3.

Jennifer Baumgardner and Amy Richards, *Manifesta: Young Women, Feminism, and the Future* [2000] (New York: Farrar, Straus & Giroux, 2010), 139–40.

Jane Birnbaum, "Bum Rap," *Entertainment Weekly*, June 12, 1992.

Laird Borrelli-Persson, "9 Unforgettable Alexander Queen Shows from the '90s and Beyond," Vogue.com, October 3, 2015.

"Botulinum Toxin Type A Product Approval Information—Licensing Action," FDA.gov, April 12, 2002.

David Brooks, *Bobos in Paradise: The New Upper Class and How They Got There* (New York: Simon & Schuster, 2000), 198–99.

DeNeen L. Brown, "Bald Truths About Women," *Washington Post*, June 8, 1999, C1, 8.

Kara Brown, "The One Good Thing That Could Come from All of This Booty Talk," *Vanity Fair*, September 2014.

Jess Cartner-Morley, "How to Wear Clothes," *Guardian*, August 4, 2001.

Susan Chandler and Theresa Ann Palmer, "Remember When Bras Were for Burning?," *BusinessWeek*, January 16, 1995.

"Cosmetic Surgery Trends, 1992, 2007, 2008," Department of Public Relations, American Society of Plastic Surgeons, Plasticsurgery.org.

Irin Carmon, "CosmoGirl to Close," WWD.com, October 10, 2008.

Graydon Carter and David Friend, eds., *Oscar Night: 75 Years of Hollywood Parties* (New York: Knopf, 2004), 21.

Bronwyn Cosgrave, *Made for Each Other: Fashion and the Academy Awards* (New York: Bloomsbury, 2007), 174–78, 182, 186, 204–5.

Sloane Crosley, "Eight Million Bodies in the Naked City," *New York Times*, August 1, 2010.

Eliana Dockterman, "Barbie for Every Body," *Time*, February 8, 2016, 48.

Ruth Doherty, " 'Hello Boys' Billboard Voted Most Iconic Advert Image of All Time," *Huffington Post* (U.K.), May 22, 2015.

Lesley Downer, "When Fashion Got Real," *Wall Street Journal Europe*, November 24, 2000.

Tamala M. Edwards and Roberta Grant, "Hair Down to There," *Time*, February 15, 1999.

James Fox, "The Riddle of Kate Moss," *Vanity Fair*, December 2012, 168.

Patty Fox, *Star Style at the Academy Awards: A Century of Glamour* (Santa Monica, CA: Angel City Press, 2000), 14, 95, 98–102.

"Gisele Bündchen," entry in Voguepedia: The World of Fashion in *Vogue*, vogue.com/voguepedia/Gisele_Bundchen.

Robin Givhan, "Ob-la-di, Ob-lad-da, Bras Go On," *Newsweek*, March 26, 2012, 73.

George Gurley, "A Sexual Standoff in the Naked City," *New York Observer*, August 30, 1998.

Elizabeth Hayt, "At Hair Salons, an Extension on Youth," *New York Times*, September 28, 2008.

Heather Hodson, "Time for Your Injections Ms Jones," *Guardian*, September 7, 2008.

bell hooks, "Selling Hot Pussy: Representations of Black Female Sexuality in the Cultural Marketplace," in Richardson, Taylor, and Whittier, *Feminist Frontiers*, 120, 124–26.

Cathy Horyn, "Changing My Mind About Marc Jacobs's Grunge Collection," *New York*, April 1, 2015.

Alexandra Jacobs, "Smooth Moves: How Sara Blakely Rehabilitated the Girdle," *New Yorker*, March 28, 2011, 60.

Barbara Kantrowitz and Nina Archer Biddle, "The Tempest in a D-Cup," *Newsweek*, March 28, 1994.

Rob Kemp, " 'And I Cannot Lie': The Oral History of Sir Mix-a-Lot's 'Baby Got Back' Video," Vulture.com, December 19, 2013.

Ruth La Ferla, "Elizabeth Hurley: The Swimsuit Issue," *New York Times*, April 10, 2005.

Diane E. Levin and Jean Kilbourne, *So Sexy So Soon: The New Sexualized Childhood and What Parents Can Do to Protect Their Kids* (New York: Ballantine, 2008), 25, 44–45, 142.

Martha Kleder, "Thongs & Freak Dancing Equal Trouble," Culture and Family Issues, CultureAndFamily.org, May 22, 2002.

Alex Kuczynski, "Now You See It, Now You Don't," *New York Times*, September 12, 2004.

Felicia R. Lee, "Cleaving to the Goal of Cleavage," *New York Times*, September 28, 1994.

Annie Leibovitz, Hollywood Issue (cover), *Vanity Fair*, April 1995.

Robert D. McFadden, "Joan Rivers, 1933–2014: A Comic Stiletto Quick to Skewer, Even Herself," *New York Times*, September 5, 2014, A1, B16.

Dave McGinn, "What's Up with Bald Celebrities?," *Toronto Globe and Mail*, September 19, 2009.

Bethany McLean, "Whose Yoga Is It, Anyway?," *Vanity Fair*, April 2012, 150.

Douglas Martin, "Corinne Day, Photography of 'Grunge' Look, Is Dead," *New York Times*, September 2, 2010, A33.

Suzy Menkes, "Now That the Pricing Dam Has Burst," *International Herald Tribune*, February 26, 2009.

"Met Gala Flashback: Princess Diana's 1996 Dior Moment," *People* StyleWatch, People.com, April 5, 2015.

Simon Mills, "Think Before You Ink," *Telegraph*, July 16, 2008.

Matthew Moberg et al. with Allan Afuah, "Sara Lee: Wonderbra" (case study), University of Michigan Business School, 1999, www-personal.umich.edu/~afuah/cases/case15.html.

Desmond Morris, *The Naked Woman: A Study of the Female Body* (New York: Thomas Dunne, 2004), 15–17, 31, 78, 94–95, 110, 174–75, 227–29.

Egan and Fareed Mostoufi, "Ass You Like It," *Time Out New York*, October 11, 2007.

Emily Nussbaum, "Last Girl in Larchmont," *New Yorker*, February 23, 2015.

Andrew O'Hehir, "Joan Rivers Gets Her (Scary) Close-Up," *Salon*, June 9, 2010.

Yumiko Ono and Craig S. Smith, "Mane Attraction: When It Comes to Hair, Extensions Stretch Clear Across the Globe," *Wall Street Journal*, October 4, 1996.

Camille Paglia, "Taylor Swift, Katy Perry and Hollywood Are Ruining Women," *Hollywood Reporter*, December 6, 2012.

Jon Pareles, "Why Sinead O'Connor Hit a Nerve," *New York Times*, November 1, 1992.

Kathy Peiss, "Feminism and the History of the Face," in *The Social and Political Body*, edited by Theodore R. Schatzki and Wolfgang Natter (New York: Guilford, 1996), 176.

Patrick Pemberton, "Rapper Doesn't Mind Legacy of the Behind," *Seattle Times*, June 12, 2006.

William Safire, "Ode on a G-String," *New York Times*, August 4, 1991.

Amy Saltzman, "The 'Tramp Stamp' Story," *Philadelphia Weekly*, May 12, 2009.

Susan Saulny, "Businessmen Who Created Fashion Café Are Hit with Fraud Charges," *New York Times*, December 2, 2000.

Charlie Scheips, *American Fashion: Council of Fashion Designers of America* (New York, Assouline, 2007), 209–10.

Mallory Schlossberg, "How Victoria's Secret's Core Customers Completely Changed," BusinessInsider.com, August 3, 2015.

Mark Seal, "The Doctor Will Sue You Now," *Vanity Fair*, March 2012, 222–23.

Kevin Sessums and Firooz Zahedi, "Bronx Belle," *Vanity Fair*, July 1998, 114–15.

Richard Severo and Peter Keepnews, "Phyllis Diller, Sassy Comedian, Dies at 95," *New York Times*, August 21, 2012, A1, B13.

Choire Sicha, "Let Me Tell You About the Most Heartfelt $200 I Ever Made," *New York*, September 16, 2013, 42–44.

Natasha Singer, "Putting Vanity on Hold," *New York Times*, December 18, 2008, E1, 3.

Pat Sloan, "It's USA or Bust for Sara Lee's Wonderbra," *Advertising Age*, March 21, 1994.

Lenore Skenazy, "Yankee Panky," *New York Sun*, May 20, 2008.

Amy Spindler, "A Death Tarnishes Fashion's 'Heroin Look,' " *New York Times*, May 20, 1997.

Natasha Stagg, "Behind, Beneath, and Between: Tracing the Thong," *DIS*, http://dismagazine.com/discussion/22772/behind-beneath-and-between-tracing-the-thong/.

Joel Stein, "The Fall of the Supermodel," *Time*, November 9, 1998.

Joshua David Stein, "Twerking, a User's Guide," *New York*, August 19, 2013, 38.

Ricki Stern and Annie Sundberg, directors, *Joan Rivers: A Piece of Work*, Breakthrough Films, 2010, produced by Stern, Sundberg, and Seth Keal.

Guy Trebay, "In His Shoes," *New York Times*, October 16, 2011, ST1, 12.

———, "Remembering a Time When Fashion Shows Were Fun," *New York Times*, September 10, 2015, D8.

Natasha Velez, Shawn Cohen, and Leonard Greene, "Joan Rivers Dead at 81," *New York Post*, September 4, 2014.

Philippe Venzano, "Corinne Day: Caution Fragile!," *Mixt(e)*, January 6, 2000.

Harriet Walker, "Gisele Bündchen: The Charmed Life of the Mega-Model," *Independent*, May 12, 2009.

Teddy Wayne, "What Will Induce Nostalgia in 2033?," *New York Times*, January 6, 2013, ST1, 6.

Megan Willett, "How the Victoria's Secret Fashion Show Has Evolved over the Last 20 Years," BusinessInsider.com, December 9, 2015.

Joan Williams, *Unbending Gender: Why Family and Work Conflict and What to Do About It* (New York: Oxford University Press, 2001), 269.

Eric Wilson, "John Casablancas, Modeling Visionary, Dies at 70," *New York Times*, July 20, 2013.

———, "When New York Met the World," *New York Times*, February 11, 2010, E1, 6.

——— and Cathy Horyn, "Alexander McQueen, Brazen Designer, Dies at 40," *New York Times*, February 12, 2010, B9.

Alex Witchel, "As 'Nail Art' Becomes the Fashion, Who's to Scrub the Broiler Pan?," *New York Times*, October 3, 1999.

Naomi Wolf, *The Beauty Myth: How Images of Beauty Are Used Against Women* [1991] (New York: Harper Perennial, 2002), 220.

Christopher Wren, "Clinton Calls Fashion Ads' 'Heroin Chic' Deplorable," *New York Times*, May 22, 1997.

Peter York, "Hair Is Just an Option and Baldness Is a Statement. So Nivea Wants Us to Get Shaving," *Independent*, March 9, 2008.

CHAPTER 17: The Bust Boom

Interviews: Michael Ciaravino, Jessica Stern Meyer, Christian Miranda, Cindi Harwood Rose, Erica Rose, Franklin Rose, Sharon St. Romain Frank, Stacy Tompkins.

"1999 Bum Steer Awards," *Texas Monthly*, January 1999.

"About Bulletgirl," Bulletgirl, http://bulletgirl.com/ABOUT.aspx.

David Baddour, "Strippers Finally Settle with Rick's Cabaret for $15 Million," *Houston Chronicle*, April 3, 2015.

"Breast Implants on Trial: Chronology of Silicone Breast Implants," *Frontline*, PBS, www.pbs.org/wgbh/pages/frontline/implants/cron.html.

Thomas Burton, "Adding Insult to Injury: The Breast-Implant Settlement Falls Short," *The Progressive*, July 1994.

Cary Castagna, "TV's Erica Rose Keeps Fit Without Daddy's Help," *Edmonton Sun*, June 15, 2009.

Face to Face with Connie Chung (transcript), CBS, December 10, 1990.

"FDA Breast Implant Consumer Handbook—2004—Timeline of Breast Implant Activities," U.S. Food and Drug Administration, FDA.gov.

Barnaby J. Feder, "Dow Corning in Bankruptcy over Lawsuits," *New York Times*, May 16, 1995.

Sander L. Gilman, *Making the Body Beautiful: A Cultural History of Aesthetic Surgery* (Princeton, NJ: Princeton University Press, 1999), 239–43, 247.

Lisa Gray, "Image Augmentation," *Houston Press*, December 30, 1999.

Nora Jacobson, *Cleavage: Technology, Controversy, and the Ironies of the Man-Made Breast* (New Brunswick, NJ: Rutgers University Press, 1999).

Joan Kron, "Implant Nation," *Allure*, February 2010, 108–13.

Alex Kuczynski, *Beauty Junkies: Inside Our $15 Billion Obsession with Cosmetic Surgery* (New York: Doubleday, 2006), 257.

M. G. Lord, "Unnatural Woman" (review of Florence Williams's *Breasts: A Natural and Unnatural History*), *New York Times Book Review*, September 16, 2012.

Earl Miller, "20th Anniversary Pet: Lynn," *Penthouse*, September 1989, 139–52.

David J. Morrow, "Settlement on Breast Implant Claims," *New York Times*, November 10, 1998.

Lawrence O'Neil, director, *Breast Men*, HBO, 1997, produced by Gary Lucchesi and Robert McMinn.

Alli Rosenbloom and Ryan Gajewski, "Bachelor Nation's Erica Rose Is Pregnant—Get the Details!," USMagazine.com, February 1, 2016.

Maura Spiegel and Lithe Sebesta, *The Breast Book: An Intimate and Curious History* (New York: Workman, 2002).

Sara Stewart, "Cup Half Full," *New York Post*, April 20, 2010.

Mimi Swartz, "Silicone City," *Texas Monthly*, August 1995, 65–69, 92–100.

Steven Thomson, "Erica Rose Lands in Princess Rehab, Reveals Self-Produced Jewish Dating Show Concept," *Culturemap Houston*, Culturemap.com, June 8, 2010.

Naomi Wolf, *The Beauty Myth: How Images of Beauty Are Used Against Women* [1991] (New York: Harper Perennial, 2002), 4, 242, 248, 253, 266.

CHAPTER 18: Celebrity Sin

Interviews: Aimée Bell, Harry Benson, Stephen Claypole, David Cogan, Richard Friend, Philip Gefter, Gary Ginsberg, Art Harris, Stephen Mayes, J. P. Pappis, Joe Peyronnin, Drew Pinsky, Luc Sante, Ben Silverman, Aidan Sullivan, Susan Zirinsky.

"Amy Fisher: 'I Feel No Sympathy' for Mary Jo Buttafuoco," FoxNews.com, February 11, 2008.

Jennifer Armstrong et al., "The 25 Biggest Scandals of the Past 25 Years," *Entertainment Weekly*, August 31, 2007, 22–31.

"Aspen Tragedy," EW.com, March 24, 2000.

Ken Auletta, "The $64,000 Question," *New Yorker*, September 19, 1994.

Dan Balz, "Legacy of Untimely Death Continues," *Washington Post*, January 2, 1998.

David Barboza, "'Too Hot for TV,' the New Video Verité Is All Too Real for Some," *New York Times*, February 2, 1998.

Jennifer Baumgardner and Amy Richards, *Manifesta: Young Women, Feminism, and the Future* [2000] (New York: Farrar, Straus & Giroux, 2010), 139–40.

Melinda Beck et al., "Video Vigilantes," *Newsweek*, July 22, 1991, 42–47.

Richard L. Berke, "Clinton Aide Dick Morris Quits over Tie to Call Girl," *New York Times*, August 30, 1996.

"Biggest Star Sex Tape Scandals," *US Weekly*, August 21, 2009.

Marie Brenner, "After the Gold Rush," *Vanity Fair*, September 1990.

Michael Brick, "Move to New York Exposed! Star to Leave Florida Home!," *New York Times*, April 25, 2003.

Nadine Brozan, "Chronicle," *New York Times*, April 17, 1996.

———, "Chronicle," *New York Times*, April 24, 1992.

———, "Chronicle," *New York Times*, July 11, 1995.

Stephen Buckley, "Gillooly Pleads Guilty, Says Harding Approved Plot," *Washington Post*, February 2, 1994.

Stephanie Bunbury, "The Rebel Princess," TheAge.com, October 8, 2003.

Mary Jo Buttafucoco, "About Me," http://maryjobuttafuoco.wixsite.com/mary-jo/about-me.

"Buttafuoco Is Released After 4 Months in Jail," *Los Angeles Times*, March 24, 1994.

Robert Chalmers, "Claudine Longet: Aspen's Femme Fatale," *GQ* (U.K.), May 7, 2013.

Bob Colacello, "A Court of His Own," *Vanity Fair*, December 2005, 348–49.

Matthew Cooper, "The Morris Meltdown," *Newsweek*, September 9, 1996.

"Court TV, 1991–2007, in Photos," *Media Decoder* (blog), NYTimes.com, January 1, 2008.

Guy Debord, *The Society of the Spectacle* [1967], translated by Ken Knabb (London: Rebel Press, 2005), 7–8, 11–15, 30, 80–85, 95–97, 118.

Alicia Dennis, "Dylan Farrow's Brother Moses Defends Woody Allen," *People*, February 5, 2014.

Lisa DePaulo, "The True Confessions of Dick Morris," *George*, January 1998.

Frank DiGiacomo, "The Gossip Behind the Gossip," *Vanity Fair*, December 2004.

Dominick Dunne, "Dominick Dunne's Courtroom Notebook: The Menendez Murder Trial," *Vanity Fair*, October 1993.

————, "Nightmare on Elm Drive," *Vanity Fair*, October 1990.

Claudia Eller and James Bates, "De Luca's Behavior Has Town Buzzing," *Los Angeles Times*, March 27, 1998.

Kelly Phillips Erb, "Anna Nicole Smith's Estate Loses Yet Another Run at the Marshall Fortune," *Forbes*, August 20, 2014.

Mary H. J. Farrell, "The Trumps Head for Divorce Court," *People*, February 26, 1990.

Mitchell Fink, "The Insider," *People*, March 2, 1992.

Neal Gabler, "The Greatest Show on Earth," *Newsweek*, December 12, 2009.

"Game, Suit, Match," *New York Times*, March 15, 1992.

David Gelman, Lydia Denworth, and Nadine Joseph, "'Outing': An Unexpected Assault on Sexual Privacy," *Newsweek,* April 30, 1990.

Mitch Gelman, "Shattered: We Know All About Mike Tyson's Release from Prison...," *Newsday* via *Los Angeles Times*, March 31, 1995.

Tom Gliatto, "Kathie Lee's Crisis," *People*, June 2, 1997.

Kevin Glynn, "Tabloid Television," Museum of Broadcast Communications, www.museum.tv/eotv/tabloidtelev.htm.

Michelle Green, "Bugged and Bedeviled," *People*, February 1, 1993.

————, "Duchess in Dutch," *People*, September 7, 1992.

Larry Gross, *Contested Closets: The Politics and Ethics of Outing* (Minneapolis: University of Minnesota Press, 1993), 2, 138, 151–52, 187–90, 207, 220, 229–30.

Guy Gugliotta, "Regarding Henry: HUD Secretary's Unforgettable Affair," *Washington Post*, October 12, 1994.

Jack Healy, "Grand Jury Urged Charges in JonBenet Ramsey Case," *New York Times*, October 26, 2013, A11.

Erik Hedegaard, "'This Show Is Good for America,'" *Rolling Stone*, May 14, 1998.

Edward Helmore, "I Did a Bad Thing and There You Have It," *Independent*, July 12, 1995.

William A. Henry III, "History as It Happens: Linking Leaders as Never Before, CNN Has Changed the Way the World Does Business," *Time* (Man of the Year), January 6, 1992, 24.

Lynn Hirschberg, "Don't Hate Me Because I'm Beautiful," *Vanity Fair*, December 1990, 222.

John Hiscock, "Hugh Grant on Prostitute Charge," *Telegraph*, June 28, 1995.

Anna Holmes, "The Disposable Woman," *New York Times*, March 4, 2011.

Walter Isaacson, "The Heart Wants What It Wants" (interview with Woody Allen), *Time*, August 31, 1992.

Sharon Isaak and Tim Appelo, "Making a Killing: The Selling of the Amy Fisher Story," *Entertainment Weekly*, September 25, 1992, 28–33.

Charles Isherwood, "Older, but No More Mature," *New York Times*, November 12, 2010, C1, 17.

Michael Janofsky, "Marv Albert Pleads Guilty and Is Dismissed by NBC," *New York Times*, September 26, 1997.

"'Jenny Jones' Talk-Show Killer Gets 20–25 Years," CNN.com, December 4, 1996.

"Joey Buttafuoco vs 'Chyna' Joanie Laurer!" (video), Fox, 2002, youtube.com/watch?v=JuLWWDoN85E.

Bernadette Johnson, "10 Most Incriminating Secret Recordings: Princess Diana's Squidgygate," People.com, people.howstuffworks.com/10-incriminating-recordings8.htm.

Paul Johnson, "British Noblesse Abandons Its Oblige," *Wall Street Journal*, March 30, 1992.

Erica Johnston, "Meet Two Activists Who Brought Sweeping Change to the Gay Rights Movement," *Washington Post Magazine*, October 3, 2014.

Tom Junod, "'Kevin Spacey?' My Mom Said. 'I Hear He's...,'" *Esquire*, October 1997.

David Kamp, "The Tabloid Decade," *Vanity Fair*, February 1999.

Michael Katz, "Mike Tyson Chews Off a Piece of Evander Holyfield's Ear During 1997 Las Vegas Bout," *New York Daily News*, June 29, 1997.

Dana Kennedy, "Scandal Inc.," *Entertainment Weekly*, March 4, 1994, 18–27.

Edward Klein, "The Trouble with Andrew," *Vanity Fair*, August 2011, 101.

Sharon LaFraniere, "Barry Arrested on Cocaine Charges in Undercover FBI, Police Operation," *Washington Post*, January 19, 1990.

Devon Leonard, "The Tabloid King's Dilemma," *Fortune*, November 1, 2004.

Irv Letofsky, "Roseanne Is Sorry—But Not *That* Sorry," *Los Angeles Times*, July 28, 1990.

Rebecca Lewin, "A Few Minutes with Fractious Fran," *Advocate*, July 3, 1990.

Ryan Linkof, "Why We Need the Tabloids," *New York Times*, July 20, 2011, A27.

Carol Lloyd, "Flynt's Revenge," *Salon*, February 1999.

Darcie Lunsford, "Taming the Tabloids," *AJR*, September 2000.

Dyan Machan, "Trash Sells," *Forbes*, April 15, 2002.

William Mader, "Britain: The Not So Merry Wife of Windsor," *Time*, March 30, 1992.

Jonathan Mahler, "The National Enquirer: A Tabloid Story," in *The National Enquirer: Thirty Years of Unforgettable Images*, edited by Charles Melcher and Valerie Virga, with David Keeps (New York: Talk Miramax, 2001), 244–53.

————, "On Williams, NBC Clings to the Past," *New York Times*, June 19, 2015, B1, 8.

————, "What Rupert Wrought," *New York*, April 11, 2005.

Heather Mallick, "The Princess and the Press," *Frontline*, PBS, October 19, 1997.

Charles Melcher and Valerie Virga, eds., with David Keeps, *The National Enquirer: Thirty Years of Unforgettable Images* (New York: Talk Miramax, 2001), 7–11, 17, 19, 76, 83.

"Mendendez Brothers Convicted in Parents' Murder 16 Years Ago," LosAngelesTimes.com, March 2012.

Lawrie Mifflin, "In This War, CNN Has Real Competition," *New York Times*, April 5, 1999.

"Mike Tyson Timeline," ESPN, http://static.espn.go.com/boxing/news/2002/0129/1319772.html.

Janice Min, "Rattled Royals," *People*, September 30, 1996.

Alex Mitchell, "The Original Hack," *Sydney Morning Herald*, July 31, 2011.

Dick Morris, *Behind the Oval Office: Getting Reelected Against All Odds* (New York: St. Martin's, 1999), xxxix, 322–24, 332–33.

David Moye, "Joey Buttafuoco Battles Amy Fisher's Husband, Lou Bellera, in Celebrity Boxing," *Huffington Post*, November 3, 2011.

"Navratilova, Former Companion Reach Settlement of Lawsuit," Associated Press via *Los Angeles Times*, March 14, 1992.

Joe Nocera, "Murdoch's Fatal Flaw," *New York Times*, July 9, 2011, A19.

Jocelyn Noveck, "A Look Back at the Allegations Against Woody Allen," Associated Press via *Denver Post*, February 4, 2014.

Lisa O'Carroll, Mark Sweney, and Roy Greenslade, "Page 3: The Sun Calls Time on Topless Models After 44 Years," *Guardian*, January 20, 1015.

"On This Day: 19 March [1992]," BBC, news.bbc.co.uk/onthisday/hi/dates/stories/march/19/newsid_2543000/2543667.stm.

"On This Day: 9 November [1993]," BBC, news.bbc.co.uk/onthisday/hi/dates/stories/november/9/newsid_2515000/2515739.stm.

"On This Day: 20 November [1992]," BBC, news.bbc.co.uk/onthisday/hi/dates/stories/november/20/newsid_2551000/2551107.stm.

Maureen Orth, "The Killer's Trail," *Vanity Fair*, September 1997.

————, "Mia's Story," *Vanity Fair*, November 1992, 214–20.

————, "Momma Mia!," *Vanity Fair*, October 2013.

Jeannie Park, "He Does, She Does—They Do!," *People*, October 21, 1991, 38–45.

Stanton Peele, "The Top Seven Kennedy Sex Scandals," *Psychology Today*, May 21, 2008.

Marcia Heroux Pounds, "National Enquirer Leaving Boca for New York," (Broward and Palm Beach) *Sun Sentinel*, May 10, 2014.

"Princess Stephanie's Divorce Is Approved," *Chicago Tribune*, October 5, 1996.

Larry Reibstein, "Trash + Class = Cash: The Battle of the TV News Magazine Shows," *Newsweek*, April 11, 1994, 60–65.

Frank Rich, "The Age of the Mediathon," *New York Times Magazine*, October 29, 2000.

————, "The 'New News,'" *New York Times*, October 28, 1998.

————, "The 'Seinfeld' Hoax," *New York Times*, May 13, 1998.

Fred Ritchin, "The Image Wars," *Dateline: Winners of the Overseas Press Club Awards* (annual bulletin), Spring 2015, 18.

David Rohde, "Son of Robert Kennedy Dies in Colorado Skiing Accident," *New York Times*, January 1, 1998.

Larry Rohter, "It Might Be News, but It's Not 'MacNeil/Lehrer,'" *New York Times*, April 25, 1993.

————, "Pee-wee Herman Enters a Plea of No Contest," *New York Times*, November 8, 1991.

Frances Romero, "Olympic Showdowns on Ice: Tonya Harding and Nancy Kerrigan," Time.com, February 25, 2010.

Alyssa Rosenberg, "In New *30 for 30* Film, ESPN to Explore the Tonya Harding–Nancy Kerrigan Rivalry and Its Tragic Results," ThinkProgress.org, July 26, 2013.

Howard Rosenberg, "He's Finally Ready for the 'Joey Buttafuoco Show,'" *Los Angeles Times*, May 29, 1995.

George Rush and Christina Boyle, "Shamed Duchess of York Steps Out Post-scandal to Hawk Her New Books in New York," *New York Daily News*, May 26, 2010.

Joal Ryan, "The Death of Eddie Murphy's Infamous Passenger," E! News, Eonline.com, May 1, 1998.

————, "Marv Pulls Rug Out from Under Wig Story," E! News, Eonline.com, November 6, 1997.

Nancy Jo Sales, "The Camera Wars," *Vanity Fair*, March 2003, 184.

Diana Jean Schemo, "Amy Fisher to Enter Guilty Plea," *New York Times*, September 23, 1992.

Karen S. Schneider, "The Donald Ducks Out," *People*, May 19, 1997.

Lisa Schwarzbaum, "Mrs. Arnold in Charge," *Entertainment Weekly*, October 25, 1991, 28.

"The Science of Covers: Celebs, Cleavage and Sparkle," *WWD*, January 4, 2008.

John Seabrook, "The Big Sellout," *New Yorker*, October 20, 1997.

Mark Seal, "The Doctor Will Sue You Now," *Vanity Fair*, March 2012, 223.

Jacqueline E. Sharkey, "The Diana Aftermath," *AJR*, November 1997.

E. R. Shipp, "Tyson Gets 6-Year Prison Term for Rape Conviction in Indiana," *New York Times*, March 27, 1992.

Michelle Singer, "Timeline: Anna Nicole Smith," CBSNews.com, February 28, 2007.

Stephanie Slifer, "Police Chief Speaks Out on JonBenet Ramsey Case, Regrets It," CBSNews.com, February 25, 2015.

Kyle Smith, "Double Trouble: A Pickup Turns Into a Drag for Eddie Murphy," *People*, May 19, 1997.

Sally Bedell Smith, "Diana and the Press," *Vanity Fair*, September 1998.

Elizabeth Sporkin, "Ooh-La-La Marla!," *People*, March 5, 1990.

———, "Pee-wee's Big Disgrace," *People*, August 12, 1991.

Alessandra Stanley, "For Some, a Search for Celebrity Is Worth Any Risk," *New York Times*, November 28, 2009, A12.

"Stephanie Humiliée: Les Dessous du Scandale—Exclusif: Les Photos," *L'illustré*, September 11, 1996.

Marlow Stern, "Mike Tyson Opens Up About His Rape Conviction, Brad Pitt, and Love of Pinkberry," *Daily Beast*, November 6, 2013.

Mimi Swartz, "How to Marry a Millionaire," *Texas Monthly*, October 1994, 126–31, 159–60.

Sam Tanenhaus, "Woody Allen's Black Magic," *Newsweek*, June 18, 2012.

Bryce Taylor, "Gym Owner Defends Princess Pictures," *Independent*, November 17, 1993.

Tracy Thompson and Elsa Walsh, "Jurors View Videotape of Barry Drug Arrest," *Washington Post*, June 29, 1990.

Jon Thurber, "Son of Acting Legend Was Guilty of Killing His Half-Sister's Lover," *Los Angeles Times*, January 27, 2008.

"Transsexual Prostitute Arrested in Eddie Murphy's Car," CNN.com, May 2, 1997.

George W. S. Trow, *Within the Context of No Context* [1981] (New York: Atlantic Monthly Press, 1997), 72–74, 78, 80–82.

David Tuller, "Uproar over Gays Booting Others out of the Closet," *San Francisco Chronicle*, March 12, 1990, in Gross, *Contested Closets*, 219–22.

Ted Turner, "Summary of ASME Members' Lunch," American Society of Magazine Editors (letter), February 5, 1997.

Tom Vanderbilt, "When Animals Attack, Cars Crash and Stunts Go Bad," *New York Times Magazine*, December 6, 1998, 50–54.

Lloyd Vries, "Joey Buttafuoco in Trouble Again," Associated Press via CBSNews.com, March 31, 2016.

Robert B. Weide, "The Woody Allen Allegations: Not So Fast," *Daily Beast*, January 27, 2014.

Allen White, "Reagan's AIDS Legacy/Silence Equals Death," SFGate.com, June 8, 2004.

Michael White and David Sharrock, "Charles and Diana to Separate," *Guardian*, December 10, 1992.

Elliott Wilk, "Findings of Fact," in Woody Allen v Maria Villiers Farrow, Supreme Court, New York County, #68738/92, 1992.

Peter Wilkinson, "Who Killed Pee-wee?," *Rolling Stone*, October 3, 1991.

Marjorie Williams, "Day of the Jackals," *Vanity Fair*, November 1996, 64–66, 88.

A. N. Wilson, "The Message in the Mourning," *New York Times*, September 3, 1997.

Michael Winerip, "Looking for an 11 O'Clock Fix," *New York Times Magazine*, January 11, 1988, 30–36.

Alex Witchel, "At Home With: Marla Maples; Cinderella, with Both of Her Shoes," *New York Times*, August 20, 1992.

James Wolcott, "U.S. Confidential," *Vanity Fair*, June 2002.

Michael Wolff, "Politico's Washington Coup," *Vanity Fair*, August 2009, 74–75.

"Woody Allen Denies Crossing Incest Line," Associated Press via *Los Angeles Times*, August 23, 1992.

Richard Zoglin, "The Fact-to-Film Frenzy," *Time*, March 29, 1993, 56–57.

CHAPTER 19: Four Moments That Changed the Narrative

Interviews: John Wayne Bobbitt, Lorena Bobbitt, Donna Ferrato, Art Harris, Anita Hill,
Paula Corbin Jones, Joel Paul.

"1995: O. J. Simpson Verdict Is Not Guilty," CNN.com, October 3, 1995, via YouTube, www.youtube.com/watch?v=rurKd569xRw.

Joel Achenbach, "A Stitch in Time," *Washington Post*, October 7, 1993.

Nikol G. Alexander and Drucilla Cornell, "Dismissed or Banished? A Testament to the Reasonableness of the Simpson Jury," in *Birth of a Nation'hood: Gaze, Script, and Spectacle in the O.J. Simpson Case*, edited by Toni Morrison and Claudia Brodsky Lacour (New York: Pantheon, 1997), 59–60, 68–69, 77–78.

Martin Amis, "Rendezvous with Rushdie," *Vanity Fair*, December 1990.

Lili Anolik, "It All Began with O.J.," *Vanity Fair*, June 2014, 108–17, 154.

Kent Babb, "How the O. J. Simpson Murder Trial 20 Years Ago Changed the Media Landscape," *Washington Post*, June 9, 2014.

Peter Baker, "Clinton Settles Paula Jones Lawsuit for $850,000," *Washington Post*, November 14, 1998.

"Battle of Sexes Joined in Case of a Mutilation," *New York Times*, November 8, 1993.

"'Baywatch' Goes Out with the Tide," *Economist*, March 4, 1999.

"Baywatch to Make 'Movie Debut,'" BBC News, August 21, 2001.

Chris Boyette, "5 Surprising Facts About O. J. Simpson's Slow-Speed Chase," CNN.com, June 10, 2014.

David Brock, *Blinded by the Right: Confessions of an Ex-Conservative* (New York: Three Rivers, 2002), 166, 193–94, 200–203, 282–84.

——, "Living with the Clintons," *American Spectator*, January 1994.

Frank Bruni, "The Invention of Outrage," *New York Times*, November 6, 2011, SR3.

Deirdre Carmody, "Time Responds to Criticism over Simpson Cover," *New York Times*, June 25, 1994.

Ellis Cashmore, *Celebrity/Culture* (Abingdon, Oxfordshire: Routledge, 2006), 157.

Andrew J. Cherlin, *The Marriage-Go-Round: The State of Marriage and the Family in America Today* (New York: Knopf, 2009), 102.

Robin Clark, "Judge Ito Said He Would Sequester Jurors, Giving Them Two Days to Prepare. They Were Grim-Faced," *Philadelphia Inquirer*, January 10, 1995.

Francis X. Clines, "Clinton, in First for a President, Testifies in Sex Harassment Suit," *New York Times*, January 18, 1998.

Tim Cornwell, "Pammy and Tommy Were Lovers," *Independent*, May 15, 1998.

Ann Coulter, "Clinton Sure Can Pick 'Em," *Jewish World Review*, October 30, 2000.

Steve Coz, introduction to *The National Enquirer: Thirty Years of Unforgettable Images*, edited by Charles Melcher and Valrier Virga, with David Keeps (New York: Talk Miramax, 2001), 10–13.

Barbara Creed, *The Monstrous Feminine: Film, Feminism, Psychoanalysis* (Abingdon, Oxfordshire: Routledge, 1993), 109.

Ann duCille, "The Unbearable Darkness of Being," in Morrison and Lacour, *Birth of a Nation'hood*, 314–15.

Dominick Dunne, "L.A. in the Age of O.J.," *Vanity Fair*, February 1995.

James Ellroy, "Sex, Glitz and Greed: The Seduction of O.J. Simpson," *GQ*, December 1994, 267.

Jodi Enda, "Simpson Bought a Knife Weeks Before Slaying, Jury Is Told," *Philadelphia Inquirer*, July 1, 1994.

Steve Erickson, "The Celebrity Sex Tape and the End of Imagination," *Los Angeles*, October 2008, 132–37, 214.

Robert C. Fellmeth, "Perspectives on Judge Ito: Just Another Nice Guy? Phooey!," *Los Angeles Times*, November 16, 1994.

Nancy Gibbs, "O.J. Simpson: End of the Run," *Time*, June 27, 1994, 28–35.

Elizabeth Gleick, "Severance Pay," *People*, December 13, 1993.

Walter Goodman, "Judge Ito, Spare That Camera," *New York Times*, November 6, 1994.

Ken Gormley, *The Death of American Virtue: Clinton vs. Starr* (New York: Broadway, 2010), 118, 259–61, 319, 323–24, 329–30, 338, 341–43, 348, 358–64, 412–17, 431, 566–67, 576–77, 598, 674.

"Grand Jury Testimony Says That Simpson Spied on Wife's Dates," *New York Times*, July 31, 1994.

Raymond Hernandez, "The Simpson Case: The Pursuit; A Spectacle Gripping and Bizarre," *New York Times*, June 18, 1994.

Jere Hester, "Porn Star: O.J. Did It; Says She Knows Plenty After Conversations with Cowlings," *New York Daily News*, September 13, 1994.

Gloria Hillard, "Ex-Simpson Juror Poses for Playboy," CNN.com, February 5, 1996.

Christian Holub, "What Is a 'Brentwood Hello'? Connie Britton & James Corden Explain," *Entertainment Weekly*, March 11, 2016.

Caroline Howe, "'Nic Leaned Over and Started Kissing Me.' Faye Resnick's Tawdry Tell-All…,'" *Daily Mail*, March 10, 2016.

"Husband Tells Court of Sexual Mutilation by Wife," *New York Times*, November 10, 1993.

"Husband Tells of Mutilation as Wife's Trial Begins," *New York Times*, January 11, 1994.

Michael Isikoff and Evan Thomas, "'I Want Him to Admit What He Did,'" *Newsweek*, June 9, 1997.

Michael Janofsky and Sara Rimer, "A Troubled Life Unfolds…Simpson: 'Baddest Cat,' a Polished Star, or Both?," *New York Times*, June 26, 1994.

"John Wayne and Lorena Bobbitt Trials: 1993 & 1994," Law Library/American Law and Legal Information, http://law.jrank.org/pages/3596/John-Wayne-Lorena-Bobbitt-Trials-1993-1994.html.

"Jones v Clinton: Special Report—Complaint," May 1994, via WashingtonPost.com.

"Jones v Clinton: Special Report—Judge Wright's Opinion," April 1, 1994, via WashingtonPost.com.

Peter Kane, *The Bobbitt Case—You Decide: Transcripts of the Sex Trial That Shocked the World* (New York: Windsor/Pinnacle, 1994), 14–16, 19–28, 201–2, 219–24, 344–47.

Sam Kashner, "Both Huntress and Prey," *Vanity Fair*, November 2014.

Daniel Klaidman, "Clinton v. Paula Jones," *Newsweek*, January 12, 1997.

Gregory Krieg, "Donald Trump Defends Size of His Penis," CNN.com, March 4, 2016.

Howard Kurtz, "Clinton on TV: Here, There and Everywhere, It Seemed," *Washington Post*, September 22, 1998.

Stephen Labaton, "Suit Accuses President of Advance," *New York Times*, May 7, 1994.

Adam Leff and Richard Rushfield, "The O.J. Emmys," *Vanity Fair*, December 1995.

Richard Leiby, "Bobbitt: A Slice of America," *Washington Post*, January 11, 1994.

Amanda Chicago Lewis, "Pam and Tommy: The Untold Story of the World's Most Infamous Sex Tape," *Rolling Stone*, December 22, 2014.

Neil A. Lewis, "Sex Harassment Suit Based on 1860's Law," *New York Times*, May 7, 1994.

"Lorena Bobbitt Goes Free," *New York Times*, March 1, 1994.

Joe Lynch, "Tommy Lee & Pam Anderson Married 20 Years Ago Today," Billboard.com, February 19, 2015.

Jim McClellan, "Wired World: Click and Pant Seth Warshavsky...," *Observer*, February 7, 1999.

Jonathan Mahler, "The National Enquirer: A Tabloid Story," in *The National Enquirer: Thirty Years of Unforgettable Images*, 250.

David Margolick, "The Enquirer: Required Reading in Simpson Case," *New York Times*, October 24, 1994.

———, "Lorena Bobbitt Acquitted in Mutilation of Husband," *New York Times*, January 22, 1994.

———, "Victims Put Up Long Fight, a Witness for Simpson Says," *New York Times*, August 11, 1995.

Kim Masters, "Sex, Lies, and an 8-Inch Carving Knife," *Vanity Fair*, November 1993, 168–72, 207–12.

Rudy Maxa, "Paula Jones: Clinton's Accuser Getting Nude and Lewd," *Penthouse*, January 1995.

———, "Paula Jones: The Nudes and Her Sleazy Past," *Penthouse*, April 1998.

Charles Melcher and Valerie Virga, eds., with David Keeps, *The National Enquirer: Thirty Years of Unforgettable Images* (New York: Talk Miramax, 2001), 21, 162.

Michaels v. Internet Entertainment Group, Inc., No. CV 98-0583 DDP (CWX), U.S. District Court, C.D. California (1998).

Toni Morrison, "The Official Story: Dead Man Golfing," in Morrison and Lacour, *Birth of a Nation'hood*, xv–xvi.

Seth Mydans, "O. J. Simpson's Ex-Wife Slain at Her Condo in Los Angeles," *New York Times*, June 14, 1994.

"Nicole Simpson's 911 Calls," Associated Press via *Los Angeles Times*, June 23, 1994.

"O.J. Simpson Trial: Transcript of Bronco Call (June 17, 1994)," CNN.com, December 11, 2007.

"The O.J. Verdict," *Frontline*, PBS, October 4, 2005, www.pbs.org/wgbh/pages/frontline/oj/etc/script.html.

Xana O'Neill, "John Bobbitt Still Swooning for Lorena," NBC San Diego, May 4, 2009, NBCSanDiego.com.

Clarence Page, "Bobbitt Tale Needs Happy Ending After the Bobbitt Salute," *Chicago Tribune*, January 19, 1994.

Camille Paglia, *Vamps and Tramps: New Essays* [1994] (New York: Knopf Doubleday, 2011), 13.

"Pamela Anderson, Tommy Lee Lawsuit Thrown Out," MTV News, April 9, 1997.

Pamela Paul, *Pornified: How Pornography Is Damaging Our Lives, Our Relationships, and Our Families* (New York: Henry Holt, 2006), 59.

"Perils of Paula Jones," *Penthouse*, November 2000.

James Poniewozik, "'The People v. O.J. Simpson': Why the Trial Matters Now," *New York Times*, April 6, 2016.

Faye D. Resnick with Mike Walker, *Nicole Brown Simpson: The Private Diary of a Life Interrupted* (Beverly Hills, CA: Dove, 1994), 46–47.

Katie Roiphe, "All the Rage," *New York Times*, November 29, 1993.

Michael Ross, "Lorena Bobbitt Testifies on Abuse Claims," *Los Angeles Times*, January 13, 1994.

———, "Lorena Bobbitt's Trial for Cutting Penis Begins," *Los Angeles Times*, January 11, 1994.

Mike Royko, "When It Comes to Trashing, Some Know How to Pile On," *Chicago Tribune*, January 14, 1997.

Carlos Sanchez, "Man Cut by Wife Indicted on Sex Assault Charge," *Washington Post*, August 4, 1993.

Howard Schneider, "Paula Jones and a House Divided," *Washington Post*, June 9, 1994.

Jacqueline E. Sharkey, "The Diana Aftermath," *AJR*, November 1997.

Stephanie Simon, "FBI Expert Says Simpson Wore Bruno Maglis in Photo," *Los Angeles Times*, November 21, 1996.

Amy C. Sims, "Trendy Lawyers Share Stage with Celeb Clients," FoxNews.com, December 16, 2003.

"The Simpson Murder Case: Nicole Simpson's 911 Calls," *Los Angeles Times*, June 23, 1994.

Allan Smith, "How O.J. Simpson's Car Chase Led to Record Sales at Domino's Pizza," BusinessInsider.com, June 17, 2014.

Dylan Stableford, "TV's Most Powerful Moments: 9/11, Katrina, O.J., Nielsen Study Finds," Yahoo.com, July 11, 2012.

George Stephanopoulos, *All Too Human: A Political Education* (Boston: Little, Brown, 1999), 273.

Benjamin Svetkey, "Advantage Marla," *Entertainment Weekly*, July 6, 1990.

Evan Thomas and Daniel Klaidman, "Clinton V. Paula Jones," *Newsweek*, January 13, 1997.

Paul Thompson, "O. J. Simpson's Ex Paula Barbieri...," *Daily Mail*, February 10, 2016.

Jeffrey Toobin, *A Vast Conspiracy: The Real Story of the Sex Scandal That Nearly Brought Down a President* (New York: Touchstone, 1999), 138.

Bill Turque et al., "He Could Run...but He Couldn't Hide,"*Newsweek*, June 27, 1994, 14–27.

Stephen Wayda, "Faye: Ms. Resnick Believes in Full Disclosure," *Playboy*, March 1997, 126–35.

Thomas E. Weber, "How Pamela Anderson Lee Became Queen of the Web," *Wall Street Journal*, April 13, 1999.

Jason Wells, "20 Year Ago Today: O. J. Simpson's Slow-Speed Chase Stopped L.A.," *Los Angeles Times*, June 17, 2014.

"Whitewater: Special Report—Timeline," WashingtonPost.com, www.washingtonpost.com/wp-srv/politics/special/whitewater/timeline.htm.

James Wolcott, "Schtuppin' with the Stars," *Vanity Fair*, February 2010, 68–69.

Buck Wolf, "John Wayne Bobbitt Remarries," ABC News, March 26, 2002.

Virginia Woolf, *The Hogarth Essays: Mr. Bennett and Mrs. Brown* (London: Hogarth, 1924), 4.

Evan Wright, "Porn.con?: Seth Warshavsky Was One of the Youngest, Brashest Entrepreneurs on the Web...," *Rolling Stone*, August 3, 2000.

CHAPTER 20: The Boomsie Twins

Interviews: Judy Bachrach, Lisa Baron, Dan Buck, Jerry Burke, Gary Ginsberg, Mary Matalin, Jean-Jacques Naudet, Joe Peyronnin, David Rhodes, Jennifer Rider, Sam Tanenhaus, Terry Teachout, James Warren.

Roger Ailes with Jon Kraushar, *You Are the Message: Getting What You Want by Being Who You Are* [1988] (New York: Crown Business, 1995), xiii, 13–16, 21, 177.

Kurt Andersen, "Meet the Press Now," *New York*, July 21, 2008, 18–19.

James Atlas, "The Counter Counterculture, *New York Times Magazine*, February 12, 1995.

Matt Bai, "Newt. Again," *New York Times Magazine*, March 1, 2009, 28–30.

Peter Baker, "If Bill Clinton Was President," *New York Times*, December 12, 2010, WK1, 4.

Fred Barnes, "Revenge of the Squares," *New Republic*, March 13, 1995.

Lisa Baron, *Life of the Party: A Political Press Tart Bares All* (New York: Citadel, 2011), 63, 153, 190–92.

Richard Blow, "Camelot's Son," *Vanity Fair*, May 2002.

Peter J. Boyer, "Bull Rush," *Vanity Fair*, May 1992, 158–59.

Taylor Branch, *The Clinton Tapes: Wrestling History with the President* (New York: Simon & Schuster, 2009), 203.

Kendall Breitman, "'Nerd Prom' Documentary Skewers White House Correspondents' Dinner," Politico.com, April 8, 2015.

David Brock, *Blinded by the Right: Confessions of an Ex-Conservative* (New York: Three Rivers, 2002), xvii, 60–61, 86, 115, 129, 151–52, 171–73, 270.

Timothey J. Burger and Owen Mortiz, "Newt Plays House with New Squeeze," *New York Daily News*, August 12, 1999.

Bryan Burrough and Kim Masters, "Cable Guys," *Vanity Fair*, January 1997.

David Carr, "How Drudge Stayed on Top," *New York Times*, May 16, 2011, B1, 8.

David Carr and Tim Arango, "A Fox Chief at the Pinnacle of Media and Politics," *New York Times*, January 10, 2010, A1, C4.

Graydon Carter, "Donald Trump: The Ugly American," *Vanity Fair*, October 2016.

Zev Chafets, "Late-Period Limbaugh," *New York Times Magazine*, July 6, 2008, 33, 37.

Amy Chozick, "Obama Is an Avid Reader, and Critic of the News," *New York Times*, August 8, 2012, A13.

Bill Clinton, *My Life* (New York: Random House/Vintage, 2004), 629, 634–35.

Gail Collins, "Eye of the Newt," *New York Times*, March 12, 2011.

———, "Opening Newt's Marriage," *New York Times*, January 21, 2012, A23.

Michael Colton, "Keeping Up with Jones: Amid the Celebrities at the White House Correspondents' Dinner, One Stood Out," *Washington Post*, April 17, 1998, C1, 8.

Jennet Conant, "L.A. Confidential," *Vanity Fair*, December 1997, 160–72.

Matthew Cooper, "Newt's Been Lutheran, Baptist, and Catholic. Is that Flip Flopping?" *National Journal*, January 19, 2012.

Frank DiGiacomo, "Paula Watches Bill Whip Out Jokes: Press, Prez Renew Old Love Affair," *New York Observer*, May 3, 1998.

Maureen Dowd, "Call Off the Dogs," *New York Times*, February 15, 2015, SR11.

———, "My Man Newt," *New York Times*, November 30, 2011, A35.

———, "Newt Loves Callista," *New York Times*, June 12, 2011, WK9.

Matt Drudge, *Drudge Manifesto* (New York: NAL, 2000), 22.

Kevin Drum, "Newt Gingrich and the Hospital Room," *Mother Jones*, May 2011.

Sarah Ellison, "Two Men and a Newsstand," *Vanity Fair*, October 2010, 247–48.

Ron Elving, "GOP's 'Pledge' Echoes 'Contract': But Much Myth Surrounds '94 Plan," NPR.org, September 23, 2010.

David Friend, *Watching the World Change: The Stories Behind the Images of 9/11* (New York: Farrar, Straus & Giroux, 2006), 103.

David Frum, "Why Rush Is Wrong," *Newsweek*, March 16, 2009, 26–32.

Joseph Gallivan, "Ted Rips Levin's Leadership of AOL TW," *New York Post*, April 16, 2001.

Jeffrey B. Gayner, "The Contract with America: Implementing New Ideas in the U.S.," Heritage Foundation, October 12, 1995.

Nancy Gibbs and Karen Tumulty, "Master of the House," *Time* (Man of the Year), December 25, 1995, 54–60, 83.

Steven M. Gillon, *The Pact: Bill Clinton, Newt Gingrich, and the Rivalry That Defined a Generation* (New York: Oxford University Press, 2008), xviii, 10–11, 27–28, 123–29, 136.

Newt Gingrich et al., "Republican Contract with America," www.house.gov/house/Contract/CONTRACT.html.

James V. Grimaldi, "Marianne Gingrich, Newt's Ex-Wife, Says He Wanted 'Open Marriage,'" *Washington Post*, January 19, 2012.

Marc Gunther, "The Rules According to Rupert," *Fortune*, October 26, 1998.

Marshall Heyman, "'Conscious' Celebrities Flock to D.C.," *Wall Street Journal*, May 2, 2011.

Geoffrey Kabaservice, "The Moderates Who Lighted the Fuse," *New York Times*, October 4, 2013, A35.

Joe Klein, *The Natural: The Misunderstood Presidency of Bill Clinton* (New York: Doubleday, 2002), 145–46.

"A Kennedy Crackup," *Newsweek*, May 12, 1997.

Helen Kennedy, "Kennedy Baby-Sitter Meets DA," *New York Daily News*, May 23, 1997.

John F. Kennedy Jr., "Editor's Letter: Don't Sit Under the Apple Tree," *George*, September 1997.

"John F. Kennedy Jr.: The Sexiest Man Alive," *People* (cover), September 12, 1988.

Ed Kilgore, "Chameleon: The Long-Buried Liberal History of Newt Gingrich," *New Republic*, March 3, 2011.

Mark Kriegel, "JFK Jr. Finally Becomes a Kennedy," *New York Daily News*, August 13, 1997.

Howard Kurtz, "A Guide to Media Behavior in the Age of Newt," *Washington Post*, February 26, 1995.

———, "Weeding Out Liberals at WTTG?; News Chief Backs Off Memo About Staff," *Washington Post*, September 9, 1993.

Rich Lacayo, "Bringing Down the House G.O.P. Guerrilla," *Time*, November 7, 1994.

Rush Limbaugh, *See, I Told You So* (New York: Pocket, 1993), 19, 25, 79, 195–96, 225.

Michael Lind, "Why Intellectual Conservatism Died," *Dissent*, Winter 1995, 42–47.

Sarah Lyall, "Murdoch Facing Parliament's Ire in Hacking Case," *New York Times*, July 2, 2011, A1, B7.

Terry McDermott, "Dumb Like a Fox," *CJR*, March/April 2010, 26–32.

Kim Masters and Bryan Burrough, "Cable Guys," *Vanity Fair*, January 1997, 76.

Tim Murphy and David Corn, "Newt in His Own Words: 33 Years of Bomb-Throwing," *Mother Jones*, April 2011.

Andrew Neil, "Murdoch and Me," *Vanity Fair*, December 1996, 192–98, 204–6.

"News America Publishing Inc. History," www.fundinguniverse.com/company-histories/news-america-publishing-inc-history/.

David Osborne, "The Swinging Days of Newt Gingrich," *Mother Jones*, November 1984.

John Podhoretz, "There Is No Republican Establishment," *Commentary*, January 22, 2016.

Frank Rich, "Separated at Birth," *New York Times*, January 12, 1995.

———, "They Got Some 'Splainin' to Do," *New York Times*, July 19, 2009, WK10.

John H. Richardson, "The Indispensible Republican," *Esquire*, November 2010, 106–12, 184–86.

Sara Rimer, "A Kennedy Faces the Fallout from a Scandal," *New York Times*, July 10, 1997.

Roxanne Roberts, "White House Correspondents' Association Dinner: A Theme Party Has Little to Do with D.C.," *Washington Post*, May 1, 2014.

George Rush and Joanna Molloy, "Ex–Ralph Reed Spokeswoman Lisa Baron Spilling Sexy Political Details for Book," *New York Daily News*, November 29, 2009.

Joe Scarborough, "The Case for Newt," Politico.com, December 5, 2011.

———, "The Newt I Know," Politico.com, January 27, 2012.

Katharine Q. Seelye, "Gingrich's Life: The Complications and Ideals," *New York Times*, November 24, 1994.

Gail Sheehy, "The Inner Quest of Newt Gingrich," *Vanity Fair*, September 1995, 154, 217.

Gabriel Sherman, "The Elephant in the Green Room," *New York*, May 22, 2011, 20–24.

———, "The Revenge of Roger's Angels," *New York*, September 5, 2016.

Hedrick Smith, *The People and the Power Game*, PBS, 1996, Hedrick Smith Productions in association with South Carolina Educational Television, produced by Pat Roddy and Barak Goodman.

Brian Stelter, "Fox News Stars Close to Renewing Deals," *New York Times*, April 20, 2012.

Sheryl Gay Stolberg, "Gingrich Stuck to Caustic Path in Ethics Battles," *New York Times*, January 27, 2012, A1, 16.

Stephen Talbot, "Newt's Glass House," *Salon*, August 8, 1998.

Sam Tanenhaus, "Conservatism Is Dead," *New Republic*, February 18, 2009, 17.

David Usborne, "Murdoch Meets His Match," *Independent*, November 24, 1996.

Juli Weiner, "An Unabridged Guide to All of Newt Gingrich's Wives," VanityFair.com, August 10, 2010.

Rachel Weiner, "C-SPAN Denied Cameras in the House of Representatives, Again," *Washington Post*, February 4, 2011.

Philip Weiss, "Watching Matt Drudge," *New York*, August 27, 2007.

James Wolcott, "Fox Populi," *Vanity Fair*, August 2011, 72–74.

Michael Wolff, *The Man Who Owns the News: Inside the Secret World of Rupert Murdoch* (New York: Broadway Books, 2008), 134, 204–9, 306–9, 314, 346.

———, "The Unbeatable Roger Ailes," *USA Today*, January 5, 2014.

Jeff Zeleny, "On the Stump, Gingrich Puts Focus on Faith," *New York Times*, February 27, 2011, A1, 21.

Jason Zengerle, "If I Take Down Fox, Is All Forgiven?," *New York*, May 30, 2011, 26–30.

CHAPTER 21: Objects in Mirror Are Tinier Than They Appear

Interviews: Lucia Brawley, Todd Brewster, David Burnett, Jack Hayford, Jesse Jackson, Michael Kimmel, Stuart Krichevsky, Bill McCartney, Eli Reed, Scott Turow.

"7 Promises," Promise Keepers, https://promisekeepers.org/about/7-promises.

Christopher Andersen, *Barack and Michelle* (New York: Morrow, 2009).

Michael Azerrad, "Here We Are Now," *Rolling Stone*, April 16, 1992.

Tara Siegel Bernard, "Vigilant Eye on Gender Pay Gap," *New York Times*, November 15, 2014, B1.

Charles M. Blow, "Fathers' Sons and Brothers' Keepers," *New York Times*, March 1, 2014, A19.

Robert Bly, *Iron John: A Book About Men* [1990] (Cambridge, MA: Da Capo, 2004), xiii–xiv, 2–6, 11–12, 23–24, 61, 80–81, 94–96, 99–100, 186, 217, 224.

Jane E. Brody, "The Challenges of Male Friendships," *New York Times*, June 28, 2016.

Ric Bucher, "Steve Javie Retiring as NBA Referee," ESPN.com, September 16, 2011.

"Bud Light—I Love You, Man" (commercial, 1995), via CANBike.org, November 7, 2013.

"Bud Light's 'I Love You, Man' Goes to the Head of the Class," *Philadelphia Inquirer*, December 19, 1995.

Stephanie Coontz, "The Myth of Male Decline," *New York Times*, September 30, 2012, SR1, 5.

Ken Corbett, *Boyhoods: Rethinking Masculinities* (New Haven, CT: Yale University Press, 2009), 7.

Hank De Zutter, "What Makes Obama Run?," *Chicago Reader*, December 7, 1995.

R. F. Doyle, "The Men's/Fathers' Movement—Present, Past, Future," Men's Movement, www.mensdefense.org/MensMovement.htm.

Tim Elliott, "A Grand Bromance," *The Age*, August 23, 2007.

Susan Faludi, *Backlash: The Undeclared War Against American Women* [1991] (New York: Three Rivers, 2006), 244, 316–19.

Ford Fessenden, "A Million Here, a Million There," *New York Times*, January 17, 2009, A13.

Robert Frost, "Mending Wall" [1914], in *The Poetry of Robert Frost*, edited by Edward Connery Lathem (New York: Holt, Rinehart & Winston, 1969), 33–34.

Michael Fumento, " 'Road Rage' Versus Reality," *Atlantic*, August 1998.

Steve Gillon, *Boomer Nation: The Largest and Richest Generation Ever and How It Changed America* (New York: Free Press, 2004), 139.

Bonnie Goldstein, "What Newt Gingrich's Three Wives Tell Us About the President He'd Be," *Washington Post*, January 2, 2012.

John Gray, *Men Are from Mars, Women Are from Venus: A Practical Guide for Improving Communication and Getting What You Want in Your Relationship* (New York: HarperCollins, 1992), 11.

"Great Mother and New Father Conference, History," http://greatmotherconference.org/about/history/.

Tim Griffin, "Did the 1990 Colorado Team Deserve the National Title?," ESPN.com, July 30, 2008.

Sebastian Junger, "Hitting the Wall," *New York Times Magazine*, August 16, 1992.

Michiko Kakutani, "Beyond Iron John? How About Iron Jane?," *New York Times*, August 27, 1993.

Michael Kimmel, *Manhood in America: A Cultural History* (New York: Free Press, 1996), 8–10, 111, 280–84, 305–9, 316.

Aaron R. Kipnis, *Knights Without Armor: A Guide to the Inner Lives of Men* (Santa Barbara, CA: Indigo Phoenix Books, 2004), 97.

Beth Ann Krier and Jeannine Stein, "Attention, Professional Shoppers!," *Los Angeles Times*, January 18, 1991.

Nicholas Kristof, "Gritting Our Teeth and Giving President Trump a Chance," *New York Times*, November 9, 2016.

Tamar Lewin, "Target of House Legislation: Procedure Doctors Rarely Use," *New York Times*, November 2, 1995.

Charles H. Lippy, "Miles to Go: Promise Keepers in Historical and Cultural Context," *Soundings: An Interdisciplinary Journal*, Summer/Fall 1997.

Myra MacPherson, "Newt Gingrich, Point Man in a House Divided," *Washington Post*, June 12, 1989.

Michael A. Messner, *Politics of Masculinities: Men in Movements* [1997] (Lanham, MD: AltaMira, 2000), 37.

Casey B. Mulligan, "A Milestone for Working Women?," *Economix* (blog), NYTimes.com, January 14, 2009.

"New York Times Best Sellers: One Hit Wonders," *New York Times* Best Seller List, nytbestsellerlist.com/authors/one-hit-wonders.

Camille Paglia, "Homosexuality at the Fin de Siecle" (*Esquire*, October 1991), in Paglia, *Sex, Art, and American Culture: Essays* (New York: Vintage, 1992), 24.

"PK History," PromiseKeepers.org/about/PK-history.

Jackie Powder, "Plunged into the Storm," *Baltimore Sun*, June 26, 2000.

"Promise Keepers Fill Washington Mall with Prayer," CNN.com, October 4, 1997.

Jack Sawyer, *On Male Liberation* (Pittsburgh: Know, 1970).

Chase Scheinbaum, "Anger Management Goes to the Doctor," *Bloomberg BusinessWeek*, August 2, 2012.

Katharine Q. Seelye, "G.O.P. Gains Allies in Move to Repeal Assault-Rifle Ban," *New York Times*, January 26, 1995.

Robert St. Estephe, "Blacklisted from History: A History of the Men's Rights Movement," GoodMenProject.com, June 30, 2012.

Alison Stewart, "Defining and Discussing the 'Man Crush'" (interview with Michael Musto), MSNBC, June 30, 2005, www.nbcnews.com/id/8406828/#.UvzulCif8lJ.

Julie Tamaki, "Jack Nicholson Accused of Breaking Man's Windshield," *Los Angeles Times*, February 23, 1994.

Lionel Tiger, *The Decline of Males: The First Look at an Unexpected New World for Men and Women* (New York: St. Martin's Griffin, 1999), 7–8, 20–21, 26, 258.

Nick Tosches, "Oedipus Tex," *Penthouse*, December 1992, 126–30, 166–70.

Scott Turow, "Embraceable You," *Vanity Fair*, June 2000, 112–14.

Teddy Wayne, "What Will Induce Nostalgia in 2033?," *New York Times*, January 4, 2013, ST1, 6.

CHAPTER 22: Shadows on the Wall of the Man Cave

Interviews: Ken Aretsky, Brian Bedol, Lucia Brawley, Jack Deligter, Phil de Picciotto, Steve Fine, Brett Forrest, Sam Friend, Joel Paul, Michael Rooney, Jane Root, Mark Seliger, Tim Zahner.

"20 Years of Adobe Photoshop," WebDesignerDepot.com, February 1, 2010.

"1998 Hall of Fame," *Vanity Fair*, December 1998.

"Absolutely Amazing: McGwire Caps Magical Season with 69th, 70th Homers," Associated Press via CNNSI.com, September 27, 1998.

"Andre Agassi Admits Long Hairstyle Was a Wig," *Telegraph*, October 31, 2009.

Ingrid Banks, "Hair Still Matters," in *Feminist Frontiers*, edited by Laurel Richardson, Verta Taylor, and Nancy Whittier (New York: McGraw-Hill, 2004), 116.

Des Bieler, "Allen Iverson Admits One of His Tattoos Is Just Covering Up an Older, Less Interesting Tattoo," *Washington Post*, May 21, 2015.

Greg Bishop, "After Drug Revelations, Defining '98 Home Run Chase," *New York Times*, July 4, 2009.

Sam Borden, "Sammy Sosa Caught Using Corked Bat in 2003 Game vs. Devil Rays," *New York Daily News*, June 4, 2003.

"Callaway Golf Company History," www.fundinguniverse.com/company-histories/callaway-golf-company-history/.

Bill Clinton, 1996 State of the Union Address, January 23, 1996, via *PBS NewsHour*.

James Collins, "High Stakes Winners," *Time*, June 24, 2001.

Rose Davis, Tina Moore, and Larry McShane, "Tiger Woods Said Elin Nordegren, Not Car Crash, Scratched Face and Chased Him with Golf Club: Report," *New York Daily News*, November 27, 2009.

Jamie Diamond, "Java Jive," *Entertainment Weekly*, April 19, 1991.

Jason Diamos, "His Head Still Shaved, Messier Still Bristles," *New York Times*, February 4, 1999.

Bruce Feiler, "Dominating the Man Cave," *New York Times*, February 6, 2011, ST2.

Mike Fish, "Successful Union: Martin, Fans Benefitting from Viagra Sponsorship," CNNSI.com, October 25, 2001.

"Former 'Home Run King' Admits Steroid Use, Reignites Scandal in Pro Sports," *PBS NewsHour*, January 12, 2010, http://www.pbs.org/newshour/bb/sports-jan-june10-mcgwire_01-12/.

Thomas Frank, *The Conquest of Cool: Business Culture, Counterculture, and the Rise of Hip Consumerism* (Chicago: University of Chicago Press, 1997), ix, 7, 233–34.

David M. Friedman, *A Mind of Its Own: A Cultural History of the Penis* (New York: Penguin, 2001), 249.

Tom Friend, "Tyson Disqualified for Biting Holyfield's Ears," *New York Times*, June 29, 1997.

Cork Gaines, "PEDs Have Destroyed Baseball's List of Career Home Run Leaders," BusinessInsider.com, August 13, 2013.

Nicci Gerard, "Innocence on the Line," *Guardian*, November 11, 1999.

Brian Grazer and Charles Fishman, "Behind the Mind, and Out-of-This-World Hair, of Legendary Hollywood Producer Brian Grazer," *Vanity Fair*, February 2015.

Tracee Hamilton, "O Sports-Themed Christmas Tree, How Thorny Are Thy Ornament Dilemmas," *Washington Post*, December 1, 2013.

James Harris, "The 10 Best Dressed Athletes of the '90s," Complex.com, December 9, 2012.

"The History of ROGAINE Products," www.rogaine.com/category/facts/our+history.do.

"Hummer Vehicles," AMGeneral.com/Vehicles/Hummer, 2014.

Roy S. Johnson, "The Jordan Effect," *Fortune*, June 22, 1998.

Tyler Kepner, "McGwire Admits That He Used Steroids," *New York Times*, January 11, 2010.

———, "Pujols Issues a Reminder of His Place in History," *New York Times*, April 26, 2014, B1, 13.

Joe Kita, "Men Riding Bicycles: The Unseen Danger," *Bicycling*, August 1997.

Eric Konigsberg, "The Real Spree," *New York*, April 19, 1999, 34, 37–39.

Raquel Laneri, "The Best-Dressed Athletes," Forbes.com, December 7, 2010.

Joe LaPointe, "Sure, He Can Dress, but Can He Coach?," *New York Times*, May 13, 1990.

"Lauder: Pleasures for Men" (ad), Estée Lauder Inc., 1997, in *George*, February 1998.

Lexa W. Lee, "Bike Seats for Men," Demand Media (Sponsored), HealthyLiving.AZCentral.com.

Robert Lipsyte, "A Day at the Races Offers a Checkup as Another Pit Stop," *New York Times*, July 1, 2001.

Joanne Lovering, "Hers and Hers Closet Is Far More Precise," *Toronto Star*, March 21, 1992.

Michael McCann, "Will Steroids Report Lead to Perjury Investigation of Sammy Sosa?," SI.com, June 16, 2009.

"McGwire Admits Nothing; Sosa and Palmeiro Deny Use," ESPN.com News Services, March 18, 2005.

"McGwire Apologizes to La Russa, Selig," ESPN.com News Services, January 12, 2010.

Willoughby Mariano and Henry Pierson Curtis, "Investigator Suspected Tiger Woods Was Under the Influence at Time of Accident," *Los Angeles Times*, December 8, 2009.

Kim Masters, "Where There's Smoke...," *Vanity Fair*, March 1996.

James Andrew Miller and Tom Shales, *Those Guys Have All the Fun: Inside the World of ESPN* (New York: Little, Brown, 2011).

———, "Game On! The Untold Secrets and Furious Egos Behind the Rise of *SportsCenter*," *GQ*, May 16, 2011.

Roger Minkow, "Bringing Ergonomics to Cycling: The Creation of the Body Geometry Bicycle Saddle," PARC Forum, Palo Alto, CA, October 31, 2002, www.parc.com/event/63/bringing-ergonomics-to-cycling.html.

Malcolm Moran, "Jordan Ran Up Golf Debts, Book Says," *New York Times*, June 4, 1993.

Ross Newman, "Rose Pleads Guilty to Two Tax Charges," *Los Angeles Times*, April 21, 1990.

Bob Nightengale, "1994 Strike Most Embarrassing Moment in MLB History," USAToday.com, August 11, 2014.

———, "Trio Gets Elected, but Hall Still Messy," *USA Today*, January 8, 2014.

Camille Paglia, "No Sex Please, We're Middle Class," *New York Times*, June 26, 2010.

Ashley Parker, "Carrying On Presidential Tradition, One Leisurely Round at a Time," *New York Times*, January 2, 2014.

"Pete Rose Timeline," *Cincinnati Enquirer*, January 6, 2004.

Julia Phillips, *You'll Never Eat Lunch in This Town Again* (New York: Random House, 1991).

Kate Pickert, "A Brief History of the X Games," *Time*, January 22, 2009.

"Police to Talk to Woods About Crash" (transcript), CNN.com, November 28, 2009.

Rick Reilly, "Last Call?" *Sports Illustrated*, May 11, 1998.

Donald Charles Richardson, "The Long Hot Summer: All About the Newest Grooming Tips and Trends," *Playboy*, April 1996, 108.

Ronale Tucker Rhodes, "Top 20 [Fitness Training] Facility Trends," AthleticBusiness.com, June 2005.

"Rogaine Company Profile," BioPortfolio.com, January 30, 2014.

Richard Sandomir, "Beyond the Fringe: The Boldly Bald," *New York Times*, May 5, 1993.

———, "Classic Sports Network Gets $20 Million in New Capital," *New York Times*, September 3, 1996.

———, "A Satisfied, Although Intense Sportscaster," *New York Times*, January 25, 1999, C10.

Joe Saraceno, "Chew on This: Ten Years On, Holyfield Still Fighting," *USA Today*, June 27, 2007.

Michael S. Schmidt, "Sosa Is Said to Have Tested Positive in 2003," *New York Times*, June 16, 2009.

Mark Seal, "The Temptation of Tiger Woods, Part II: Losing Control," *Vanity Fair*, June 2010.

Mark Simpson, "Here Come the Mirror Men: Why the Future Is Metrosexual," *Independent*, November 15, 1994.

Natasha Singer, "Selling That New-Man Feeling," *New York Times*, November 24, 2013, BU1, 6.

"Sosa Catches McGwire Again with Nos. 61, 62," Associated Press via CNNSI.com, September 13, 1998.

"Sosa's Ego a Problem...Again," Comcast SportsNet Chicago, November 29, 2012.

"Sosa Pulls Even with McGwire," Associated Press via *Sun Journal* (New Bern, NC), September 14, 1998.

John Strege, "Not Everyone Agrees with Clinton Receiving PGA Distinguished Service Award," *Golf Digest*, August 7, 2014.

Jeff Summitt, "Why Ti? Explaining the Importance of Titanium Face Irons," blog.hirekogolf.com, May 2010.

Richard Todd, *The Thing Itself: On the Search for Authenticity* (New York: Riverhead, 2008), 85, 88, 95.

Adam Tschorn, "Death of the Man Cave (1992–2012)," *Los Angeles Times*, March 16, 2012.

"Unleaded Coffee," *New York Times*, April 12, 1991.

Nathan Walker, "The NBA's Top Five Baldheaded Ballers Ever," Yahoo.com, June 2, 2009.

Ralph Warner and Jose Martinez, "Wanna Be a Baller? The History of Songs Dedicated to NBA Players," Complex.com, April 21, 2011.

Rick Weinberg, "Sammy Sosa Gets Caught with Corked Bat," ESPN.com, August 4, 2004.

David Westin, "Spieth Wins Wire to Wire, Becomes Second-Youngest Masters Champion," Augusta.com, April 13, 2015.

Alex Williams, "From 'Wolf' to Sheepish Clothing," *New York Times*, December 26, 2013, E1, E6.

Duff Wilson, "McGwire Offers No Denials at Steroid Hearings," *New York Times*, March 18, 2005.

Eric Wilson, "Stretching a Six-Pack," *New York Times*, May 13, 2010, E1, 10.

Michael Wise, "Bald Facts: Pacers Can't Stop O'Neal," *New York Times*, May 26, 1995.

———, "N.B.A. Star Who Choked Coach Wins Reinstatement of Contract," *New York Times*, March 5, 1998.

Gene Wojciechowski, "Jordan Hit on Gambling," *Los Angeles Times*, June 3, 1993.

Peter York, "Peter York on Ads," *Independent*, March 8, 2008.

CHAPTER 23: Dudes and Subdudes

Interviews: Michael Douglas, Bruce Feirstein, Sam Friend, Mark Kotfila, Donald Liebenson, Rosie Nalle, Alanna Nash, Lester Schwalb, Jim Windolf.

David Ansen, "Gross-Out Comedies," *Newsweek*, October 31, 2008.

Ken Auletta, "What Won't They Do?," *New Yorker*, May 17, 1993.

"Basic Breakup: Michael Douglas's Marriage Is Off Again," *People*, July 10, 1995.

Peter Biskind, "The Return of Quentin Tarantino," *Vanity Fair*, October 2003, 315.

Rhys Blakely and Will Pavia, "Zeta-Jones 'Was Crumbling' as Husband Fought Cancer," *Times* (U.K.), April 14, 2011.

K. C. Blumm, "Michael Douglas: I Lied—I Actually Had Tongue Cancer," *People*, September 23, 2016.

Xan Brooks, "Michael Douglas on Liberace, Cannes, Cancer and Cunnilingus," *Guardian*, June 2, 2013.

———, "Natural Born Copycats," *Guardian*, December 19, 2002.

Amy Chozick, "Presidents, Real and Imagined, Bond: Bill Clinton and His 'House of Cards' Counterpart Pal Around," *New York Times*, February 22, 2015, AR28.

Susan Churcher, "Michael Douglas: My Night with Two Mrs. Robinsons at Age 16," *Daily Mail*, April 24, 2010.

Nancy Collins, "Michael's Full Disclosure," *Vanity Fair*, January 1995.

Gareth G. Cook, "The Dark Side of Camp," *Washington Monthly*, September 1995.

Sharon Cotliar, "Michael Douglas Clarifies Remarks About Cancer and Oral Sex," *People*, June 3, 2013.

Steve Daly, "Battle Royale: Sincerity vs. Irony," *Entertainment Weekly*, Spring 2000, 68–75.

David Denby, "The Real Rhett Butler," *New Yorker*, May 25, 2009, 75.

"Despite U.S. Campaign, a Boom in Pornography," *New York Times*, July 4, 1993.

Eliana Dockterman, "*The Wolf of Wall Street* Breaks F-Bomb Record," Time.com, January 3, 2014.

Diana Douglas Darrid, *In The Wings: A Memoir* (New York: Barricade Books, 1999), 231.

Kirk Douglas, *Let's Face It: 90 Years of Living, Loving, and Learning* (Hoboken, NJ: Wiley, 2007), 97.

Roger Ebert, "Basic Instinct" (review), *Chicago Sun-Times*, March 30, 1992.

Susan Faludi, *Backlash: The Undeclared War Against American Women* [1991] (New York: Three Rivers, 2006), 125–30, 134–35.

Scott Feinberg, "Kirk Douglas: 'I Am Always Optimistic,'" *Hollywood Reporter*, June 6, 2012.

Margalit Fox, "Henry Hill, Mobster and Movie Inspiration, Dies at 69," *New York Times*, June 14, 2012, B19.

Nancy Gibbs, "What's Next for Bill and Hillary?," *Time*, February 15, 1999.

J. J. Gould, "A Brief History of Dude," *Atlantic*, November 2013.

Mike Hale, "Once Upon a Time, a Real Leading Man," *New York Times*, July 31, 2009, C1, 11.

Val Hennessy, "In the Hype Market," *You* (Australia), March 6, 1988.

Stephen Holden, "Perfect Plan: Kill My Wife. Please," *New York Times*, June 5, 1998.

Desson Howe, "New Powers Generation," *Washington Post*, June 11, 1999.

Benjamin Hufbauer, "How Trump's Favorite Movie Explains Him," Politico.com, June 6, 2016.

Mary Huhn, "Cooper's Art-iculated Contempt for Maxim," *New York Post*, March 19, 1999.

Kay S. Hymowitz, *Manning Up: How the Rise of Women Has Turned Men into Boys* (New York: Basic Books, 2011), 112–15.

Dave Itzkoff, "The Refined Art of Tastelessness," *New York Times*, August 17, 2008.

Jim Jerome, "Michael Douglas—Second Chances," *AARP*, March/April 2010.

Pauline Kael, "The Man from Dream City," *New Yorker*, July 14, 1975.

Dave Kehr, "Jim Carrey as the Id Unleashed a Bit Before Its Time," *New York Times*, February 27, 2011, AR13.

Rita Kempley, "Basic Instinct" (review), *Washington Post*, March 20, 1992.

Zara Kessler, "Michael Douglas Can Be the Indecent Angelina Jolie," BloombergView.com, June 4, 2013.

Judy Kurtz, "Hillary Binging on 'House of Cards,'" TheHill.com, September 4, 2015.

Dave Lake, "The 10 Most Controversial 'South Park' Episodes," MSN.com, tv.msn.com/controversial-south-park-episodes/.

Anthony Lane, "Mein Camp: *Brüno*" (review), *New Yorker*, July 20, 2009, 70–72.

Dennis Lim, "Mortification Man: Noah Baumbach's 'Greenberg' Crystallizes the Ben Stiller Persona," *New York Times*, March 14, 2010, AR1, 9.

Janet Maslin, "A Chief Executive in Love in the White House," *New York Times*, November 17, 1995.

———, "Sure, She May Be Mean, but Is She a Murderer?," *New York Times*, March 20, 1992.

"Michael Douglas Cancer Oral Sex Claim: Transcript and Audio," *Guardian*, June 3, 2013.

"Michael Douglas' Throat Cancer Caused by Oral Sex, Not Smoking or Drinking," *Huffington Post*, June 3, 2013.

Ruth Morris, "Michael Douglas: This Man Is Not a Sex Addict," *Independent*, June 27, 1999.

Nina Munk, "Dennis the Menace," *Vanity Fair*, May 2001.

Maureen Orth, "Not Your Average Joe," *Vanity Fair*, April 1996.

Evgenia Peretz, "Michael Douglas, Take Two," *Vanity Fair*, March 1, 2010.

David Plotz, "Joe Eszterhas: How Did a B-Movie Screenwriter Become an A-List Celebrity?," *Slate*, March 15, 1998.

Terrence Rafferty, "Woman on Top," *New Yorker*, December 19, 1994, 107.

Mark A. Reid, ed., *Spike Lee's Do the Right Thing* (Cambridge: Cambridge University Press, 1997), 150.

Dean Schabner and Susan Donaldson James, "Michael Douglas Says His Tumor's Gone, Throat Cancer Likely Beaten," ABCNews.com, January 11, 2011.

Mark Seal, "Cinema Tarantino: The Making of *Pulp Fiction*," *Vanity Fair*, March 2013, 382, 387.

Michael Shnayerson, "Natural Born Opponents," *Vanity Fair*, July 1996, 98–105, 141–44.

Kathy Shwiff, "How Sherry Lansing Learned to Trust the Audience," *Wall Street Journal*, April 4, 2013.

Max Sparber, "Drinker's Cinema: The Big Lebowski," *The Bottle Gang: The Twin Cities' Guide to Sophisticated Drinking*, February 3, 2007, bottlegang.blogspot.com.

Zach Stafford, "A-One, a-Two-hoo, a-HPV!," *Huffington Post*, June 7, 2013.

Alessandra Stanley, "Men with a Message: Help Wanted," *New York Times*, January 3, 2010, AR22.

Hilary Stout, "Viagra: The Thrill That Was," *New York Times*, June 3, 2011.

Peter Travers, "Basic Instinct" (review, 1992), RollingStone.com, (reposted) February 7, 2001.

Scott Turow, "Something's Up," *Vanity Fair*, September 1999, 168–78.

Bernhard Weinraub, "'Basic Instinct': The Suspect Is Attractive, and May Be Fatal," *New York Times*, March 15, 1992.

Robert W. Welkos, "Director Trims 'Basic Instinct' to Get R Rating," *Los Angeles Times*, February 11, 1992.

CHAPTER 24: Porn Goes Pop

Interviews: Debby Applegate, (formerly known as) Danni Ashe, Anthony Haden-Guest, Dian Hanson, Samir Husni, Rob Klug, Nancy Libin, Frank Rich, Robert Rosen, Kirsten Swinth, Zak Tanjeloff.

"3 Deny Distributing Pornographic Material," *Deseret News*, February 4, 1998.

"Backgrounder—Crossroads of the World," www.crossroadsoftheworldla.com/overview.html .

Brian Alexander, "Women on Top: Female Execs Rise in Porn Biz," MSNBC.com, December 3, 2008.

Martin Amis, "A Rough Trade," *Guardian*, March 17, 2001.

Bill Asher, "Adult Firm Vivid Hopes to Win Over Blushing Investors in IPO," *Billboard*, August 19, 2000.

Bill Braun, "A Long Love Affair with Magazines," *AJR*, August/September 2012.

Susannah Breslin, "Adult Director Max Hardcore Released from Prison," Forbes.com, July 7, 2011.

Kathee Brewer, "Can We Chat?," *AVN Online* (supplement), April 2010.

Frank Bruni, "Reconstructing Marky Mark," *New York Times*, August 31, 1997.

Edward L. Carter, "Movie Buffs Prosecutor Has Few Regrets Despite Acquittal, Porn Trial Was a Success, He Says," *Deseret News*, September 6, 1999.

"Child Online Protection Act (COPA)," Center for Democracy & Technology, CDT.org/speech/copa/.

Children's Online Privacy Protection Act of 1998, FTC.gov/ogc/coppa1.htm.

"CPPA, COPA, CIPA: Which Is Which?," American Library Association, ALA.org/offices/oif/ifissues/issuesrelatedlinks/cppacopacipa.

Joe D'Angelo, "Snoop Dogg Wins Porn Awards for 'Doggystyle' Flick," MTV.com, January 2002.

Jancee Dunn, "The Rock-Porn Connection," *Rolling Stone*, August 19, 1999.

Martin Edlund, "Hip-Hop's Crossover to the Adult Aisle," *New York Times*, March 7, 2004.

Susan Faludi, "The Money Shot," *New Yorker*, October 30, 1995.

Mark Gimein, "Sex Sells, Doesn't It?," *Salon*, December 1, 1999.

Ben Greenman, "Naked Truth," *New Yorker*, November 30, 2009.

William L. Hamilton, "The Mainstream Flirts with Pornography Chic," *New York Times*, March 21, 1999.

Dian Hanson, ed., *The Big Book of Breasts* (Cologne: Taschen, 2006), 43–44.

Eric Hayden, "Larry Flynt Sells Hustler HQ Building for $89 million," *Hollywood Reporter*, May 15, 2013.

Erik Hedegaard, "The X-Rated Redemption of Mark Wahlberg," *Rolling Stone*, October 30, 1997.

Lynn Hirschberg, "His Way," *New York Times Magazine*, December 19, 1999.

Steve Hochman, "Goodby Jane's Addiction, Hello Porno for Pyros," *Los Angeles Times*, March 22, 1992.

Wendy Kaminer, "Feminists Against the First Amendment," *Atlantic*, November 1992.

"Khan Tusion Interview," AVN.com, January 31, 2000, business.avn.com/video/Khan-Tusion-Interview-34233.html.

John Leland, "Madonna's 'Sex' Book: The New Voyeurism," *Newsweek*, November 1, 1992.

Ariel Levy, *Female Chauvinist Pigs: Women and the Rise of Raunch Culture* (New York: Free Press, 2006), 2, 8.

Donald Liebenson, "Mr. Skin's Naked Enthusiasm," *Los Angeles Times*, December 6, 2009.

Ian Lovett, "Condom Requirement Sought for Sex-Film Sets," *New York Times*, February 10, 2011, A18.

Seth Lubove, "Obscene Profits," *Forbes*, December 12, 2002.

———, "See No Evil," *Forbes*, September 17, 2001.

Steve Mikulan, "Hustler After Dark: Flynt Building to Turn Off Lights Saturday," *L.A. Weekly*, March 27, 2009.

Chadwick Moore, "Man's Best Friend: From Tom of Finland to Big Penises, Dian Hanson Is on a Mission to Rehabilitate Old-School Masculinity," *Out*, September 4, 2013.

Andrew Adam Newman, "Site That Bills Itself as a Movie Reviewer Finds That Sex Sells," *New York Times*, July 23, 2007.

Dan Pacheco et al., "Screening Cyber Smut: Censorship or Sensible?," WashingtonPost.com, September 11. 1997.

Pamela Paul, *Pornified: How Pornography Is Damaging Our Lives, Our Relationships, and Our Families* (New York: Henry Holt, 2005), 5–8.

Degen Pener, "You Know It When You See It, and You're Seeing It More," *New York Times*, May 10, 1992.

"Playboy History," www.playboyenterprises.com/about/history/.

Brett Pulley, "The Porn King," *Forbes*, March 7, 2005.

Frank Rich, "Finally, Porn Does Prime Time," *New York Times*, July 27, 2003.

———, "Naked Capitalists," *New York Times Magazine*, May 20, 2001.

Matt Richtel, "Lights, Camera, Lots of Action. Forget the Script," *New York Times*, July 8, 2009.

Dennis Romboy, "Movie Buffs Cost Taxpayers Some Big Bucks...," *Deseret News*, April 2, 1999.

Robert Rosen, *Beaver Street: A History of Modern Pornography* (London: HeadPress, 2010), 181.

William Safire, "Money Quote," *New York Times*, March 13, 2005.

R. V. Scheide, "Viagra and the Culture of Manhood," *Sacramento News and Review,* January 12, 2006.

Marshall Sella, "The Soho Love Goddess," *New York*, January 31, 2000.

Elina Shatkin, "Dian Hanson—Sexy Book Editor" (interview), *The Believer*, January/February 2015.

T. I. Stanley, "'Surreal Life': Porn Crosses Over to Media Mainstream," *Advertising Age*, January 26, 2004.

Brad Stone, "Craigslist to Remove 'Erotic' Ads," *New York Times*, May 14, 2009, B1, 6.

Rosalinda Stone, "Porn Yesterday: True Confessions of a Celebrity Skin Editor," *Village Voice*, July 27, 1999.

Paul Sullivan, "13 Strikeouts Do Nothing to Cool Down Wood Fever," *Chicago Tribune*, May 30, 1998.

"Supreme Court Won't Revive Online Content Law," Yahoo.com, January 21, 2009.

J. Tinsley, "'Doggystyle' Turns 20: How Snoop Dogg Transformed from Accused Murderer to American Idol," Uproxx.com, November 22, 2013.

Fred Turner, *From Counterculture to Cyberculture: Stewart Brand, the Whole Earth Network, and the Rise of Digital Utopianism* (Chicago: University of Chicago Press, 2007), 13.

Matt Tyrnauer, "Unbridled Taschen," *Vanity Fair*, October 2000.

"Wall Street Meets Pornography," *New York Times*, October 23, 2000.

David Foster Wallace, "Big Red Son" [1998], in *Consider the Lobster and Other Essays* (Boston: Back Bay, 2005), 5, 7, 20–28.

"We Got Wood: Catch-22," *Baseball Heckler* (blog), May 18, 2006, https://mlblogsbaseballheckler.wordpress.com/2006/05/18/we-got-wood-catch-22/.

Mary Elizabeth Williams, "Woof! There It Is!: Snoop Dogg Asks Not What Porn Can Do for Him, but What He Can Do for Pornography," *Salon*, March 15, 2001.

James Wolcott, "Debbie Does Barnes & Noble," *Vanity Fair*, September 2005, 249.

Naomi Wolf, *The Beauty Myth: How Images of Beauty Are Used Against Women* [1991] (New York: Harper Perennial, 2002), 162–64.

Evan Wright, "Porn.con?," *Rolling Stone*, August 3, 2000.

Jen Yamato, "The N.W.A. Member Turned Pornographer," *Daily Beast*, August, 11, 2015.

CHAPTER 25: Chez Fleiss

Interview: Heidi Fleiss.

Richard Abowitz, "Heidi's Suds Farm," *Los Angeles Times*, April 7, 2007.

"Accused Madam Heidi Fleiss Opens Clothing Store," *Los Angeles Times*, July 21, 1994.

Eric Benson, "The Sheen Stimulus," *New York*, December 12, 2010.

Brendan Bernhard, "Heidi Fleiss Dreams of a Brothel," *New York Sun*, July 17, 2008.

Edward J. Boyer, "Former Clients Testify as Heidi Fleiss Trial Begins," *Los Angeles Times*, June 30, 1995.

Henry Brean, "Heidi Fleiss Gives Up on Plan for Brothel for Women," *Las Vegas Review-Journal*, February 10, 2009.

Paul Brownfield, "TV's Big Noisemaker—And Proud of It," *Los Angeles Times*, November 20, 2002.

Mark Cina, "Charlie Sheen: 5 Craziest Things He's Said in the Past 24 Hours," *Hollywood Reporter*, February 28, 2011.

Dominick Dunne, "L.A. in the Age of O.J.," *Vanity Fair*, February 1995.

Heidi Fleiss, *Panderings* (Los Angeles: 1 Hour Entertainment, 2002).

John M. Glionna and Javier Panzar, "In Nevada, There Is Little Love Left for Brothels," *Los Angeles Times*, October 14, 2015.

Erin Goldmeier, "Exotic Pet Crisis," RadarOnline.com, June 10, 2016.

"Heidi Fleiss, Charlie Sheen Prostitution Scandal: Both Made Mistakes," *Huffington Post*, April 27, 2013.

"Heidi Fleiss Booted from Celebrity Rehab for One Night After Battle with Tom Sizemore," RadarOnline.com, July 18, 2009.

Lynn Hirschberg, "Heidi Does Hollywood," *Vanity Fair*, February 1994, 88–94, 122–25.

Bill Hoffman, "Charlie's a Self-Proclaimed Sex Ma-Sheen," *New York Post*, September 19, 2000.

" 'Hollywood Madam' Heidi Fleiss Abandons Plans for Stud Farm," FoxNews.com, February 10, 2009.

Shawn Hubler, "Actor Says He Got Call Girls from Fleiss," *Los Angeles Times*, July 21, 1995.

———, "Fleiss Case Opens Window on World of L.A. Call Girls," *Los Angeles Times*, December 13, 1993.

———, "Fleiss Sentenced to 37 Months for Tax Evasion," *Los Angeles Times*, January 8, 1997.

———, "For Former Madam of Beverly Hills—A Final Indignity," *Los Angeles Times*, December 14, 1992.

——, "Heidi Fleiss Faces Post-prison Life with a New Face," *Los Angeles Times*, August 31, 2000.

Eun Kyung Kim, "Charlie Sheen Reveals He's HIV Positive in Today Show Exclusive," *USA Today*, November 17, 2015

Jesse Kornbluth, "I'm Alex. Call Me," *Vanity Fair*, November 1989.

Annie Leibovitz, "Hall of Fame" (1993), *Vanity Fair*, December 1993.

"Life and Times of Heidi Fleiss" (interview with Heidi Fleiss), *Larry King Live*, CNN, February 8, 2002, http://edition.cnn.com/TRANSCRIPTS/0202/08/lkl.00.html.

Michael Martinez, "Nevada Brothels: Things to Know in Wake of Lamar Odom's Collapse," CNN.com, October 15, 2015.

Jim Rutenberg, "Charlie Sheen's Redemption Helps a Studio in Its Struggles," *New York Times*, February 4, 2002.

Mark Seal, "Charlie Sheen's War," *Vanity Fair*, February 2011.

———, "Reality Kings," *Vanity Fair*, July 2003.

Alessandra Stanley, "A Madam's New Consorts," *New York Times*, July 28, 2011.

Gary Strauss, "There's More to Heidi Fleiss Than a Shady Past," *USA Today*, July 21, 2008, 2D.

CHAPTER 26: Hard Currency

Interviews: Douglas Brinkley, Brett Forrest, Scott Gutterson, Art Harris, Hana Jakrlova, Michael Levine, Sunny Mindel, Fawnia Mondey, Michael J. Peter, Iva Roze Skoch, Madonna Swanson, Don Waitt, Neil Wexler, anonymous friend in "finance," anonymous "sports executive."

"20 Damn Good Reasons to Go to EXPO 20…: #12 State of the Union, from Tell-It-Like-It-Is Joe Redner," *Gentlemen's Club Owners EXPO: 20 Year Reunion* (program), August 26–29, 2012, 6.

Lizette Alvarez, "Strip Clubs in Tampa Are Ready to Cash In on G.O.P. Convention," *New York Times*, July 27, 2012.

Katherine P. Avgerinos, "From Vixen to Victim: The Sensationalization and Normalization of Prostitution in Post-Soviet Russia," *Vestnik, The Journal of Russian and Asian Studies*, www.sras.org, October 23, 2006.

Peter Baker, "Obama Says Budget Nominee Is Fit for 'Hall of Fame,' " *New York Times*, July 14, 2010, A13.

Michael Barbaro, "For Mayoral Hopeful Who Lost Fight to Remove Art, No Regrets," *New York Times*, March 28, 2013, A1, 25.

Anne Berryman, "Letter from Atlanta: The Seamy Gold Club Trial," *Time*, June 15, 2001.

Ralph Blumenthal and Carol Vogel, "Museum Says Giuliani Knew of Show in July and Was Silent," *New York Times*, October 5, 1999.

David Brooks, *Bobos in Paradise: The New Upper Class and How They Got There* (New York: Simon & Schuster, 2000), 10–11, 110.

———, "An Innovation Agenda," *New York Times*, December 8, 2009.

———, "The Next Culture War," *New York Times*, September 29, 2009.

E. S. Browning, "The Bull Turns 10, but Will It Reach 11?" *Wall Street Journal*, October 10, 2000.

Russ Buettner, "Ruling Against Zoning Law Regarding X-Rated Material," *New York Times*, August 21, 2012, A24.

Elisabeth Bumiller, "In Wake of Attack, Giuliani Cracks Down on Homeless," *New York Times*, November 20, 1999.

Brian Cabell, "NBA Star Ewing Testifies at Strip Club Trial," CNN.com, July 24, 2001.

"Canadian Court Rules Lap Dancing Indecent," *Toledo Blade*, June 27, 1997.

Graydon Carter et al., "The New Establishment," *Vanity Fair*, October 1994, 32, 209.

"Clinton Projects $1.9 Trillion Surplus," ABCNews.com, December 23, 2000.

Eric Conrad and Warren Richey, "Hedonism on High Seas: Nude Cruise Isn't NFL's Idea of Fun" (Broward and Palm Beach) *Sun Sentinel*, January 24, 1995.

"The Economics of Sex," *World of Work* (International Labor Organization), September/October 1998.

"Exotic Dancer Magazine Turns 20" (press release), EDpublications.com, July 2011, www.edpublications.com/the-magazine/ed-turns-20.

Manny Fernandez, "Strip Clubs and Their City Call a Truce," *New York Times*, January 2, 2014.

David Firestone, "In Testimony, Patrick Ewing Tells of Favors at Strip Club," *New York Times*, July 24, 2001.

———, "Mayor Removes the Gloves and Laces Into Messinger," *New York Times*, September 19, 1997.

Ben Fountain, "Naked Capitalism," *New York Times*, January 9, 2011.

Thomas L. Friedman, "The Post-Binge World," *New York Times*, October 11, 2008.

Andrew S. Garib and William Sherman, "Famed Sex Den Scores, Once a Top Moneymaker, Can't Jiggle Out of Financial Troubles," *New York Daily News*, December 10, 2008.

Deena Guzder, "The Economics of Commercial Sexual Exploitation," Pulitzer Center, August 25, 2009.

———, "A Move to Register Sex Offenders Globally," *Time*, September 7, 2009.

Stuart Haggas, "The Many Pleasures of Prague," PassportMagazine.com, December 17, 2010.

Art Harris and Jim Polk, "Ex-Gold Club Owner Gets 16 Months," CNN.com, January 8, 2002.

Jed Heyman, "Three's Company," *New York*, August 31, 2004.

Carl Hiaasen, *Strip Tease* [1993] (New York: Grand Central, 2005), 269–71.

Jonathan P. Hicks, "Giuliani in Accord with City Council on X-Rated Shops," *New York Times*, March 14, 1995.

Larry Keller, "Owner of Nude Bars Accused of Mob Ties, Violence" (Broward and Palm Beach) *Sun Sentinel*, November 15, 1991.

Andrew Kirtzman, *Rudy Giuliani: Emperor of the City* (New York: Harper Perennial, 2001), 215.

Nicholas D. Kristof, "A Sexy Economic Feud of No Interest to the I.M.F.," *New York Times*, June 17, 1999.

———, "What About American Girls Sold on the Streets?," *New York Times*, April 24, 2011, WK10.

Craig Horowitz, "The Fall of Supermayor," *New York*, April 19, 1999, 24–31.

Jose Lambiet, "The Man Who Would Be King," (Broward and Palm Beach) *Sun Sentinel*, November 10, 1997.

David Leonhardt and Geraldine Fabrikant, "After 30-Year Run, Rise of the Super-Rich Hits a Sobering Wall," *New York Times*, August 21, 2009, A1, 16.

Alex Frew McMillan, "Bucks Naked: Here's the Bottom Line on Running a Topless Club," AllBusiness.com, April 1, 1996.

Steven Lee Myers, "Giuliani Proposes Toughening Laws on X-Rated Shops," *New York Times*, September 11, 1994.

"Michael J. Peter" (bio), Solid Gold Ft. Lauderdale, solidgoldftl.com/bio/php.

Kathleen Nadeau, "The Impact of Colonization on Asia and the Pacific: Re-examining the Prostitution Question," *East Asian Pastoral Review* 45, no. 2 (2008).

Kathleen Nadeau and Sangita Rayamajhi, *Women's Roles in Asia* (Santa Barbara, CA: Greenwood, 2013), 66, 71–72.

Degen Pener, "You Know It When You See It, and You're Seeing It More," *New York Times*, May 10, 1992.

Michael J. Peter, "Keynote Address, EXPO '96," *Exotic Dancer Bulletin*, Fall 1996, 17–19.

Nick Ravo, "Topless Bars for a Crowd in Pinstripes," *New York Times*, April 15, 1992.

David Remnick, ed., *The New Gilded Age: The New Yorker Looks at the Culture of Affluence* (New York: Random House, 2000), xi–xiii.

Noah Remnick, "Court Rejects New York City's Efforts to Restrict Sex Shops," *New York Times*, July 22, 2015.

David Rohde, "Judge Deals a Blow to City's Campaign Against Sex Shops," August 29, 1998.

———, "Sex Shops Try to Obey Law, as Written," *New York Times*, August 6, 1998.

Ron Rosenbaum, "Hurricane Hiaasen," *Vanity Fair*, September 1993.

H. Luke Schaefer and Kathryn Edin, "Extreme Poverty in the United States, 1996–2011," National Poverty Center (policy brief), February 2012.

Eric Schlosser, "The Business of Pornography," *U.S. News & World Report*, February 10, 1997.

Matt Schudel, "Michael J. Peter: The Solid Gold Touch," (Broward and Palm Beach) *Sun Sentinel*, October 3, 1993.

Peter Schwartz and Peter Leyden, "The Long Boom: A History of the Future, 1980–2020," *Wired*, July 1997.

"Sex, Sports and the Mob: The Gold Club Trial," CNN.com, June 15, 2001.

Jeffrey Shields, "Ruling May Clear Strip Club Mogul," (Broward and Palm Beach) *Sun Sentinel*, November 1, 2002.

Bill Simmons, "Idiot's Guide to Gold Club Trial," Page 2, ESPN.com, September 27, 2001.

Iva R. Skoch, "Special Report: Gay-4-Pay in Prague," Globalpost.com, March 24, 2010.

Michael Specter, "Contraband Women—A Special Report: Traffickers' New Cargo: Naive Slavic Women," *New York Times*, January 11, 1998.

Joseph E. Stiglitz, *Roaring Nineties: A New History of the World's Most Prosperous Decade* (New York: Norton, 2003), xxxvi–xxxvii, xl–xli, xlv, 6, 10–11, 56–57.

"Strip Club Owner Agrees to Plea Deal," ABCNews.com, August 2, 2001.

Susan G. Strother, "2 Orlando Strip Clubs to Be Sold," *Orlando Sentinel*, January 18, 1997.

Lisa Taddeo, "Rachel Uchitel Is Not a Madam," *New York*, April 4, 2010.

Vivian S. Toy, "First Store Is Padlocked Under Sex-Shop Law," *New York Times*, September 20, 1997.

Louis Uchitelle, "The Richest of the Rich, Proud of a New Gilded Age," *New York Times*, July 15, 2007.

Stephen Van Drake, "Court Clears Businessman of Charges," *South Florida Business Journal*, October 31, 2002.

Rebecca Wakefield, "Strip Wars: The Politics of Selling Sex Entertainment on SoBe," *Miami New Times*, May 2, 2002.

Kassia R. Wosick-Correa and Lauren J. Joseph, "Sexy Ladies Sexing Ladies: Women as Consumers in Strip Clubs," *Journal of Sex Research*, 2008, 201–16.

Roger Yu, "Trump Taj Mahal Closes After Years of Losses," *USA Today*, October 10, 2016.

CHAPTER 27: The Lowest-Hanging Fruit

Interviews: Patrick Carnes, Susan Cheever, "Geraldine," Heidi Fleiss, Sam Kashner, Elisabeth Owen, Drew Pinsky, "Tiffany," Cara Tripodi, Jill Vermeire.

Ann Louise Bardach, "A Fever in the Blood," *Vanity Fair*, January 1991, 24–34.

Martin Barron and Michael Kimmel, "Sexual Violence in Three Pornographic Media: Toward a Sociological Explanation," *Journal of Sex Research* 37, no. 2 (May 2000): 161–68.

Jane Brody, "Cybersex Gives Birth to a Psychological Disorder," *New York Times*, May 16, 2000.

Frank Bruni, "The Bleaker Sex," *New York Times*, March 31, 2012.

Patrick Carnes, *Don't Call It Love: Recovery from Sexual Addiction* (New York: Bantam, 1991), 3, 37, 75–76, 94–95, 104–5, 210, 218, 384.

———, *Facing the Shadow: Starting Sexual and Relationship Recovery* [2001] (Carefree, AZ: Gentle Path, 2010), ix, 7, 32, 87–88, 97.

———, *Out of the Shadows: Understanding Sexual Addiction* [1983, published as *The Sexual Addiction*] (City Center, MN: Hazelden, 1994).

Susan Cheever, *Desire: When Sex Meets Addiction* (New York: Simon & Schuster, 2008), 17–18, 45, 49, 53–54, 65, 77, 153–55.

Barbara Dolan, "Behavior: Do People Get Hooked on Sex?," *Time*, June 4, 1990.

Ross Douthat, "Is Pornography Adultery?," *Atlantic*, October 2008, 80–86.

Murray Dubin, "Sexual Healing: Addictions to Drugs and Alcohol Are Familiar…," *Philadelphia Inquirer*, April 5, 1995.

"Earthly Concerns: The Catholic Church in America," *Economist*, August 18, 2012.

Ann Friedman, "Too Much or Too Little: DSM-V's Gray Area on Sex Addiction," The Cut, NYMag.com, May 23, 2013.

Daniel Goleman, "Some Sexual Behavior Viewed As an Addiction," *New York Times*, October 16, 1984.

D'Arcy Jenish, "Obsessed with Sex," *Maclean's*, January 21, 1991.

Jennifer Joseph et al., "Mary Kay Letourneau Fualaau, Vili Fualaau Detail Their Path from Teacher-Student Sex Scandal to Raising Teenagers," ABCNews.com, April 10, 2015.

Chris Lee, "The Sex Addiction Epidemic," *Newsweek*, December 5, 2011, 50.

Kelly McDaniel, KellyMcDanielTherapy.com, 2014.

Jim Orford, "Hypersexuality: Implications for a Theory of Dependence," *British Journal of Addiction* 73, no. 3 (1978).

"Our Staff," S.T.A.R. (Sexual Trauma and Recovery Inc.), http://starhealing.org/about-star-healing-sexual-trauma-and-recover/our-staff/.

Pamela Paul, *Pornified: How Pornography Is Damaging Our Lives, Our Relationships, and Our Families* (New York: Henry Holt, 2005), 20, 163, 166–67, 267.

Drew Pinsky, interview with Gennifer Flowers, *Loveline*, June 13, 2008, lovelinedownloads.com/ddl2008.htm.

Eric Pooley et al., "Kiss but Don't Tell," *Time*, March 23, 1998.

Stephanie Rosenbloom, "Ambition + Desire = Trouble," *New York Times*, June 19, 2011, ST2.

Davy Rothbart, "He's Just Not That Into Anyone," *New York*, February 7, 2011, 39–41, 88.

Michael Ryan, *Secret Life: An Autobiography* (New York: Vintage, 1996).

Allen Salkin, "No Sympathy for the Sex Addict," *New York Times*, September 7, 2008, ST12.

Jeremy Scahill, *Blackwater: The Rise of the World's Most Powerful Mercenary Army* (New York: Nation Books, 2007), 301–3.

Lauren Slater, "How Do You Cure a Sex Addict?," *New York Times*, November 19, 2000.

George Stephanopoulos, *All Too Human: A Political Education* (Boston: Little, Brown, 1999), 268.

Ian Urbina, "New Guidelines May Sharply Increase Addiction Diagnoses," *New York Times*, May 12, 2012, A11.

"Jill Vermeire MFT," mytherapistjill.com.

Stacey Wilson and Stephen M. Silverman, "Mary Kay Letourneau Gets Married," *People*, May 21, 2005.

Naomi Wolf, *The Beauty Myth: How Images of Beauty Are Used Against Women* [1991] (New York: Harper Perennial, 2002), 162.

Wesley Yang, "The Sex Diaries," *New York*, November 2, 2009, 32.

CHAPTER 28: Culture Wars, Part II

Interviews: Richard Friend, William Hultberg, Douglas MacKinnon, Steven Mauldin, Carol J. C. Maxwell, Kate Michelman, Dee Dee Myers, Ian Osterloh, William Stayton, Gay Talese, Joan Williams.

Jonathan Alter, "Thinking of Family Values," *Newsweek*, December 30, 1996.

Laura Bassett, "U.S. Abortion Rate Hits Lowest Point Since 1973," *Huffington Post*, February 2, 2014.

Emily Bazelon, "The New Abortion Providers," *New York Times Magazine*, July 18, 2010, 32.

Jo Becker, "The Road to Championing Same-Sex Marriage," *New York Times*, August 19, 2009, A1, 14.

Dallas A. Blanchard, *The Anti-Abortion Movement and the Rise of the Religious Right: From Polite to Fiery Protest* (New York: Twayne, 1994), 29, 40–41, 53–59, 118.

Charles M. Blow, "The G.O.P.'s Cynical Gay Ploy," *New York Times*, June 20, 2016, A19.

Fred Brock, "A Dose of Sense from Viagra's Spokesman," *New York Times*, June 4, 2000.

John M. Broder, "Dole Castigates Hollywood for Debasing U.S. Culture," *Los Angeles Times*, June 1, 1995.

Frank Bruni, "Marriage and the Supremes," *New York Times*, March 24, 2013, SR3.

———, "Same-Sex Sinners?," *New York Times*, April 5, 2015, SR3.

George Chauncey, "The Long Road to Marriage Equality," *New York Times*, June 27, 2013, A31.

Andrew J. Cherlin, *The Marriage-Go-Round: The State of Marriage and the Family in America Today* (New York: Knopf, 2009), 15.

Adam Clymer, "House, in a 395–28 Vote, Reprimands Gingrich," *New York Times*, January 22, 1997.

Ross Douthat, "The Changing Culture War," *New York Times*, December 6, 2010.

———, "The Orphaned '90s," *New York Times*, February 14, 2016, SR9.

———, "The Unborn Paradox," *New York Times*, January 3, 2011, A21.

Jon Frandsen, "Gingrich Reportedly Resigning as Speaker, Leaving House," Gannett News Service via *Detroit News*, November 6, 1998.

Richard A. Friend, "From Surviving to Thriving: Lessons from Lesbian and Gay Youth" (lecture), American Educational Research Association, Chicago, March 25, 1997.

———, "Power, Pleasure, and the Social Context of Sexuality" (lecture), April 21, 1998.

John Gallagher and Chris Bull, *Perfect Enemies: The Religious Right, the Gay Movement, and the Politics of the 1990s* (New York: Crown, 1996), via WashingtonPost.com (chapter 1 excerpt).

Nicole Gaudiano, "At Anti-abortion Rally, Mike Pence Is a Beacon of Hope," *USA Today*, January 27, 2017.

Andrew Gelman, Jeffrey Lax, and Justin Phillips, "Over Time, a Gay Marriage Groundswell," *New York Times*, August 22, 2010.

"Getting Marriage Straight," *Economist*, September 7, 1996.

Steven M. Gillon, *The Pact: Bill Clinton, Newt Gingrich, and the Rivalry That Defined a Generation* (New York: Oxford University Press, 2008), 175.

Laurie Goodstein, "New Poll Suggests Decline in Support of a Woman's Right to Have an Abortion, *New York Times*, October 2, 2009, A16.

Jennifer Haberkorn, "Gorsuch Pick Affirms Trump Vow to Pick 'Pro-Life' Justice," Politico.com, January 31, 2017.

Christopher Hitchens, "Fetal Distraction," *Vanity Fair*, February 2003, 84–88.

Molly Ivins, "Nobody Gets Cut Any Slack for Their Political Passion," *Fort Worth Star-Telegram*, June 16, 1994.

"Judge Orders Gay Marriage Ban Unconstitutional," Associated Press via *New York Times*, July 8, 2010.

Christie Keith, "Queerly Beloved," AfterElton.com, May 11, 2008.

"The Killing of a Doctor," *New York Times*, June 2, 2009, A14.

Joe Klein, *The Natural: The Misunderstood Presidency of Bill Clinton* (New York: Doubleday, 2002), 153–55, 160.

Howard Kurtz, "How Newt Gingrich Crashed and Burned When He Was House Speaker," *Daily Beast*, December 27, 2011.

David Leonhardt, "Why Abortion Is Not Like Other Issues," *New York Times*, July 14, 2013, SR4.

"Let Them Wed," *Economist*, January 4, 1996.

Adam Liptak, "'Equal Dignity': 5–4 Ruling Makes Same-Sex Marriage a Right Nationwide," *New York Times*, June 27, 2015, A1, 11.

Meika Loe, *The Rise of Viagra: How the Little Blue Pill Changed Sex in America* (New York: New York University Press, 2004), 56–57.

Carol J. C. Maxwell, *Pro-Life Activists in America: Meaning, Motivation, and Direct Action* (Cambridge: Cambridge University Press, 2002), 3, 9, 14–15, 74–75, 78–86, 190–91, 230–31.

Jon Meacham, "The End of Christian America," *Newsweek*, April 13, 2009.

Kate Michelman, *With Liberty and Justice for All: A Life Spent Protecting the Right to Choose* (New York: Hudson Street, 2005).

Claire Cain Miller, "The Divorce Surge Is Over, but the Myth Lives On," *New York Times*, December 2, 2014.

David Moats, *Civil Wars: The Battle for Gay Marriage* (New York: Harcourt, 2005), 198–99, 217, 241–42.

Partial-Birth Abortion Ban Act of 1995: H.R. 1833 (104th) (House of Representatives Bill, defeated), June 4, 1995, www.govtrack.us/congress/bills/104/hr1833.

Randall Patterson, "Students of Virginity," *New York Times Magazine*, March 30, 2008, 40.

Kate Pickert, "What Choice?: Abortion-Rights Activists Won an Epic Victory in *Roe v. Wade*. They've Been Losing Ever Since," *Time*, January 14, 2013, 38–46.

Phil Reeves, "Dole Turns His Fire on Hollywood 'Depravity,'" *Independent*, June 2, 1995.

Jamie Reidy, *Hard Sell: The Evolution of a Viagra Salesman* (Kansas City: Andrews McMeel, 2005), 199.

Frank Rich, "40 Years Later, Still Second-Class Americans," *New York Times*, June 28, 2009, WK8.

———, "The Culture Warriors Get Laid Off," *New York Times*, March 15, 2009, WK12.

———, "I Got You, Babe," *New York Times*, May 25, 1996.

Sam Roberts, "Counting Layoffs, Bowlers and Other Bits of U.S. Life," *New York Times*, December 20, 2009.

Tina Rosenberg, "The Stealth War Against Abortion," *Rolling Stone*, June 27, 1996.

Philip Roth, *The Human Stain* (New York: Vintage, 2001), 3.

Julie Rovner, "'Partial-Birth Abortion': Separating Fact from Spin," NPR, February 21, 2006.

William Saletan, "This Is the Way the Culture Wars End," *New York Times*, February 22, 2009, WK11.

Dan Schnur, "Gingrich, We Hardly Newt Ye," *Salon*, November 11, 1998.

Somini Sengupta, "Trump Revives Ban on Aid to Groups That Discuss Abortion," *New York Times*, January 24, 2017.

Jennifer Senior, "The Abortion Distortion: Just How Pro-Choice Is America, Really?," *New York*, December 7, 2009, 44–49, 105.

Paul Solotaroff, "Surviving the Crusades," *Rolling Stone*, October 14, 1993.

Liam Stack, "Trump Victory Alarms Gay and Transgender Groups," *New York Times*, November 11, 2016.

Brian Stelter, "Doctor's Killer, Some Say, Is Not Alone in the Blame," *New York Times*, June 2, 2009, A14.

Seth Stephens-Davidowitz, "The Return of the D.I.Y. Abortion," *New York Times*, March 6, 2016, SR2.

Sheryl Gay Stolberg, "In Fight for Marriage Rights, 'She's Our Thurgood Marshall,'" *New York Times*, March 28, 2013, A19.

———, "A Pregnant Pause," *New York Times*, November 29, 2009, WR1, 6.

Daniel Strauss, "Hillary and Bill Clinton Hail Supreme Court Ruling on DOMA," TheHill.com, June 26, 2013.

Joe Stumpe and Monica Davey, "Abortion Doctor Slain by Gunman in Kansas Church," *New York Times*, June 1, 2009, A1, 3.

Andrew Sullivan, "Why Gay Marriage Is Good for Straight America," *Daily Beast*, July 18, 2011.

Sabrina Tavernise, "Married Couples Are No Longer a Majority, Census Finds," *New York Times*, May 26, 2011, A22.

"Tom and Walter Got Married," Talk of the Town, *New Yorker*, December 20, 1993.

Gary Wills, "George Bush, Prisoner of the Crazies," *New York Times*, August 16, 1992.

Naomi Wolf, "Scenes from a Gay Marriage," *George*, February 1998, 48–49.

CHAPTER 29: The Hardener's Tale

Interviews: David Brinkley, Simon Campbell, Nicole Daedone, Peter Ellis, Clive Gingell, Irwin Goldstein, Michael Mendelsohn, Ian Osterloh, Nick Terrett.

AA Illustrated Guide to Britain (London: Drive Publications, 1975), 104, 146–47.

"About Viagra: Frequently Asked Questions" (includes disclaimer notice), 2000, Viagra.com/consumers/about/index.asp?n=0.

Jay Baglia, *The Viagra Ad Venture: Masculinity, Media, and the Performance of Sexual Health* (New York: Peter Lang, 2005), 73, 169.

Andrew S. Bell, David Brown, and Nicholas K. Terrett, United States Patent 5,250,534, Pyrazolopyrimidinone Antianginal Agents, Pfizer Inc., May 14, 1992 (filed), October 5, 1993 (date of patent).

Simon F. Campbell, "Science, Art and Drug Discovery: A Personal Perspective," *Clinical Science* 99, no. 4 (2000): 255–60.

Geoffrey Chaucer, *The Canterbury Tales* [1394], translated by R. M. Lumiansky (New York: Washington Square, 1971), 14–15.

Kevin Cook, "The Magic Little Blue Pill," *Playboy*, May 2015, 112.

"Did You Know?," VisitBristol.co.uk.

Canaan Downs, "Yohimbe Bark & Prostate Health," Livestrong.com, June 6, 2011.

Peter Ellis and Nicholas Kenneth Terrett, United States Patent 6,469,012 B1, Pyrazolopyrimidinones for the Treatment of Impotence, Pfizer Inc., May 13, 1994 (filed), October 22, 2002 (date of patent).

David M. Friedman, *A Mind of Its Own: A Cultural History of the Penis* (New York: Penguin, 2001), 47–48, 254–57, 260–61, 297.

Joseph Hooper, "Sex Science Timeline," *Men's Journal*, August 1998.

Larry Katzenstein and Eric B. Grossman, *Viagra: The Remarkable Story of the Discovery and Launch* (New York: Medical Information Press, 2001), 2, 6–7, 11–17, 38–39.

"King Henry VIII's Kentish Roots," BBC News, October 8, 2009.

Jim Kling, "From Hypertension to Angina to Viagra," *Modern Drug Discovery* 1, no. 2 (November/December 1998): 31–38.

Gina Kolata, "Drugs That Deliver More Than Originally Promised," *New York Times*, April 5, 1998.

———, "U.S. Approves Sale of Impotence Pill: Huge Market Seen," *New York Times*, March 28, 1998.

R. J. Krane, I. Goldstein, and I. Saenz de Tejada, "Medical Progress: Impotence," *New England Journal of Medicine* 321, no. 24 (1989): 1648–59.

Meika Loe, *The Rise of Viagra: How the Little Blue Pill Changed Sex in America* (New York: New York University Press, 2004), 11–13, 36–37, 50.

Michael E. Mendelsohn, "Viagra: Now Mending Hearts," *Nature Medicine* 11 (February 2005): 115–16.

Ian Osterloh, "How I Discovered Viagra," *Cosmos*, June 2007.

Elizabeth Palmer, "Making the Love Drug," *Chemistry in Britain* 35, no. 1 (January 1999): 24–26.

Michael Parrish, "Up, Up & Away," *Playboy*, June 1997, 92–96.

Lois Rogers, "Viagranation," *Times* (U.K.), July 15, 2007.

R. V. Scheide, "Viagra and the Culture of Manhood," *Sacramento News and Review*, January 12, 2006.

David Stipp, "Why Pfizer Is So Hot," *Fortune*, May 11, 1998.

——— and Robert Whitaker with Alicia Hills Moore, "The Selling of Impotence," *Fortune*, March 16, 1998.

Nick Terrett, "Love Chemistry: The Science Behind Viagra" (lecture), Ensemble Discovery, October 2009.

CHAPTER 30: Homo Erectus

Interviews: Pravin Agravat, James Balog, Susie Bright, David Brinkley, Simon Campbell, Peter Ellis, Clive Gingell, Irwin Goldstein, Michael Mendelsohn, Jean-Jacques Naudet, Michael O'Brien, Ian Osterloh.

Pravin Agravat, *A Guide to Sexual and Erectile Dysfunction in Men* (London/Bournemouth: Quay, 2010).

Jay Baglia, *The Viagra Ad Venture: Masculinity, Media, and the Performance of Sexual Health* (New York: Peter Lang, 2005), 8, 20, 45–47, 53, 78, 84, 164, 200.

M. Boolell et al., "Sildenafil: An Orally Active Type 5 Cyclic GMP-Specific Phosphodiesterase Inhibitor for the Treatment of Penile Erectile Dysfunction," *International Journal of Impotence Research* 8, no. 2 (June 1996): 47–52.

Susie Bright, "Viagra Calls, II: Curse of the Trophy Wives," *Salon*, July 31, 1998.

Marlene Cimons, "Pill to Treat Impotence Is OKd by FDA," *Los Angeles Times*, March 28, 1998.

Chris Conway, "Viagra: Recalling the Madness," *New York Times*, March 30, 2008, WK5.

Caroline Daniel, "Beyond Sugarcoating: New Colors, Shapes and Names Are Cures for the Common Pill," *Washington Post*, November 11, 1998.

Brian Deer, "Viagra: Sex Drugs & Rock 'N' Roll," *Sunday Times Magazine* (U.K.), September 6, 1998.

Peter Elkind and Jennifer Reingold with Doris Burke, "Inside Pfizer's Palace Coup," *Fortune*, July 28, 2011.

David M. Friedman, "A Real Growth Stock," *Salon*, April 23, 1998.

———, *A Mind of Its Own: A Cultural History of the Penis* (New York: Penguin, 2001), 286.

Bruce Handy, "The Viagra Craze," *Time*, May 4, 1998.

Diedtra Henderson, "Sex Drugs Called Avenue to HIV," *Boston Globe*, September 26, 2005.

Jack Hitt, "The Second Sexual Revolution," *New York Times Magazine*, February 20, 2000.

Larry Katzenstein and Eric B. Grossman, *Viagra: The Remarkable Story of the Discovery and Launch* (New York: Medical Information Press, 2001), 16, 28–33, 35, 45, 50.

Julie Kirkwood, "What's in a Name?," *Eagle-Tribune* (North Andover, MA), September 1, 2003.

Gina Kolata, "Impotence Is Given Another Name, and a Drug Market Grows," *New York Times*, April 18, 2000.

Alex Kuczynski, "Curious Women Are Seeing if Viagra Works Wonders for Them," *New York Times*, May 17, 1998.

John Leland, "A Pill for Impotence?," *Newsweek*, November 17, 1997.

Meika Loe, *The Rise of Viagra: How the Little Blue Pill Changed Sex in America* (New York: New York University Press, 2004), 24, 56, 65, 171, 176–77.

Lynne Luciano, *Looking Good: Male Body Image in Modern America* (New York: Hill & Wang, 2001), 200.

Daniel McGinn and Anjali Arora, "Viagra's Hothouse," *Newsweek*, December 21, 1998.

Selina McKee, "Shock as Pfizer Prepares to Exit Sandwich R&D Site," PharmaTimes.com, February 3, 2011.

Donald G. McNeil Jr, "Variations on 'Vital': The Science of Naming Drugs (Sorry, 'Z' Is Already Taken)," *New York Times*, December 28, 2003.

Elizabeth Palmer, "Making the Love Drug," *Chemistry in Britain* 35, no. 1 (January 1999): 24–26.

Tara Parker-Pope, "Viagra Is Misunderstood Despite Name Recognition," *Wall Street Journal*, November 11, 2002.

"Pfizer Halts Development of Alond for Diabetic Neuropathy," Doctor's Guide Publishing, August 13, 1999, PSL Group.com.

"The Pilgrim's Way," North Downs Way/National Trail, NationalTrail.co.uk.

Andrew Pollack, "F.D.A. Panel Backs 'Viagra for Women,'" *New York Times*, June 5, 2015, A1, 3.

"Prescription Drugs Trends," Fact Sheet 3057, Kaiser Family Foundation, September 2000.

Jack Reidy, *Hard Sell: The Evolution of a Viagra Salesman* (Kansas City: Andrews McMeel, 2005), 145–53, 161–62, 200.

Debs Rooney, *The Young Person's Guide to Canterbury Cathedral* (Canterbury, Kent: Cathedral Enterprises, 2003), 34.

R. V. Scheide, "Viagra and the Culture of Manhood," *Sacramento News and Review*, January 12, 2006.

"Sildenafil Submission's Celebration Party," *Pfizer Insite* (in-house magazine), November 1997.

Alessandra Stanley, "Still Hung Over from the '90s," *New York Times*, January 6, 2012, C1, 15.

Louise Stewart, "Pfizer's Closure Will Have Huge Impact on Kent," BBC News, February 1, 2011.

David Stipp, "Why Pfizer Is So Hot," *Fortune*, May 11, 1998.

Hilary Stout, "Viagra: The Thrill That Was," *New York Times*, June 5, 2011, ST8.

"Viagra Receives Positive Opinion from European Regulatory Committee," Doctor's Guide Publishing, May 29, 1998, PSLGroup.com.

"Viagra Usage in U.S., March 2000," USRF.org/breakingnews/viagra-usage2000.html.

"Viagra vs. Cialis: What Hidden Messages Does a Brand Name Send?," www.lexicon-branding.com.

Duff Wilson, "Big Push of Pill to Marketplace Stirs Debate on Sexual Desire," *New York Times*, June 17, 2010, A1, 3.

CHAPTER 31: The Internet and the Intern

> *Interviews: Molly Friend, Daniel Gerstein, Anita Hill, Monica Lewinsky, Mark McKinnon, Dee Dee Myers, Mike Murphy, Drew Pinsky.*

Renata Adler, "Decoding the Starr Report," *Vanity Fair*, December 1998.

Peter Baker, "Lasting Effects of Political Poison," *New York Times*, December 13, 2008.

—— and John F. Harris, "Clinton Admits to Lewinsky Relationship, Challenges Starr to End Personal 'Prying,'" *Washington Post*, August 18, 1998.

—— and Susan Schmidt, analysis, "Starr Alleges 'Abundant' Lies; President Denies Impeachability," in *Washington Post*, eds., *The Starr Report: The Findings of Independent Counsel Kenneth W. Starr on President Clinton and the Lewinsky Affair* (New York: PublicAffairs, 1998), x.

Dan Balz, "A Crisis with No Parallel," *Washington Post*, January 26, 1998.

Susan Wise Bauer, *The Art of the Public Grovel: Sexual Sin and Public Confession in America* (Princeton, NJ: Princeton University Press, 2008), 171–74.

Greg Beato, "Criminal Verite," Reason.com, April 2009.

Richard Berke, "Once a Nemesis, Jackson Has Become the President's Spiritual Adviser," *New York Times*, March 6, 1998.

"Best Sellers Plus," *New York Times* Best Seller List (expanded), NYTimes.com, October 18, 1998.

Julian Borger, "Monica's Revenge: Lewinsky Testifies Against Woman Who Exposed Affair with Clinton," *Guardian*, December 16, 1999.

Dale Bumpers, U.S. Senate, Clinton Impeachment Trial (transcript), January 21, 1999, via CNN.com.

George W. Bush, Campaign Rally, Grand Rapids, Michigan (transcript), November 3, 2000, via CNN.com.

Megan Carpentier, "Monica Lewinsky's Story Is a Scandal of Americans' Double-Standards," *Guardian*, May 8, 2014.

"A Chronology: Key Moments in the Clinton-Lewinsky Saga," CNN.com, 1998, www.cnn.com/ALLPOLITICS/1998/resources/lewinsky/timeline/.

Bill Clinton, *My Life* (New York: Random House/Vintage, 2004), 808.

"A Clinton Timeline," CBSNews.com, January 8, 2001, www.cbsnews.com/news/a-clinton-timeline/.

Hillary Rodham Clinton, *Living History* (New York: Scribner, 2003), 245, 446.

Matthew Cooper, "A Saddam Souvenir," *Time*, May 29, 2004.

"Direct Access: Rev. J. Philip Wogaman," *Washington Post*, December 16, 1998.

Marc Fisher, "Tripp's Tapes: Listening In on a Betrayal," *Washington Post*, November 18, 1998.

Matt Flegenheimer, "Bill Clinton, After a Year of Restraint, Unleashes an Impassioned Self-Defense," *New York Times*, September 9, 2016.

Evan Forster, "Fast Times at Beverly High: When Monica Lewinsky's Sex Life Became the World's Biggest Scandal, Her Former Classmates Made Sure No Story Was Left Unsold," *Details*, April 1998.

John Fund, "Tom DeLay Saga Ends—Conviction Reversed," *National Review*, October 1, 2014.

"Gingrich Admits Having Affair in '90s," Associated Press via MSNBC.com, March 9, 2007.

Erving Goffman, *The Presentation of the Self in Everyday Life* (New York: Anchor, 1959).

Laurie Goodstein, "The Counselors: Clinton Selects Clerics to Give Him Guidance," *New York Times*, September 15, 1998.

Ken Gormley, *The Death of American Virtue: Clinton v. Starr* (New York: Broadway, 2010), 352–58, 369, 373, 568, 573–74, 668.

Vanessa Grigoriadis, "Monica Takes Manhattan," *New York*, March 19, 2001.

Alexander Hamilton, *Federalist* (No. 65, 439–45), March 7, 1788, via "The Founders' Constitution: Impeachment Clauses," UChicago.edu, press-pubs.uchicago.edu/founders/documents/a1_2_5s9.html.

Michael Isikoff, *Uncovering Clinton: A Reporter's Story* (New York: Crown/Three Rivers, 2000), 311–16, 339.

———, "Lewinsky vs. Clinton," *Newsweek*, August 10, 1998, 26–32.

———, "The Tripp Trap?," *Newsweek*, July 13, 1998.

Michael Isikoff and Evan Thomas, "Clinton and the Intern," *Newsweek*, February 2, 1998.

Robert G. Kaiser, "One Senator's Journey," *Washington Post*, February 13, 1999.

Joe Klein, *The Natural: The Misunderstood Presidency of Bill Clinton* (New York, Doubleday, 2002), 5, 177–79, 182.

David Kravets, "Starr Report Showcases Net's Speed," Wired.com, September 11, 2009.

Christopher Lasch, *The Culture of Narcissism: American Life in an Age of Diminishing Expectations* [1979] (New York: Norton, 1991), 3.

Judd Legum, "What We Now Know About the Men Who Led the Impeachment of Clinton," ThinkProgress.org, May 30, 2015.

Monica Lewinsky, "The Price of Shame," TED Talk, TED2015, March 2015, www.ted.com/talks/monica_lewinsky _the_price_of_shame.

———, "Shame and Survival," *Vanity Fair*, June 2014.

"Lewinsky-Tripp Tapes" (1997–98), from *American Experience*, "Clinton," PBS, www.pbs.org/wgbh/american experience/features/primary-resources/lewinsky-tripp/.

Joseph Lieberman, Senate speech, September 3, 1998, via CNN.com, www.cnn.com/ALLPOLITICS/1998/09/03/ lieberman/.

Aamer Madhani and John Bacon, "Judge Sentences 'Serial Child Molester' Hastert to 15 Months," *USA Today*, April 27, 2016.

Alexis Madrigal, "How Frictionless Sharing Could Undermine Your Legal Right to Privacy," *Atlantic*, March 2012.

Joshua Micah Marshall, "Kenneth Starr's $70 Million Bag of Garbage," *Salon*, March 13, 2002.

Chris Matyszczyk, "Zuckerberg: I Know That People Don't Want Privacy," CNET.com, January 10, 2010.

Mayo Clinic, "Personality Disorders," www.mayoclinic.org/diseases-conditions/personality-disorders/symptoms-causes/ dxc-20247656.

Dick Morris, *Behind the Oval Office: Getting Reelected Against All Odds* (New York: Random House, 1999), xxxii.

Andrew Morton, *Monica's Story* (New York: St. Martin's, 1999), 12–14, 219–25, 247–49.

Kate Murphy, "We Want Privacy, but Can't Stop Sharing," *New York Times*, October 4, 2014.

"President Clinton's Videotaped Testimony," August 17, 1998 (released by House Judiciary Committee, September 21, 1998), www.cnn.com/icreport/.

Jamie Reidy, *Hard Sell: The Evolution of a Viagra Salesman* (Kansas City: Andrews McMeel, 2005).

Frank Rich, "All Monica All the Time," *New York Times*, January 24, 1998, A15.

———, "Scandal Loves a Clinton," *New York*, April 7, 2014, 37.

Jeffrey Rosen, *The Unwanted Gaze: The Destruction of Privacy in America* (New York: Random House, 2000).

Hanna Rosin, "Ministers to Give Clinton 'Pastoral Care,'" *Washington Post*, September 16, 1998.

Gregg Russell, "Pandora's Web?: Clinton-Lewinsky Allegations Fuel Debate About Journalism and the Internet," CNN.com, January 30, 1998.

Jonathan Schell, "Land of Dreams," *Nation*, July 11, 1999.

Arthur M. Schlesinger Jr., *Journals: 1952–2000* (New York: Penguin, 2007), 832.

Aaron Sorkin, "*V.F.* Portrait: David Fincher," *Vanity Fair*, December 2011.

Kenneth W. Starr et al., *The Starr Report: The Findings of Independent Counsel Kenneth W. Starr on President Clinton and the Lewinsky Affair* (New York: PublicAffairs, 1998).

"The Starr Report: Full Text of Findings Sent to Congress," *New York Times*, September 12, 1998.

Gloria Steinem, "Why Feminists Support Clinton," *New York Times*, March 22, 1998.

George Stephanopoulos, *All Too Human: A Political Education* (Boston: Little, Brown, 1999), 440–41.

Caroline Daniel Washington, "Beyond Sugarcoating," *Washington Post*, November 11, 1998.

Marjorie Williams, "Clinton and Women," *Vanity Fair*, May 1998, 194–97, 250–53.

AFTERWORD: *The Trumpen Show*

Interviews: Emily Jane Fox, Jon Kelly, Cullen Murphy, Henry Schuster, Tim Zahner.

"6th Republican Debate Transcript, Annotated: Who Said What and What It Meant," WashingtonPost.com, January 14, 2016.

"2016 Presidential Debate Fast Facts," CNN.com, October 24, 2016, www.cnn.com/2015/07/27/us/2016 -presidential-debates-fast-facts/.

"2016 Presidential Primary Election Schedule," WashingtonPost.com, March 1, 2016, www.washingtonpost.com/ graphics/politics/2016-election/primaries/schedule/.

Jill Abramson, "Hillary Clinton Conspiracy Theories Are a Generation in the Making," *Guardian*, December 6, 2016.

Claire Atkinson, "Marvel Executive Set to Join Trump's Veterans Affairs Staff," *New York Post*, January 7, 2017.

Justin Baragona, "'Rope. Tree. Journalist.': Trump Supporter Wears Shirt Supporting Lynching Reporters," Mediaite.com, November 6, 2016.

Martin Baron, Acceptance Speech, Hitchens Prize Ceremony, New York City, November 29, 2016, www.vanityfair.com/news/2016/11/washington-post-editor-marty-baron-message-to-journalists.

Peter Beinart, "Why America Is Moving Left," *Atlantic*, January/February 2016.

Brian Bennett, "Can Donald Trump Really Round Up and Deport 11 Million People?," *Los Angeles Times*, August 23, 2016.

Laura Bennett, "What Trump Really Meant When He Said That Megyn Kelly Had 'Blood Coming Out of Her Wherever,'" *Slate*, August 10, 2015.

Noah Bierman, "A New Favorite Chant Has Overtaken Donald Trump's Rallies," *Los Angeles Times*, October 17, 2016.

Kyle Blaine, "Trump Did Four Interviews on Sunday—No One Asked Him About His Campaign Manager," BuzzFeed.com, March 13, 2016.

Jacob Brogan, "The Best Lines of the CNN GOP Debate," *Slate*, February 25, 2016.

Jonah Engel Bromwich, "Donald Trump's Star on Hollywood Walk of Fame Is Smashed," *New York Times*, October 26, 2016.

Nina Burleigh, "The Presidential Election Was a Referendum on Gender—And Women Lost," *Newsweek*, November 14, 2016.

Alexander Burns, Maggie Haberman, and Jonathan Martin, "Donald Trump Apology Caps Day of Outrage over Lewd Tape," *New York Times*, October 7, 2016.

Sue Carswell, "Trump Says Goodbye Marla, Hello Carla," *People*, July 8, 1991.

Susan Chira, "Trump's Vision of Manhood," *New York Times*, October 25, 2016.

Niraj Chokshi, "How the American Electorate Is Changing," *New York Times*, November 25, 2016.

Amy Chozick, "A Duel of Political Operatives," *New York Times*, May 24, 2016, A1, 13.

Stephen Collinson, "Trump: Clinton 'Has to Go to Jail,'" CNN.com, October 13, 2016.

Sopan Deb, "Trump Scorns the Pop Culture World He Once Cultivated," *New York Times*, January 31, 2017.

Lisa de Moraes and Anita Busch, "Donald Trump Names Steven Mnuchin New Treasury Secretary," Deadline.com, November 29, 2016.

"Donald Trump: 'We Are Going to Win Big-League'" (video), Associated Press via *Guardian*, May 4, 2016.

"Donald Trump's Taped Comments About Women," *New York Times*, October 8, 2016.

C. Eugene Emery Jr., "Priorities USA Ad Rips Trump's 'F——Themselves' Quote Way Out of Context," Politifact.com, May 18, 2016.

Susan Faludi, *Backlash: The Undeclared War Against American Women* [1991] (New York: Three Rivers, 2006), 9–13, 243.

———, "Not Their Mother's Candidate," *New York Times*, February 14, 2016, SR3.

———, "How Hillary Clinton Met Satan," *New York Times*, October 29, 2016.

Marc Fisher and Will Hobson, "Donald Trump Masqueraded as Publicist to Brag About Himself," *Washington Post*, May 13, 2016.

Clare Foran, "Women Aren't Responsible for Hillary Clinton's Defeat," *Atlantic*, November 13, 2016.

David Gergen, "For Trump, It's a Wrestling Match," CNN.com, September 16, 2015.

Anne Godlasky, "Half of Republicans Think Trump Won Popular Vote; Clinton Won by 2.86 Million," *USA Today*, December 19, 2016.

Don Gonyea, "F-Bomb On a T-Shirt: At Trump Rallies, Profanity Comes Onstage and Off," NPR.org, June 17, 2016.

Michael M. Grynbaum, "An 'Apprentice' Role for Trump Opens Door Wide for Questions," *New York Times*, December 9, 2016.

Josh Hafner, "Donald Trump Loves the 'Poorly Educated'—And They Love Him," *USA Today*, February 24, 2016.

Daniel Henninger, "The Trumpen Proletariat," *Wall Street Journal*, July 6, 2016.

Michael Hirschorn, "How to Take Back the Counterculture," *New York*, November 28, 2016, 34.

Jan Hoffman, "The Ego Behind the Ego in a Trump Gamble," *New York Times*, November 18, 1999.

Ben Jacobs, "Julian Assange Gives Guarded Praise of Trump...," *Guardian*, December 24, 2016.

Glenn Kessler, "When Did McConnell Say He Wanted to Make Obama a 'One-Term President?,'" *Washington Post*, September 25, 2012.

Nicholas Kristof, "When a Crackpot Seeks Office," *New York Times*, September 15, 2016, A27.

Judd Legum, "This French Philosopher Is the Only One Who Can Explain the Donald Trump Phenomenon," ThinkProgress.org, September 14, 2015.

Michael Lewis, "Obama's Way," *Vanity Fair*, October 2012.

Jonathan Martin, "Donald Trump's Anything-Goes Campaign Sets an Alarming Political Precedent," *New York Times*, September 17, 2016.

Jonathan Martin, Maggie Haberman, and Alexander Burns, "Lewd Trump Tape Is Breaking Point for Many in G.O.P.," *New York Times*, October 9, 2016, A1, 26.

Ben Mathis-Lilley, "Trump Was Recorded in 2005 Bragging About Grabbing Women 'By the Pussy,'" *Slate*, October 7, 2016.

Stephanie Mencimer, "How Paula Jones Paved the Way for Donald Trump to Be Repeatedly Dragged into Court as President," *Mother Jones*, November 15, 2016.

Stephen L. Miller, "How Pro Wrestling Taught Donald Trump to Be the Perfect Showman," *National Review*, April 4, 2016.

Suzanne Moore, "Why Did Women Vote for Trump? Because Misogyny Is Not a Male-Only Attribute," *Guardian*, November 16, 2016.

Alexis Okeowo, "Hate on the Rise After Trump's Election," *New Yorker*, November 17, 2016.

George Orwell, *1984* [1949] (New York: NAL, 1961), 54.

Frank Pallotta, "The 'P-word' Problem: Trump's Comments Pose Issue for News Outlets," Money.CNN.com, October 7, 2016.

Ashley Parker, "Trump's Rallying Cry: 'Our System Is Rigged,'" *New York Times*, October 14, 2016, A16.

Chris Perez, "Pam Anderson Can't Get Enough of 'Sexy' Julian Assange," *New York Post*, March 10, 2017.

Amber Phillips, "Why the News Networks Let Donald Trump Phone It In (Literally)," WashingtonPost.com, August 10, 2015.

James Poniewozik, "The New TV Reality: All Trump," *New York Times*, December 12, 2016, C5.

Jonathan Mahler, "CNN Had a Problem. Donald Trump Solved It," *New York Times Magazine*, April 9, 2017.

"President Clinton's Deposition," *Washington Post*, March 13, 1998, www.washingtonpost.com/wp-srv/politics/special/clinton/stories/clintondep031398.htm#willey.

Michael Putney, "Trump Campaign Rallies Feed the Vitriol Machine," *Miami Herald*, August 17, 2016.

James Rainey, "WME-IMG Chief Financial Officer Chris Liddell Joins Donald Trump's White House Team," Variety.com, January 17, 2017.

Katie Reilly, "Here Are All the Times Donald Trump Insulted Mexico," Time.com, August 31, 2016.

David Remnick, "Donald Trump and the Enemies of the American People," *New Yorker*, February 18, 2017.

Frank Rich, *The Greatest Story Ever Sold: The Decline and Fall of Truth, from 9/11 to Katrina* (New York: Penguin, 2006), 141.

Janelle Ross, "So Which Women Has Donald Trump Called 'Dogs' and 'Fat Pigs'?," WashingtonPost.com, August 8, 2015.

Edward Rothstein, "For the Media's Dupes, Perhaps Thinking Makes It So," *New York Times*, June 8, 1998, E2.

Avik Roy, "Donald Trump on Obamacare on '60 Minutes': Everybody's Got to Be Covered and 'The Government's Gonna Pay for It,'" Forbes.com, September 28, 2015.

Ale Russian, "Trump Boasted of Avoiding STDs While Dating: Vaginas Are 'Landmines…It Is My Personal Vietnam,'" People.com, October 28, 2016.

John Saward, "Welcome to Trump County, U.S.A.," VanityFair.com, February 24, 2016.

Anna R. Schecter et al., "Trump Doctor Wrote Health Letter in 5 Minutes as Limo Waited," NBCNews.com, August 26, 2016.

Nell Scovell, "Trump's Real Tragedy for Women," VanityFair.com, November 16, 2016.

Katharine Q. Seelye, "Flash? President Bush Says He Reads Papers," *New York Times*, December 25, 2006.

Michael D. Shear and Maggie Haberman, "From Trump's Mar-a-Lago to Facebook, a National Security Crisis in the Open," *New York Times*, February 13, 2017.

Stephen S. Roach, "Donald Trump Is Right About Globalization: It's a Broken System," MarketWatch.com, July 25, 2016.

Alex Ross, "The Frankfurt School Knew Trump Was Coming," *New Yorker*, December 5, 2016.

Scott Shane, "In Trump, Populist Provocateur Found the Man for His Mission," *New York Times*, November 28, 2106, A1, 14–15.

Michael Tomasky, "It's Time for the Media to Step Up and Call Out Donald Trump's Many Lies," *Daily Beast*, September 8, 2016.

Jeffrey Toobin, "The Dirty Trickster," *New Yorker*, June 2, 2008.

Donald Trump, @realDonaldTrump, Twitter, February 13, 2016.

Isabel Vincent, "Melania Trump's Girl-on-Girl Photos From Racy Shoot Revealed," *New York Post*, August 1, 2016.

Josh Voorhees, "The *New York Times* Drops an F-Bomb, but Was It the Grey Lady's First?," *Slate*, August 26, 2013.

James Warren, "A Social Media Extravaganza," Poynter.org, November 23, 2016.

Peter Wehner, "What Wouldn't Jesus Do?," *New York Times*, March 1, 2016.

Tina Witherspoon, @shop_grrl, Twitter, September 29, 2016.

Index

Aarons, Slim, 55
Abel, Richard, 208
abortion, 59, 152, 198–99, 457–62
Abramovic, Marina, 231
Abramson, Jill, 90n, 91, 96–97, 545
Academy Awards, 246, 247–48, 247n
Access Hollywood (TV show), 286, 525
Acconci, Vito, 231
Acker, Kathy, 238
ACLU v. Reno, 419n
ACT UP, 232
Adams, Eric, 370n
Adler, Polly, 414
Adler, Renata, 521
Adorno, Theodor W., 554
Against the Wall (Hardy and Hough), 353
Agee, James, 188
Agenda, The (Woodward), 54, 55, 154
Agravat, Pravin, 500–501
Aguilera, Christina, 412
AIDS, 136, 152, 159, 163, 232, 288, 448n, 473
Ailes, Roger, 27, 333–35, 334–35n, 337
Albert, Marv, 280
Albright, Madeleine, 63, 308
Al-Fayed, Dodi, 280, 280n
Alford, Mimi, 42n
Allen, Joan, 140
Allen, Mike, 481, 482, 487, 489, 491
Allen, Woody, 277, 399, 402n
Alley, Kirstie, 124
All in the Family (TV show), 341
All's Fair (Carville), 31–32
All Too Human (Stephanopoulos), 28, 31, 523
"alpha female," 349n
Al-Qaeda, 6, 543

Alter, Jonathan, 282n, 470
alt-politics, 336–37
alt.sex.bondage (asb), 171n
amateur porn tapes, 294–97, 415, 415n
American Beauty (movie), 402–4
American decorum, 292
American Express, 184n, 259n
American Family, An (documentary), 230n
American male, 339–404
    Clinton as new masculine archetype,
        40–41, 43–44, 48–50, 53–58, 341
    in movies, 382–404
    in sports, 368–81
American Pie (movie), 88n, 140, 402
American President, The (movie), 392n
American Psycho (Ellis), 238
Ames, Mark, 429n
anal bleaching, 252n
Anatomy of Love (Fisher), 12
Andersen, Kurt, 237n
Andersen, Mark, 68
Anderson, Pamela, 227, 294–97, 294n, 555
Andersson, Per, 482
Andreessen, Marc, 172
Angel, Katherine, 138n
"angry white male," 72n, 331, 350–51, 353n
"animal hoarding," 422n
Aniston, Jennifer, 228
Anne, Princess Royal, 274
Anolik, Lili, 303–4
Ansen, David, 402
antiabortion movement, 459–62
antipornography movement, 62, 409, 409–10n
AOL, 170–72

Apatow, Judd, 402*n*
Applegate, Debby, 222, 414–15
Apprentice, The (TV show), 549–50
Archer, Anne, 386–88
Architect of Desire, The (Lessard), 237
Aretsky, Ken, 372–73
Armani, Giorgio, 248
Armstrong, Lance, 380
Arora, Anjali, 502
Arsenio Hall Show, The (TV show), 54, 326
art, 231–35
Art of the Public Grovel, The (Bauer), 109, 110
Aspin, Les, 63–64, 204, 205
Assange, Julian, 555
Athey, Ron, 233
Atlas, James, 333
Atwater, Lee, 107, 329*n*
Aubry, Erin, 251–52
Aucoin, Kevyn, 257*n*
Auletta, Ken, 169*n*, 334*n*
Austin Powers (movie), 183, 401–2, 402*n*
Avgerinos, Katherine, 428
AVN Awards, 416
Azerrad, Michael, 351

Babbage, Charles, 185*n*
Baby Boomers, 3–4, 9, 44, 106, 350
"Baby Got Back" (song), 253, 253*n*
Bachrach, Judy, 327
Backlash (Faludi), 71–72, 387, 546–47, 547*n*
Baglia, Jay, 510
Bai, Matt, 111*n*
Baiul, Oksana, 278
Baker, Nicholson, 238
Baker, Peter, 521
Bakker, Jim, 110
Bakker, Tammy Faye, 110
bald heads, 250–51, 367
Baldwin, Alec, 56
Baldwin, James, 348
Ballentine, Debra, 305
Ballentine, Sandra, 249
Balog, James, 504
Banks, Ingrid, 249–50, 368, 368*n*
Bannister, Roger, 114
Bannon, Steve, 107*n*, 336–37, 552
Baranco, Victor, 144
Baratta, Tommy, 130

Barbie, 249, 249*n*
Barbieri, Paula, 300–301
Barkley, Charles, 241
Barney, Matthew, 233–34, 233*n*
Barnlund, Dean, 142*n*
Baron, Lisa, 330, 330*n*, 334
Barr, Bob, 466
Barr, Roseanne, 237, 276
Barron, Martin, 453
Barry, Marion, 113, 276
Barry, Richard, 455
Barrymore, Drew, 237–38, 326
Basic Instinct (movie), 382–83, 385, 388–89, 390
Basinger, Kim, 56
Basson, Rosemary, 138–39
Bauer, Susan Wise, 109, 110
Baumgardner, Jennifer, 60, 252
Baumgarten, Craig, 299*n*
Baywatch (TV show), 226–27, 294
Bazelon, Emily, 461–62
Beatty, Warren, 53, 81–82, 129*n*, 328
Beauty Myth, The (Wolf), 72–73, 73*n*, 141, 453–54
beauty tips, 257
Beavis and Butt-head (TV cartoon), 400
Begala, Paul, 27, 32, 104, 520
Behind the Oval Office (Morris), 32, 49–50, 56*n*, 329*n*
Beinart, Peter, 544
Belkin, Aaron, 209
Bell, Andrew, 477*n*
Bellamy, Bill, 224
Bellow, Saul, 298
belly shirts, 251
Benedikt Taschen, 405–7
Bening, Annette, 392*n*, 403
Bennett, Jessica, 529*n*
Bennett, William J., 40*n*, 216–17*n*, 216–18
Bennetts, Leslie, 76*n*, 244–45*n*
Benson, Harry, 43, 289
Bentley, Toni, 119*n*, 241
Bergen, Candice, 155–58
Bergner, Daniel, 138–39
Berkley, Elizabeth, 435
Berlin Wall, 41, 431
Berman, Michael, 326
Bernard, Tara Siegel, 349*n*
Berners-Lee, Tim, 172

Bernstein, Richard, 548*n*
Berryman, Anne, 440–41
Bess, Carrie, 302
Betamax, 169, 169*n*
Biden, Joe, 90, 93, 95, 200, 419*n*, 555
Biggs, Jason, 402
Big Lebowski, The (movie), 392–94
Bikini Kill, 67–68, 68*n*
"bimbo eruptions," 24–25
Bindel, Julie, 432*n*
Birth of a Nation'hood (Morrison, ed.), 300
Bissinger, Buzz, 201*n*
Björk, 238
Black, Rob, 416*n*
Black Hawk Down (Bowden), 358
Black Lives Matter, 239, 544
Blakely, Sara, 257
Blanchard, Dallas A., 460*n*
Blank, Joani, 136–37*n*
Blinded by the Right (Brock), 96, 165–66
Blitt, Barry, 237
Bloodworth-Thomason, Linda, 159
Bloom, Stanley, 507
Bloomberg, Michael, 444*n*
blowjobs, 225–26*n*
Blumenthal, Sidney, 25, 26–27
Bly, Robert, 45, 50, 354–55
Blythe, W. J., Jr., 44–45
Bobbitt, John Wayne, 5, 312–21, 313*n*
Bobbitt, Lorena, 5, 312–21
Boehner, John, 57
Bogle, Kathleen A., 223–24
Bonauto, Mary, 464
Bond, Rich, 163
Boogie Nights (movie), 411
Boolell, Mitra, 489–90, 491, 494
Boomsie twins, 324
Boorstin, Daniel, 16
booty, the, 251–53
"booty rap," 252
Bork, Robert, 90, 92, 93*n*, 108*n*, 184*n*, 239
Bosson, Paul, 47
Botox, 249, 270
Bowden, Mark, 358
Bowles, Erskine, 522*n*
Boxer, Barbara, 203
Boyer, Peter J., 332
Boys Don't Cry (movie), 201*n*
Boyz n the Hood (movie), 351, 392

Bozell, L. Brent, III, 227
Branch, Taylor, 207, 207*n*, 337
Brand, Stewart, 178, 181, 191*n*
Brando, Christian, 276
Brandweek, 184
Brantley, Ben, 233
bras, 255–56
Braun, Carol Moseley, 97*n*
Brawley, Lucia, 350–51, 368
Brazilian bikini waxes, 122–31
Brazilian Sexy (Padilha), 132
Breaking Bad (TV show), 397*n*
breast cancer, 261, 261*n*
breast implants, 261–73
Breast Men (movie), 262–63, 268
Breitbart, Andrew, 336
Breitbart News, 337, 552
Breslin, Jimmy, 444
Bridges, Jeff, 393–94
Bright, Susie, 191–93, 515, 534*n*
Brilliant, Larry, 191*n*
Brin, Sergey, 173*n*
Brindley, Giles, 483–84, 486
Brinkley, David, 473–74, 497–500, 502,
    507, 508, 511, 514–15
Brinkley, Douglas, 430*n*
Broad, William, 137
Brock, David, 26, 77, 96, 163, 165–66,
    305–6, 310, 332–33, 333*n*, 336
Brody, Jane E., 448
"bromance," 342
Bronson, Po, 175*n*
Brooklyn Museum, 234–35
Brooks, David, 15*n*, 52*n*, 256, 331, 349*n*,
    544*n*
Brothers, Joyce, 314
Brown, David, 477*n*, 495
Brown, Divine, 278
Brown, Jerry, 155
Brown, Mark, 305
Brown, Tina, 74, 237
Browner, Carol, 63
Browning, Dolly Kyle, 447
Brownmiller, Susan, 62*n*
Bruni, Frank, 78*n*
"Bub," 54*n*
Bubba Boomers, 40, 44, 54–55, 54*n*
Buchanan, Patrick, 152, 161, 162, 164–66,
    165*n*, 313*n*

Buckley, William F., Jr., 43, 166
Bumpers, Dale, 538
Bündchen, Gisele, 259
Bunim, Mary-Ellis, 230
Burke, Edmund, 337
Burleigh, Nina, 556
Burning Man, 177
Burn Rate (Wolff), 170–74
Burroughs, William, 168
Burslem, Frank, 478
Burton, Jeff, 413*n*
Buscemi, Steve, 393
Bush, George H. W., 4, 40–42, 323,
      328–29*n*, 331
   election of 1992, 21, 37, 40–42, 158–59,
      162, 166–67
   Thomas nomination, 89–90
Bush, George W., 3, 9, 37, 543–44
   election of 2000, 2–3, 335*n*, 411*n*, 540
   Iraq War, 165*n*, 212–13, 543
   partial-birth abortion ban, 199*n*
Bushnell, Candace, 15, 237
Buttafuoco, Joey, 277
Buttafuoco, Mary Jo, 277
Byrd, James, Jr., 201*n*
Byrd, Robert, 206–8

Cabaret (musical), 235–36
Cabot, John, 488
Cadenet, Amanda de, 255
Callaway Bertha, 361
Calvin Klein, 1, 82
Camelot myth, 42, 43
Camilla, Duchess of Cornwall, 275, 282
Campbell, Naomi, 257
Campbell, Simon, 475–77, 479, 480, 481–82,
      487–88, 497, 504–7, 512, 515
Campolo, Tony, 520
Cannon, David G., 54–55
Caplan, Arthur, 502
Caprino, Mariann, 508
Cardura, 475, 498
Carlesimo, P. J., 375
Carlson, Margaret, 411*n*
Carlson, Tucker, 76
Carnes, Patrick, 445–46, 446*n*, 450,
      451–52*n*, 451–53, 455–56
Carnie, Davie, 342
Carolla, Adam, 239–40

Carr, David, 114*n*
Carrey, Jim, 401, 401*n*, 552
Carter, Graydon, 55, 55*n*, 213, 327–28
Carter, Jimmy, 40*n*, 43*n*
Caruso, David, 227
Carvey, Dana, 51
Carville, James, 26, 52, 53, 54, 101*n*, 107*n*,
      308, 555
   Clintons' *60 Minutes* interview, 27–28,
      30–32, 35–36, 37, 39
   election of 1992, 103–4, 105
   "It's the economy, stupid," 158, 158*n*
Casablancas, John, 257
Cassidy, James Eldridge, 46*n*
Casual Friday, 372–73
Cattrall, Kim, 16, 140, 515
Celebrity Rehab (TV show), 277, 421
celebrity sex tapes, 294–97
celebrity sin, 274–91
Chamberlain, Wilt, 238
Chapman, Jake and Dinos, 234
Charnas, Dan, 253
Chastain, Brandi, 66
Chaucer, Geoffrey, 474
Cheever, Susan, 448*n*
Cherlin, Andrew J., 8–9, 300, 467*n*,
      468–69, 469*n*
Cheryan, Sapna, 185, 185*n*
Chevalier, Haakon, 147
chick flicks, 64–65
chick lit, 64
Child Internet Protection Act, 419
Child Online Protection Act, 419, 419*n*
child porn, 419, 419*n*, 453
Child Pornography Prevention Act, 419
Childs, Timothy, 175
China Syndrome, The (movie), 385
Chung, Connie, 261
Cialis, 497
Ciaravino, Michael, 264
cigars, 361–62
Civil Rights Acts, 344
Clarke, Torie, 329*n*
Classic Sports Network, 374*n*
Clinton, Bill, 7, 8–10, 20–58, 269,
      326–27
   background of, 44–48
   charisma of, 51–53
   cigar smoking, 361*n*

culture wars and, 153–62, 199, 457–58, 461, 465, 469–71
economy, 434, 440
election of 1992, 8, 21, 37, 40–42, 75, 166–67, 197–98
    Democratic National Convention, 159–62
    New Hampshire primary, 20, 21, 102–10, 104*n*
empathy of, 57–58
favorability ratings, 539, 539*n*
as first black president, 197–98*n*
Flowers scandal, 20–21, 23–24, 29–30, 34–35, 50, 99–102, 105, 109*n*, 211, 447–48
gays in the military and, 7, 200–210, 211–12
Gingrich and, 337–38, 3222
golf, 375, 375*n*
Hollywood and, 55–56, 56*n*, 403–4
impeachment proceedings, 403–4, 522–24, 535–40
Jones lawsuit, 5, 292–93, 304–12, 332–33, 446*n*, 518
Kennedy handshake, 48, 48*n*
LAX tarmac haircut, 367*n*
Lewinsky affair, 2, 3, 5, 8–9, 78, 98, 311, 445–46, 518–21, 527, 528–29
lies of, 211–12, 214–18
as new masculine archetype, 40–41, 43–44, 48–50, 53–58, 341
nickname of, 51
school uniform policy, 370–71
sex addiction of, 445–48
sex rumors about, 8–9, 24–27
shifting public attitude toward, 106–10, 113–15
60 Minutes interview, 20–21, 22, 28–39, 37*n*, 99, 108–9, 109*n*, 110, 112–13, 115, 211
Clinton, Chelsea, 25, 27, 158
Clinton, Hillary Rodham, 5, 9, 20–39, 74–80
background of, 21–22
culture wars and, 153–54
election of 2008, 57*n*, 79
election of 2016, 10, 77, 80*n*, 543, 545–48, 551, 554–56

as empowerment icon, 74–80
favorability ratings, 539*n*
First Lady role, 49, 77–80
lies of, 213, 214, 216–17
personal attacks on, 75–77
60 Minutes interview, 20–21, 22, 28–39, 37*n*, 99, 108–9, 109*n*, 110, 112–13, 115
on "vast right-wing conspiracy," 78, 333, 541
Clinton, Roger, 45, 46
Clinton, Virginia Blythe, 44–48
Clinton Foundation, 547, 547*n*
Clooney, George, 253, 382
Close, Glenn, 118, 382, 386–88
"Closer" (song), 219–20
CNN, 286–87, 333
Cobain, Kurt, 68, 68*n*, 351
Cock & Bull (Self), 238
Coen brothers, 392–94, 398
Cognard-Black, Jennifer, 246*n*
Cohen, Stefanie, 223
Colbert, Stephen, 212, 212*n*
Combs, Sean, 368
"coming out," 85–86, 133, 201
Communications Decency Act, 419
Complicated Man, A (Takiff), 103, 104, 204, 206
Contested Closets (Gross), 288
contraception, 458–59
Contract with America, 323–24, 329
Conway, George, III, 555
Conway, Kellyanne, 555
Cook, Ryan, 239–40
Cooper, Al, 448
Cooper, Art, 400
Cooper, Chris, 403
Cooper, Gary, 44, 55, 55*n*, 382
Corallo, Mark, 523
Corbin, Bobby, 305
Corcoran Gallery, 232, 232*n*
Cosgrave, Bronwyn, 248, 254, 255*n*
CosmoGirl (magazine), 257
Costner, Kevin, 382
Coulter, Allen, 397*n*
Coulter, Ann, 311, 333, 555
Coupland, Douglas, 7, 241, 372*n*
Couric, Katie, 120
Court TV, 286

Cowlings, Al, 297, 300–301
Cox, David, 495n
Craigslist, 184, 195
Crawford, Cindy, 326
Cremaster Cycle, The (Barney), 233–34, 233n
Crichton, Sarah, 61–62
Crimes and Misdemeanors (movie), 399
Cronin, Thomas, 263
Cross, Charles R., 68n
Cruel Intentions (movie), 228
Cruise, Tom, 236, 382
Crystal, Billy, 134
Csikszentmihalyi, Mihaly, 146n
Culture of Narcissism, The (Lasch), 526
culture wars, 4, 10, 152–67, 457–71, 534, 544–45
Cumming, Alan, 69–70n, 235–36
Cunt (Muscio), 120
Cuomo, Mario, 100
Current Affair, A (TV show), 227, 285, 427
Currin, John, 234
cybersex, 168–75, 182–94

Daedone, Nicole, 127–28n, 141–51
Dafoe, Willem, 235
Dallek, Robert, 43
Darrach, Brad, 229n
date rape, 61–62
dating sites, 194–96
David, Larry, 228
Davis, Geena, 65
Davis, Kristin, 14
Davis, Lanny, 111n
Dead Right (Frum), 167
Death of American Virtue, The (Gormley), 305, 306–7, 307n
Death of Outrage, The (Bennett), 217, 218
Decline of Males, The (Tiger), 341–42n, 348–48
Defense of Marriage Act (DOMA), 466–67, 469, 470
DeGeneres, Ellen, 5, 85–87, 86n, 464n
Dell'Abate, Gary, 241
De Luca, Mike, 280
Demi Moore's law, 220–21
Democratic National Convention
1992, 159–62
1996, 279
Desai, Ken, 491

designer vaginas, 121–22
Destiny's Child, 69n
Devine, L. Franklin, 32–33
Devine, Tad, 103
Diana, Princess of Wales, 1, 74, 255n, 274–75, 280, 280n, 281, 420
Diaz, Cameron, 295n, 401
Dick, Philip K., 176n, 525n
Dionne, E. J., 111
DiSanto, Tony, 169n
Disclosure (movie), 385, 389–91
Disneyland, Gay Days, 200n
divorce rates, 8, 8n, 468, 468n
DIY porn, 415, 415n
Dobell, Byron, 411n
Dobson, James, 194
Dodson, Betty, 118–19, 122, 134
Doherty, Shannen, 64
Dole, Bob, 203–4, 328, 466, 469, 470–71
Domke, Todd, 101n
Don't Ask, Don't Tell (DADT), 200–210, 211–12
Don't Call It Love (Carnes), 452
Doonesbury (cartoon), 41
Dorsey-Rivas, Amylia, 253n
Do the Right Thing (movie), 397n
double entendres, 3n
Douglas, Diana Dill, 383
Douglas, Kirk, 383
Douglas, Michael, 351, 382–92
Douthat, Ross, 397n, 455, 470
Dow Corning, 261–62
Dowd, Maureen, 33–34, 79, 280n, 325
Downey, Robert, Jr., 398
Drinking: A Love Story (Knapp), 237
Drollet, Dag, 276
Drudge, Matt, 328n, 333n, 335–36, 518, 555
Drudge Report, 189, 307, 335–36, 553, 555
Ducruet, Daniel, 278–79
"dude," 393n
Dukakis, Mike, 21, 27, 41, 197
Duncan, David Ewing, 6n, 179–80n
Dunham, Lena, 15n
Dunne, Dominick, 299n
Durkheim, Émile, 539n
Dworkin, Andrea, 62, 409

Eastwood, Clint, 524n
ECHO, 190–91

ED (Exotic Dancer), 435–36
Edwards, Edwin, 102
Edwards-Beal, Sian, 186–87
EEOC (Equal Employment Opportunity
    Commission), 90–91, 93, 97, 98
eHarmony.com, 194–95
Eikenberry, Jill, 141
Elders, Joycelyn, 136–37, 136*n*
Eliot, George, 70–71
Elizabeth II, 274–75
Ellen (TV show), 5, 85–86, 87*n*, 464*n*
Ellin, Abby, 186
Elliott, Tim, 342
Ellis, Bret Easton, 238
Ellis, John, 335*n*
Ellis, Peter, 477*n*, 478–82, 487–91, 496,
    497, 502–3, 512
Ellison, Ralph, 348
Ellroy, James, 299
Elmer-Dewitt, Philip, 183–84
Elving, Ron, 338
Emanuel, Ari, 552
embryonic stem cells, 6
EMILY's List, 97
e-monks, 187
empowerment icons, 74–98
Engelbart, Douglas, 181
English, Diane, 156
Ensler, Eve, 5, 116–20
Ephron, Nora, 134
Equal Rights Amendment, 348
erectile dysfunction, 138, 471, 476–77,
    481–517
Erickson, Paul, 313*n*
Erikson, Marianne, 421–22
Eros and Civilization (Freud), 11
erotic economy, 428–44
ESPN, 368–70, 370*n*, 373, 374
ESPN The Magazine, 366*n*, 367, 374
Esquire, 62, 62*n*, 84, 235, 372*n*
estrogen supplements, 4, 139–40, 221
Eszterhas, Joe, 383, 389
Etcoff, Nancy, 73*n*
Ethical Spectacle, 110
Evangelista, Linda, 257
"event glamour," 298
Eviva, 497*n*
evolution, 12, 17–18, 19
Ewing, Patrick, 442

"Express Yourself" (song), 83–84
eyebrows, 249
Eyes Wide Shut (movie), 236

Facebook, 196, 531
Facebook Effect, The (Kirkpatrick), 188
Falling Down (movie), 351, 391*n*
Faludi, Susan, 71–72, 318*n*, 387, 546–47,
    547*n*
Falwell, Jerry, 86, 202, 463
Family and Medical Leave Act, 199
Family Guy (TV show), 400*n*
Family Reinforcement Act, 323
Farber, Jim, 84
Fargo (movie), 396, 398
Farrakhan, Louis, 343, 343*n*
Farrelly brothers, 401, 401*n*
Farrow, Dylan O'Sullivan, 277
Farrow, Mia, 277
Fast Times at Ridgemont High (movie), 393*n*
Fatal Attraction (movie), 383, 385, 386–88
fatherhood, 363–64
"fathers' rights" associations, 352
"feeding the ducks," 314*n*
Feig, Paul, 402*n*
Feiler, Bruce, 369, 370*n*
Feinstein, Dianne, 203
Feirstein, Bruce, 395*n*
female bonding, 17–18, 246*n*
Female Chauvinist Pigs (Levy), 62*n*, 412
female sexual dysfunction (FSD), 138–39
"feminist," 61
Ferguson, Sarah, 274, 275
Ferrato, Donna, 315–16, 315*n*
Ferrell, Will, 401
fertility, 73, 88, 137, 489*n*, 497
fertility treatments, 4
fetal tissue research, 198, 198*n*
Field of Dreams (movie), 57*n*
Fields, Dexter, 250–51
Fight Club (movie), 382, 396*n*
Finley, Karen, 233
Finley v. NEA, 233*n*
First in His Class (Maraniss), 25, 44–45
First Wives Club, The (movie), 65
Fisher, Amy, 277
Fisher, Helen, 12–14, 16–19, 221–22, 313–14
Fiske, Robert, 306
Fleiss, Heidi, 130*n*, 420–27

Fleiss, Mike, 421
Fleming, Alexander, 480
"flow," 146*n*
Flowers, Eura Gean "Gennifer," 20–21, 23–24, 24*n*, 29–30, 34–35, 50, 99–102, 105, 109*n*, 211, 447–48
Fly Fishing Through the Midlife Crisis (Raines), 353
Flying Boy, The (Lee), 353–54
Flynt, Larry, 287*n*, 410, 411
Foley, Mark, 333*n*
Fonda, Jane, 118, 145, 333–34, 364
Forbes, Steve, 51
Forman, Miloš, 287*n*
Forrest, Brett, 363, 374, 428–30
Fortensky, Larry, 277
Foss, Krista, 122
Fox, Emily Jane, 546
Fox, Patty, 248
Fox News, 328, 333–35, 335*n*, 531–32, 553
Francis, Joe, 226
Frank, Barney, 111–12, 205*n*
Frank, Nathaniel, 202, 203*n*, 205*n*, 208, 210
Freaks and Geeks (TV show), 402*n*
Freedom of Access to Clinic Entrances Act, 461
Freud, Sigmund, 10–11, 360, 454, 526
Fried Green Tomatoes (movie), 127
Friedman, Ann, 70
Friedman, David M., 483, 508, 513
Friedman, Thomas, 431
Friend, Richard, 463, 464–65
Friends (TV show), 227–28
Frost, David, 43*n*
Frost, Robert, 357
Frum, David, 166–67, 333
"fuck," 9
Fuck Me Blind (zine), 68
Fuhrman, Mark, 302, 533*n*
Full Monty, The (musical), 235
Fumento, Michael, 359
Furchgott, Robert, 487
Future Sex (magazine), 189–90

Gaitskill, Mary, 238
Gallagher, Peter, 404
Galliano, John, 255*n*
Gandy, Kim, 313
Gauthier, Rand, 295–96

gay marriage, 7, 463–66
Gayner, Jeffrey, 338
gay outings, 288–89
gays in the military, 200–210, 211–12
Gay-Straight Alliances, 222
Geffen, David, 404
Geldof, Bob, 141
gender bias, 185, 185*n*, 546–47
Gender Equity in Education Act, 66, 200
Generation X (Coupland), 7
Generation X (Gen Xers), 341, 369*n*, 372
gentlemen's clubs, 434–42
George (magazine), 326–27, 331
George, Ken, 463
Gepi-Attee, Sam, 491, 493
Gergen, David, 49, 550–51
Gerow, Frank, 263
Gerstein, Daniel, 535–38, 536*n*
Getting It Through My Thick Skull (Buttafuoco), 277
Gibson, Mel, 382
Gibson, William, 176–77*n*, 525*n*
Gifford, Frank, 279
Gifford, Kathie Lee, 279
Gilbey, James, 274
Gillon, Steven, 322, 323–24, 338, 344*n*, 350, 522*n*
Gillooly, Jeff, 278
Gilman, Sander L., 246
Gingell, Clive, 488–92, 493, 500, 501
Gingold, Alfred, 354*n*
Gingrich, Jackie, 325
Gingrich, Newton "Newt," 2, 9, 165*n*, 287*n*, 322–25, 337–38, 344, 353, 469, 469*n*, 470, 521, 522
Ginsberg, Gary, 33, 326–27
Ginsburg, Faye, 460*n*
Ginsburg, Ruth Bader, 64
Girard, René, 526*n*
Girls (TV show), 15*n*
Girls Gone Wild (videos), 226
girls' schools, 65–66
Girls to the Front (Marcus), 59, 67–68
Giuliani, Rudy, 9, 113, 234–35, 442–43*n*, 442–44
Givens, Robin, 277
Gladys Knight and the Pips, 53
Glaser, Elizabeth, 159
Gobie, Steven, 112

Goffman, Erving, 530
Goldberg, Arthur, 43
Goldberg, Vicki, 82
Gold Club (Atlanta), 440–42
GoldenEye (movie), 1
Golden Shower, 259*n*
Goldin, Nan, 258
Goldman, Ronald, 297–98, 533
Goldstein, Irwin, 484–86, 490*n*, 494, 502, 506
Goldwater, Barry, 166, 202, 338
gonzo porn, 407
GoodFellas (movie), 395, 397–98
Goodman, John, 393–94
Good Vibrations, 136–37, 136–37*n*
Google, 173–74, 531
Gore, Al, 2–3, 55, 158–59, 335*n*, 540
Gormley, Ken, 25–26, 305, 306–7, 307*n*
gossip, 17–18
GQ (magazine), 365, 366–67, 400
Graham, Billy, 47
Gran Fury, 232
Grant, Hugh, 278
Grathwohl, Casper, 213*n*
Gray, John, 354
Grazer, Brian, 367
Greatest Generation, 56–57
Greatest Story Ever Sold, The (Rich), 212–13
Green, Fiona J., 122
Greenberg, Paul, 51, 214
Greenberg, Stan, 31, 103
Greenfield, Jeff, 332
Greenman, Ben, 171
Greenspan, Alan, 7*n*
Greenstone, Michael, 349*n*
Greer, Germaine, 73, 119
Grey's Anatomy (TV show), 116*n*
Grigoriadis, Vanessa, 534–35*n*
Grimes, William, 248*n*
Gross, Larry, 288
Grossman, Lawrence K., 533*n*
grunge look, 257–58
Grunwald, Mandy, 31, 50, 328
Guccione, Bob, 130, 267
Gulf War, 41, 287, 524*n*
Gurley, George, 254, 351*n*
Gutterson, Scott, 441*n*
"guy cry" pictures, 57*n*
Guy Rules, 187

Haden-Guest, Anthony, 408
Hadza, 17
Hahn, Jessica, 110
hair, 249–50, 366–68
hair extensions, 250
Hair Matters (Banks), 249–50, 368
Hall, Fawn, 328
Hall, Leslie, 122
Hamilton, George, 277*n*
Hamilton, Linda, 66
Hamilton, Ursaline, 265
Hamilton, William L., 413
Handy, Bruce, 85, 507
Hanks, Tom, 382
Hanna, Kathleen, 67–68, 68*n*, 70
Hannity, Sean, 334, 555
Hanson, Dian, 405–7, 409
Harding, Tonya, 278, 282*n*
Hard Sell (Reidy), 511
Hardy, Marshall, 353
Harrelson, Woody, 398
Harris, Art, 287, 301, 441–42
Harris, Jonathan, 174*n*
Harris, Maxine, 47
Harrison, Kathryn, 237
Hart, Gary, 110–11, 111*n*, 115, 283*n*, 328, 467*n*
Hart, Veronica, 408–9
Hastert, Dennis, 522
Hatch, Orrin, 94, 417*n*
Hate Crimes Prevention Act, 200, 201*n*
Hayford, Jack, 346*n*
Hayman, Fred, 248, 248*n*
Healy, Bernadine, 505–6*n*
Heather Has Two Mommies (Newman), 332
Heathers (movie), 228
Heavenly Creatures (movie), 235
Heche, Anne, 86*n*
Hefner, Christie, 410
Hefner, Hugh, 271, 409, 411, 411*n*
Helms, Jesse, 232
Hemingway, Ernest, 32
Henderson, Diedtra, 513–14
Hendrix, Blake, 99
Hennessy, Val, 386
heroin chic, 258
Herz, J. C., 182
Herzigová, Eva, 256
Hess, Amanda, 187

Hewitt, Don, 28, 30, 30*n*, 33, 35–36
Hewitt, James, 1, 274
Hewitt, Jennifer Love, 64
Hey, Bubba! (Cannon), 54–55
HGH (human growth hormone), 378*n*
Hiaasen, Carl, 435
High Noon (movie), 55*n*
Higonett, Anne, 363–64*n*
Hill, Anita, 5, 9, 59, 73, 89–98, 332–33, 535*n*
Hill, Jonah, 402*n*
Hilton, Paris, 294*n*, 297, 303
Hirst, Damien, 234
Hitchens, Christopher, 123*n*, 154*n*, 225, 293*n*
Hitt, Jack, 490*n*, 503
HMOs (health maintenance organizations),
    503–4
Hof, Dennis, 422*n*
Holmes, Eugene, 102
Holmes, John, 411
Holyfield, Evander, 375
homoeroticism, 362–63
"hooking up," 223–24
Hooking Up (Bogle), 223–24
hooks, bell, 252
Hooper, Joseph, 483
Hooters, 1
Hopper, Grace, 185*n*
Horyn, Cathy, 258–59
Hot Springs, Arkansas, 46–47, 46*n*
Hough, John, 353
House of Cards (TV show), 404
Houston, and breast implants, 261–73
Houston Rockets, 268, 270, 272
Howard, Hilary, 135
Howard Stern Show, The 101, 136*n*,
    240–43, 313, 552*n*
HSX.com, 247*n*
Huffington, Arianna, 329
Huffington, Michael, 333*n*
Hultberg, William, 468*n*
human genome, 6
Human Stain, The (Roth), 471
Hummer, 360–61
Hungry Duck (Moscow), 429–30*n*
Hurley, Elizabeth, 278
Hurricane Katrina, 543–44
Husni, Samir, 410*n*
Hussein, Saddam, 287
Hustler (magazine), 287*n*, 410, 410*n*, 412

Hutton, Lauren, 139
Hyde, Henry, 163, 200*n*
Hymowitz, Kay S., 66, 66*n*, 399–400
"hysteria," 62

Ickes, Harold, 29
Ignarro, Louis, 486, 487
image.net, 174–75
In Bed with Manhattan (TV pilot), 186
Industrial Revolution, 18, 19
Ingraham, Laura, 328, 333*n*
Internet, 168–96, 419, 527–28, 532
In the Wings (Douglas), 383
Into the Wild (Krakauer), 358
Invisible Man, The (Ellison), 348
Iraq War, 165*n*, 212–13, 543
Ireland, Patricia, 59
Iron John (Bly), 354–55, 355*n*
"irrational exuberance," 7, 7*n*
Isaacson, Walter, 6–7, 185*n*
Isikoff, Michael, 306, 446, 518
Islands of Privacy (Nippert-Eng), 531
It Takes a Village (Clinton), 75
Itzkoff, Dave, 400–401
Iverson, Allen, 371
Ivins, Molly, 165

Jackson, Jesse, 342–45, 520
Jackson, Michael, 277, 278, 285
Jackson, Samuel L., 396–97
Jacobs, Alexandra, 257
Jacobs, Marc, 257–58
Jakrlova, Hana, 433*n*
Jameson, Jenna, 242, 411, 422
Jane (magazine), 257
Jenner, Brody, 303
Jenner, Caitlyn, 303
Jenner, Kris, 303
Jennings, Peter, 26
Jen-X (McCarthy), 238, 242
Jeremy, Ron, 411
Jerry Springer Show, The (TV show), 285, 526
Jeter, Derek, 372
Jigsaw (zine), 68
Jobs, Steve, 181
Johnson, Andrew, 536
Johnson, Gerald, 263*n*
Johnson, Jenna, 551*n*
Johnson, Lyndon, 23–24, 43, 214

Johnson, Lynn, 267, 267*n*
Johnson, Richard, 65, 229
Johnson, Sabrina, 408
Johnson, Suzen, 279
John Wayne Bobbitt Uncut (porn), 313, 318*n*
Jones, Abigail, 230–31
Jones, Alex, 552
Jones, Chuck, 276*n*
Jones, Paula Corbin, 5, 292–93, 304–12, 328*n*, 332–33, 446*n*, 518, 555
Jones, Reese, 144–45*n*, 147, 151
Jones, Tommy Lee, 158, 382
Jordan, Barbara, 159
Jordan, Michael, 340, 340*n*, 375
Joyner, Mario, 229*n*
J Sisters, 122–31
Junger, Sebastian, 357–59

Kabaservice, Geoffrey, 322
Kadrey, Richard, 171*n*
Kakutani, Michiko, 82
Kamp, David, 282, 283*n*, 284, 397*n*
Kane, Sarah, 233
Kaplan, Dick, 99
Kaplan, Steve, 441–42
Kara, Siddharth, 431
Kardashian, Kim, 297, 303
Kardashian, Robert, 303
Kashner, Sam, 449
Katen, Karen, 499
Katzenberg, Jeffrey, 404
Katzenstein, Larry, 493–94
Kaysen, Susanna, 237
Keen, Sam, 353
Kehr, David, 401*n*
Keitel, Harvey, 396–97
Kelley, Raina, 295*n*
Kellogg, Stuart, 289
Kemp, Jack, 329
Kemp, Rob, 253
Kennedy, Carolyn Bessette, 328*n*
Kennedy, D. James, 164
Kennedy, Edward "Ted," 95, 164, 206, 207, 276
Kennedy, Jim, 38
Kennedy, John F., 23–24, 30*n*, 42, 42*n*, 48, 56*n*, 106
Kennedy, John F., Jr., 326–27, 328*n*
Kennedy, Joseph P., Sr. "Joe," 326

Kennedy, Michael, 327
Kennedy, Robert F., 279
Kent, Anne, 251
Kerouac, Jack, 180*n*
Kerrey, Bob, 100, 103, 536
Kerrigan, Nancy, 278, 286
Kerry, John, 203
Kesey, Ken, 178
Khan Tusion, 408
Kidman, Nicole, 235, 236
Kiesling, Scott F., 393*n*
Kimmel, Michael, 352–53, 355*n*, 453
King, Larry, 471
King, Martin Luther, Jr., 343–44, 397*n*
King, Stephen, 52*n*
Kinsey, Alfred, 138*n*, 485
Kinsley, Michael, 56
Kipnis, Aaron, 353
Kipnis, Laura, 76, 77
Kirkpatrick, David, 188
Kirkpatrick, John, 496
Kiss, The (Harrison), 237
Klein, Joe, 21, 77*n*, 104, 108*n*, 153, 214–15, 215*n*
Kling, Jim, 478, 481
Klug, Rob, 417–18
Knights Without Armor (Kipnis), 353
Kolata, Gina, 483
Komisaruk, Barry R., 137
Koons, Jeff, 234
Koppel, Ted, 165
Kotler, Steven, 146*n*
Krakauer, Jon, 358
Kristof, Nicholas, 79, 156–57*n*, 213, 349*n*, 432
Kristol, William, 90*n*, 155, 552
Kroft, Steve, 22, 28–30, 32–39, 109*n*, 111*n*, 112–13, 115, 211
Kruse, Michael, 37*n*
Kubrick, Stanley, 236
Kuczynski, Alex, 263
Kushner, Jared, 552
Kuwait, 41, 42, 287

L.A. Confidential (movie), 289*n*
L.A. Law (TV show), 141
L.A. Story (movie), 366
labiaplasties, 121–22

lad culture, 366*n*, 400
Ladd, Alan, 55
Landers, Ann, 106–7
Lanier, Jaron, 188–89
Lansing, Sherry, 65, 387
Larry's Party (Shields), 238
Lasch, Christopher, 526
Law, Jude, 235
Lawrence, Jennifer, 297, 531
Lawrence, Robert, 137
Lear, Norman, 341
Lebowitz, Fran, 289
Lee, John, 353–54
Lee, Spike, 397*n*
Lee, Tommy, 294–97, 294*n*
Legum, Judd, 551
Leibovich, Mark, 10, 187
Leibovitz, Annie, 87–89, 124
Leland, John, 486*n*
Leno, Jay, 278–79, 309, 508
Leoni, Téa, 1
Lerner, Alan Jay, 330
Lerner, Michael, 77
"lesbian chic," 86
Lessard, Suzannah, 237
Letourneau, Mary Kay, 449
Letterman, David, 156, 444*n*
Levin, Gerald, 334*n*
LeVine, Steve, 213*n*
Levy, Ariel, 62*n*, 78, 412
Lewinsky, Monica, 2, 3, 5, 8–9, 78, 98,
 307, 311, 445–46, 518–21, 527–35,
 540–41
Lewis, Amanda Chicago, 295–96
Lewis, Juliette, 398
Lewis, Michael, 368
libido, 10–11
Libin, Nancy, 419*n*
Lieberman, Joseph, 535–38
Liebling, A. J., 178–79
lies (lying), 211–18
Life of the Party (Baron), 330, 331*n*
Life on the Screen (Turkle), 183
Lilith Fair, 70
Lilla, Mark, 353*n*
Limbaugh, Rush, 90*n*, 331–32
Lind, Michael, 332
lingerie, 254–55
Lippert, Barbara, 78*n*

Little, Paul F., 407
Little Girl Lost (Barrymore), 237–38
Little Rock Nine, 48
Living History (Clinton), 27, 75
Livingston, Bob, 287*n*, 522, 523
Locklear, Heather, 294*n*
Loe, Meika, 120–21, 484, 486*n*, 504, 514
Lofton, Kathryn, 114*n*
Lolita (Nabokov), 449
London, Jack, 358
Longet, Claudine, 284
Lonstein, Shoshanna, 229–30
Looney, Adam, 349*n*
Lopez, Jennifer, 253
Lords, Traci, 411
Los Angeles riots of 1992, 164–65
Love, Courtney, 68*n*, 69, 120, 255, 410
Lovelace, Ada, 185*n*
Loveline (radio show), 239–40
Lovell, Cyndi, 262
Lovell, Melissa, 262
Lovering, Joanne, 373
Love Story (movie), 158–59
Lowe, Rob, 295*n*
Lucas, Sarah, 234
Luciano, Lynne, 486*n*
Lust for Life (movie), 383
Lynch, David, 398–99
Lyne, Adrian, 387

McCarthy, Jenny, 238, 242
McCartney, Bill, 345–47
McCurry, Mike, 103
McDaniel, Kelly, 452
McDaniel, Wanda, 248
MacDonald, Gordon, 520
McDowall, Roddy, 277*n*
McGinn, Daniel, 502
McGovern, George, 57, 166, 207*n*
McGuigan, Patrick, 90*n*
McGwire, Mark, 376–79
McKinlay, John, 485
MacKinnon, Catharine, 62, 409
MacKinnon, Douglas, 471
McKinnon, Mark, 37, 112, 540
McLuhan, Marshall, 178
McMahon, Linda, 552
McMahon, Vince, 550–51
McMillan, Terry, 64

McPeak, Merrill "Tony," 204, 206, 206*n*
McQueen, Alexander, 253, 258–59
Macy, Bill, 398
Maddow, Rachel, 165
Made for Each Other (Cosgrave), 248, 255
Madonna, 5, 68, 81–85, 235, 426
Magowan, Margot, 341
Mahler, Jonathan, 284*n*
Mailer, Norman, 23, 84, 233*n*, 235, 238
Maines, Rachel P., 135
Making the Body Beautiful (Gilman), 246
male bonding, 341–42, 341–42*n*, 368
male fitness, 364–65
male grooming, 362–63, 366–67*n*
Mallon, Thomas, 284
"man caves," 373–74
Man from Hope, The (video), 159
Manhood in America (Kimmel), 352–53
man hugs, 340–42
Manifesta (Baumgardner and Richards), 60, 252
Man in the Gray Flannel Suit, The (Wilson), 348
Mann, Sally, 233
Manning Up (Hymowitz), 66, 399–400
Mano, D. Keith, 435
Man Show, The (TV show), 400*n*
Manson, Marilyn, 238
Maples, Marla, 2, 276, 276*n*, 308, 327*n*, 328
Mapplethorpe, Robert, 82–83, 231–32, 413
Maraniss, David, 25, 44–45
March for Women's Lives (1992), 59
Marcus, Sara, 59, 67–68
Marcuse, Herbert, 11, 348
Marie Claire (magazine), 257
marijuana, 154–55, 154*n*
Maris, Roger, 376
"marketplace feminism," 61, 61*n*
Markoff, John, 179–80
Markowitz, Sari, 125–26
Marmion, Shannon, 88
Marmor, Michael, 512
Márquez, Gabriel García, 124
Marquis, John, 126, 128*n*
"marriage crisis," 467–68*n*
marriage equality, 7, 463–66
Marriage-Go-Round, The (Cherlin), 8, 468–69, 470*n*

Marsh, Kathy, 285
Marshall, J. Howard, II, 278
Marshall, Thurgood, 89
Martin, Steve, 366
Maslin, Janet, 389
Masters, Kim, 314, 315, 362
Mastro, Randy, 443
Masturbate-A-Thon, 137
masturbation, 136–37, 136*n*
Matalin, Mary, 31*n*, 37–38, 39, 155, 161–62, 328–29*n*
matchmaking services, 194–96
Mathews, Larry, 130
Matlock, David, 122
Mauldin, Steven, 464–65, 464*n*
Maxim (magazine), 366*n*, 400, 413
Maxwell, Carol J. C., 459–60, 459–61*n*
Mayer, Jane, 90*n*, 91, 96–97, 335*n*
Mayes, Stephen, 193–94
Maynard, Joyce, 237
"mean girl," 228
Meese, Edwin, 409
megachurches, 344, 344*n*, 346*n*, 452*n*
Meisel, Steven, 82
Melendez, John "Stuttering John," 100–101, 101*n*
Melich, Tanya, 162–63
Mellinger, S. H., 204–5
Mellody, Pia, 452
Mencken, H. L., 538
Mendelsohn, Michael, 139, 506*n*
Mendes, Sam, 403
Menendez, Lyle and Erik, 278
menopause, 4, 139
Men's Liberation, Inc., 352
menstruation, 18
Merkin, Daphne, 237
Messner, Michael A., 352
Metcalfe, Jane, 169, 175–79
"metrosexual," 365–66, 365*n*
Metzenbaum, Howard, 210
Michelman, Kate, 458, 459, 462
"MILF," 7, 88*n*
Milk, Harvey, 222
Miller, Stephen L., 550
Million Man March (1995), 5, 343–44, 343*n*
Mills, C. Wright, 348
Mindel, Sunny, 234–35, 443–44

Mind of Its Own, A (Friedman), 483, 508, 513
Minoxidil, 366–67
Miss America (Stern), 2
Mitchell, Joni, 158
Mitchell, Nance, 130
mixed martial arts (MMA), 374–75*n*
Mnuchin, Steven, 552
Mobilization of Responsible Tulane Students (MORTS), 325*n*
mojo, 382
Money, John, 450
"money shot," 411–12
Monkhouse, Bob, 508–9
monogamy, 12, 387, 468
Monroe, Marilyn, 42*n*
Montgomery, John, 180
Moore, Demi, 5, 87–89, 87*n*, 220–21, 247, 250, 390–91, 435
Moore, Gordon, 220
Moore, Julianne, 394
Moore, Lorrie, 74
Moore, Suzanne, 545
Moore's law, 220–21
"moral relativism," 4
Morone, James, 40*n*
Morris, Desmond, 249, 251, 252*n*
Morris, Dick, 32, 49–50, 56*n*, 279, 279*n*, 329*n*, 469–70
Morrison, Toni, 197–98*n*, 300
Morrow, Lance, 166, 324*n*
Mortensen, Viggo, 391
Moskos, Charles, 205*n*
Moss, Kate, 256, 258
Moynihan, Daniel Patrick, 156–57*n*, 444*n*, 536
Mrs. Doubtfire (movie), 157*n*
Mrskin.com, 412
MSNBC, 328, 532, 533*n*
MTV, 54, 81, 230–31, 238, 253, 413
Mugler, Thierry, 411
Mundy, Carl, 204
Munford, Rebecca, 69–70
Murad, Ferid, 486
Murdoch, Rupert, 108, 241, 242*n*, 283–84, 284*n*, 333, 335*n*, 555
Murdoch, Wendi Deng, 335*n*
Murphy, Eddie, 279
Murphy, Kate, 531

Murphy, Mike, 520
Murphy Brown (TV show), 155–58, 160
Murray, Jonathan, 230
Muscio, Inga, 120
Muskie, Edmund, 57
My American Journey (Powell), 1–2
Myers, Dee Dee, 21, 37, 39, 50, 63, 65, 102, 103–4, 104*n*, 106, 215, 458, 505–6*n*, 523
Myers, Mike, 183, 382, 401–2, 402*n*
My Life (Clinton), 45, 46*n*, 48*n*, 155*n*, 447

Nabokov, Vladimir, 449
Nadeau, Kathleen, 432
Naked Truth, The (TV show), 1
Napolitano, Chris, 126
narcissism, 526, 526*n*
NASCAR, 374, 510, 510*n*
National Child Protection Act, 200
National Enquirer, 279*n*, 283–84, 283*n*, 299*n*
National Organization for Women (NOW), 59, 313, 462
National Pay Inequity Awareness Day, 200
Natural, The (Klein), 104, 108*n*, 215*n*
Natural Born Killers (movie), 398
navel rings, 251
Navratilova, Martina, 276
Navy Tailhook scandal, 61, 61*n*
Ndegeocello, Meshell, 250
NEA Four, 233
Nelson, Judy, 276
Nerve.com, 186, 194–95
NetGuide, 170–74
New England Patriots, 379*n*
New Hampshire primary of 1992, 20, 21, 102–10, 104*n*
Newton, Helmut, 406
Newton, Isaac, 168
New York Post, 276, 284, 284*n*, 556
Nicholson, Jack, 56, 130, 359, 424, 513
Nightline (TV show), 27–28, 28*n*, 102
Nine Inch Nails, 219–20, 239
Nippert-Eng, Christena, 531
Nirvana, 68, 68*n*, 223, 351
Nixon, Cynthia, 14, 16
Nixon, Richard, 30*n*, 43*n*, 164, 312, 409
Nobel Prize, 4, 487, 517
Nolan, Martin, 379*n*

Noonan, Peggy, 197
Nordegren, Elin, 380–81
Noriega, Manuel, 41
North, Oliver, 328
Notorious B.I.G., 238*n*
Nunn, Sam, 206
Nussbaum, Emily, 84, 245–46*n*
NYPD Blue (TV show), 227

O: The Oprah Magazine (magazine), 257
Obama, Barack, 9, 52*n*, 213*n*, 343, 544–45
   abortion aid, 198*n*
   DNC speech (2004), 160*n*
   election of 2008, 79, 210, 370*n*
   Hillary and election of 2016, 80*n*
O'Brien, Michael, 509–10, 509–10*n*
Occupy Wall Street, 544
O'Connor, Sinéad, 250
Ofili, Chris, 234–35
Ogden, Gina, 137–38*n*
Ogletree, Charles, 302
Olbermann, Keith, 369–70
O'Leary, Hazel, 63
O'Neal, Ron, 368*n*
O'Neal, Shaquille, 372
One-Dimensional Man (Marcuse), 348
One Flew Over the Cuckoo's Nest (movie),
   383, 387
OneTaste, 144–45*n*, 144–51
online dating, 194–96
On Location Tours (New York City), 16–17
On Our Backs (journal), 189, 191
On Photography (Sontag), 221
On the Edge of the Bed (Palac), 190
Operation Desert Storm, 287
Operation Rescue, 152
Oppenheimer, Mark, 114*n*
Oppenheimer, Robert, 147, 150
Oprah Winfrey Show, The (TV show),
   114–15*n*, 116–17*n*, 250
oral sex, 225–26, 225–26*n*
O'Reilly, Bill, 334, 555
orgasmic meditation (OM), 143–51
orgasms, 134–51
O'Rourke, P. J., 333
Osterloh, Ian, 481–82, 492–96, 501–3,
   507, 508–9, 512
Out of Sight (movie), 253
Out of the Shadows (Carnes), 452

Owen, Elisabeth, 454–55
Oxford American (magazine), 49*n*

Pact, The (Gillon), 322, 323–24, 338,
   522*n*
Padilha, Janea, 123–31
Padilha, Jonice, 123, 125, 128, 133
Padilha, Joyce, 123, 126, 131–32
Padilha, Pedro, 124
Page, Larry, 173*n*
Paget, L. Lou, 225–26*n*
Paglia, Camille, 63, 70–71, 81, 84–85*n*,
   120, 178, 253, 313, 349
Palac, Lisa, 189–91, 191*n*
Paley, Maggie, 249*n*
Palin, Sarah, 525*n*
Palladino, Jack, 24*n*
Palm Center, 209*n*
Paltrow, Gwyneth, 124, 126*n*, 255*n*, 391
paparazzo, 289–91
Parker, Sarah Jessica, 15, 16, 126
Park Place Baptist Church (Hot Springs), 47
Passion and Betrayal (Flowers), 99, 102
Patrick, Dan, 369
Patrick, Jon, 371–72
Paul, Henri, 280
Paul, Joel, 91, 92, 362–63
Paul, Pamela, 224, 294, 412, 413, 455
Paulsen, Amy, 227–28
Paumgarten, Nick, 195
Payne, Dan, 101–2*n*, 112
PayPal, 184–85
Pearl Jam, 223, 351
Pelosi, Nancy, 76*n*
Pence, Mike, 466, 466*n*
penicillin, 480
Penn, Mark, 470*n*
Penthouse (magazine), 130, 267, 267*n*, 296,
   305, 308, 310–11, 410*n*, 513
People and the Power Game (documentary), 26
People vs. Larry Flynt, The (movie), 287*n*,
   410
People Weekly, 283, 283–84*n*
Pepitone, Julianne, 68*n*, 69
Perel, Esther, 467*n*
Peretz, Evgenia, 386
Perfect Murder, A (movie), 385, 391
Perfect Storm, The (Junger), 358
Perlmutter, Ike, 552

Perot, Ross, 25, 161, 197
Personal Responsibility Act, 323
Peter, Michael J., 437–39
Peterman, Larry, 417
Peters, Jon, 130n
Pfizer, 473–82, 486–517. *See also* Viagra
Phair, Liz, 69
Phillips, Julia, 364–65
Phillips, Mark, 274
Pickert, Kate, 459
piercings, 251
Pine Bluff Commercial, 51
Pinsky, Drew, 225–26, 239–40, 447–48, 525–28, 526n
Pipher, Mary, 66–67
Pippen, Scottie, 340
Pitt, Brad, 382
Planned Parenthood v. Casey, 457–58, 462
Playboy (magazine), 126, 271, 294, 301, 409, 410, 412
Pleasantville (movie), 140
Pleasure Chest (New York City), 13–14, 18, 136
Podhoretz, John, 331
political correctness, 548, 548n
Politics of Masculinities (Messner), 352
Pollack, Eileen, 185, 185n
Pollitt, Katha, 76
Poniewozik, James, 212n, 302, 552
porn, 168–75, 182–85, 405–19, 453, 455
porn envy, 122
Pornified (Paul), 294, 412, 455
Porno for Pyros, 412
"post-fact syndrome," 212–13
Powell, Colin, 1–2, 203, 204, 205–6
Presley, Elvis, 44, 159, 283n
Pretty Woman (movie), 424
Previn, Soon-Yi, 277
priapism, 489, 489n
Private Parts (Stern), 241, 242–43
Probst, Ken, 413n
Pro-Life Activists in America (Maxwell), 459–60, 459–61n
Promise Keepers, 5, 345–47
Prozac Nation (Wurtzel), 237
"psychic coitus," 137–38n
puberty, 4–5, 65n, 66–67
Pulp Fiction (movie), 396–97, 396n
Puzo, Mario, 225

Quayle, Dan, 155–58, 160
Queen, Carol, 136–37
Quindlen, Anna, 62n
Quivers, Robin, 241

R. Kelly, 1
Rabbit, the, 135–36
Rafferty, Terrence, 390
Raines, Howell, 353
Ramsey, JonBenét, 279
Rauch, Jonathan, 79–80, 215–16
Ray, Anthony, 252–53, 253n
Read, Howard, 82–83
Reagan, Nancy, 43, 420
Reagan, Ronald, 4, 41, 43, 90, 106, 288, 524n
Real World, The (TV show), 230–31
Red Hot Chili Peppers, 238
Reed, Ishmael, 52n
Reed, Ralph, 330, 330n
Regan, Judith, 241–43
ReganBooks, 242n
Reich, Robert, 199, 338
Reich, Wilhelm, 183
Reidy, Jamie, 510–11
Reingold, Anne, 28
Reinisch, June, 225
Reno, Janet, 63, 306, 461
Republican National Convention
　1992, 7, 154, 162–67, 323
　2016, 551
Republican War Against Women, The (Melich), 162–63
Resnick, Faye, 301, 303
Restless Virgins (Jones), 230–31
Reubens, Paul, 276
Reviving Ophelia (Pipher), 66–67
Reznor, Trent, 219–20
Rice, Donna, 110, 308, 328
Rich, Frank, 107, 212–13, 283, 287, 324, 413–14, 470
Richards, Amy, 60, 252
Richards, Ann, 37, 41–42
Rick's Cabaret (Houston), 267–68
Rider, Jennifer, 328–29
Riesman, David, 348
Rifkin, Arnold, 281
RigiScan, 490–91, 493
Ringwald, Molly, 534n
Riot Grrrl, 67–70

Rise of Viagra, The (Loe), 484, 486*n*, 504, 514
Ritts, Herb, 326
Rivers, Joan, 244–48
Rivers, Melissa, 247
road rage, 359
Roaring Nineties, The (Stiglitz), 434
Robb, Chuck, 206
Roberts, Dave, 475
Rock, Chris, 198*n*, 402*n*, 439*n*
Rodman, Dennis, 371, 371*n*
Roe v. Wade, 59, 198, 457, 462
Rogaine, 366–67
Rogen, Seth, 402*n*
Roiphe, Katie, 61, 61*n*, 313
Romney, George, 40*n*
Romney, Mitt, 544
Rooney, Michael, 367
Rose, Cindi Harwood, 264–68, 265*n*,
    269*n*, 272–73, 273*n*
Rose, Erica, 265, 265*n*, 272
Rose, Franklin, 262–73
Rose, Pete, 375
Rosen, Jeffrey, 215, 530–31, 539*n*
Rosen, Robert, 408
Rosenberg, Alyssa, 86
Rosenberg, Tina, 461
Rose Ribbon Foundation, 264–65
Rosin, Hanna, 349*n*
Rossetto, Louis, 175–78
Roth, Andrew, 429–30*n*
Roth, Gabrielle, 149
Roth, Philip, 225, 238, 471
Rowlands, Sherry, 279
Royko, Mike, 308
Russell, Jane, 44
Russia (Soviet Union), 6, 428–30
Rutenberg, Jim, 78*n*
RU-486, 199, 458 59
Ryan, Meg, 134
Ryan, Michael, 448, 448*n*
Ryzik, Melena, 70

Sabich, Spider, 284
Sachs, Arnie, 48*n*
safe sex, 8, 225
Safire, William, 54*n*, 214
St. Claire, Jasmin, 408, 408*n*
St. Romain-Frank, Sharon, 268–69
Salinger, J. D., 237

Salomon, Rick, 294*n*
Salon (website), 194–95
Salt-N-Pepa, 69*n*, 238
same-sex marriage, 7, 463–66
Samuels, Gill, 478
Sancton, Julian, 222–23
Sanders, Bernie, 544
Sandler, Adam, 401
Sanford, Mark, 114
Sarandon, Susan, 65, 118
Saturday Night Live (TV show), 552
satyrion, 483, 483*n*
Saward, John, 547
Scheide, R. V., 415, 508
Schell, Jonathan, 524, 533
Schiffer, Claudia, 326–27
Schlesinger, Arthur, Jr., 327, 521
Schmidt, Susan, 521
Schmidtke, Diana, 366*n*
Schmitt, Eric, 204
Schneider, Howard, 305
Schuster, Henry, 555, 556
Schwarzenegger, Arnold, 360*n*
Schwimmer, David, 228, 262–63, 268
Scorsese, Martin, 397–98
Scott, Janny, 522*n*
Scott, Wilbur J., 202*n*
Secret Life (Ryan), 448, 448*n*
Segal, Erich, 158
Seinfeld (TV show), 228–30, 228*n*
Seinfeld, Jerry, 228–30
Self, Will, 238
Sellers, Victoria, 426, 426*n*
serial monogamy, 12, 468
Sex (Madonna), 82–83, 83*n*
sex addiction, 445–56
Sex and the City (TV show), 13–16, 19, 123,
    126, 135, 140, 259, 515
sex chats, 170–71
sex drive, 10–11, 12
sex-positive feminism, 62–63, 62*n*
Sex Tape (movie), 295*n*
Sextasy, 513
sex toys, 13–14, 134–37
sex trafficking, 429–33
Sex Trafficking (Kara), 431
sexual assault, 61–62
sexual dysfunction, 138–39, 138*n*. *See also*
    erectile dysfunction

sexual harassment, 91, 97–98. *See also* Hill, Anita

sexual mores, 3, 428, 532–33

Sexual Personae (Paglia), 70–71, 71*n*, 120

Shacove, Gene, 129–30

Shakespeare in Love (movie), 255*n*

Shakur, Tupac, 238*n*

Shalala, Donna, 63

Shampoo (movie), 129–30, 129–30*n*

Shanklin, Douglas, 261

shapewear, 256–57

Sheehy, Gail, 30, 36–37, 47, 78, 325, 446

Sheen, Charlie, 424, 425, 425*n*

Shepard, Matthew, 201*n*

Sherman, Cindy, 231, 233

Sherrill, Martha, 74

Shields, Brooke, 81*n*

Shields, Carol, 238

"shock art," 233

Showgirls (movie), 435

Siegel, Richard, 500

sildenafil. *See* Viagra

Simon, Josh, 220

Simon, Paul, 159

Simpson, Alan, 94–95

Simpson, Mark, 365–66, 366*n*

Simpson, Nicole Brown, 297–98, 300–301, 533

Simpson, O. J., 9, 242, 292–93, 297–304, 524, 527, 533

Simpsons, The (TV cartoon), 400

Singleton, John, 351, 392

Sischy, Ingrid, 82–83, 83*n*, 231–32

60 Minutes (TV show), 20–21, 22, 28–39, 37*n*, 99, 108–9, 109*n*, 110, 112–13, 115, 211

Skoch, Iva Roze, 432–33

Slouching Towards Gomorrah (Bork), 184*n*, 239

Slow Sex (Daedone), 144–45

Smith, Anna Nicole, 1, 263*n*, 278

Smith, Krista, 226*n*

Smith, Will, 382

Smith, William Kennedy, 276

Smoking Gun, 189

Snoop Dogg, 252, 368, 412

Snowden, Edward J., 530, 531

Snyder, Gabriel, 336

social identity and self-identity, 530

Soderbergh, Steven, 253

Sohn, Amy, 237

Solotaroff, Paul, 461

Sontag, Susan, 221

Sopranos, The (TV show), 397*n*

Sorkin, Aaron, 392*n*, 529–30

Sosa, Sammy, 376–79

South Park (TV cartoon), 400, 400*n*

South Park: Bigger, Longer & Uncut (movie), 401–2

Spacey, Kevin, 403–4

Spanish fly, 483

Spanx, 257

Spears, Britney, 238, 251, 412

Specter, Arlen, 95, 97

Specter, Michael, 430, 431

Spice Girls, 10, 64, 69–70*n*

Spielberg, Steven, 403–4

sports bras, 256

Sprewell, Latrell, 375

Stagliano, John, 407

Stahl, Jerry, 237

Staller, Ilona, 234

Stanley, Alessandra, 387*n*

Stanley, Angela, 467–68*n*

Stanley, Sandra Carson, 202*n*

Star (tabloid), 22–24, 26, 29, 99, 102, 279, 283

Stark, Koo, 411

Starkman, Dean, 213*n*

Starr, Kenneth, 57*n*, 306, 307, 307*n*, 518–19, 520–21

Starr Report, 521, 555

Star Style at the Academy Awards (Fox), 248

Star Wars (movie), 395

Stayton, William, 463

Steele, Patricia, 104–5

Steere, Bill, 497, 508, 512

Stegner, Wallace, 180*n*

Steinem, Gloria, 66, 73, 118, 245, 411*n*

Stephanie, Princess of Monaco, 278–79

Stephanopoulos, George, 25, 27–31, 35, 53, 103, 105, 205, 207, 523, 555

Stephenson, Neal, 177*n*

Sterling, Bruce, 177*n*, 212*n*

Stern, Howard, 2, 101, 136*n*, 240–43, 313, 552*n*

steroids, 375–80

Stevens, Stuart, 544

Stewart, Jon, 86*n*
Stewart, Martha, 77
Stiglitz, Joseph, 434
Stiller, Ben, 401
Sting, 140–41
Stipp, David, 485
Stolberg, Sheryl Gay, 323
Stolley, Richard, 283–84*n*
Stone, Oliver, 237, 398
Stone, Robert, 78
Stone, Roger, 555–56
Stone, Sharon, 383, 388–89
Stout, Hilary, 514
Strange Justice (Mayer and Abramson), 90*n*, 91, 96
Streisand, Barbra, 130*n*
strip clubs, 434–42
Strip Tease (Hiaasen), 435
Striptease (movie), 435
Strother, Raymond, 113–14
Stryker, Jeff, 411
Stubbs, Robert, 122
Sturges, Jock, 233
Styler, Trudie, 140–41
sublimation, 10–11
Suleman, Nadya "Octomom," 295*n*
Sullivan, Aidan, 174–75
Sultan, Larry, 413*n*
Summers, Ann, 135
Super Bowl XXVI, 19, 20, 22, 33
Super Fly (movie), 368
supermodels, 257
Surfing on the Internet (Herz), 182
Swaggart, Jimmy, 110
Swartz, Mimi, 157, 262
Swinth, Kirsten, 60, 62–63, 409–10*n*
Swisher, Kara, 86
Syme, Rachel, 257*n*

Tabloid Decade, 282–85
Taibbi, Matt, 429*n*
Tailhook scandal, 61, 61*n*
Take Back the Night marches, 62
Take Our Daughters to Work Day, 66
Takiff, Michael, 103, 104, 204, 206
Talbot, Margaret, 15*n*, 539*n*
Tanenbaum, Leora, 529*n*
Tanenhaus, Sam, 329–30*n*, 331, 335, 336–37

Tanjeloff, Zak, 418
Tantric sex, 140–41
Tarantino, Quentin, 396–96, 396*n*, 398
tattoos, 251, 371
Taylor, Elizabeth, 277
Teachout, Terry, 330–31
Tea Party, 90*n*, 332, 544
Technology of Orgasm, The (Maines), 135
Teena, Brandon, 201*n*
Terrett, Nick, 477–79, 477*n*, 481–82, 486–88, 495
Thelma & Louise (movie), 64–65, 314, 382
There's Something About Mary (movie), 401
Thiel, Peter, 552
third-wave feminism, 59–73
Thomas, Clarence, 5, 59, 89–97, 390
Thomas, Evan, 308
Thomas, Virginia, 90*n*, 96, 96*n*
Thomason, Harry, 159
Thompson, Hunter S., 107*n*, 446–47*n*
thong, the, 253–54
"threading," 249
Thurmond, Strom, 94, 94*n*
Tiger, Lionel, 341–42*n*, 348–49
Tiller, George, 460–61
TinySex, 183
Title IX, 66, 66*n*
Todd, Richard, 160
Tomasky, Michael, 213
Tom Green Show (TV show), 400*n*
Tom of Finland, 406
Tompkins, Stacy, 269–71
Toobin, Jeffrey, 90*n*, 298*n*
Topless (Mano), 435
Tornaghi, Anna Maria, 131
Tosches, Nick, 352, 353–54
Tough Guys Don't Dance (Mailer), 23
Tower, John, 108*n*
Towne, Robert, 129*n*
Travolta, John, 396–97
Tribe Called Quest, A, 252
Tripp, Linda, 307, 312, 447*n*, 518–19, 518*n*, 521
Trivial Pursuit, 282*n*
Trudeau, Garry, 41
True Compass (Kennedy), 207
Truman, Harry, 40*n*
Truman Show, The (movie), 553

Trump, Donald, 9, 10, 332, 336–37, 545–56
  affairs of, 2, 276, 276*n*, 308, 311*n*, 327*n*,
    328
  "angry white male," 72*n*
  Clinton and women, 311*n*
  election of 2016, 77, 105*n*, 165, 324*n*,
    335*n*, 338*n*, 349*n*, 379*n*, 543, 545–56
  lies of, 213, 213*n*
  reality TV and, 9, 379*n*, 525, 548–54
  reproductive choice and, 466*n*
  Stern interviews, 241, 552*n*
  working class voters and, 349*n*
Trump, Ivana, 2, 276
Trump, Ivanka, 335*n*
"truthiness," 212, 212*n*
Truth or Dare (documentary), 81–82, 84
Tsongas, Paul, 105, 106
Tucker, Michael, 141
Tulgan, Bruce, 222
Tuller, David, 288
Turkle, Sherry, 183
Turlington, Christy, 257, 327
Turner, Fred, 191*n*
Turner, Kathleen, 388
Turner, Ted, 287, 333–34, 334*n*
Turnley, David, 229
Turow, Scott, 340–41
TV newsmags, 285–86
"twerk," 252
Twin Peaks (TV show), 398–99
Two and a Half Men (TV show), 425*n*
Twohey, Megan, 24*n*
Tyrnauer, Matt, 406
Tyson, Mike, 277, 375

UK-92480, 475, 479–82, 486–98
Unbending Gender (Williams), 260
Unfriendly Fire (Frank), 202, 203*n*, 205*n*,
    208, 210
Unwanted Gaze, The (Rosen), 215, 530–31

vagina, 116–33
Vagina: A New Biography (Wolf), 119*n*
vagina dentata, 120
vaginal rejuvenation surgery, 121–22
Vagina Monologues, The (play), 5, 116–20
Vail, Tobi, 67–68
"vajayjay," 116*n*
Van der Leun, Gerard, 168, 171*n*, 178

Vanity Fair's Hollywood, 55–56
V-chip, 418–19, 470
V-Day, 118
Veblen, Thorstein, 281*n*
Velvet Revolution, 433*n*
Venzano, Philippe, 258
Verhoeven, Paul, 383, 388–89
Versace, Gianni, 280
Vetterlein, Ray, 144
VHS, 169, 169*n*
Viagra, 4, 221, 472–517
  clinical studies, 495–97, 500–501, 512–13
  discovery of, 474–96
  Dole and, 471
  Douglas and, 383
  gay men and, 514–15
  marketing and sales, 472–74, 506–12
  naming, 497–501
  porn use of, 415
  public rollout of, 501–9
  side effects, 472–73, 496
Viagra Ad Venture, The (Baglia), 510
vibrators, 13–14, 135–37
Victoria's Secret, 255
video games, 350*n*, 524*n*
Vietnam War, 43, 56, 102–3, 154–55, 178,
    180, 203, 324
Vile Body, 330–31
Violence Against Women Act, 200, 300, 313
VIP rooms, 439–40
Vitter, David, 114
Vox (Baker), 238
VRtube, 183*n*

Wahlberg, Mark, 363, 411
Waiting to Exhale (McMillan), 64
Waitt, Don, 435–36
Wallace, Ben, 415*n*
Wallace, David Foster, 3*n*, 416, 416*n*
Wallace, George, 165
Wallace, Mike, 32–33
Wall Street (movie), 385, 386, 391*n*
Walters, Barbara, 280
Wanderer, Nancy, 37*n*
Ward, Elizabeth, 25
War of the Roses, The (movie), 385, 388
Warren, James C., 333*n*
Warren, Jim, 180
"war room," 107, 107*n*

War Room, The (documentary), 25, 101–2*n*
Warshavsky, Seth, 296, 407
Washington, Denzel, 382
Washington, Desiree, 277
Wasserstein, Wendy, 79
Watergate, 24, 111*n*, 212, 306, 530*n*
Waters, John, 283*n*
Watts, Alan, 142*n*
Wayne, Teddy, 365*n*
webcams, 173, 173*n*
Weber, Thomas E., 296
Webster, Jamieson, 15*n*, 51–52
Weigel, Moira, 396*n*, 548*n*
Weiner, Anthony, 556
Weinraub, Bernard, 389
Weldon, Fay, 73
We Live in Public (documentary), 173*n*
WELL, The, 191–93, 191*n*
Wenner, Jann, 51*n*
Weyrich, Paul, 10, 90*n*
What the Dormouse Said (Markoff), 179–80
When Harry Met Sally (movie), 134
Whipple, Beverly, 137
Whitaker, Robert, 485
White, Teddy, 40*n*
Whitehead, Barbara Dafoe, 157
White House Correspondents' Association
    Dinner, 327–28
"whitelash theory," 72*n*, 353*n*
Whyte, William H., 348
Why Women Should Rule the World (Myers), 65
Wicker, Pierre, 501*n*
WikiLeaks, 525, 555
Wild Man, 354–56
Wild Things (movie), 228
Wilhelm, David, 26–27
Will, George, 332
Willey, Kathleen, 522
Williams, Joan, 75–76, 197–98, 260
Williams, Marjorie, 54
Williams, Robin, 157*n*
Williams, Venus, 250
Willis, Bruce, 87
Wilson, Eric, 258–59
Wilson, Marie, 66
Wilson, Sloan, 348
Wilson, William Julius, 156–57*n*
Winchester, Simon, 184*n*
Windolf, Jim, 396*n*, 398–99

Winerip, Michael, 285
Winfrey, Oprah, 114–15*n*, 116–17*n*, 200,
    250, 548*n*
Winter, Rachel, 196
Wired (magazine), 168, 169, 171*n*, 175,
    177–79, 183*n*
Wojnarowicz, David, 232
Wolcott, James, 81*n*, 228, 283*n*, 289*n*,
    398*n*, 415*n*
Wolf, Naomi, 72–73, 73*n*, 119*n*, 141, 453–54
Wolfe, Tom, 368
Wolff, Bill, 369–70
Wolff, Michael, 107*n*, 170–74, 173*n*, 195
Wolfson, Evan, 463–64*n*
women empowerment icons, 74–98
women in the workplace, 348–49, 350–51
women's movement, 59–73
Wonderbra, 255–56
Wood, Kerry, 411
Woodcock, Janet, 507
Woods, Tiger, 269, 380–81, 445
Woodstock '94, 219–20
Woodward, Bob, 54, 55, 111*n*, 154, 214
Woolf, Virginia, 77, 292
Wooten, Jim, 26
working class voters, 349*n*
workplace sexual harassment, 91, 97–98.
    See also Hill, Anita
World Wrestling Entertainment (WWE),
    550–51
Wright, Betsey, 24–25, 50
Wright, Susan Webber, 305, 307, 446*n*
Wurtzel, Elizabeth, 237

X Games, 374–75

YBAs (Young British Artists), 234
Year 2000 (Y2K) problem, 3
yoga, 121, 145–46
You Are Not a Gadget (Lanier), 188–89
Young Widow, The (movie), 44
"You Remind Me of Something" (song), 1

Zahedi, Firooz, 253
Zahner, Tim, 369, 552*n*
Zane, Matt, 407
Zeisler, Andi, 61, 61*n*
Zeta-Jones, Catherine, 383
Zuckerberg, Mark, 531

About the Author

DAVID FRIEND, *Vanity Fair*'s editor of creative development and the former director of photography of *Life* magazine, is a journalist, curator, Emmy-winning producer, and the author of *Watching the World Change: The Stories Behind the Images of 9/11.*